26th April 2000

Daddy,
Happy Tra[vels]
Happy Birthday
All my love
C[harles]

AUSTRALIA'S
WORLD HERITAGE

Australia's
WORLD HERITAGE

First published in 1997 by World Heritage Publishing Pty Limited

© Copyright OZ-LOCATIONS PUBLISHERS, 1997

Based on an original works
© Copyright OZ-LOCATIONS PUBLISHERS, 1996

All rights reserved. No part of this publication may be reproduced, stored in a retrieval system or transmitted in any form or by any means, electronic, mechanical, photocopying, recording or otherwise without the prior written permission of OZ-LOCATIONS PUBLISHERS.

Produced by World Heritage Publishing Pty Limited
P.O.Box 423, Glebe, NSW, 2037, Australia.
E-mail Address: whp@s054.aone.net.au

Managing Editor: Robert Osborne

Senior Consulting Editor: Peter Prineas

Editors: Dr Jim Thorsell (IUCN), Tony Duffy

Graphic Design & Illustrations: Scott Jordan Design

Production Assistants and
Photographic Research: Kay Osborne, Tony Duffy, Sharyn Driscoll

Production Consultants: Gordon Liu, Brian Kinsela, Brett Cullen

Writers: Vincent Serventy, William Lines, Vivienne Courto, Robert Levitus, John Sinclair, David Lergessner, Rod Wells, Dirk Megirian, Joan Domicelj, Atticus Fleming

The publishers would like to give special thanks to the following individuals and organisations for their invaluable assistance in the production of this book: Dr Jim Thorsell, Head, Natural Heritage Programme, IUCN - The World Conservation Union; UNESCO's World Heritage Centre, Paris and in particular Dr Bernd von Droste and Sacha Goldman; Rolf Hogan, IUCN; Drs Warren Nicholls and Daryl King, Directors, Australia's World Heritage Unit (AWHU), Canberra; Stuart Read (AWHU); Elizabeth Bilney; The World Conservation Monitoring Centre (WCMC) and the International Council on Monuments and Sites (ICOMOS).

ISBN 1-57769-007-9

Pre-press Production: Fancy Graphic Production Ltd, Hong Kong

Printed in Hong Kong by Inter Scan Limited from new growth plantation forest.

Captions:
Front end paper: Kata Tjuta
Page 1: Central Eastern Rainforest
Page 2-3: Wet Tropical Rainforest
This page: Tall Mulla Mulla, Uluru

CONTENTS

FOREWORD	6
INTRODUCTION	8
TIME LINE AND GLOSSARY	10
CHAPTER 1 The Great Barrier Reef	12
CHAPTER 2 Kakadu National Park	36
CHAPTER 3 Willandra Lakes Region	60
CHAPTER 4 Tasmanian Wilderness	80
CHAPTER 5 Lord Howe Island Group	104
CHAPTER 6 Uluru - Kata Tjuta National Park	120
CHAPTER 7 Central Eastern Rainforest Reserves	144
CHAPTER 8 Wet Tropics of Queensland	172
CHAPTER 9 Shark Bay	196
CHAPTER 10 Fraser Island	224
CHAPTER 11 Australian Mammal Fossil Sites (Riversleigh and Naracoorte)	248
CHAPTER 12 Heard & McDonald Islands	272
APPENDICES AUSTRALIAN TENTATIVE LIST Macquarie Island	288
Sydney Opera House In Its Harbour Setting	300
Australian World Heritage Properties Conservation Act (1983) - An Overview	312
INDEX	315
PHOTO CREDITS	321

FOREWORD

Here is a book which takes us to ancient Gondwanan rainforests, to the arid heart of the Australian continent and on to the bounty of the surrounding seas. In this journey through landscape and time, we come upon places, landforms, fossils, rocks, animals, plants, communities of life and things that are familiar and unfamiliar, as well as ancient and rich cultures.

The places we visit have been recognised by the international community as special ones to be preserved for all humanity, and for all time. The adoption, in 1972, of the Convention Concerning the Protection of the World Cultural and Natural Heritage, (popularly known as the World Heritage Convention), by the General Conference of the United Nations' Education, Scientific and Cultural Organisation (UNESCO) was the most significant act of its kind since the scribes drew up a list of the Seven Wonders of the Ancient World.

The Convention was innovative. It introduced the notion of a universal shared responsibility. It aimed to promote co-operation among nations to protect natural and cultural heritage which is of such outstanding universal value that its conservation is of concern to all people of the world. This international or universal value distinguishes places on the World Heritage List from those on other lists that recognise values of national or local conservation significance, that exist, for example, in national parks and other reserves with national, regional or local heritage designations.

How does a place gain World Heritage Listing?

The Convention provides a number of criteria which are used to judge whether or not a site nominated by a State Party to the Convention is of universal and outstanding value. Nominated sites are referred to a body called the 'World Heritage Bureau' representing the 21 member elected State Parties known as the World Heritage Committee. The Secretariat of the Bureau, based in Paris, then refers each site for assessment by one or more of three international non-government organisations: IUCN -The World Conservation Union which reviews natural site nominations; the International Council on Monuments and Sites (ICOMOS) and the International Centre for the Study of the Preservation and Restoration of Cultural Property (ICCROM) which, together, assess cultural nominations.

The nominations are evaluated to see if they meet any one of the prescribed cultural or natural criteria set out under the Convention, always remembering that its key words are "outstanding universal value".

Article 1 of the Convention defines cultural heritage as being:

(i) monuments, architectural works, works of monumental sculpture and painting, elements or structures of an archaeological nature, inscriptions, cave dwellings and combinations of features, which are of outstanding universal value from the point of view of history, art or science; or

(ii) groups of buildings: groups of separate or connected buildings which, because of their architecture, their homogeneity or their place in the landscape, are of outstanding universal value from the point of view of history, art or science; or

(iii) sites: works of man or the combined works of nature and man, and areas, including archaeological sites, which are of outstanding universal value from the historical, aesthetic, ethnological or anthropological points of view.

Article 2 of the Convention defines natural heritage as being:

(i) natural features consisting of physical and biological formations or groups of such formations, which are of outstanding universal value; or

(ii) geological and physiographical formations and precisely delineated areas which constitute the habitat of threatened species of animals and plants of outstanding universal value from the point of view of science; or

(iii) natural sites or precisely delineated natural areas of outstanding universal value from the point of view of science, conservation or natural beauty.

World Heritage is a comparatively well-recognised idea in Australia where it has been the focal point for much publicity and success in the conservation of natural areas such as Fraser Island and the Western Tasmanian Wilderness. It has also enjoyed the support, in the main, of the major political parties - from the Whitlam Government which was one of the first in the world to sign the Convention, to the Fraser Government which offered a huge compensation package to the Government of Tasmania to entice it to stop the building of a hydro-electric dam that threatened natural heritage areas. Significantly, the first major piece of legislation introduced into the federal parliament by the Hawke Government was the Australian World Heritage Properties Act, 1983.

World Heritage is denying the economic rationalists. Recent examples of this can be seen in the USA and Canada where governments have acted to stop mining activities worth US$2 billion, in each case, affecting Yellowstone National Park and the last wild rivers in North America - the Alsek -Tatshenshini River system.

My friends in conservation caution me about the dangers of trying to quantify the value of natural heritage. Yet, I have been struck by the compelling economic arguments put forward by the reports of the United States Congress's bipartisan committee responsible for the Government Accounting Office (GAO) which reports to Congress on the affairs of their various bureaucracies. They arrived at an economic model to measure the economic impact, including their contribution to employment, of their national parks and their World Heritage sites. I have applied their model to many of our Australian World Heritage Areas based on visitor information supplied by relevant park authorities. The results are graphically illustrated opposite.

We should carefully consider the fact that the life of our natural heritage, which the Convention aims to extend to perpetuity, dwarfs the life of any mine, and so do the economic benefits. As the world is more and more affected by development, the value of World Heritage areas must increase. How is it possible to compare the 20 or 30 year life of a mine with the hundreds or thousands of years of a World Heritage Area? How can any government ignore the $3 trillion dollar economic value of the Great Barrier Reef over 100 years and the four thousand present jobs that depend on its integrity, when considering oil exploration permits or shipping routes?

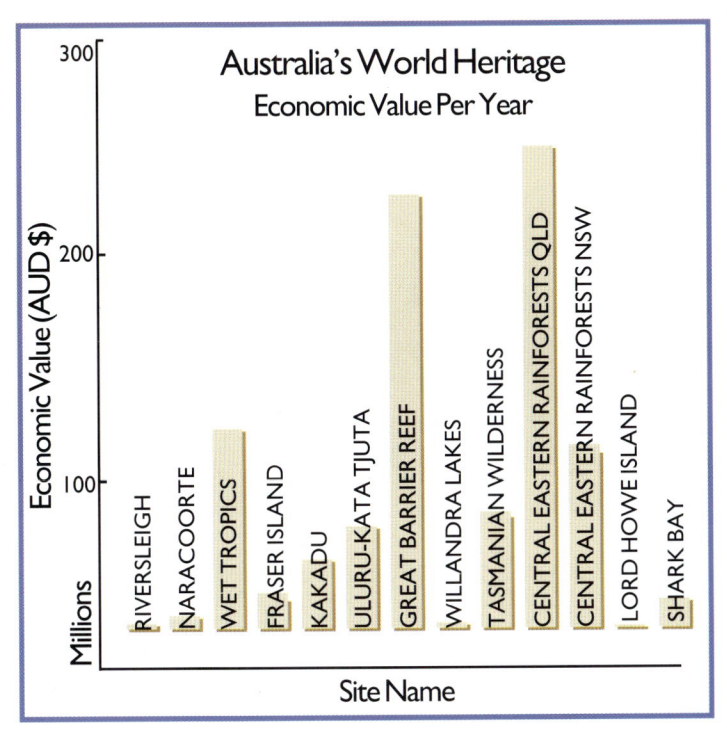

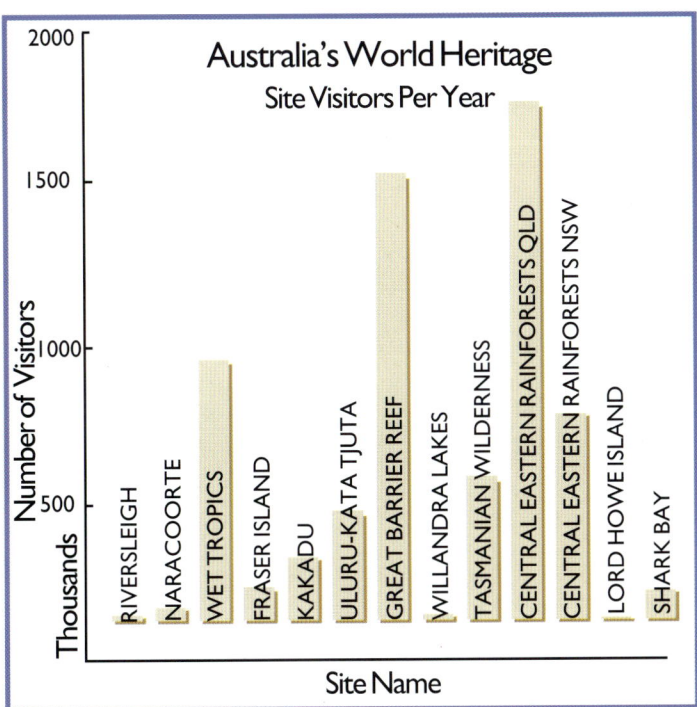

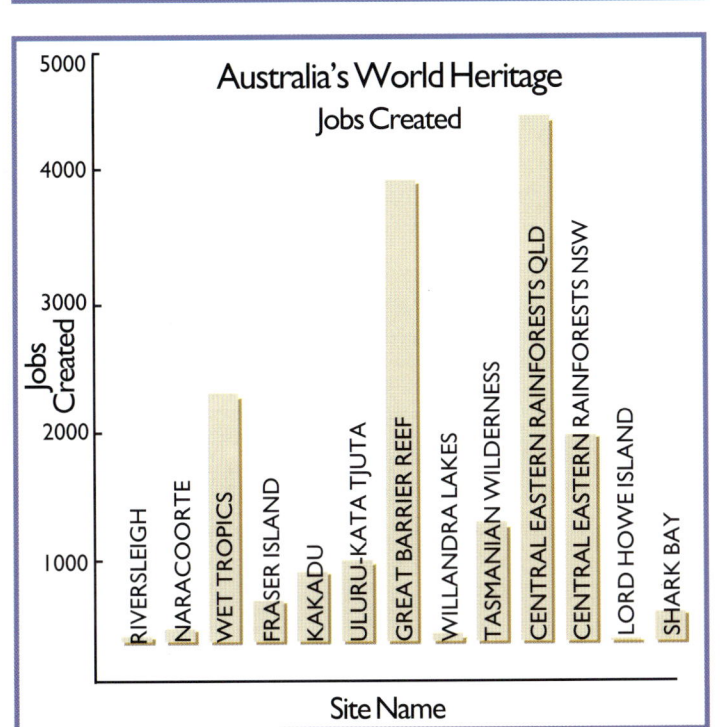

Australia's World Heritage
Economic Value Per Year

[Bar chart showing Economic Value (AUD $) in Millions by Site Name: Riversleigh, Naracoorte, Wet Tropics, Fraser Island, Kakadu, Uluru-Kata Tjuta, Great Barrier Reef, Willandra Lakes, Tasmanian Wilderness, Central Eastern Rainforests QLD, Central Eastern Rainforests NSW, Lord Howe Island, Shark Bay]

Australia's World Heritage
Site Visitors Per Year

[Bar chart showing Number of Visitors in Thousands by Site Name]

Australia's World Heritage
Jobs Created

[Bar chart showing Jobs Created by Site Name]

Equally important is the consideration that some other development or economic activity within a World Heritage Area may be carried on and not significantly affect its values. The World Heritage Convention recognises this possibility.

Since the early days of the Convention, both in Australia and globally, inscription of areas on the World Heritage List has brought with it tangible benefits beyond preservation. In addition to local employment opportunities, local communities have benefited from improved planning and management of the resources, and additional state and Commonwealth funding. Recognition of a place as a World Heritage Area is also a major foreign currency earner.

What are the implications of World Heritage listing?

Contrary to popular belief, a range of activities is permissible within a World Heritage Area, as long as the activities do not threaten its values. For example, in many World Heritage places, tourism continues and, indeed, increases; normal community activities, including recreational fishing, commercial fishing and, in some areas, grazing, also continue.

Private rights of ownership of land are not affected by inclusion of an area on the World Heritage List and, in fact, Article 6(1) of the Convention states that "sovereignty" and "property rights" must be "fully respected".

Worldwide, there are numerous examples where private properties have been listed. They include Monticello, the home of Thomas Jefferson, in the USA, and Blenheim Palace in the United Kingdom. State and local laws continue to apply and control does not pass to another body, whether it be the state or Commonwealth Government or any international body or foreign power. The Convention requires consent from Federal, state and local governments, and private citizens owning and controlling relevant lands, before a nomination to the World Heritage List can proceed.

These principles also recognise indigenous peoples' rights to land, and require their support, before a nomination can be successful.

I have been privileged to attend the last four annual World Heritage Committee Meetings and to work with the World Heritage Centre in Paris, as well as with IUCN-The World Conservation Union to increase my knowledge of our world's natural and cultural heritage.

It is my hope that the work of editors, writers and photographers in creating *Australia's World Heritage* will further stimulate Australians' interest in their World Heritage Areas and ensure even greater public support for their protection.

Robert Osborne
Managing Editor and Publisher

INTRODUCTION

When Captain Cook charted the east coast of Australia in 1770, the whole continent was like a national park and its small human population lived within the limits of the available resources. Since then, Australia's landscape has undergone substantial transformation but it is a country that still finds itself in a position to avoid many of the more devastating and unsustainable effects that accompany human exploitation of the Earth's natural heritage.

Like many other people who had never been to Australia, my early impressions of the country were dominated by deserts. After ten visits over the past thirty years, I have grown to appreciate just how varied and rich the continent is in its scenery, animals and plants. Australia has, in fact, been included in the Megadiverse Group of Seven. This means that Australia is one of the seven countries in the world that, between them, contain over half of all the biological species still existing on Earth (the other six countries are Brazil, Colombia, Mexico, Zaire, Madagascar and Indonesia).

This means that Australia has a major responsibility to ensure that this natural diversity is maintained. It means, too, that Australia's 'report card' is of great interest to the conservation community world-wide. After all, Australia is the only developed country that has significant remaining natural tropical habitats such as mangroves, coral reefs and tropical forests. The view of the IUCN is if that we cannot conserve these habitats in Australia, this must reflect poorly on our chances of doing so in the other megadiverse countries, none of which enjoys the same level of affluence.

The World Heritage Convention has been a particularly effective tool in conserving outstanding natural sites in Australia. Since making its first nominations to the prestigious World Heritage List in 1981, the number of listed sites in Australia has grown to eleven. This is the second highest number of listed natural heritage sites, (after the USA with twelve) of all 150 state parties to the Convention. Another site is to be considered for listing in 1997.

I have been privileged to act as the IUCN examiner for each of Australia's nominations and have presented reports on the nominated areas to the annual meetings of UNESCO's World Heritage Committee. This work has taken me to the furthest corners and the most wondrous parts of the Australian continent, and the world, but it has not always been easy.

Indeed, IUCN, as technical adjudicator under contract to UNESCO's World Heritage Committee, sometimes finds itself in a difficult position when called upon to conduct evaluations in Australia. Not only are nominations very complex, but IUCN examiners can find themselves in the uncomfortable role of arbiters between interests that are polarised, and involving issues that are politically loaded. Not being accustomed to dealing with Australia's media, IUCN's representatives have sometimes been pursued and misrepresented, to the detriment of the organisation's role as a quasi-judicial and independent scientific body. This is not to say that it hasn't been worthwhile in terms of results and it is pleasing to note that those more confrontational days are behind us.

Having an area inscribed on an honours list is, of course, not the end of the matter. The need to ensure effective management and to establish world-class standards for all Australian sites has not been overlooked. Indeed, exemplary projects that have been carried out within World Heritage sites, and that have earned recognition world-wide, include:

- involvement of local people in park management through the Aboriginal training programme in several of the areas;
- rescue of the Lord Howe Island woodhen from the brink of extinction;
- establishment of the Wet Tropics Management Authority and its approach to planning and management on a regional scale;
- elimination of exotic species such as mimosa and buffalo in Kakadu;
- rehabilitation of trails in South-west Tasmania and provision of supplementary management funds from the Commonwealth to strengthen state efforts;
- acquisition of key sections of forest lands and additions to the rainforest parks in New South Wales;
- preparation of management plans for all sites;
- development of visitor information facilities which help to explain the work of the World Heritage Convention to the public.

This sample list of achievements demonstrates Australia's commitment to World Heritage and shows both a recognition of the advantages of World Heritage listing and an acceptance of the obligations that go with it.

Nevertheless, there are still misconceptions in Australia about the World Heritage Convention and what it means. That is why IUCN strongly supports the publication of this exceptional book. It will do much to promote the World Heritage concept in Australia and the need to attain the highest standards of stewardship in listed areas.

There are few goals worth pursuing more than the one academics refer to as 'intergenerational equity', that is, ensuring the next generation is able to inherit the natural treasures of the present generation. This was recognised in 1982 by the presiding Premier of New South Wales, Neville Wran. When commenting on the conclusion of the long battle to protect what is now the Central Eastern Rainforest Reserves World Heritage Area, Mr Wran said:

> "One hundred years from now, after we are all dead and gone, the one single act for which our government will be most remembered will be our action to protect these forests".

The Premier's statement reflected one of the eight moral laws of humankind: that is, that we have a duty to posterity. This, of course, is the essential idea behind the concept of World Heritage - it implies there is something of great value to be inherited by the generations to follow. This book sets out to remind us of what has been done to pass on this inheritance, undiminished, through the operation of the World Heritage Convention in Australia.

Dr Jim Thorsell, Head, Natural Heritage Programme,
IUCN - The World Conservation Union

WORLD HERITAGE PROCESS

Australian Government submits a nomination to the World Heritage Committee Secretariat in Paris

World Heritage Committee Secretariat refers the nomination to the World Heritage Bureau for assessment

World Heritage Bureau obtains advice from IUCN-The World Conservation Union (natural heritage places) and/or ICOMOS and ICCROM (cultural heritage places)

Nomination is assessed at a meeting of the World Heritage Bureau

World Heritage Bureau makes a recommendation to the World Heritage Committee on the place's suitability for listing.

Additional information may be sought from the Australian Government

Decision on nomination at the annual December meeting of the World Heritage Committee

Nomination rejected for World Heritage List

Decision on the nomination is deferred

Nomination is accepted for the World Heritage List

Place is inscribed on the World Heritage List

Monitoring reports

GLOSSARY

TIME LINE

Era	Period/Epoch	Age
CAINOZOIC	HOLOCENE	10 000 YEARS
CAINOZOIC	PLIOCENE	5.2 MILLION YEARS
CAINOZOIC	MIOCENE	23.3 MILLION YEARS
CAINOZOIC	OLIGOCENE	35.4 MILLION YEARS
CAINOZOIC	EOCENE	56.5 MILLION YEARS
CAINOZOIC	PALAEOCENE	65 MILLION YEARS
MESOZOIC	CRETACEOUS	145.6 MILLION YEARS
MESOZOIC	JURASSIC	210 MILLION YEARS
MESOZOIC	TRIASSIC	245 MILLION YEARS
PALAEOZOIC	PERMIAN	290 MILLION YEARS
PALAEOZOIC	CARBONIFEROUS	363.5 MILLION YEARS
PALAEOZOIC	DEVONIAN	408.5 MILLION YEARS
PALAEOZOIC	SILURIAN	439 MILLION YEARS
PALAEOZOIC	ORDOVICIAN	510 MILLION YEARS
PALAEOZOIC	CAMBRIAN	520 MILLION YEARS
PRE-CAMBRIAN	PROTEROZOIC	2000 MILLION YEARS
PRE-CAMBRIAN	ARCHAEAN	4500 MILLION YEARS

acacia A genus of leguminous shrubs or trees, sometimes known as mimosa.
alabaster A fine-grained, white, opaque or translucent form of gypsum.
alga (pl. algae) A non-flowering, stemless water plant.
alluvial Pertaining to deposits of sand, soil, etc left by rivers or streams.
angiosperm Any plant which produces flowers and reproduces from seeds enclosed in a carpel.
aquifer A layer of rock or soil that contains or conducts water.
arboreal Pertaining to trees.
archipelago A group of islands.
atoll A coral island with a ring-shaped reef which encloses a lagoon.
bettong A small *marsupial*; also known as the rat kangaroo.
bêche-de-mer A kind of sea slug eaten as a delicacy in some Asian countries.
boodie A burrowing rat kangaroo.
bryophyte A member of any of the phylum Bryophyta being non-vascular plants, including true mosses and liverworts.
calcareous Of, containing or like calcium carbonate; chalky.
Cainozoic Pertaining to the present era of geological time, beginning 65 million years ago and characterised by the ascendancy of mammals.
canopy The cover formed by the leafy upper branches of the trees in a forest.
carbon dating A method of determining the age of an organic object by measuring the ratio of isotopes present as the result of the decay of carbon 14, a radioactive isotope of carbon. Also referred to as *radiocarbon dating*.
carnivore An animal that eats flesh.
carpel The female reproductive organ of flowering plants.
cay A small, low island; variation of key.
conifer Any plant of the class Pinopsida, chiefly of evergreen trees and shrubs, including those of the pine and cypress families, that bear both seeds and pollen on dry scales arranged as a cone.
cycad Any of several palm-like gymnospermous trees of the order Cycadales, having a thick, unbranched trunk, a crown of leathery pinnate leaves and large cones.
cyclone A system of winds rotating inwards to an area of low barometric pressure, often of a violent and destructive nature.
dasyure A small, carnivorous Australasian *marsupial*.
Dreaming An English term used to denote the ancient time of the creation of all things by the sacred ancestors of Australian Aborigines.
dugong A plant-eating marine mammal of Australasian seas and coasts, also known as a sea cow.
echinoderm Any marine invertebrate animal of the phylum Echinodermata, including starfish, sea urchins and sea cucumbers, characterised by a five-part, radially symmetrical body and a *calcareous* endoskeleton.
ecosystem A system formed by the interaction of a community of organisms with its environment.
endemic Belonging exclusively, or confined, to, a particular place.
epiphyte A plant that grows above the ground and is supported non-parasitically by another plant or object, and deriving its nutrients and water from rain, the air, dust, etc; air plant.
escarpment A long, steep slope, usually on the edge of a plateau or the like.
eucalypt Any tree of the genus Eucalyptus, of the myrtle family, native to Australia and the adjacent islands, having aromatic, evergreen leaves.
exotic Not native; introduced from abroad; foreign.
feral Descriptive of a domestic animal, individual or species, that has gone wild.
fungus Any of a group of unicellular, multicellular or multinucleate non-photosynthetic organisms that feed on organic matter, including moulds, yeast, mushrooms and toadstools.
furious fifties Blustery ocean winds occurring between the latitudes 50° and 60° South.
gecko Any small, mostly nocturnal tropical lizard of the family Gekkonidae, usually having toe pads that can cling to smooth surfaces.
global warming The increase in temperature of the Earth's atmosphere brought about by the greenhouse effect.
Gondwana A hypothetical supercontinent formed at the end of the *Palaeozoic* era, consisting of the modern landmasses of South America,

Africa, Antarctica, Australia and peninsular India.
guano The excrement of birds or bats, sometimes extracted commercially and used as fertiliser.
gypsum A soft, mineral, hydrous calcium sulphate that occurs in massive or fibrous form and also as alabaster and selenite: used to make plaster of Paris and as a fertiliser.
Holocene Pertaining to the present geological epoch which originated about 10 000 years ago at the end of the last glacial period, and forming the latter part of the *Quaternary* Period; also known as the *Recent* period.
Homo Sapiens The species of bipedal primates to which modern humans belong, characterised by a brain capacity averaging 1400 cubic centimetres (85 cubic inches) and by dependence upon language and the creation and utilisation of complex tools.
hydro-electricity Electricity generated by utilising the power of moving water, usually by means of large turbines.
hydrology The science of the properties of water.
Ice Age The geologically recent *Pleistocene* Epoch, during which much of the northern hemisphere was covered by great ice sheets; also called the glacial epoch.
Jurassic The second period of the *Mesozoic* Era, occurring between 195 and 135 million years ago.
karst An area of *limestone* terrain characterised by *sinkholes*, ravines and underground streams.
krill Tiny planktonic crustaceans found in the seas around the Antarctic and forming the staple diet of baleen whales.
lek Gaelic for 'grouse'. An area in which males of any species maintain courtship territories to attract and mate with females.
lichen Any complex organism of the group Lichenes, composed of a *fungus* in symbiotic union with an *alga*, most commonly forming crusty patches on rocks and trees.
limestone A sedimentary rock consisting mainly of calcium carbonate.
lunette A crescent-shaped dune formed on the sheltered side of a lake basin.
macropod Any plant-eating mammal of the family Macropodidae, including kangaroos and wallabies.
mallee Any of the various dwarf Australian *eucalypts*, such as *Eucalyptus dumosa* and *oleosa*, that sometimes form large tracts of brushwood.
mangrove Any tropical tree or shrub belonging to the genus *Rhizophora*, of the family Rhizophoraceae, the species of which are mostly low trees growing in marshes or tidal shores, noted for interlacing, above-ground roots.
marsupial Any animal of the order Marsupialia, comprising mammals having no placenta and bearing immature young that complete their development in a pouch on the mother's abdomen including possums, kangaroos, phalangers and dasyures.
megafauna A range of very large marsupial species which became extinct in Australia during the late *Pleistocene* and early *Holocene* epochs. Some, but not all, have modern, though much smaller, counterparts.
Mesozoic Pertaining to a geological era occurring between 230 and 65 million years ago, characterised by the appearance of flowering plants and by dinosaurs.
midden A dunghill or refuse heap.
Miocene Pertaining to an epoch of the Tertiary period of geological time occurring between 25 and 10 million years ago, when grazing animals became widespread
mollusc Any invertebrate of the phylum Mollusca, typically having a *calcareous* shell of one, two or more pieces that wholly or partly enclose the soft, unsegmented body, including chitons, snails, bivalves, squids and octopuses.
monolith A single block or piece of stone of considerable size.
monotreme An egg-laying mammal of the order Monotremata, comprising only the platypus and the echidnas of Australia and New Guinea.
monsoon The seasonal wind of the Indian Ocean and south Asia, blowing from the south-west in summer and from the north-east in winter; the season during which the south-west monsoon blows, commonly marked by heavy rains; rainy season.
moss Any tiny, leafy-stemmed, filamentous *bryophyte* of the class Musci, growing in tufts, sods or mats on moist ground, tree trunks, rocks, etc.
Oligocene Pertaining to the third epoch of the *Tertiary* period of geological time, between 38 and 26 million years ago; characterised by evidence of the first primates.
ophiolite A sub-aerial body formed by a portion of exposed ocean crust.
overgrazing The practice and result of running a greater number of grazing animals on a piece of pasture land than that land is ecologically able to sustain.
palaeomagnetism The study of magnetism found in ancient rocks.
palaeontology The study of life in the geological past.
Palaeozoic Pertaining to a geological era occurring between 570 and 230 million years ago, when fish, insects and reptiles first appeared.
pelagic Pertaining to the upper layers of the open sea.
phalanger An Australasian arboreal *marsupial* characterised by dense fur and a long tail.
plate tectonics A geological theory that describes the Earth's crust as divided into a number of rigid plates, movement of which accounts for such phenomena as continental drift and the distribution of earthquakes.
Pleistocene Pertaining to the epoch of the Quaternary period of geological time beginning about two million years ago and ending 10 000 years ago, being the time of the last Ice Age and of the advent of modern humans.
Pliocene Pertaining to a geological epoch of the *Tertiary* period, occurring from 10 to 2 million years ago, when mammalian life was proliferating and the climate began to cool.
Precambrian Pertaining to the earliest era of geological time which ended 570 million years ago and, during which, the Earth's crust formed and life first appeared in the seas.
Proteaceae A family of shrubs with cone-like flower heads native to the southern hemisphere.
pteridophyte Any of the division of flowerless plants including ferns, clubmosses and horsetails.
Quaternary Pertaining to the present geological period, forming the latter part of the *Cainozoic* Era, which began about 2 million years ago, and including the *Recent* and *Pleistocene* Epochs.
quoll A ferocious carnivorous *marsupial* about the size of a small cat.
radiocarbon dating See *carbon dating*.
Recent See *Holocene*.
relict species Any animal or plant species which has survived in a primitive form since an earlier geological age.
roaring forties Blustery ocean winds occurring between the latitudes 40° and 50° South.
rufous Of an animal, to be reddish-brown in colour.
salinity Pertaining to the amount of salt contained in a body of water.
savannah A plain characterised by coarse grasses and scattered tree growth.
scleromorphy An adaptation of plants resulting in leathery, hard, spiny or reduced leaves with the purpose of reducing moisture loss.
sclerophyll Pertaining to those plants exhibiting the characteristic of *scleromorphy*.
seismic Pertaining to an earthquake or vibration of the earth.
selenite A glassy form of gypsum.
siltation The process by which a water channel becomes blocked with sediment.
sinkhole A hole formed in soluble rock by the action of water, serving to conduct surface water to an underground passage.
skink Any small lizard of the family Scincidae.
sphagnum Any spongy moss of the genus *Sphagnum* occurring chiefly in bogs; used for potting and packing plants.
spinifex Australian grass with pointed leaves and spiny seed-heads.
stalactite A deposit, usually of calcium carbonate, shaped like an icicle, hanging from the roof of a cave or the like, and formed by the dripping of percolating *calcareous* water.
stalagmite A deposit, usually of calcium carbonate, resembling an inverted *stalactite*, formed on the floor of a cave or the like by the dripping of percolating *calcareous* water.
stromatolite A body formed by the mineralisation of an aggregation of ancient microbial organisms.
tectonic Pertaining to the structure of the Earth's crust; referring to the forces or conditions within the Earth that cause movements of the crust. See *plate tectonics*.
Tertiary Pertaining to the earlier period of the *Cainozoic* Era, beginning about 65 million years ago, during which, mammals gained ascendancy.
travertine A form of limestone deposited by springs.
trawling Fishing by means of a large, wide-mouthed net dragged along the bottom of a body of water.
wallaby Any of various *marsupials* of the family Macropodidae, being smaller than kangaroos and having large hind feet and long tails.
wetland (Often, wetlands) land that has a wet and spongy soil, such as a marsh, swamp or bog.

The Great Barrier Reef
Queensland

The Great Barrier Reef has no equal among the Earth's coral reefs. The reef is the most extensive in the world and its nearly pristine environments support fauna of breathtaking diversity. The reef waters hold major populations of the endangered dugong and its islands provide vital nesting sites for the endangered green and loggerhead turtles. In addition to the visual spectacle of the coral reefs, the area contains a living laboratory of micro-organic colonies and geological processes. More than 4000 publications describe the reef and its environments, testifying to its great natural and cultural interest. These features, as well as the reef's cultural significance to both indigenous and non-indigenous Australians, led to the Great Barrier Reef being inscribed on the World Heritage List in 1981.

Location

The Great Barrier Reef covers an area of 348 700 square kilometres (134 600 square miles) off the north-east coast of Australia between the latitudes 24°30' South and 10°41' South. Lying off the Queensland coast, the reef extends some 2000 kilometres (1250 miles) from Fraser Island just below the Tropic of Capricorn, northwards to Cape York and the coastal waters of Papua New Guinea. The marine park includes the Capricorn-Bunker Group National Park but excludes the islands which form part of the State of Queensland. The Capricorn-Bunker Group National Park constitutes a land component of the marine park, represented by Hoskyn, Heron, Fairfax and Lady Musgrove Islands, although the latter two are coral cays.

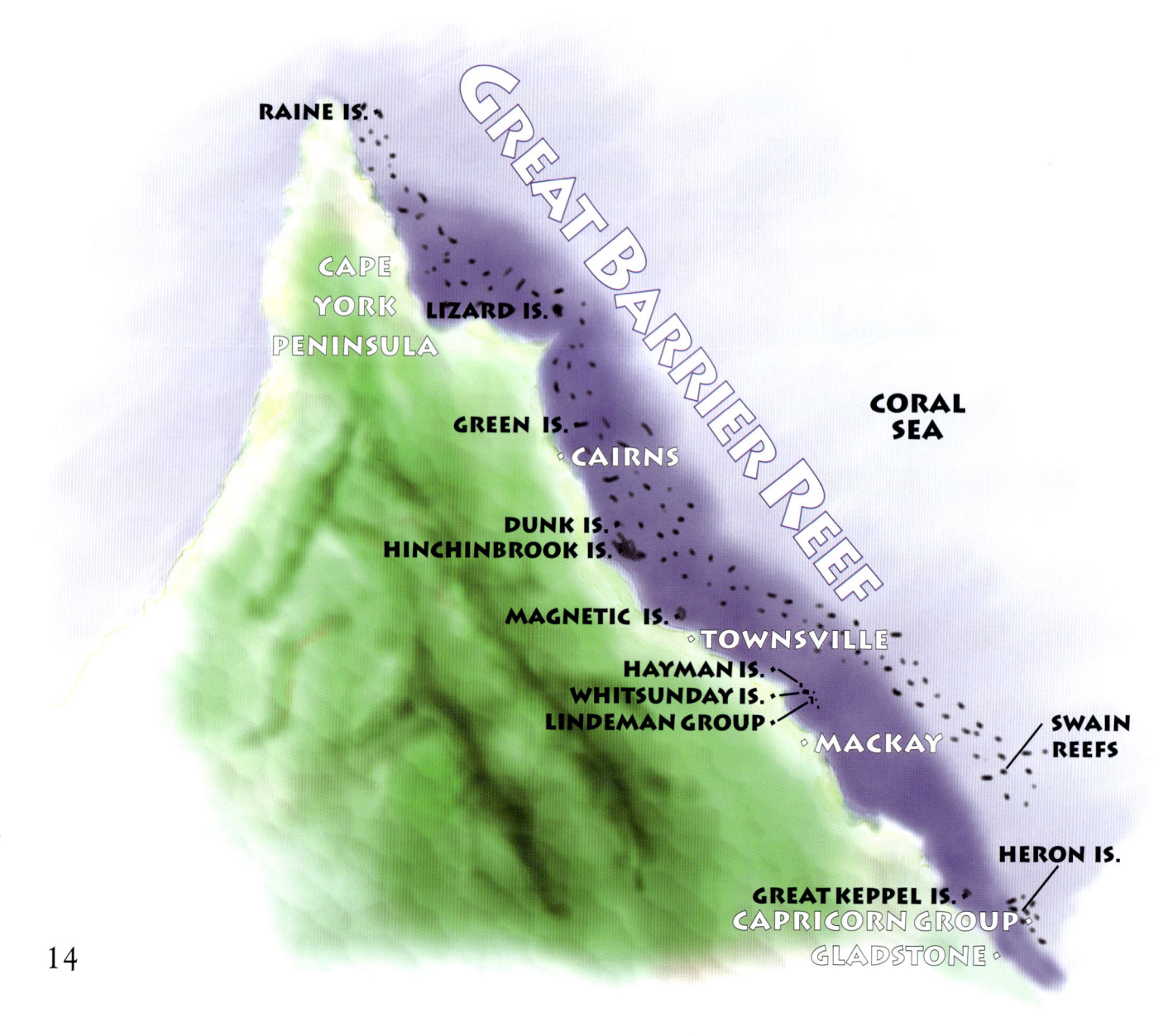

The Great Barrier Reef
by Vincent Serventy

The Great Barrier Reef is more a maze than a barrier. Perhaps Captain Cook is to blame for the name, as he wrote:

"It is a wall of Coral Rock rising almost perpendicular out of the unfathomable ocean...".

This maze of more than 2900 individual reefs stretches 2000 kilometres (1240 miles) from near Fraser Island in the south to the tip of Cape York in the north. Some of the reefs are separated by channels only a few hundred metres wide, some are 20 kilometres (12 miles) apart and they range from less than a hectare to a 100 square kilometres (40 square miles) in extent.

There are three basic coral reef structures. Platform, or patch reefs, develop when the corals grow out in all directions, while wall reefs grow vertically, aided by strong currents that bring plentiful food. Some reefs are exposed at low tide but a too-long exposure to sun and air is fatal to most corals and nature's pruning keeps them below water. Small islands of sand may form with time and develop a plant cover. These are the true coral cays. Seventy-one cays are known, including the popular holiday resorts of Green Island and Heron Island. Closer to the coast are the continental islands; pieces of the mainland cut off by rising sea levels at the end of the last Ice Age some 10 000 years ago. Many of these islands also develop fringing reefs of great beauty and diversity.

Geologists believe that the reef began to grow about two million years ago but it was not the permanent feature it seems today. The waxing and waning of Ice Ages led to rising and falling sea levels. The last melting of the ice caps, some 10 000 years ago, saw the sea advance and push back the Aborigines who had hunted over the land where coral reefs now grow.

The great maze of reefs fall into three sections. The northern one is narrow and shallow, most of it less than 30 metres (100 feet) deep. The few breaks in it are well known as they offer an escape from the stormy oceans into sheltered waters. The central section has deeper water, ranging from 36 to 55 metres (120 to 180 feet) with a 15 kilometres (9 miles) wide channel in the north, and a 50 kilometres (30 miles) wide channel in the south. There are fringing reefs and many platform reefs along the islands. The southern section is the widest and deepest and has an aggregation of patch reefs with the Capricorn and Bunker groups of islands at its southern end.

The wealth of organic growth makes this region unlike any other. In the words of its nomination for World Heritage listing:

"... the largest collection of coral reefs in the world. Biologically it supports the most diverse ecosystems known to man...".

Reef-building corals have existed for more than 400 million years, although as already mentioned, the present Great Barrier Reef is very young, and has grown for only about 8000 years. The hard coral polyps have built the largest living structure in the world, either on land or in the sea. Although the coral polyps are the major architects, limy algae make an indispensable contribution in binding the skeletons of all the marine creatures that live here.

Some 340 species of coral are described from the region; their forms are branching like the staghorn or massive like brain shaped corals. Some grow as huge plates, some as crusts on other reef material. Mushroom corals live as single polyps and look like overturned brown or pink mushrooms. The soft corals lack limy skeletons. Some species, aptly called dead man's fingers, hang limp at low tide. Sea fans and sea whips are created by various kinds of polyps.

The coral animals grow rapidly in the warm, clear water. One piece was observed to develop 25 000 new polyps in a thousand days. Corals like temperatures of between 20° and 30° Celsius (68° and 86° Fahrenheit) and water from 5 to 28 metres (16 to 92 feet) deep. Clear water allows sunlight to reach their tissues. The living flesh of corals has myriads of tiny green plants that are the major reason for their productivity. Corals are tiny and a single lump of living reef may weigh tonnes and contain millions of individuals.

These creatures grow in the direction their food comes from. They are carnivores, as fierce in their way as a flesh-eating tiger quoll or a dingo, but they must wait for their prey to come close to their stinging tentacles. Some eat tiny fish while others eat their neighbours.

Many new individuals are budded from the parent but polyps can also reproduce sexually. Eggs develop in one parent and are released at the same time as the male sperm. Spawning corals are one of the great spectacles of the reef. Release times vary, although near Orpheus Island the season is short - four or five nights after a late spring full moon.

The steady trade winds blow most of the year so the visitor may find the winter a cool 18° Celsius (66° Fahrenheit). The winds lose strength in spring and summer, although this season may bring cyclones. Summer is also the time of seabird breeding and the time when turtles come ashore to nest.

Awe-inspiring is the best way to describe the return of the female green turtle to lay her eggs well above high water mark on a coral cay beach. Her nesting ritual stretches back for millions of years, to the age of the dinosaurs. The turtle first digs a large hollow with her front flippers, then she delicately scoops out an egg chamber with her hind flipper. She lays around 100 eggs, although as many as 182 have been recorded. Finally she covers the hole and heads back to sea. In one season a female might lay as many as ten egg-batches at two-week intervals, although she may not nest again for five years.

An extraordinary fact about the incubation of green turtle eggs is that when the sand temperature is below 30° Celsius (86° Fahrenheit) most of the hatchlings are male, around 30° Celsius (86° Fahrenheit) there are even numbers of both sexes, and above 30° Celsius (86° Fahrenheit) most are female.

The green turtle, the more agile loggerhead turtle and the beautiful hawksbill turtle nest along the length of the reef. The flatback turtle prefers to nest on continental islands as well as the mainland. Raine Island has the world's greatest concentration of breeding female green turtles, over 11 000 having been recorded in the one night. Their young hatch out after two months, usually at night, to avoid land predators like crabs and birds. Hunters such as sharks are waiting for them in the sea but, to keep the population stable, a pair need have only two surviving young, so nature makes allowance for the losses.

After nesting, green turtles may migrate a 1000 kilometres (620 miles). Their main food appears to be sea grasses and algae but baby turtles reared in captivity are comprehensive in their tastes and will eat small animal life. The loggerhead and hawksbill turtles are carnivores, which perhaps explains why the flesh of the vegetarian green turtle is more acceptable to human tastes. The giant of the tribe, the leathery turtle, browses on floating life in the sea, particularly jellyfish.

Uncountable numbers of microscopic plants, nourished by sunlight and fertilisers in the ocean, sustain the huge amount of animal life in the sea, 60% living in the upper surface. Like a rainforest, a coral reef ecosystem is self-sustaining. This explains its huge productivity in normally impoverished tropical oceans. Some nutrients are washed down in rain but most come up from the deeper layers, brought to the surface by currents and washed through the maze of coral reefs.

Tidal movements are crucial and currents of two metres (six feet) a second provide the force which pulls up the deep water and with it, the nutrients.

This floating life of the sea is not all microscopic. There is a bewildering variety, with some giants such as certain species of jellyfish. Blue is the dominant colour as it provides the best camouflage. Portuguese men-of-war or bluebottles, and the deadly box jellyfish, are a danger to people swimming in northern Australian seas (although the danger is near the coast, rather than around coral cays).

Creatures living in the reef are abundant, even in 'dead reefs' of coral rubble. Many of the molluscs are treasured as ornaments. There are the beautiful volutes (sea snails), and the potentially dangerous cone shells; some 4000 species are already described but many more are still in need of scientific examination. There are also the sea slugs, many of which are spectacular, like the Spanish dancer which waves its scarlet folds. The cuttlefish, squid and octopus are unusual molluscs that have almost, or entirely, discarded their shells.

The giant clam is the most famous mollusc. Its shell can be a metre long and weigh as much as 200 kilograms (440 pounds). A giant clam can grow from egg to commercial size in only two years. It grows rapidly because, like a coral polyp, it has single-celled algae in its tissues. This makes clams valuable for marine farming. Clam circles are being 'planted' on some Pacific islands. Dr Richard Braley, working with the Great Barrier Reef Marine Park Authority, has shown that clam densities as high as 100 per hectare may bring useful results for the peoples of the Pacific and Indian Oceans.

The crown-of-thorns starfish is a dangerous reef animal. It can be up to half a metre (one and a half feet) in diameter, and have from seven to 23 arms armoured with menacing spines. This starfish spreads its stomach out of the body, surrounds the food and digests it, then withdraws the stomach and moves on.

Coral polyps are an attractive and plentiful food supply. Once the seastar was uncommon on the reef, but a series of population explosions have devastated vast areas of reef. A seastar may lay 20 million eggs and such irruptions are common in nature. Why this particular seastar has become a serious problem on the reef is a hotly debated topic and the subject of continuing research.

This seastar is not the only threat to the reef. In 1925 a cyclone dumped so much freshwater on an exposed reef that it was destroyed. Forty years later the corals have recolonised but this is a span of time that is too long for a dependent tourist industry.

Seabirds nest in huge colonies. The most obvious is the sooty tern, a bird which likes to be close to the sea, and which nests in the thousands on suitable cays. Common noddies share coral cays with sooties but the black noddies prefer to nest in trees. Visitors admire the glorious red-tailed tropicbirds and those rakish pirates, the fast-flying frigatebirds, that force other birds to disgorge some of the food they are carrying home to their hungry chicks.

Captain James Cook made the reef known to the world of eighteenth century Europe but his exploration in 1770 almost came to an abrupt end when his ship the *Endeavour* hit coral. Cook was unaware of the danger, not realising he was sailing through a maze. He limped into an inlet where Cooktown now stands, repaired his ship and, laden with natural history specimens new to science, sailed north to Possession Island where he claimed this vast country for England. A few years later Captain Bligh, cast adrift by mutineers, made his extraordinary open boat voyage through the reef to safety and fame.

Others followed but it was scientists who revealed the wonders of this region. In 1928-29 the British-Australian Great Barrier Reef Expedition spent a year on Low Isles, bringing back so many specimens that some of them await study even now. The leader, now Sir Maurice Yonge, returned to his old site some years ago and said to me that the reefs had deteriorated so much he could never repeat his work.

That sort of warning caused conservationists to do battle to save the reef. Eventually a Royal Commission made a study of its future and the Great Barrier Reef Marine Park was set up. Research stations were founded at Lizard, Heron and One Tree Islands, and the Australian Institute of Marine Science was established near Townsville. The reef was added to the World Heritage List and scientists methodically developed management zones extending over its entire length.

Constant vigilance is needed if the reef is not to be destroyed. A decline in water quality in many regions has been noted and attributed to nutrients and pollutants coming from the mainland. Agriculture, forestry and sewage all add to this load. A recent estimate is that 25 million tonnes (24.6 million tons) of sediment, 77 000 tonnes (75 770 tons) of nitrogen and 11 000 tonnes (10 800 tons) of phosphorus find their way into Queensland waters each year. Studies into the affects has begun and may throw light on the problems this causes in conserving the reef. Even the crown-of-thorns starfish explosions may be due to influences such as these.

Earlier this century the scientist Professor Wood Jones referred to a remark made by an old sailor: ". . . Nobody can sail through Hinchinbrook Pass and not believe in God . . .". I believe that any person visiting this great wonder of the world must be changed for the better, and will become determined to protect the Great Barrier Reef.

ABOVE A blue seastar budding.

RIGHT A green turtle leaves a sandy coral cay for the sea. This highly endangered species feeds mainly on sea grasses growing in shallow and tropical waters. Female green turtles return to the beach where they were born to lay their eggs. Buried in beach sand and warmed by the sun, their eggs incubate for periods of 48 to 80 days before hatching.

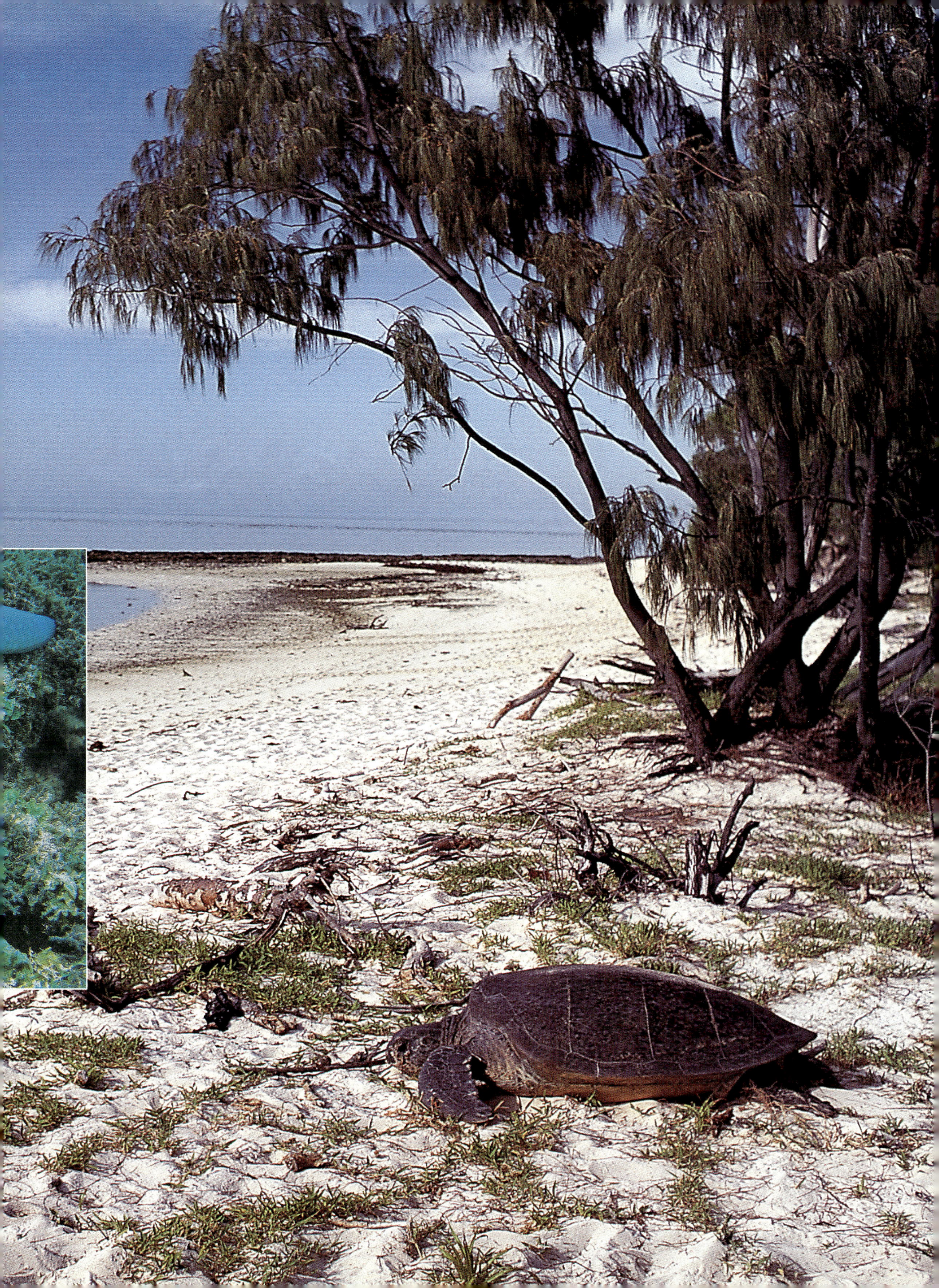

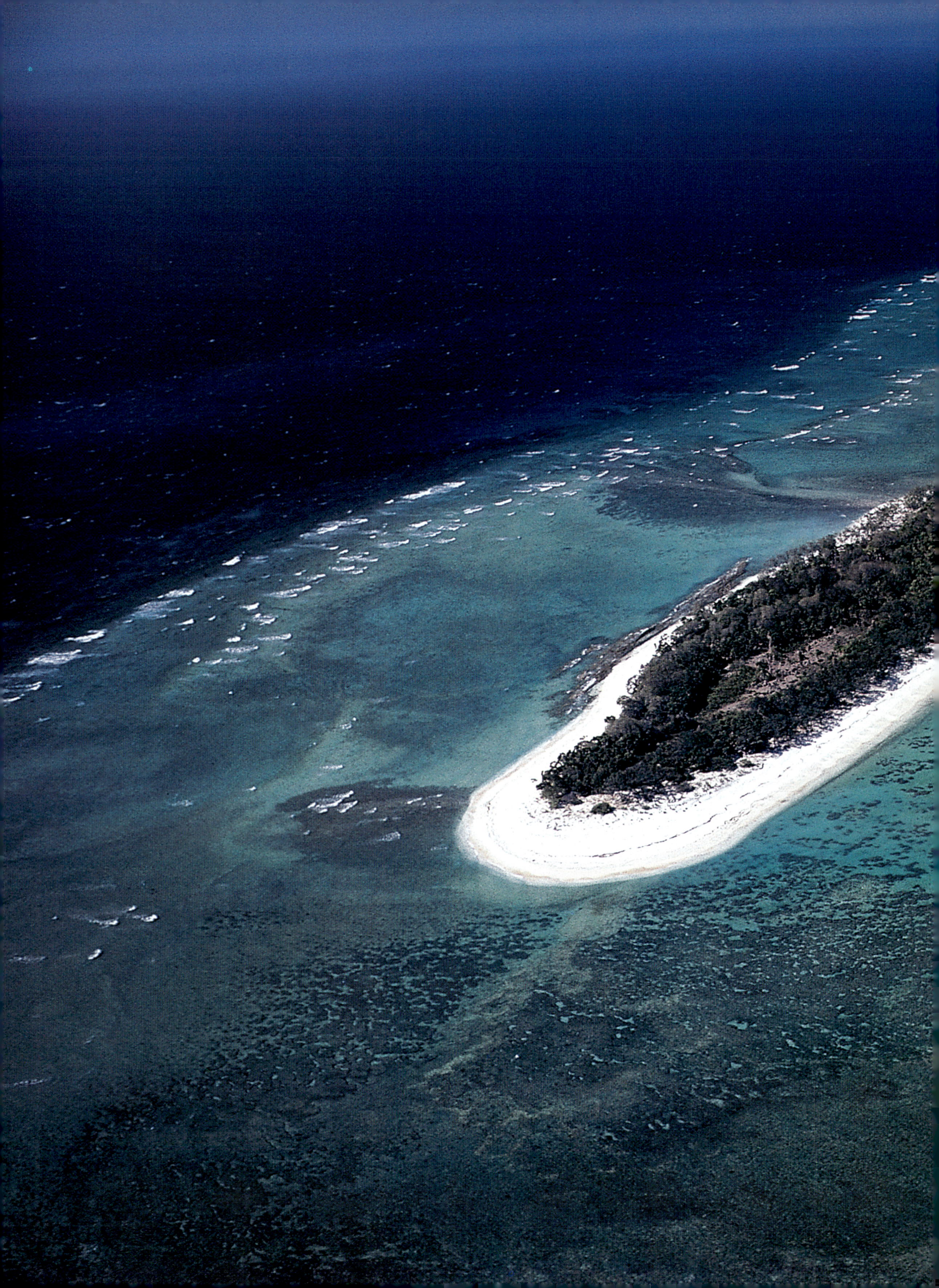

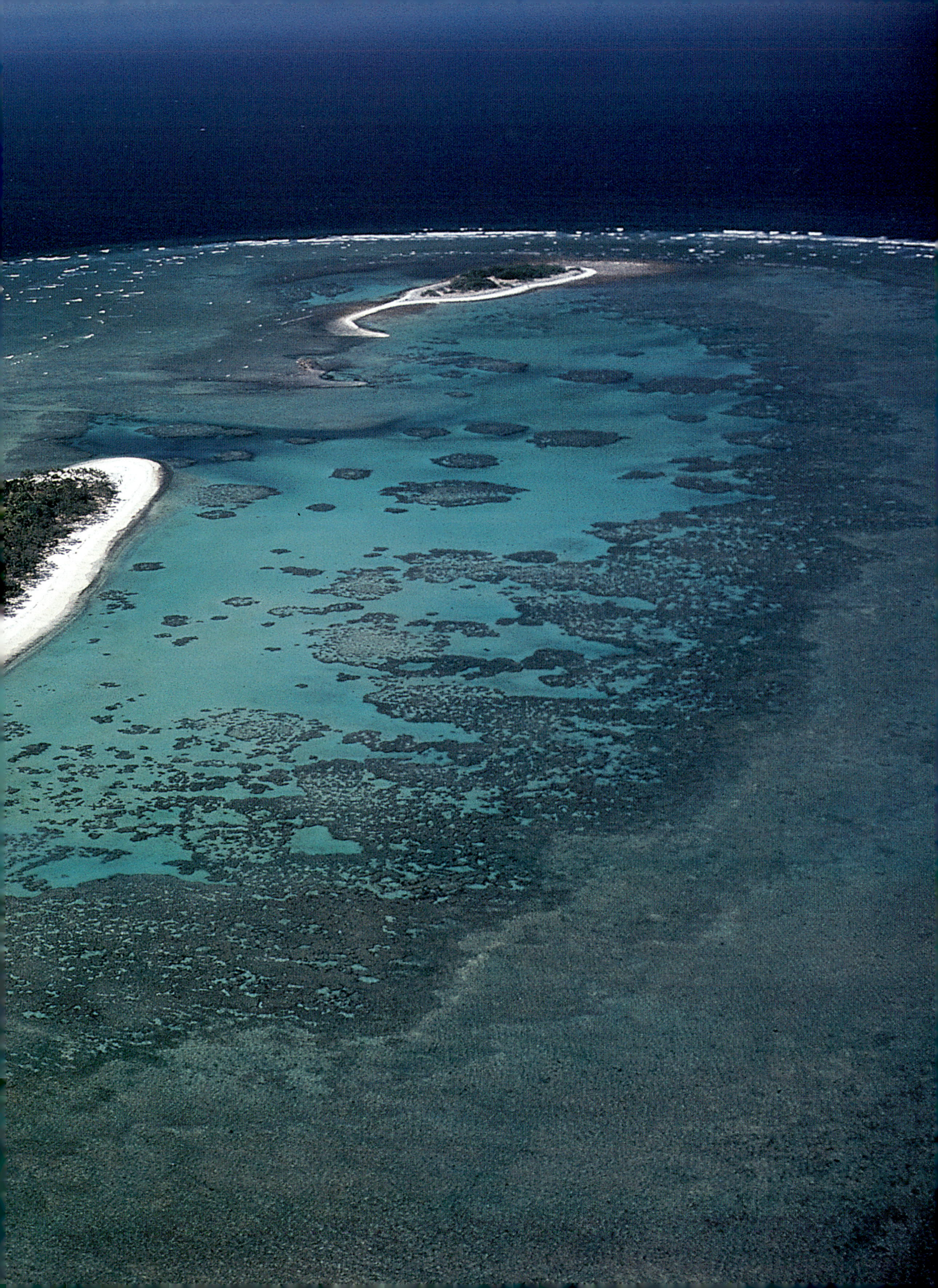

Physical Features

The Great Barrier Reef extends along most of the Queensland coastline and through a range of latitudes, giving it a large geographic and environmental variation. Marked differences occur with changes in latitude, allowing the park to be divided into three distinct sectors.

The northern sector, comprising all the reefs north of latitude 16° South, is distinguished by the shallowness of the water covering the continental shelf, which is usually less than 36 metres (120 feet) deep. Running along the edge of the continental shelf is an almost unbroken line of wall reefs, with numerous patch reefs lying between it and the Queensland coast. Many of these reefs form cays, some of which support communities of mangroves.

Between 16° South and 21° South is the park's central sector. Here, in considerably deeper water (36 to 55 metres or 120 to 180 feet), is a scatter of platform reefs that are separated from one another by distances of 5 to 10 kilometres (3 to 6 miles). They are separated from the mainland coast and coastal islands by a channel that is 15 kilometres (9 miles) wide in the north and widens out to 50 kilometres (30 miles) in the south. The park's southern sector (21° South to 24° South) has the deepest waters of all, extending down to 145 metres (475 feet). The northern part of this sector contains a maze of jagged reef-masses that are separated by channels as narrow as 100 metres (330 feet), with powerful tidal currents coursing through them. To the south, the tidal range is less extreme; here the outer continental shelf is dominated by small, tightly-packed patch reefs known collectively as the Swain Reefs. The Capricorn and Bunker Island groups emerge from a submerged ridge in the far south of this sector, half way between the mainland and the edge of the continental shelf. These island groups include many well-vegetated coral cays, amongst which Fairfax Island and Lady Musgrove Island are the most significant.

The climate of the Great Barrier Reef area is tropical, with warm temperatures, high humidity and a variable rainfall. It is influenced primarily by equatorial low pressure during summer months and by the sub-tropical high pressure zone during winter.

The air temperature ranges between 30° Celsius and 24° Celsius (86° Fahrenheit and 75° Fahrenheit) in mid-summer, dropping to 23° Celsius to 18° Celsius (73° Fahrenheit to 64° Fahrenheit) in July. The water temperature similarly peaks in summer and is at its lowest in July.

Rainfall varies greatly from year to year and in geographical distribution, but most comes during the summer months with the monsoon season and occasional tropical cyclones. Areas in the southernmost part of the park sometimes receive good rainfall in winter associated with winter depressions. Wind patterns are dominated by the south-east trade winds for most of the year, with monsoonal north-westerlies prevailing in the north of the park during summer. Huge waves and howling winds brought by cyclones can destroy fragile reef and coral cay environments, whilst freshwater run-off after very heavy rain may reduce sea-water salinity to levels that kill living corals.

PREVIOUS PAGE Fairfax Island is one of 71 cays slowly emerging from a coral base on the Great Barrier Reef. This aerial view suggests the important role of the fringing reef in the cay's protection.

RIGHT This balloon-shaped plant anchored to the coral floor is called Valona algae. It exemplifies the strange directions in evolution taken by life on the reef.

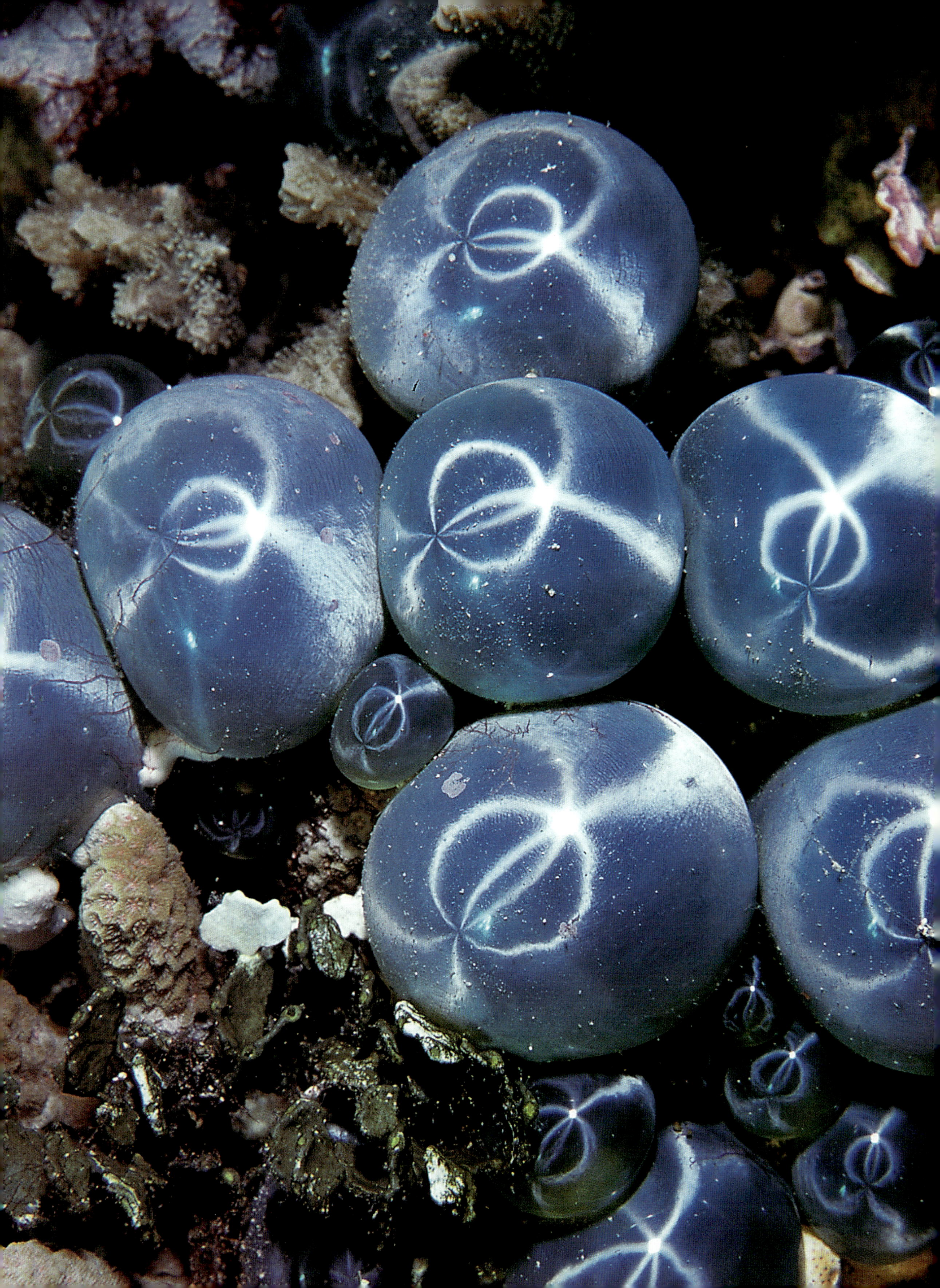

Special Features

The most remarkable and studied feature of the park is the famous Barrier Reef. Rather than forming a continuous barrier along the coast as the name suggests, the Great Barrier Reef is made up of 2900 individual reefs with a great variety in their form and structure. The reefs extend in a maze along the coastline and some 760 of them are fringing reefs, which vary in shape, and range in size from less than one hectare (2.47 acres) up to 10 000 hectares (24 700 acres). They provide some of the Earth's most breathtaking marine scenery.

The reefs are formed and maintained by the tiny calcareous skeletons of marine plants and animals. Some tropical marine organisms have the ability to produce substantial skeletons of calcium carbonate. This ability is most highly developed in the corals and results from the association between the coral polyps and plant cells found in their tissues. There are believed to be 400 coral species on the Great Barrier Reef, the majority of which produce calcareous skeletons. Depending upon the hydrology and the exposure of the area in which they develop, corals have a variety of growth forms and may occur as branching corals, rounded brain corals or plate-like corals. Some grow on other organisms or on reef debris, whilst unattached single polyps may form mushroom corals. Whatever their shape, these brilliantly coloured living corals make a display exceeding the most picturesque flower-garden.

There is much more to the Great Barrier Reef than its striking physical presence. The natural history of the reef is a continuing tale of life, death and deposition stretching back over 15 000 years. Between that time and 6000 years ago, the sea level on the north-east continental shelf of Australia rose 45 metres (150 feet) to reach its present-day level. As the rising waters covered sites suitable for colonisation by corals and other organisms, reefs began to form there. Suitable sites often included weathered limestone hillocks - the remains of reefs formed millions of years before. Typically, a modern reef consists of a veneer of living organisms overlaying a stratum of recent rapid coral growth one to five metres (3 to 16 feet) thick, all atop an ancient structure. The abundant and varied living veneer of the reef usually extends from the water's surface to a depth of about 40 metres (130 feet) where there is not enough light to sustain plant growth.

The coral reefs in the Great Barrier Reef are mainly of two types: platform or patch reefs, which are the result of radial growth; and wall or ribbon reefs resulting from elongated growth, typically in areas of strong water currents. Fringing reefs occur where reef growth is established on sub-tidal rocks off the mainland coast or a continental island.

Seventy-one of the reefs have formed coral cays, which represent a further stage in the life of a coral reef. Cays form most frequently on platform reefs, when sand and rubble are deposited by wind and water and accumulate there. Once a cay has reached the level where it remains exposed at high tide, it becomes a welcome resting place for sea birds. Over time, guano, or bird waste, builds up to form a layer of organic material in which salt-resistant seeds that have been washed onto the cay may lodge and germinate. When the cay has grown so large that not all fresh water runs off into the sea, a more varied plant life can take hold. The amount and variety of plant and animal life on a coral cay is almost entirely reliant upon the amount of rainfall it receives.

RIGHT Small tropical fish swim in the park waters in great abundance.

NEXT PAGE Green turtles mating in the shallow waters of a coral cay.

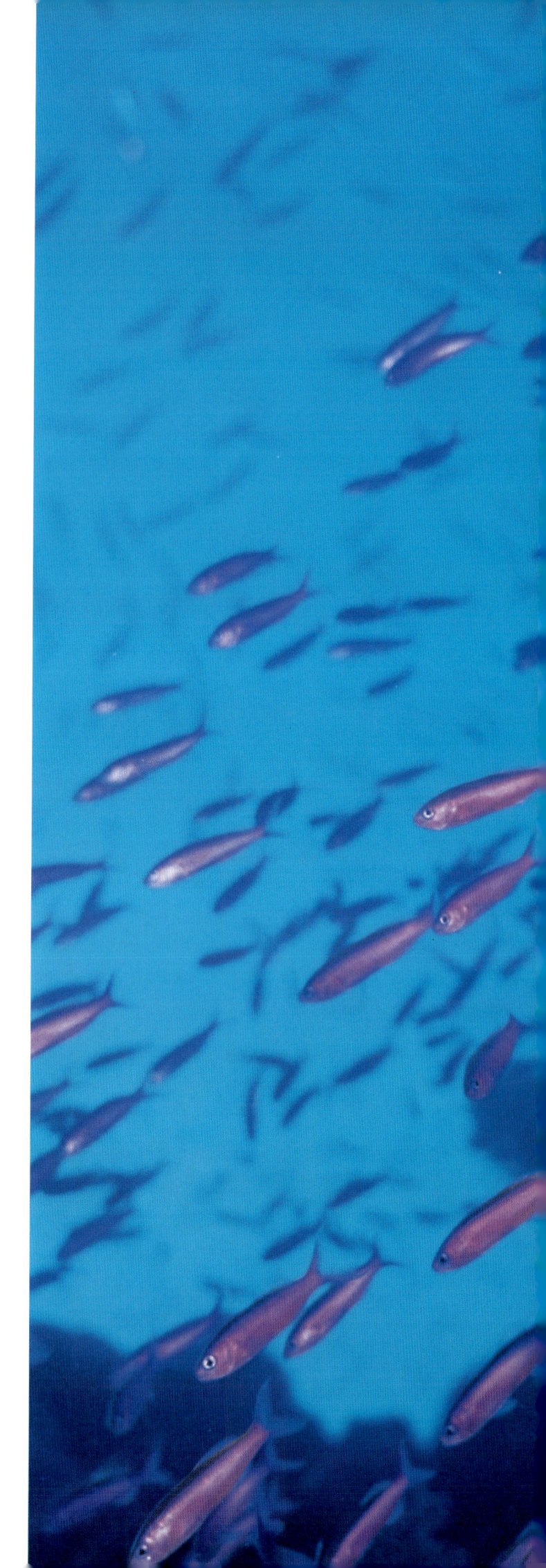

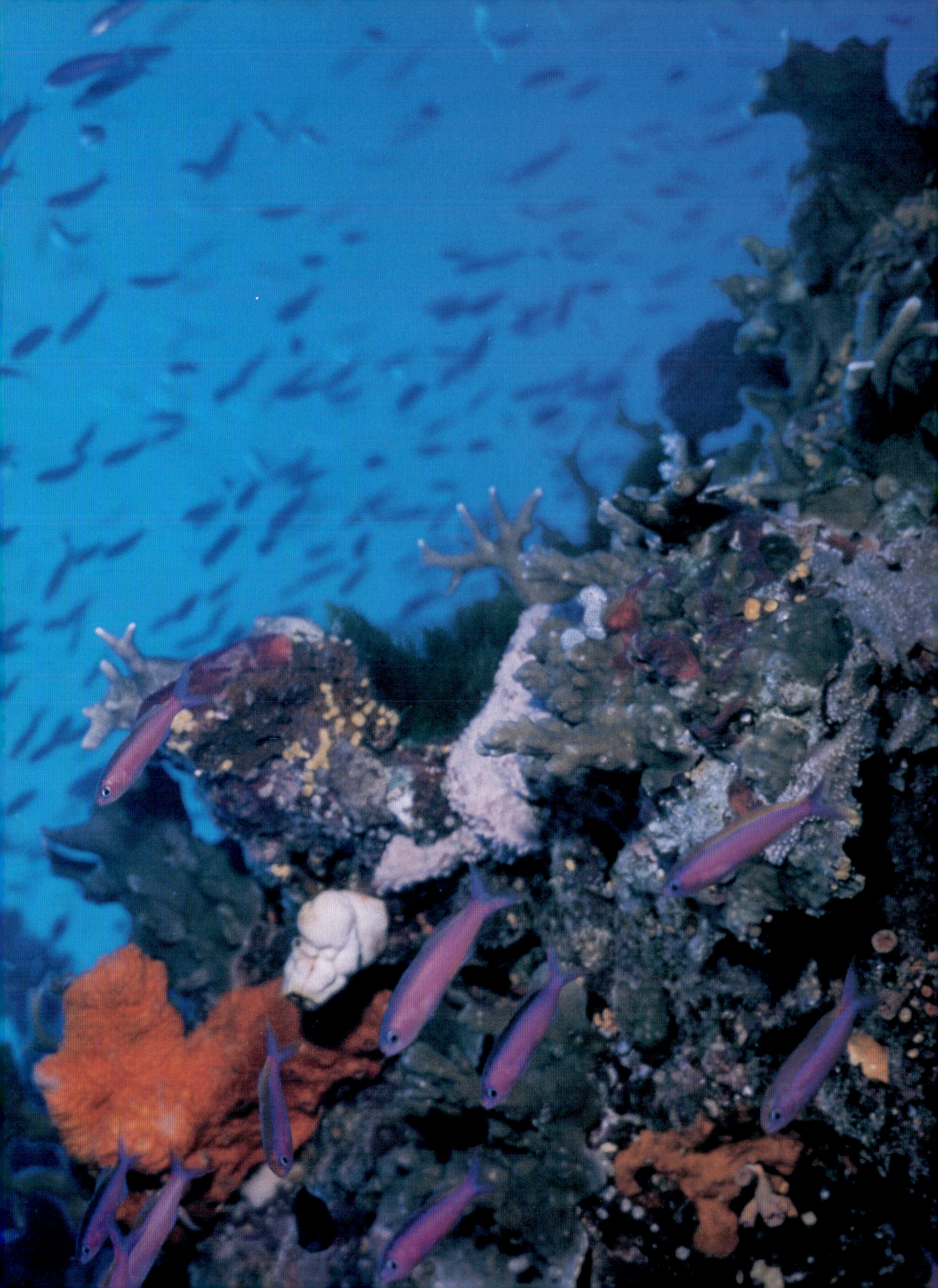

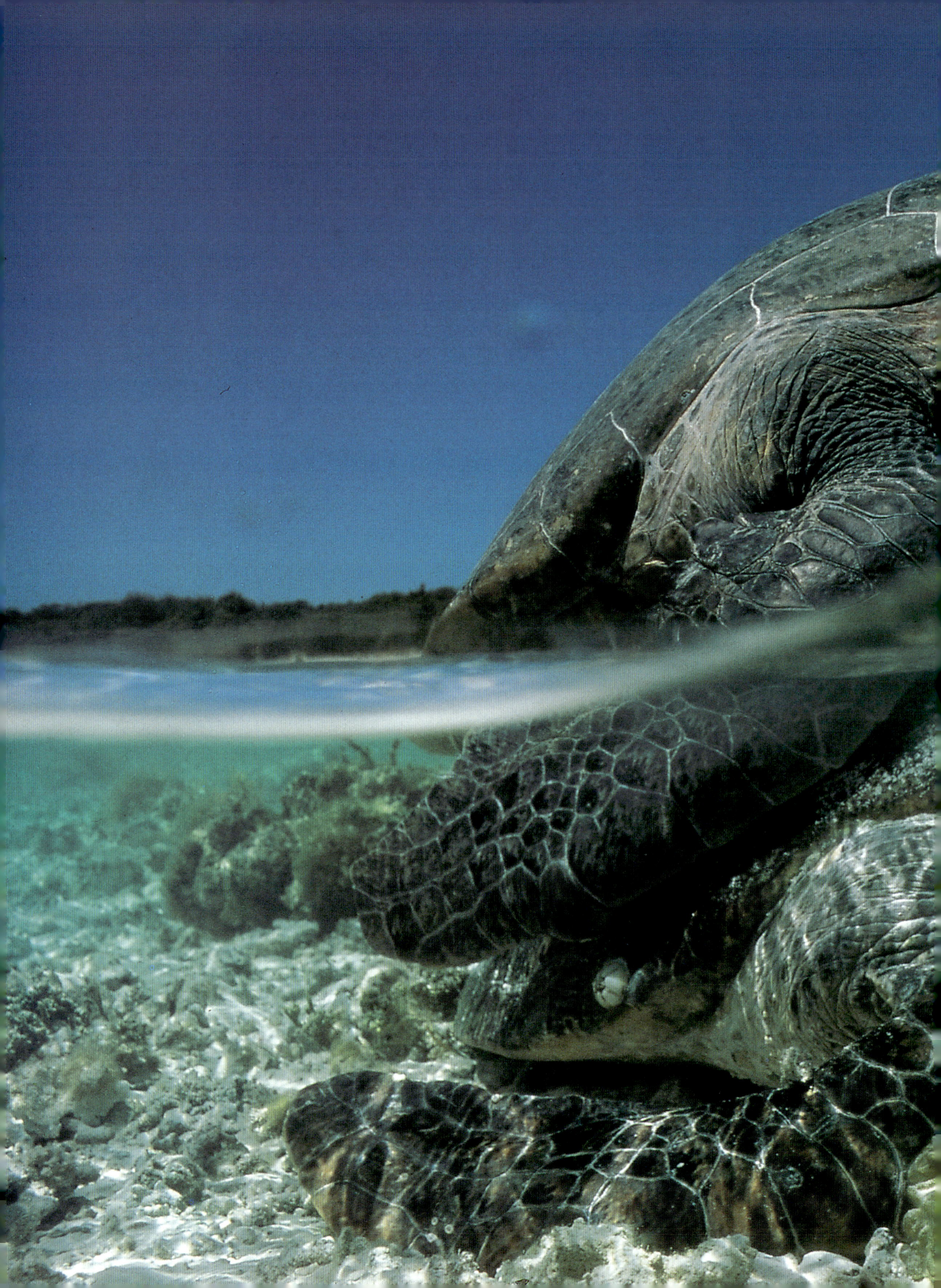

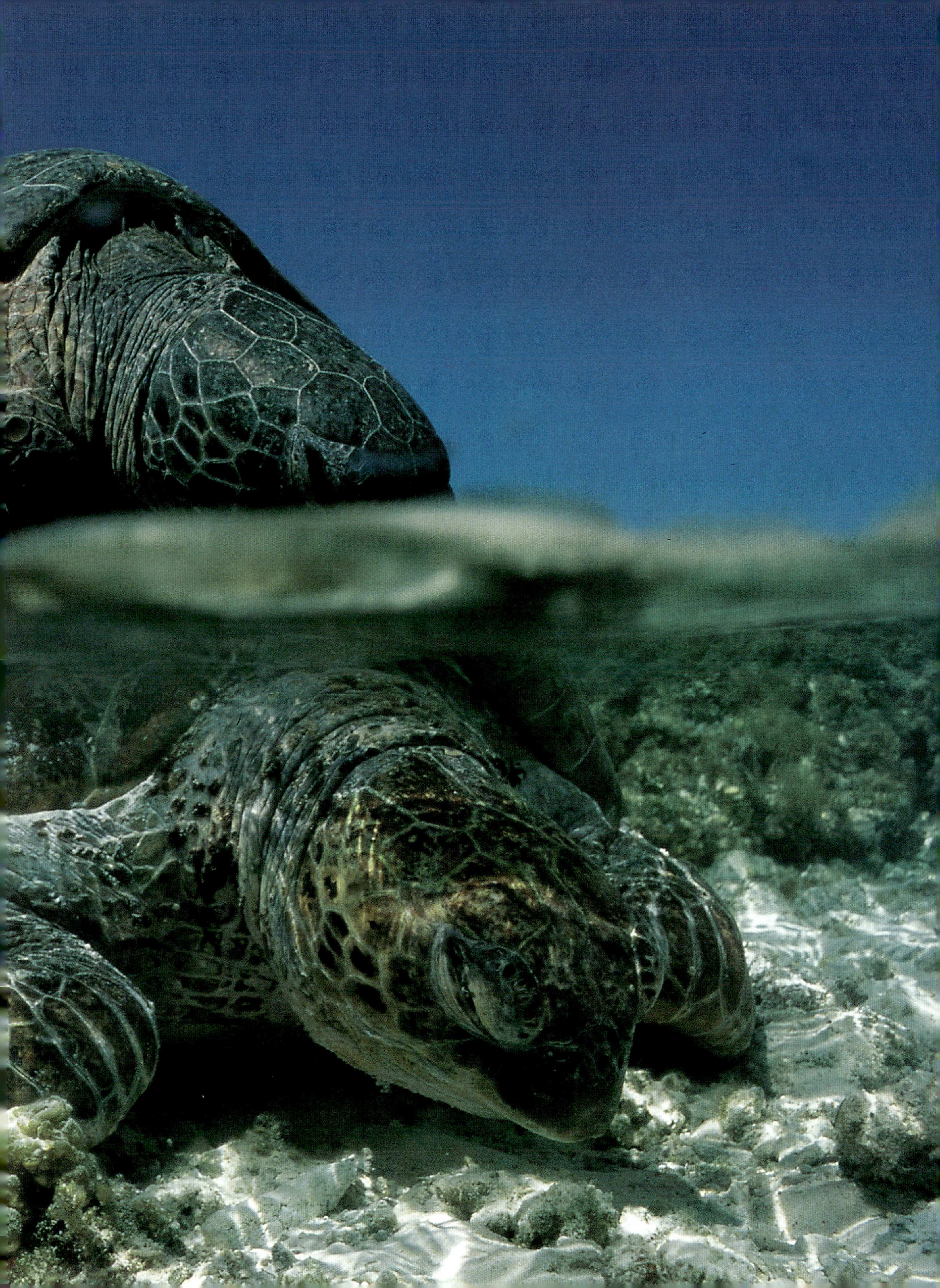

Flora

The Great Barrier Reef is predominantly a sea environment and so the flora of the reef is mainly a sea flora, with the groups best represented being the algae and sea grasses. The reef supports a great variety of fleshy algae, many of which are small and inconspicuous, but which provide an important food source for turtles, fish, molluscs and sea urchins. The two major algal groups found in the park are the Chlorophyta (green algae) and the Rhodophyta (red algae). Of the red algae, there are five genera, or groups of related species, which are calcareous, meaning they have a closely textured skeleton structure. This characteristic helps them to contribute to the formation of a resistant crust on the reef, adding to its protection from heavy and continuous wave action, as is often experienced during cyclones. The green algae types are not so important in protecting the reef from wave damage, but they do help to build up the reef by contributing sediment.

Sea grasses occur in small pockets throughout the length of the Great Barrier Reef. These grasses contribute to the diet of grazing animals such as fish and turtles. Extensive sea grass meadows are found only in some inshore coastal areas, where they are vital feeding grounds for the dugong.

NEXT PAGE A face-to-face meeting with a large potato cod.

BELOW Yellow coral.

RIGHT The view from Shaw Peak in the Whitsunday group.

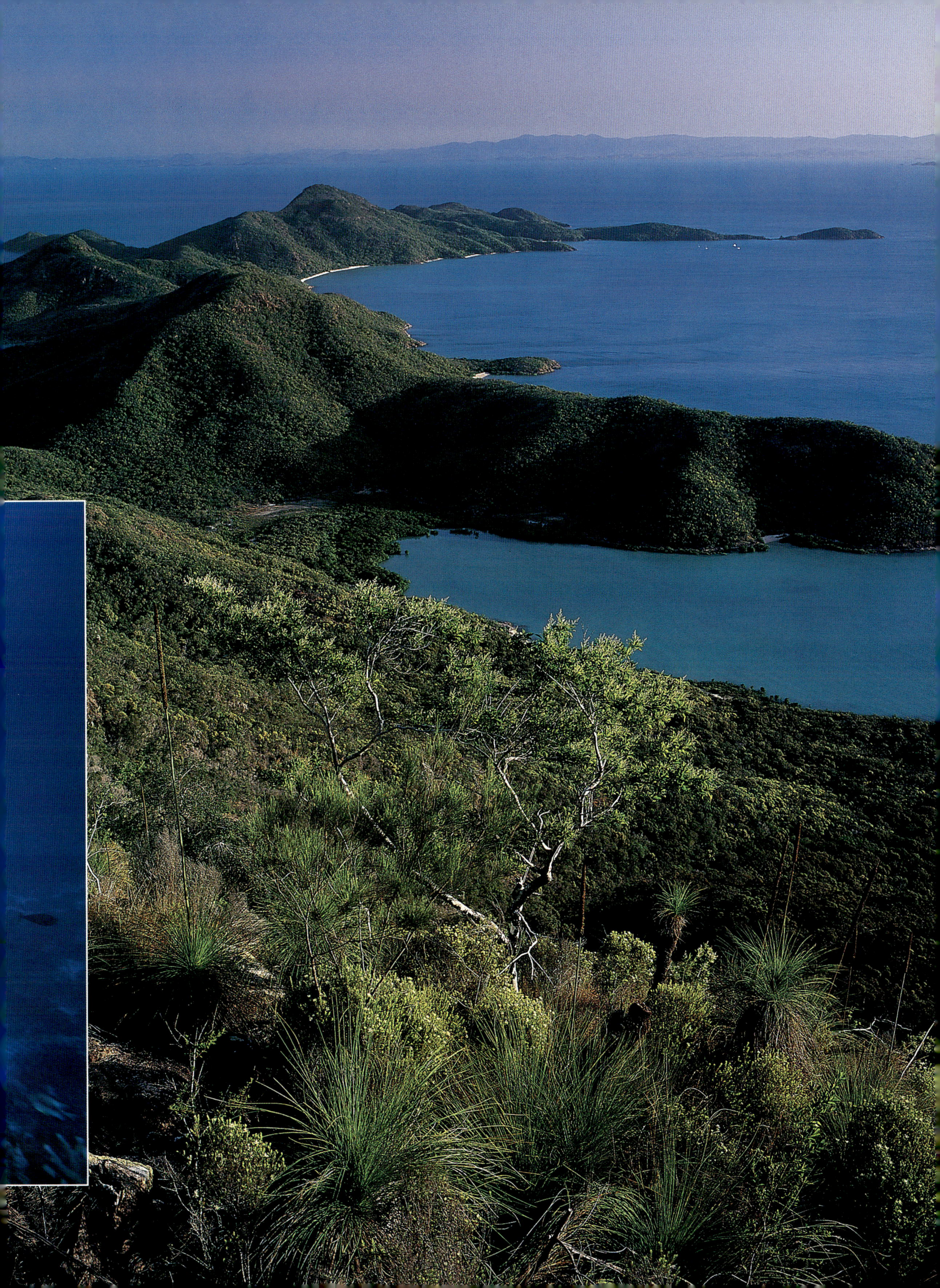

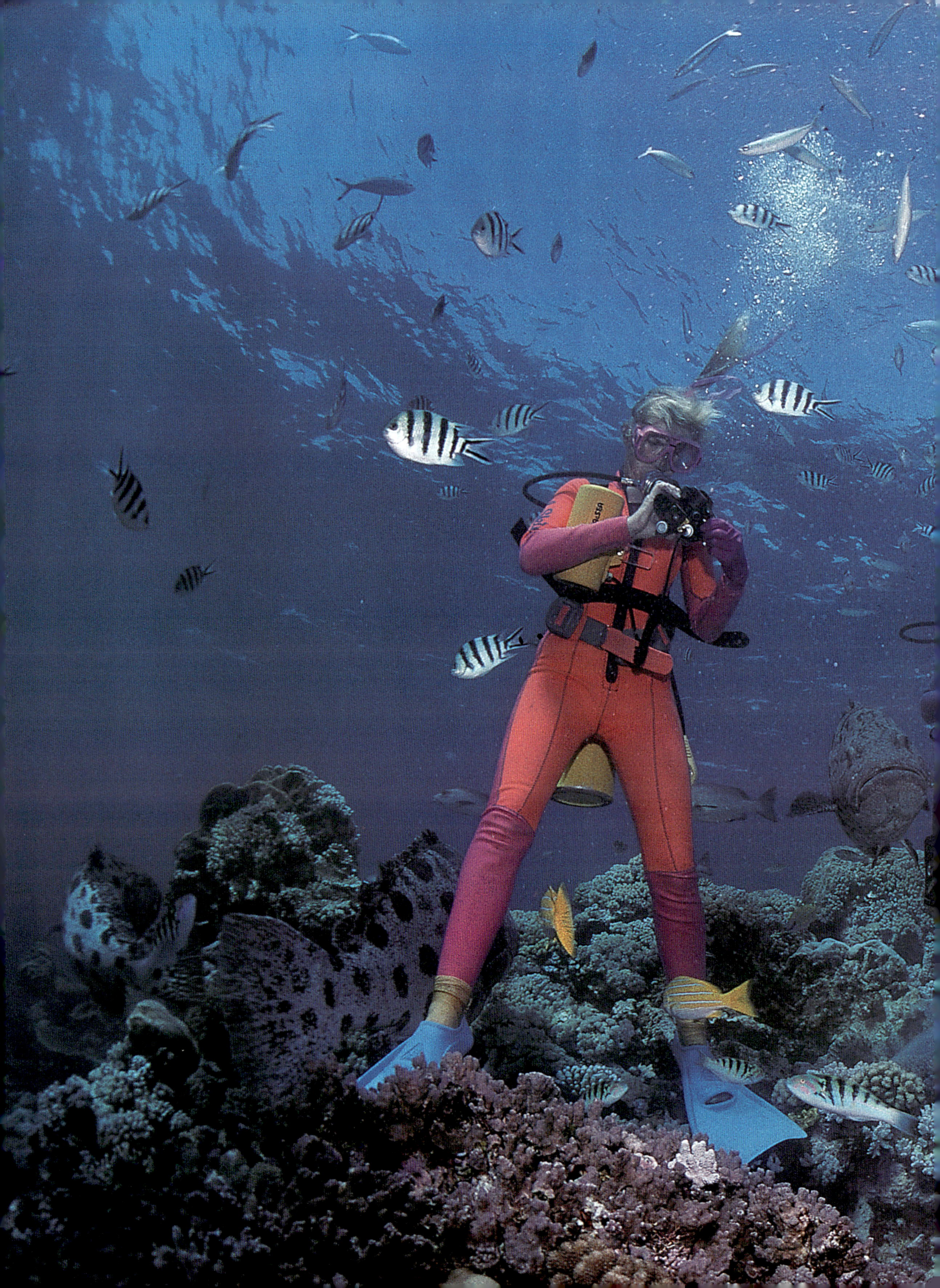

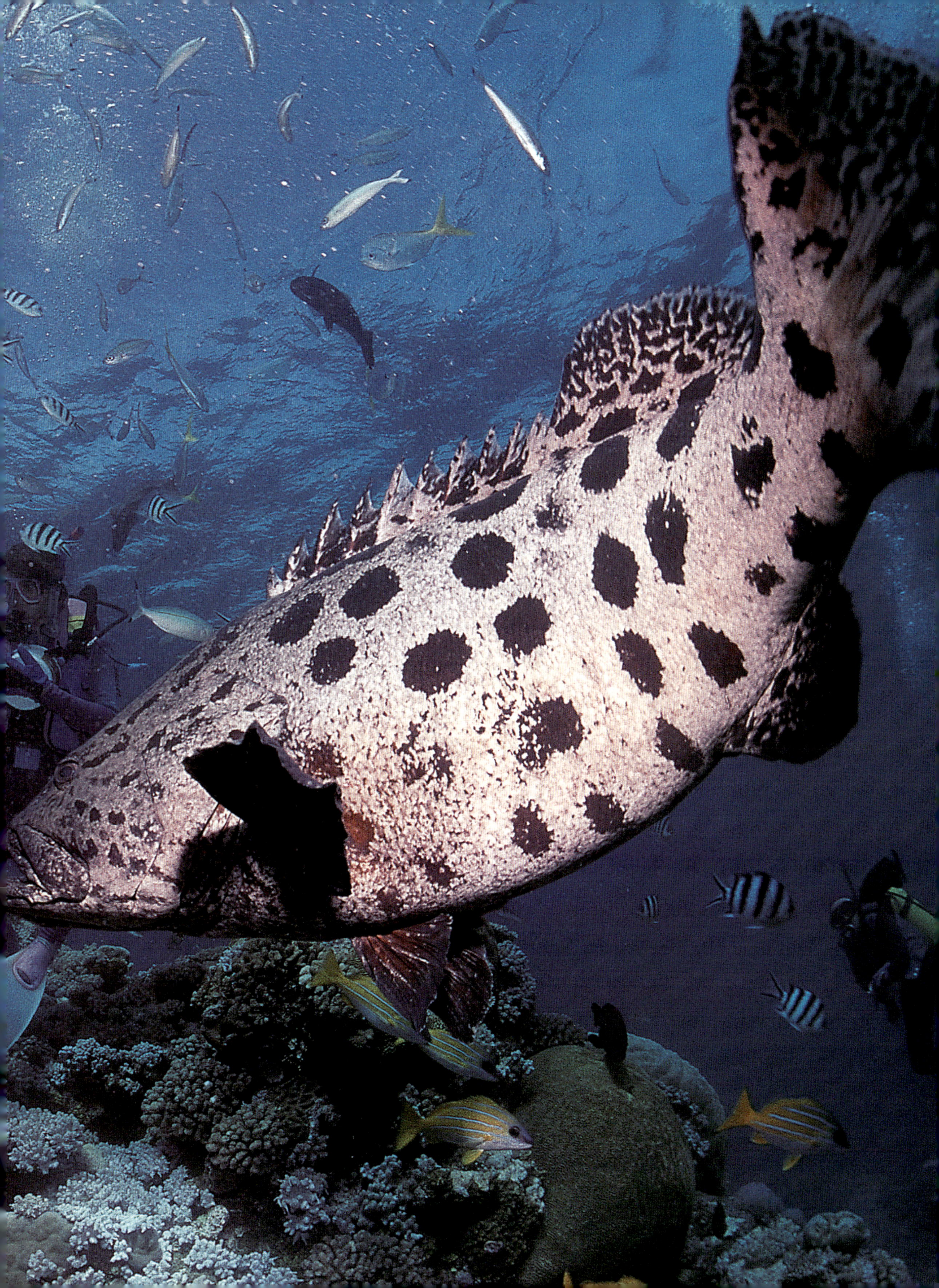

Fauna

The fauna of the Great Barrier Reef are extraordinary in their diversity and this is so at all levels from micro-organisms to mammals. Apart from the corals, reef invertebrates (animals without backbones) include sponges, molluscs, echinoderms, anemones and marine worms. These are essential to the growth and survival of the reef as they penetrate and break up coral and other structures, producing large amounts of debris.

Of the 4000 mollusc species which have so far been collected from the reef, some of the better known are trochus shells, helmet shells, cowrie shells and the weighty and impressive giant clams.

The echinoderms include the beautiful and brightly coloured starfish, sea urchins of many shapes and sizes, and the sea slug, or bêche-de-mer, which was sought after in Asia in earlier times and was probably the Australian continent's first exported product.

The Great Barrier Reef supports some 1500 fish species. Among the pelagic, or open-water dwelling fish, are the marlin - highly prized among sport fishermen - and the mackerel. Bottom-dwelling fish include large and colourful species such as the coral trout, sweetlip, red emperor, snapper and cod, all of which live in and around the reefs. Territorial species like the butterfly fish and damsel fish spend most of their adult lives on the few square metres of reef which form their home. Small, and coloured brightly in all imaginable hues, these elegant-looking fish often feature in home aquariums but they are seen at their best defending their little domains amongst the coral.

The reef area plays an important part in the life-cycles of several turtle species, including the endangered green and loggerhead turtles which nest in some areas. Other turtle species found in the area are the leatherback, flatback, hawkbill and Pacific Ridley. All are protected under both Australian Commonwealth and state laws.

Large marine mammals occur in the park, although the range of species is not fully known. Sizeable populations of the endangered dugong graze on the inshore seagrass beds which are considered a major feeding ground for this species. Humpback, minke and killer whales are also found in the area, as well as bottlenose, Irrawaddy and Indo-Pacific humpback dolphins. Spinner dolphins are occasionally sighted.

Some of the earliest research in the area that now forms the Great Barrier Reef Marine Park was carried out by ornithological expeditions, which were drawn to the reef by the variety of birdlife to be seen there. Amongst the larger sea birds, these early researchers recorded the stately reef heron, the osprey, the ungainly pelican, frigate birds and majestic sea eagles, as well as the more common terns, gulls and shearwaters. In all, the reef's cays and islands support 242 bird species including 40 sea-birds. The area's importance as a nesting habitat is considerable, with 21 species of sea-bird maintaining breeding colonies and the breeding sites of 109 land-birds recorded there.

ABOVE Hermit crabs are 'squatters' that make their home in abandoned sea snail shells or the hollows of coral skeletons. As they grow, they are forced to move into larger premises, but unlike other crabs, they have a soft abdomen of modest proportions which can be shaped to fit each new home.

RIGHT Specimens of black coral, pink sponge and yellow fine coral are prevalent on the outer reef, off Cairns.

BELOW The Great Barrier Reef anemonefish is common on the reef and makes its home amongst one of the reef's four species of anemone. These tiny tropical fish grow to four centimetres (two inches) in length and enjoy an immunity to the poisons of the anemone which are deadly to most other fish.

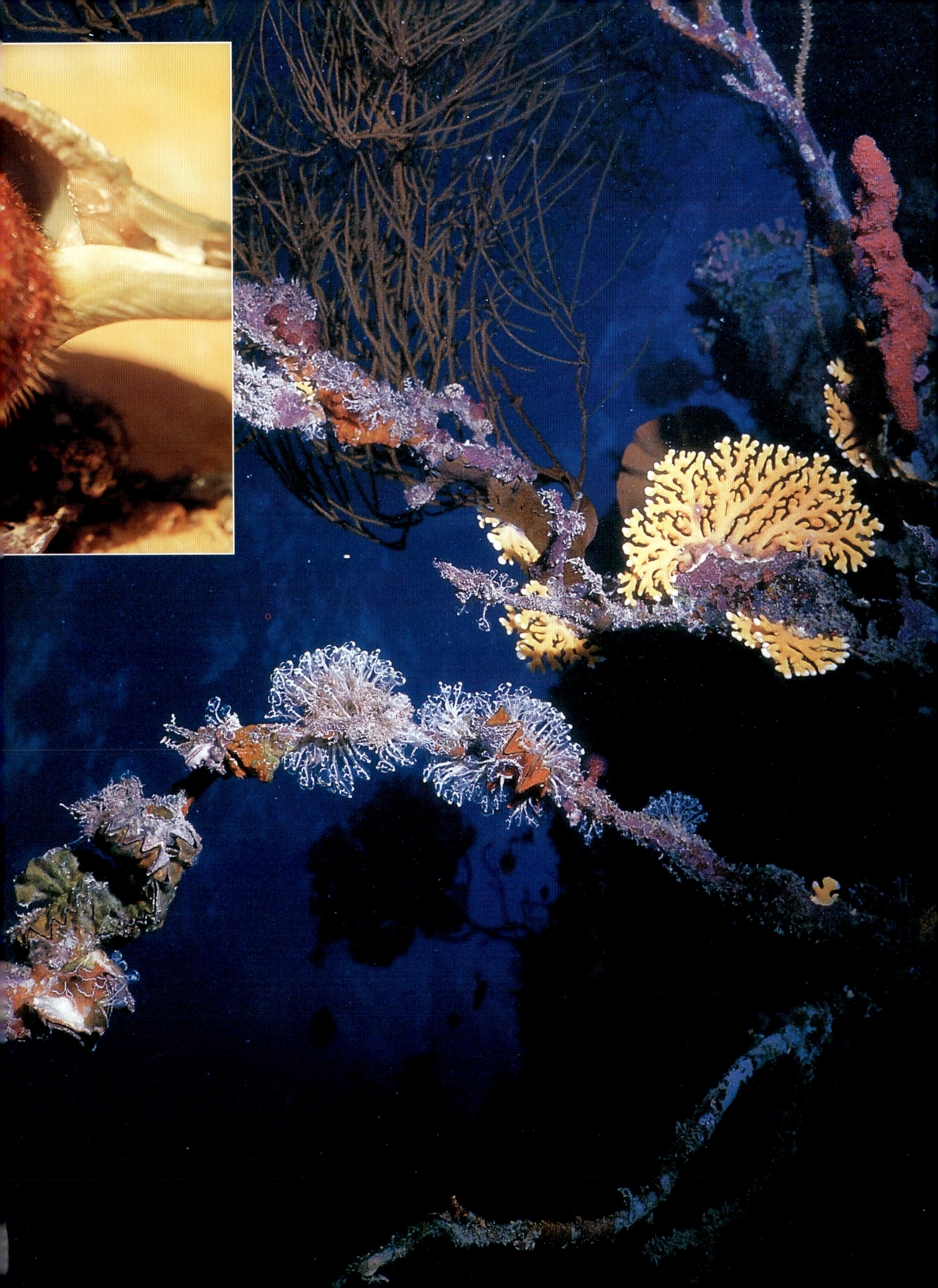

Cultural Heritage

The Great Barrier Reef is an important element in the history and culture of many of the Aboriginal groups of coastal north-eastern Australia. Aboriginal people ranged over the continental shelf before the sea submerged it at the end of the last Ice Age. This was before the development of the present-day reef began, some 15 000 years ago. Aborigines used the marine ecosystems from the beaches of the coastal mainland to the offshore islands and fringing reefs. In the north they used single and double outrigger canoes which could carry up to four adults and served both as a hunting platform and for transport.

The coastal peoples spent most of the year in a fairly small area, moving only 500 metres (a third of a mile) or so at a time when they needed a clean campsite or wished to be closer to a seasonal abundance of foods such as yams or crabs. Every two to three years, large gatherings would be held at long-established sites where ceremonies and trade would take place.

There is evidence that the Barrier Reef region was visited by non-indigenous peoples before the 1770 voyage of the *Endeavour* under Captain James Cook. Chinese, Portuguese and Spanish mariners are known to have visited Timor and other areas to Australia's near north in the fifteenth and sixteenth centuries, and fishermen from Macassar (now Ujung Pandang, Indonesia) visited the coast of what is now the Northern Territory in search of bêche-de-mer from the mid-eighteenth century up to 1906. It has been suggested that some sixteenth century French maps show a portion of the north-east Australian coast and that these maps were drawn from information collected on a Portuguese voyage in 1522-24.

In June 1770 Captain James Cook's ship the *Endeavour* ran aground on a reef near modern-day Cooktown in the course of an exploration of the Australian coast. Cook was able to beach his ship, repair it and returned to England safely.

The Great Barrier Reef has always posed a danger to shipping. Some 30 historically significant wrecks lie within the marine park area, including the *Pandora* which sank in 1791 while carrying prisoners involved in the notorious mutiny on Captain Bligh's ship, the Bounty. Another notable wreck is the *SS Yongala* which capsized in a cyclone with the loss of 122 lives.

Navigation difficulties led to the erection of numerous lighthouses, some of which are of historical importance. The Raine Island lighthouse was constructed by convict labour in 1844. Now derelict, it has been listed by the National Trust of Queensland. The lighthouses on Lady Elliott and North Reef islands remain in operation and are fine examples of nineteenth century riveted steel plate construction.

The Great Barrier Reef is a striking natural feature on a massive scale and as such has been the subject of innumerable scientific expeditions since the time of Cook. These began with Matthew Flinders in the *Investigator* (1802-03) and continue today in the work of various tertiary institutions and research bodies such as the Australian Institute of Marine Science and the Australian Museum.

European exploitation of the reef for economic purposes reached a peak during the late nineteenth century. During this time a number of cays on the reef were mined for guano or phosphate rock. Many of these operations involved a substantial workforce, such as that at North West Island which in 1897 employed 112 people. In some instances, large quantities of topsoil were taken from the cays: it is estimated that mining at Lady Elliott Island removed a layer of material 2.5 metres (8 feet) thick.

Today, oil exploration permits are in force over most of the reef between Cairns and Rockhampton. It is, however, Commonwealth and State government policy to prohibit any drilling which may damage the reef. In 1971 all companies holding petroleum exploration permits in the area agreed to a suspension of their operations.

Industry, therefore, has not been allowed to spoil the reef. The outstanding beauty and incalculable scientific importance of the area was quickly recognised and the region has a corresponding history of conservation and preservation action. Some 160 of the region's islands were gazetted as National Parks under the State Forests and National Parks Act 1903 - 1948 (Queensland), including parts of Green Island (1937) and Heron Island (1943). In 1914 the taking of coral was restricted in declared areas and in 1974 two heavily used sites at Heron-Wistari reef and Green Island reef were declared marine parks.

Except for recreational line fishing, the taking of fish, shells, coral and other marine organisms is prohibited on the reef. Whaling in Australian waters was outlawed by the 1960 and 1989 Commonwealth Whaling Acts. The Queensland Fisheries Act 1976 prohibits the taking of turtles, marine mammals, clams and triton shells, as well as restricting the taking of pearl oysters, pearls, green snails, trochus, coral, shell grit, coral limestone and star sand, and placing size restrictions on the catching of some fish. All fauna on the islands of the Great Barrier Reef are protected by the Queensland Fauna Conservation Act 1974-79 and the Forestry Act 1959-79.

By late 1981 when 98.5% of the Great Barrier Reef region had been brought within the marine park, IUCN -The International Union for the Conservation of Nature determined that the park met all the required criteria for World Heritage Listing and the area was subsequently inscribed on the list.

ABOVE Lizard Island.

RIGHT The Indo-Pacific batfish. These very tame and curious fish are noted for their long, flowing fins. They are among the most graceful and friendly of coral reef inhabitants, and one of the species most likely to benefit from hand-feeding by divers.

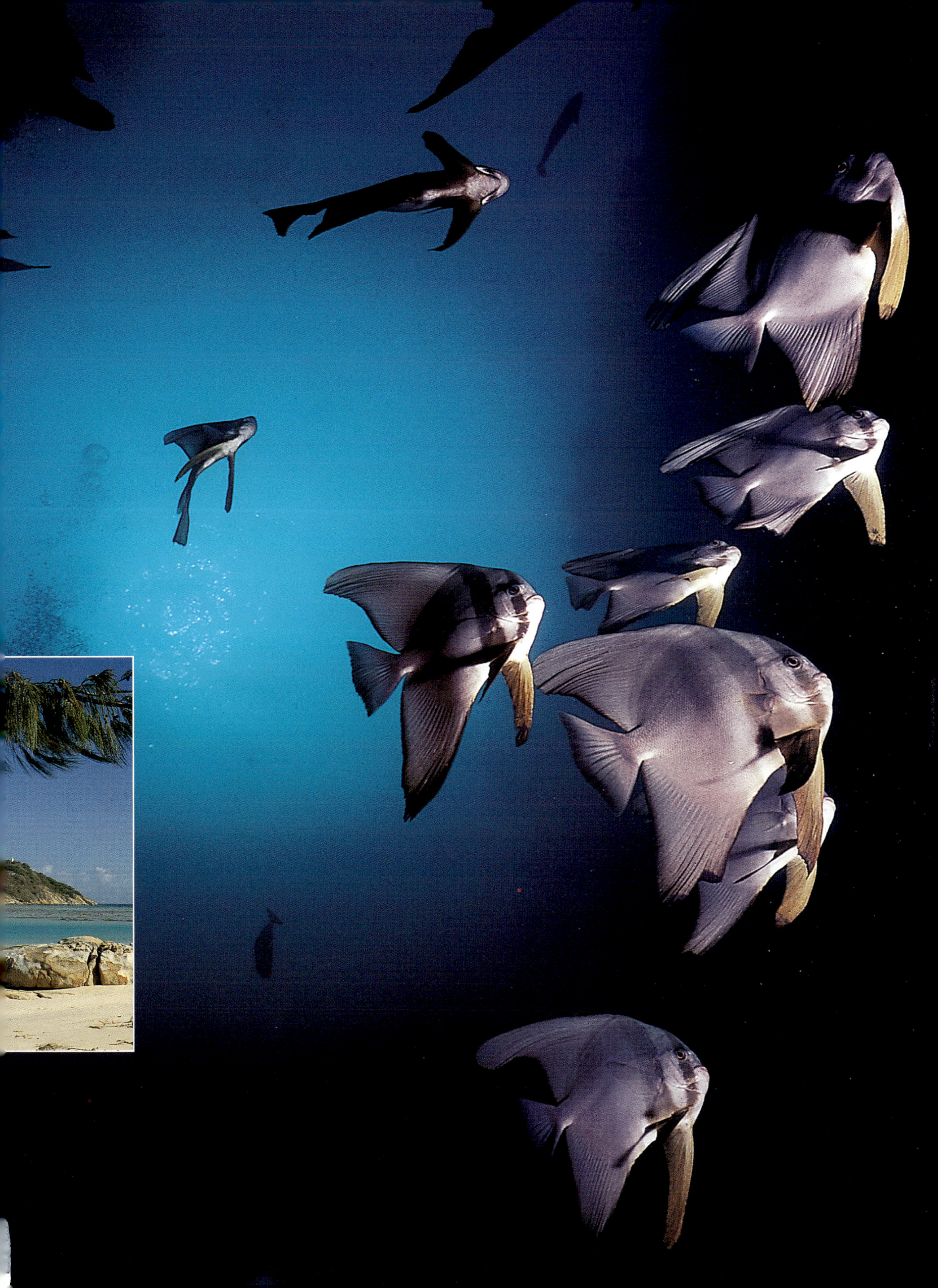

Human Impact

The marine and near-shore resources of the Great Barrier Reef have formed an important part of the traditional economy of the region's indigenous peoples for many thousands of years. The continuation of this sustainable use of the reef by Aboriginal people is permitted under State and Commonwealth law. This activity does not impact substantially on the reef environment.

Non-Aboriginal people live on various islands within the World Heritage Area, many of them employed in the region's flourishing tourist industry. Barrier Reef tourism is the largest industry in the region. Expenditure at island resorts for commercial boating trips and on private recreational boating exceeds A$250 million per annum. The economic benefits of heavy tourism are, however, counterbalanced by the impacts that this activity has on the reef environment.

At present, commercial fishing continues in the region around the Great Barrier Reef and there are concerns that some of the methods used, such as bottom trawling for prawns, are reaching harvesting levels that are unsustainable.

Facilities

The number of people who visit the Great Barrier Reef each year is now well over half a million. Together, these people spend over 2.2 million visitor days annually on the reef and its islands. There are hundreds of tourist resorts up and down the Queensland coast designed to suit a wide range of budgets, located in both mainland urban centres and on the Great Barrier Reef islands. Visitors to these resorts may make extensive use of the marine park's reefs and waters for a variety of recreational activities, including fishing, diving, and snorkelling, water sports, sightseeing, reef walking and shell collecting. Overall, tourism is permitted in 99.8% of the park, that is, in all except designated preservation and scientific research zones.

Threats

The natural marvels of the Great Barrier Reef Marine Park are easily accessible to tourists and are a 'must see' for all those lucky enough to have the opportunity. However, the increasing demands placed upon the reef environment by tourist operations have produced a range of problems. A number of impacts arise from reef-based tourism operations, including the discharge of waste, litter and fuel from pleasure craft; direct physical damage caused by anchors and by people snorkelling, diving and reef-walking; and the disturbance of fauna, either by direct interference or through over-fishing and collecting. Researchers continue to monitor the effect of human activities on reef ecosystems with the aim of minimising impact through design, prohibition or limitation.

Although oil exploration in the region has been suspended, there are concerns that this situation will not continue indefinitely, especially in the face of rising oil prices. There are five areas covered by offshore petroleum exploration permits and these, in total, comprise almost half the area of the park. Oil tankers and other ships that navigate the reef waters represent a threat to the reef from accidents and wrecks.

Deteriorating water quality is also a concern for park managers. Run-off from the mainland and populated islands contains suspended solids, herbicides, pesticides, nutrients and other materials which may have an adverse effect on the reef. At this stage, the extent of this damage is not known, but the problem is exacerbated by increasing development in the area.

A direct threat to the reef has emerged in the form of the coral-eating crown of thorns starfish, Acanthaster planci. Between 1965 and 1974, large populations of this predator killed large areas of reef corals, particularly in the central sector. It is believed that sporadic outbreaks of starfish populations are the result of ecological imbalances caused by human activity in the park.

Management

Management of the Great Barrier Reef Marine Park is the responsibility of the Great Barrier Reef Marine Park Authority, which was established in 1973 to administer and manage the area. The Authority is comprised of the chairman and members from each of the Queensland and Commonwealth governments, and is advised by a 15-member consultative committee. The Authority controls the issue of permits for a wide range of activities pursued within the park, including tourist facilities, education and research programs, aircraft operations, waste disposal, mooring operations and traditional hunting and fishing.

The day-to-day management of the park is undertaken by officers of the Queensland National Parks and Wildlife Service (NPWS) and the Queensland Fisheries Service. These officers have authority to prevent and repair damage in the park, and to impose penalties, seize equipment and recover costs from those who offend against park regulations. To exercise these powers, the NPWS has approximately 60 staff working within the park. Some seven field officers are available on any given day to patrol 800 kilometres (500 miles) of coastline and, consequently, their capacity to protect the park is limited.

Given the size of the park and the difficulties of protecting such a vast area, a large part of the NPWS management budget is devoted to education. The Great Barrier Reef Marine Park Authority has an education and information section which produces programs for public education. These assist tour operators in the development of activity programs which encourage tourists to exercise care for the environment while enjoying the park.

RIGHT Tropical fish swarm to investigate visitors to their underwater garden. These divers are using motorised scuba propulsion units, enabling them to explore a greater area of the coral reef beds.

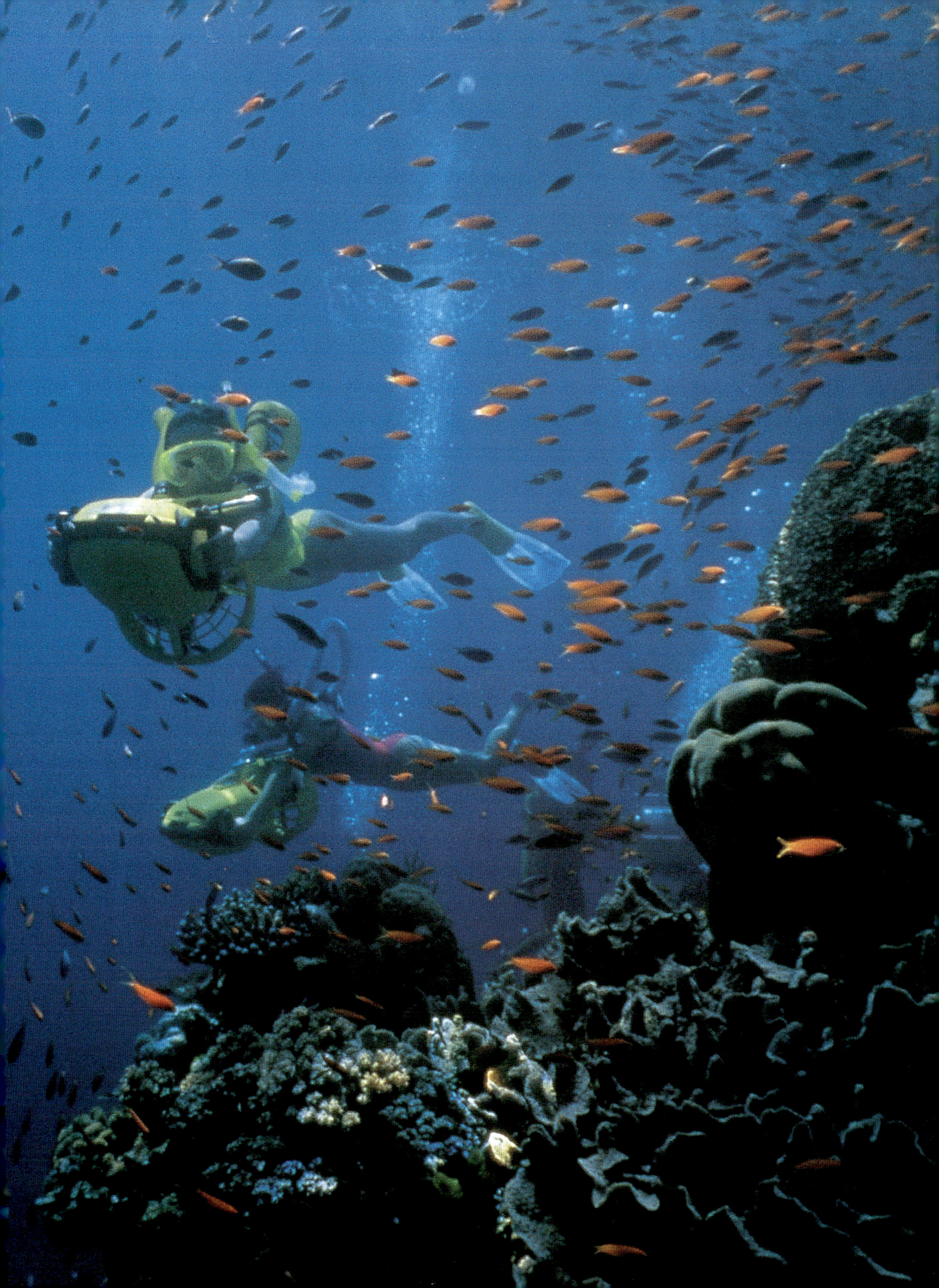

KAKADU
National Park

Kakadu National Park is esteemed for its biological diversity and for the great wealth of cultural sites contained within its boundaries. The largest park on the Australian continent, it has a greater variety of land systems than any other park. It is also one of the few parks to contain an entire major river basin. Kakadu was inscribed on the World Heritage List in three stages in 1981, 1987 and 1991.

Rare natural phenomena or places of exceptional natural beauty are features which may qualify a place for listing under the World Heritage Convention. These qualities can be seen in Kakadu's internationally important wetlands and the breathtaking escarpment over which spectacular waterfalls cascade during the wet season. The park's huge size, its environmental diversity and its location in a part of Australia that has not been altered substantially by European settlement have made it a vital refuge for many habitats and species.

Kakadu exemplifies major stages in the Earth's evolutionary history with its outstanding examples of both recent and ancient geological changes, its relict faunal species that have become much diminished in their range or status, and species representing various stages in Australia's biological evolution. Much of the park is relatively unaffected by modern-day human influences and its native ecosystems remain largely intact; it therefore provides an opportunity for the continuing study of large-scale evolutionary processes.

Humanity's long relationship with the Kakadu landscape is shown in the abundant domestic and ceremonial sites and the park's magnificent rock art. Collectively they attest to a physical and spiritual relationship between Aboriginal people and the changing environment of Kakadu which began many thousands of years ago and continues to this day.

Location

Situated between the Wildman and East Alligator Rivers, 200 kilometres (125 miles) east of Darwin in Australia's Northern Territory, Kakadu National Park covers an area of 19 804 square kilometres (7644 square miles). The park is outstanding in that it incorporates almost all the South Alligator River system and all major habitat types and landforms of northern Australia.

PREVIOUS PAGE Sunrise over the South Alligator River finds a flock of magpie geese, a species that is very common on the floodplains of the area and named for its black and white colouring.

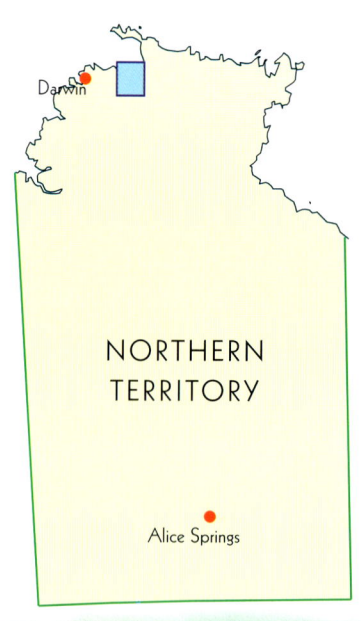

NORTHERN TERRITORY

Darwin
Alice Springs

KAKADU NATIONAL PARK

FIELD ISLAND
VAN DIEMAN GULF
ARNHEM LAND
FINKE BAY
EAST ALLIGATOR RIVER
UBIRR
SOUTH ALLIGATOR RIVER
MUNMARLARY
COOINDA
NOURLANGIE-MT BROCKMAN MASSIF
DEAF ADDER CR
JIM JIM FALLS
TWIN FALLS
MARY RIVER RANGER STATION

The Natural World Heritage Values of Kakadu

by William Lines

In 1976, the head of the Ranger Uranium Inquiry, Justice Fox, prescribed a set of incompatible uses for the Alligator Rivers region in the Northern Territory: uranium mining, the establishment of a national park, the use and occupation of the land by Aboriginal people, tourism and pastoral activities.

The recommendations, and their acceptance by the federal government, reflected a modern belief that humans can continue to make contradictory demands upon the Earth. A utilitarian creed, which holds that everything humans consider worthy and desirable is ultimately connected and compatible, is the ethos that governs Kakadu National Park.

Kakadu grew out of Woolwonga Aboriginal Reserve, established in 1964 as a wildlife sanctuary of just over 500 square kilometres (200 square miles). Conservationists continued to fight for the creation of a major national park in the region. However, the discovery in the early 1970s of some of the richest and most extensive uranium deposits in the world raised the stakes. Developers saw uranium as a source of tremendous wealth. Conservationists opposed mining for its disruptive and polluting effects and for the larger problems that uranium use generates.

Nevertheless, the government believed Kakadu could have both use and preservation. Mining was allowed and the park was established in stages, to eventually encompass almost two million hectares (five million acres) excluding Stage III.

In 1981, Kakadu was included on the World Heritage List, the first Australian property to be listed. Kakadu qualified on the basis of both its natural and cultural significance. Listing recognised the extent and richness of Kakadu's wetlands and waterfowl habitats, as well as the park's nearly 5000 Aboriginal art sites, which may constitute the oldest and greatest collection of preserved early human artistic effort.

More than 200 kilometres (125 miles) from north to south and 100 kilometres (60 miles) from east to west, Kakadu contains 500 kilometres (300 miles) of spectacular sandstone escarpment. These cliffs, which run 500 kilometres (300 miles) east and south across the park and mark the edge of the Arnhem Land plateau, record a geological history dating back almost 2000 million years. In comparison, the riverine and coastal floodplains are very recent landforms.

When Aborigines first settled in the area, 50 000 or more years ago, much of the world's water was locked up in the polar ice caps, the sea level was considerably lower and the seashore was 300 kilometres (200 miles) further north. Kakadu was part of a dry inland plain. As global temperature increased, the ice caps melted, the sea level rose, the river valleys became flooded and rainfall increased.

Flooding led to siltation and vast mangrove swamps spread in the river estuaries from about 7000 years ago. When sea levels stabilised around 6000 years ago, freshwater swamps and floodplains formed in the back areas. New plant and animal communities evolved.

Europeans recognised two annual climatic periods, the dry and wet. Aboriginal people discerned six. The dry season lasts from May to September and the wet from November to March. April and October are transitional months. High temperatures prevail throughout the year and, on average, range between 20° and 35° Celsius (68° and 95° Fahrenheit). They rarely fall below 17° Celsius (62° Fahrenheit).

In October, temperature and humidity increase. Black thunderclouds roll across the sky and spectacular lightning displays foreshadow the wet to come. Violent thunderstorms crash over the land in November. Torrential rains begin in December or January and last through March. About 135 centimetres (50 inches) falls each year.

Water starts moving across the plateau, which rises about 300 metres (900 feet) over the neighbouring lowland hill country. The plateau's gorges and depressions shelter rainforest, heathland and scrub.

The carved and weathered edge of the plateau - the escarpment - features sheer cliffs, overhangs, caves and steep rock promontories with long talus slopes of broken rock. In the wet, sheets of water cascade over the escarpment. Some streams persist throughout the year, including Jim Jim Falls, which drop 200 metres (620 feet) into a deep, boulder-strewn pool.

The streams and rivers that collect at the bottom of the escarpment flow through a region of lowland hills, above undulating plains of grassland, savannah and open eucalypt woodland. Although the soils are acidic, shallow and infertile, the plant and animal communities are rich. These forests and woodlands cover more than half the park. A ground cover of tall annual grasses provides fuel for dry season fires. In pockets free from fire, dense monsoon rainforest persists.

Many of the fires are deliberately lit by the park managers as they seek to recreate the pattern of Aboriginal fire that resulted, at the end of each dry season, in a mosaic of unburnt patches interspersed with small patches of low and medium intensity burns.

Below the lowland hills, Kakadu's four major rivers have created a complex of billabongs, creeks, freshwater floodplains and backwater swamps, which are flooded from three to nine months of the year. The wetlands attract large numbers of tropical water birds. Up to two and a half million birds congregate in Kakadu in the dry season. Magpie geese and wandering whistling-duck are the most abundant.

Out of the wetlands, the rivers cross tidal flats, formed of sea and river deposited alluvial mud. In the dry season, the slow-moving rivers meander in great loops across the mud towards the coast. Here a dark strip of mangrove swamps - containing over 20 species of mangrove - fringes the coast, tidal river margins, offshore mud banks and islands.

Over a third of Australia's bird species, 289 species in all, can be found in Kakadu. Species that are unique to the area are mainly restricted to the escarpment and its outliers, where deep rock gorges and forested gullies provide habitat for banded pigeons, rock pigeons and grass wrens. Birds of prey range widely over the park and include wedgetailed eagles and collared sparrowhawks.

Bustards and emus inhabit the drier areas along with parrots and lorikeets, red-tailed black cockatoos and sulphur-crested cockatoos. Kingfishers, kookaburras, rainbow bee eaters, flycatchers and many other birds prefer wetland margins. When in flower, the floodplains' paperbarks attract nectar-eating birds such as honeyeaters and lorikeets.

Coastal bird fauna include boobies, cormorants, curlews, egrets, greenshanks, herons, ospreys, oyster catchers, plovers, rails, stilts, sandpipers, terns and turnstones.

Kakadu includes representatives from all the rich and varied groups of reptiles that inhabit Australia: skinks, geckoes, lizards and venomous and non-venomous snakes. Venomous snakes include taipans, king browns and death adders. Both species of Australian crocodile are recovering after years of hunting depleted their numbers throughout northern Australia.

Over 60 species of mammals live in the park. Dingoes range widely. Wallabies inhabit open woodland. Mobs of antilopine kangaroos frequent stony ridges and open woodland.

Twenty-six of the 65 species of Australian bats live here, ranging from large, fruit-eating flying foxes to small, mouse-sized animals. There are also four uncommon bat species: ghost bats, orange horseshoe bats, lesserwary-nose horseshoe bats and white-striped sheathtail bats, probably confined to Kakadu.

Feral pigs, cats, dogs, European honey bees and water buffalo have disrupted and are disrupting the park ecology. Cane toads may become established in the near future as they migrate west from Queensland. About 70 introduced plant species (5% of the total) have been identified in the park. Dense, thorny thickets of *mimosa pigra* are widespread on neighbouring properties. The aquatic fern *salvinia molesta* threatened to clog waterways and absorb most of the nutrients from water but has been stabilised by an introduced biological control agent - a tiny leaf-eating weevil.

To these threats are added a variety of pressures: tourism, resort development, improved access to the park sites and uranium mining.

Many people see joint management between the Australian Nature Conservation Agency and Aboriginal owners as the solution to resolving conflicting demands. Others see the arrangement as perpetuating contradictions at the heart of Kakadu National Park.

The aggressive promotion of tourism has meant that park visitor numbers have increased by more than 450% in just 14 years - from 45 000 in 1982 to over a quarter of a million. Joint management may be exacerbating this growth as Aboriginal members of the management board - who form the majority - have an interest in promoting existing and future tourist facilities.

Not all threats arise within the park. The federal government's plans for expanded uranium mining - with associated threats of widespread contamination - illustrate the contradictory and potentially destructive demands Australians place on their land.

ABOVE Traditional Aboriginal face painting is practiced for religious ceremonies.

RIGHT One of many spectacular sheer rock faces of the Kakadu escarpment.

Kakadu - The Human Landscape
by Robert Levitus

The features that make Kakadu National Park a spectacular scenic experience and a diverse ecological domain also make it a field for the interpretation of human life in ancient Australia. Located against the undeveloped tropical north coast of the continent, Kakadu contains places that were probably among the earliest to be colonised by people traversing the islands and land bridges of what is now the Indonesian Archipelago. The cultural heritage of Kakadu began with the works and lives of those people as they extended their range to the south when sea levels were lower. Estimating that beginning point is itself a large concern. For the Aboriginal colonisers and their descendants, the rock shelters of the Kakadu escarpment and outliers provided large and protected living spaces. Today their floors are seen as deep, rich archaeological deposits, the lower layers of which have given radio-carbon dates of 20 000 to 25 000 years; beneath them are layers dated at 50 000 to 60 000 years using less certain methods. These dates currently frame debates about the first human occupation of the Australian continent.

The pronounced ecological zones of the park, from freshwater wetland to escarpment outliers and plateau valleys, are reflected in its archaeology. There are diverse aggregations of Aboriginal artefacts and material remains left in the upper layers of rock-shelter deposits and scattered widely across the edges of the floodplains. In the past, archaeologists might have interpreted differences in this material as reflecting the activities of separate Aboriginal groups occupying and exploiting each ecological zone. However, the surrounding landscape of Kakadu and the productivity of its varied habitats for foraging bands of Aborigines suggest that these sites were used in succession by groups moving from one to the other.

Seasonality was the key. The dry season is known more intimately in the Aboriginal calendar as the cooler period of Yegge, the cold weather of Wurrgeng, the hot dry time of Gurrung and the humid pre-monsoonal Gunumeleng. Rivers and streams gradually stop flowing in the dry and expansive sheets of water over the wetlands, reducing to a small number of remnant swamps. Plant and animal food sources, especially packed and noisy crowds of magpie geese, concentrate here as the dry season wears on. In traditional times, hundreds of Aborigines concentrated in large camps around them, exploiting this rich and transient resource, exchanging goods and arranging dealings with other people that they may not have seen for months and engaging in ceremonies.

As wet season storms arrived in Gudjewg, these people broke into smaller bands and began dispersing across the landscape. Rivers rose again, billabongs re-filled, water washed across ridges and flood plains disappeared under a seasonal sea that lasted into the post-monsoonal time of Bang Gerreng. People travelled widely now, re-visiting home estates, searching out foods that were less abundant and less easily procurable, moving out to the edges of their social range to meet with people of different languages visiting from farther regions, and returning to the swamps for another briefer harvest, this time of goose eggs laid after the last floods had passed. This seasonal pattern allowed the diverse archaeological sites of the park to be comprehended as components of a single system of human ecology.

Yet another artefact of human activity, paintings on rock surfaces, presents contemporary Aboriginal observations not only on that system of human ecology, but on those that preceded it, even before the wetlands formed. The hundreds of kilometres of sandstone escarpment and outliers that feature in the public imagination of Kakadu are host to an enormous body of art in thousands of rock galleries. The art works range from monotone figures, such as a red-ochred wallaby painted in a small hollow on the underside of a boulder in the scrub, to hundreds of motifs, varied in style and subject, overlain and crowded along a back wall and extending onto an overhanging roof. The rock art of Kakadu transforms the geological heritage of sandstone cliffs and caves into an exhibition place for schools of ancient artists, an archive of local history and religion, and a repository of human observations of ecology and environmental change. Over the last 25 years, especially since the establishment of the park, the Kakadu region has been recognised as equalling the pre-eminent rock art provinces of other continents.

Studying these paintings has been an inter-disciplinary enterprise but the beginnings of insight came from pioneering investigations based on tireless visiting and the recording of thousands of motifs in hundreds of galleries spread through the gorges and outliers of western Arnhem Land. Myriads of running figures, hunting scenes, internally-segmented and detailed fish and kangaroo, items of human manufacture, mythical heroes and encounters with Europeans are abundantly presented across the rock faces. Extensive and careful recording and analysis allowed scholars to move beyond purely aesthetic appreciation to a chronology that paid close attention to the order of layering: which style and subject was always found underneath or superimposed upon another. This laid the ground for an exciting interpretive leap that sought to learn more about the art and, from it, by going outside the art. Researchers looked closely at the contents of the images - which animals and implements are represented in each period - and argued that they illustrated successive periods of environmental change and local Aboriginal adaptation.

Under this careful study, the rock art revealed: the hunting of large macropods that was possible when the Kakadu lowlands were hundreds of kilometres from the coast, rainfall was lower and vegetation more sparse; the barramundi that swam upstream from tidal estuaries formed by post-glacial inundation of ancient river valleys; and the goosewing fans made from the plumage of birds nesting on new freshwater wetlands that formed within walking distance of the sandstone shelters. Geomorphology provided dates for this grand succession from about 20 000 years ago and gave a frame of reference from which to infer the age of each style of art. The abundance of art has allowed detailed and divergent chronologies to be compiled. Ultimately, competing interpretations of rock art as environmental history may be overtaken by the use of mineral chemistry to directly date layers of paint forming the art works, or layers of protective silica over the paint.

As well as illustrating the park's ecology, the art of Kakadu also points to some of the founding ideas of Aboriginal culture. In some paintings, artists have represented Dreamtime beings, creator figures that travelled across an ancient formless landscape, left behind topographical features, social groups and languages and instituted relationships between them that are cited now as cultural charter by knowledgeable people. Languages are therefore owned by particular groups, people inherit responsibilities for tracts of country and special places located in them, and those places retain power from the actions or immanence of Dreamings. Access to the paintings, or to the meanings secreted within their designs, may be restricted to particular classes of persons. Relationships of this order today guide the process of consultations over park developments and have, at times, formed the grounds upon which Aborigines have tried to limit or prevent the entry of outsiders into their estates.

The whites that first sought a living from the Alligator Rivers flood plains in the late nineteenth century found a local Aboriginal society already in rapid population decline due to introduced infectious diseases. Some of the local language groups, each traditionally responsible for its own area of land and the mythical sites upon it, ultimately disappeared, as did their languages. Other groups were reduced to remnants. When one of the first generation of whites, Paddy Cahill, entered his third decade in the Alligator Rivers region in the 1910s, he recorded the continuing decline of Gagudju-speaking people with whom he had worked. Those people, from whom Kakadu takes its name, are now reduced to a tiny number and their language is on the verge of disappearing.

Kakadu's modern history left signs that are now also regarded as heritage. The last generation of Aboriginal artists added another class of motifs to the work of their ancestors: items of European technology and scenes from the new narrative of contact with white strangers. A subject of these recordings was the buffalo. Introduced by the British, it began colonising the Kakadu area from the north-east in the nineteenth century, spreading across a congenial new habitat of swamps, flood plains and savannah woodland. Shooters began taking hides in the 1880s, gradually drawing Aborigines from many areas and language groups into this work. The industry that they joined was seasonal and mobile and the camps were places of hard work rewarded mostly in kind, with clothes, cooking utensils, swag covers, mosquito nets and, most important of all for retaining Aboriginal labour, tobacco. Cash payments came late and only a few years before the industry, depressed by synthetic substitutes, poor processing and exporting restrictions, came to an end in 1956.

The shooters stalked the buffalo on foot or chased them on horseback, bringing down single animals in the scrub or running down a line of them across open flood plains. Skinners came behind, removing every usable inch of the thick and slippery hides and heaving them onto horses for the journey to camp, where they were cured and prepared for shipment to Darwin. In a region earlier abandoned by ambitious pastoralists and agriculturalists, it was this sort of rough and opportunistic work, supplemented by crocodile shooting, prospecting, poisoning dingos for bounty or mustering wild cattle, that made up a shifting and seasonal industry. The relics of this era are still scattered through the bush: disused buildings, rusting vehicles and overgrown tracks. The Aboriginal role in Kakadu now is different. Forming the majority on the Board of Management, Aborigines oversee the work of Parks Australia in managing Kakadu's environment, its heritage values and the industry of tourism and recreation that those things have fostered. As early colonisers, foragers, artists and bush-workers, their forebears used the park. This generation has been handed new roles, as managers, custodians and rangers, within a new regime that seeks to preserve and present the values of old systems, natural and cultural.

RIGHT This Aboriginal rock painting is in a style known as "X-ray" because it shows the internal structure of the subject. The painting depicts a silver barramundi, an important food resource for Aborigines and now the basis of a local fishing industry.

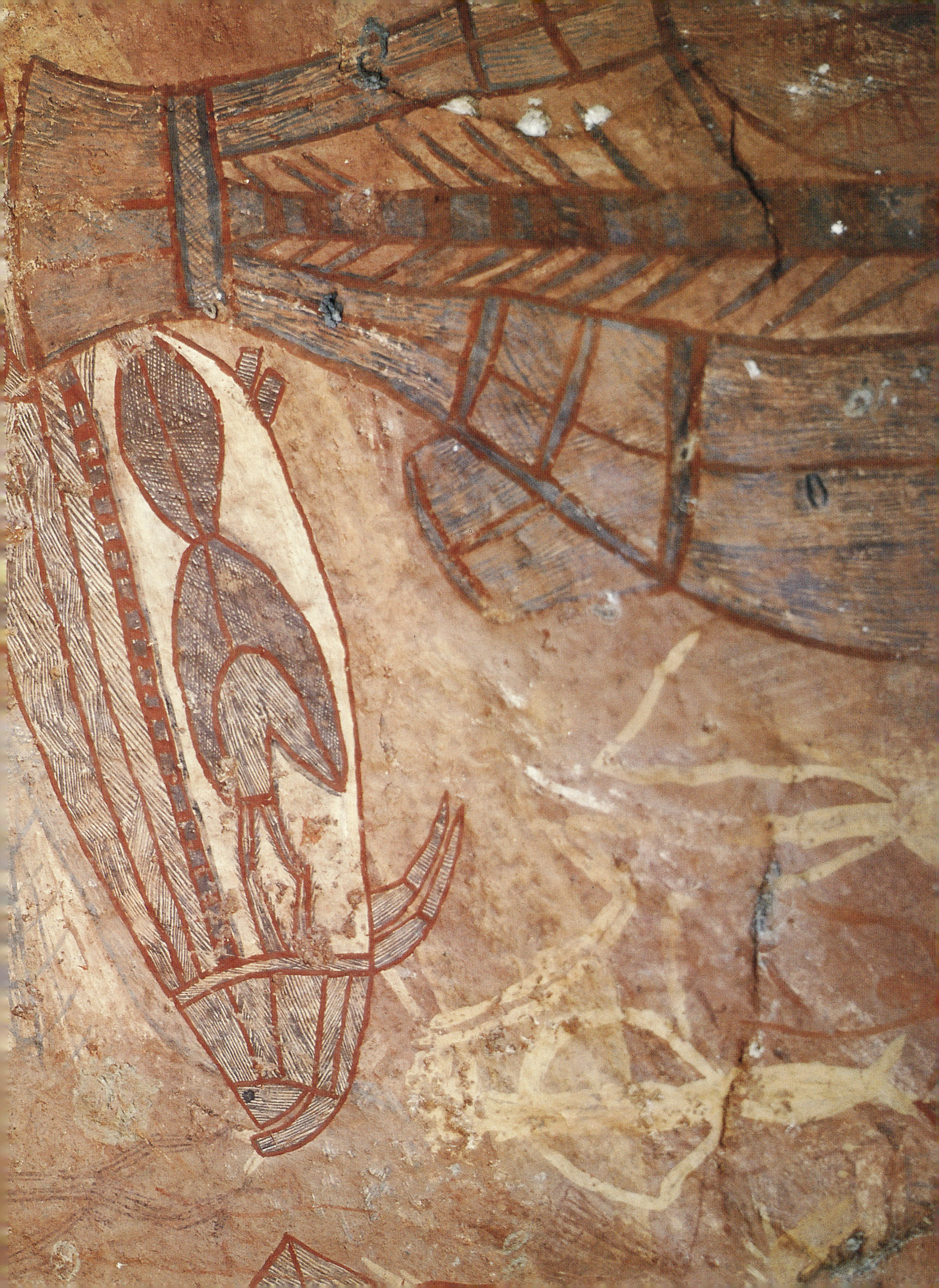

Physical Features

The Kakadu landscape includes formations of great antiquity as well as some that even now are in the process of formation and change. The landforms of the park fall into four major groups. The most spectacular of these is the Arnhem Land plateau and its escarpment, which is wild and inaccessible, with treacherous sheer cliffs, waterfalls and forbidding overhangs and caves. The southern hills and basins are characterised by rounded, pebble-covered hills and ranges. The landscape known as the Koolpinyah Surface is made up of repeatedly weathered and deposited gravels, sands, silts and clays. The coastal riverine plains are associated with the tidal reaches of all the major Kakadu river systems; these are relatively recent features of the landscape and are still in the process of forming. In addition to these four major landforms, the park contains some 473 square kilometres (183 square miles) of coastal, intertidal and estuarine areas, and two islands.

The park is within a region of tropical monsoon climate which is characterised by a marked wet season that starts in December and lasts four to five months and is followed by a dry season which produces near drought conditions. This climate has been a major factor in determining the distribution of water, plants and animals and in shaping the park's distinctive landforms over the aeons. The average annual rainfall is approximately 130 centimetres (51 inches), with 34 centimetres (13 inches) falling in January and hardly any rain falling in June. The land begins to dry out in April and by August the seasonal streams have disappeared. November is the hottest month, although temperatures are consistently warm, with an average of 34°Celsius (93°Fahrenheit) in summer and 30°Celsius (86°Fahrenheit) in winter.

ABOVE The man-eating saltwater or estuarine crocodile has been found up river where it poses a threat to both visitors and local people. This species grows up to 10 metres (33 feet) in length and can be distinguished from the much less dangerous freshwater crocodile by its size and its wider and more rounded head.

RIGHT Nourlangie Rock escarpment and waterlilies in the Angbangbang Billabong.

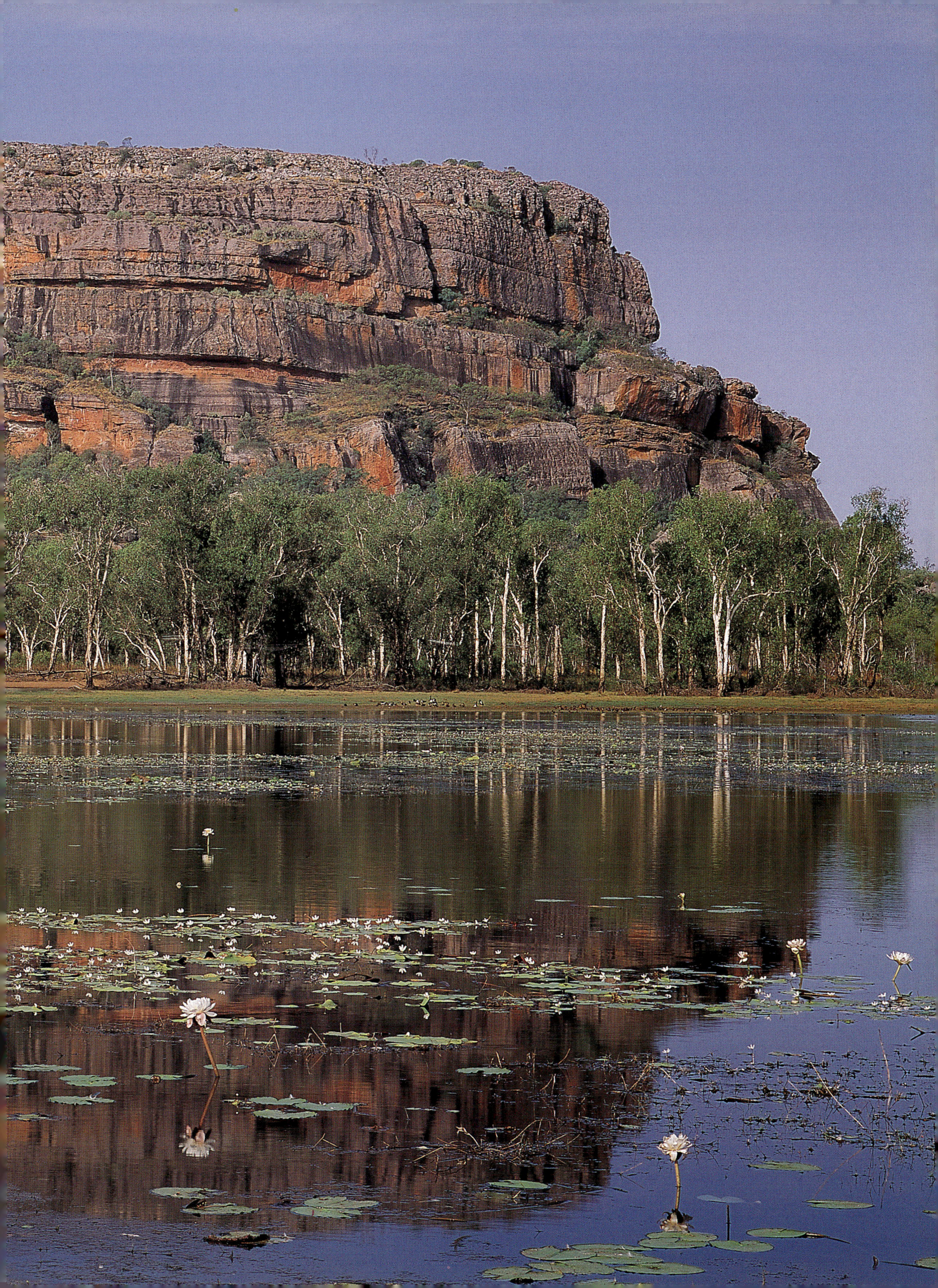

Special Features

Kakadu is inscribed as both a natural and cultural site on the World Heritage List. Many visitors are drawn to the park by its unparalleled cultural features. More than 50 000 years of human interaction with this fascinating and changing environment, together with the record which this association has left scattered on the ground or painted on the rock faces, sets Kakadu apart from other nature reserves.

Evidence for human occupation of the region dates back to at least 50 000 years ago, which is the oldest record of a human presence in Australia. More astonishing still are the pieces of faceted ochre and ochre-stained grinding stones found in the lower levels of a number of archaeological sites dated to between 18 000 and 30 000 years ago. From these fragments comes the awe-inspiring knowledge that forms of artistic expression were already taking place at this early period and that this constitutes evidence of human artistic expression that is amongst the earliest known in the world!

Archaeological evidence has also revealed that the ancient residents of Kakadu made edge-ground axes and tools with handles some 20 000 years ago. Once again, this is one of the earliest records for this kind of technology in the world.

In the archaeological deposits at Kakadu, evidence has been found of major environmental changes and the strategies used by people to cope with these changes. Researchers have been able to determine the nature of these adaptations from the evidence of changing tool kits and changes in the types and amounts of foods consumed. Remarkably, this knowledge has been supplemented by the record of changes in lifestyles and beliefs represented in the various artistic styles and techniques of Kakadu rock art. At this stage, research suggests that the rock art in Kakadu can be classified into four periods, each of which can be related to an era of change in the environment. The artistic periods are the pre-estuarine, over 8000 years ago; the estuarine, 8000 to 1500 years ago; the freshwater, 1500 to 200 years ago; and the period of European contact dating from 200 years ago to the present. Each period corresponds with a particular art style: macropods and human figures with boomerangs dominate the art of the pre-estuarine, when the land was drier and large game was abundant; in the estuarine period macropods and emus are less evident in the art, while naturalistic representations of fish such as barramundi are common.

There are over 7000 rock art sites in the national park, 3500 of which have been registered by park managers. Many sites contain large numbers of paintings - the number of individual paintings in the park is estimated to be in the millions. Areas of particularly intensive artistic activity include the Nourlangie-Brockman massif, Ubirr (Rock) and Deaf Adder Creek. The majority of sites contain paintings but there are also engravings and designs made in bees wax. Although the subject of some debate, it is thought that the earliest paintings are at least 10 000 years old and probably much older. One of the significant aspects of Kakadu's cultural heritage is the continuing residence of Aboriginal people within the area now included in the park for over 50 000 years. The long heritage of traditional beliefs and practices remains a powerful force in the daily lives of local Aboriginal people who continue to act as custodians and curators of their sacred landscapes.

ABOVE A Galawan, one of Kakadu's largest monitors or sand goannas.

RIGHT The lotus flower is prominent in the aquatic vegetation of the floodplains and billabongs of Kakadu. The seeds of the red lotus lily are a traditional food source for Aborigines.

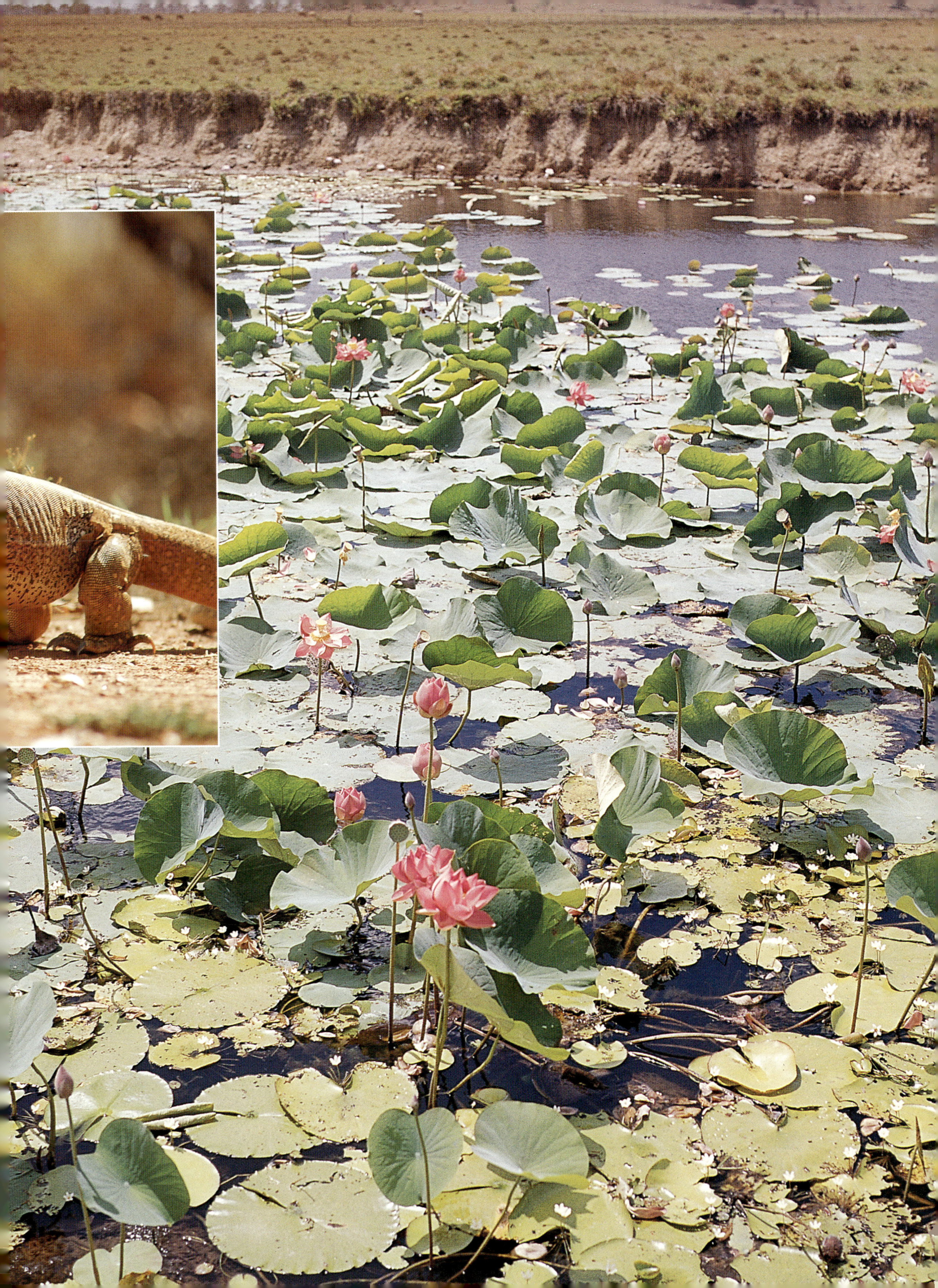

Flora

Kakadu National Park is the most floristically diverse area of northern Australia with over 1600 plant species recorded; of these, 46 are considered rare or threatened and nine are not found beyond the park. This great variety reflects the diversity of the area's landforms and the many habitats they support. Kakadu's vegetation can be classified into 13 broad groups. Of these, seven are dominated by particular species of eucalyptus, while the remaining categories are characterised by mangrove, samphire, lowland rainforest, paperbark swamp, seasonal floodplain and sandstone rainforest.

The flora of the sandstone formations of the western Arnhem Land escarpment are particularly important, as many of these species are not found elsewhere. Most of Kakadu is covered by an open woodland dominated by eucalyptus trees, with an understorey of tall grass - a vegetation type that is known as savannah in many parts of the world. However, Kakadu's floristic features are many: it is famous for its extensive wetlands; for the heaths, woodlands and rainforest of the western Arnhem Land sandstone escarpment and for pristine tracts of eucalypt representing the largest expanses of such forests in Australia. In addition, Kakadu contains six of the Northern Territory's 16 monsoon rainforest types which serve as an important refuge for migratory birds and for other species during the dry season.

ABOVE This brilliant flower is from the eucalypt, Darwin woollybutt.

RIGHT A view from Ubirr, an Aboriginal rock art site that looks over the Kakadu floodplain. This panorama has inspired countless generations of indigenous artists who have painted in these rocky galleries for thousands of years.

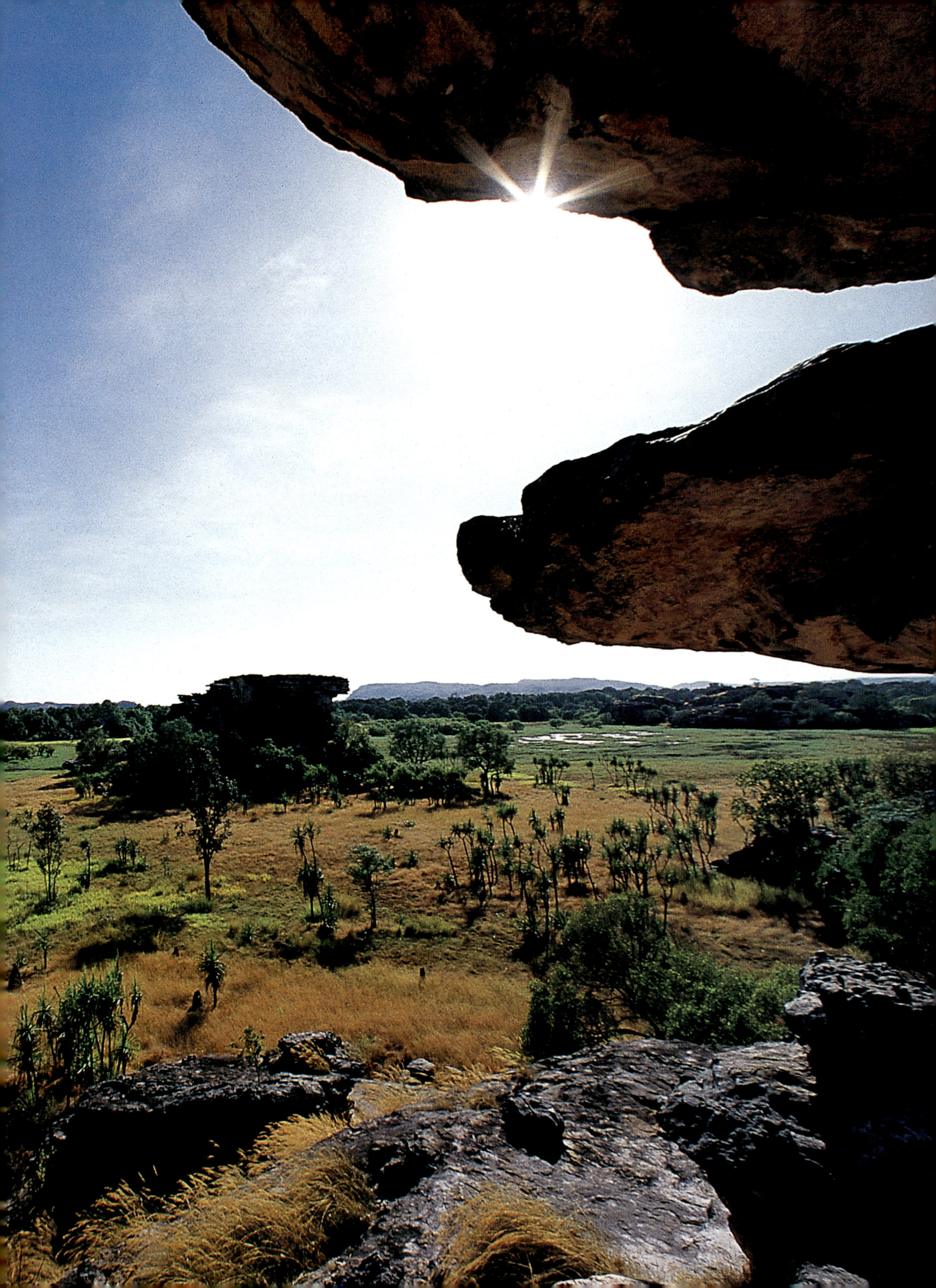

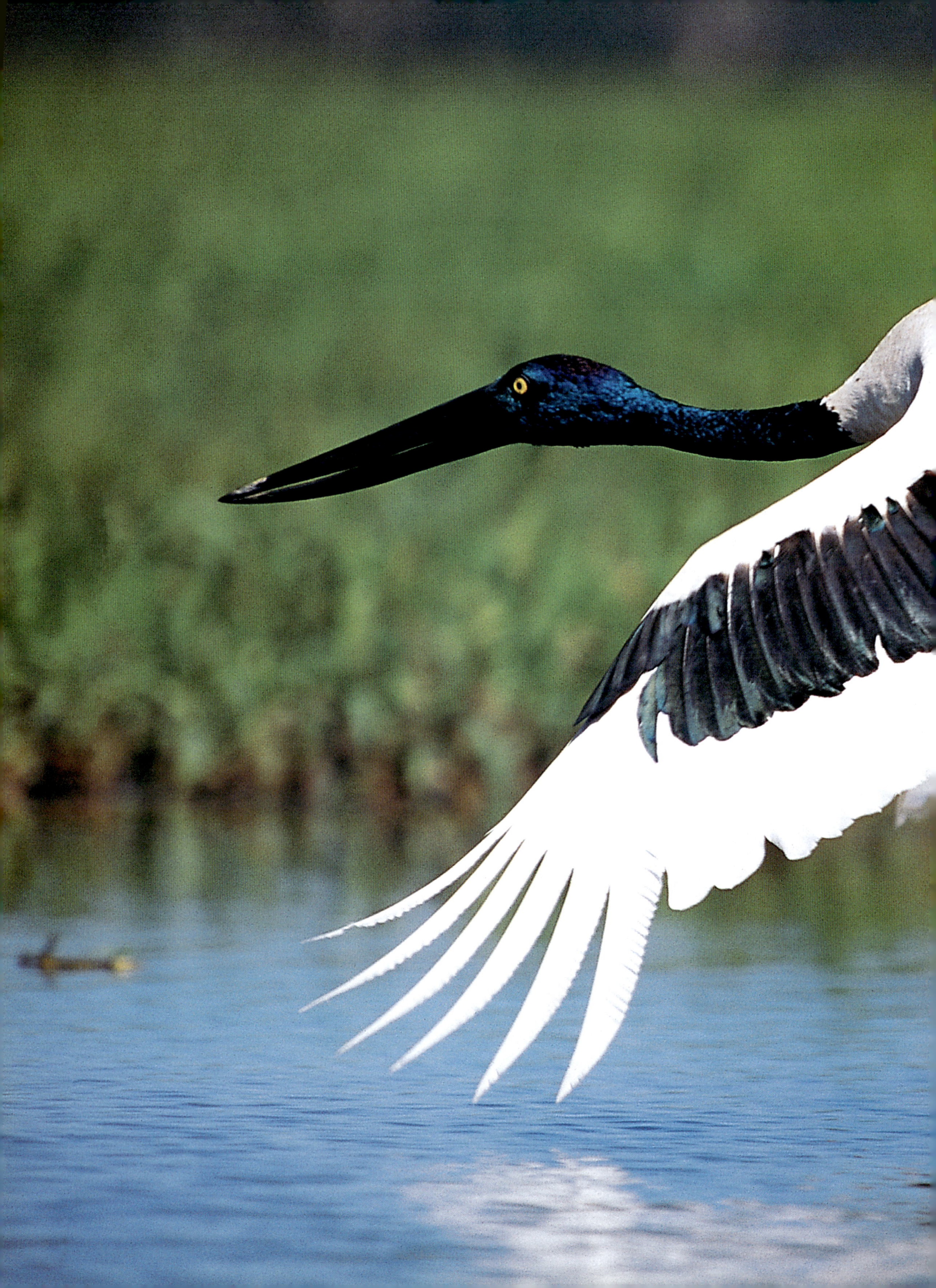

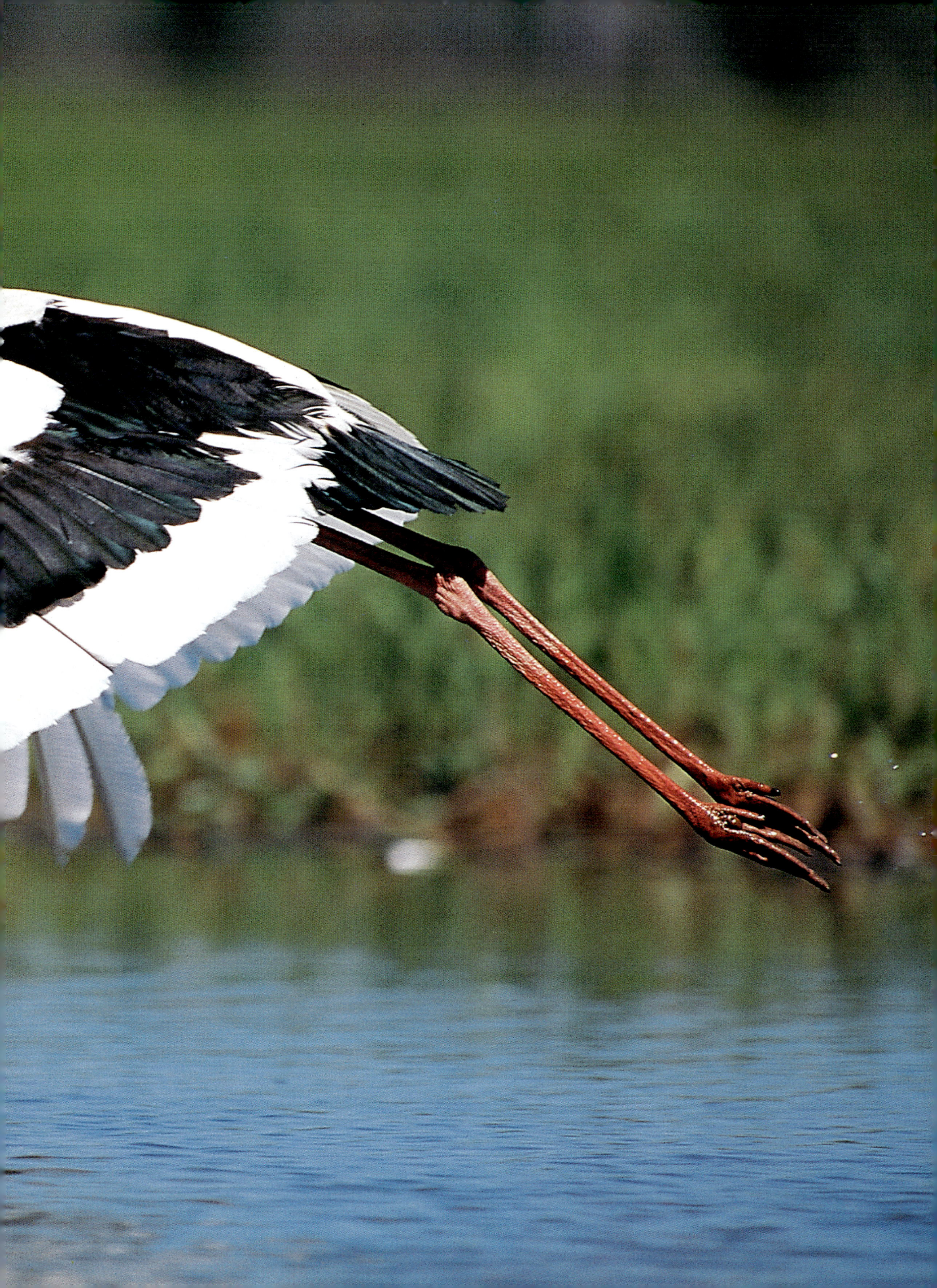

Fauna

Owing to the diversity of its land systems, from marine and coastal habitats to the arid sandstone escarpment, Kakadu is one of the world's most species-rich wildlife parks. It contains over 64 species of mammals, including 26 of the 65 species of Australian bats, 289 bird species, 128 reptiles, 25 frogs and 59 freshwater and estuarine fish species. Thirty three percent of Australia's bird species and 25% of its fish species are represented in the park.

Many species of fauna found here are limited to the region. The mammals include 19 marsupials and one monotreme, the echidna. Among the marsupials are species found only in the Arnhem sandstone, such as the black wallaroo, and species from the wider northern monsoon region, such as the rock ringtail possum and the narbalek. The largest group of mammals in the park are the bats, represented by 28 species.

The little red flying-fox and the black flying-fox are widespread, roosting in large, noisy colonies and feeding by night on fruit and nectar. These creatures play an important role in the pollination of eucalypts and paperbarks and in the dispersal of some monsoon forest plants.

The birds of Kakadu are astonishing in their diversity, with one third of all Australian bird species represented. Distinct groups of birds are to be seen within the park's various habitats, with the greatest variety of birdlife in the open forests and woodlands. Dense flocks of waterbirds can be seen thronging on the famous Kakadu wetlands, which support no less than 60 species, including herons, egrets, ibises, bittern, ducks, geese, spoonbills, darters, cormorants and brolgas, the last performing graceful and intricate courtship dances during the mating season. The waterbirds gather in the park in vast numbers, reaching a peak of more than two-and-a-half million in August and October. Numerous bird species are permanent residents, depending upon the park for their survival; they include the endemic banded fruit dove, the rare red goshawk and the endangered Gouldian finch.

Kakadu's reptile fauna is as noteworthy as its birdlife. The park is home to two crocodile species; five freshwater turtle species; five species of sea turtle; 77 types of lizard, including geckos, legless lizards, dragons, monitors and skinks; and 39 species of snake. Kakadu contains the most important breeding habitat in the world for the saltwater crocodile and the pig-nosed turtle. The pig-nosed turtle is also of scientific significance as a relict species - the sole surviving member of its family. Nesting sites of endangered green and loggerhead turtles and of the flatback turtle are located on West Alligator Beach and on Field Island.

Kakadu's great faunal diversity extends to the invertebrate kingdom. Although there is still much research to be done, it is estimated that there are more than 10 000, and possibly as many as 100 000, insect species living in the park, including over 100 species of butterfly, 503 species of wasps and bees and some 1000 species of flies.

RIGHT Plumed whistling ducks are a common sight in Kakadu. This light brown duck with a pink bill and creamy-coloured feathers on its flanks is named for the whistling noise it makes in flight.

PREVIOUS PAGE The abundant lagoons and pools of the Kakadu floodplain are an ideal habitat for the magnificent jabiru, Australia's only stork. The jabiru's wingspan extends to 2.2 metres (over 7 feet) and it grows to a height of 120 centimetres (4 feet).

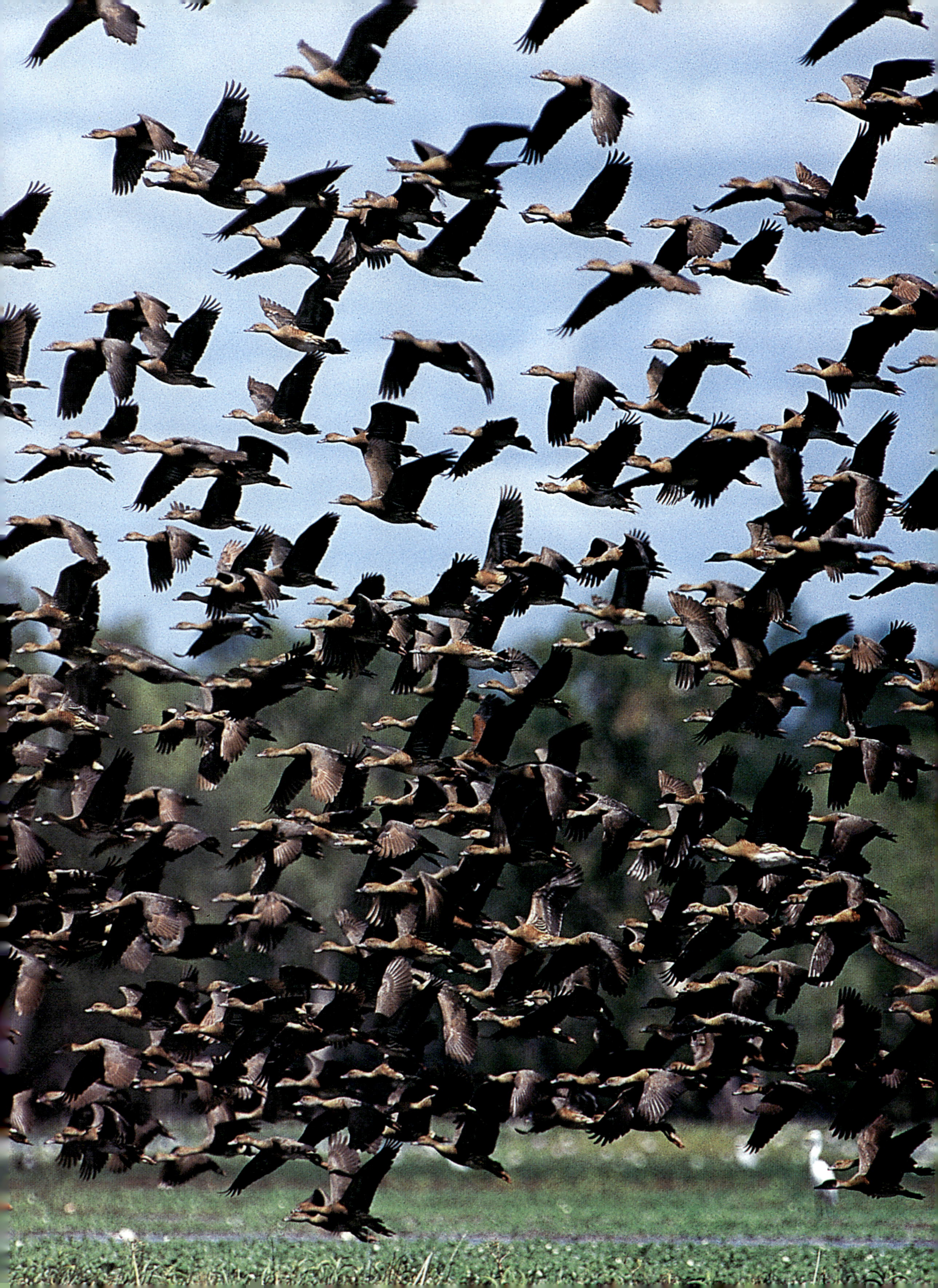

Cultural Heritage

Combined with its great natural assets, the outstanding cultural attributes of Kakadu National Park give it a value unsurpassed by any other protected area on earth. The archaeological and rock art sites found in the park are of major significance to world culture and their number, age and excellent state of preservation make them some of the most important sites in Australia.

Archaeological evidence suggests that people first came to the Australian continent from Asia during periods of low sea level which occurred some 52 000 to 70 000 years ago during the Pleistocene era. At this time, Australia and New Guinea formed a single land mass and were separated from what is now the Indonesian Archipelago by narrow sections of open sea no more than 70 kilometres (44 miles) across.

Traditional Aboriginal life in Kakadu was a complex mixture of hunting and gathering and of ceremonial and recreational activities which were carried out in accordance with the dictates of the seasons. The environment was rich in plant and animal foods and the vegetation also provided fibres for ropes, hulls for canoes and shafts for spears. There was plenty of stone suitable for making into tools, and ochre for paint.

The Aborigines of the region had a good standard of living and they enjoyed leisure to devote to social and spiritual pursuits. Today Kakadu is rich in sites associated with events of the Aboriginal creation era and with the lives and journeys of their ancestral beings. Some of these sites are prominent features in the landscape while others are hidden and considered dangerous to all except those of appropriate status. Apart from these sacred sites, there are numerous ceremonial sites, commonly identified by elaborate stone arrangements or bone mounds, which are associated with initiations, seasonal rituals or burials.

Contact between indigenous Australians and other people can be dated back to the seventeenth century, when Macassan fishermen from Ujung Pandang in modern day Indonesia made annual visits to the north Australian coast to fish for bêche-de-mer. Late in that same century, the north Australian coastline became familiar to Dutch mariners but the first detailed explorations by the colonising British did not take place until almost a century later in 1799.

The first European to explore the Kakadu region by land was the ill-fated German explorer Ludwig Leichhardt, who, during 1844-45, undertook an epic journey from Moreton Bay (now Brisbane) to the military outpost at Port Essington on the northern coastline.

Military outposts were established in the north from the 1820s and these were the gateway for the introduction of water buffalo, large numbers of which escaped or were left behind as the settlements were abandoned. Water buffalo became an economic resource to both indigenous and European people in the region but also caused considerable damage to the environment.

TOP RIGHT An Aboriginal rock painting in "X-ray" style depicts a female and family members, with barramundi.

RIGHT The frill-necked lizard or dragon with its characteristic neck frill which spreads menacingly when the reptile is alarmed and changes colour.

Although early explorers were optimistic about the prospects of agriculture in the north, the climate proved unsuitable and, by the 1890s, the industry was in decline. However, running cattle and harvesting buffalo continued as viable activities into the twentieth century.

From 1870, some small-scale gold mining took place in areas south and west of the park but it was not until the 1950s and 1960s that the mineral wealth of the region was fully explored. In the 1960s and 1970s, mining interests turned to the north-east, where extensive uranium deposits had been discovered. The Ranger uranium mine, although specifically excluded from the World Heritage Area, continues to operate and the land will be included in the park when mining ceases. Mining operations at South Alligator River ceased in the early 1980s but continued at Coronation Hill and El Sharana until 1991 when the federal government took a decision to add Coronation Hill to the Kakadu National Park Area.

The dedication of the Kakadu area for conservation purposes began in 1964 when the 505 square kilometres (195 square miles) Woolwonga Aboriginal Reserve was proclaimed a wildlife sanctuary. Subsequently, an investigation was made of the feasibility of establishing a national park in the Alligator Rivers region. This led in 1972 to the declaration of the Alligator Rivers Wildlife Sanctuary and Protected Area.

In 1977, the commissioners of the Ranger Uranium Environmental Inquiry recommended that a national park be created to protect rare species of flora and fauna, rare habitats and significant Aboriginal cultural sites. The commissioners thought it desirable to include the entire catchment area of at least one large river in a regional national park and identified the South Alligator River as the most suitable. In 1978, the Commonwealth acquired the land that now forms Kakadu National Park and Stage I of the park, incorporating the former Woolwonga and Alligator Rivers wildlife sanctuaries, was proclaimed in April, 1979.

Stage I of the park was inscribed on the World Heritage List in October 1981, with Stage II being added as an extension to the property in December 1987. Most of Stage III was incorporated into the park between 1987 and 1989, with the final components being listed in June, 1991.

Human Impact

Due to the extremes of the monsoonal climate, the unsuitability of northern Australian soils for agriculture and the inaccessible nature of large parts of the park, Kakadu is largely unaffected by present human activities. Damage has been done to the park environment in the past by grazing and mining but this has largely been restored or mitigated and feral animals continue to be removed.

Approximately 300 Aboriginal people live in the park, including traditional owners and people with recognised social and traditional attachments to the area. Some Aboriginal people live in Jabiru township or at ranger stations while others have established outstations within the park boundaries. Traditional land use within the park is sustainable and does not impact adversely on the environment.

The township of Jabiru lies within the park and serves the Ranger uranium mine and is increasingly a centre for tourist development.

Facilities

Each year, Kakadu receives around 220 000 visitors, many of whom are attracted by the wealth of Aboriginal art and culture found within the park. Access to the park is by road and air. The park is most commonly reached via the Arnhem Highway from Darwin, where tourism to Kakadu and other parks in the region contributes substantially to the economy. Kakadu can also be reached from the south via Pine Creek Road. There are several airstrips suitable for light aircraft in and around the park. Entry restrictions apply only to potentially dangerous sites, such as abandoned mine shafts, and to areas set aside for Aboriginal use, or for management, research or conservation purposes. A range of accommodation is available in the park, from hotels at Jabiru to the campsites and picnic areas provided at many locations. Other conveniences for visitors include car parks, toilet facilities, access trails, viewing platforms and interpretive signs.

Threats

Threats to the biological integrity of the park include invasion by aggressive exotic weeds, most notably *mimosa pigra* and *salvinia molesta*. *Mimosa* has been controlled rigorously by a team working full-time on its eradication since 1984, however, *Salvinia* continues to grow uncontrolled in some areas. Strenuous efforts continue to be made to remove this plant, including the release of a biological control insect, the use of appropriate herbicides, mechanical harvesting and the quarantining of affected areas until the risk of the species spreading becomes negligible.

Kakadu has also suffered from invasion by exotic animals, one of the most destructive being the water buffalo which destroys native vegetation by tramping and wallowing. They also disrupt surface scatters of cultural materials such as stone artefacts, and may damage Aboriginal ceremonial sites. A program to control buffalo numbers in the park was begun in 1979 and this had removed some 100 000 buffalo by the end of 1990.

A further threat to Kakadu National Park is the possibility of radioactive contamination from a uranium mine which operates within an enclave in the park. Although, to date, controls have been effective, the long term problems of containing mining wastes and their disposal are cause for concern. In addition to the Ranger uranium mine, there are two other leases: Koongarra and Jabiluka, the latter of which is located close to an important floodplain inside the park. Although the threat of mining in the headwaters of the South Alligator River was diminished with the inscription of the third stage of Kakadu National Park on the World Heritage List, there is no guarantee this deposit will not be developed. There also still remain potential effects on Kakadu from uranium mining outside the park and from within the enclave which require ongoing attention.

A major challenge facing park managers is the conservation of Kakadu's many cultural sites, particularly the rock art. Damage may be done to Aboriginal rock art sites by dust, by encroaching vegetation, by animals and humans touching the surfaces, by termites and mud-building wasps and by the effects of water flow and chemicals. Art sites can be protected from deterioration by a number of quite simple means, such as diverting water flow from the surface, pruning away vegetation, removing insect nests and fencing sites to protect them from feral animals and people. Deliberate vandalism of cultural sites is very rare within the park and passive control devices such as the provision of pathways and barriers at frequently visited sites are effective in controlling inadvertent damage caused by visitors.

Management

One half of Kakadu National Park belongs to traditional Aboriginal owners, who lease it to the Commonwealth Government to be managed as a national park. The remaining area is vested in Parks Australia.

The park is controlled by a board of management, which was established in 1989 and comprises 10 Aboriginal people nominated by the park's traditional owners, two officers of Parks Australia, an employee of the Northern Territory Tourist Commission and a prominent nature conservationist.

The park is managed to prevent and minimise damage caused by weeds, feral animals, fire, mining operations and tourism, and to restore land affected in the past by mining and pastoralism. Management strategies include a strong visitor education program, research and monitoring activities, the restoration of former grazing and mine site areas, eradication of introduced species and the development of a controlled burning regime intended to reflect former Aboriginal burning-off practices.

Kakadu National Park attracts park management experts from many countries to review the experience gained there. Compared to most other parks, it has a substantial budget (around $9 million) and 38 full-time staff, including 12 Aboriginal members.

Aboriginal residents of the park are actively involved in park management. Aboriginal cultural advisors and rangers work towards the preservation of art sites and play an important role in visitor education.

RIGHT Sunset over the South Alligator River.

NEXT PAGE The magnificent Jim Jim Falls in full flow over the Kakadu escarpment.

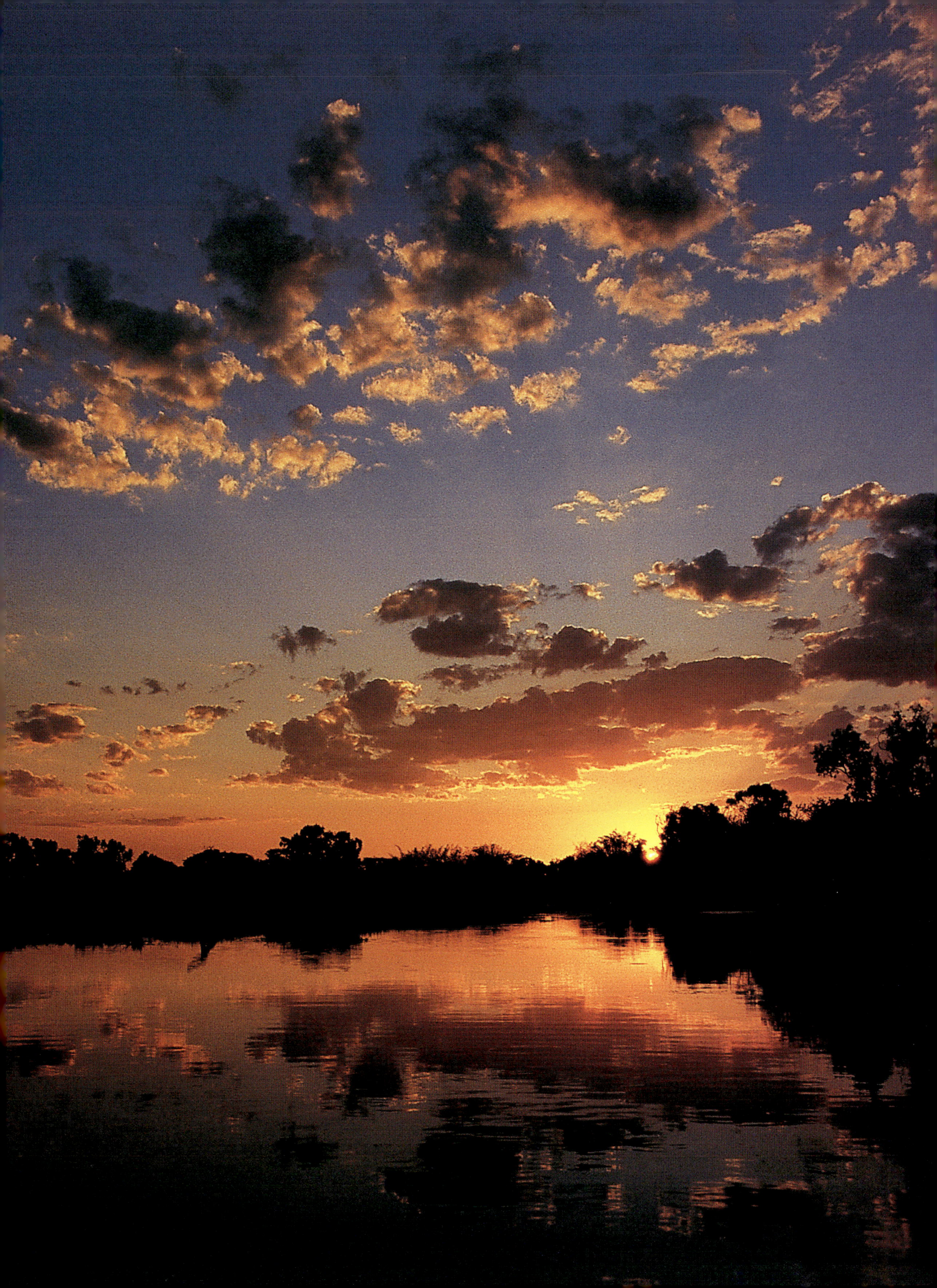

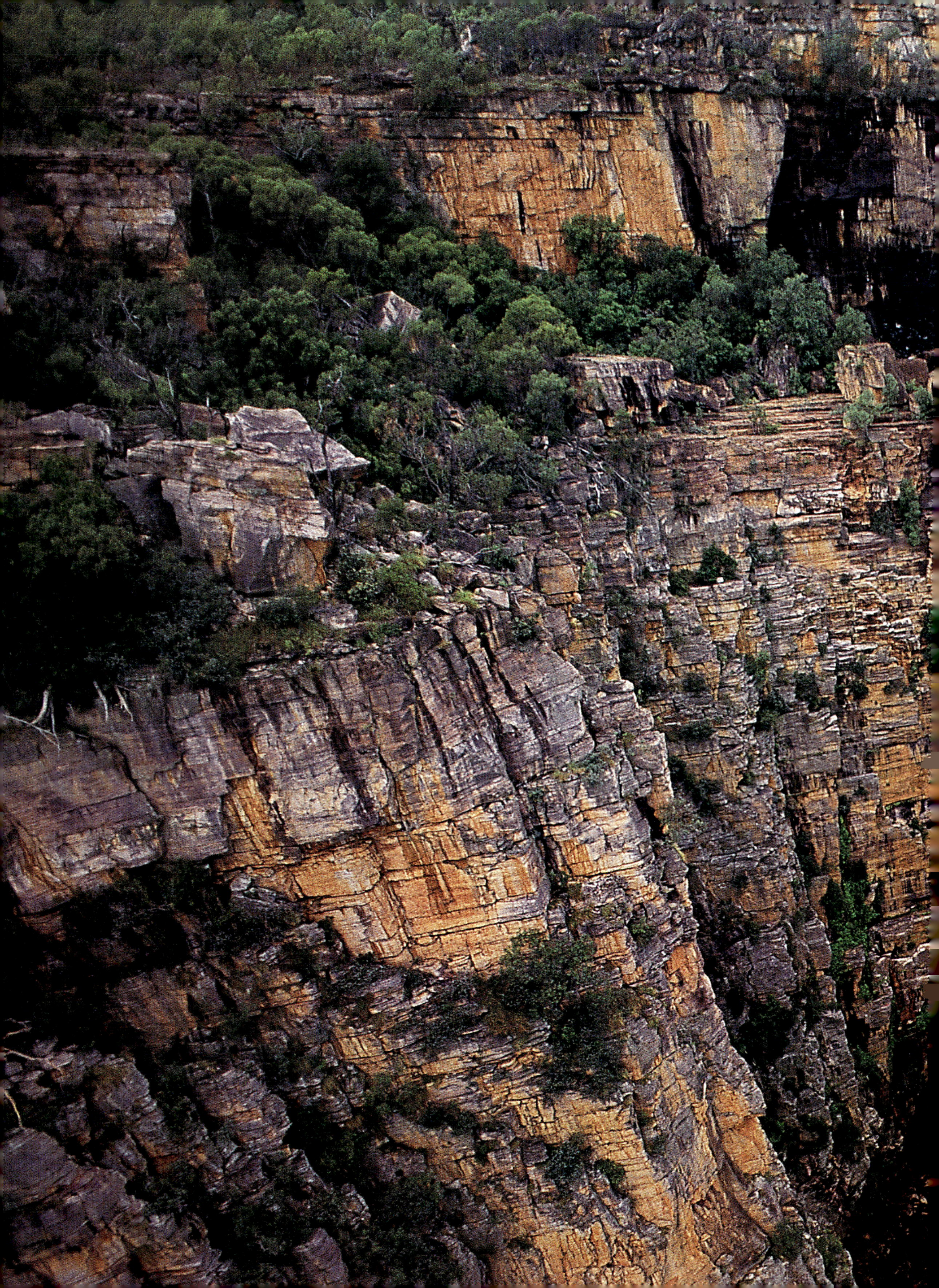

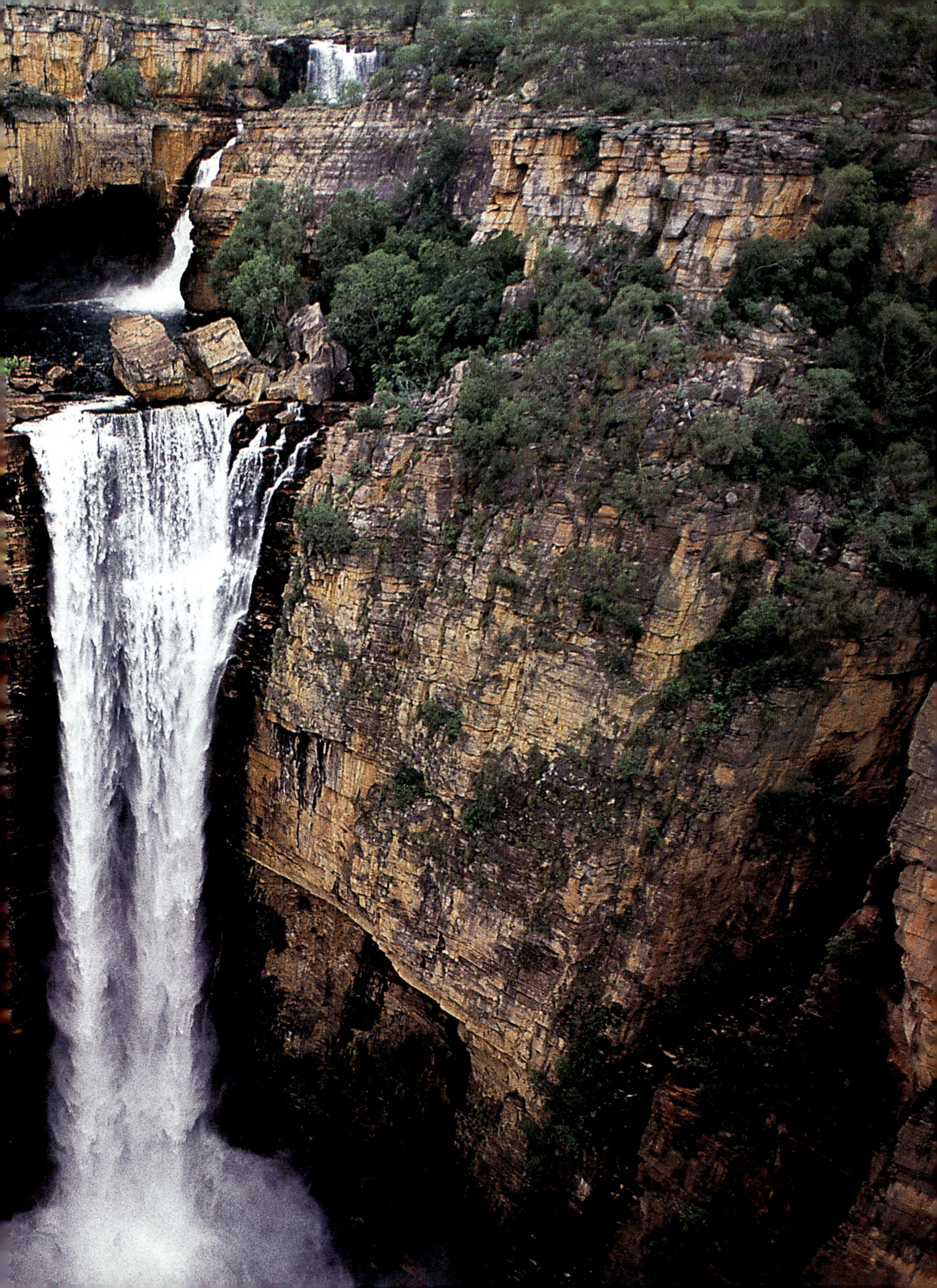

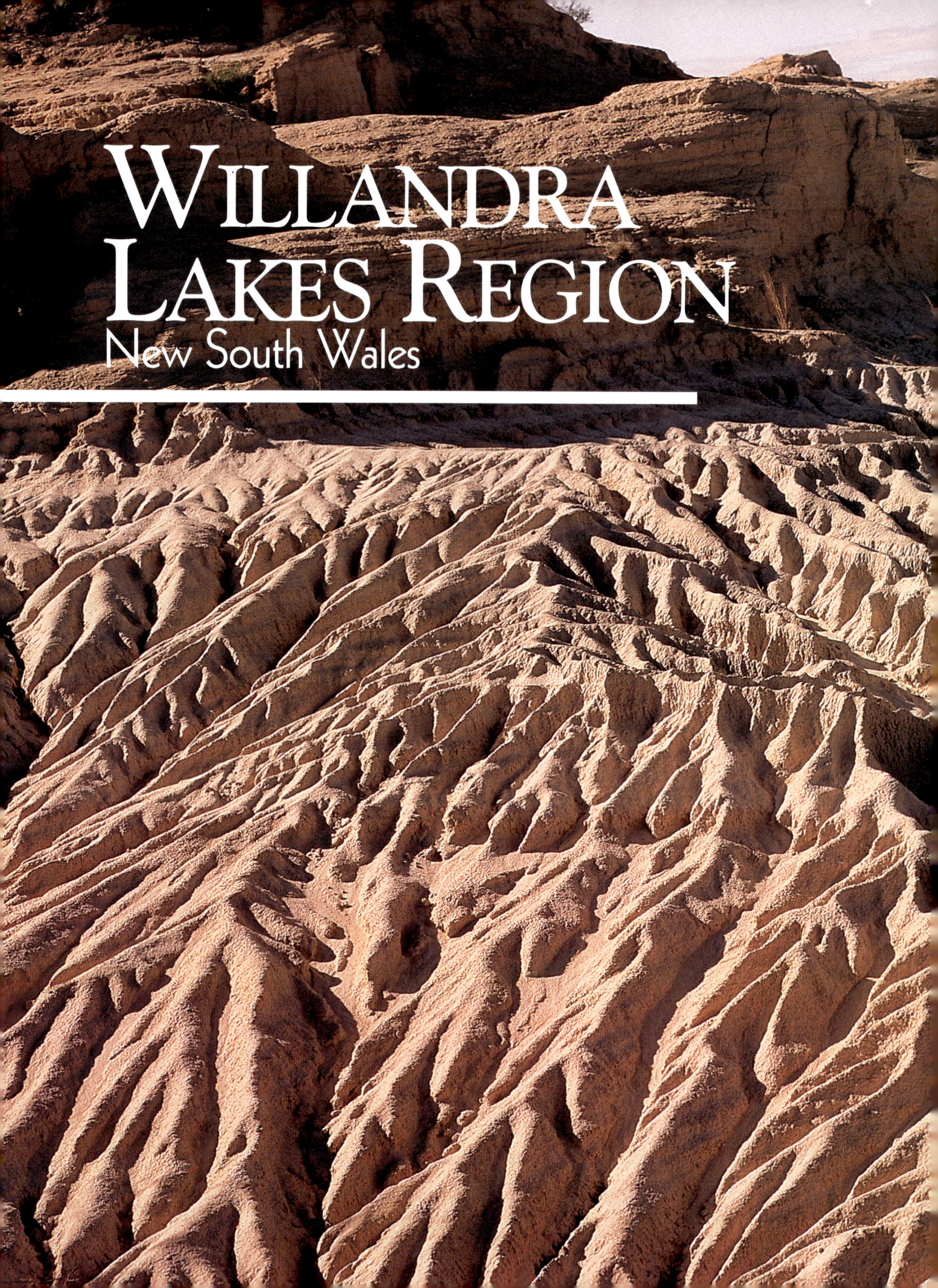

WILLANDRA LAKES REGION
New South Wales

Although somewhat neglected and the least visited of Australia's World Heritage areas, the Willandra Lakes Region has one of the most absorbing of all stories to tell. The focus of this site is a fossil lake system in the arid south-west of New South Wales where the landforms and sediments have preserved with unmatched veracity, events from 10 000 to 40 000 years ago during the last Ice Age. The area contains a plethora of ancient cultural and human remains and has yielded dates for the presence of modern humans which are among the oldest in the world. For these reasons, the Willandra Lakes Region was listed in 1981 as one of a few World Heritage areas recognised for both its natural and cultural values.

Location

The Willandra Lakes Region lies in the Murray Basin in remote south-west New South Wales. The site covers an area of around 239 000 hectares (590 000 acres), of which 27 847 hectares (68 813 acres) are contained within Mungo National Park. With the exception of the national park (which is administered by the New South Wales Parks and Wildlife Service), the land is controlled by the Western Lands Commission of NSW and has been leased for pastoral purposes.

PREVIOUS PAGE The wind-blown dunes known as the Walls of China are a prominent feature of the Willandra Lakes Region. These sand and clay structured dunes are termed 'lunettes' because the wind has fashioned them into a crescent-moon shape.

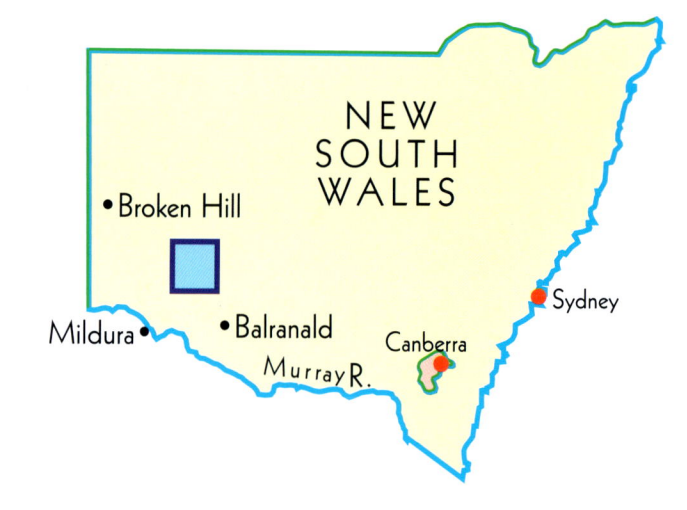

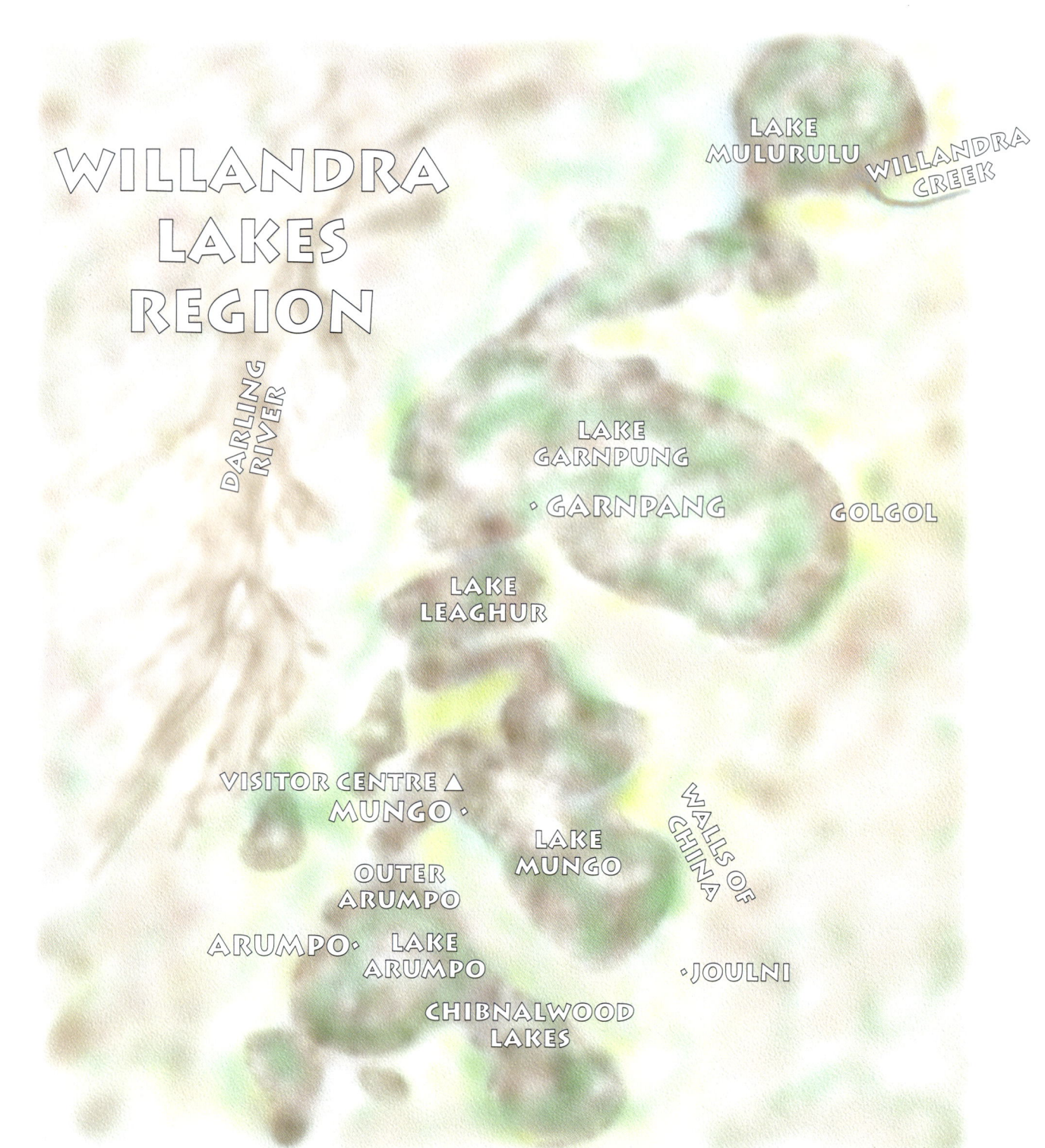

Willandra Lakes
By William Lines

I have always been fascinated by origins and this fascination is not mine alone. We are all curious about where we have come from and how the world came to be what it is. The story of the genesis of life and of the human family exerts a powerful hold over our imaginations.

Clues to the story about the spread of human beings over the face of the planet and their adaptation to different climates and locales have been found in Australia. In 1969, the skeleton of a young woman, cremated and buried 26 000 years ago, was discovered in a sand dune near dry Lake Mungo in south-west New South Wales. In 1974, another skeleton, of a man laid out in a grave 30 000 years ago and decorated with ochre, was found nearby.

These two individuals from the Willandra Lakes are the oldest securely dated humans in Australia. Later Willandra discoveries have enabled archaeologists and prehistorians to reconstruct the context of their lives. The resulting story raised the scientific and heritage importance of the Willandra Lakes to an international level and the area was listed as a World Heritage Area in 1981.

The World Heritage nomination claimed: "The Willandra Lakes System stands in the same relation to the global documentation of the culture of early *Homo sapiens* as the Olduvai Gorge relates to Hominid origins."

Is this claim justified?

Archaeologists and geneticists generally agree that humans, or *Homo sapiens*, arose in one place as a small population (with about 7500 males) in Africa about 270 000 years ago and later spread throughout the world. The exodus from Africa began about 100 000 or so years ago. All non-Africans (including Europeans, Asians and Australian Aborigines) have descended from this migrant population.

Between 40 000 and 100 000 years ago, some of these out-of-Africa migrants entered Australia, almost certainly from the north. Although the exact time and place of entry is unknown and is a matter of speculation, what is certain is that every part of Australia, from Cape York to the Kimberley Ranges, from Darwin to southern Tasmania and the south-west tip of Western Australia, had been occupied by 20 000 to 24 000 years ago. People were even camping in the centre of the continent over 22 000 years ago.

The first Australians entered a land dried out by the Ice Ages, a place of desert winds and gradually drying lakes, but humans are no strangers to Ice Ages or to aridity.

At least 18 separate ice advances and retreats have occurred in the last 2 million years or so, at roughly 100 000 year intervals, and the severity and size of the glaciers produced during each cycle has increased.

The last glacial advance and retreat began about 35 000 years ago and ended about 10 000 years ago.

The Ice Ages changed global climate. More of Australia became permanently arid. Aridity also struck southern Africa, where it reduced tropical forest cover and increased the forest fringe and savannah grasslands. Human-like beings or Hominids evolved on the margins of forest and grassland. Thus, the onset of the Ice Age coincided with the appearance of the first species of human or *Homo* almost 2.5 million years ago. The first stone tools also date from this time. We are creatures of the Ice Age even if we do not willingly seek arid places.

Although a relatively long arid period occurred across much of Australia between 75 000 and 35 000 years ago, the constant dry conditions did not affect the Murray Basin. There, from about 60 000 years ago, the catchments on the southern half of the Great Dividing Range, which supplied water to the Murrumbidgee and Murray and the south-east rivers, were moist. By 55 000 years ago all the lakes in the Murray Basin were full.

Into this well-watered land walked the first Australians. Some of these people settled around the shores of the freshwater Willandra Lakes, situated in present-day south western New South Wales, some 400 kilometres (250 miles) from the Southern Ocean, and 70 metres (230 feet) above sea level.

Consisting of six major lakes and numerous smaller depressions, and covering an area of 1088 square kilometres (420 square miles), the Willandra Lakes ranged in size from small ephemeral ponds up to Lake Garnpung, which was 500 square kilometres (190 square miles) in area and more than 10 metres (33 feet) deep. The Willandra Creek, now an anabranch or great billabong of the Lachlan River, once connected and replenished the lakes.

The lakes once overflowed through an outlet channel that can still be seen winding southwards through dunefields to the Murrumbidgee River west of Balranald, its banks clearly discernible for much of the way. Dry for at least 15 000 years, the survival of this ancient channel shows the great stability of the landscape through which it passes.

Fringed by hundreds of kilometres of lush shoreline, the lakes offered ideal hunting and foraging opportunities. At one camp on the shores of Lake Mungo, around 26 000 years ago, a young woman died. Survivors lit a fire and cremated the corpse. After the fire burnt out the charred bones were smashed and swept together into a shallow pit that eventually became covered with sand.

In 1969, archaeologists recovered those bones eroding from a block of soil carbonate in a sand dune marking the shores of the once full lake. A few years later, another burial, from around 30 000 years ago, was located eroding from sediments a few hundred metres from the cremation site. Here the remains of a tall man lay extended in a grave, the hands clasped. Deep red staining on the bones and in the soil indicated that the corpse had been coated thickly with red ochre, but to what purpose is not known.

The contrasting modes of burial and the care and attention lavished on the bodies provided grounds for plenty of speculation. Archaeologists and prehistorians began relating the story of these people who had lived by Willandra Lakes. The treatment of the bodies, they said, indicated intricate ritual concepts and social attitudes. These people were modern humans. They were us.

The discoveries triggered intense scientific interest in the Willandra Lakes - and not just from archaeologists. The area has since generated a large number of academic studies and doctoral dissertations in palaeochemistry, climatology, various branches of earth sciences, archaeomagnetism, radiocarbon dating, palaeoecology and faunal extinction. The Willandra Lakes Region offers such rich clues about the past that it represents a landmark in Pleistocene research for the Pacific and Australasia.

Today the lakes are dry. Outlined on their eastern margins by arching, ancient dunes, their basins lie on a wide, semi-arid plain that is open to the sky and punctuated by low ridges and dry creeks.

Most of the reconstructed history of the lakes and their occupants comes from debris and material buried in the lunette dunes formed on the downwind side of lakes.

When the lakes were full, westerly winds blew across the waters and stirred up waves that created sandy white beaches on their eastern sides. During dry summers, the wind blew the sand from the beaches into crescent-shaped sand dunes, known as lunettes. Lunettes lie at right angles to the wind direction and their ends curve downwind in two horns in response to the wind sweeping round, as well as over them, and they build up to a height at which they become stable.

The first lunettes formed during the late stage of the previous glacial period, possibly 120 000 years ago. No evidence of human occupation has been detected in any of these early exposed lunettes. Thereafter the lakes dried out.

Nevertheless, the climate changed again and, between 75 000 and 35 000 years ago, the lakes filled and lunette building resumed.

Even within this wet period there were droughts. During a dry period about 36 000 years ago, water levels dropped, lake water salinity increased and saltpans formed in the drying margins. Lake Mungo, in particular, shrank, became increasingly saline and almost dried up. Westerly winds carried a great deal of salt from the saltpans into the surrounding landscape and turned it saline.

Following a return to wetter conditions, the lakes refilled and remained at moderate levels until about 25 000 years ago. For about 7 000 years, to around 18 000 years ago, the lake levels fluctuated, although the general trend was for levels to become lower and the water saltier.

Around 18 000 years ago, the lakes were replenished but 1000 years later, the lakes began to dry again in response to the most intense period of global cooling.

As the lakes dried successively from south to north, they became increasingly salty. Enormous volumes of salty dust and sand piled over the lunettes and travelled across the land. At Lake Chibnalwood between 18 000 and 16 000 years ago, the wind picked up clay pellets and formed them into a clay lunette. Clay lunettes are relatively rare and the 30 metre (100 feet) high specimens at the Chibnalwood Lakes are amongst the largest clay dunes in the world.

As the lunettes formed, they slowly covered the living areas and burial places of hundreds of generations of people.

By 14 000 years ago, only Lake Mulurulu, the uppermost lake, contained water. Thereafter it dried, lunette building ceased and shrubs and trees grew on the lake bed.

The lakes did not refill. The Lachlan River has changed its course and Willandra Creek no longer carries any water as far as the Willandra Lakes, except during the heaviest floods.

These cycles, clearly marked in the layers of soil in the lunettes, reveal clues to the pattern of climatic change that has affected Australia over the past 100 000 years. The Willandra Lakes testify to periods in the past that were at times both wetter and drier than today.

Before the lakes finally dried up, people lived everywhere in the region. All the lakes, large and small, as well as areas adjacent to Willandra Creek, show signs of occupation.

However, as archaeologists depend upon natural erosion of lunette slopes for the exposure of material evidence of the past, the most eroded lunettes provide the most material. Most finds have been made around Lake Mungo.

ABOVE Eroded lunette dunes of Mungo Lake at dusk. Grazing in the area has exacerbated the erosion.

Mungo lunette is about 25 kilometres (15 miles) long and was once up to 40 metres (130 feet) high. Over one third of the lunette is eroded, exposing 600 hectares (1500 acres) of its core. Finds in this area indicate intensive occupation between about 32 000 and 25 000 years ago when the lake was at its maximum: up to 10 metres (33 feet) deep and 135 square kilometres (50 square miles) in area.

By contrast, Lake Garnpung's lunette has partially eroded over only a few hundred hectares of its 5700 hectare (1400 acres) area and there is practically no erosion of Lake Leaghur lunette.

Of the total area of all the Willandra lunettes, approximately eight per cent are extensively eroded, 20% partly eroded, while 72% remain vegetated and intact. Stabilising vegetation includes several species of low, multi-stemmed mallee eucalypts and, on sandy areas, white cypress pine. Porcupine grass or spinifex grows among the trees.

Erosion at Mungo lunette has produced a long white hill, visible from several kilometres away, above the sombre green and brown plains. This striking scenic feature is known as the Walls of China.

Sculpted shapes along its face expose successive phases of lunette building. Colours range from deep red to green-grey. Layers of clean quartz sand alternate with bands of clay-rich sediment and reveal the history of the wet and dry phases of the lake.

The remains of the cremated young woman found in 1969 - now known as Mungo Lady - lay on the southern end of the Mungo lunette. The second human find lay nearby. By 1989, the remains of 135 individuals had been identified. Three of the remains were complete.

Erosion, particularly by water and gullying, not only exposes sediments but rapidly moves large amounts of soil and causes the loss, scattering, removal or reburial of archaeological material. Rain and wind exacerbate the situation by moving fragments of bone down slopes.

Most remains, because they are not associated with soil layers that can be identified and of a determined age, cannot be accurately dated. However, all the individuals found in situ were from the southern end of the Lake Mungo lunette and were associated with the soil zone considered to have ended about 36 000 years ago. This means that human occupation certainly predates 30 000 years ago and is probably of the order of 40 000 years ago. Accordingly, since human occupation goes back to around 40 000 years ago, while the end of lunette formation and the final drying of the Willandra Lakes occurred around 15 000 years ago, there is a vast period of time over which recovered human remains around the Lakes could extend.

Most of the skeletons recovered are incomplete. The condition of the bones varies. Some are highly mineralised and hard, others delicate and friable, breaking at the slightest touch. Some bones are burnt, many are encrusted with calcium carbonate, others stained with manganese.

Missing and degenerated bone make many standard post-mortem observations impossible. Surface erosion and carbonate incrustation of bones compound the problem. Because of a lack of remaining teeth, determining the age to which the individuals lived has also been difficult. Most are simply identified as adult.

Even sexing the remains has been difficult. Of 135 individuals found, 15 males and 36 females have been identified. Nonetheless, as inadequate as they are, the bones provide significant clues about the Willandra Lakes people. Although there were undoubtedly hard times, starvation or poor nutrition was probably rare. Abundant, quality food promoted body growth and good health. Skeletal remains confirm quick and accurate healing of fractures. The strong structural composition of long bones attests to well-built limbs. Prominent areas of muscle attachment attest to ample muscle development.

Fortunately, we do not have to rely only on bones for clues about the life of these people. The lunettes contain other material that reveal the story of the long occupation of Willandra Lakes.

Stone tools eroded from the lunettes suggest they were used in many ways. Tools are relatively large, consisting either of heavy pieces used for chopping, smashing or planing, or flakes shaped for cutting, sawing and scraping. Notched and concave flakes probably smoothed wooden shafts; broad, curved specimens could flense skins.

The tools from Lake Mungo form a type of reference collection and belong, in the language of formal archaeology, to The Australian Core Tool and Scraper Tradition. Similar tools of a similar age have been unearthed elsewhere in Australia and in South-east Asia. Thus, these tools may constitute the technology possessed by the first Australian immigrants who crossed the deep waters that separate Asia from Australia.

Shell middens, or refuse heaps, testify to an abundant supply of shellfish and reveal a picture of people camping on the beaches, fishing and eating the freshwater mussels that abounded. The hearths of their fireplaces have been excavated to disclose the remains of fish feasts during which hundreds of fish were eaten.

Surviving remains of fish and crustaceans look almost as fresh as they were on the day they were caught in the waters of the now-dry lake, which then lapped only a few metres from a camp. Meals included Murray cod and golden perch.

However, the Willandra inhabitants ate more than fish. The remains of small mammals, birds, emu eggs and lizards in fireplace hearths and shell middens dated to before 34 000 years ago, attest to a varied and protein-rich diet. Material from these sources provided archaeologists with over 100 dates, most of them between 10 000 and 40 000 years ago. One excavation uncovered lumps of red pigment sealed well below the ashes of a fire lit around 32 000 years ago. The presence of the colouring materials, brought intentionally into the area, and the ochred burial of the second recovered skeleton hint at the existence of an aesthetic sense.

Aesthetics, ritual and concern for deceased kin are considered hallmarks of humankind. Further, because there is no reason to question that these humans were the ancestors of present-day Aborigines, their remains establish the great antiquity of Aboriginal culture.

Not all significant remains are confined to middens and hearths or other obviously human created sites.

Lunettes at Lake Tandou and Lake Menindee contain the remains of extinct megafauna such as the giant *Diprotodon*, the giant kangaroo *Protemnodon*, the browsing kangaroo *Sthenurus*, the marsupial lion *Thylacoleo*, and the giant browsing kangaroo *Procoptodon*. There are also remains of hare-wallabies, nailtail wallabies, bettongs, pig-footed bandicoots and bilbies. Lunettes at Lake Menura and Lake Victoria contain koala remains, indicating that these creatures lived in the riverine forest in the seasonally dry habitat just as they do in parts of Queensland today.

The lunettes hold great potential for the recovery of more extinct giant marsupial species. So far, remains of large animals and megafauna have been conspicuously absent from shell midden and hearth food debris. However, if the bones of megafauna were to be found in association with human sites, Willandra would help establish a link between hunting by humans and the extinction of the giant marsupials.

ABOVE Wind, rain and the effects of channelled water have created some interesting forms over the last few hundred years.

Other animal remains indicate the previous presence of now locally extinct species including the rat kangaroo, hairy-nosed wombat, Tasmanian devil and Tasmanian tiger. The latter two species are now extinct over continental Australia.

The lunettes do not only preserve biological material. The Willandra Lakes Region is one of the benchmarks in world-wide studies of changes in earth magnetism.

Magnetic strength and direction can change, even reverse, with north becoming south and south becoming north. Sometimes the polarity starts to change and the strength of the field fluctuates, as if a reversal were about to take place, before returning to normal. When Lake Mungo was full, there were two fluctuations in which the magnetic field was stronger than usual: one between 31 000 and 28 000 years ago, and a weaker one at 26 000 years ago.

Stones from hearths reveal the two magnetic field shifts. When they formed part of Aboriginal fireplaces, the stones underwent heating to the point where their magnetic minerals became unlocked and aligned themselves in the direction of the Earth's magnetic field at the time.

Modern European occupation of the Willandra Lakes began in the 1850s. By 1860, when the Burke and Wills expedition crossed the Willandra area, pastoral settlements had been established at Balranald and Menindee. In 1869, Chinese labourers helped build a huge woolshed, still standing, of local Murray pine. Presumably, the naming of the dune formations as 'The Walls of China' derives from that link.

In the 1860s, Lake Mungo was part of Gol Gol station. In 1922 Lake Mungo became a separate 16 000 hectare (40 000 acres) holding and was given the name Mungo from a picture of an old Scottish church. In 1978, the New South Wales National Parks and Wildlife Service took over the property and made it the nucleus of Mungo National Park, dedicated in 1979.

When placed on the World Heritage List in 1981, the Willandra Lakes Region covered 370 000 hectares (915 000 acres). In 1995, following criticism from the World Heritage Committee, the Australian government revised the boundaries and reduced the area to 239 000 hectares (590 000 acres).

Nominated for World Heritage listing on the basis of both its natural and cultural values, the Willandra Lakes Region preserves an outstanding set of clues to the major stages of the Earth's ice age history. These clues are cumulative and interconnected and reveal geological processes, biological evolution and human interaction with the natural environment.

Information on water level fluctuations in the lakes, tied closely to radio-carbon dating and other methods, provides clues about the water regime across south-east Australia and the climates that controlled it. These clues also contribute to the reconstruction of past global conditions.

Mungo Lady is the earliest record of cremation in the world. Other human remains found at Willandra Lakes provide insights into past care for the dead.

Because the lakes dried out some 15 000 years ago, they offer virtually unmodified landscapes for investigation. Lake Mulurulu, the northern-most lake and the last to dry, contains the most recent archaeological evidence.

Occupation of the area has been continuous but as nature changed the environment from freshwater lakes to semi-arid conditions, the lacustrine economy also changed.

The Willandra Lakes provide evidence of the most distant point of dispersal around the Earth reached by humans during the climax of the last Ice Age.

The 30 000 years of human occupation revealed at Willandra Lakes has few parallels for its time span anywhere in the world and throws much light on the origins of human life on the Australian continent.

Special Features

The Willandra Lakes Region is an example of a semi-arid environment which has remained unaltered by the effects of glaciation, sea-level fluctuations or movements in the Earth's crust since the Pleistocene epoch. It is an invaluable resource for research into the past which can contribute to a better understanding of the present, offering evidence for changes in climate and related environmental changes over the past 100 000 years.

Among Willandra's 1000 square kilometres (390 square miles) of dried-out lake basins and dunes, the 30 metre (100 feet) high Chibnalwood 'lunette' dunes - so described because of its crescent-moon shape - is a prominent landmark. Formed by wind-blown clay particles around 18 000 to 16 000 years ago, these lunettes are among the largest known clay dunes in the world.

ABOVE Apostle birds drinking at a waterhole.

RIGHT Wind and water erosion have hewn these fluted towers, a feature at the Walls of China.

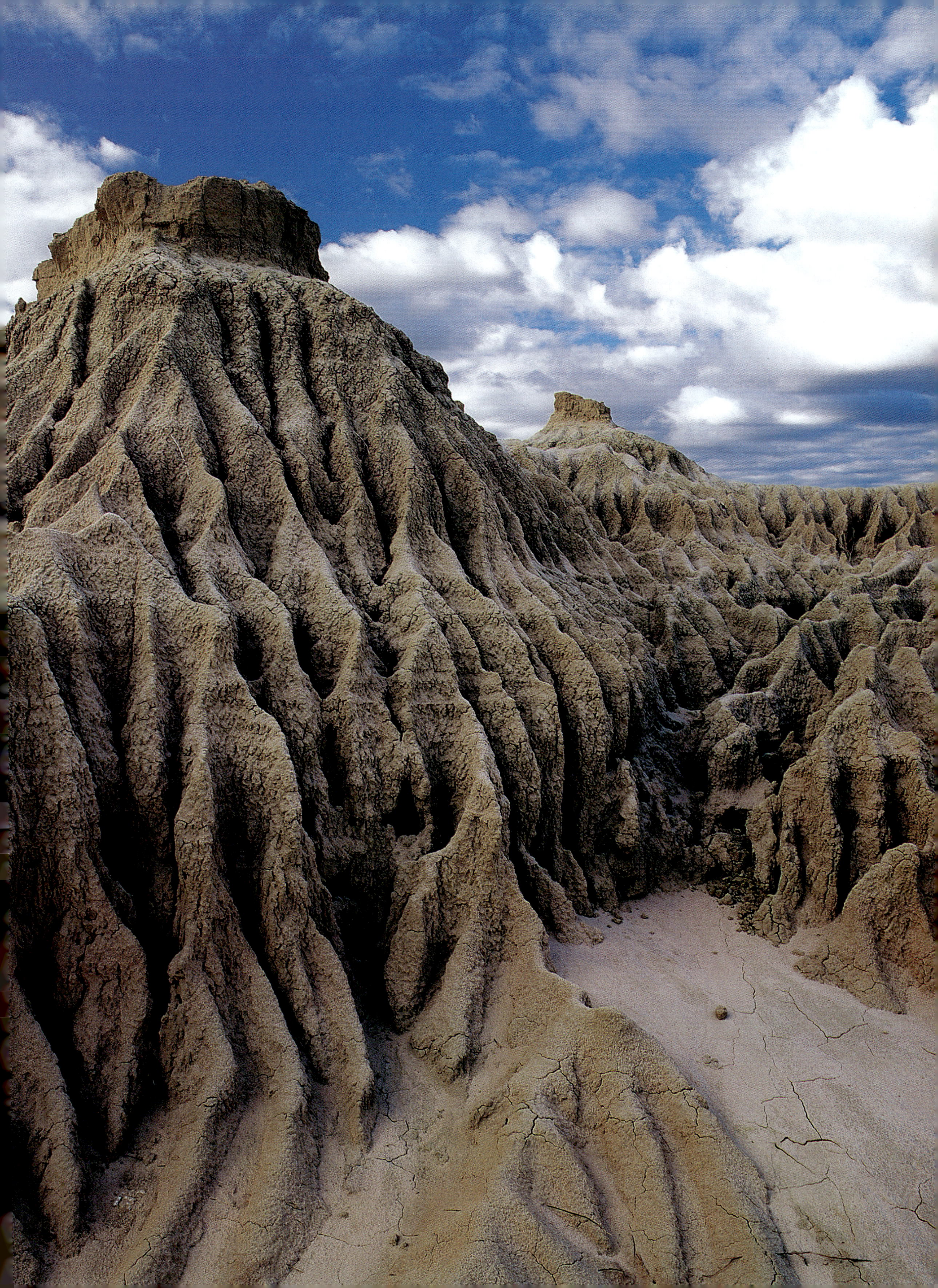

Flora

This semi-arid region is dominated by plant species that have been able to survive high temperatures and prolonged periods without rain, and that have adapted to soils with a high saline or limestone content. These include saltbushes, bluebushes, bluebells and groundsel bushes growing in the ancient lakebeds.

The sandplains and dunes are vegetated by a variety of herbs and grasses such as spinifex, speargrass and copper burrs, as well as a few hardy mallees and tree species which include: the cypress pines, more common fruit bearing berrigan and native apricot trees, belah and rosewood trees and dillon-bush. Most species are common to semi arid regions of Australia.

ABOVE A dust storm at Lake Mungo.

RIGHT The visitor centre at Mungo, near the old homestead and woolshed, holds many of the Aboriginal artefacts discovered in the area and displays reconstructions of the area's now extinct species including the giant prehistoric 'wombat' or *Zygomaturus*.

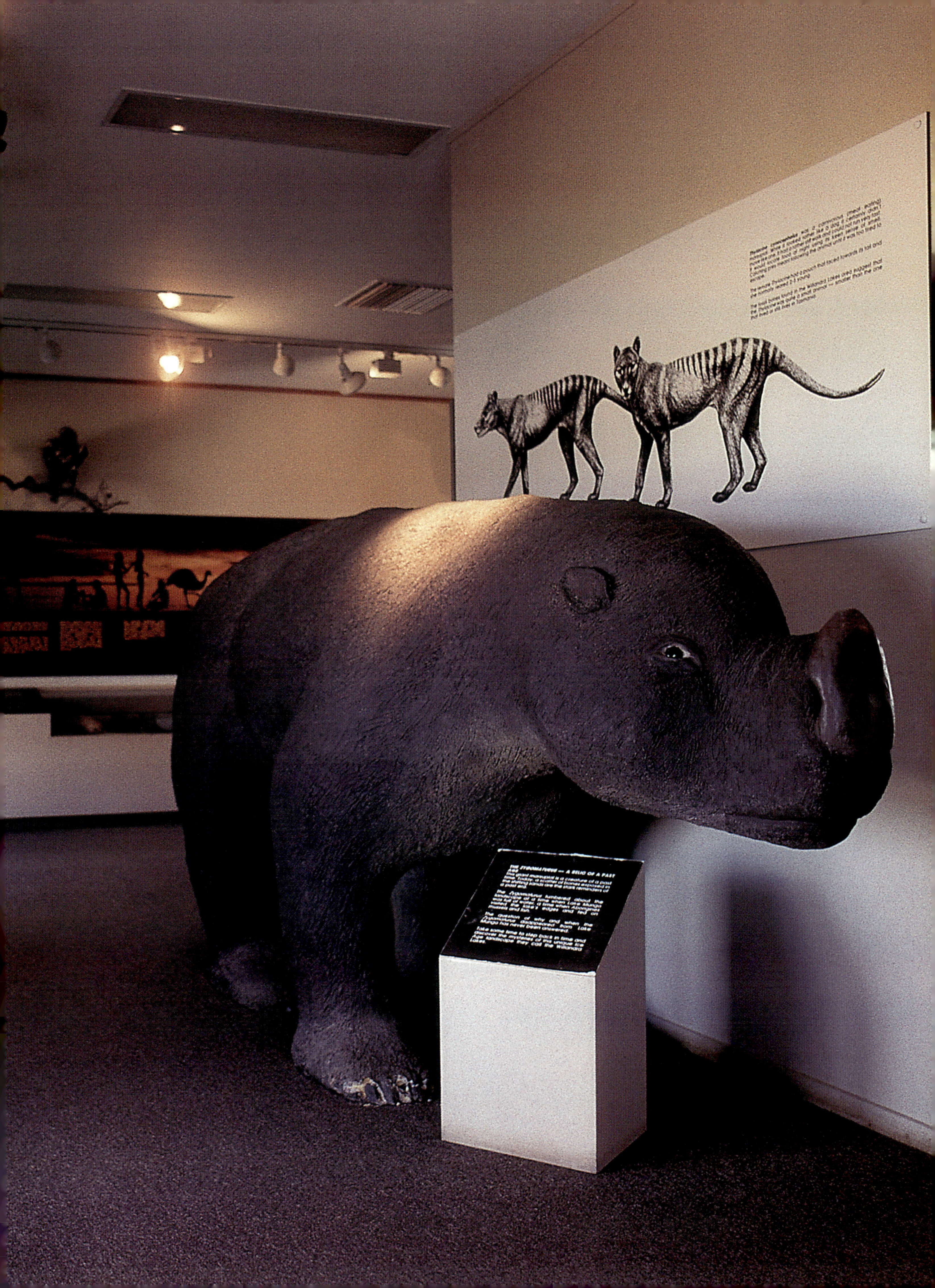

ABOVE The skeletal remains of a burrowing bettong.

Fauna

Animal species at Willandra Lakes are typical of the semi-arid western region of New South Wales. The area is inhabited by a number of marsupials including the red and western grey kangaroos who graze on the spartan grasses and mallee scrub vegetation. Others are the common fat-tailed dunnart and planigales, a fierce carnivore on a miniature scale to the Tasmanian Devil who eat insects associated with the vegetation. The dry scrub trees also host termites and ants which provide ample food resources for the short-beaked echidna, one of Australia's two egg laying mammals or monotremes. There are also nine species of bat living within the region, amongst whom are the rarer greater long-eared bat.

Several introduced species have also ravaged the native wildlife and vegetation over the years, including sheep. Feral species which have wreaked destruction include the European rabbit, red fox and goat.

There are also several bird species living in this area which include the pink cockatoo, emu, apostle bird, crested pigeon, chestnut quail-thrush, red-capped robin and the colourful mulga parrot.

However, best adapted to this arid land are the numerous native reptile species including the ugly looking shingleback lizard and the legless Burton's snake lizard which is often mistaken for a snake.

RIGHT Lake Mungo lunette. The dunes of the area are gradually moving eastward under the influence of the westerly winds.

RIGHT INSET Hardy saltbush and bluebush shrubs dominate the dry ancient lake beds of the Willandra Lakes System and provide grazing for wildlife.

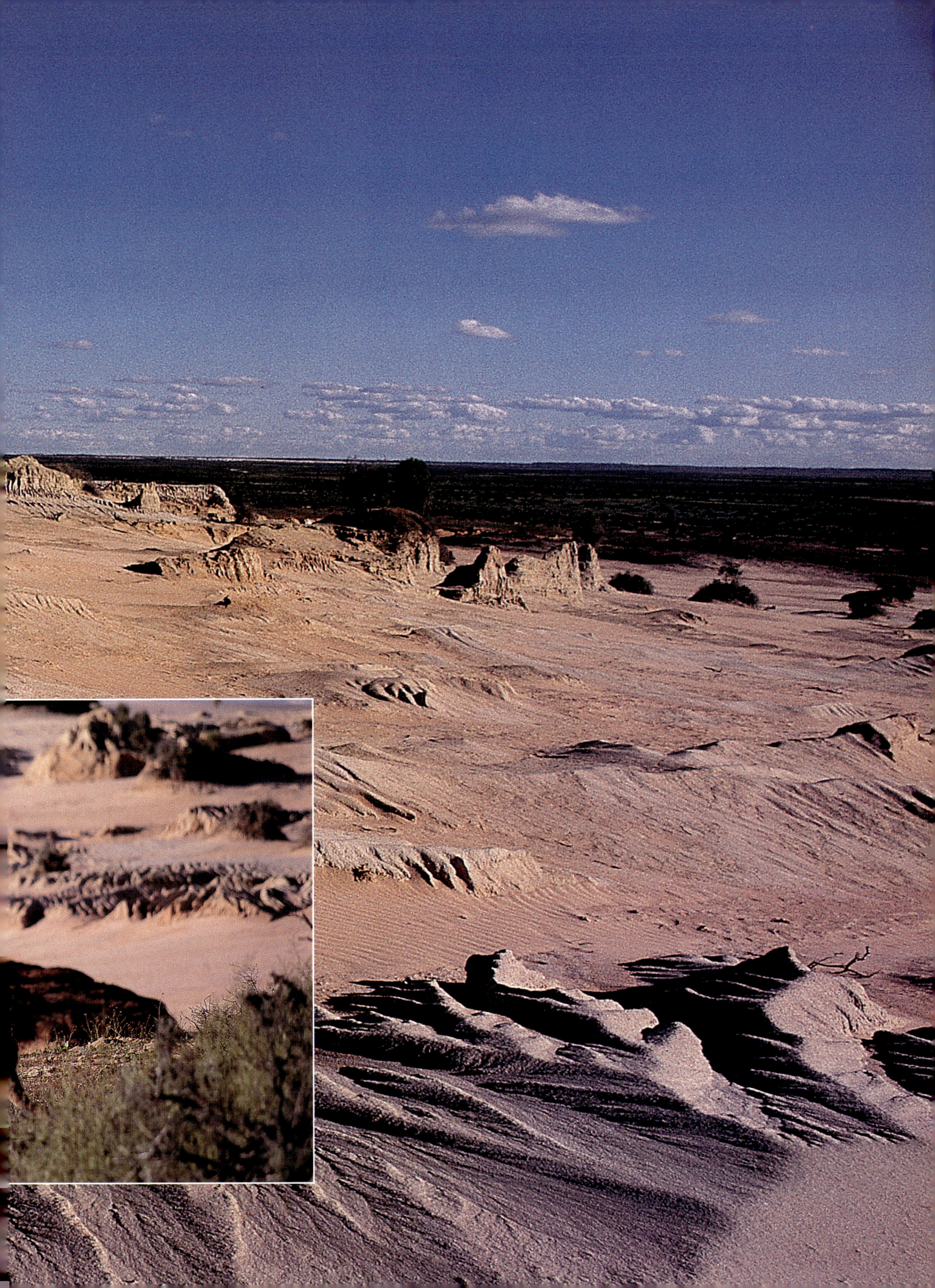

Cultural Heritage

As well as being an outstanding natural museum of the earth sciences, the Willandra Lakes Region forms a dramatic chapter in the world's cultural history. Archaeological remains found at the eroding lunette sand dunes of the region hold evidence of the world's oldest known cremation and a 30 000 year-old ochre burial site, which are comparable in age to ancient sites discovered in France. The remains, interred with care and ceremony, show that these people were fully modern human beings. Their presence in the Willandra area some 30 000 years ago marks the most distant point on the Earth reached by humans during the height of the last Ice Age. Grind stones and mortars have been found from more recent times. Used to grind wild grass seeds into flour, these tools are evidence of one of the world's earliest seed-grinding economies.

The Willandra Lakes Region has also yielded well-preserved remains of Australia's ancient megafauna, such as the giant kangaroo *Procoptodon*. The extinction of these creatures has long been a mystery: was hunting by humans the cause of their demise? The Willandra Lakes Region may yet yield the answer.

The Willandra Lakes Region also holds the ashes of many long-extinguished fire-place hearths, some as much as 30 000 years old. These hearths provide fascinating insights into the state of the Earth's magnetic field in the past and have revealed fluctuations and reversals in the Earth's polarity. Measurements made at Willandra have revealed that 30 000 years ago, there was a variation in the Earth's magnetic field of 120°, making the region a benchmark in studies of palaeomagnetism around the world.

TOP RIGHT The first large scale excavation undertaken as seen here was to gain information about the occupation of the region by the people to which the cremated remains of the `Mungo lady' and `Mungo man' finds belonged. The red-brown Mungo soil corresponds to a period when Willandra Lakes contained fresh water more than 25 000 years ago. Stone artefacts were found as far down as the scientists standing in the bottom of the trench.

BOTTOM RIGHT An aboriginal fireplace containing meal remains of golden perch which radiocarbon dating puts at 34 000 years ago.

BELOW A ground-edge chisel artefact found at Lake Mungo made from stone material imported from outside the region.

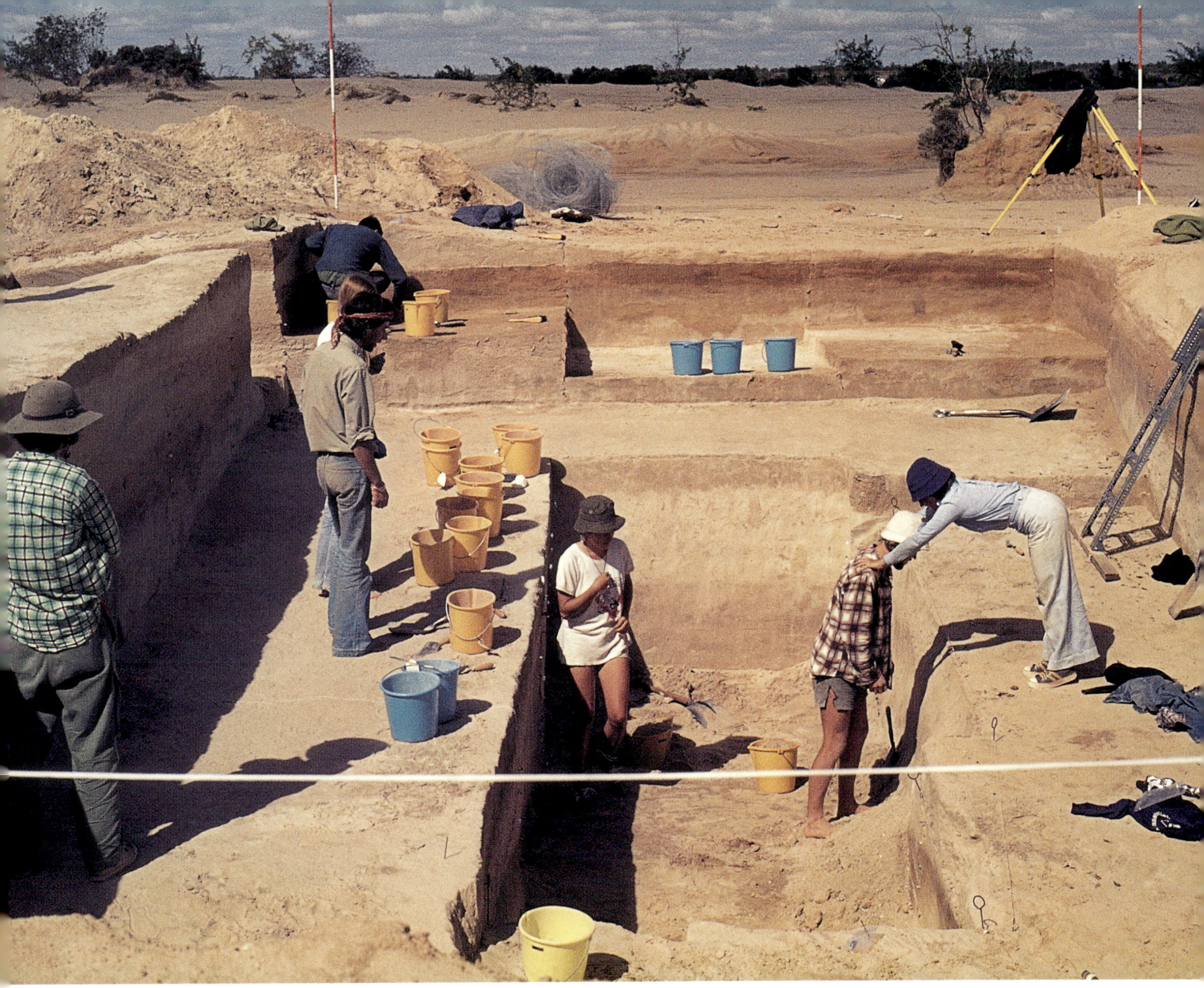

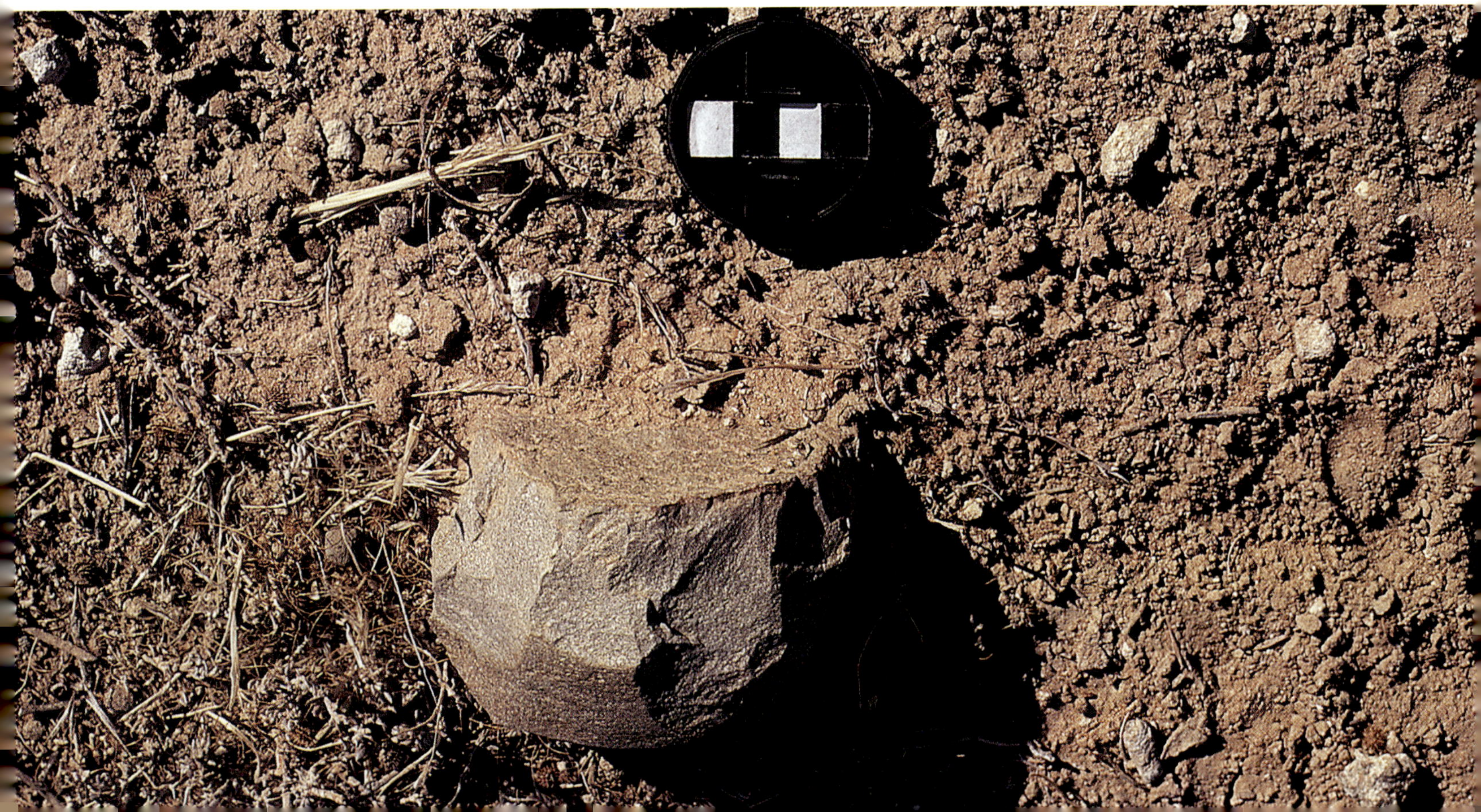

ABOVE The striking colours of the mallee ringneck contrast strongly with the barren, desert landscape.

RIGHT The historical Mungo Lake wool shearing shed.

76

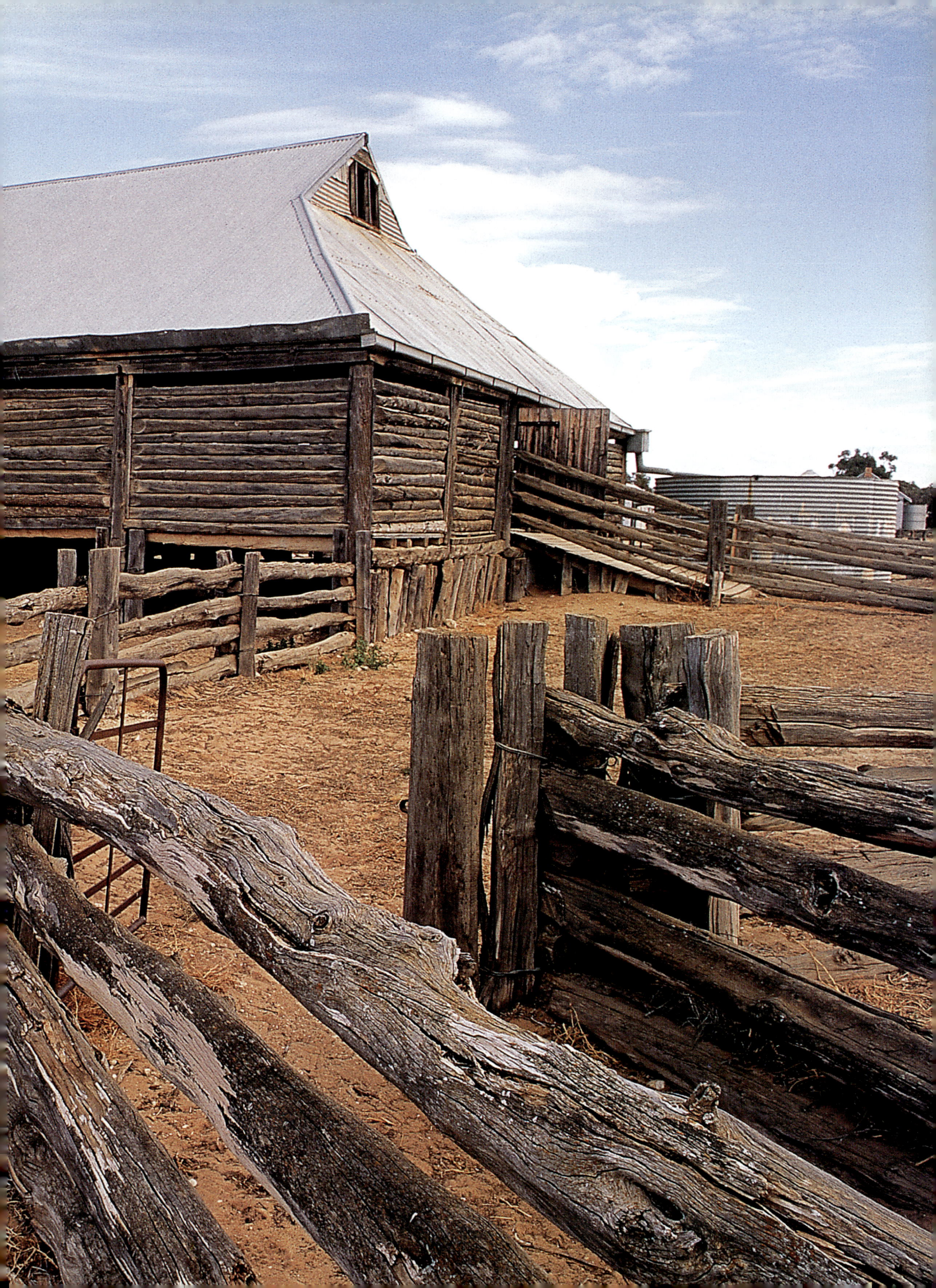

Threats

Lacking spectacular features and located in a dry and remote corner of Australia, the Willandra Lakes Region receives few visitors compared with other World Heritage areas. The little tourism that occurs is mainly confined to the Mungo National Park, where travellers are rewarded by the stark - almost otherworldly - splendour of the lunette dunes called the Walls of China. The greatest threat to the integrity of the Willandra Lakes Region is that the site has long been overlooked and under-funded. In April 1994, IUCN-The World Conservation Union arranged a field visit to Willandra Lakes and concluded that it was the most neglected of all Australia's World Heritage sites and in urgent need of attention.

Additional problems have arisen from long-standing conflicts involving graziers pasturing their flocks on leases within the site, local Aboriginal groups and various government agencies. In the 1994 IUCN visit, it was noted that despite Aboriginal concerns and the problems with graziers, no management plan for the site had been concluded 13 years after the inscription of Willandra Lakes on the World Heritage List. Work subsequently began on a management plan for the area. A plan was finally made in 1996.

Prungle Lakes, the southernmost dry lakes in the chain, have partially been sown to wheat.

Sheep grazing for wool occurs on surrounding land but the main danger to the environment is from feral animals.

Feral grazing animals cause vegetation loss and soil erosion and, through habitat destruction, diminish wildlife, while feral predators destroy native animals more directly. Ferals in Willandra include rabbits, foxes, goats and cats. Droughts reduce their numbers drastically but they multiply in good seasons.

Tourism is not a significant pressure at Willandra but is increasing. The remoteness of the area, the summer heat and poor roads - almost impassable in wet weather - mean that the most important areas within Willandra Lakes receive few visitors.

RIGHT An eroded lunette at sunset, Mungo Lake.

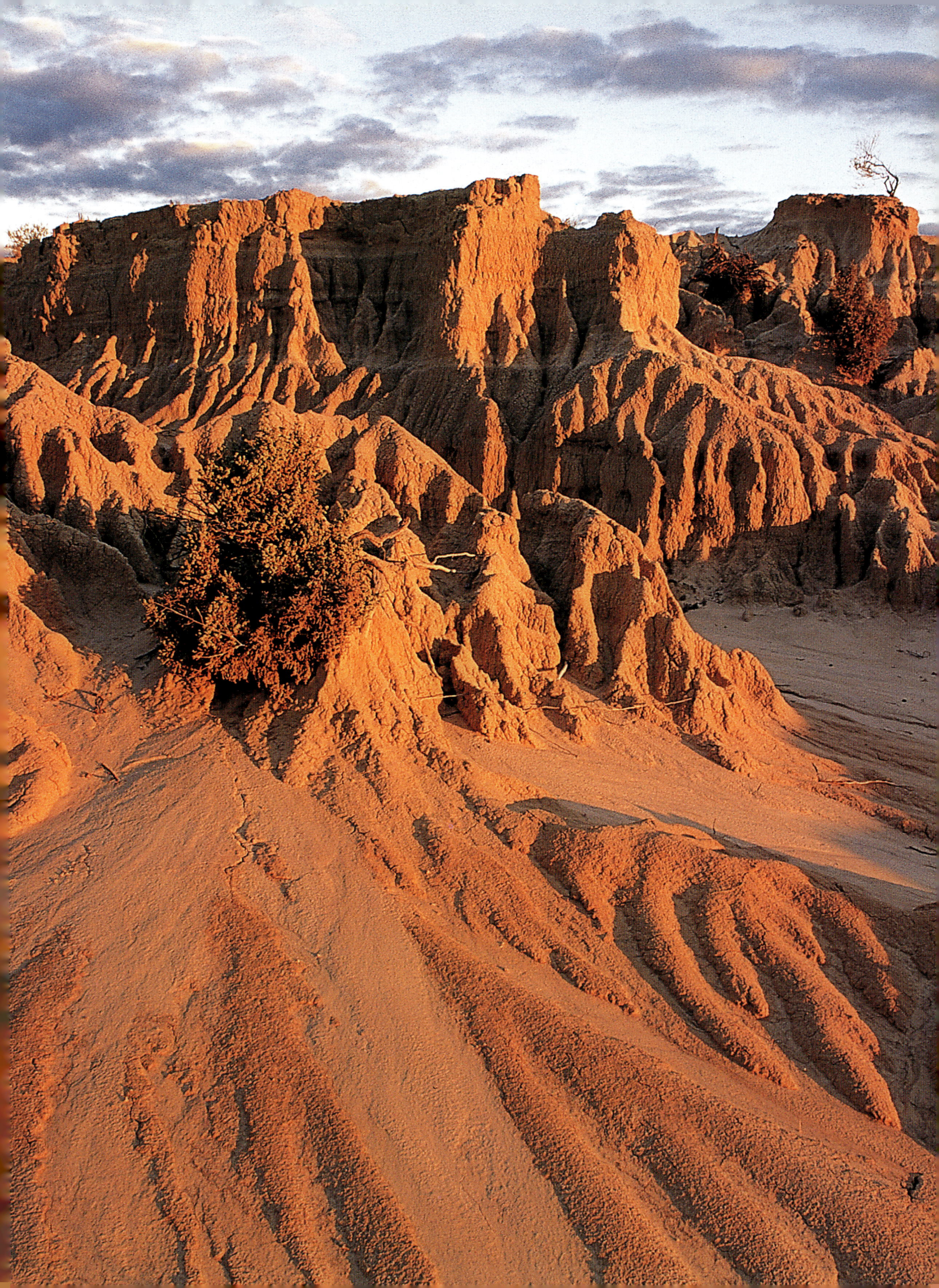

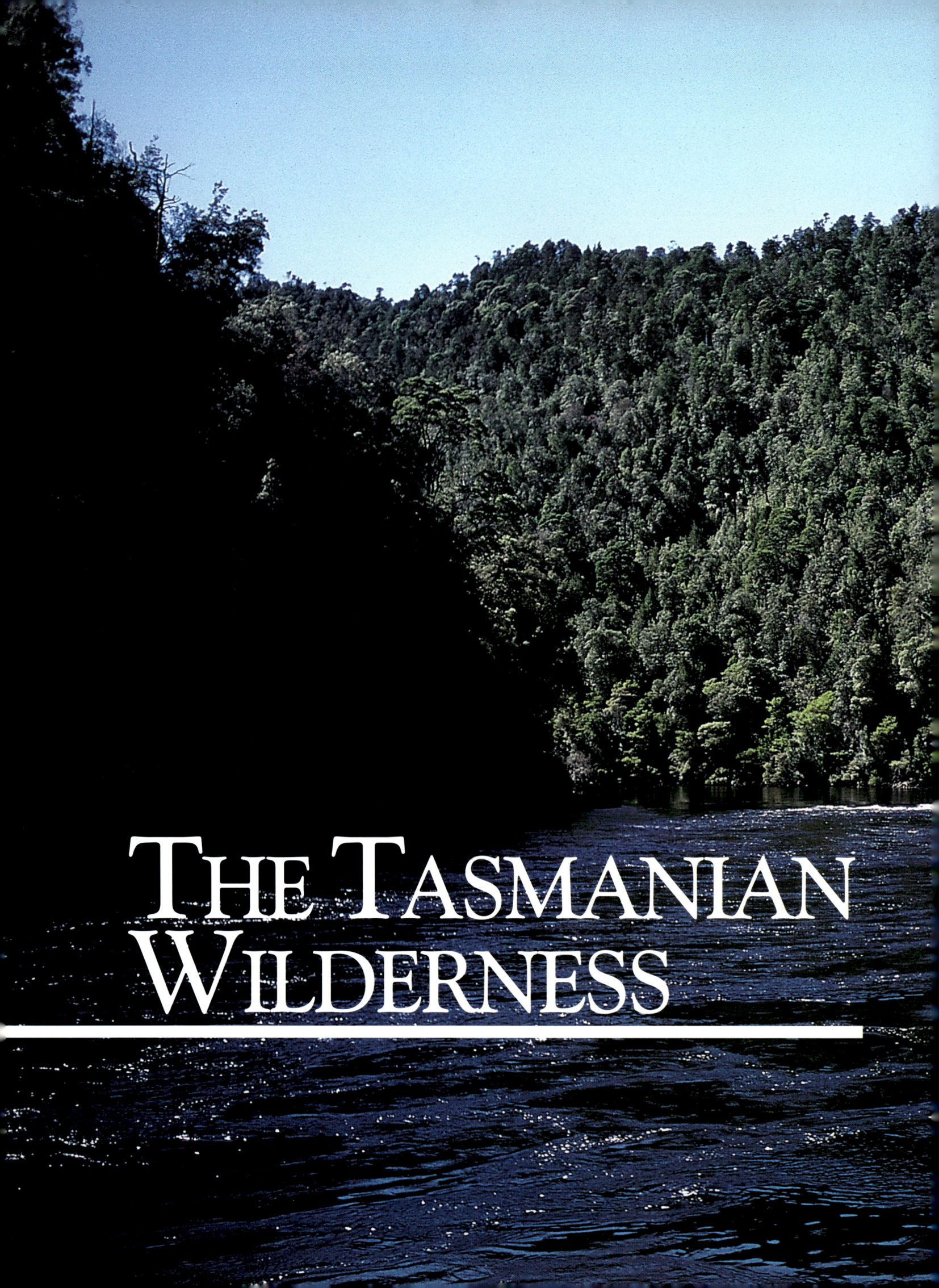

The Tasmanian Wilderness

There is no place in Australia like the wilderness of South-west Tasmania. It is set apart by its combination of dramatic scenery, extensive coastal habitats, geological features, wild rivers, countless lakes, specialised alpine and rainforest plants, as well as some 30 native animal species that are found nowhere else. In addition, it holds important evidence of human occupation during the last Ice Age. The Tasmanian Wilderness World Heritage Area is one of the five largest conservation units in Australia and offers a conjunction of biophysical and cultural qualities that make it a very significant region for both science and conservation. The site was inscribed on the World Heritage List in 1982 after it was judged to meet all four natural criteria as well as three of the prescribed cultural criteria.

Location

The Tasmanian Wilderness World Heritage Area incorporates a wealth of conservation areas including five national parks: Cradle Mountain-Lake St.Clair, Southwest, Franklin-Lower Gordon Wild rivers, Walls of Jerusalem, Hartz Mountains; six state reserves: Devils Gullet, Marakoopa Cave, Exit Cave, Liffey Falls, Port Davey, Sarah Island Historic Site; four conservation areas: Central Plateau; Oakleigh Creek State Forest, South-west State Forest, St. Clair Lagoon; a number of forest reserves: Meander, Liffey, Drys Bluff; land areas vested in the Hydro-Electric Commission: Franklin-Lower Gordon Leased Reserve, Strathgordon-Scotts Peak Area, Middle Gordon-Denison Area, Lake Augusta, Nelson Valley Area, Lake McKenzie Area; 5270 hectares (13 000 acres) of unallocated Crown land; and Maatsuyker Island. Together, these areas extend over 1 374 000 hectares (3 400 000 acres) of south-west and central Tasmania.

PREVIOUS PAGE The wild Gordon River has cut its way through mountain ranges to create spectacular gorges.

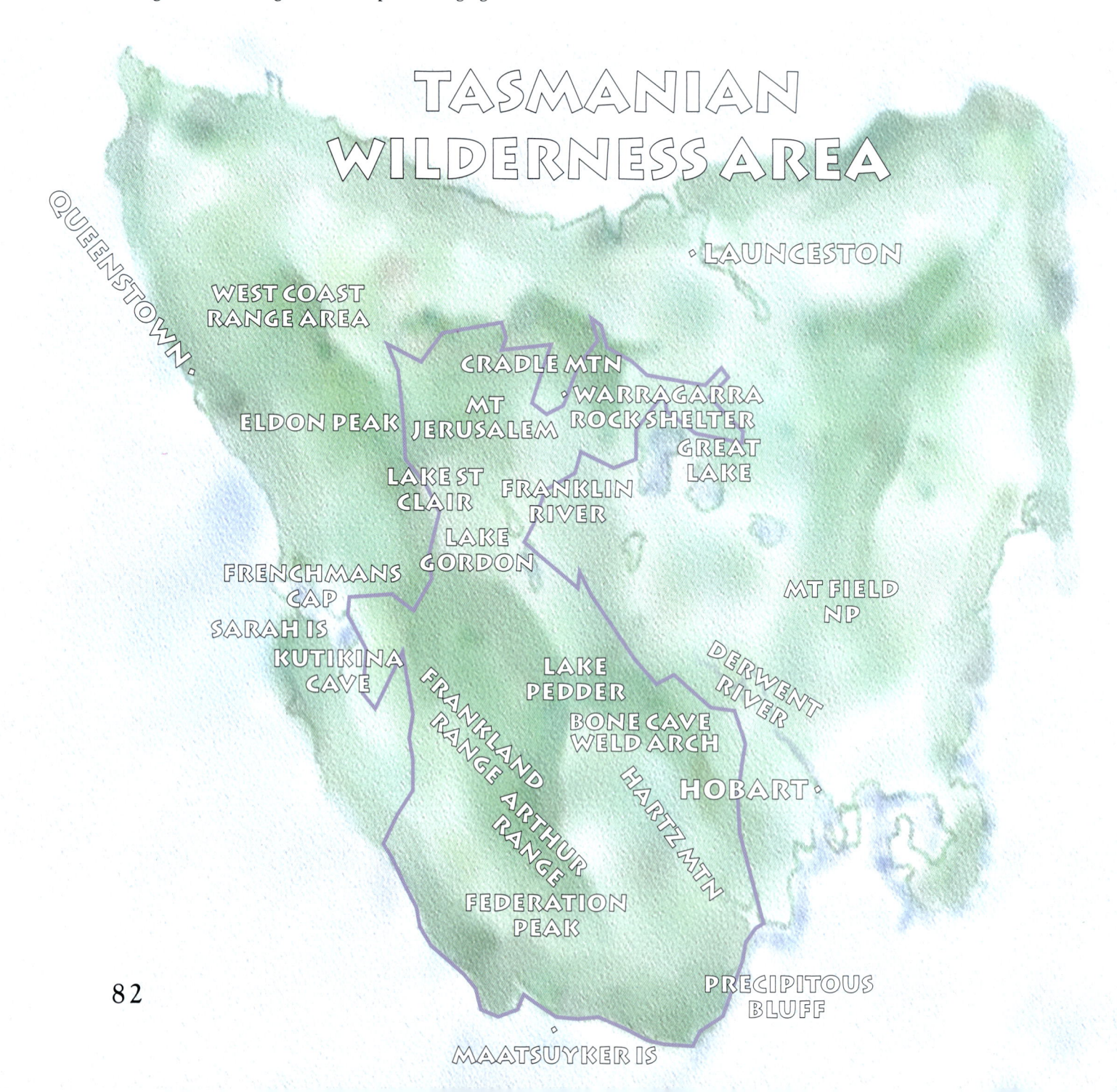

The Tasmanian Wilderness
A Landscape Peopled Long Ago

by William Lines

At the time of the first British settlement in 1804, Tasmania was the home of about 5000 Aboriginal people. They were descendent from the most isolated humans on the planet. Apart from fleeting contact with passing ships during the previous 200 years, their ancestors had lived for 500 generations without encountering another human group.

Within 30 years of the arrival of the British, most of Tasmania's tribal Aborigines were dead and their way of life had been shattered. By 1855, only three men, two boys and eleven women remained alive. The men died first and the last tribal Aboriginal woman, Truganini, died in 1876. The culture and identity of the group has not been entirely lost, however, and is kept alive by Tasmanians of mixed descent, who identify as Aborigines.

Part of the legacy of the Tasmanian Aborigines is preserved in caves, rock art, fireplace hearths and the heaps of shell wastes called middens to be found in the remote wilderness of Western Tasmania. These remains and artefacts are so significant and so rich that they form part of World Heritage. Here are undisturbed archaeological sites which date back over 30 000 years and excavated material, as well as the cave paintings, which point to an Ice Age society that has disappeared.

South-west Tasmania is a region where mountain ridges rise above extensive tracts of rainforest or wet eucalypt forest, and a place of rivers, lakes and buttongrass plains. During the coldest phase of the last Ice Age, about 20 000 years ago, the scene was different: glaciers sat in the high mountain valleys and alpine vegetation covered plains and slopes; the cold conditions forced the rainforest to retreat to sheltered valleys. Elsewhere, shrublands, herbfields, grassy plains and open forests provided excellent grazing for marsupials similar to the wallabies that inhabit some parts of the area today, as well as giant marsupials, known as megafauna, that have since become extinct. The presence of so much game undoubtedly attracted hunters.

The hunters dragged their kill, mostly red-necked wallaby, back to caves in the now densely forested valleys of the Junee-Florentine Rivers, as well as to caves in the Gordon Limestone cliffs that line both the Gordon and Franklin Rivers. Hundreds of flaked stone tools and fossil wallaby bones have been found in these caves.

In Beginner's Luck Cave in the Florentine Valley, stone tools date to about 20 000 years ago.

The richest finds, however, have been made at Kutikina (or Fraser) Cave some 35 metres (115 feet) above the banks of the Franklin River. Excavation has uncovered fireplace hearths, broken animal bones, stone tools and other material. In fact, initial excavation yielded more than one hundred times the number of stone artefacts recovered up to that time from all other Tasmanian Ice Age sites put together. One cubic metre (one cubic yard) of material dug from the floor of the cave yielded about 40 000 stone artefacts and 35 kilograms (77 pounds) of bone in some 250 000 fragments.

First occupied about 20 000 years ago, Kutikina is a large limestone cave with easy access and a level floor. It was obviously a major base camp. Here, hunters cut up wallaby carcasses with a rock called 'Darwin-glass' that came from a meteor crater about 50 kilometres (30 miles) to the north-west.

The inhabitants of Kutikina Cave were the most southerly human beings on Earth and they lived just 1000 kilometres (600 miles) from the edge of the great Antarctic ice sheet which, at the height of the last Ice Age some 15 000 years ago, approached much closer to Tasmania than it does today.

The first humans arrived in southern New Zealand only about 1000 years ago; the oldest evidence of human occupation in southern Patagonia, at the southern extremity of the South American continent, dates from 10 000 years ago. Nevertheless, on the evidence of Kutikina Cave alone, humans were in south-west Tasmania at least 10 000 years before this. Other evidence suggests they may have been there even earlier.

Bone Cave, in the Weld River Valley, has yielded rock art, stone tools and the remains of eastern grey kangaroos. Radio-carbon dating suggests the cave was first occupied 29 000 years ago.

Rock art is not confined to Bone Cave but has been found in several locations in South-west Tasmania, most famously at Judds Cavern (also known as Wargata Mina) on the Cracroft River.

One of the longest river caves in Australia, with over three and a half kilometres (two and a quarter miles) of explored passages, Judds Cavern was first discovered in 1896 by explorer Henry Judd. Further investigation over the last two decades has uncovered several art panels about 50 metres (160 feet) inside the cavern, at the very limit of daylight penetration.

One of these art panels is eight metres (26 feet) long and three metres (10 feet) high. All the paintings are hand stencils which were made by the artist blowing red ochre from the mouth onto a hand pressed against the rock face. There are also large areas of smeared pigment. Human blood was used as a fixative.

Other decorated surfaces are almost certainly present in the cave but concealed behind a calcium carbonate wash, which now stains the cave walls, or by stalagmites which have grown up from the cave floor.

The antiquity of these paintings is comparable to that of the famous cave paintings of south-west France and Spain and, within Australia, they are unique both because of their age and because they were painted deep within subterranean passages.

Artwork in Bone Cave, as well as Nanwoon Cave in the Florentine Valley, appears comparable in age to that in Judds Cavern and the caves on the Franklin and Maxwell Rivers.

At Ballawinne Cave on the Maxwell River, red hand stencils appear on the walls in total darkness between 20 and 30 metres (70 and 100 feet) inside the cave at the end of a narrow, twisting entrance passage. Smears of ochre mark the entrance.

About 15 000 years ago, the world's climate warmed, the glaciers melted and rainforests spread over the valleys and up the slopes of the hills. The wallabies became much less plentiful and the hunters abandoned Kutikina Cave. Their fireplace hearths became covered with thin stalagmites.

Melting of the Earth's ice caps caused a rise in sea levels 12 000 years ago, which formed Bass Strait and cut Tasmania off from the Australian mainland. From that time, the people of Tasmania appear to have had no further contact with other people in Australia. Their isolation is the longest known for any human group.

Archaeological sites from this period of isolation are especially valuable in documenting cultural change among Tasmanian Aborigines.

Although the Franklin River sites appear to have been last inhabited about 12 000 years ago, some bone fragments from Nanwoon Cave in the Florentine Valley date to 7200 years ago. They indicate that people at least visited these sites in later times.

Raw materials for stone tools and ochres for paint were brought from sites elsewhere and indicate the existence of trade and migratory routes through the Lemonthyme area.

Certainly, people moved into Tasmanian highland areas following the disappearance of the glaciers. They left stone artefacts, stone quarries and rock shelters. Open campsites dot the western Central Plateau, particularly around lakes, rivers and forest margins.

Cave paintings from Warragarra rock shelter in the upper Mersey valley, which have been dated to nearly 10 000 years of age, indicate that Aborigines lived in the extended forest areas. This inland area became more important as the climate warmed. Stones from outside the area, found at Warragarra, indicate habitation 2000 years ago.

On the coast, Aborigines braved the rigours of the Southern Ocean. At South Cape Bay, shell middens, rock shelters and open sites with stone artefacts indicate occupation from the last 3000 years or so. The finds also show the importance of seafoods as well as land foods in the Aboriginal diet. People began to occupy and use offshore islands as well as marginal rainforest.

Most archaeological investigation is recent. In the 1970s, surveys of coastal areas were undertaken. In the 1980s, archaeologists investigated the inland river valleys.

They found 37 caves that indicated occupation, all of it dated to between 11 500 and 30 000 years ago.

Owing to the large area of the southern forests, difficulty of access, the rugged nature of the country and the short time allowed for ground survey, only a small portion of the region has actually been looked at in the field. First findings, however, are of international significance.

Much of the initial investigation was done under pressure. The Tasmanian Hydro-Electric Commission planned to dam the Gordon-Franklin Rivers, inundating river valleys and flooding cave sites. When archaeologists found evidence of great antiquity, the Commission attempted to discredit the finds and claimed that other sites, equally significant, existed outside the planned flooded area. The Hydro-Electric Commission was unsuccessful, both in discrediting the initial findings, which have since been confirmed and extended, and in its attempts to dam the Gordon-Franklin river system.

South-west Tasmania, one of the last great temperate wildernesses in the world, was accepted for World Heritage listing in 1989. The World Heritage inscription was also substantially supported by its high cultural values evident as a result of the long Aboriginal occupation of the area.

The archaeological sites of South-west Tasmania illustrate a hunter-gatherer way of life in a harsh and rugged landscape. Moreover, they indicate changes in ways of life made in accordance with changes in climate. The fact that these sites lie in a landscape relatively undisturbed by European settlement and occupation adds to their universal significance.

RIGHT The sheer quartzite crags of the Eastern Arthur Range provide spectacular vistas to those who scale them.

NEXT PAGE Peaks of the rugged Arthur Ranges lift their heads above a blanket of low cloud.

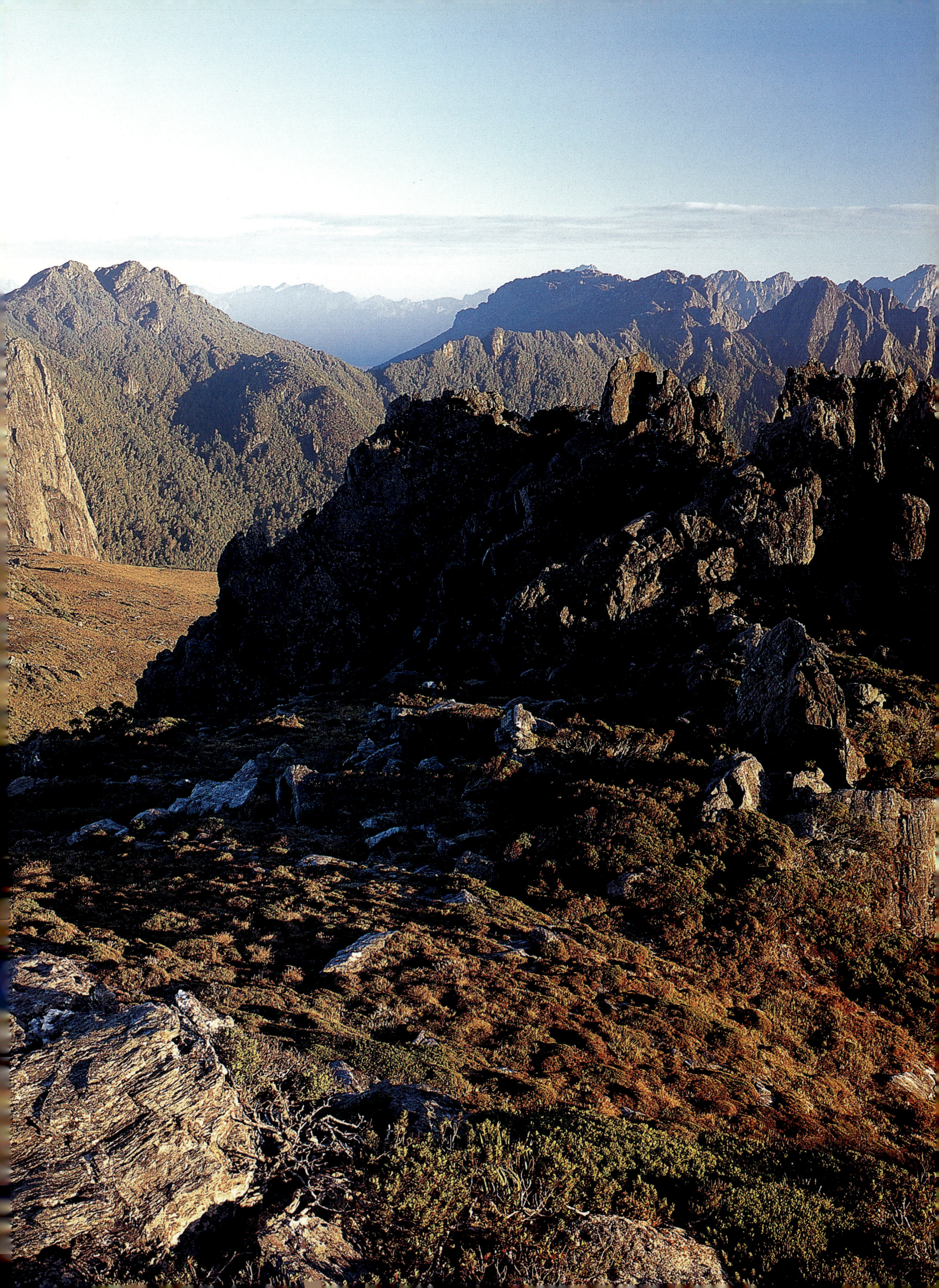

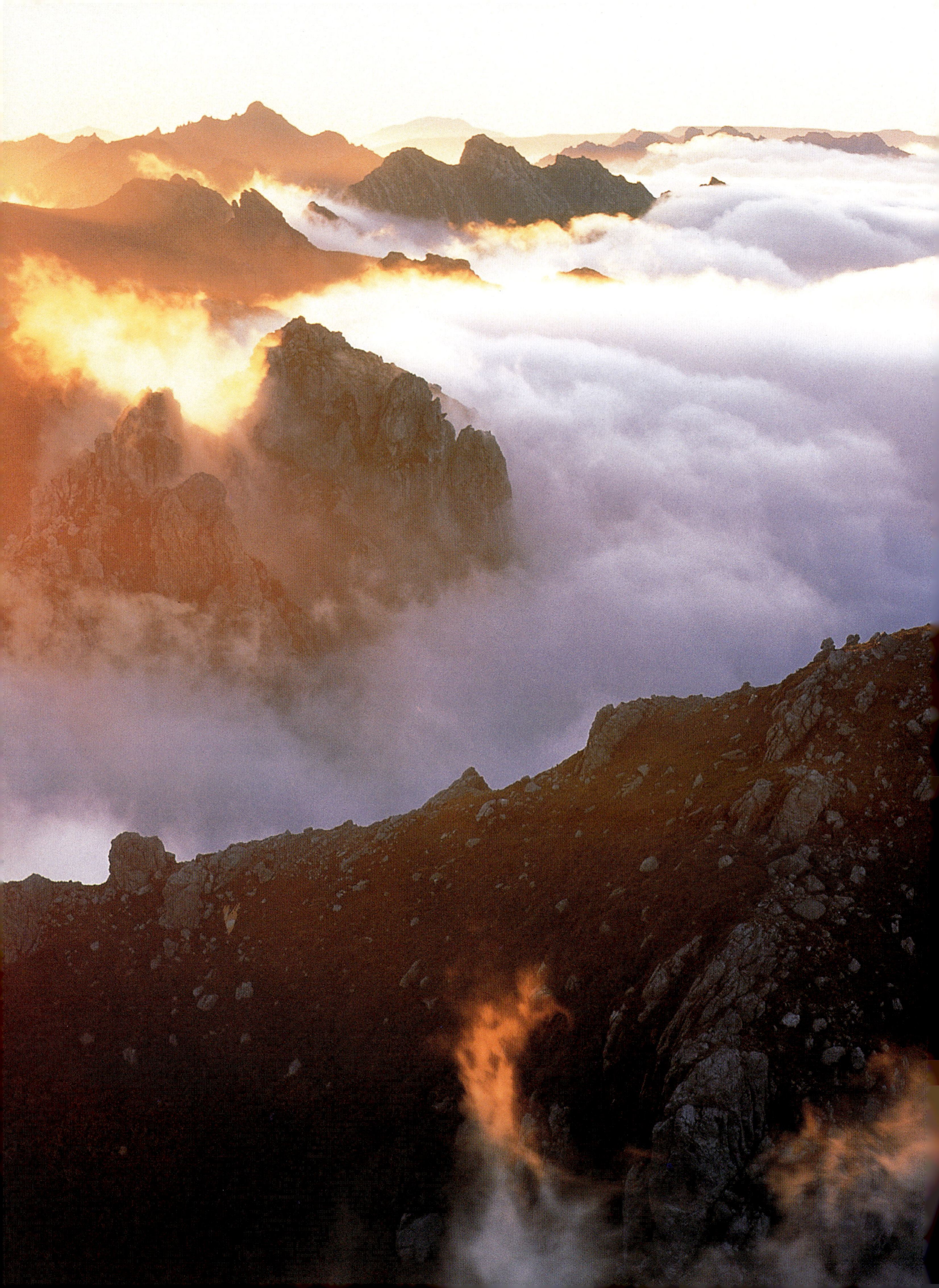

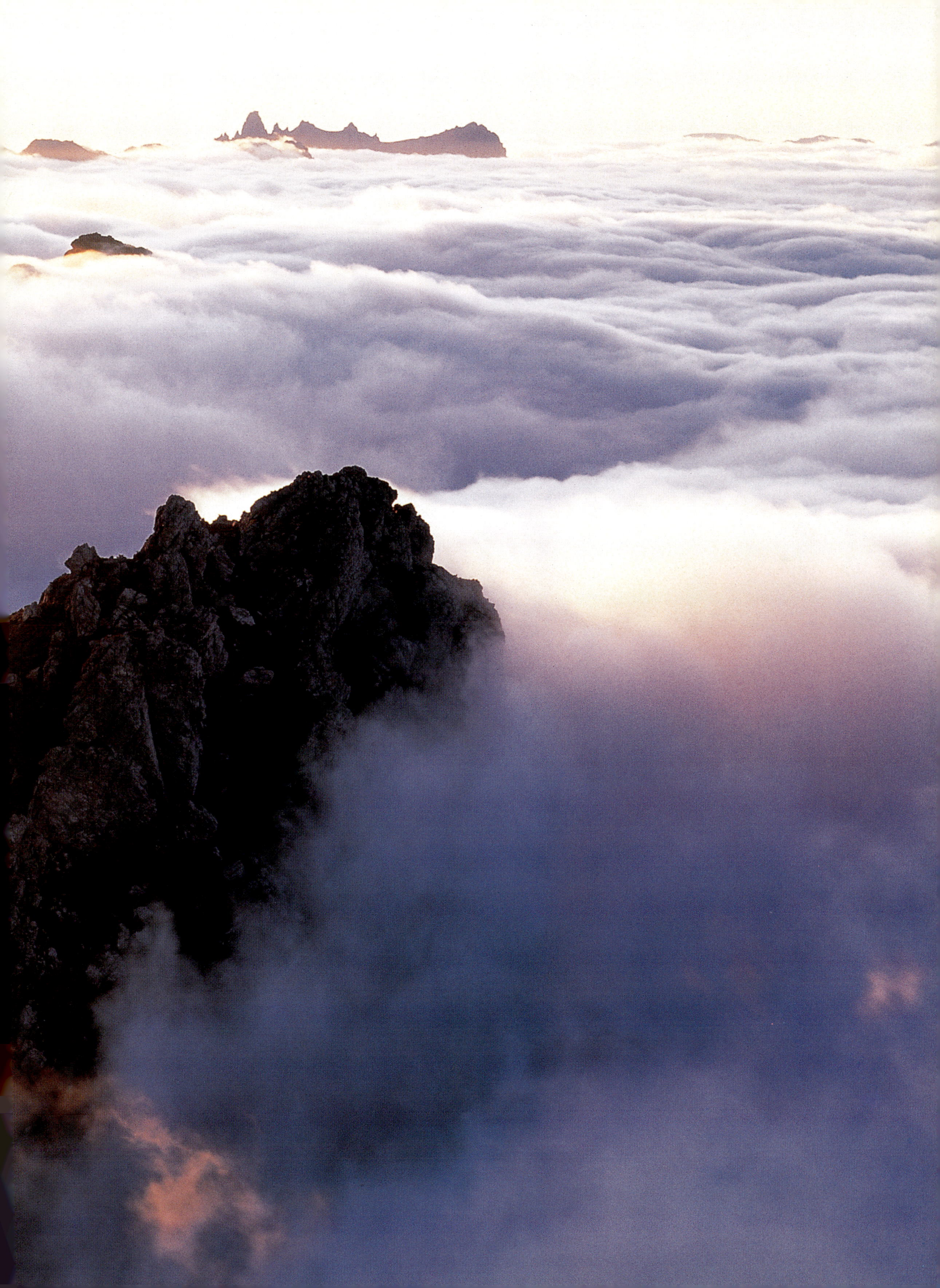

Physical Features

South-west Tasmania is the most consistently wet place in Australia. Set in the path of the blustering winds known as the Roaring Forties, the region has a very high annual rainfall and a high incidence of cloud and cool temperatures. The damp and misty climate accentuates the landscape's look of ancient isolation. In contrast with mainland Australia, South-west Tasmania is a region of true fold mountains and cloud-covered plateaus and is dominated by vistas of craggy peaks and glacial lakes. The altitudinal range of the World Heritage Area is impressive, beginning at sea level and rising to 1617 metres (5304 feet) at the summit of Mount Ossa, Tasmania's highest peak.

Geologically, Tasmania is one of the world's most diverse land masses. The island is corrugated by fold structures in the west and by fault structures in the east, both of which are represented in the World Heritage Area. Across these two major provinces there are changes in land, soil and vegetation types.

The fold structure province lies on very ancient rocks laid down in Precambrian time from 4500 million to 600 million years ago. This province stretches from the south coast to Cradle Mountain and is characterised by the extraordinarily rugged and densely vegetated terrain typified by the Arthur Ranges, where jagged quartzite peaks rise above rainforested valleys, slopes tangled with scoparia and streams flowing between bauera thickets.

During the last Ice Age, glaciers formed and eroded spectacular landforms such as horns, aretes, cirques, 'U'-shaped valleys and countless rock basins which filled with water to become the glacial lakes. Most of these features are seen at Frenchman's Cap and in the Frankland, Arthur, Prince of Wales and Ironbound ranges. One of the most dramatic examples of glaciation is the ice-scoured face of The Font in the Spires Range.

During the glaciations, the sea-level fluctuated and, at the end of the Ice Age, the sea rose dramatically. The present coastline is typical of a drowned landscape: the coast is very exposed with rocky, wave-cut platforms, steep slopes, forbidding cliffs, treacherous gulches, blowholes and arches.

The south-west of the World Heritage Area is a karst, or cave-bearing, landscape which has been formed by groundwater percolating through and eroding the underlying dolomite and limestone rock strata. This process results in the formation of extensive underground passages, caves, sinkholes, arches, pinnacles and blind valleys. Among the karst features of South-west Tasmania are Exit Cave, which at 19 kilometres (12 miles) is the longest measured cave system in Australia, and Anne-a-kananda which is the deepest cave at 373 metres (1224 feet).

The fault structure province is represented above 600 metres (2000 feet) elevation in the east and north of the World Heritage Area. Over a prolonged era, sediments were laid down. This was followed in the Jurassic Era (from 135 to 65 million years ago) by a dramatic period of igneous activity, when molten rock formed deep within the Earth under great pressure and pushed up towards to the surface. This was probably the result of tensions between the different segments of the ancient 'supercontinent' known as Gondwana, of which the Australian continent once formed a part. These pressures forced massive amounts of dolerite to the surface and this volcanic rock can now be seen at Mount Anne and Cradle Mountain and in other prominent features of the World Heritage Area. Faulting, or fracturing of the rock strata, which also occurred around this time, gave rise to the distinctive plateaus and residual hills which characterise the fault structure province. Features of the fault landscape include Lake St. Clair - the deepest lake in Australia - the Hartz Mountains and the Walls of Jerusalem.

RIGHT Native pines and the giant heath Pandani shrouded in snow on the Du Cane Range, Lake St. Clair National Park.

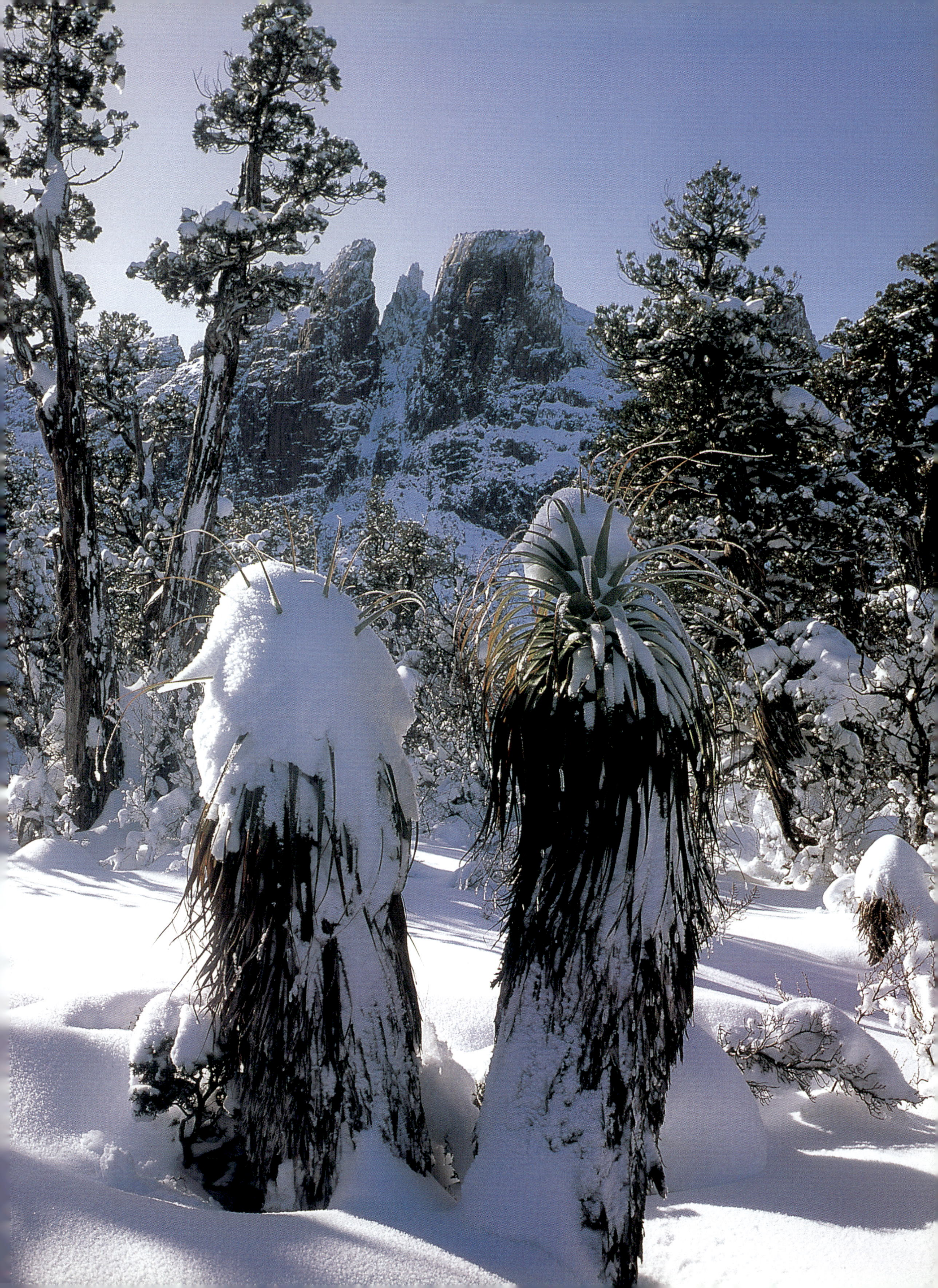

Flora

The vegetation of the Tasmanian Wilderness World Heritage Area is unusual in having as much in common with the vegetation of South America and New Zealand as it does with the rest of Australia. The higher peaks and plateaux support a type of alpine vegetation that is peculiar to the locality. Unlike the alpine flora of the mainland, which is dominated by tussock and herb grasses, the Tasmanian alpine flora consists almost entirely of shrubby plants, of which up to 60% of the species are not found elsewhere.

Although pockets of cool-temperate rainforest occur on the continental mainland, Tasmania contains the largest and most pristine tracts of this forest type in Australia. Some 30% of the area below the treeline is covered by rainforest which is dominated by species termed 'Antarctic', because they are descendants of the flora of the 'supercontinent', Gondwana. Ancient relicts include the King's holly, which is found in only a one square kilometre (one third of one square mile) patch and has been identified as genetically the same as a 43 000 year old fossil leaf from Antarctica and the oldest living plant in the world. The shrub has reproduced itself from root suckering and the layering of stems. Other features associated with tropical rainforests, such as drip-tip leaves, buttressing and the presence of epiphytes, are not to be seen in Tasmania's temperate rainforests. Trees commonly found in the Tasmanian rainforest include ancient myrtle beech, sassafras, Huon pine, King Billy pine which lives to 1200 years old, and leatherwood which is famous for the delicious, pale honey produced from its flowers.

There are also large areas of forest dominated by eucalypt species. Tall messmate stringybark and Smithton peppermint are to be seen growing in the midst of the rainforests and emerging high above the rainforest canopy over large areas. In addition to this mixed forest type, eucalypts are dominant in the sub-alpine woodlands and also in the forest types classed as sclerophyll (hard-leaved) and dry sclerophyll communities. Of particular significance are the magnificent stands of tall pristine forest to be found in the area; swamp gum or Regnans - the world's tallest flowering plant - here forms a canopy that is 80 to 90 metres (240 to 300 feet) high and well above the canopy of the wet sclerophyll forest which serves as a mere understorey to these towering trees.

Of the identified vegetation communities in Tasmania, the World Heritage Area contains at least 33 of the 43 alpine communities and 30 of the 34 temperate rainforest communities, the latter being dominated by Gondwana species. The area boasts 31 of the 65 wet sclerophyll communities, 15 of the 35 dry eucalypt communities, 19 of the 25 buttongrass moorland communities and 9 of the 37 grassland and grassy woodland communities.

The size and diversity of the area ensures that it protects a great variety of habitats which support many unusual plant types and communities. In addition to the vegetation types mentioned, there are coastal wet and dry scrubs, important wetlands and some of Tasmania's best developed sphagnum bogs, as well as plant types that are peculiar to salt marshes, coastal cliffs and coastal sand dune habitats and also to sea-bird breeding colonies.

RIGHT Pandani is almost exclusively confined to Tasmania and is among the world's tallest heath species.

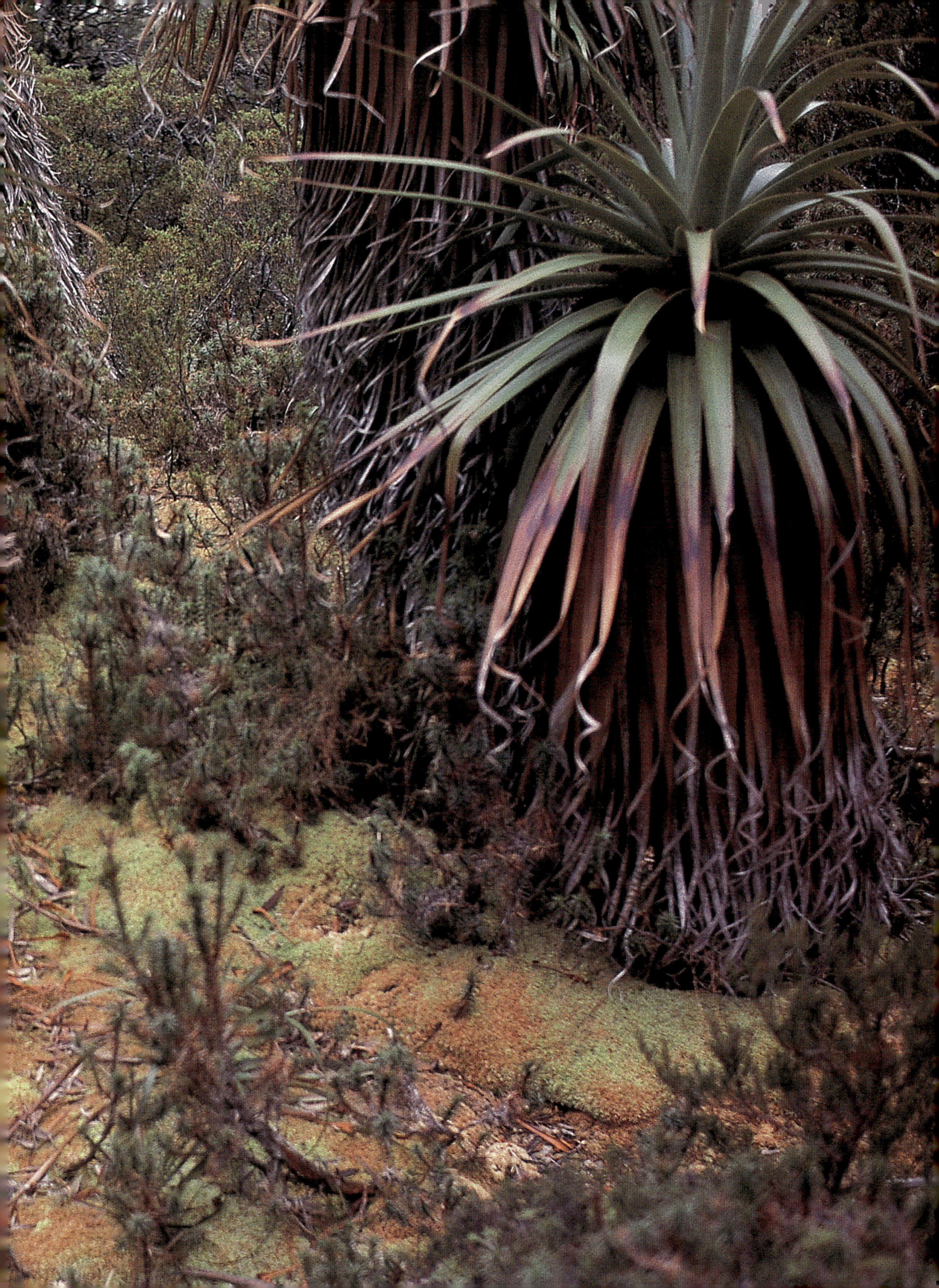

ABOVE The native green rosella is found in the region's eucalypt forests.

RIGHT Tasmanian cool temperate rainforest is distinctive in having a low number of dominant species and a relative absence of clinging plants, or epiphytes, apart from mosses and lichens. Rainforest adaptations such as stem flowering, buttressing and drip tip leaves are also not prominent. Rotting logs, moss-covered rocks and leaf litter provide an important microhabitat for many species such as land snails, flatworms, onycophorans, spiders, centipedes, millipedes, collembola and beetles.

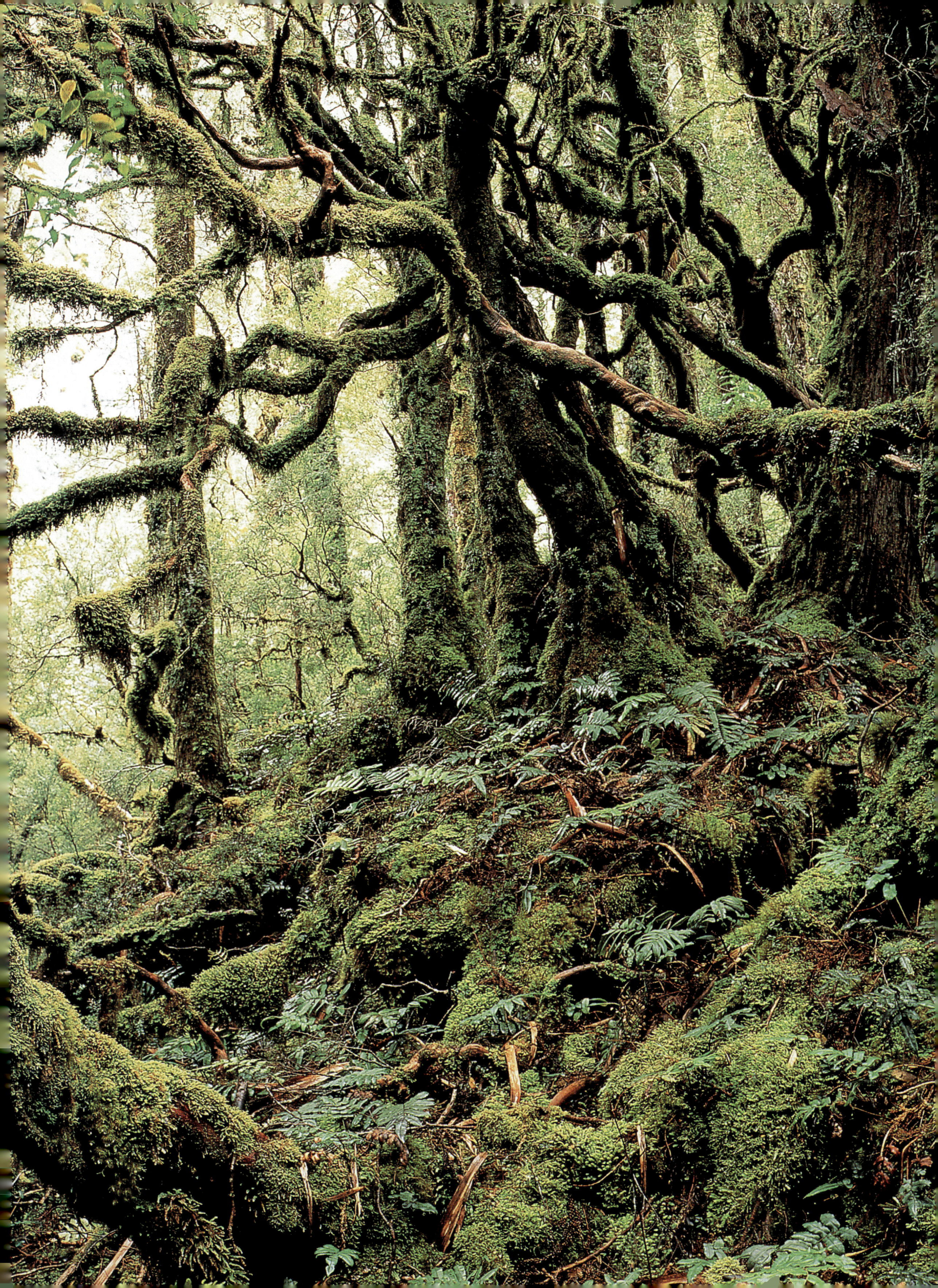

ABOVE King Billy pines growing on Cradle Mountain.

RIGHT Storm clouds over New River Lagoon and the Ironbound Range. The south and south-west coasts are a spectacular landscape of bold headlands, sweeping sandy beaches, rocky coves, secluded inlets, wave-cut platforms, blowholes and rock arches. Sea caves 10 metres (33 feet) above the present sea level are evidence of higher sea levels long ago.

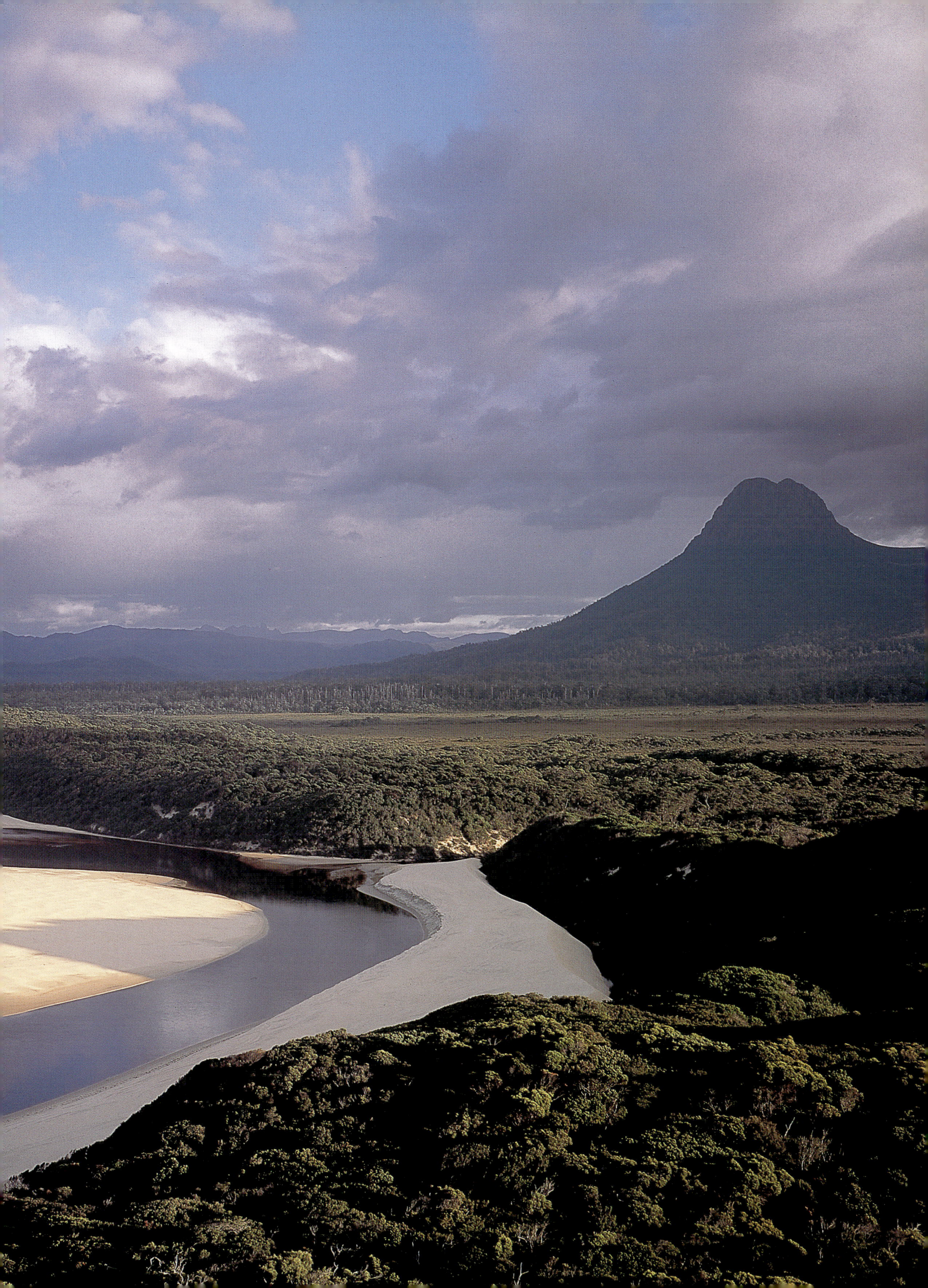

Fauna

Tasmania's fauna are significant because they include an unusually high proportion of species that are endemic - not found anywhere else - and groups which are relict - much reduced in status or distribution since an earlier time - as well as species which are of ancient origin. The proportion of animals that are endemic is very high in Tasmania and is especially high among the invertebrates, or animals without backbones, such as insects. The region's diverse topography, geology, soils and vegetation, combined with its harsh and variable climatic conditions, have created a wide array of animal habitats, with a fauna that is correspondingly diverse. The insularity of Tasmania and of the south-west wilderness area in particular, has helped protect it from the impact of introduced species, such as the fox which has taken such a heavy toll on mainland fauna.

The native fauna of the World Heritage Area fall into two main groups. The first, comprising the marsupials and the burrowing freshwater crayfish, are relict survivors of a richer and more widely distributed fauna that once existed on the ancient 'supercontinent' of Gondwana. The second group, including rodents and bats, is made up of species which entered Australia from Asia after Gondwana broke up into the continents and subcontinents of the southern hemisphere.

Of Tasmania's 32 mammal species, 27 are present in the World Heritage Area. Four of these are restricted to Tasmania and include the Tasmanian devil, the largest carnivorous marsupial species still surviving. A larger marsupial carnivore, the Tasmanian tiger, or (*thylacine*), is thought to have become extinct in 1936, although unconfirmed sightings continue to be made.

Of the 150 bird species found in the World Heritage Area, 13 are endemic to Tasmania. They include the orange-bellied parrot which inhabits the moorland buttongrass and is one of Australia's rarest and most threatened birds.

There are 11 reptile species of which four are restricted to Tasmania, one of these being the Pedra Branca skink which is found only on the small, rocky offshore island of Pedra Branca. There are also six frog species, including two that are endemic. The bright green Tasmanian tree frog is restricted mainly to the World Heritage Area.

Four of the 15 freshwater fish species are found only in Tasmania and two of these are rare outside the World Heritage Area. Unfortunately, introduced fish such as trout and salmon have played a part in the decline of native fish species. The freshwater crustaceans are of global significance as many are relict species whose origins can be traced back to the ancient fauna of Gondwana.

Introduced animals are rare in the World Heritage Area. Species that do occur include feral cats, rabbits, fallow deer, the black rat, the house mouse and the sugar glider. Exotic birds include the starling and kookaburra. Introduced invertebrates include the honey bee and European wasp. Exotic fish such as brown trout, Atlantic salmon, rainbow trout and brook trout have been introduced to, or have invaded, lakes and streams.

TOP INSET The Tasmanian tiger is thought to be extinct, although unconfirmed sightings are occasionally reported.

CENTRE INSET Black currawong.

BOTTOM INSET Of the 37 mammal species present in the South-west Tasmanian Wilderness, six are found only in Tasmania. One of these is the Tasmanian devil (pictured) which, if the Tasmanian tiger is accepted to be extinct, is the world's largest carnivorous marsupial. The Tasmanian devil subdues its prey with powerful jaws and sharp incisor teeth.

FAR RIGHT Cold lakes formed by glacial erosion are common in the area, perched high on the mountain ranges. These lakes provide habitat for rare native fish species, the galaxias and freshwater crustaceans.

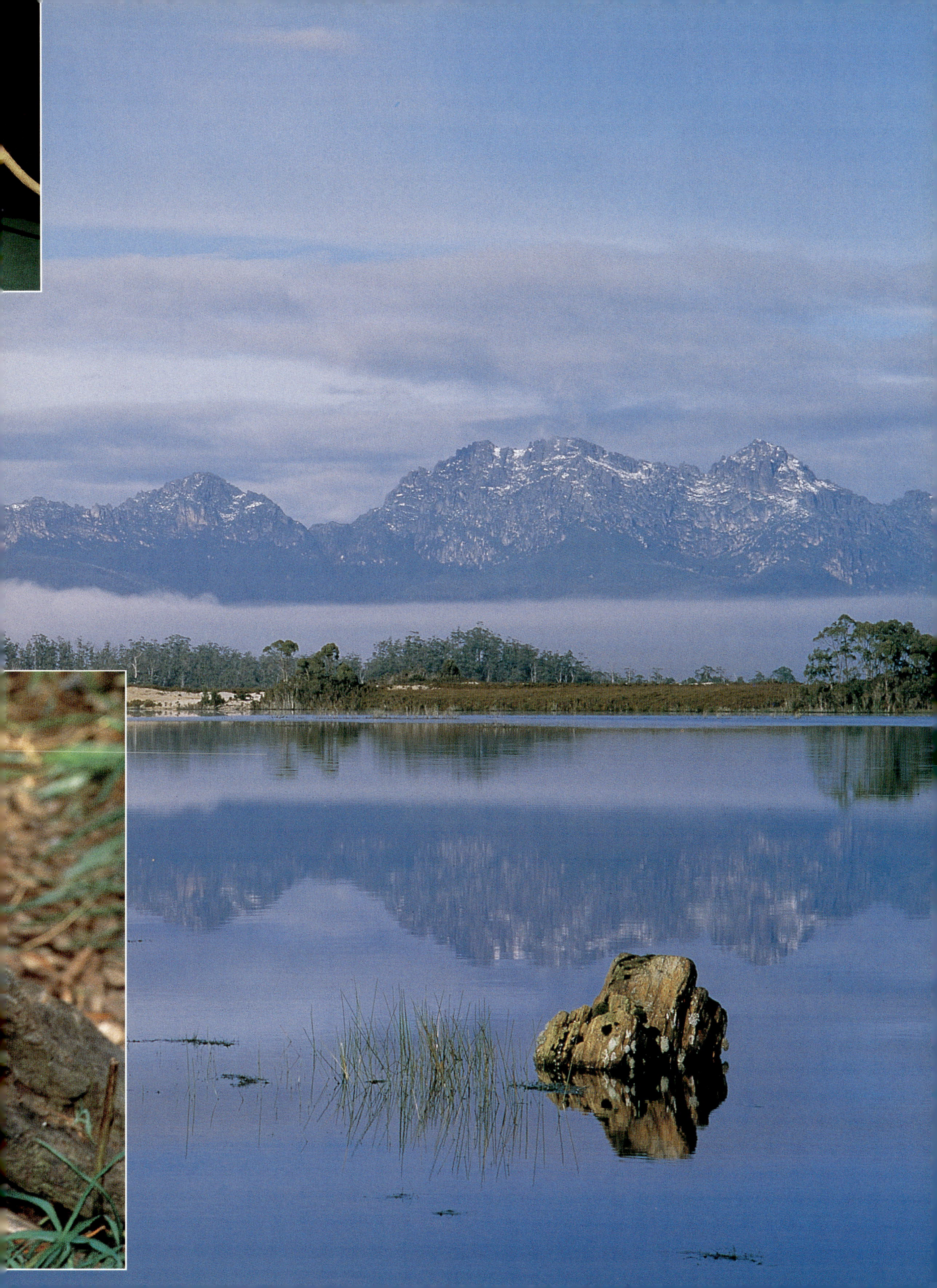

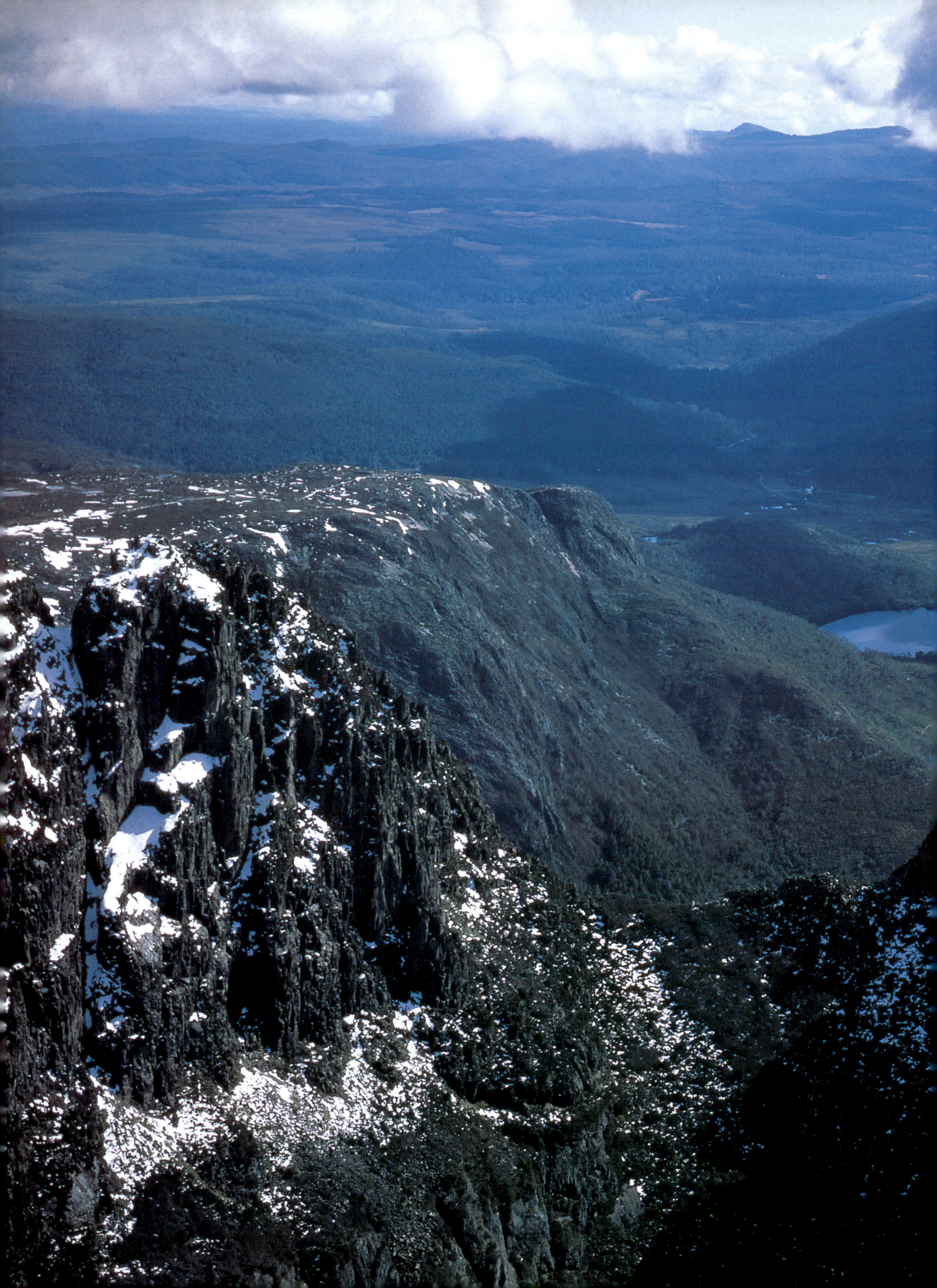

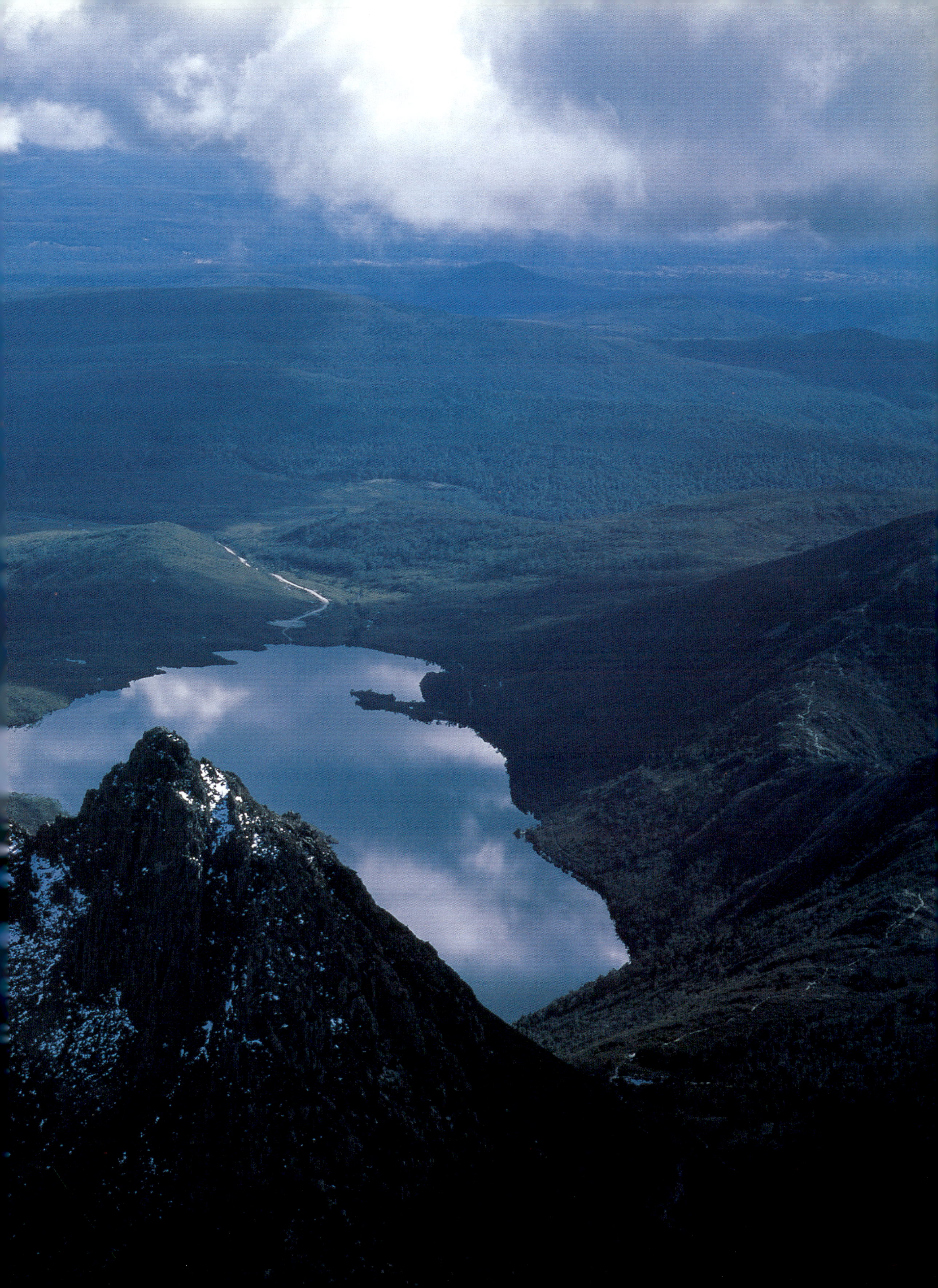

Cultural Heritage

Until the arrival of the Dutch explorer Abel Janszoon Tasman in 1642, Tasmania was possibly the most isolated place on Earth. Cut off from the Australian mainland 8000 years before by the flooding of Bass Strait, the Tasmanian Aborigines lived without any outside influences.

Archaeological evidence has shown that a hunter-gatherer society flourished in the inland south-west of Tasmania during the last Ice Age from at least 30 000 years ago until the start of the present climatic era around 11 500 years ago. The climatic change heralded a new warmer age in which the vegetation of the south-west changed from open woodlands and grasslands where game was plentiful, to dense temperate rainforests where game was scarce. This forced Aboriginal people to move to the coasts and adopt new survival strategies.

Some 37 caves used by Aborigines in the remote past have been located in Tasmania's south-west. The first cave site where Ice Age occupation was recognised and investigated was Kutikina Cave in the Franklin River Valley. This one site was found to contain exceptionally rich evidence of over 5000 years of continual human habitation, including a large proportion of bone belonging to the red-necked wallaby, which revealed the importance of this species in the diet of the former inhabitants. Recently, rock art has been discovered at three sites in the Maxwell, Cracroft and Weld river valleys. These finds are of great importance as they demonstrate that art and presumably ceremony were an integral part of this ancient society. Judds Cavern (or Wargata Mina), which is one of the largest river caves in Australia, is the most richly decorated of these sites. It contains over 3.5 kilometres (2.2 miles) of explored passages and is the southernmost painted site known in the world.

Research has shown that Aboriginal people were established on South-west Tasmania's coast 3000 years ago, although it seems likely that their occupation would date back to 6000 years ago when the sea stopped rising and stabilised at its present level. The south coast and Port Davey contain a range of sites including rock shelters, quarries and an immense array of large and complex shell waste heaps, or middens, which have been little disturbed since the coming of Europeans early in the nineteenth century.

After several decades of colonisation blighted misunderstandings and appalling bloodshed, the native people who still survived were persuaded by the missionary George Robinson to move to a settlement in the Bass Strait islands. Their descendants live on throughout Tasmania today.

European incursions into lands within the present World Heritage Area began in the early 1800s when felling of valuable Huon pine and whaling formed important elements in the colonial economy. Whaling ceased before the turn of the century but pine logging continued on in some areas up to recent times.

The remoteness of the area exactly suited the requirements of the British penal system. A convict settlement was built at Sarah Island in 1821 and operated until 1833, accommodating the most hardened convict re-offenders. The harsh climate, severe conditions and the heavy labour of felling Huon pine along the Gordon River made Sarah Island a place of dread that came to be synonymous with the cruelty of the colonial penal system. The ruined remains of the penitentiary and other buildings can still be seen there.

With its romantic and rugged beauty, the Tasmanian Wilderness Region has a substantial history of preservation. Cradle Mountain was originally established as a scenic reserve in 1922 under the Scenery Preservation Act, 1915. This park was extended in 1936 to include Lake St Clair and the Oakleigh Creek Conservation Area. Other areas received protection throughout the 1970s, culminating in the establishment of the South-west National Park as a biosphere reserve in October 1977.

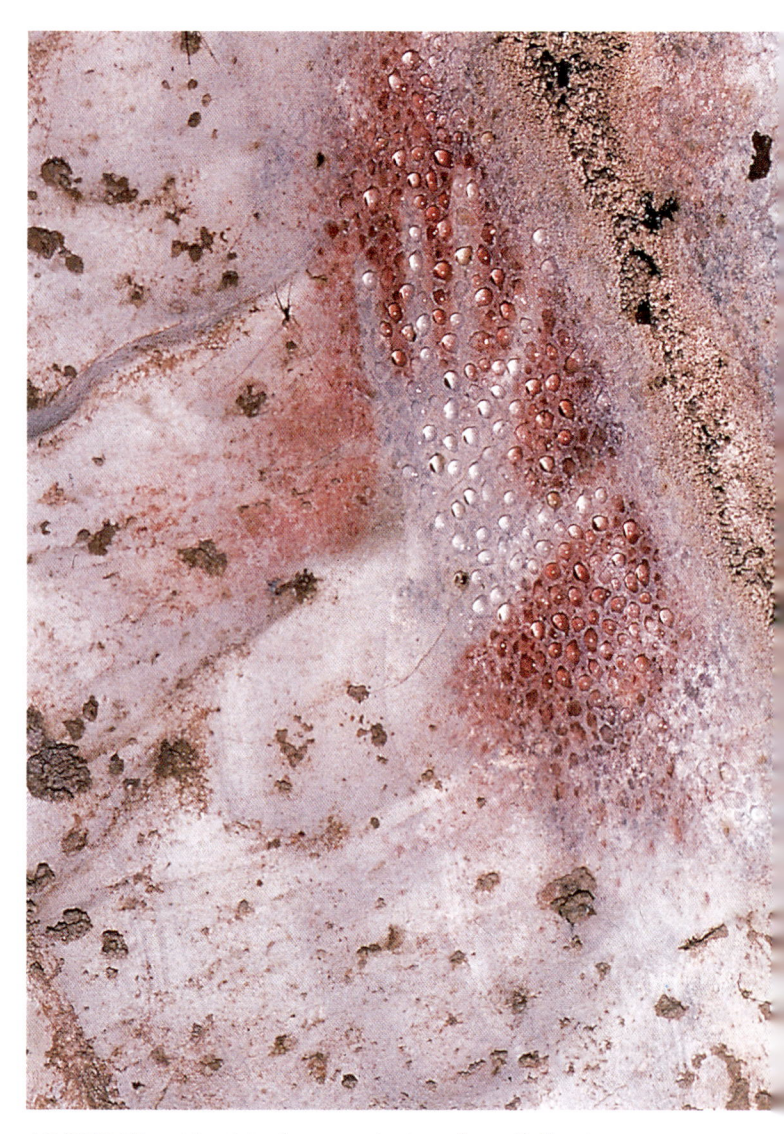

ABOVE The Aboriginal cave paintings from Ballawinne Cave, Maxwell River, are all red hand stencils. They are situated in total darkness between 20 and 30 metres (66 and 100 feet) inside the cave at the end of a narrow, twisting entrance passage smeared with ochre. Radio-carbon dating on the rock art pigment shows them to have been painted in the Pleistocene Ice Age between 30 000 and 11 500 years ago. Chemical analysis of the pigments revealed that blood was a constituent of the ochre used in the paintings.

RIGHT The dolerite-capped Mt Anne is one of the highest peaks in the Tasmanian Wilderness. The Judds Glacier has scoured the mountain's face and formed Judds Lake, on the foreshores of which grow King Billy pines.

PREVIOUS PAGE An aerial view looking down on Cradle Mountain, Dove Lake and glacier-sculpted valleys beyond.

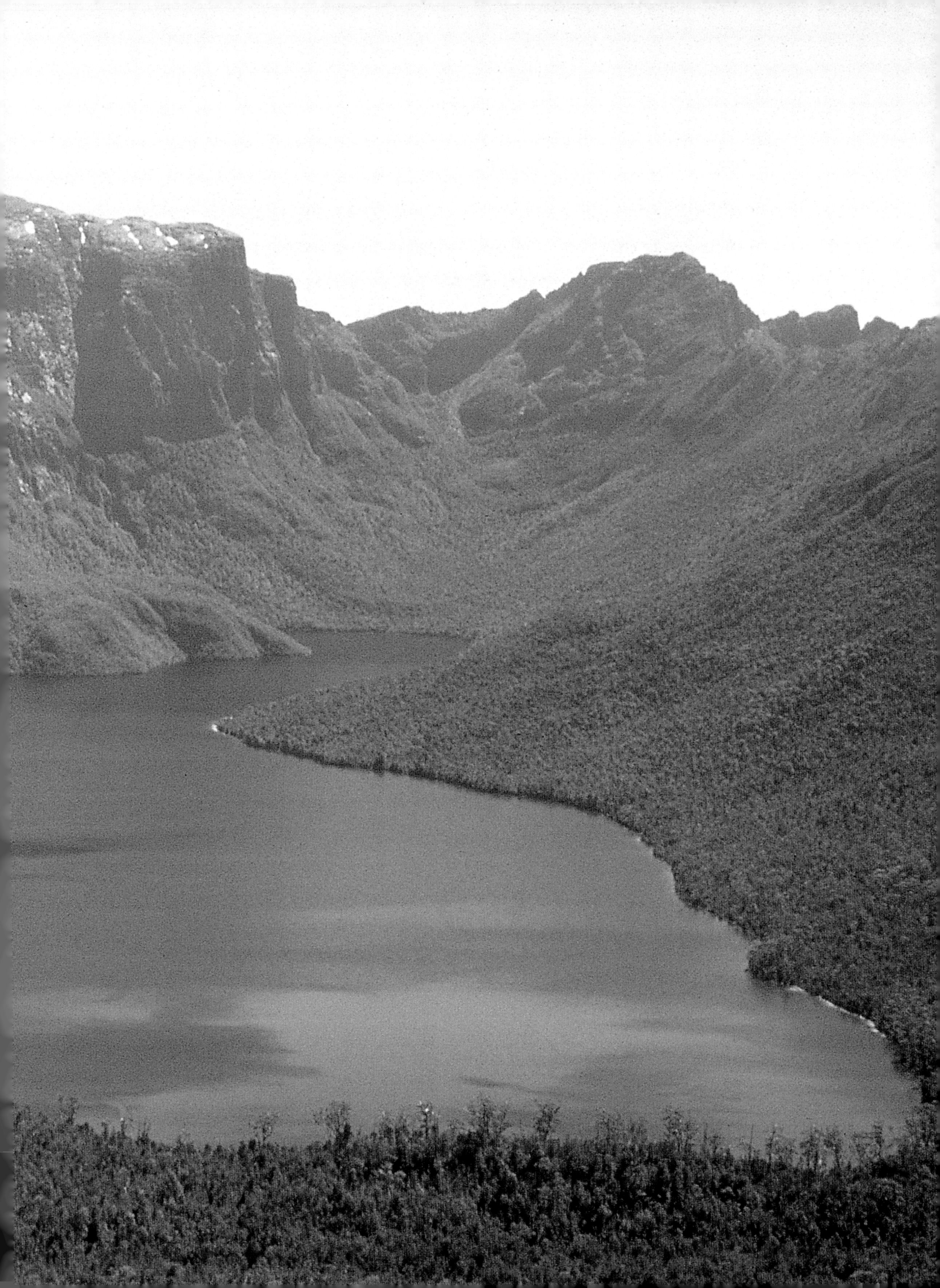

Human Impact

Despite the efforts of earlier Tasmanian Government administrations to the contrary, the Tasmanian Wilderness World Heritage Area remains relatively undisturbed by human activity. The only permanent residents within the area today are the Department of Lands, Parks and Wildlife officers at the Lake St Clair and Cradle Valley ranger stations, and the light-house keeper at Maatsuyker Island.

The area is subject to a number of industrial uses, including two small-scale mines, limited mineral exploration, two quarries, hydro-electric power development and transmission, and telecommunications.

The Middle Gordon Hydro-Electric Scheme, an ill-conceived project sponsored by the Tasmanian Government in the 1970s, has caused considerable damage to the area's natural values by damming the Gordon River, drowning Lake Pedder, establishing the village of Strathgordon and opening up the south-west to motor traffic using the new Gordon River and Scotts Peak roads.

Port Davey is used for shelter by professional fishermen. Beekeeping occurs along the Lyell Highway, Mount McCall Track and on roadsides in the southern forests, the small, white bee-hives presenting an unexpectedly domestic spectacle dotted amidst the uncompromisingly wild scenery.

Facilities

The Tasmanian Wilderness World Heritage Area offers a range of facilities and activities for visitors and caters to the needs of casual picnickers as well as experienced bushwalkers. Large numbers of visitors travel to Cradle Mountain and Lake St Clair, and along the Lyell Highway, the Gordon River Road and the Scotts Peak Road. Special tours to the area can be arranged from major towns in both the north and south of the state.

Many visitors to Tasmania travel to the west coast port township of Strahan to enjoy a cruise up the tranquil and beautiful Gordon River. The hydro-electricity impoundment created over the drowned Lake Pedder and the numerous lakes of the Central Plateau are famous for their excellent trout fishing. A scenic flight in a conventional or amphibious light aircraft is another way to experience the region's stunning scenery.

Small huts are available for rental in both the Cradle Mountain and Lake St Clair national parks. The more adventurous will go prepared for tent camping in the accessible camping areas while the truly hardy will venture out into the vast wilderness areas. Increasingly, tourists visit this area to enjoy active forms of recreation such as bushwalking, caving, mountaineering, climbing, rafting, canoeing and cross-country skiing.

Long-established walking tracks such as the Overland Track and South Coast Track provide walkers with a challenging and very rewarding wilderness experience.

Threats

The Tasmanian Wilderness World Heritage Area contains most of the last great temperate wilderness remaining in Australia. The relative isolation of the area has meant that most of the land has been preserved in a natural or near-natural condition. However, just beyond the boundaries of the listed World Heritage Area, logging operations continue with their associated clear-felling of trees, road building and the risk of escaping fire, all of which threaten to degrade scenic and wilderness values.

A major modification of the World Heritage Area was imposed by the construction of the Middle Gordon Hydro-Electric Scheme in the early 1970s. This power scheme involved the damming of part of the Gordon River, now excluded from the World Heritage Area, and the flooding of Lake Pedder and its unique white quartzite beach. As part of this operation, the Gordon River and Scotts Peak roads were built into the very heart of the South-west Conservation Area and the hamlet of Strathgordon was built just outside the boundaries of the South-west National Park.

In the early 1980s, the threat of similar damage on a larger scale came with the proposal to flood the lower reaches of the Gordon and Franklin Rivers, also as means of increasing Tasmania's supply of hydro-electric power. If carried out, this project would have inundated huge tracts of pristine forest and caused the permanent loss of internationally significant cultural sites including Kutikina Cave. The plans for the Gordon-below-Franklin Dam were approved by the Tasmanian government in 1982 but met with unprecedented opposition, both nationally and internationally. The inscription of the Tasmanian Wilderness region on the World Heritage list was a great boost to the conservation case. Following the recommendations of the World Heritage Committee, the Australian Federal Government intervened, passing the World Heritage Properties Conservation Act in 1983. A Tasmanian Government challenge to the validity of this Act was rejected by the High Court of Australia on July 1, 1983, thus preventing the destruction of an irreplaceable natural treasure.

Damage to vegetation caused by trampling by walkers poses some threat to the park but is localised to accessible areas and is easily remedied by the improvement of paths and other passive control measures. Root rot fungus which selectively attacks tree and shrub species is widespread along some access routes and is believed to be carried on the soles of walkers' boots.

Mineral exploration leases are still current at Adamsfield and some gravel quarrel activities continue.

Management

Only about 100 hectares (247 acres) of the Tasmanian Wilderness World Heritage Area is privately-owned land. The remainder of this vast property is vested in the Crown and administered by the Tasmanian Government through the Department of Lands, Parks and Wildlife and the Forestry Commission. The state's Hydro-Electric Commission controls 15 300 hectares (37 808 acres), of which all but 1 175 hectares (2904 acres) are leased to the Department of Lands, Parks and Wildlife which has day to day management control of the area.

ABOVE Green and golden frog.

RIGHT The tussock and heathland-covered foreshore of Dove Lake with Cradle Mountain rising in the background.

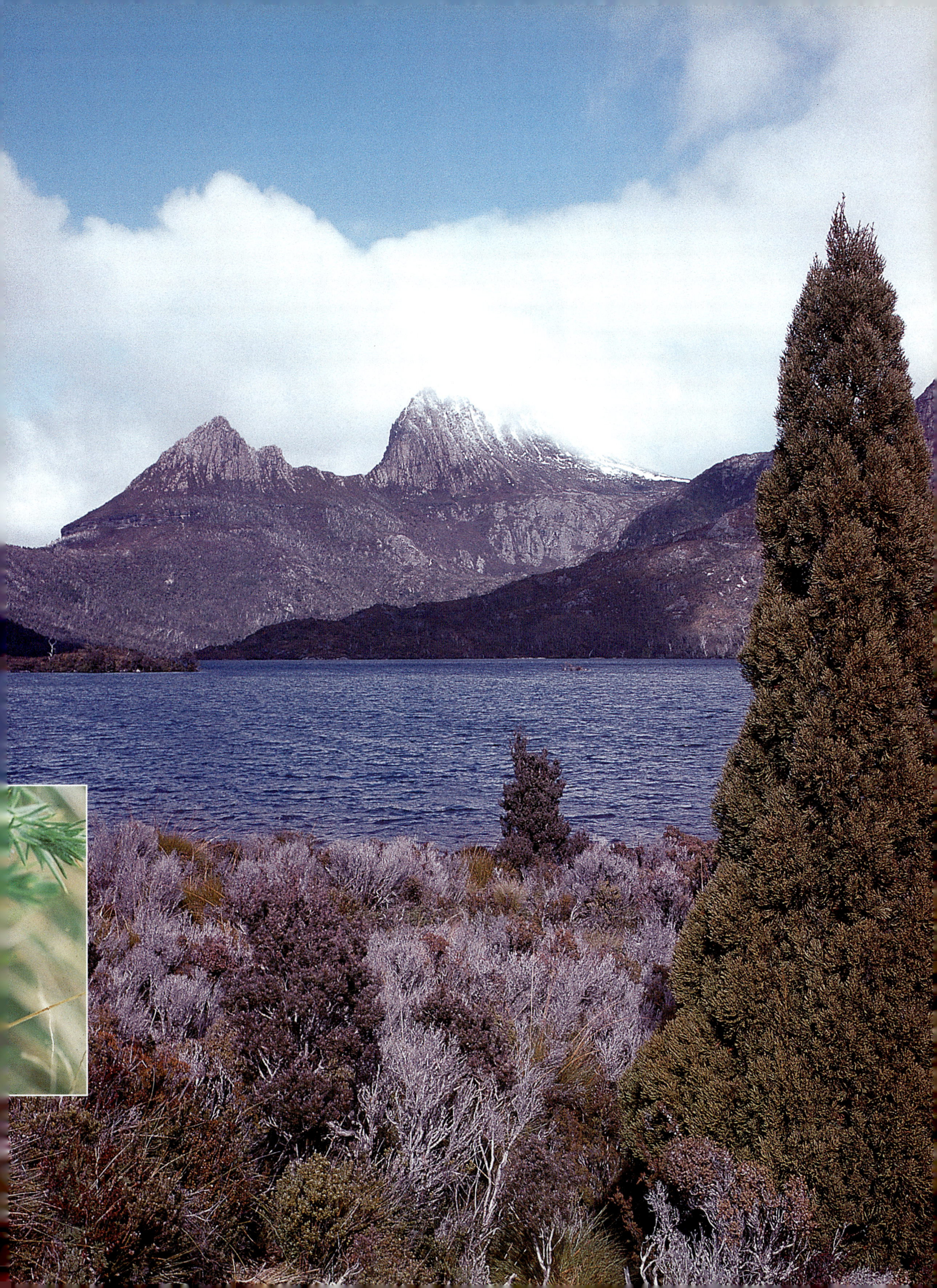

The Lord Howe Island Group

Jutting out of the waters of the South Pacific Ocean like a row of broken teeth, the Lord Howe Island Group are the eroded remnants of an ancient and long-extinct volcano which rises some two kilometres (one and a quarter miles) up from a ridge on the ocean floor. Lord Howe Island takes its place among the World Heritage areas as an example of a high island born out of volcanic activity and the site of the southern-most true coral reef in the world. Lord Howe is also significant due to its truly unique flora and fauna which adapted to the island environment by forming new species. Seventy-five of the plants found on the island occur nowhere else and, of these, 73 are considered by IUCN-The World Conservation Union to be rare or endangered. In addition, several species of rare and endangered animals make their home on the island, including the Lord Howe Island woodhen, one of the world's rarest creatures.

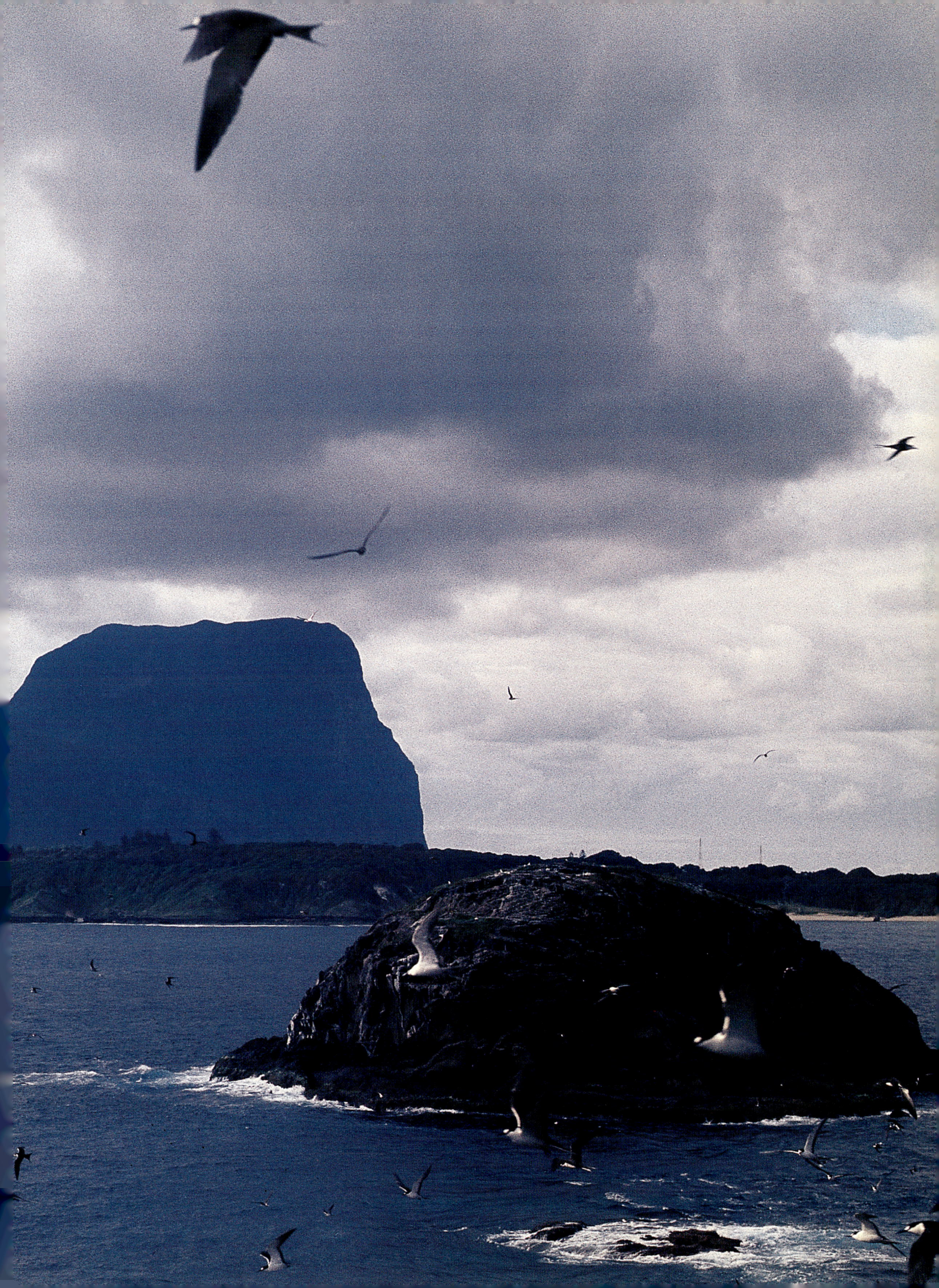

Location

The Lord Howe Island Group World Heritage Area is located in the South Pacific Ocean, 700 kilometres (435 miles) north-east of Sydney. The World Heritage Area comprises some 75% of the land of Lord Howe Island and all of the surrounding offshore islands and rocks of significant size. Outlying islands include the Admiralty Group, lying immediately north-east of Lord Howe Island; Mutton Bird and Sail Rocks to the east; Blackburn (Rabbit) Island, which lies in the lagoon on the western side of Lord Howe Island; Gower Island, just off the southern tip; and the awesome tower of rock known as Balls Pyramid, some 25 kilometres (15 miles) south-east of the island.

PREVIOUS PAGE Looking south towards Lord Howe Island's Mount Lidgbird and Mount Gower. These great peaks rise dramatically from the ocean and are a dominant feature of the landscape in almost every corner of the island.

The Lord Howe Island Group

By Vincent Serventy

"When I was in the woods amongst the birds I could not help picturing to myself the Golden Age as described by Ovid..." wrote Surgeon Arthur Bowes in 1788 while exploring Lord Howe Island. His response has been echoed over the years by many visitors enchanted by the island's exquisite scenery and its fascinating and abundant wildlife.

Lord Howe Island, its surrounding rocky islets and the 650 metre (2130 feet) spire of Balls Pyramid, make up the Lord Howe Island Group in the South Pacific Ocean, some 700 kilometres (435 miles) north-east of Sydney.

Lord Howe Island is a green and mountainous crescent, fringed with reefs, about 10 kilometres (six miles) long and varying from 300 metres (990 feet) to six kilometres (four miles) wide. Almost half of the island is taken up by the southern mountains. Most of the rock is basalt and the island's fertile soils are derived from this mineral and nutrient-rich volcanic material.

Most visitors appreciate the refreshing naturalness of Lord Howe, an impression that deepens as the wealth and diversity of the landscapes of the island group are gradually explored. The island's subtropical climate, with a mean temperature of 16°Celsius (61°Fahrenheit) in winter and a comfortable 23°Celsius (74°Fahrenheit) in summer, attracts visitors all year round.

The nomination of the Lord Howe Island Group for the World Heritage List recognised: "... exceptional natural beauty. The diversity of endemic animals, plants and invertebrates makes them an outstanding example of independent evolutionary processes from the point of view of science and conservation."

This isolated natural treasure house is a classic example of a land mass raised above the sea by volcanic activity. Lord Howe and its companion islets and rocks are the crown of an undersea volcano that built up from a ridge on the floor of the Pacific Ocean. Balls Pyramid, even though it is 25 kilometres (15 miles) to the south of Lord Howe Island, is part of the same volcanic complex.

The undersea ridge from which the volcano emerged is known as the Lord Howe Rise. Dr Lin Sutherland and Dr Alex Ritchie of the Australian Museum, in outlining the geological history of the area, have described this vast rise as being between 18 and 29 kilometres (11 to 18 miles) thick, and being made of a section of continental crust which was left behind when the basin now containing the Tasman Sea was formed some 70 million years ago.

The volcano which created the island group emerged later and produced two distinct lava flows, the last creating the dramatic peaks of Lord Howe Island, Mount Gower and Mount Lidgbird. The crown of the volcano rose above the surface of the ocean but the battering of the sea reduced it to a shallow rim of rubble, which was then colonised by many different marine creatures, forming the rich undersea community that now enthrals visitors.

Different creatures colonised the land and both the plants and animals of the Lord Howe Group show strong relationships with eastern Australia as well as links with New Zealand and New Caledonia. It is possible that in earlier times, undersea mountains - remnants of other volcanoes - could have served as 'stepping stones', helping land plants and animals to reach Lord Howe from neighbouring land masses. Spores and seeds would have drifted across on the wind and storm-driven logs may have brought other cargo. New plant and animal colonists are still arriving by these means today.

The first people to visit Lord Howe may have been intrepid Polynesian voyagers who stopped for a time but found the island too small for a permanent settlement. For Europeans, the island was a happy discovery made by chance. The settlement of Sydney was just a fortnight old when Governor Phillip dispatched Lieutenant Lidgbird Ball in February 1788 to investigate the prospects for settlement of Norfolk Island to the north-east. On the way Ball found and named Lord Howe Island. He sailed on to Norfolk but returned to explore this intriguing place on his way back to Sydney, reporting an abundance of bird life and vegetation, with many turtles in the sea.

Ball's report encouraged a stream of visitors. Surgeon Arthur Bowes rhapsodised over the birds which provided a great meal: "... supp'd on part of our game, ... sweet and good, the pidgeons were the largest I ever saw...". Sadly, the island's pigeons - hunted by hungry sailors - soon went the way of the dodo. By 1834, the island was often visited for fresh food and water and there was a settlement of four men, three women and two children thriving on a diet of fish and birds. Some years later, Lord Howe was growing vegetables for the Sydney market, with onions a major crop. The seeds of the Howea (formerly kentia) palm became an important export. The island was proclaimed a botanic reserve in 1883 and a board of control was created in 1913. The attraction of the place for holiday visitors outstripped the island's poor anchorage, leading to the development of a flying boat service which used the lagoon for landings; in the 1970s an airstrip was built.

Two mountains, Lidgbird and Gower, dominate the landscape. Clouds often wreath the summits of both peaks, creating a moist environment which favours the growth of ferns and epiphytes. There is a wealth of greenery, with lush rainforest in sheltered areas. Forest trees some 20 metres (65 feet) high interlace their branches to form a continuous canopy in the valleys. Palms, scalybarks, blue plums, screw palms and liana vines add to the fascination. The aerial roots of banyan figs anchor in the soil around the parent tree, always expanding its perimeter, so that the islanders call these 'walking trees'. As one ascends the mountains, the vegetation changes until finally tea tree and other hardy shrubs dominate.

About a third of Lord Howe's 180 species of flowering plants are found only on this island, with the others displaying influences from New Zealand, Australia and New Caledonia. During Lord Howe's long isolation, new species and varieties of plants evolved, making the island a magnet for botanists. Unfortunately, a great deal of damage has been done since humans began visiting and settling the island. There have been introductions of exotic species. Some, such as the asparagus fern, bitou bush and cherry guava, have the potential to be serious pests. Controls are now in place to stop any more dangerous introductions of plants and animals. Inevitably, the first settlers cleared some of the land for crops and pasture. The demand for palm plants has been constant and the palm seed industry continues, with residents harvesting four kilograms of seeds from each tree. Rats and insects take the rest.

In 1918, the ship *Makambo* went aground at Lord Howe. The ship's rats spread over the island, taking a heavy toll of birds and other animal life. While their numbers are now controlled by poisoning, a permanent solution to the rat problem still eludes wildlife managers. Researchers at the Australian Museum have studied all aspects of the island's natural history. It is a sad catalogue of losses. There were once 15 species of breeding land birds, of which 14 species were found nowhere else. Nine species have become extinct and two are endangered. Sailors hungry for meat, and invading rats, are only part of the story of extinction. Dogs and cats played a part, and goats and pigs added to the disaster. Fortunately, today the remaining wildlife is more secure.

The seabirds, which breed mainly on the smaller and less accessible islets, have fared better. One species of particular interest is the providence petrel, so named because this bird's arrival to breed on Norfolk Island was timely enough to save the first settlers from starvation. Within a few years, the providence petrel was exterminated on Norfolk but the colony on Lord Howe has flourished to the extent that its numbers are estimated at 40 000 birds. The fleshy-footed shearwater, whose burrows are a risk to walkers, is also common. The arrival of the breeding shearwaters at dusk makes a spectacular sight. There are many breeding species on the offshore islands, with the sooty terns the most abundant at around 100 000 birds.

Lord Howe Island's most famous bird is the woodhen, a flightless member of the group of birds known as rails. Fearless, or perhaps ingenuous, like so many island rails, the woodhen was easily killed. Captain Thomas Gilbert wrote: "... several of these I knocked down and, their legs being broken, I placed them near me as I sat under a tree. The pain they suffered caused them to make a doleful cry, which brought five or six dozen of the same kind to them, and by that means I was able to take nearly the whole of them ...". In this manner woodhens were diminished in number, with dogs and pigs adding to the slaughter. There was consternation when John Disney, an ornithologist at the Australian Museum, found there were only about 20 adult woodhens left, living on the summits of Mount Lidgbird and Mount Gower where they were reasonably safe from pigs. Pressure from conservationists, particularly the Wild Life Preservation Society of Australia, caused research to be abandoned in favour of a breeding programme. This was successful and, by 1981, four of the young birds were released into the wild. Today, all the wild pigs have been removed and the woodhens are reasonably abundant once more.

Lord Howe Island's surrounding reefs represent the most southerly development of significant reef corals, which extend for five-kilometres (three miles) along the western side of the island. There are 57 species of corals, a small number compared to the 400 species of the Great Barrier Reef. However, many of them are among the major reef building organisms. The animals and plants of the reefs here are a mix of tropical and cold water forms. Fish species number around 480 and seastars, sea urchins, molluscs, marine worms and a host of other sea creatures are plentiful.

An interesting relic among the land animals is a giant stick insect that survives on Balls Pyramid where it is safe from rats. Landings on Balls Pyramid are controlled to avoid damage to the wildlife, mainly the breeding seabirds. The surrounding seas teem with fish and visitors take their catches back to be cooked by the various tourist lodges on the main island.

Lord Howe Island has some 250 residents and around 4000 visitors a year. Controls are in place to maintain the island's quality of wildlife and landscape, and planning measures are designed to keep all buildings at lower than palm tree height so that, from a distance, the island will be seen as the green paradise that welcomed the first visitors.

The World Heritage listing provides 11 reasons why this island group was added to the world's 'natural crown jewels', but no mere summation can do justice to Lord Howe. Visitors walking through the forests or along the grassy roads, climbing to the high points, exploring the reefs or cycling over the few island roads know something of its fascination. As the sun sets and the cloud blanket on Gower and Lidgbird is tinged with rose and gold, the scene is breathtaking. Truly this is one of the most beautiful islands in the world.

RIGHT Lord Howe Island is the home to three species of palms found nowhere else. They are the plentiful Howea or Kentia palm and, shown here, the *Hedyscepe* and *Lepidorrhachis* palms.

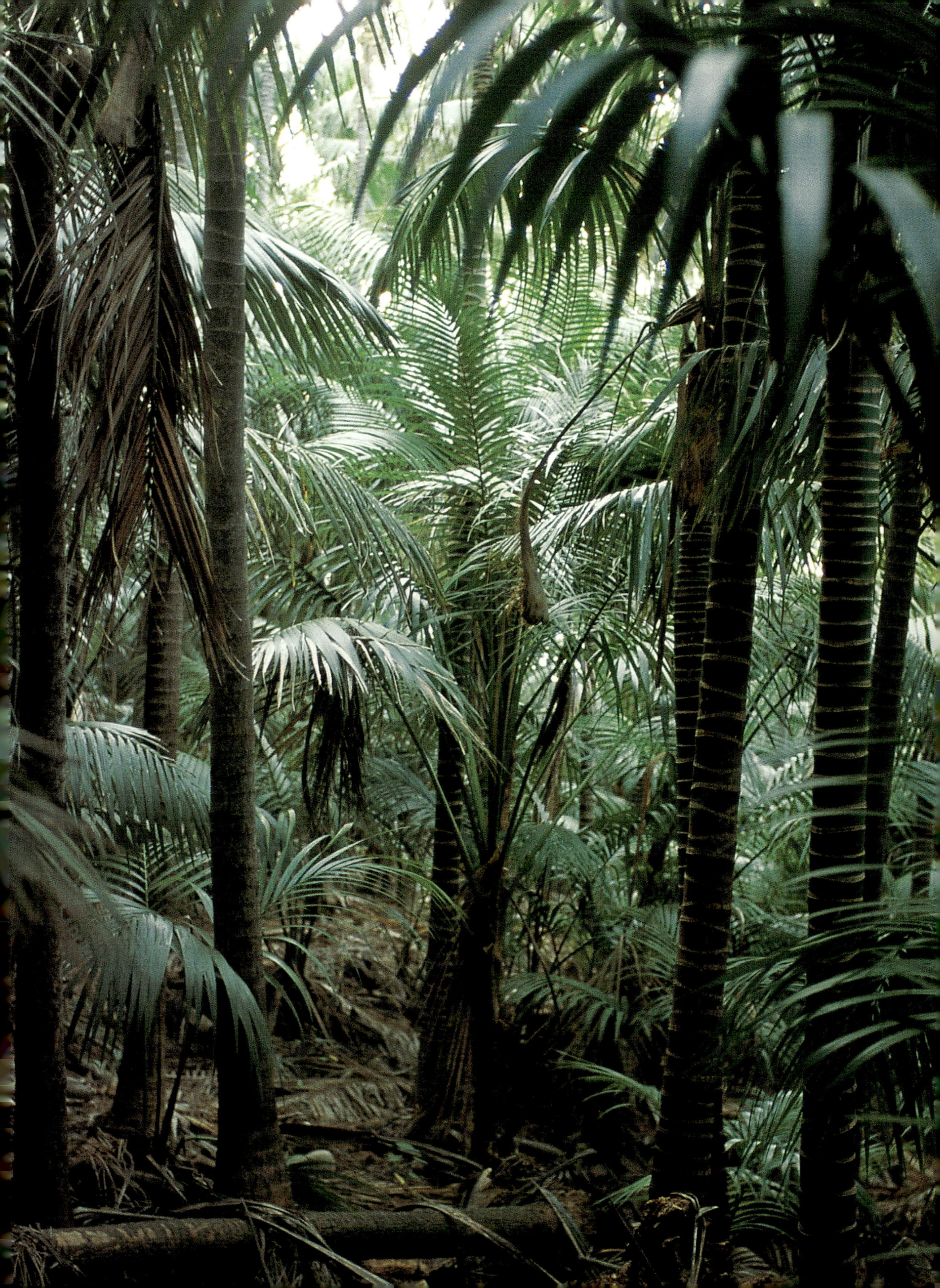

Physical Features

The Lord Howe Island Group is one of the most beautiful World Heritage sites and also one of the smallest. The main island of Lord Howe covers a diminutive 1455 hectares (3500 acres), measures just 10 kilometres (6 miles) in length from north to south and is little more than two kilometres (one and a quarter miles) wide. The tiny islets surrounding it add another 885 hectares (2185 acres) to the total area. Echoing the shape of the long-gone volcanic crater from which it was born, Lord Howe Island is roughly crescent-shaped and encloses a coral reef lagoon on its south-west side.

The island's craggy topography makes it a spectacular sight. Dominating the southern part of the island are the twin cloud-capped peaks of Mount Gower and Mount Lidgbird, which rise to 875 metres (2870 feet) and 777 metres (2549 feet) respectively. The seaward flanks of Mt Gower are formed by precipitous cliffs several hundred metres in height. The northern tip of Lord Howe Island consists of steep hillsides which also culminate in impressive cliffs dropping steeply into the sea. There are many smaller islands and steep rocks scattered around the main island. The most distant - and striking - of these is the group of islets and rock stacks clustered around the 650 metre (2132 feet) pinnacle of Balls Pyramid.

In this scene of tossing ocean waves and craggy peaks, a narrow strip of low-lying land in the central part of the main island forms the only habitable area in the Lord Howe Island Group.

Lord Howe Island, the Admiralty Islands and Balls Pyramid are the eroded remnants of a large volcano which erupted from the sea floor intermittently for about half a million years some 6.5 to 7 million years ago. During this period, the volcano measured about 50 by 16 kilometres (30 by 10 miles) and rose some 1700 metres (5600 feet) above sea level. The existing island and rocky islets represent only a small part of the original volume of the volcano. However, they are still impressive and they form the peaks of a sea mount 65 kilometres (40 miles) long and 24 kilometres (15 miles) wide which rises almost two kilometres (one and a quarter miles) from the ocean floor. The entire island group has remarkable volcanic features not seen anywhere else on Earth.

Precipitous Balls Pyramid represents a nearly complete stage in the destruction of a volcanic island, while Lord Howe Island's rich volcanic soils have yielded important palaeontological finds, including interesting fossils: the shells of ancient land snails, bird bones and the giant horned turtle. This creature, which probably became extinct more than 20 000 years ago, had clawed feet rather than flippers and therefore is assumed to have been a land-dweller.

The region has a humid, subtropical climate with temperatures averaging 16° Celsius (61° Fahrenheit) in August and 23° Celsius (74° Fahrenheit) in February. Annual average rainfall in the lowlands is almost 1700 millimetres (67 inches) but in some years it has been known to reach as high as 2870 millimetres (113 inches) and fall as low as 1000 millimetres (40 inches). The islands are also characterised by a high relative humidity and strong winds.

RIGHT Balls Pyramid, 25 kilometres (15 miles) to the south-east of Lord Howe Island, is a rocky pinnacle rising from the ocean floor some 2000 metres (6580 feet) beneath the surface to a height of 650 metres (2140 feet) above sea level. Like Lord Howe Island, Balls Pyramid is a remnant of the vast shield volcano that loomed above the ocean here eight million years ago and which is now in the final stages of erosion.

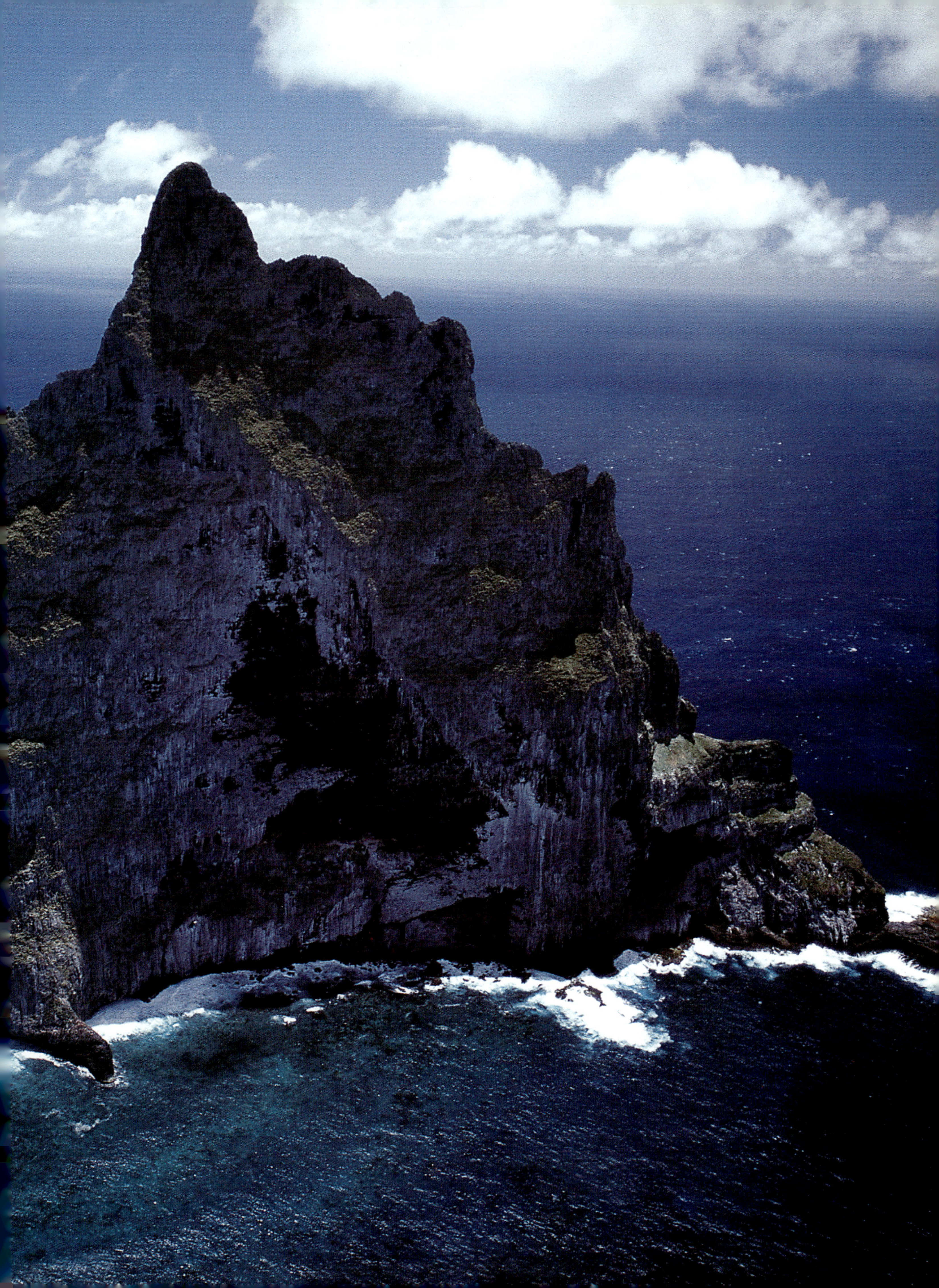

Special Features

Apart from its breathtaking natural beauty and its immense importance as a repository of endangered species, Lord Howe Island is the site of the world's southern-most coral reef, a structure which began to form during the Pleistocene epoch which commenced some 500 000 years ago. The reef is like no other in that it exemplifies a transition between an algal reef (built up by calcareous algae) and a coral reef (built up by corals), changing with fluctuations of warm and cold water around the island.

The corals found in the reef include 57 species grouped into 33 genera, which are few when compared with the splendid array found off the coast of Queensland. However, it is more than the number found off the northern New South Wales Coast around the Solitary Islands and includes two species not known from the Great Barrier Reef.

The corals of Lord Howe Island display very different characteristics from their northerly counterparts. This is due in part to the growth forms peculiar to the dominant species and in part to the limited range of species. The corals are periodically stripped bare by cold, sub-antarctic currents and then recolonised by larvae washed down from the tropics. The existing coral communities are the result of a balance between these two processes.

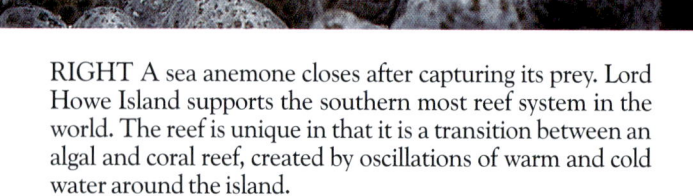

RIGHT A sea anemone closes after capturing its prey. Lord Howe Island supports the southern most reef system in the world. The reef is unique in that it is a transition between an algal and coral reef, created by oscillations of warm and cold water around the island.

ABOVE Cook's scorpionfish.

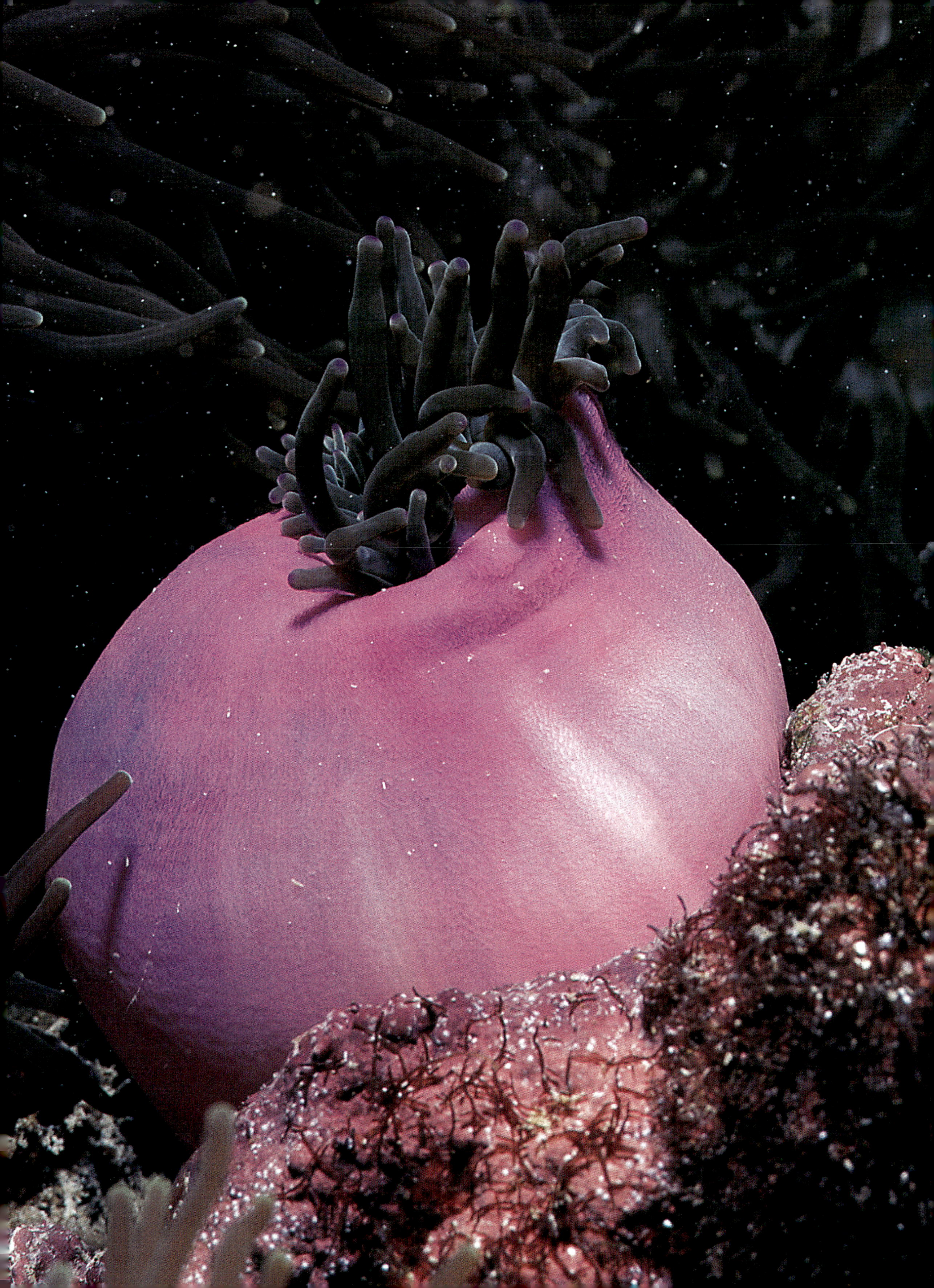

Flora

A range of vegetation types has been identified in the island group, corresponding with different environments, including lowland, valley, ridge and mountain areas, as well as habitats exposed to the sea. Exposure to wind and salt spray appears to be the determining factor in the range, structure and types of plants found in the location. Lord Howe Island is one of those very few small Pacific Islands with mountains high enough for the development of true cloud forest on their summits.

There are 241 native species of plants on Lord Howe Island. An astonishing 75 of these species do not occur anywhere else and 116 are considered to be rare or endangered. Many plants found on the island have a very restricted distribution; an example is the herb *Chinoconchloa conspicua* which is known only from a single clump found high on Mt Lidgbird.

Of the 48 species of native ferns, 19 are restricted to these islands. Of 180 species of flowering plants, 56 grow only here. Some of these plants suggest new species formed locally and in comparatively recent times, making them important to the study of plant evolution.

The vegetation of the Lord Howe Island group has links with subtropical and temperate rainforest found in other parts of the world. It shares 129 plant genera with Australia, 102 with New Caledonia and 75 with New Zealand. There are 160 introduced plant species but these are found mostly in the lowland settlement area. Several weed species are currently causing concern within the World Heritage Area, including bitou bush and kikuya grass.

RIGHT Mt. Lidgbird and the lagoon with Howea palms in the foreground. Weathering of these volcanic masses has produced a complex system of valleys and ridges. Here, a wide array of vegetation communities has developed under the influence of the maritime environment.

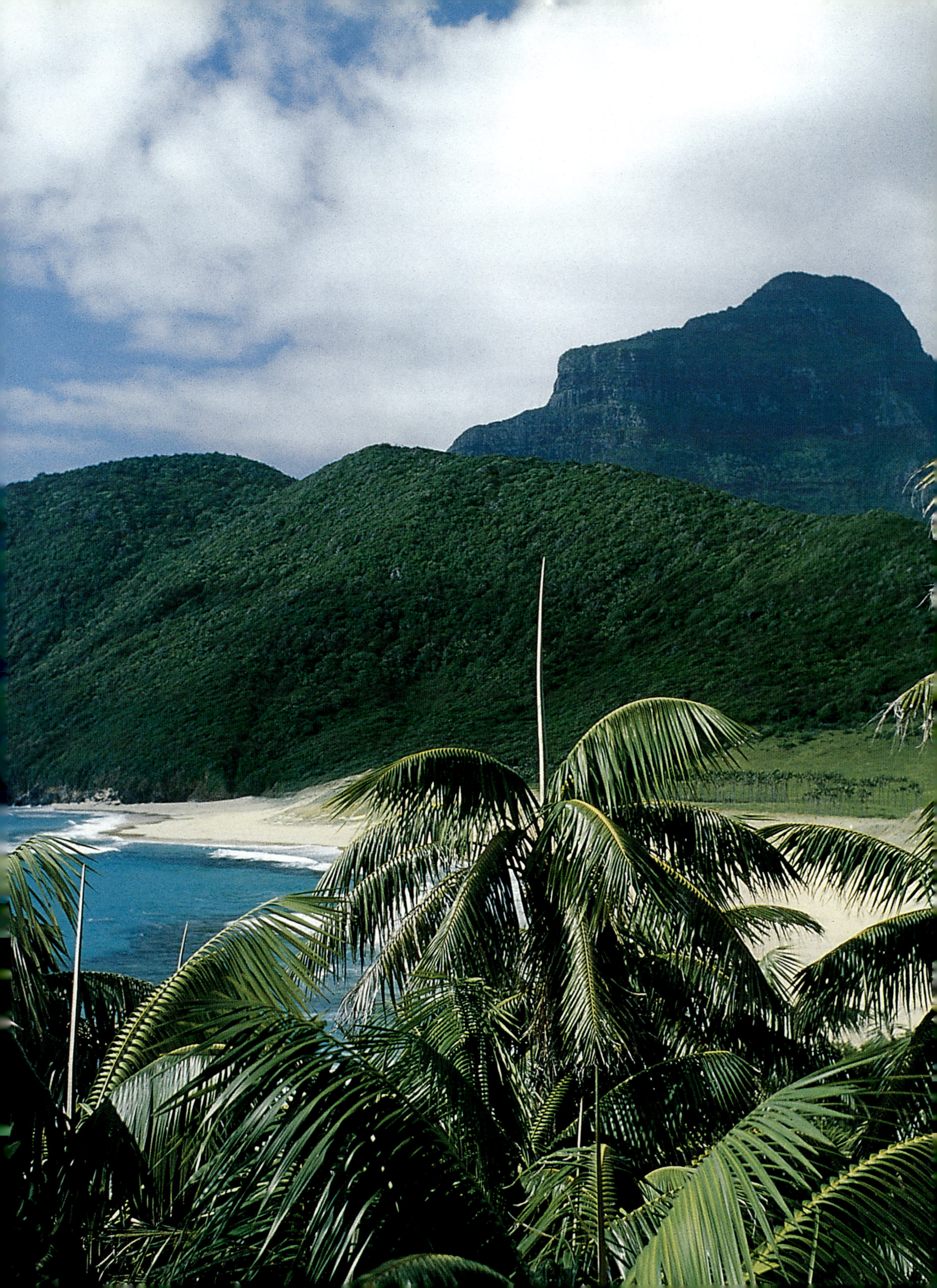

Fauna

The islands are home to four species of birds not found elsewhere. Significant among these is the Lord Howe Island woodhen. For some time, this flightless rail lived on the brink of extinction. With a population of only 16 individuals in 1975, the woodhen was one of the world's rarest animals. A successful captive breeding program has since increased the population to over 250. The rarity of the woodhen is almost equalled by the Lord Howe Island currawong, a species which numbers less than 300 birds. The other land birds unique to these islands are the relatively abundant silver-eye and the Lord Howe Island golden whistler.

For their size, the islands support a very abundant and diverse bird life. There are at least 129 native and introduced bird species, of which 27 breed here regularly. Lord Howe Island is now the only known breeding ground for the providence petrel, although it may also breed on Balls Pyramid. The fleshy-footed shearwaters which breed in substantial numbers on Lord Howe represent probably half the world's population of this species. Other breeding species include the Kermadec petrel, black-winged petrel, wedge-tailed shearwater, little shearwater, white-bellied storm petrel, masked booby, red-tailed tropic bird, sooty tern, noddy and grey ternlet. These species occur in greater concentrations here than in any other place on Earth. Among the migratory species which visit the island group regularly are the double-banded dotterel, the eastern golden plover, turnstone, whimbrel and bar-tailed godwit.

The island group supports two species of land reptile. These are threatened with extinction on the main island but remain abundant on other islands in the group.

There are many invertebrates, or animals without backbones. Small land-dwelling gastropods, such as the snails and slugs, number nine species and 16 subspecies, which is a greater number of subspecies than found on the Australian mainland. Of 100 species of spider recorded on Lord Howe Island, over half are thought to be limited to the area. A species of leech and ten earthworm species are thought to be confined to this island group.

The only indigenous mammal known to survive on Lord Howe Island is a bat: the large forest *eptesicus*. A fossil bat skull found in a cave in 1972 has been described as a new species and may have occurred in modern times but is no longer in existence. Introduced species include the mouse, rat, cat and goat.

The waters around Lord Howe Island provide a fascinating and unusual mixture of temperate and tropical organisms. Some 477 species of fish in 107 families have been recorded, of which a small proportion is limited to these waters and those of Norfolk Island and Middleton Reef.

ABOVE A pair of masked booby birds nesting at Muttonbird Point.

RIGHT The endangered Lord Howe Island woodhen, a flightless rail, is one of the rarest birds in the world. The main surviving population lives on the plateaux of Mounts Gower and Lidgbird. Woodhen numbers have steadily increased since the introduction of a captive breeding program in 1980 and now total around 250 birds.

FAR TOP RIGHT The Lord Howe group is the only known breeding place of the providence petrel. There are over 100 000 breeding pairs on the islands.

FAR BOTTOM RIGHT The vulnerable Lord Howe Island pied currawong survives on the island.

Cultural Heritage

Lord Howe's natural splendour is due in part to its unusually short period of contact with humans. No evidence of Polynesian or Melanesian occupation has been found and it appears that the earliest human use of the island was made in 1788 by the British naval vessel, *HMS Supply*. It was not until the nineteenth century that a small permanent settlement was established. The island's population fluctuated over the years but grew and consolidated into a distinctive social structure and culture. Although World Heritage listing was not made on cultural criteria, the island is an interesting example of restricted island settlement.

There has been considerable scientific interest in Lord Howe Island since its discovery. A succession of scientific expeditions in the nineteenth century established the international significance of the island's natural history. In the 1970s, the Australian Museum undertook a survey of the land environment for the Lord Howe Island Board. This survey recommended the establishment of an extensive land reserve for the protection of the local plants and animals.

On 1 January 1982, the natural areas at the northern and southern ends of Lord Howe Island, as well as the offshore islands, were established as a Permanent Park Preserve, which can be revoked only by an Act of Parliament; this reservation provides a standard of protection similar to that of a national park in New South Wales.

Human Impact

The World Heritage Area currently supports a resident population of between 250 to 300 people, almost all of whom live in the relatively flat lowlands in the central part of Lord Howe Island. The local economy is based upon tourism, followed by public administration and community service. Approximately 10% of the vegetation of the main island has been cleared for agriculture and a further 10% has been subjected to physical disturbance. Commercial activities carried out within the Park Preserve include collection of palm seeds, especially those of the kentia or Howea palm, and the cutting of Pandanus foliage for the production of baskets and other craft items. These activities are monitored and controlled by the administrative body, the Lord Howe Island Board.

Management

The Lord Howe Island Group is administered as part of the State of New South Wales. The managing agency is the Lord Howe Island Board, composed of five members, of whom three are elected island residents, one is the head of the New South Wales Department of Land and Water Conservation and one is the Director-General of the New South Wales National Parks and Wildlife Service.

The Board has adopted what is known as a 'land use policy set', based on a model which divides the region into two components: the World Heritage reserve and the settlement area. Fundamental management aims are to maintain the natural land-forming processes, to protect significant landforms, to maintain and avoid disruption to plant and animal populations and habitats, to eliminate human disturbance, to control or remove exotic species, to restore disturbed areas, to preserve the natural scenery and character of the region, to promote appreciation and enjoyment of the preserve, to maintain the full range of genetic diversity among the reserve's plants and to guarantee the continued livelihood of the island residents.

Much capital and labour (some 30% of the Board's budget) has been devoted to reducing weed infestations and feral animal pests. So far, limited resources have required efforts to be directed towards control of pests rather than their elimination. Successful projects have included the removal of goats from the northern hills of the main island and the elimination of feral pigs.

Facilities

In summer, up to 400 tourists may visit the island group at the one time. The principal means of access is by light aircraft. There are four licensed guest houses providing full board, and 13 self-contained apartment complexes. The major recreational activity is walking, often for nature study, bird watching or photography. There is an extensive system of walking tracks throughout the reserve and a guide service is available. Scenic flights are provided over the island group and several operators offer boat tours. Interpretation and environmental education activities are currently being developed.

Threats

Since the arrival of people on Lord Howe Island, nine of the 15 land birds recorded upon discovery - seven of which were restricted to the region - have become extinct. Their destruction was the result of hunting, the introduction of the black rat, owl and cat, or due to environmental changes caused by the introduction of goats and pigs. The size of some seabird colonies has also declined. Although exact details are not known, the region's unique land snails are now less abundant and are confined to isolated colonies, and the two native lizards are very restricted - if not extinct - on the main island.

In the settled parts of Lord Howe Island, the destruction of the native vegetation has been virtually complete after many years of clearing for settlement, grazing and agriculture. Introduced plants number 175 species and, although these exotics tend not to invade the undisturbed native vegetation communities, they do take over re-growth on cleared areas. Perhaps the greatest threat to the long-isolated environment of the Lord Howe Island Group World Heritage Area is the destruction of native plants, animals and their habitats by introduced animals.

THIS PAGE The weathered slopes and shores of Lord Howe island have yielded fossils of prehistoric creatures such as the giant horned turtle.

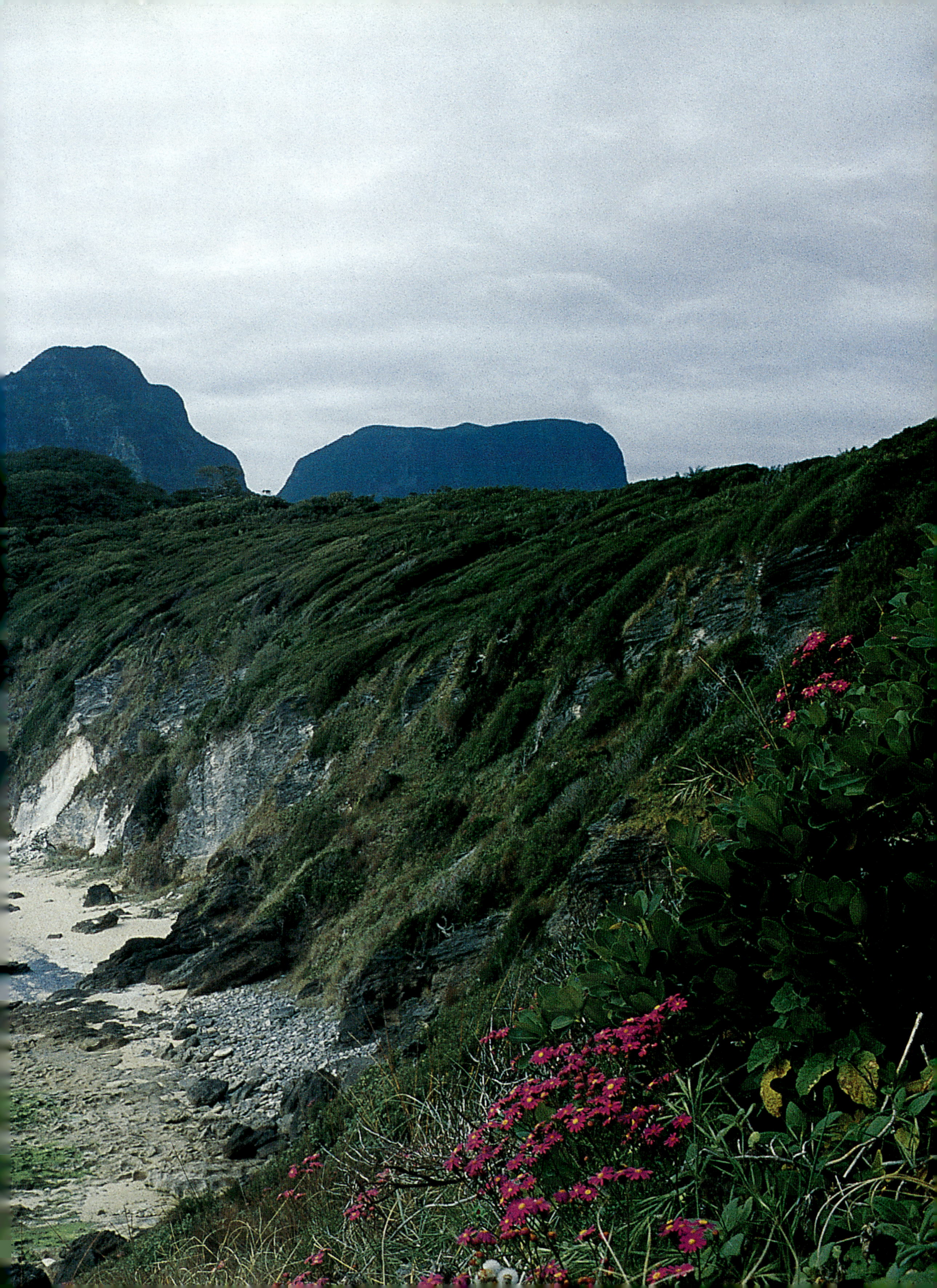

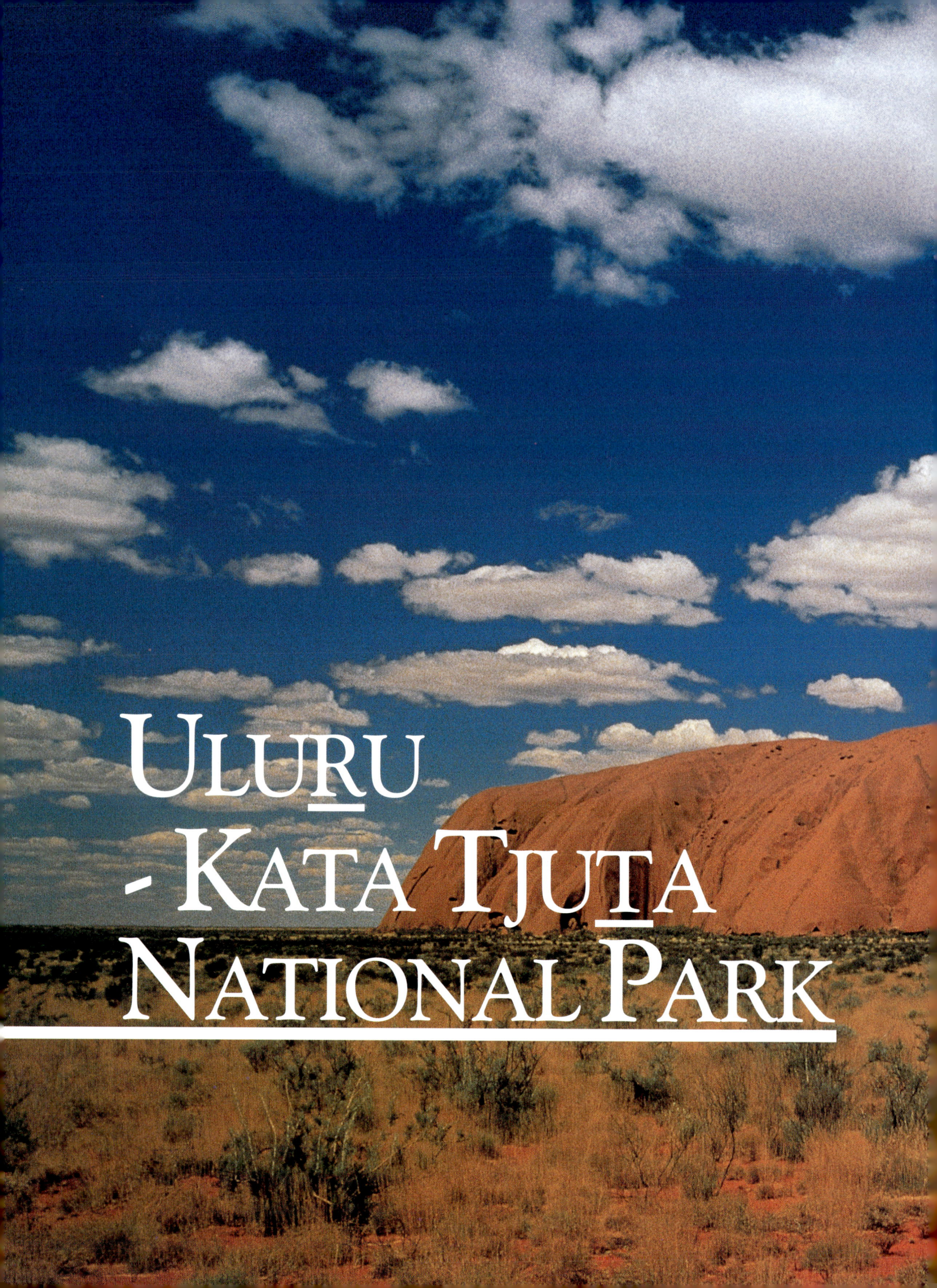

Uluru - Kata Tjuta National Park

Australia's 'Red Centre' is a place of harsh beauty, forming, in different ways, part of the mythic geography of Aboriginal and non-Aboriginal Australians. It is also a tourist attraction that draws many thousands of visitors each year. The Uluṟu - Kata Tjuṯa (Ayers Rock - Mount Olga) National Park is a landscape of sweeping red sand plains and rolling dunes, punctuated by the immense monolithic formations of Uluṟu and Kata Tjuṯa. Many thousands of years of Aboriginal occupation of lands within and around the park are a testimony to the durability of traditional Aboriginal society and the hunting and gathering economy which sustained it. The land of Uluṟu - Kata Tjuṯa is invested with significance by the local Yankunytjatjara and Pitjantjatjara speaking peoples through their religious philosophy. The physical features of the park form an integral part of their spiritual life, social customs and traditions.

Location

Uluṟu - Kata Tjuṯa National Park is situated in the south-west corner of the Northern Territory close to the centre of the Australian continent and within Australia's Western Desert. It is some 335 kilometres (210 miles) west of Alice Springs. The park encompasses 132 566 hectares (327 584 acres) of arid country. Much of the landscape is relatively featureless, so the boundaries of the park are not defined by reference to physical features but by geographical co-ordinates: 25°05' to 25°25' South and 130°40' to 131°22' East. The Yulara tourist resort is about 4 kilometres (2.5 miles) north of the park's boundary.

PREVIOUS PAGE Aerial view of Uluṟu with Kata Tjuṯa in the background. Mountain-building forces about 450 million years ago raised the central Australian region above sea level. Over time much of the land was worn down to form a great plain. Resistant rocks such as Uluṟu and Kata Tjuṯa remained to dominate the desert landscape and eventually to assume great spiritual significance among the local Aboriginal people.

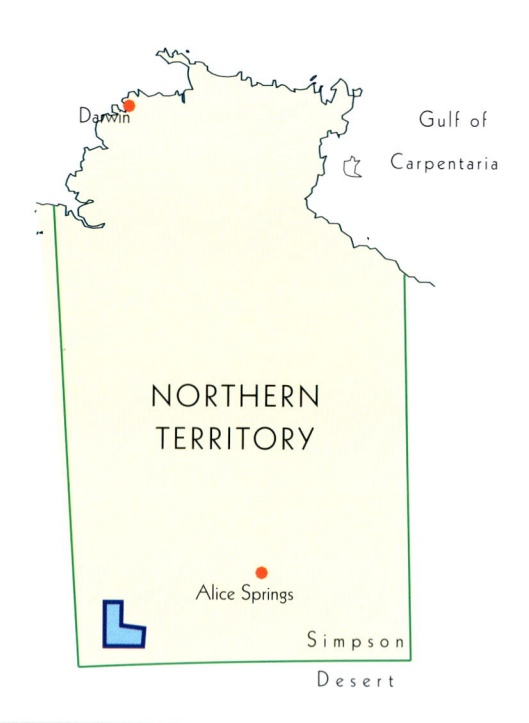

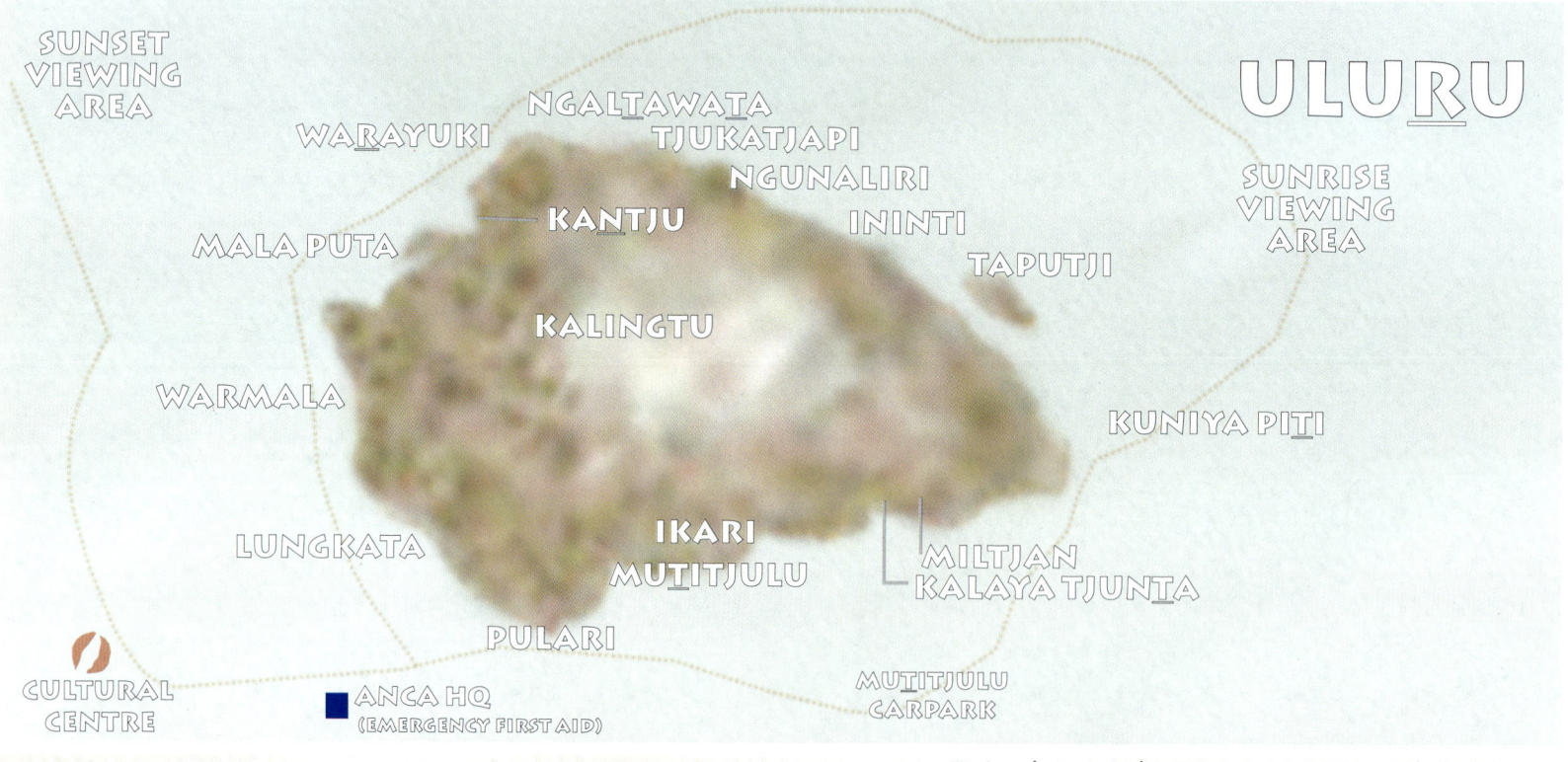

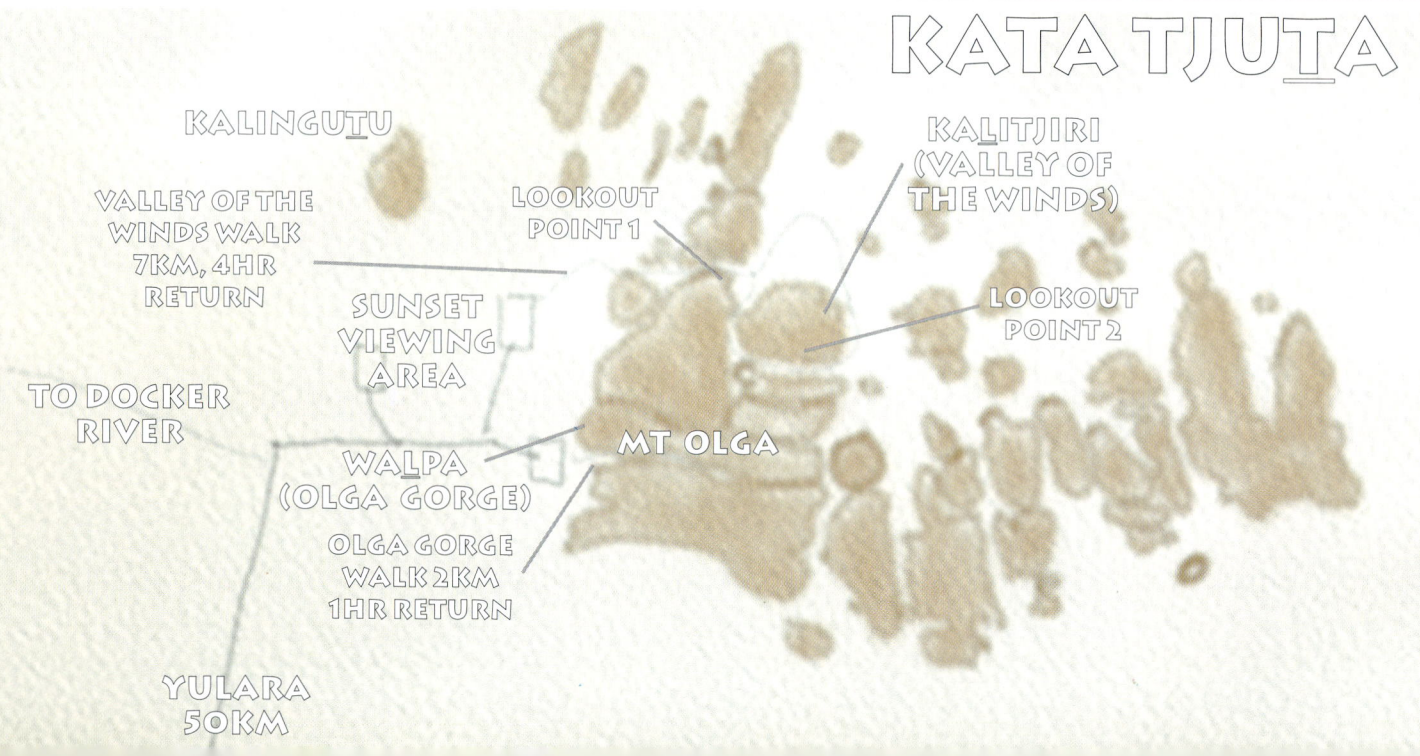

The Cultural Heritage of Uluru - Kata Tjuta National Park

by William Lines

When evaluating the Australian government's nomination of Uluru National Park to the World Heritage list in 1989 on the basis of the area's cultural values, the IUCN warned of the possible erosion of Aboriginal culture. It was suggested that this would undermine and degrade Uluru's cultural significance.

When the Australian government renominated Uluru - Kata Tjuta National Park in 1994 for its cultural values, the park management claimed the area's traditional Aboriginal culture was intact. The granting of freehold title to the traditional owners, the use of Aboriginal nomenclature, the application of Aboriginal fire practices to the landscape and the care of waterholes in park management ensured the continuity and vibrancy of Aboriginal culture.

People have lived in central Australia for 30 000 years or more. Traditional life was based on the religious philosophy, Tjukurpa. Tjukurpa describes how a network of tracks, marking the journeys of ancestral beings, came to crisscross the park and connect such monoliths as Uluru and Kata Tjuta and other sites both inside and outside the present park. These stories bind the people socially, spiritually and historically to the land (ngura). Tjukurpa regulates how the country is used, what foods are eaten and how they are prepared, where people live and where they move, whom people marry and the affiliation of their children, how tools are manufactured, and how people relate to each other. For example, when rain falls in one area, Tjukurpa requires its inhabitants to host visitors from neighbouring areas. When rain falls elsewhere, these hosts take their turn as the guests of other groups.

Water is crucial. Accordingly, group territories tended to focus on the ranges, where there are more rock holes and soaks in the otherwise dry beds of the creeks. Uluru, which takes its name from Uluru rock hole, high up on the monolith, and Kata Tjuta, which means 'many heads', are both traditional base camps because of their reliable supplies of water.

Uluru stands in the territory of a people who speak a dialect called Yankunytjatjara. This is closely related to Pitjantjatjara, the other principal dialect spoken in Uluru - Kata Tjuta. Speakers refer to themselves as Anangu to distinguish themselves from the people of other places. Soon after birth, every Anangu person is identified with a specific ancestral being, partly based on the birth-place's association with a particular ancestor and partly on physical features and character that reveal the child's Tjukurpa. Pointing to a cliff face on Uluru, one Anangu said, "That's a rock but that's got to have something else, because that's got all those old men's memories inside".

Several stories describe the creation of Uluru. One of them, the Wiyai Kutjara story, tells how two boys built Uluru during the creation era while playing in the mud after rain. When they finished, they travelled south to Wiputa, on the northern side of the Musgrave Ranges, where they killed and cooked a euro, a western species of kangaroo (tjukurpa palya). After this, the boys turned finished, they travelled south to Wiputa, on the northern side of the Musgrave Ranges, where they killed and cooked a euro, a western species of kangaroo. After this, the boys turned north again towards Atila (Mount Conner). On the way, at Anari, one boy threw his tjuni (wooden club) at a hare wallaby, but the club struck the ground and made a fresh-water spring. He would not reveal this source of water to the other boy who nearly died of thirst. The boys fought and made their way to table-topped Atila where their bodies are preserved as boulders on the summit of the mountain.

Twelve major painting sites are among the hundreds to be seen in rock shelters around the base of Uluru. Paintings up to 9000 years old display geometric forms such as circles, arcs and human and animal footprints. Later paintings employ human and animal silhouettes. All express the ideas (kulini, or physical thinking) of the Tjukurpa. They were made as teaching tools to record, for example, an actual emu hunt by the artist or the story of Lungkata, Blue Tongue Lizard Man, who stole an emu hunted by the Bell Bird Brothers in the heroic past. Norman Tjalkalyiri, one of the park's Anangu rangers, describes the rock art as an 'Anangu blackboard'. Present-day Anangu consider it inappropriate to continue painting in rock shelters out of respect for those of their grandparents' generation who were the last to paint there. The artistic tradition continues, however, in the form of sand drawings, body painting and acrylic paintings on canvas.

Devastating changes to Anangu culture began in the 1930s when their traditional lands were taken and developed as cattle stations. Cattle grazing monopolised the major water sources by developing them as bores and tanks; stock trampled and polluted soaks and rock holes; cattle reduced the quantity and diversity of vegetation; and many local animals became extinct, particularly the smaller ones that formed the prey of introduced feral predators. Anangu found it impossible to live off the land as they had always done. The pastoralists made the region part of a much wider economy; they were not interested in a self-sufficient local one. Anangu economy and culture was further undermined in the 1940s when a dirt road reached Uluru. Anangu began to sell carvings to tourists. While this gave them some independence from government food rations introduced to tempt them into settlements, they became more dependent on the outside world. By 1950, the ancient ways of living had been largely obliterated, although Anangu continued to live around Uluru.

In 1983, the traditional owners secured title to Uluru National Park under an agreement which provided for an immediate lease-back of the land to the Commonwealth Government so that it would continue to be managed as a national park. About 150 Pitjantjatjara and Yankuntjatjara people now live in the Mutijulu community close to the rock. Their involvement in park management provides a precedent for similar parks elsewhere. Anangu commercial activity includes the Ininti store and garage and the Maruku Arts and Crafts retail outlet. Some Anangu work as park staff and rangers.

Before the 1930s, Anangu regularly fired the vegetation and cleaned and protected soaks and waterholes. Both practices are now part of park management. Patch-burning of spinifex, mostly in winter when fires never carry far, creates a mosaic of vegetation of different ages. Large spinifex hummocks persist alongside burnt ground fertilised with ash, where edible plants can grow. Breaks in fuel cover limit the spread of summer wildfires and protect fire-sensitive plants. Many small animals shelter in the protective hummocks and feed on the plants that grow in recently burnt country.

The regular maintenance of the Anangu once ensured that wells, soaks and rockholes did not silt up and were free of stagnation. They kept them clean so that the precious water would not be fouled by dung and dead animals. They cleared away the vegetation so that the wells would not be overgrown. These water sources enabled wildlife to occupy country where no other source of surface water was available. Senior Anangu women have now revived these traditional practices.

Nevertheless, such a small group of people, subjected to a massive invasion by government, park management, modern technology, commerce and thousands of tourists, face an almost overwhelming challenge to their distinct culture. Tensions will inevitably arise between the Northern Territory's emphasis on tourism as a source of profit and Anangu who in their traditional culture had no interest in making money from the rock, only in protecting it. Moreover, as Anangu economic interests increase, traditional interests may decrease. Even the land rights legislation may subvert traditional ways as it makes Aboriginal ownership too closely resemble the European notion of freehold title with its emphasis on exclusive rights to parcels of land, rather than recognising that sets of complementary rights and responsibilities exist over each site.

Modern methods of hunting are quite different from the traditional Anangu ways. Hunting from the back of a four-wheel drive with a high-powered rifle has replaced tracking prey on foot armed only with a spear. These different methods give rise to very different relationships with the land.

The World Heritage cultural values of Uluru - Kata Tjuta relate to the religious and mythic beliefs of the past and present native Aboriginal population. The land is literally - through millennia of firing of the vegetation, camping, use and, metaphorically, through Tjukurpa and the creation stories - an artefact of Anangu culture.

Uluru, the rock, is undoubtedly the most distinctive landscape symbol of Australia. Its striking features, and those of Kata Tjuta, convey to Anangu the durability of the Tjukurpa, their Dreaming. Other people made aware of this can appreciate its significance and they readily see in these great monoliths the aeons of evolution and erosion that have formed the Australian continent.

The Natural Heritage of Uluru - Kata Tjuta National Park

by William Lines

Arid lands cover about two-thirds of the Australian continent. Arid, however, does not mean absence of life. Australia's arid regions support a rich plant and animal life well adapted to the dry climate and poor soils.

Uluru-Kata Tjuta National Park, an area of 132 538 hectares (327 369 acres) close to the centre of Australia in the Northern Territory, preserves a sample of arid zone life. The park also contains two striking rock monoliths that rise sheer from the sandy plain.

In separate expeditions in the 1870s, explorers William Gosse and Ernest Giles came upon and gave European names to the monoliths long known to the Aborigines as Uluru (Ayers Rock) and Kata Tjuta (The Olgas). The country around the two monoliths was made an Aboriginal Reserve in 1920. In 1958, following a decade of increasing tourism, an area of land including Uluru and Kata Tjuta was excised from the Aboriginal Reserve and gazetted as the Ayers Rock - Mount Olga National Park. In 1977, the park was renamed Uluru National Park. Eight years later, the local Aboriginal land trust received title to the land in the national park, which was immediately leased back to the Commonwealth Government so that it continued to be managed as a national park, but henceforth under joint management arrangements, as agreed to by the Aboriginal owners. In 1987 Uluru-Kata Tjuta was inscribed on the World Heritage List.

Nine hundred million years ago, Uluru-Kata Tjuta was part of a vast depression called the Amadeus Basin, an arm of a shallow sea that then covered most of Central Australia. Sediments, mostly sand and fine mud, washed into the basin and formed a deposit 3000 to 4000 metres (10 000 to 13 000 feet) thick. Compressed and cemented, these sediments gradually turned into rock. Five hundred and fifty million years ago, this rock was pushed up from the ancient seabed to form a mountain range 2500 to 3000 metres (8800 to 10 000 feet) high. Over the years, this range was eroded almost flat, the rock being turned into sand and mud again. Once more, this debris was compressed and consolidated and turned back into rock.

About 400 million years ago, the whole of the Central Australian region was pushed up permanently above sea level. Erosion wore down most of the high points but two masses of particularly resistant rock remained - Uluru and Kata Tjuta. Winds and rain sculpted and smoothly rounded the shapes of Uluru and Kata Tjuta but, while Uluru remained a single monolith, Kata Tjuta was made into a series of domes intersected by passages and canyons.

Uluru is one of the largest monoliths in the world and has a fine, even texture. The rock is composed of a sandstone called arkose which contains feldspar minerals often found in the Earth's crust, and the most common of all minerals, quartz. Uluru's surface is covered in large, angular, sometimes overlapping scales, the result of heat and water acting on the rock surface. The scales are coloured rust red by oxidisation and, when they flake off, the rock's true colour, a muddy grey, can be seen. Kata Tjuta's surface is coarse and composed of a type of rock known as conglomerate. This rock is made up of an aggregation of rocks, ranging from tiny pebbles to boulders, which are cemented together within finer materials such as sand and mud.

As Uluru and Kata Tjuta took shape, the climate changed. Over the millennia the Australian continent has experienced several periods of extreme aridity. At these times it was so dry and so cold that all but the hardiest plants perished over vast areas. The last extremely arid period occurred only 15 000 to 30 000 years ago. The area around Uluru and Kata Tjuta was then virtually bare and wind blew the sand into the long ridges that form the dunes and swales to be seen there today.

The present climate of Central Australia is wetter and warmer than in the past but rainfall is erratic and the seasons are variable. One year, 900 millimetres (35 inches) of rain might fall in just a few days, while the whole of the next year may see only 50 millimetres (2 inches). The annual average at Uluru is 220 millimetres (8.6 inches). In a true desert, rainfall averages less than 120 millimetres (4.7 inches) a year. Uluru-Kata Tjuta is therefore not a desert and this can be seen in its red dunes which are not wind-blown, but stable and covered in vegetation.

Shrubs, grasses and annuals grow on the dunes and these include desert grevilleas with nectar-rich orange brushes, rattlepods with white, sweet-scented flowers, and many other plants that bloom following rains. At the base of the monoliths grow desert oaks and mulga trees. Between the shrubs grow circular clumps of an arid zone grass, the prickly spinifex. Spinifex is the most common plant to be seen at Uluru-Kata Tjuta and four species grow in the park. Hummocks of spinifex cover more than a fifth of the arid region and plant communities with spinifex as a component cover as much again. The perennial, or long-lived, plants of the region are crowded in favourable seasons by ephemerals - mostly members of the daisy and pea families - which are stimulated into growth by rain. They are lush, grow quickly, flower profusely, then set their seeds before dying away. Three hundred and sixty-three plant species are found within the park, representing a large proportion of the plant-life to be found in Central Australia.

All the plants are adapted to the erratic rainfall and to the ancient soils of the region which are of low fertility, containing half the levels of phosphorous and nitrogen found in the soils of arid zones in other continents. The sandy soils do not hold moisture and the rainwater rapidly percolates down to the water table where it is out of reach of most plants. Moreover, life has to adapt to great fluctuations in temperature ranging from 46° Celsius (113° Fahrenheit) in the height of summer to the frequent frosts of winter.

To minimise the effects of long dry spells, extremes of temperature and poor soils, plants have developed small, grey-blue and spiky leaves. Gnarled trees testify to a slow and tortured growth imposed by frequent droughts, their bark thick and fibrous, their wood hard and close-grained. The harsh conditions of Central Australia have bred a hard and brittle array of plants.

Few birds are especially adapted to the arid zone and most of the 150 species found at Uluru-Kata Tjuta occur throughout Australia. The numbers of birds to be seen depend on the conditions: in good years they are abundant; in poor years they become scarce. The mulga groves - woodlands of small wattle trees, vigorous and bushy - are especially attractive to birds, and in a year favoured with good rains they will support many species including white-backed swallows, woodswallows and crested bellbirds.

The major grazers of spinifex are insects: the termites or white ants. They are unaffected by heat, cold or drought because they create their own microclimate in their nests: a constant temperature of 32° to 35° Celsius (89° to 95° Fahrenheit) and over 90 % humidity. In Uluru-Kata Tjuta there are as many as 800 termite mounds to the hectare. Ants, scavengers and gatherers of nectar and other plant exudates are as numerous as the termites.

Australia's arid zone supports a more diverse array of reptile life than any other habitat in the world, including the tropical rainforests. With 72 species, Uluru-Kata Tjuta has more reptiles than any other area of land on earth of equal size. Most feed on the abundant termites and other insects.

Large native mammals are few in the arid zone. At Uluru - Kata Tjuta there are only dingoes and kangaroos (the red kangaroo and the euro). Within living memory, there were 44 species of smaller native mammals roaming the plains and dunes of Uluru - Kata Tjuta. By the late 1980s, half had disappeared, not just from the park but from the face of the Earth. Extinct mammals of the region include the pig-footed and desert bandicoots, the crescent nailtail wallaby, two species of hopping mice and the lesser sticknest rat.

A severe drought occurred in the 1930s at a time when traditional Aboriginal burning practices were being suppressed and new predators (cats and foxes), competitors (rabbits) and grazers (sheep and cattle) were introduced. This ravaged the environment not only at Uluru but throughout the Australian arid zone. The long-existing relationships between Aboriginal communities, plants and animals in the region were severely disrupted. Instead of surviving in small numbers until the end of the drought, entire populations of many medium-sized mammals were wiped out over vast areas.

Threats to the area remain. Grazing and burrowing by rabbits endanger vegetation communities around the base of the monoliths where soils are prone to erosion and many of the plants have restricted distributions. Thirty-four exotic plant species have been introduced and one of them, Rosy dock, has the potential to become a problem of great magnitude.

Further threats may arise from the management philosophy that prevails at Uluru-Kata Tjuta National Park. The priority of the Northern Territory Conservation Commission - the body responsible for Uluru - is to increase the 'productivity' of the Territory's national parks and reserves. The Northern Territory government sees conservation primarily as a means of furthering economic development. The aim is not so much conservation as to provide recreation facilities for the growing population and to establish an expanding base for the tourist industry.

Physical Features

Uluru-Kata Tjuta National Park is on the southern edge of the extensive Amadeus sedimentary basin. It contains extensive sand plains, dunes and desert, as well as the remarkable monoliths from which it takes its name. Distant ranges to the south and west of the area and Mount Connor (Atila) to the east challenge the dominion of the monoliths.

The landscape of Uluru-Kata Tjuta is characterised by gently sloping sand plains and vast dunes, some of which are up to 30 metres (99 feet) high. The sands are coloured a deep orange-red, which, combined with the searing heat, turn the park into a midday inferno, sending small native animals and tourists alike scuttling into the shade of the rocks.

While there are drier and hotter places on Earth, Uluru-Kata Tjuta's unpredictable cycle of drought and rainfall is remarkable. Annual rainfall is highly variable, although the peak generally occurs during winter. This corresponds with peak humidity which reaches around 67% in June and July. Surface water is largely restricted to seasonal pools fed by run-off from the monoliths. The dune formations contain no defined water courses, although the swales are moister than the surrounding areas and ponds may sometimes form in them. Two aquifers have been located in the area which, if tapped, could supply the region with a total of 870 000 cubic metres (31 000 000 gallons) of water per annum.

The park experiences two marked seasons: winter from April to October and summer from November to March. The air temperature ranges between 4° and 20° Celsius (40° and 68° Fahrenheit) in winter and 22° and 38° Celsius (72° to 100° Fahrenheit) in summer. Frosts are not uncommon throughout June and August but during the dry summer months there is a constant threat of bush fires.

TOP INSET Central netted dragon.

CENTRE INSET Lungkata, blue tongue lizard.

BOTTOM INSET The spinifex hopping mouse, a nocturnal marsupial, lives in deep and extensive burrows made up of interconnecting tunnels.

FAR RIGHT Uluru (the Pitjantjatjara name for a rock hole at Ayers Rock), in the distance, is Australia's best-known geographical feature, rising abruptly 348 metres (1145 feet) from the surrounding sand plains and dunes. The Rock's location in the heart of Central Australia, its semi-desert setting and the rich red tones of the rock surface combine to make it a distinctive symbol of outback Australia. Uluru is formed of steeply dipping sandstone and has a smooth, rounded appearance with steep sides and a relatively flat but heavily fissured top surface. The Rock is nine and a half kilometres (six miles) in circumference. When it rains, water cascades down the fissures in the sides of the rock forming waterfalls up to 100 metres (330 feet) in height. In the sides and base of the rock there are many caves, inlets and overhangs.

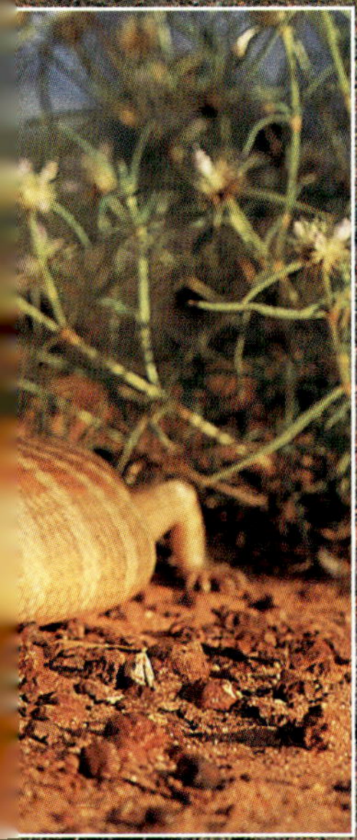
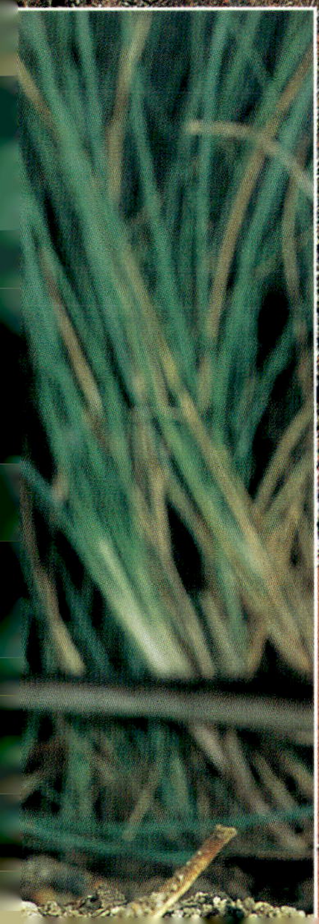
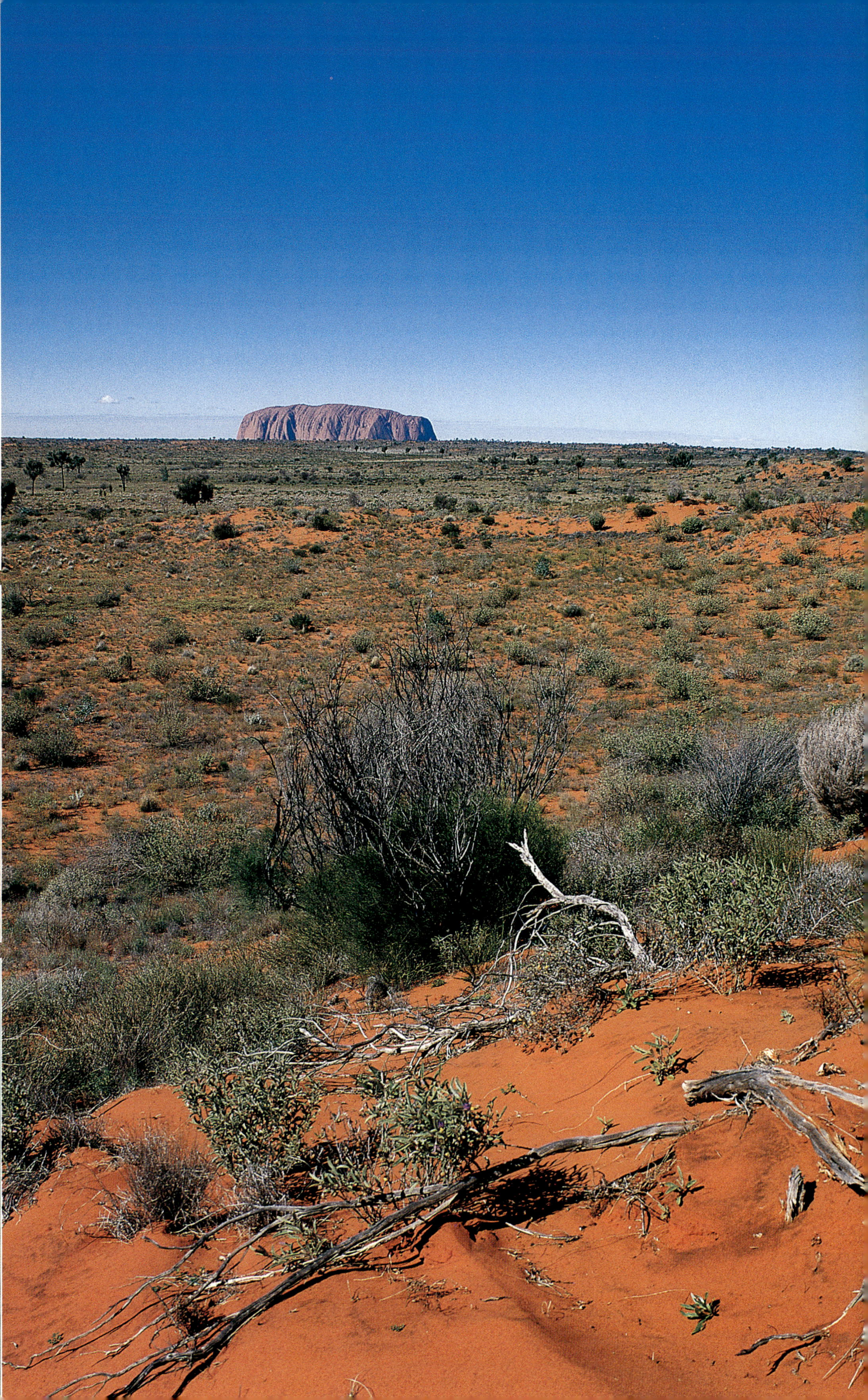

Special Features

Looming up from a barren landscape, Uluru or Ayers Rock is a cultural icon to all Australians. It rises a gigantic 348 metres (1145 feet) above the surrounding plain and reaches an elevation of 862.5 metres (2829 feet) above sea level. The rock is composed of steeply dipping sandstone which has been exposed as a result of folding, faulting and erosion of the surrounding rock and infill. This natural monument has steeply sloping sides leading to a relatively flat top. The circumference of its base is 9.4 kilometres (6 miles). Sheet erosion has caused the breaking away of layers of rock one to three metres (three to ten feet) thick parallel to the existing rock surface. The numerous caves, inlets and over-hangs at the base have been caused by chemical degradation and erosion.

Kata-Tjuta (The Olgas) lies 32 kilometres (20 miles) to the west of Uluru. Extending over some 3500 hectares (8649 acres), this feature is composed of 36 steep-sided rock domes of gently dipping conglomerate. Resembling giant bee-hives, these domes have rounded summits and were formed by the same processes which shaped Uluru. Mount Olga rises 546 metres (1791 feet) above the surrounding land and its summit is 1069 metres (3507 feet) above sea level.

The bare sandstone monoliths of Uluru and Kata-Tjuta are notable not only for their geological formation and scenic values, but also for the profound spiritual and cultural significance of the landscape to the local Aboriginal people. A thousand generations of Aboriginal people have imbued this place with a wealth of sacred sites and song lines, archaeological sites, rock art sites and engravings, making it significant at a global level.

The natural elements of the Uluru-Kata Tjuta National Park are also highly valued. The fragile arid lands ecosystem that exists here supports a surprising abundance of indigenous plants and animals.

RIGHT A sunset view of Kata Tjuta.

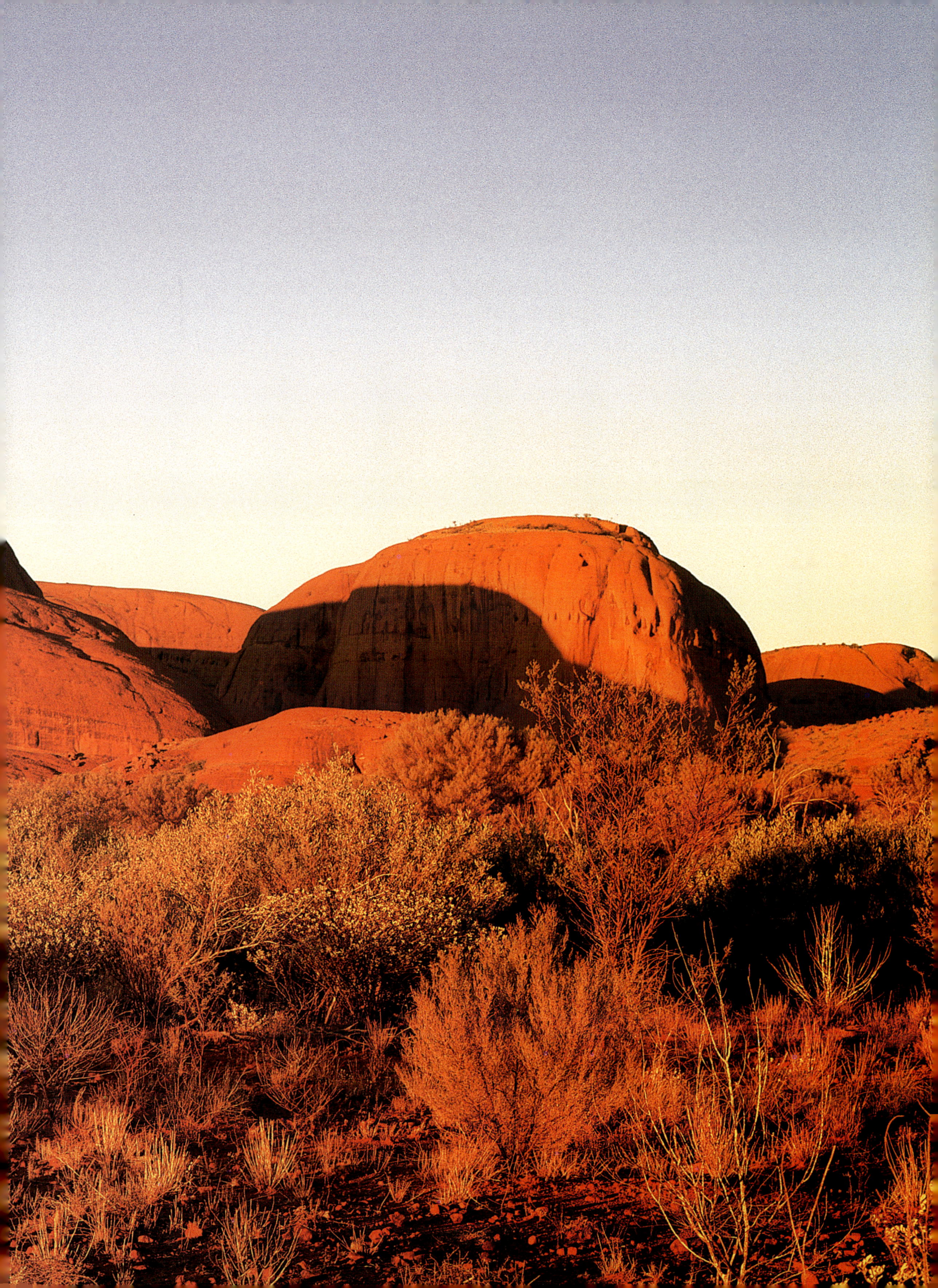

Flora

Twenty-four species of acacia or wattles, nine species of eucalypts and 16 species of grasses are prominent among over 500 plant species native to Uluru - Kata Tjuta. The distribution of plant life in the region is determined by factors such as the stability of the soil (sand being particularly mobile), microclimates, moisture, fire patterns and Aboriginal food and firewood gathering practices.

Vegetation in the park can be grouped into five major ecological zones which are arranged in a pattern of approximately concentric circles around the great monolith formations. Each zone supports a distinctive plant community.

Uluru supports hardy perennial grasses and sedges growing on shallow patches of soil, while occasional deeper pockets support stands of acacia and eucalyptus. At Kata Tjuta, the discontinuous plant cover consists almost entirely of spinifex, although wattles, cassia and hakea grow on some of the more gentle slopes.

The foothills of Kata Tjuta support grasses such as mulga grass and oat grass, with some low acacias and shrubs. Eucalypts, perennial grasses and shrubs can be found in drainage courses.

Pockets of sand and earth, washed down from the huge stone formations and deposited around their bases, have given rise to a distinct vegetation community. These areas are home to a complex of open grassland, low trees and shrubs, including bloodwood, tea-tree, acacias and lamb's tails. This vegetation can be quite luxuriant during rainy periods.

The plains support dense groves of mulga, other acacias and native fuschia, with an understorey of perennial grasses, but very little grows between these groves.

The sand dunes, rises and plains support an outlying zone of vegetation dominated by spinifex grasses, open eucalypt scrub, acacia and broom bush, interspersed in moister locations with occasional desert oaks.

'Spinifex', a group of spiky, perennial grasses, dominates the sandy dunes and plains. This group of plants is unique to Australia and is an especially important part of the park environment. It provides a habitat for a remarkable range of creatures, including a variety of marsupials and lizards. The soil in the park is of extremely low fertility but spinifex grows vigorously despite the lack of nutrients. When mature, the plants form hemispherical hummocks which may be several metres in diameter and up to 0.75 metres (2.5 feet) high. The densely massed needle-like leaves provide excellent shelter for small reptiles, invertebrates, birds and mammals from the blistering sun and also from predators.

RIGHT INSET Aboriginal people of the central deserts, like those in other parts of Australia, manage their environment by using fire, a practice known as 'fire stick farming'.

RIGHT Uluru Kata Tjuta's landscape has several vegetation communities. Beneath the great monoliths, along drainage courses and on deeper soils, grow eucalypts and shrubs, tall Mulla Mullas and wildflowers.

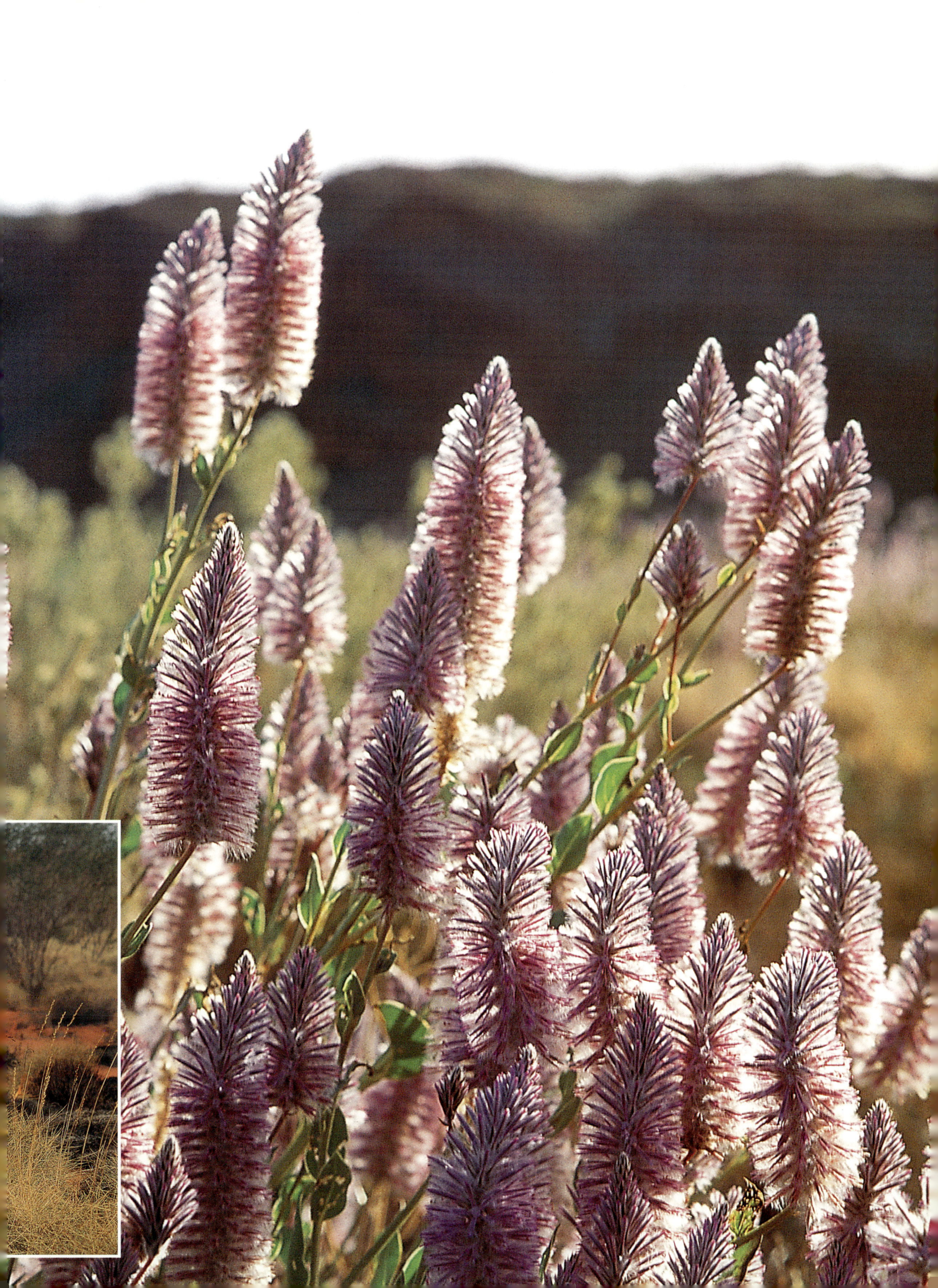

Fauna

The seemingly hostile environment does not prevent Uluru - Kata Tjuta from providing a home for many species of native animals. There are 22 native mammal species including dingo, red kangaroo, common wallaroo, marsupial mole, spinifex hopping mouse and the short-nosed echidna. There are also several species of bat, the Australian false vampire bat being particularly noteworthy. Among the small rodents and marsupials is the rare mulgara, a carnivorous marsupial about the size of a small guinea-pig, which lives only within established spinifex hummocks. The park management is studying the possibility of re-introducing the rufous hare-wallaby, the burrowing bettong and the common brush-tail possum, all of which have been lost from the area over the past 70 years.

More than 150 species of birds have been recorded in the park, 66 of which are thought to be residents. These permanent dwellers include parrots, wrens, thornbills and birds of prey such as the majestic peregrine falcon. Uluru - Kata Tjuta is also one of the few places where the patient bird-watcher may be rewarded with a glimpse of the small and elusive striated grass wren. This wren species disappeared from the park after devastating bush fires in 1976 but a survey conducted in 1989 found that the birds were once again inhabiting the spinifex hummocks which dominate the park landscape.

All five Australian reptile families are represented in the park. Among these, the species present include the monitor lizard, thorny devil, western brown snake, Ramsay's python and numerous others. Unusual aestivating amphibians such as water-holding frogs can also be found. These creatures retain water in their bodies during times of drought and burrow into the ground to await the rainy season. Little is known about the park's invertebrates but those of particular interest include the fairy shrimp and shield shrimp which exploit seasonal rock pools.

ABOVE Aquatic crustaceans manage to survive in this arid region by exploiting rock pools like those on the summit of Uluru. The northern shield shrimp is believed to have existed in its present form for over 150 million years. It perpetuates its species by producing thousands of eggs in a short period of time. The fertilised eggs are resistant to drying out and remain dormant in the soil until the next rain falls.

RIGHT Soft knob-tailed gecko. Reptiles have adapted well to this arid environment. This species will use its tongue to keep its eye moist.

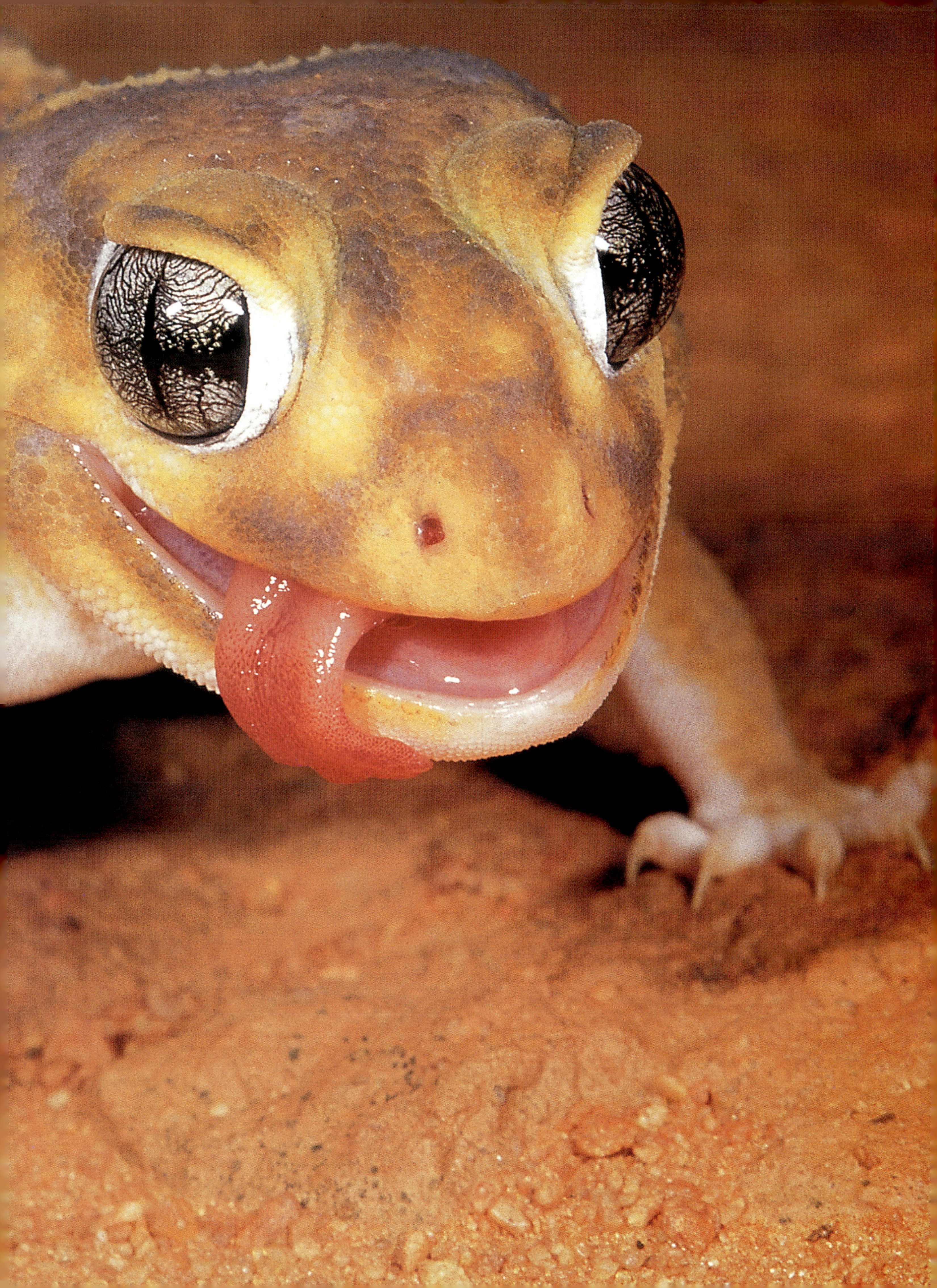

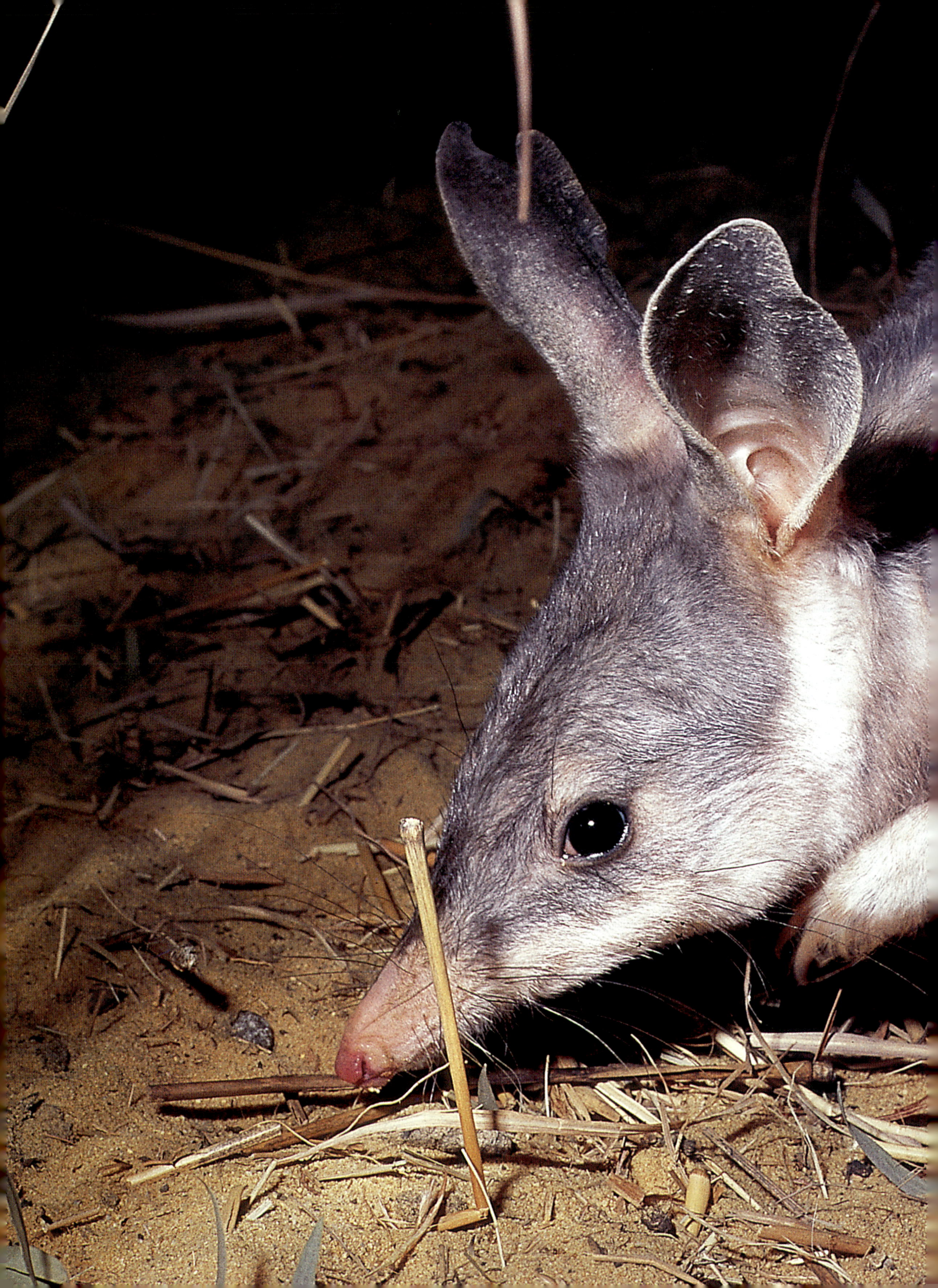

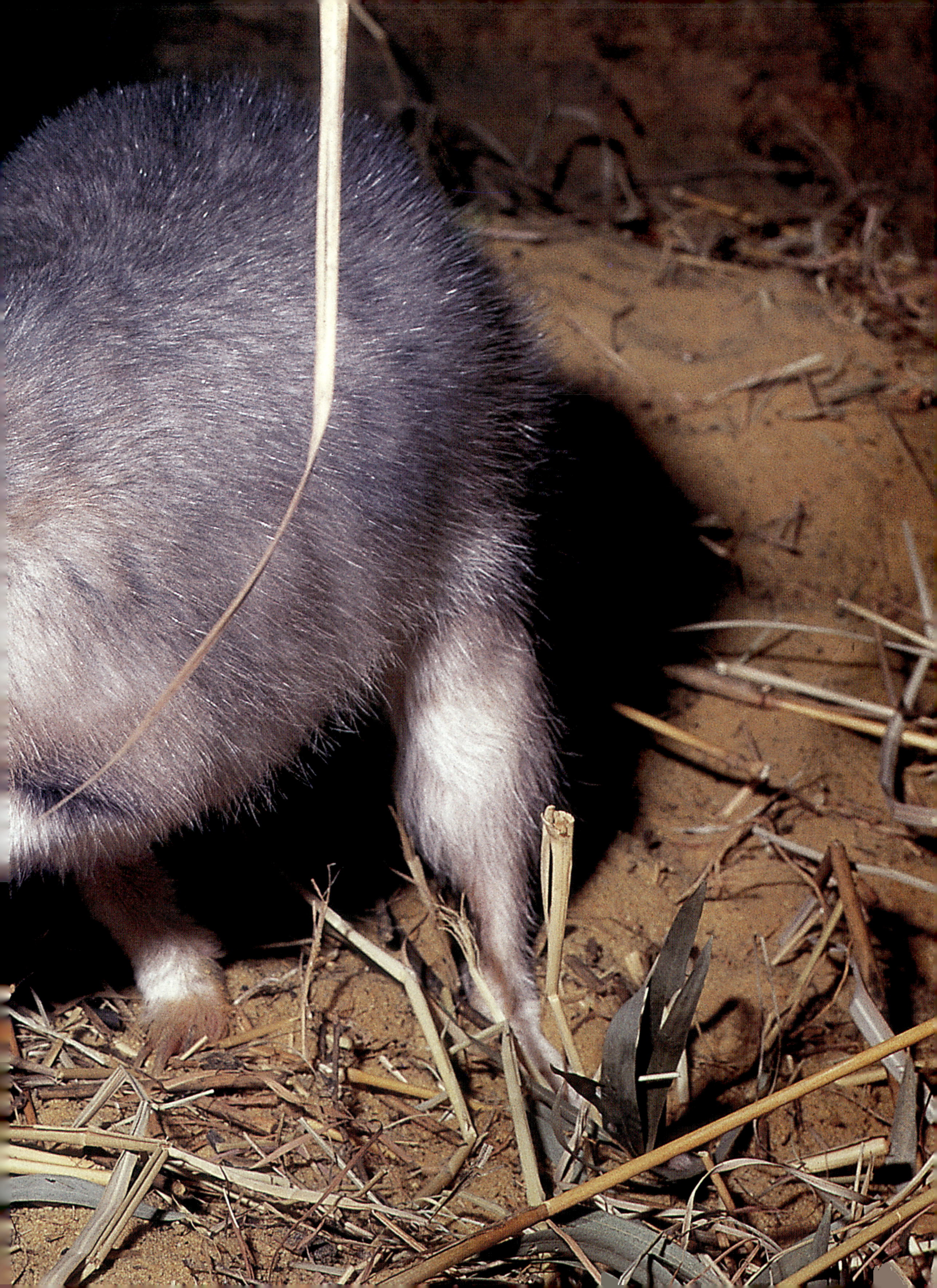

ABOVE Pink cockatoo

RIGHT Spotted bowerbird.

FAR RIGHT A Black-footed rock wallaby and her joey seen in a narrow gorge near Kata Tjuta's Valley of the Winds.

PREVIOUS PAGE The endangered bilby, a nocturnal marsupial, lives in burrows during the day and feasts on insects at night. Once common throughout much of Central Australia, its range is now reduced to remote parts of Australia's arid zone.

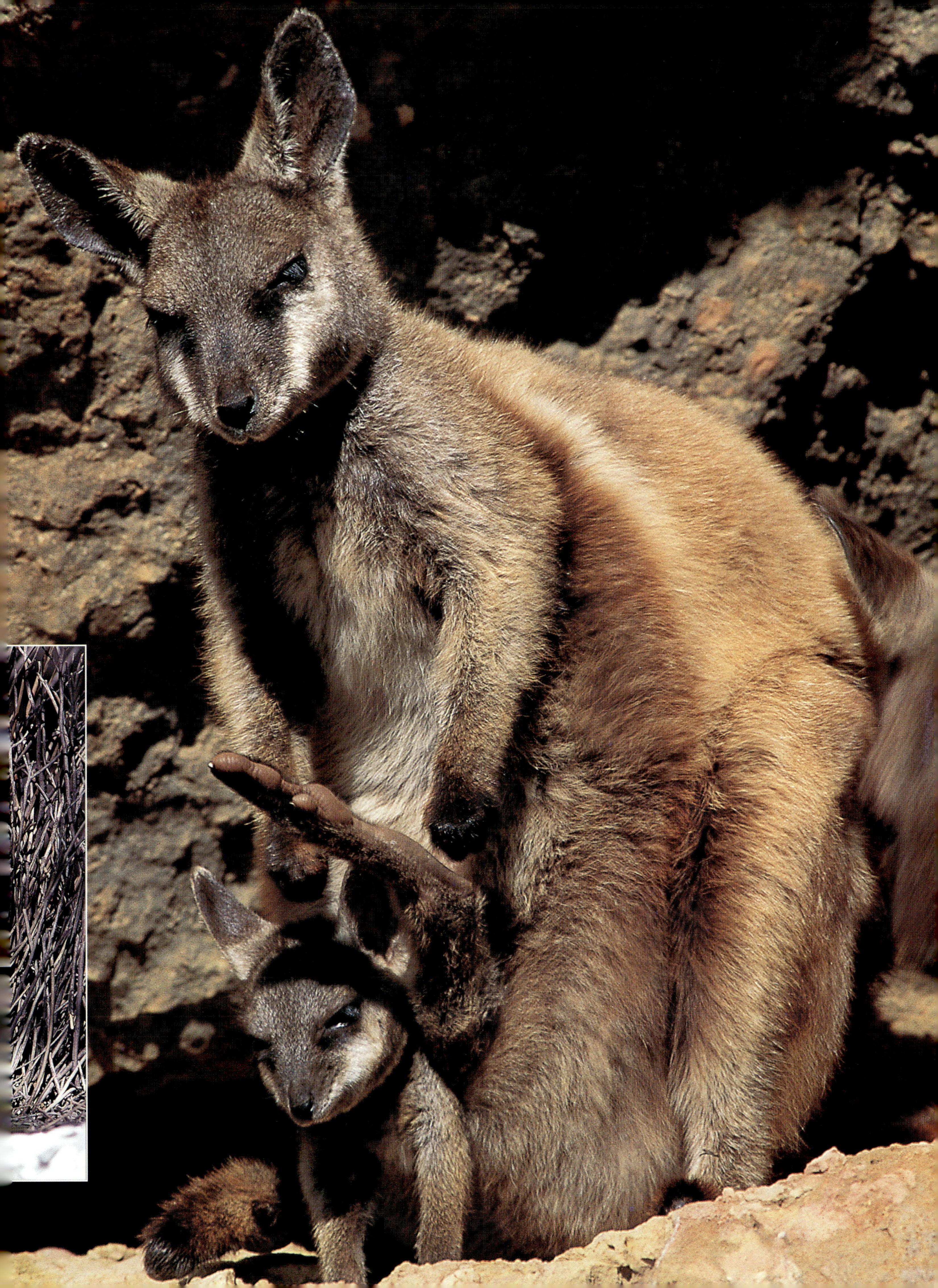

Cultural Heritage

Archaeological evidence shows that parts of Central Australia have been inhabited by Aboriginal people for at least 30 000 years.

The people of the Uluru - Kata Tjuta region have for almost all of this time lived as hunter-gatherers. Their adoption of new stone tool technologies around 4000 to 5000 years ago allowed them to more efficiently exploit their environment, leading to a substantial increase in population. The use of small stone tools such as the adze facilitated the production of hunting tools such as spear throwers and this in turn made for more effective hunting. The use of grinding stones meant that their diet could be supplemented with seed-based foods during ceremonial gatherings or at times when other foods were scarce.

Common misconceptions about the opportunistic nature of hunter-gatherer societies are dispelled by evidence from Uluru - Kata Tjuta. Aboriginal people did not simply exploit the limited desert resources, rather they actively managed their environment. They maintained a network of wells and waterholes over much of the country and they protected these water sources from pollution by animals or from becoming overgrown by vegetation. They also practised the regular burning of spinifex grasses. This activity not only promoted the growth of edible plants for their own consumption but also attracted game animals. In addition, burning served to minimise the devastating effects of bush fires through the creation of fire breaks across the plains. These practices were combined with the development of a social system which permitted reciprocal rights to resources between neighbouring groups, a method which ensured the best use of resources at times of abundance. This harmonious and successful system of land management was sustained for many thousands of years.

For the Aboriginal inhabitants of Uluru - Kata Tjuta, the landscape forms the narratives, songs and art of the Tjukurpa, or the 'Dreaming' as it is known to non-Aboriginals. The park is one of several important and interconnected centres of spiritual significance for Aboriginal people located throughout western Central Australia. The World Heritage Area is criss-crossed by a complex network of tracks marking the journeys taken by ancestral heroes. Each Aboriginal group resident in the area is accountable for celebrating and maintaining the traditions and ceremonies of the beings who created the sites within their country.

Ancient rock art at Uluru is indicative of the long history of Aboriginal life and spirituality in the region. Many of the rock shelters and overhangs in the park are decorated, with designs painted over the top of each other in many places. There are also a number of rock engraving sites.

INSET TOP Ancient Anangu rock art at Uluru.

RIGHT Cooked goanna is a popular meal in the red desert country.

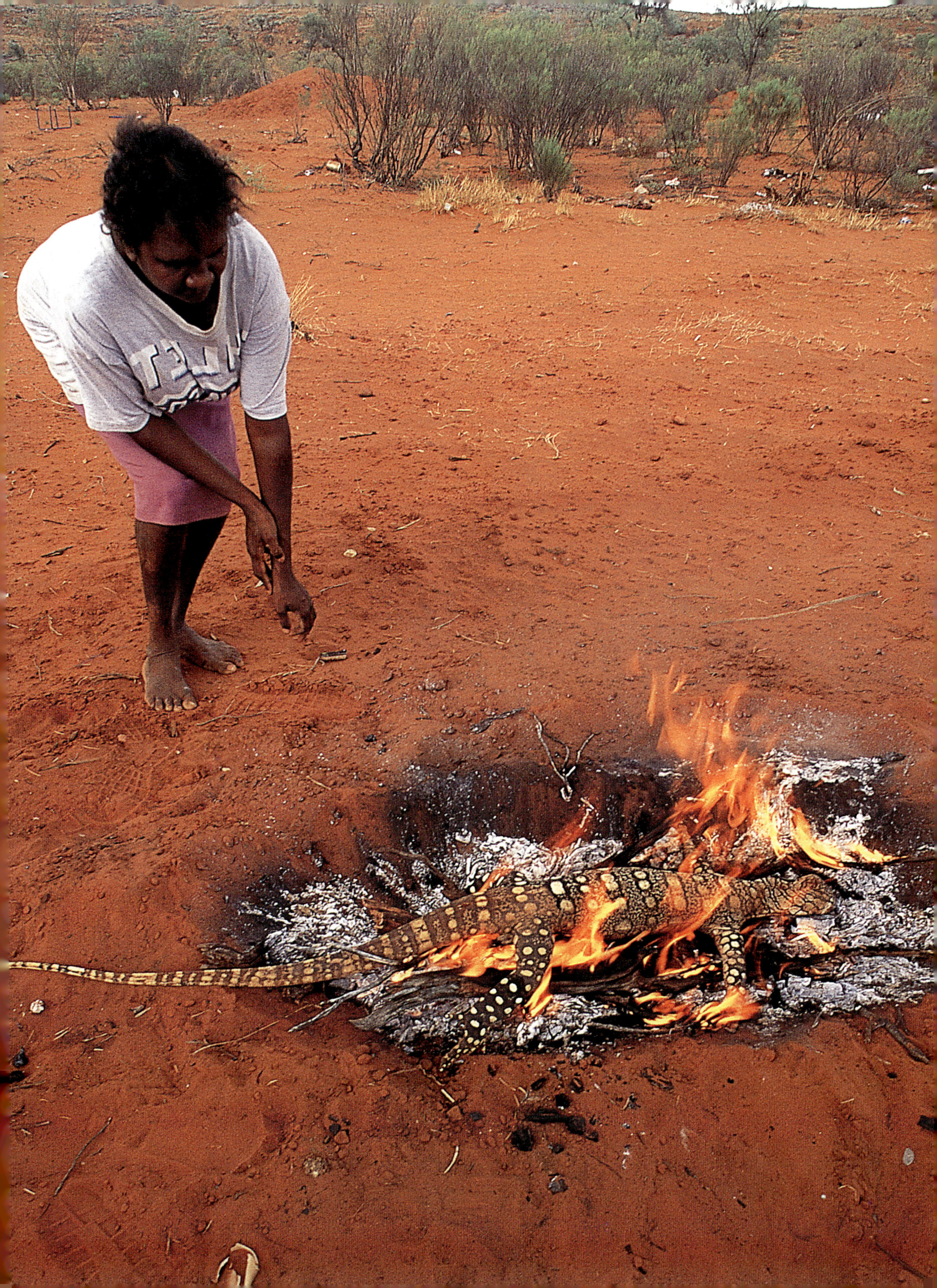

Europeans first became aware of Uluru and Kata Tjuta in the late nineteenth century. The construction of the Overland Telegraph during the 1870s opened the land to colonists. The first scientific expedition to the region, headed by William Gosse, reached Uluru in 1873. This was followed by a brief period of intensive exploration during which Europeans investigated the possibilities for extending settlement into the desert. In less than 20 years, the sponsors of such expeditions decided that the arid country was unsuitable for human habitation - a testimony to the success of the Aboriginal culture which had flourished there for many millennia.

Although early exploration had little impact on the local Aboriginal people or the land, the same was not true of development, which spread out from the telegraph line during the 1880s and 1890s. Government policy of the day promoted the 're-settlement' of Aboriginal people on mission stations, where they were strenuously encouraged to abandon their former lifestyle, beliefs and language. Introduced livestock, which was poorly adapted to the desert environment, fouled waterholes and decimated plant life. Furthermore, prolonged droughts from the 1930s to '50s and a government ban on hunting within the park made it difficult for Aboriginal people to continue their customary way of life. Despite these adversities, Aboriginal people maintained their ties with Uluru, resisting the erosion of their culture.

In 1948, a dirt road reached Uluru. The Aboriginal people began to make distinctive wood carvings to sell to the ever-increasing number of tourists arriving at the rock. In 1958, the Ayers Rock - Mount Olga area was excised from the South West Aboriginal Reserve and was declared a national park. Administrative responsibility fell to the Northern Territory Reserves Board. Tourist accommodation was built soon after and, whilst Aboriginal activity in the park was strongly discouraged, an Aboriginal-owned enterprise called the Ininti Store was established. In 1977, UNESCO declared the park a Biosphere Reserve and in 1984, tourist facilities were moved to a location outside the park's boundaries for environmental reasons.

In an historic move in accordance with the Aboriginal Land Rights (Northern Territory) Amendment Act 1985 and the National Parks and Wildlife Conservation Act 1985, inalienable freehold title to the land in the park was passed to the Aboriginal Uluru - Kata Tjuta Land Trust on 26 October, 1985. The land was then leased back to the Commonwealth Government for a period of 99 years. In 1993, the official name of the park was changed to Uluru - Kata Tjuta National Park in order to better reflect the Aboriginal significance of the park and its cultural landscape. In 1995, to commemorate the tenth anniversary of the handback, the Uluru - Kata Tjuta Cultural Centre was completed and opened, creating new opportunities of interpretation of Aboriginal culture for visitors.

RIGHT Malu, Red Kangaroo.

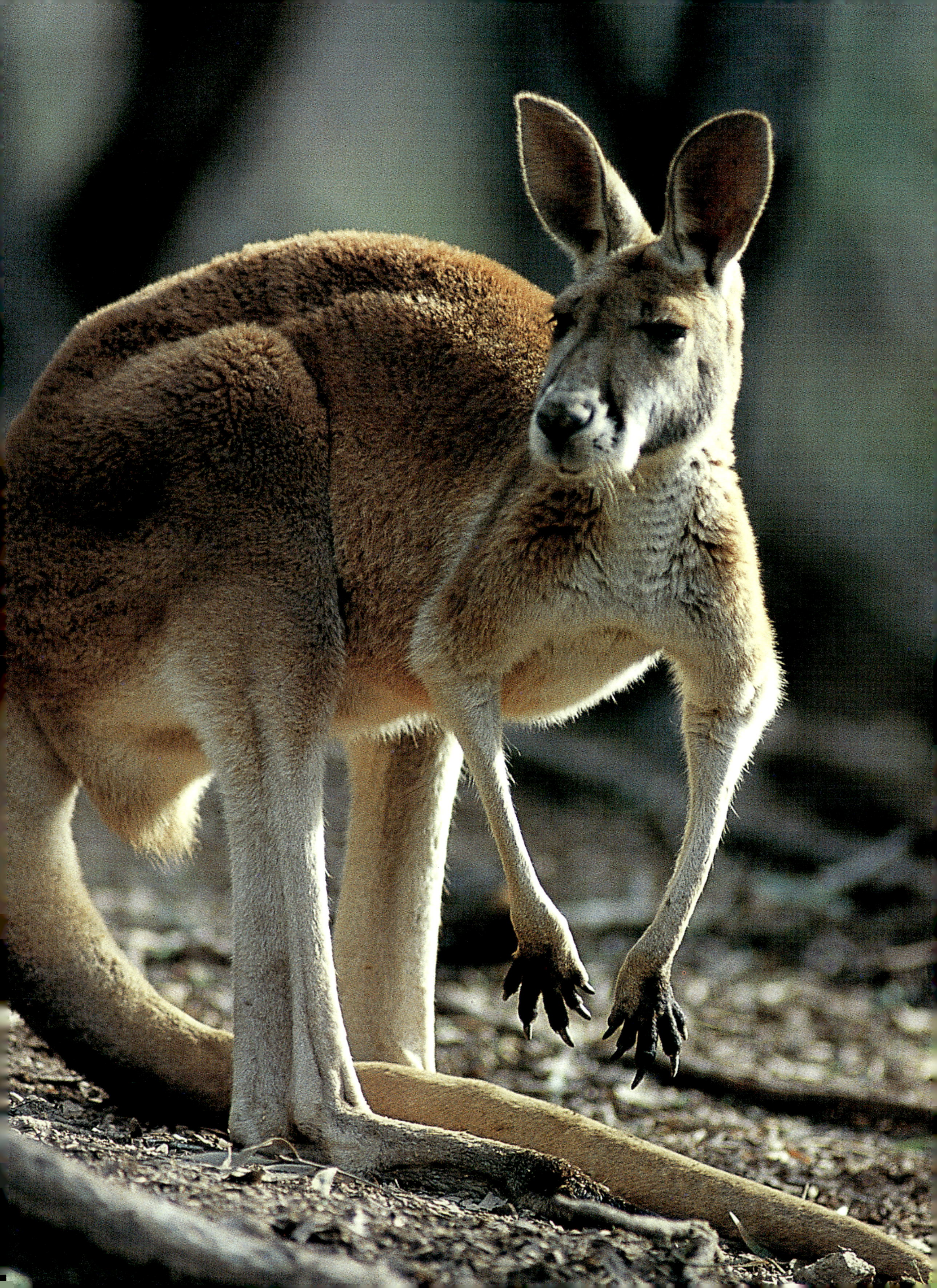

Human Impact

At a glance, the landscape at Uluru - Kata Tjuta appears little affected by humans. Nothing could be further from the truth. A deeper investigation into the interaction between the fragile desert habitat and its Aboriginal custodians reveals an ecosystem which is, in part, reliant upon a particular kind of human intervention.

For thousands of years, the Aboriginal inhabitants of Uluru - Kata Tjuta have practised patch burning of spinifex. Usually done during winter, the burning allows edible plant forms to grow in the areas denuded by fire and creates firebreaks against wildfires. Patch burning was discouraged by Europeans who mistakenly believed it to be a dangerous and useless practice. The discontinuation of the practice led to destructive wildfires in 1950 and 1976.

Regular burning was reintroduced by the Uluru - Kata Tjuta park management in 1985. A mosaic pattern of vegetation has been produced which provides food and shelter for a host of small creatures. It appears that patch burning is essential for the continued existence of many endemic plant and animal species.

Europeans arriving in the region brought with them feral animals and exotic plants which have spread into the park. Introduced animals such as the red fox, feral cats and dogs, the common house mouse, the European rabbit and feral camels either compete with, or prey upon, the indigenous animals. These foreign species are particularly hardy and tenacious and present a real threat to the native fauna. Among the plants, several native species have been lost from the park while introduced species such as Mossman River grass are establishing a strangle-hold in some areas.

At present the park is home to employees of the Australian Nature Conservation Agency and to members of the Mutitjulu Aboriginal community including Pitjantjatjara and Yakunytjatjara people. Preferring to be known as 'Anangu', they have traditional rights of occupation and live close to Uluru itself. The population of the Mutitjulu community varies, with people continually coming and going, and numbers increasing during ceremonies. Today, about a fifth of the people living at Mutitjulu are visitors from other communities.

In the past, indigenous people tended to emigrate from their traditional homelands to find paid employment. In recent times, this trend has been reversed as local Aboriginal people are becoming increasingly involved in the management of the park, working as park rangers and providing information and souvenirs for tourists. Many Aboriginal people are employed as guides and in the presentation of appropriate elements of the Tjukurpa to visitors.

Facilities

One of the most popular and spectacular tourist destinations in Australia, Uluru - Kata Tjuta National Park is accessible by both road and air. Although accommodation within the park has been closed for over a decade, the Yulara resort provides accommodation close to the park and offers campsites as well as hotel and lodge facilities. Tracks, paths and some sealed roads provide access to the monoliths and other sites. Overnight camping is not permitted inside the park and numerous sites sacred to the local people are closed to the public.

Tourism within the park is well-managed, with an emphasis on education. Visitors to the park may take one of the ranger-guided tours or may choose to explore by themselves using the information provided by the park management. A range of activities can be pursued in the park and the most popular include sightseeing, bushwalking, climbing to the top of Uluru, scenic flights, sunrise viewings of the rock, picnicking and photography. The number of visitors to the park reached 130 000 per year in the mid 1980s, has tripled since then and continues to increase at a rate of about 7% per annum.

Threats

The decline in Aboriginal culture which began at the turn of the century has been checked by the granting of freehold title over the land to local Aboriginal custodians and their involvement in the management of the national park. While inappropriate tourist developments are being controlled, tourism remains a threat to the integrity of Uluru - Kata Tjuta.

ABOVE A tiny carnivorous marsupial, the Mulgara, with offspring.

The attractions of the park are a lure to tourists, photographers and film makers but the eagerness of people to see and record the sights has led to the use of vehicles off roads, causing destruction and damage to walking tracks. Visual intrusions and disturbance caused by tourists can impinge upon the daily lives and the ceremonies of the Aboriginal people and there is also a risk that rock art might be damaged or sacred sites disturbed by visitors.

Environmental hazards such as drought and fire are ever-present. The spread of exotic plants and feral animals into the fragile desert habitat also jeopardises the indigenous plants and animals.

The late 1990s have raised a further cause for concern about the future of Uluru - Kata Tjuta National Park, as the Federal Government opens up the possibility of commercial activities such as mining within listed World Heritage Areas.

Management

The management of Uluru - Kata Tjuta National Park involves complex issues. The fragile arid land and the spectacular rock formations need to be protected; Aboriginal sacred sites and art sites must be shielded from interference; and the rights of the traditional Aboriginal community to privacy and autonomy must be maintained. At the same time, the reasonable expectations of the many thousands of Australian and international tourists who visit the park each year must be met.

Protected under a number of statutes since 1958, responsibility for the park is currently vested in the Board of Management and the Director of the NPWS. The Director and his staff are responsible for day-to-day management of the park and have the authority to restrict access to certain areas and to protect traditional Aboriginal land use. Work is carried out by officers of Parks Australia. Its staff is responsible for implementing a wide variety of conservation measures set out in the jointly developed plan of management.

Management of the park is a testimony to successful co-operation between Aboriginal and non-Aboriginal people and to the integration of traditional land management strategies with modern scientific techniques. A fire control program based on traditional Aboriginal burning practices has been introduced and measures have also been taken to control feral animals and to restrict the importation of exotic plants. Aboriginal people have a role in the education of visitors to the park.

To protect cultural rights and values, entry restrictions apply to Aboriginal living areas and to specific sites in accordance with Aboriginal law. Sacred sites have been identified and visitors are notified of access restrictions in these areas. Entry to areas set aside for special management, research or conservation purposes is also restricted.

Overnight camping within the park is prohibited. Tourist accommodation and airport facilities have been moved outside the park and the access road has been re-routed so that it approaches Uluru from a direction more sensitive to the natural environment. Some restrictions have also been placed upon still photography and cinematic or video photography within the park in accordance with the wishes of the traditional owners. Elevated walkways have been constructed for the protection of art sites and archaeological sites from damage by visitors.

ABOVE Splendid fairy wren.

143

Central Eastern Rainforest Reserves
(Australia)

Extending like a string of emeralds along the east coast of continental Australia, the Central Eastern Rainforest Reserves occupy an intermediate position between the wet tropical forests of far north Queensland and the temperate rainforests of Tasmania. These central eastern forests are mainly of the subtropical type but include limited areas of warm temperate, cool temperate, dry rainforest scrubs and littoral, or coastal, rainforest. Although the central eastern rainforests share some characteristics with the rainforests of the north and the south, they are nonetheless distinctive in their structure, composition and flora.

The NSW sites making up the Central Eastern Rainforest Reserves were inscribed on the World Heritage List in 1986 and, in 1994, the World Heritage listing was revised to include rainforest sites in south-east Queensland. The rainforests are listed mainly on the basis of their special floristic characteristics. Collectively, they contain high numbers of rare and threatened species, exhibit outstanding geological features and are a living illustration of the evolution of Australian plant life during and after the break-up of the ancient 'supercontinent' Gondwana, of which Australia once formed a part.

Location

The Central Eastern Rainforest Reserves consist of about 50 separate sites scattered in eight clusters through the north-east of New South Wales and south-east of Queensland. The areas of rainforest lie between 27° - 37° South and 151° - 154° East and from Barrington Tops in New South Wales to the Main Range in south-east Queensland. They comprise a total area of 366 507 hectares (905 272 acres).

PREVIOUS PAGE Brindle Creek in Border Ranges National Park.

CENTRAL EASTERN RAINFORESTS

QUEENSLAND

- MT MISTAKE NP
- MAIN RANGE NP
- BEAUDESERT
- BOONAH
- RATHDOWNEY
- SPRINGBROOK NP
- LAMINGTON NP
- MT BARNEY
- MT CHINGHEE NP
- NUMINBAH NR
- MT CLUNIE FR
- LIMPINWOOD NR
- KILLARNEY
- MT NOTHOFAGUS FR
- AMAROO FR
- WILSONS PEAK FR
- BORDER RANGES NP
- MT WARNING NP
- ACACIA PLATEAU FR
- TOONUMBAR NP
- NIGHTCAP NP

NEW SOUTH WALES

- TOOLOOM NP
- CAPTAINS CREEK FR
- BUNGDOOZLE FR
- RICHMOND RANGE NP
- MALLANGANEE FR

MAP CONTINUED PAGE 147

Central Eastern Rainforests

By William Lines

At several points on the coast between Newcastle and Brisbane, you can look west to a dark mass of rainforest covered mountains. From the coastal plain the mountains rise, one beyond the other, to merge into shadowy depths of peaks and mists.

Captain James Cook, from his ocean vantage, noted some of these mountain ranges in his journal and called them "high and hilly". Cook sailed round a high point of land he named Cape Byron and sighted a conspicuous and apparently isolated peak. Avoiding treacherous reefs soon after, he named the peak, Mount Warning.

Captain Cook might be forgiven some thoughts of foreboding as he contemplated the Australian landscape; he was, after all, halfway through a very long voyage of exploration and he and his crew yearned to be home. Nor was his apprehension of something menacing in nature, especially the forests, unusual for his time, or for ours.

For the last 10 000 years, since humans began to give up their nomadic hunting and gathering existence for a settled, farming life, forests have defined the limits of civilisation. Western civilisation literally cleared its living space in the midst of European forests that once extended everywhere. People have been clearing forests ever since. After denuding Europe, colonising nations started on the New World. Usually, they had much forest to clear, but not in Australia.

At the time of European settlement, Australia was the least forested of all habitable continents. Open forests dominated by eucalypt trees occupied a small proportion of the total area. Rainforest accounted for even less, covering about one per cent of the continent, or about 80 000 square kilometres (30 880 square miles). Two hundred years of clearing for timber, agriculture and settlement reduced the rainforest to little more than 20 000 square kilometres (7 720 square miles) or a quarter of its former extent. Most of the cleared rainforest grew in valleys, on tablelands and on relatively good soils. Even before this clearing however, the rainforest in Australia was distributed as a chain of disjunct islands from Cape York to Tasmania. The areas that remain are usually confined to steep or inaccessible terrain, unsuited for cultivation or timber getting, and on poor soils.

Even before this clearing however, rainforest in Australia was distributed as a chain of disjunct islands from Cape York to Tasmania. Most surviving islands of rainforest are now protected, many of which are included on the World Heritage List. World Heritage rainforest in Australia consists of three distinct blocks: the Tasmanian Wilderness in the far south (inscribed on the World Heritage list in 1989); the Wet Tropics in the far north (inscribed 1988); and the areas lying in between, which are known as the Central Eastern Rainforest Reserves.

The original World Heritage listing of the Central Eastern Rainforest Reserves in 1986 only covered a limited number of reserves within New South Wales. The boundaries were then enlarged and the rainforests relisted in 1994 to include additional areas in New South Wales adjoining other areas in Queensland, including some of the land Captain Cook described as "high and hilly". Each of the inscribed blocks conserves a separate, though complementary, record of the evolution of Australian rainforests.

During the Jurassic period, Australia was still part of the 'supercontinent' known as Gondwana. Early types of flowering plants, or ancestral angiosperms started to evolve, invading the conifer forests that were dominant at the time. After Australia split from Antarctica - the final break up of Gondwana - about 45 million years ago, these new types of plants dominated the Australian flora and covered much of the continent in rainforest.

Australia drifted north, with the rainforest vegetation it had inherited from Gondwana flourishing in a warm wet climate. As a result of the continental drift, the climate changed. The seas separating Antarctica from other lands became deeper. Cold water and cold air began circulating from west to east. These cold currents chilled Antarctica and a vast ice cap developed there, wiping out its vegetation. Most of Australia became colder too, and drier. Winter rainfall replaced summer rainfall and pronounced dry seasons became the norm. Fires became more frequent. This climatic change sifted and sorted animals and plants into suitable niches. The great tracts of rainforests became fragmented. Generalist species which were adaptable usually flourished. Species that were too specialised to adjust to the new conditions often became extinct.

Present day Australian rainforest represents the living legacy of that original Gondwanan flora and includes plants that were formerly more widespread, even in the northern hemisphere where they now no longer survive. At first sight, the rainforest appears unrelated to the typical Australian vegetation that surrounds its well-defined habitats, but this is misleading. Typical Australian plants are characterised by scleromorphy, a term meaning 'hard form". This describes an adaptation which produces leathery, hard, spiny or reduced leaves and gives plants the advantage of reduced moisture loss. This is important on the driest of all continents where permanently moist environments are few. Most sclentonmic plants however, evolved from rainforest ancestors. The Myrtaceae family of plants, to which *eucalyptus* belongs, includes many rainforest plants. Members of the Proteaceae family, which includes banksias, grevilleas (spider flowers) and other sclerophylbus, or hard-leaved plants, are also found in the rainforest. For example, the macadamia nut is from a rainforest tree of the Proteaceae family found in the region.

Scleromorphic plants cover the driest of all continents, Australia, where permanently moist environments are few. The wettest areas lie along the several thousand kilometres of discontinuous escarpments that overlook the coastal plains of much of eastern Australia. The abrupt rise of the escarpments, approaching 1 600 metres (5 250 feet) in places, presents a barrier to rain-bearing clouds from the east, so that the escarpment crests and their foothills receive, by Australian standards, very high rainfall. In any event, precipitation - in the form of mists and fogs as well as rain - is sufficiently reliable and plentiful to sustain rainforests and it is here that most of the Central Eastern Rainforests grow though the average rainfall may be as little as 700 millimetres (less than 30 inches) in the gorges which support dry rainforest.

New South Wales and south-east Queensland rainforests receive annual rainfall in excess of 1500 millimetres (60 inches). Average rainfall may be as high as 2100 millimetres (84 inches) at Point Lookout at the head of the Bellinger Valley and 2500 millimetres (98 inches) on the Tweed and Nightcap Ranges. Much of the rain falls in late summer. In high altitude escarpment rainforests, persistent low clouds and fogs make up for low rainfall seasons and keep these places permanently moist.

The Central Eastern Rainforest Reserves World Heritage Area covers 366 507 hectares (905 272 acres). It consists of around 50 individual sites comprising national parks, environmental parks, nature reserves, flora reserves, state forests, Rabbit Board paddocks, various road reserves and two areas which buffer a prison. Many of the reserves are contiguous or nearly contiguous and together the sites form eight clusters. The bulk of the protected area, some 307 284 hectares (758 990 acres) lies in New South Wales. The Queensland portion covers an area of 59 223 hectares (146 280 acres).

In NSW, six principal regions of rainforest existed at the time of European settlement and the World Heritage sites represent the major remaining viable parts of five of them; the sixth area, the Illawarra rainforest, which once covered the Wollongong coast and escarpments, is all but gone. The sites in Queensland represent the major remaining areas of rainforest in the south-east of that state. Most of the protected areas have had little or no human disturbance. Although some small areas have been logged, most of the disconnected sites are naturally occurring islands and have not been reduced to that state as a result of past clearing. A few small areas are weed-infested and need rehabilitation.

In accepting the nomination, IUCN, the World Conservation Union expressed reservations concerning the viability of several of the sites. Most biologists believe that conserved areas require a minimum size, below which biological diversity suffers irreversible decline. Several of the Central Eastern Rainforest 'islands' are below this critical, self-sustaining size. At least for the present, the reigning feature of the Central Eastern Rainforests is diversity. Other habitats, such as mangrove wetlands, are more productive and other forests, such as the coniferous forests of western North America, contain more living matter and taller timber but no habitat rivals rainforest for sheer numbers of species.

Although largely subtropical, the Central Eastern Rainforest Reserves contain at least three other types: warm temperate, cool temperate and dry. Another type is littoral rainforest, so named because it grows in proximity to the ocean on coastal sand dunes and headlands. Littoral rainforest has features of both the subtropical and dry rainforest types and is represented by the 136 hectares (336 acres) Iluka Nature Reserve in New South Wales. Each rainforest type differs in climate, soil, leaf character and special life forms. Together, they extend in a discontinuous strip over 500 kilometres (310 miles) in length, fringing eastern Australia. Notwithstanding its geographic spread, there are many similarities.

Despite type differences, all Central Eastern Rainforest Reserves support a dense canopy of tree crowns that blocks out at least 70% of the sky from the forest below. This canopy reduces light levels, ensures an even temperature, minimises air movement and contributes to continuous high humidity. Only the canopy receives a full range of light and experiences fluctuating humidities and temperatures and buffeting by winds and storms. A forceful wind may move through the treetops and sway the giant trunks, while 40 metres (130 feet) below on the rainforest floor, there will be scarcely a breeze.

Many rainforest trees are buttressed, with spreading flanges at the base that can extend several metres vertically and run up to 10 metres (33 feet) laterally. Carabeen, tulip oak and mature strangler figs all sport buttresses. Buttresses may help in strengthening against strong winds or they may assist in the uptake of oxygen and nutrients from shallow soils. Strangler figs start life when a bird or other animal drops a seed in the fork of an existing tree. The seedling sends out roots that descend to the earth and then slowly wrap, intertwine and self-graft together as they become anchored and consolidated into a sinuous composite trunk which encloses and eventually kills the host tree.

Larger trees have ramrod straight trunks that taper smoothly and scarcely branch until they reach the canopy. Below them, palms and tree ferns reach up like giant umbrellas. Liana vines, some as thick as a man's arm, contort and twist about each other, while others plaster themselves flat against tree trunks or anchor their claw-like holdfasts in the fissures of the bark. Together, these woody structures form a lattice on which an even richer array of plants flourishes, itself part of a miniature rainforest.

RIGHT The buttressed bole of the Yellow Carabeen, Lamington National Park.

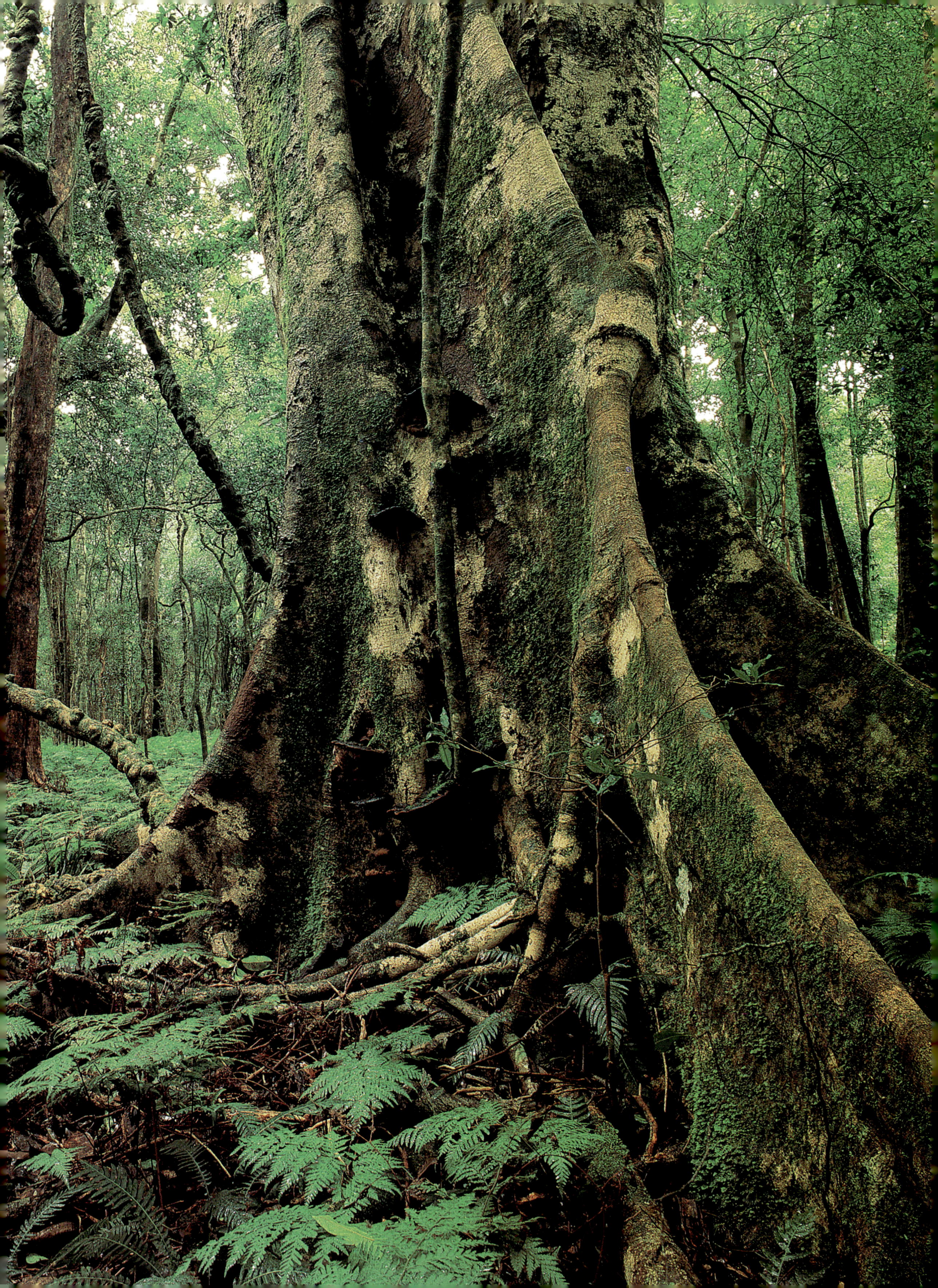

ABOVE A native rodent, the fawn footed melomys, lives in subtropical and tropical wet eucalypt forests and rainforests along the east coast of Australia.

Under conditions of high rainfall and enormous leaching, it is the sponge-like, soft, absorbing layer of decaying material, on the forest floor that absorbs and holds the water, preventing rapid runoff and soil loss and impounding the nutrients where tree roots can assimilate them. From canopy to forest floor, the rainforest enfolds worlds within worlds. A botanist once counted 50 species of plants growing on one tree. This frenzy of life depends on a few centimetres of moist humus and vegetation being constantly replenished by organic debris filtering down from the trees above and being alive with fungi, bacteria and insects. Take away the mulch of leaves and decaying material and you take away the whole life of the forest.

The constant recycling enables rainforests to thrive on nutrient-poor soils. In fact, cycling is so efficient there is relatively little interchange between the actively cycling nutrients and the underlying mineral soil. Adaptations make the most of the nutrients in the living plant material: there are leaves that return nutrients to the plant before they fall, lower leaves that capture the nutrients washed down from upper leaves and aerial roots that tap nutrients in organic matter held in the canopy.

Some plants, the epiphytes are botanical hitchhikers that grow on the branches of most rainforest trees. They live on what the air brings them: dust, fibres, dead leaves, animal waste and water. Bacteria and fungi break down the organic debris until it forms a protective mulch around an epiphyte's exposed roots and stems. This layer of humus keeps water in and contributes trace amounts of mineral salts.

Orchids are the most successful epiphytes. Nearly 70% of some 28 000 species of orchids worldwide grow only as epiphytes. About 140 different orchids grow in the Central Eastern Rainforest Reserves. The most unusual is a rare subterranean orchid that lacks leaves and chlorophyll and lives in association with a fungus. It is one of two subterranean species unique to Australia. These orchids spend their entire life, including flowering, underground.

Altogether, the Central Eastern Rainforest Reserves support a very diverse flora: 170 families, 695 genera and 1625 species of vascular plants have been recorded. About 150 species representing 100 genera occur nowhere else. In fact, most of the reserves contain rare or restricted species or rare and unique plant communities.

Animals find in the rainforests a more equable, stable and predictable habitat than is provided by most plant communities. Moreover, there is a greater variety of fruit and flowers for fruit-eaters and pollinators. The eastern rainforests are particularly rich in bird life. More than 270 species have been recorded, about 38 % of all Australian birds. Two species of lyrebirds and the rare rufous scrub-bird are particularly conspicuous. All male lyrebirds are accomplished mimics and often undertake elaborate courtship displays. Another ground-dwelling species found in the Central Eastern Rainforest Reserves is the critically endangered eastern bristlebird. Other rare or endangered species surviving in the rainforest include the Coxen's fig parrot and the marbled frogmouth.

Fruit-eating pigeons are particularly common in the rainforests. These include the topknot pigeon and the wonga pigeon. The wonga's strong legs mark it as a ground bird. It eats fallen seeds, berries and fruits. Generally shy, keeping well hidden and freezing on the spot when an intruder approaches, wongas will suddenly rise with a loud clap of wings to fly swiftly to safety. Other rare or endangered species surviving in the rainforests include Coxen's fig-parrot and the plumed frogmouth. Bowerbirds, too, are commonly seen. The males of the three species that occur in the rainforest construct bowers for courtship rituals.

Birds and other animals that live in the canopy have no trouble negotiating tree crowns; they do not find the canopy a haphazard mishmash of branches - the jungle of the human imagination. Indeed, tree crowns do not actually interlock but, in a sense, rub shoulders across a gap of about one metre (three feet). These gaps form a network of carefully memorised flight paths which speed birds and other flying animals on their way through the rainforest. Many canopy hunters, such as owls and small hawks have short stubby wings that give them great power and agility in these tight spaces.

The rainforests do not exist in isolation and a number of wide-ranging Australian animals can also be found in them. These include bandicoots, marsupial mice, native rodents, carnivorous marsupial quolls or tiger cats, the dingo, platypus and echidna. The Central Eastern Rainforest Reserves also provide habitat to 31 species of bats - half of all Australia's bat species.

The rare parma wallaby is restricted to north-east New South Wales and finds suitable habitat in the rainforests. The short-eared bobuck (or mountain possum) is found in most of the higher rainforest country. The rufous ringtail possum, a colour variant of the common ringtail, is restricted to the rainforests of south-east Queensland and north-east New South Wales.

During rain, frogs fill the nights with their mating calls. Tree frogs and ground species, including the deep-voiced great barred frog are present. In fact, some 45 species of frogs - about 25% of Australia's total frog fauna, and the most diverse - live in the eastern rainforests. Unusual species include the hip-pocket frog, which raises its tadpoles in skin pouches on the 'hips' of the males. There is also a frog called the harmonious frog because of the tuneful quality of its collective calls.

The eastern rainforests harbour about 110 species of reptiles, including, lizards, snakes and turtles, many of them restricted to rainforest and wet sclerophyll forest. The world's largest skink, the land mullet, a big shiny black lizard, and several exquisitely-patterned smaller skinks abound, together with rainforest dragons, tree goannas and water dragons. True rainforest reptiles are generally so well camouflaged they are not easily seen. They include the southern angle-headed dragon, the northern leaf-tailed gecko, burrowing skinks and the diamond python. Carpet pythons are common and, like the green tree snake, fairly harmless.

Due to the overlap of tropical and temperate elements in the eastern rainforests, the area is rich in insects, including butterflies. Fireflies, together with luminous fungi, light up at night. There are also some giants. The king cricket has a body length of up to 80 millimetres (three inches) and the pine weevil reaches 50 millimetres (two inches) in length and breeds in fallen logs of hoop pine. Leeches are active in the wet areas and scrub ticks in the dry.

Rainforests are not static. They respond to climate changes but the response is so slow that the forest creates an illusion of stability and invariability. In fact, most changes are imperceptible even over a period of 100 years. Even the rapid changes which may occur over the next 30 to 40 years as a result of global warming may not see immediate dramatic modifications. Unless the climate changes are sufficiently severe to kill standing vegetation, the buffering effect of the closed canopy and the long life span of rainforest trees - measured in centuries - ensure that the forest response to climate change will be slow.

The most conspicuous and rapid changes in rainforest are caused by major natural events or human interventions such as cyclones, logging and fire. Cyclonic winds may occasionally flatten areas of rainforest and initiate a series of recovery and recolonisation phases. Intense rain can cause landslips on steep slopes, further disturbing rainforests. When a tree falls due of the effects of wind, or after it has died due to disease or insect attack, it often brings down other trees in its path and the interlaced lianas may tear branches from neighbouring trees or pull them down. The result is a gap that allows sunlight to reach deep down into the rainforest. Stimulated by the sunlight fast-growing, weedy pioneer plants like bleeding heart, forest nightshades and native wild raspberry, together with ferns, grow profusely in areas cleared by storm damage or alongside walking tracks. Nevertheless, light gaps are short lived. Taller, woody trees are hardier than pioneers and the gap is eventually filled by their shady crowns. However, a rainforest may take centuries to recover fully from the damage inflicted by storms or logging.

The greatest threats to rainforests come from human activity. Agriculture, burning, mining, logging, road building and real estate development menace remnant rainforests the world over. Destruction has reached such a frenzy that economist Herman Daly has remarked that the contemporary fixation with growth and expansion treats the Earth as if it were 'a business in the course of liquidation'.

Conservationists are opposed to the liquidation of nature and see the destruction of rainforests as a symbol for the plundering of the planet. During the 1970s and 1980s, as Australian governments stepped up the exploitation of forests, rivers, reefs and oceans in their rush to make Australia a resource-based economy, rainforests became the focus of an intense conservation effort. Campaigners lobbied politicians and fought the logging industry in the courts and the media. Protesters dug themselves into the ground in front of bulldozers, sat in trees marked for felling, formed human chains across logging roads and marched in city streets.

Governments procrastinated; protests continued. Eventually, most rainforest logging in the public forests was halted, reserves declared and much of the remaining rainforest was placed under World Heritage protection.

The people who fought for the forests found in them a special reality, sculpted and detached from water, carbon and dust. The spectre of multitudinous life forms, breathing, growing and reproducing, as well as the close fusion of life and death, affirmed a felt kinship and unity with all things.

Whatever the origins of the forests or of humanity, the rainforests could not have evolved through aeons only to meet their demise at human hands. If civilisation was repelled by forests then civilisation would have to change. The great antiquity of the rainforests opened, to those who experienced this, the possibility of a world without human presence. No other way of seeing so emphasised the passing nature of species. The rainforests existed for aeons without human presence; they could do so again.

ABOVE The freshwater Lamington spiny blue crayfish, found in Lamington National Park, traces its origins back to the ancient supercontinent known as Gondwana of which Australia once formed a part. When encountered by walkers on a track, the crayfish retreats, sometimes emitting a distinct hissing sound.

RIGHT Rainforest cascade in Springbrook National Park.

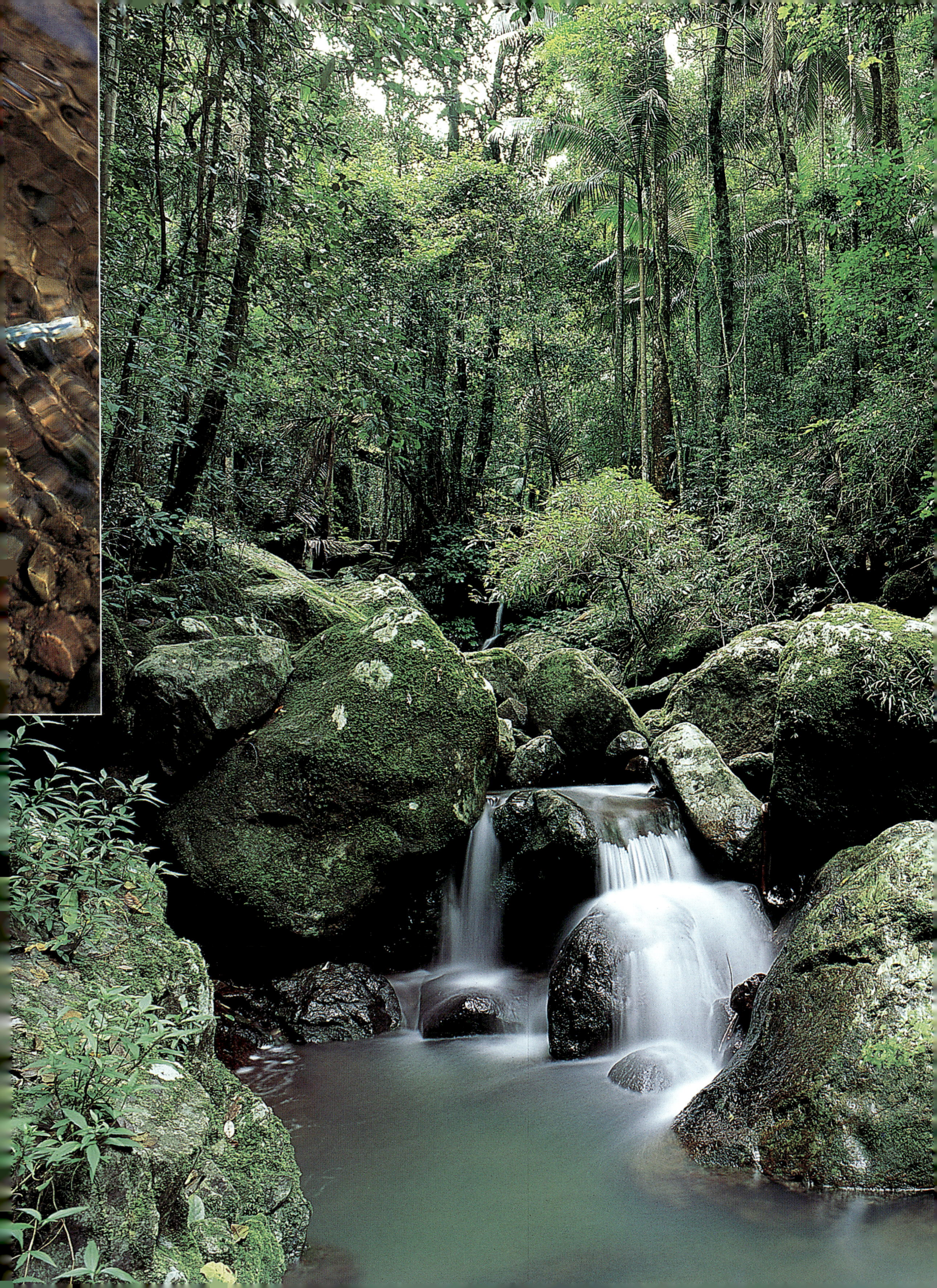

Physical Features

Oases of green on a dry island continent, Australia's rare rainforests are now even rarer, covering only 2 000 000 hectares (5 000 000 acres). In many ways, the Central Eastern Rainforest Reserves are the terrestrial equivalent of the Galapagos Islands, consisting, as they do, of numerous separated, but related, units spread across a wide geographical area. Like the famous archipelago, the rainforests combine to reveal a singular pattern of evolution which is of inestimable scientific worth. Considered together, the sites display great biological richness. As a group, they tell the fascinating story of the evolution of the rainforests on Australia's central eastern coast.

Although singular in their form and composition, Australia's rainforests share many of the characteristics of classical rainforests. Their canopies which provide a dark, heavy covering for the creatures and plants beneath; the forest floor is relatively clear; and the flora varies greatly in both form and species. Rainforests are easily distinguishable from the dominant eucalypt forests but are themselves extremely diverse. A major determinant of rainforest development is soil parent material and rainfall. While most of the continent receives less than 500 millimetres (20 inches) of rain each year, precipitation levels in the rainforest are generally three times as high though rainforests may survive in drier areas where fogs and mists are common.

Rainforests reach their greatest luxuriance on the most fertile soils, derived from volcanic rocks such as basalt. Volcanic activity occurred in several distinct areas along what is now Australia's Great Dividing Range between 10 and 24 million years ago. Seven of the eight clusters of the Central Eastern Rainforest Reserves are found on the basalt caps and gorges surrounding the remnants of these long-extinct volcanoes. The largest of these were the Focal Peak, Mount Warning and Ebor volcanoes. The eighth 'cluster' is found on coastal sands at Iluka.

RIGHT   Mount Warning National Park at sunrise photographed from Border Ranges National Park. The Mountain is the erosion-resistant plug of the extinct Tweed shield volcano which was active between 24 and 21 million years ago. The caldera-shaped valley that surrounds it was formed by the erosion of the softer lava flows down to the underlying pre-volcanic rocks. The caldera is significant for its age and size, and is rich in rare and threatened plant and animal species.

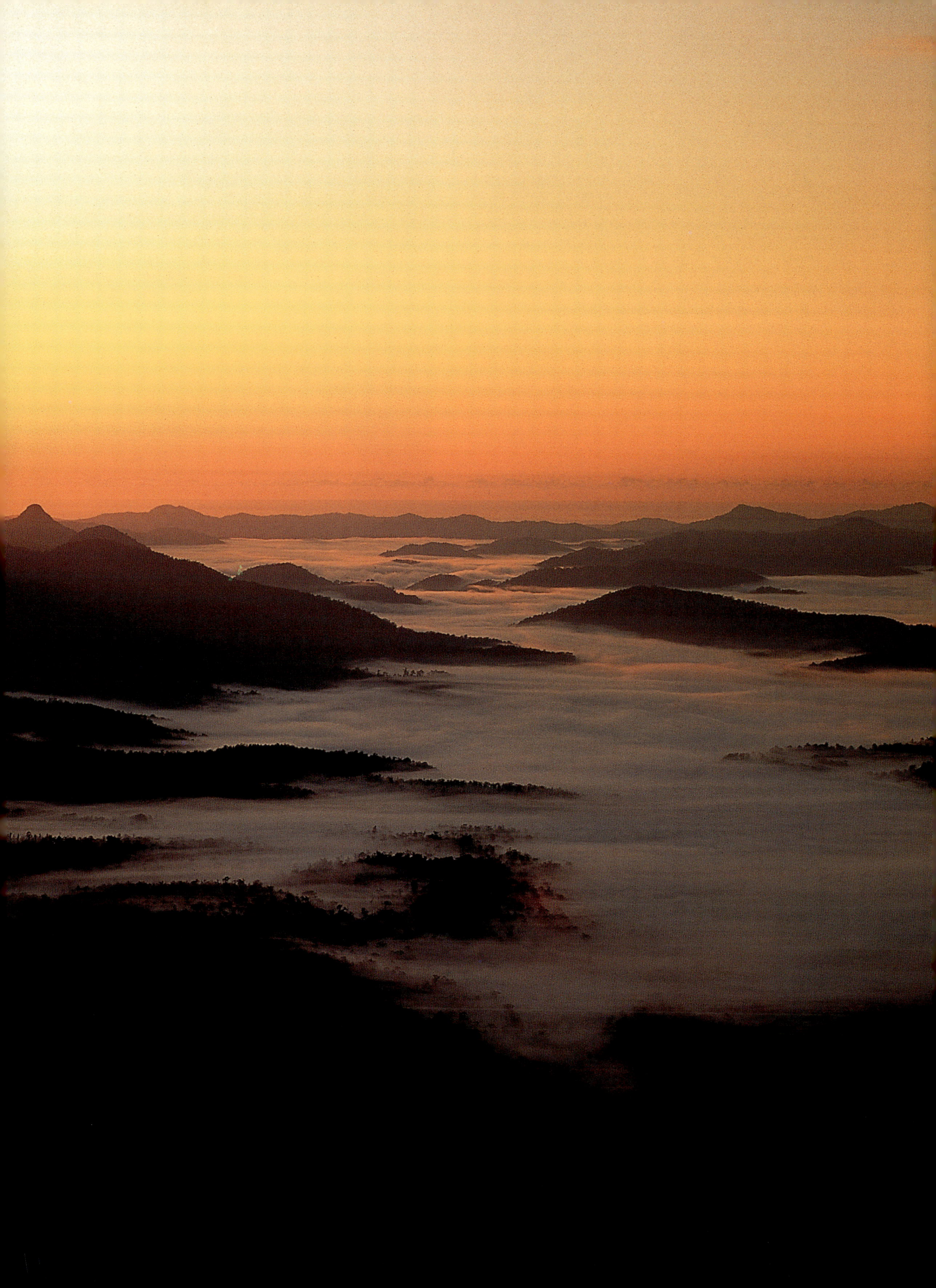

Flora

As in all rainforests, diversity is a key feature of the Central Eastern Rainforest Reserves environment, with 1625 species of vascular plants. Vines are a prominent component of the lofty canopy, tumbling in crazy loops towards the forest floor. Epiphytes, most notably the large ferns and the orchids, are one of the most visually striking and distinguishing features of the forests. Palms, strangler figs and wide-buttressed carabeens are other distinctive forms.

The non-vascular plants such as the mosses, lichens and fungi are almost an archetype of the rainforest environment. With their fantastic variations in colour and form, these sometimes overlooked species cling to fallen trunks and rocks, adding to the atmosphere of fecund and primordial grandeur which pervades the forests.

A feature of great scientific significance in the Central Eastern Rainforest Reserves is the high proportion of 'primitive' plants to be found in them. Such plants might be described as the 'living fossils' of the botanical world. Species such as the Antarctic beech are Australia's inheritance from its parent continent, Gondwana. They are success stories of evolutionary survival and the direct result of the continuation in these forests of ancient environmental conditions.

TOP Bracket fungus.

ABOVE The endangered Hastings River mouse is one of over 200 rare or threatened species found in the Central Eastern Rainforest Reserves. Between the 1840's and 1969, this species was not sighted and was presumed extinct. Populations have now been found in several locations in the World Heritage Area, including Barrington Tops, Werrikimbe and Lamington National Parks.

RIGHT Bangalow palms, or piccabeens, and brushbox trees at Desert Creek in Washpool National Park.

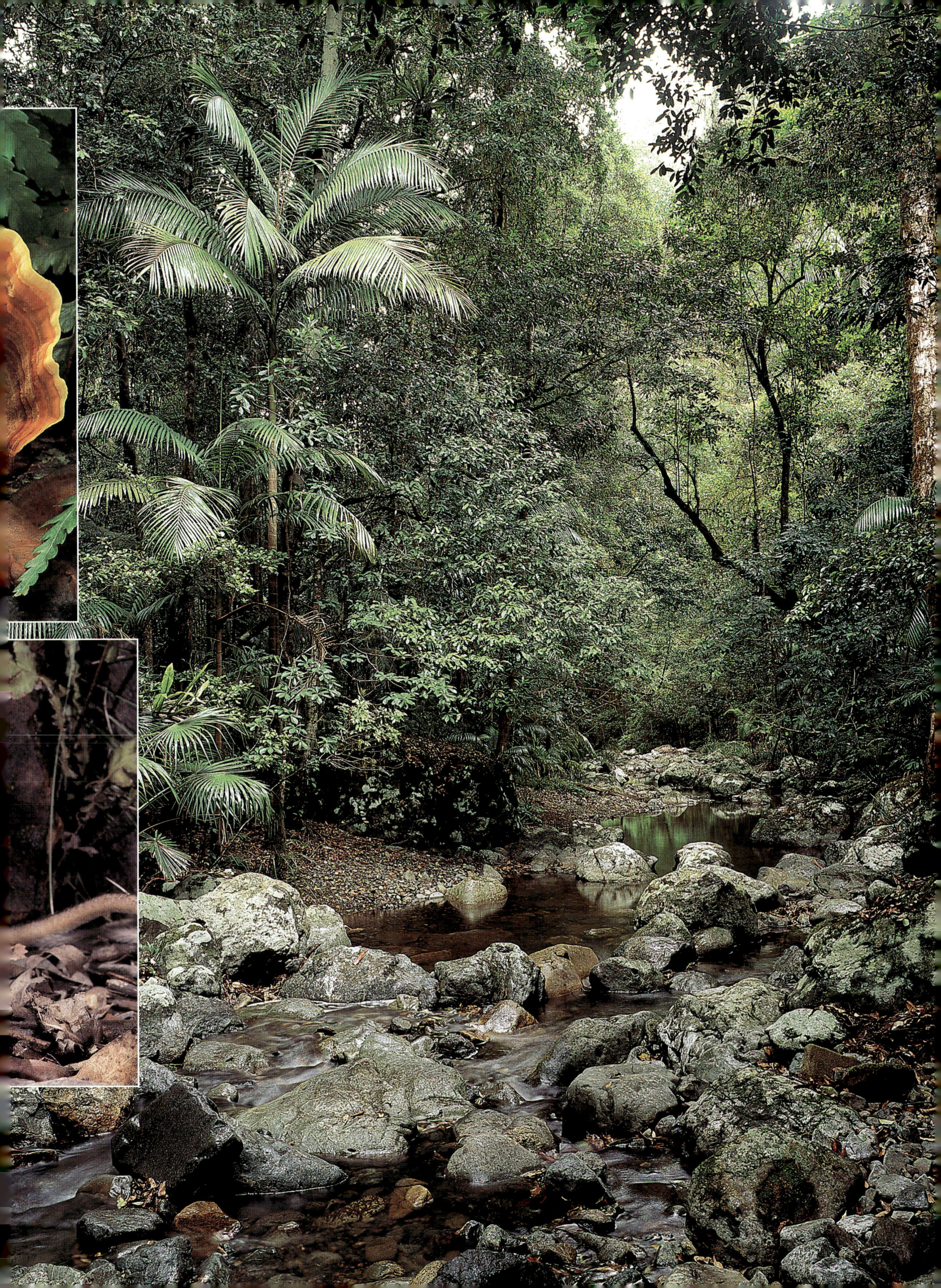

ABOVE TOP This extremely rare bluebell is an herbaceous plant found growing on the cliff faces at Mt Lindesay on the border between Queensland and New South Wales.

ABOVE *Aristolochia* (or native Dutchman's pipe) is a rainforest vine found in warm, low altitude, subtropical rainforest. Australia's second largest butterfly, the spectacular Richmond birdwing butterfly, lays her eggs on this vine - the only food plant for her caterpillars. It is threatened by the presence of the introduced Dutchman's pipe which is toxic to her caterpillars.

RIGHT A magnificent vista unfolds from the Pinnacle in Border Ranges National Park. Here, the abrupt walls of the Great Escarpment are densely covered with tall forest.

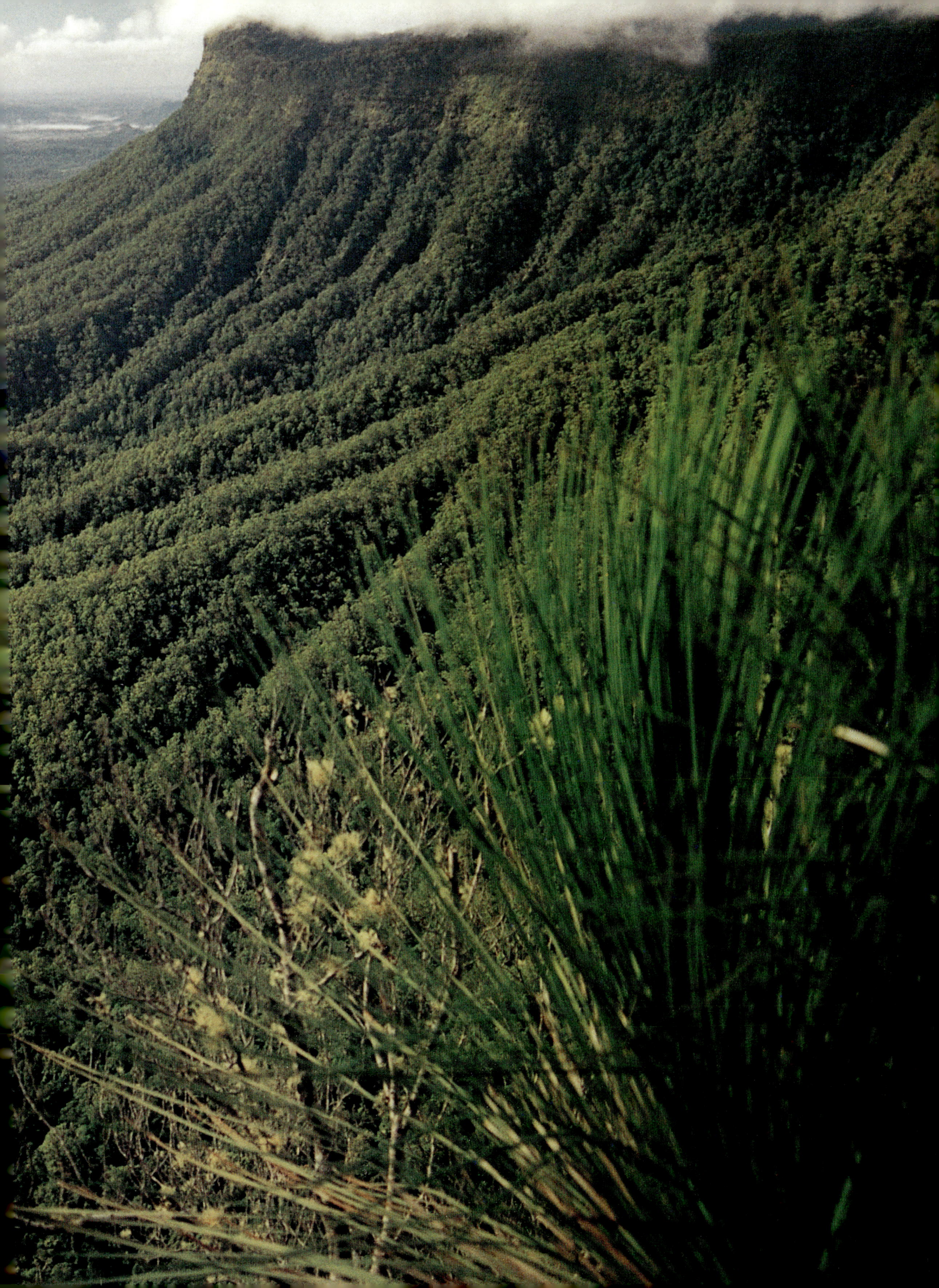

Fauna

The Central Eastern Rainforest Reserves provides habitat for a plentiful and diverse fauna. Australia's zoological marvels, the egg-laying mammals known as the monotremes, are found in some of the areas. Two species of this group, the spiny ant-eating short-beaked echidna and aquatic duck-billed platypus, are represented.

A number of species of marsupials occur throughout the reserves, including several species of macropods-literally big foot-the group includes kangaroos, wallabies and potoroos. Arboreal or tree-climbing marsupials include the mountain brush-tailed possum.

Insectivorous, blossum feeding and fruit-eating bats are a major part of Australia's mammal fauna and the Central Eastern Rainforest Reserves provide the largest habitat for these species outside of the wet tropical rainforests in northern Queensland.

Many birds flock to the reserves to feast on the fleshy fruits of the abundant rainforest flora. Common species include pigeons, bowerbirds and the noisy channel-billed cuckoo. Other, mainly ground-dwelling, birds such as noisy scrub-birds, brush turkeys and lyrebirds scratch through the leaf litter which lies thick on the forest floor in search of the countless insects to be found there.

ABOVE White nymph butterfly hatching on a stinging tree.

RIGHT The southern angle-headed dragon is a secretive rainforest inhabitant which can change colour to match its environment.

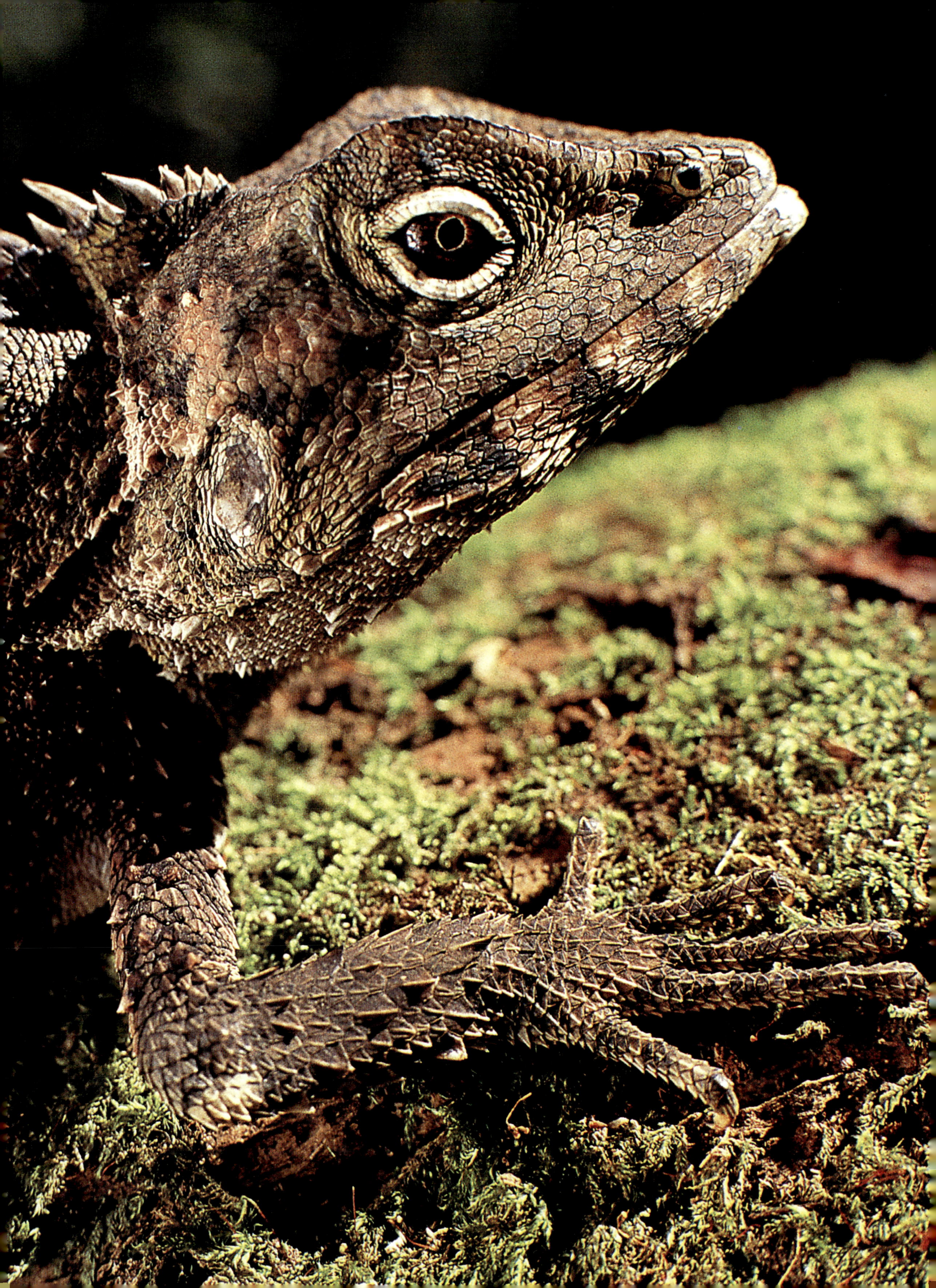

TOP Daymoth on a firewheel flower.

RIGHT Large-billed scrubwren.

FAR RIGHT A green catbird feeds its chicks. Although not readily seen, it has a drawn out wailing call that gives it its name and makes it a well-known resident of the rainforests. It belongs to the bowerbird family but instead of constructing a bower, it decorates a display area with leaves turned upside down on the forest floor.

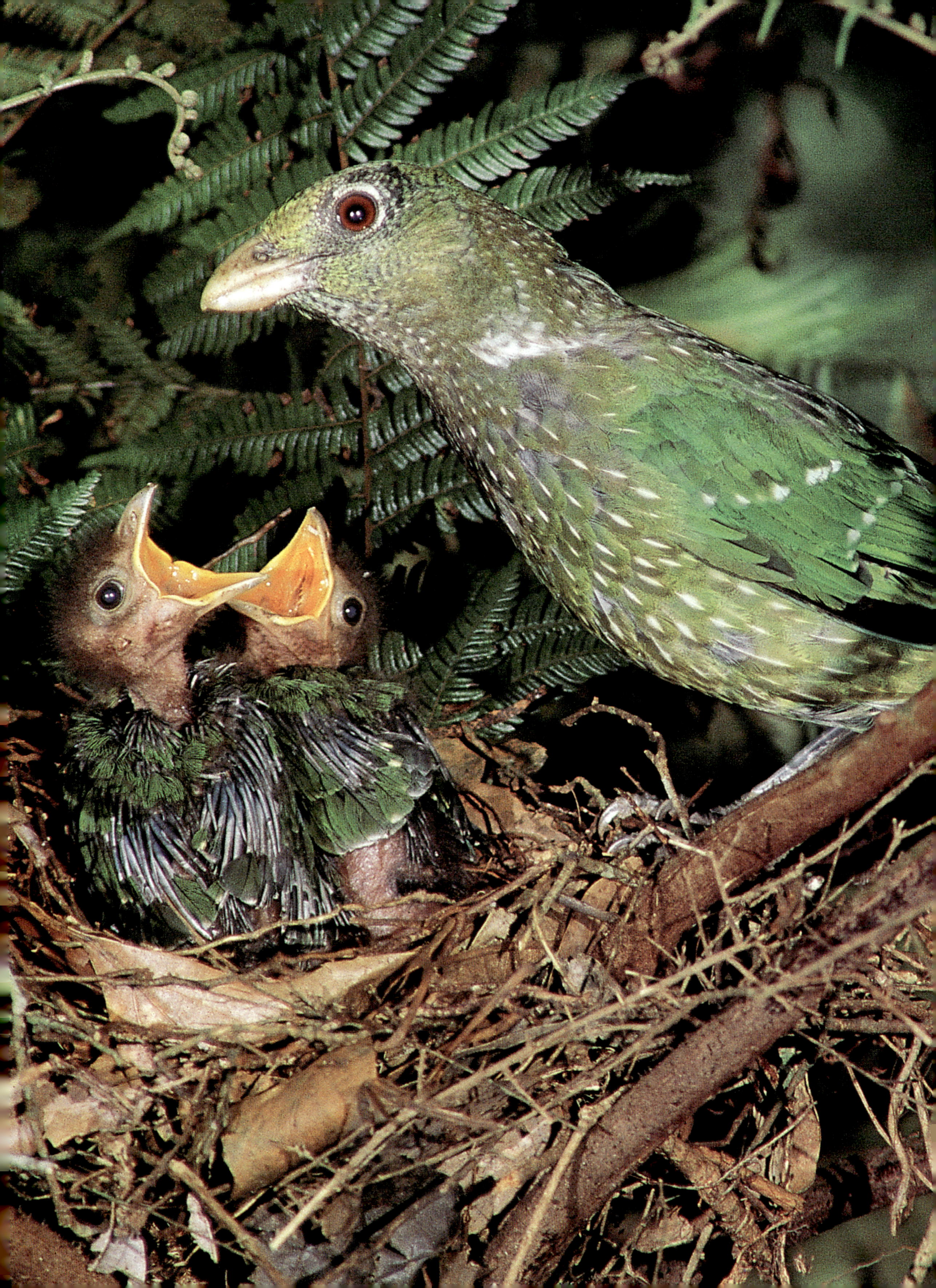

TOP Swamp wallaby.

RIGHT Golden orb spider, Washpool National Park.

FAR RIGHT Female pardalote carrying a thrip.

164

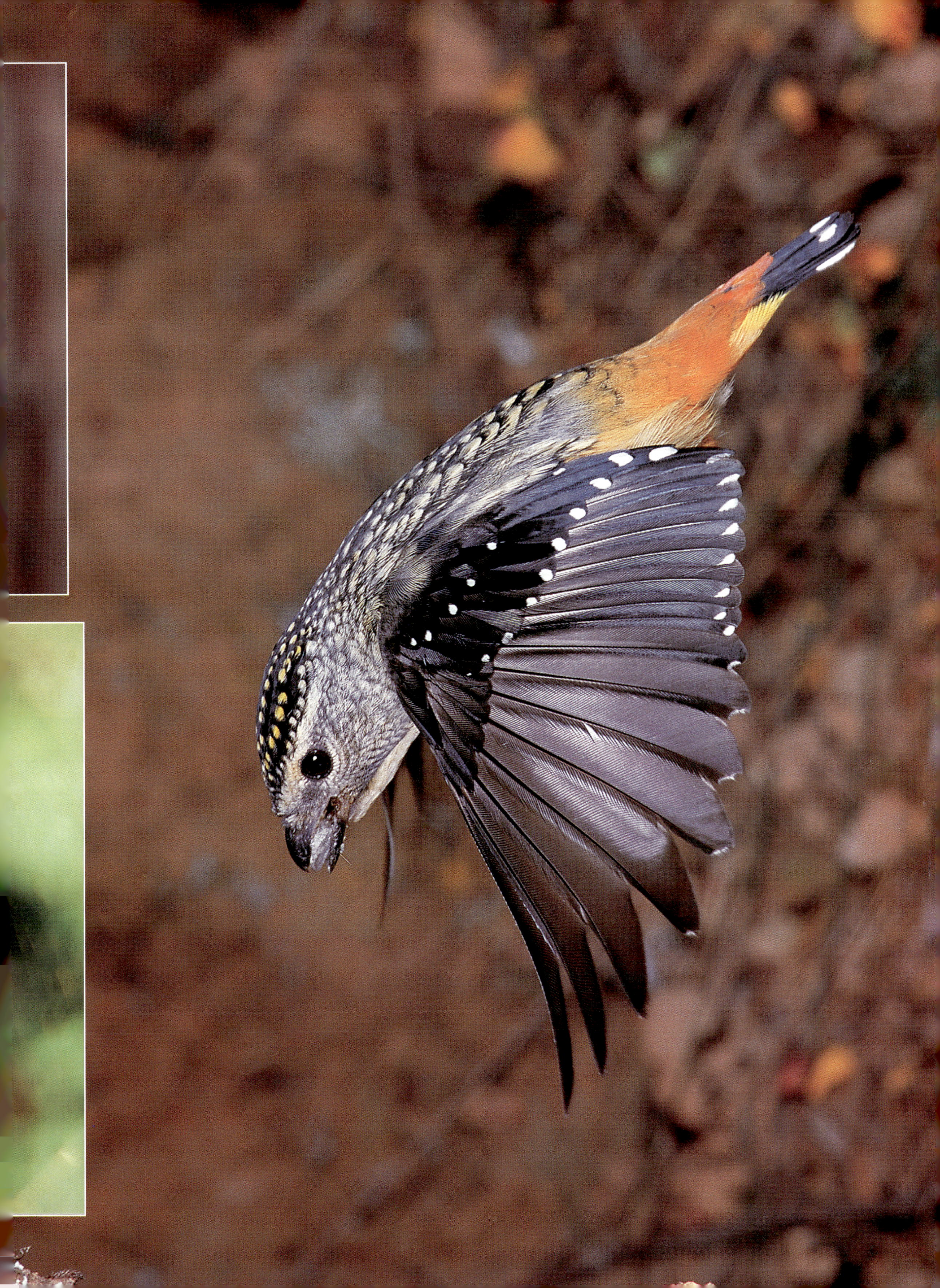

ABOVE Snowgums in Barrington Tops National Park grow adjacent to stands of Antarctic beech rainforest.

RIGHT Strangler fig.

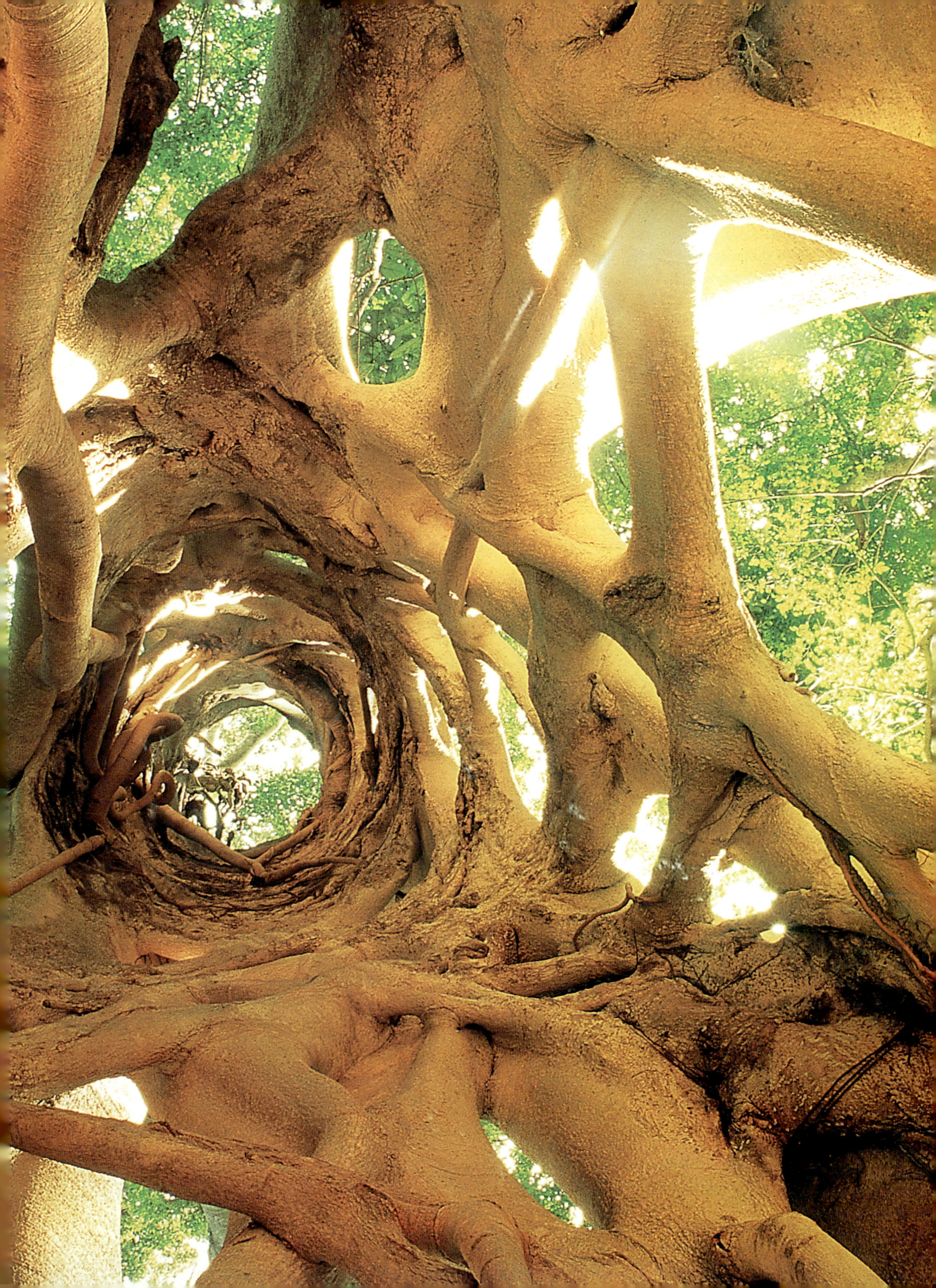

Human Impact

Most of Australia's rainforest is located along the heavily populated east coast of the continent and human impact on the forests has been severe. The remaining rainforests were once surrounded by vast and undisturbed tracts of eucalypt forest. These buffering forests have been eroded steadily since 1788 due to the effects of clearing for agriculture and logging. Much of the lowland subtropical rainforest on the floodplains has been cleared for agriculture and settlement. The logging of mountain and plateau rainforests began on a small scale in the nineteenth century. Logging intensified during the Second World War, especially in the warm temperate rainforests where coachwood trees provided timber suitable for peeling into veneer to make plywood. Large quantities of plywood went into aircraft frames such as the famous Mosquito bomber. The sustained economic boom of the post-war years continued the demand on rainforest timbers for building veneers and great volumes were consumed for such low-value uses as formwork for laying concrete. Today, the area of undisturbed mountain rainforest is very limited. Where the terrain permitted agriculture such as on the Dorrigo and Comboyne Plateaus, rainforest was cleared for agriculture, as happened in an earlier period to the lowland rainforests of the Big Scrub and the Illawarra.

Threats

The major threat to the survival of the Central Eastern Rainforest Reserves is the continuing logging of rainforest areas outside the protected areas. There are many patches of rainforest on private land. Although the remaining pockets of rainforest are often difficult to access, this is no guarantee of their safety against disturbance. The state forest areas adjacent to many of the protected World Heritage sites contain areas of rainforest, some of which continue to be logged or which remain available for logging in the future.

The small size of some of the sites making up the World Heritage Area gives cause for concern. Twenty-two of the 50 odd sites are less than 2000 hectares (4900 acres) in area, which may be too small to ensure their environmental integrity over the long term. It is a general principle of conservation biology that large areas should be set aside as reserves to help ensure the maintenance of the full range of plants and animal species that make up a protected ecosystem. However, the required area for the long-term conservation of plant communities is accepted to be considerably smaller than the area required for the maintenance of animal species. As the Central Eastern Rainforests were nominated mainly on the basis of their floristic values and many of the areas are naturally limited in size and not as a result of human modification, the small area of some fragments may not prove to be such an issue. Moreover, several of the sites adjacent to each other occur in clusters, which adds to their viability.

Management

As the protected areas of the Central Eastern Rainforests are small and scattered, management has to be tight and efficient. Day to day management remains the responsibility of the state conservation and forestry agencies, however, co-ordination of management efforts and policy is accomplished through inter-state committees on which the Commonwealth Government is also represented. Most of the sites making up the World Heritage Area are managed within national parks and nature reserves. Management efforts to strengthen and secure the integrity of the World Heritage Area have included securing the cessation of rainforest logging in the Queensland areas not already reserved as national park. Measures have also been undertaken to halt the spread of exotic weeds such as mist flower, bitou bush, camphor laurel and Kahill ginger.

RIGHT Antarctic beech is a prominent species in the cool temperate rainforests generally found in the high altitudes between Border Ranges and Barrington Tops National Parks where rainfall is augmented by fog-drip. Characteristic features are ground ferns, tree ferns, lichens and mosses.

NEXT PAGE Short-beaked echidna.

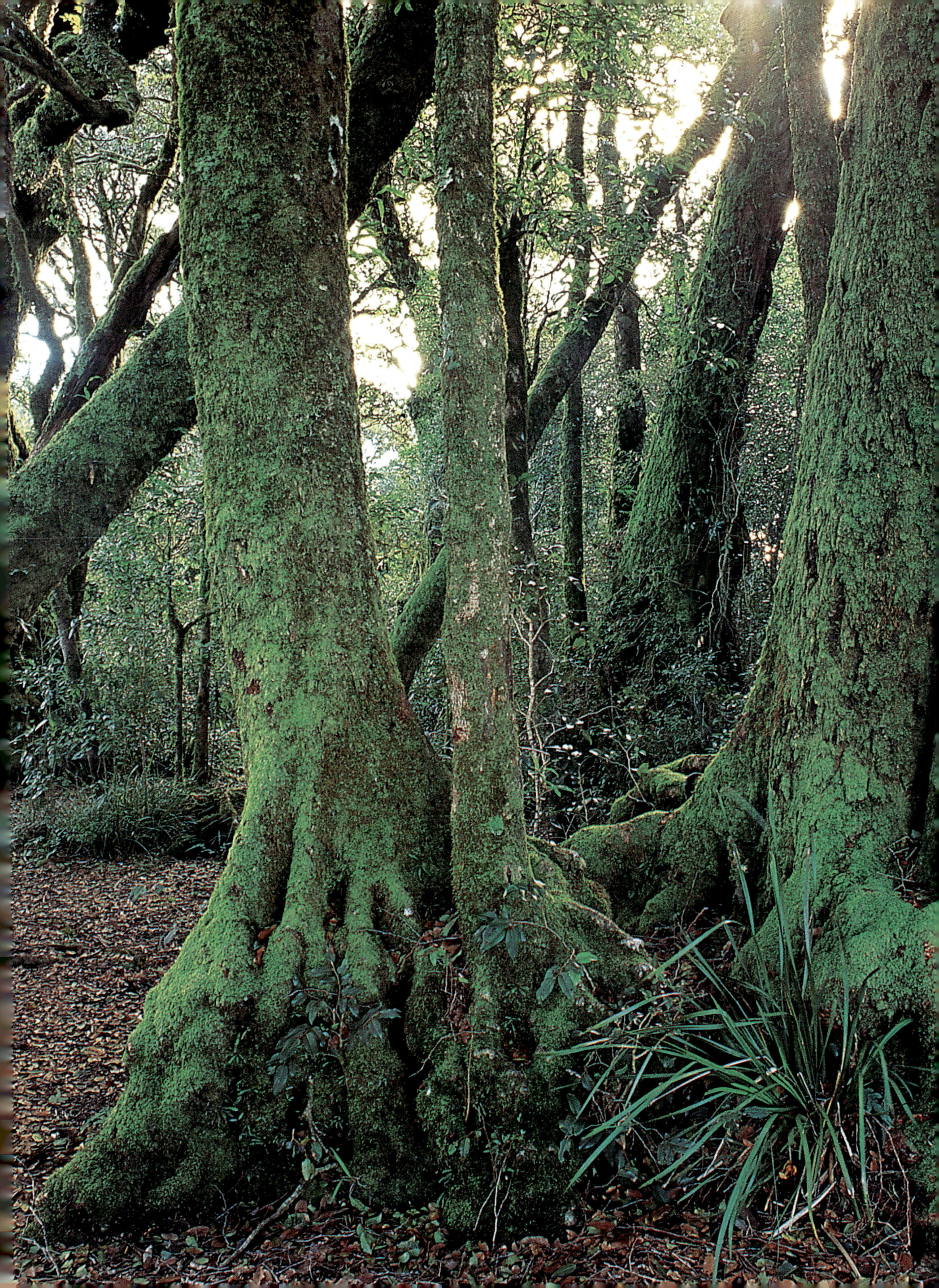

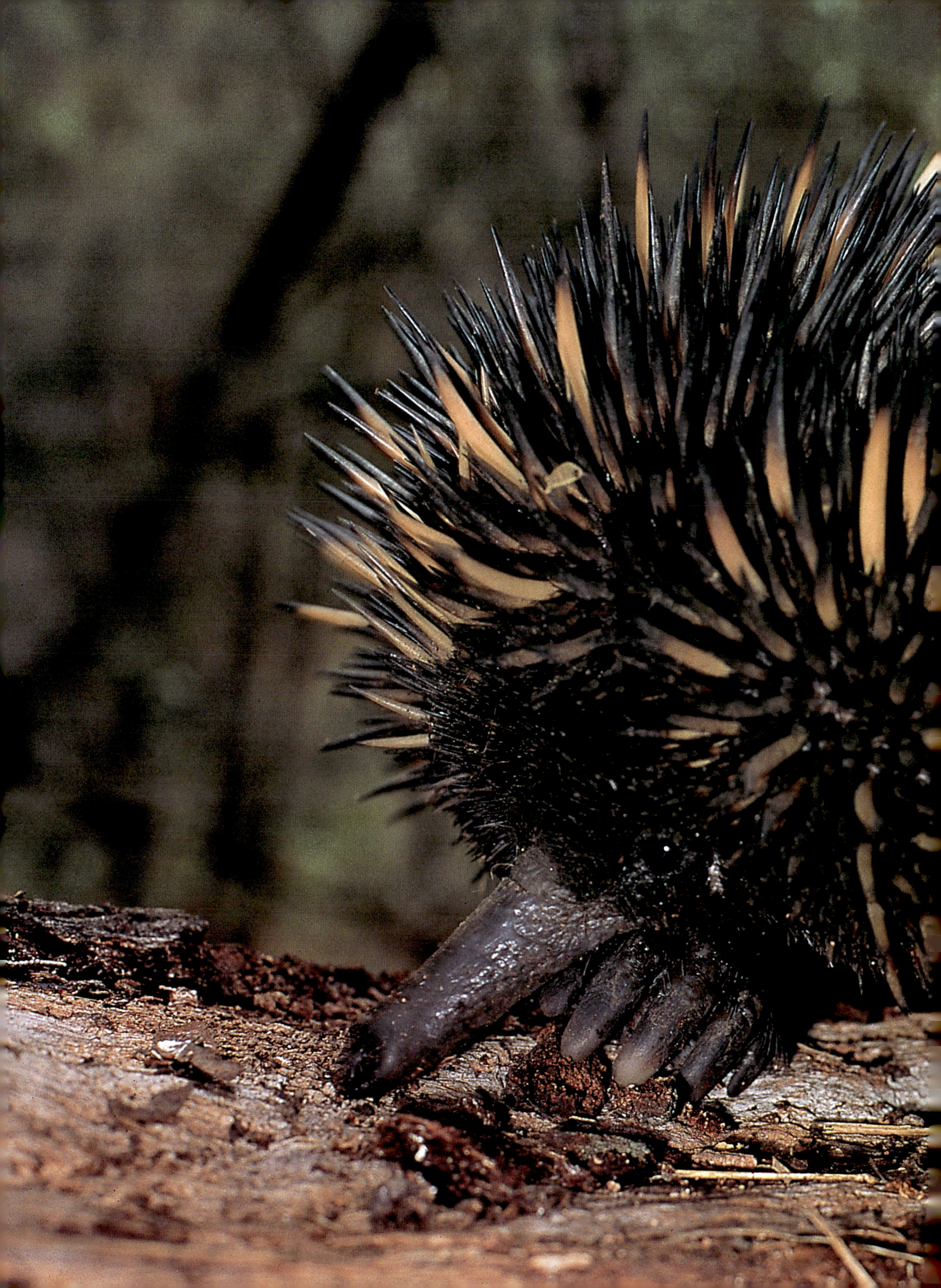

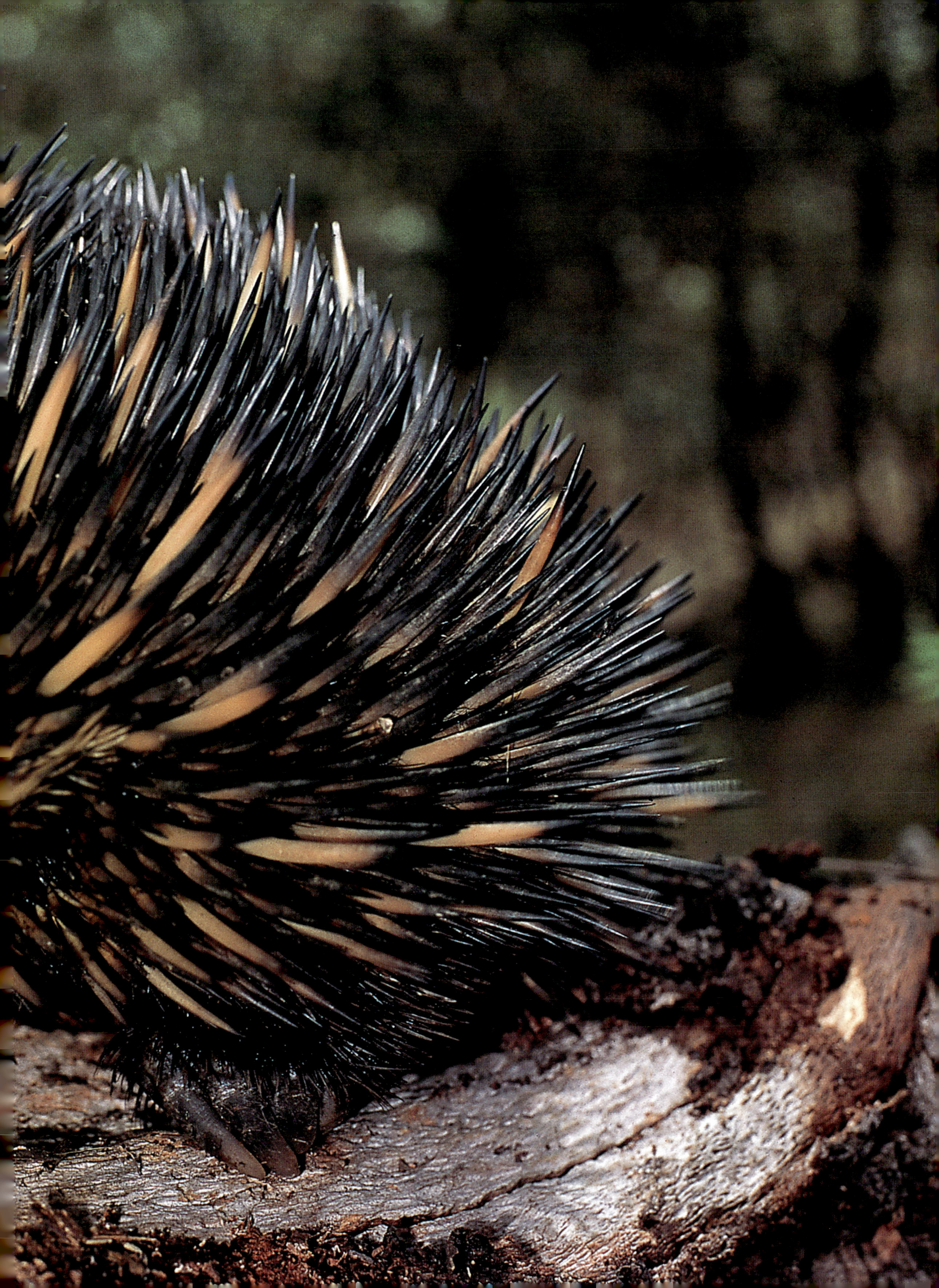

THE WET TROPICS
OF QUEENSLAND

Humid, lush and diverse, the Wet Tropics region of north-east Australia is a place of outstanding natural beauty. With its verdant forests, cascading waterfalls, crystal-clear rivers, sparkling white beaches and spectacular fringing reefs, it is the archetypal tropical paradise.

This region has features of great scientific significance. The rainforests cover a multitude of landforms and have a varied and complex evolutionary history. They are recognised as being the most diverse rainforests in Australia, both in the variety of plant life they embrace and in terms of forest structure. The slow drift north into warm and moist tropical latitudes after Australia's break with the ancient 'supercontinent' of Gondwana, some 80 million years ago, allowed these wet forests to survive and to preserve ancient life forms that have long since passed into extinction in other parts of the world, including surviving populations of the earliest spore-producing plants. The enclosing green canopy of the forest shelters the only habitats of many species that are rare, threatened or endangered.

The region also supports an ancient human culture that is sustained by the rainforests, a culture that is unique within Australia and believed by some experts to represent a first wave of Aboriginal occupation of the Australian continent.

Location

The Wet Tropics World Heritage Area extends along the north-east coast of Queensland stretching 450 kilometres (280 miles) from just north of Townsville almost to Cooktown. The boundary of the area corresponds approximately with the remaining tropical forest cover and is defined by the latitudes 15°39' to 19°17' South and longitudes 144°58' to 146°27' East. The total extent of the World Heritage Area is 894 420 hectares (2 210 200 acres) and it incorporates land tenures including 19 national parks, 31 state forests, 5 timber reserves and several Aboriginal and Islander reserves.

PREVIOUS PAGE   One of the many picturesque waterfalls found in the area.

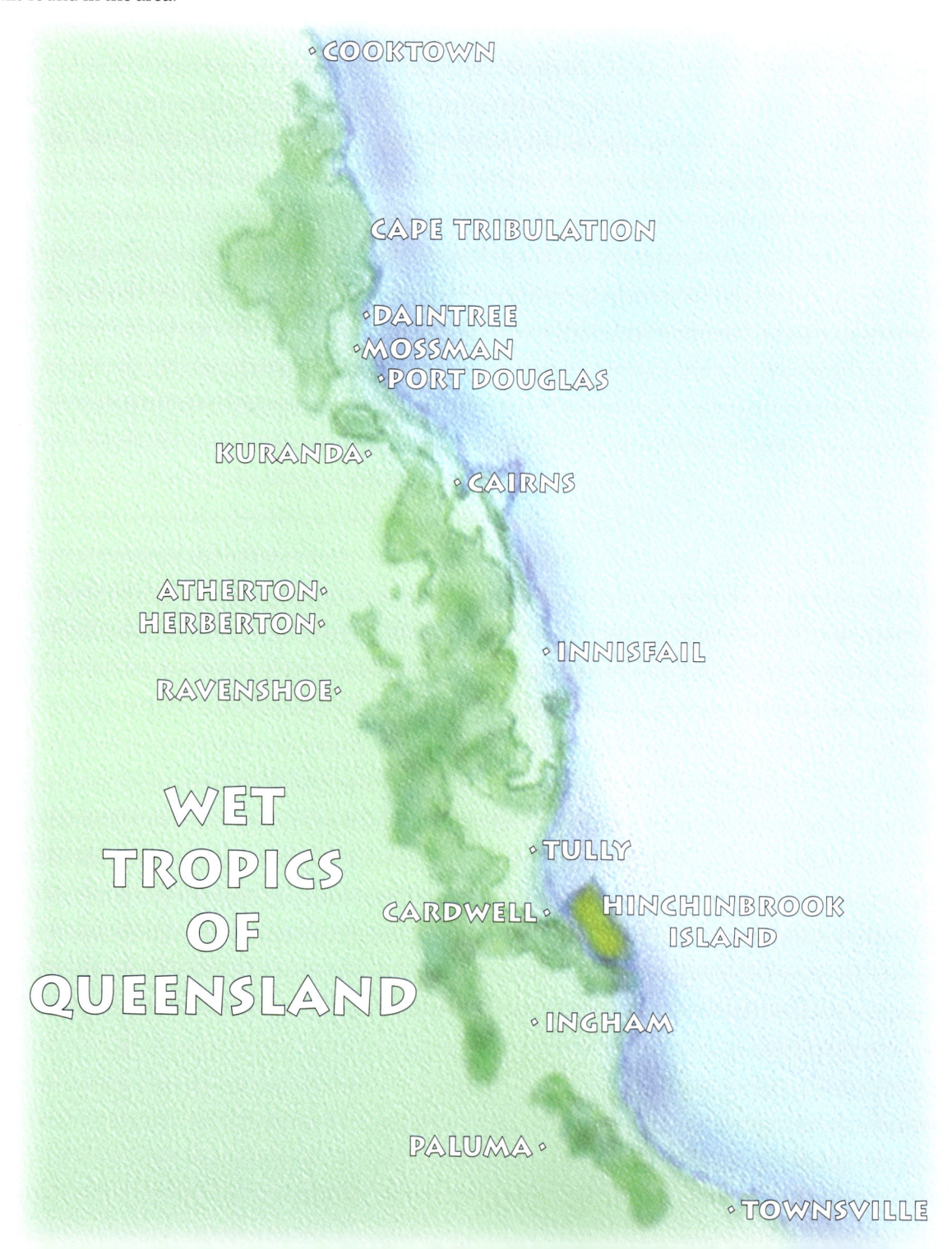

Wet Tropical Rainforests of Queensland

by David Lergessner

For many Australians, and especially Queenslanders, 1988 is remembered as the year when a protracted conflict came to an end with the inscription of Queensland's Wet Tropical Rainforests on the World Heritage List. The debate for and against the listing saw disagreements between the Commonwealth and Queensland Governments and a sometimes bitter struggle between timber workers and conservationists; the issue divided communities and even families. The argument about how Queensland's northern rainforests ought to be managed could not be separated from the social implications. World Heritage listing led some years later to the management of the World Heritage Area being placed under the auspices of the Wet Tropics Management Authority, a Commonwealth-State funded body specially established to co-ordinate its protection.

The Wet Tropics World Heritage Area is a discontinuous tract of rainforest almost 900 000 hectares (2 223 000 acres) in extent. The land consists of a mixture of tenures including national parks, state forests, timber reserves and one Aboriginal and Islander reserve, and extends from Townsville to Cooktown. About 14% of the area is freehold or various forms of leasehold. The main uses are nature conservation, tourism and recreation, forestry and defence manoeuvres. The nomination under the World Heritage Convention submitted that the area met all four of the key criteria for inscription on the World Heritage List as 'natural heritage'.

The listing of these wet tropical rainforests recognised their importance in " representing the Earth's evolutionary history ". The area provides a living record of the ecological and evolutionary processes that have shaped the Earth's flora and fauna over the last 415 million years. During that time Australia was part of Pangea, the global 'supercontinent' then part of Gondwana, the great southern continent and finally Australia. This island continent has been largely isolated from the rest of the planet for 50 million years. The outstanding significance of the area is that it contains many species representing long, distinct lineages, and therefore preserves a greater degree of evolutionary heritage than places with greater numbers of species of more closely allied forms.

The rainforests were well-established millions of years before Australia broke away from the 'supercontinent' of Gondwana. The spore-producing plants were joined by the cone bearing cycads and conifers and these were followed by flowering plants some 200 million years later. The separation of the Australian continent from Gondwana allowed for the development, during millions of years of isolation, of a unique flora and fauna. This raft of diverse plants and animals was marked for extinction during subsequent Ice Ages but it was saved from the cold and arid conditions by the northward drift of the Australian continent into a warmer, moister climate. Mixing with other floras and faunas at last occurred when sea level fluctuations, and the uplift of the New Guinea land mass due to the collision of continental plates, brought Asian floras and faunas into contact with Australia's Wet Tropics.

The listing of the Wet Tropics World Heritage Area recognised its significance as "an outstanding example of ongoing geological processes, biological evolution and man's interaction with his natural environment". Volcanic eruptions twenty million years ago almost destroyed the rainforests. Those on the Atherton Tablelands were buried under outpourings of volcanic basalt. The basalt rocks weathered to provide fertile soils which were quickly colonised by rainforest plants. The colonisers, however, were more recently evolved and vigorous rainforest species and their expansion was at the expense of the original rainforest species which failed to regain much of their former territory.

The limited areas of refuge for these earliest rainforest species included the narrow coastal plain built up by material eroded from the coastal ranges. This low-lying area was threatened periodically by advances and retreats of the Coral Sea across the plain. Within the Wet Tropics World Heritage Area, the lowland rainforests of the Daintree region are one of the few refuges of the ancient plant communities of Gondwana. Similar ancient floras can be found only on the islands of Madagascar and New Caledonia.

Because of its unusual natural history, many of the plants and animals of the region, some 43 plant genera encompassing 500 species, are found nowhere else on Earth. The region therefore contains much genetic material that is unique and which represents one of the longest time spans known for plant life on land.

The listing of the Wet Tropics also noted the area's "superlative natural phenomena" and "formations or features or areas of exceptional natural beauty". Millions of tourists are drawn to this part of the world to see its many attractions. For many people, foremost among these is the Daintree with its rainforest walks, mangrove board walk and beaches fringed by coral reefs and backed by towering rainforest-clad mountains. Nevertheless, the Wet Tropics are more than the Daintree: they are also the magnificent Barron Gorge and the Mossman Gorge, the spectacular Curtain Fig Tree, the Goldsborough Valley, the ancient volcanic sites of Lakes Eacham, Barrine and Hypipamee, Wallaman Falls - the longest single drop waterfall in Australia. There are waterfalls to be seen wherever the vigorous Wet Tropics streams plunge over the edge of the tableland and flow down to the coastal lowlands. Bordering the land is the beautiful Coral Sea and the great mangrove forests of the Hinchinbrook Channel.

The Wet Tropics World Heritage Area is a region containing important and significant natural habitats. Here, threatened species of plants and animals of outstanding universal value from the point of view of science and conservation still survive.

The plants and animals which are restricted in their distribution to parts of the Wet Tropics and, as such, are considered rare, vulnerable or endangered, make a very extensive list. The area has over 3000 species of vascular plants which have evolved over the past 100 million years.

The area also provides habitat for some distinctive native animals including the masked white-tailed rat, the musky-rat kangaroo and the southern cassowary; these are all species with either a very particular or limited distribution within the rainforests of the Wet Tropics.

The fragmented nature of the Wet Tropics region reflects over a century of European settlement. Cities and towns like Cairns, Mossman, Port Douglas, Innisfail, Tully, Cardwell and Ingham, and thousands of hectares of sugar cane farms on the lowlands, have taken the place of the natural landscape. Not so very long ago, all the land on the coastal plains between Townsville and Cape Tribulation was covered by wet tropical rainforest.

For more than 40 000 years, this region has been the home of Aboriginal people who lived in harmony with the land and sea from which they derived their living. Their environment was bountiful and, for the Kuku-Yalanji, one of the major tribal rainforest people who have retained their language and culture, it remains so. They are to be found living on the Bloomfield River and in the Mossman Gorge, although they no longer live in their distinctive 'waruns' or grass huts as traditional Kuku-Yalanji once did.

Edmund Kennedy, who journeyed from Rockingham Bay to Cape York in 1848, was the first European to enter the Wet Tropics region by an overland route. He was not followed until the 1870s, when men came in search of gold and tin. In just three years, 1400 Europeans and 17 000 Chinese had set up camp on the Palmer River gold fields just north-west of the Wet Tropics Area. The Aborigines initially resisted this invasion of their land but they were eventually subdued and most were resettled in or near mission stations established by various religious denominations. The gold miners left. The tin miners stayed and worked the many rivers throughout the region where alluvial tin could be found. The towns continued to grow, although some, like Cooktown, never regained the glory of their early mining days.

The real damage to the tropical rainforests was done by farmers and pastoralists who cleared the land in the hope of profit and the benefits for posterity they imagined would naturally follow. Much of this clearing was carried out almost a hundred years ago. The clearing has continued up to more recent times for settlement purposes, meeting a demand for 2.5 hectares (six acres) blocks of land in the rainforest. The coastline and coastal plains between Cardwell and Cairns once looked like the country between Daintree and Cooktown today, with unbroken rainforest extending from the ranges to the sea.

Logging of the wet tropical forests began in the first years of settlement. The valuable cedar forests of the Daintree were discovered in 1874. By 1878, reports in the Port Douglas Times decried the rape of the forests, claiming they would take over a hundred years to regenerate. We can see now that the cedar forests did not regenerate. In the 1930s, a Royal Commission was held into land use practices in the region. The Government of the day dismissed Edward Swain, the Conservator of Forests, whose efforts to protect large areas of rainforest from development were unpopular. It was not until the 1980s that public attitudes to the development of the wet tropical rainforests, in particular, those of the Daintree area, swung the other way. Surprisingly, the change was triggered not by a logging operation, but the building of a road. In December 1983, protesters erected blockades, chained themselves to trees and dug foxholes to prevent the construction of a 31 kilometre (19 mile) section of road through rainforest between Cape Tribulation and the Bloomfield River. The road was intended to further open up the Daintree rainforests to tourism and provide the people of the Bloomfield community - including the Kuku-Yalanji people - an alternative access to Cairns in the south. The protesters were not successful in stopping the construction of the road. The road has led to a great increase in the number of people entering the region. Opposition to the Daintree road was based in part on concerns that wet conditions in the region would make it liable to erosion and soil slippage, and that runoff from the road would greatly increase the silt load of creeks which discharged onto the coastal reefs of the Coral Sea. These concerns have proved to be justified, although the corals do not yet appear to have been affected.

The World Heritage listing on December 9, 1988 was not universally welcomed in the region. Some communities, especially those reliant on the timber industry, opposed the curtailment of logging in the rainforests and the withdrawal or reduction of log supplies. After the listing, negotiations between the Commonwealth and Queensland governments led to the establishment of the Wet Tropics Management Authority in 1992. Legislation was passed through the federal and state parliaments to provide for the protection and management of the rainforests.

A plan for the management of the Wet Tropics World Heritage Area was gazetted in 1997. The goal of the plan is to "protect, conserve, present, rehabilitate and transmit to future generations the Wet Tropics World Heritage Area within the meaning of the World Heritage Convention". The day-to-day management of the area is the responsibility of the land managers. It is also a responsibility for people who visit the area. The role of the Wet Tropics Management Authority is to co-ordinate funding, planning and management and to monitor activities to ensure the goal is achieved. The Authority has expressed the view that the plan will achieve 'protection through partnerships' and has stated that today, 80% of local people support the listing of the area as World Heritage - a large improvement on the situation in 1988.

The concept of 'partnerships' in the management and protection of rainforests will be fully tested in the Wet Tropics World Heritage Area. Some development interests continue to express disagreement with the principles of World Heritage. The Kuku-Yalanji Aboriginal community has recently lodged a native title claim over a large part of the rainforests in the northern section of the World Heritage Area.

RIGHT Herbert River ringtail possum.

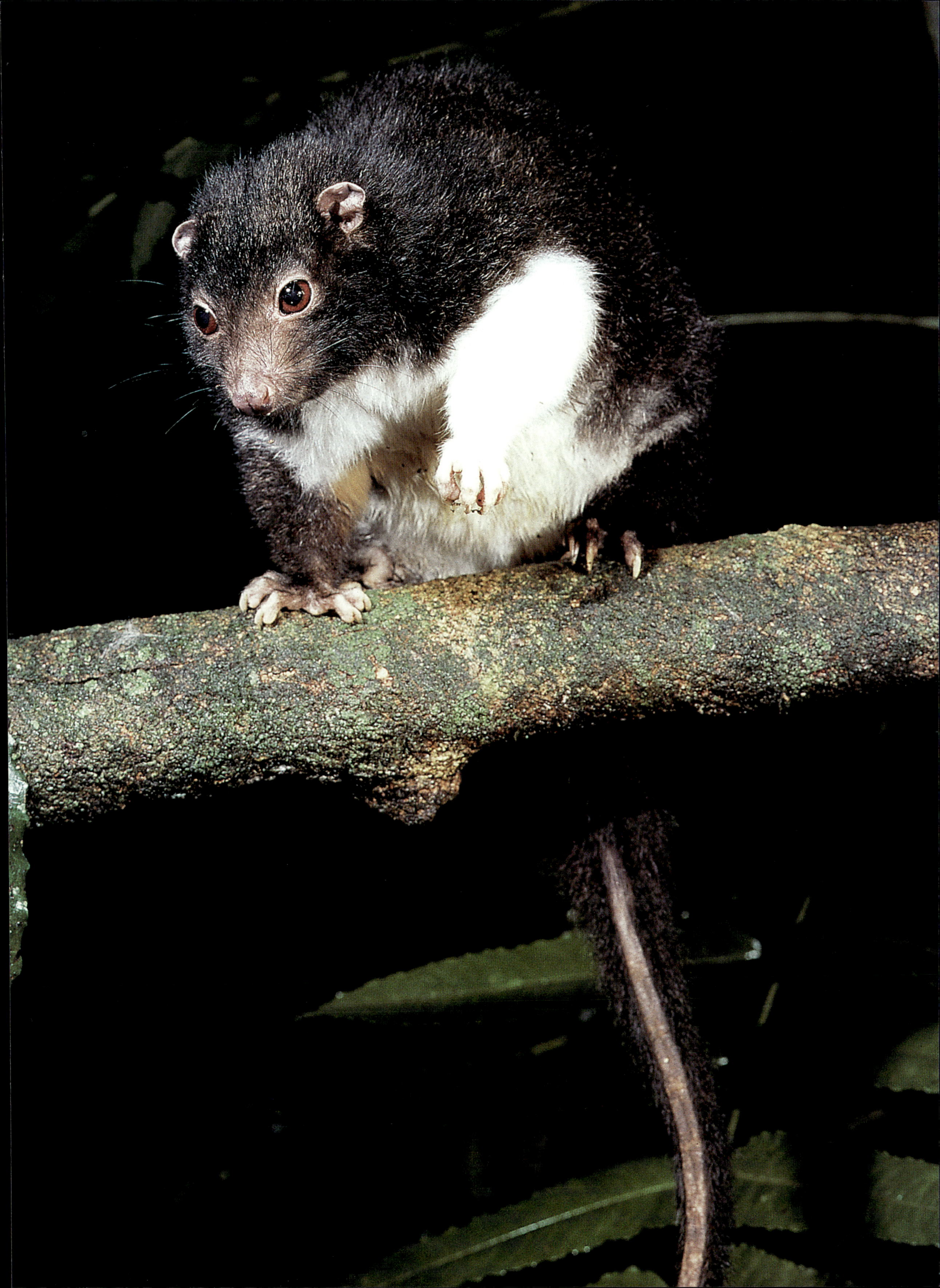

ABOVE An orchard butterfly. Brightly-coloured butterflies are abundant in the Wet Tropics.

RIGHT The flightless, giant southern cassowary. Amongst cassowaries, the work of incubating the eggs and rearing the chicks falls to male birds.

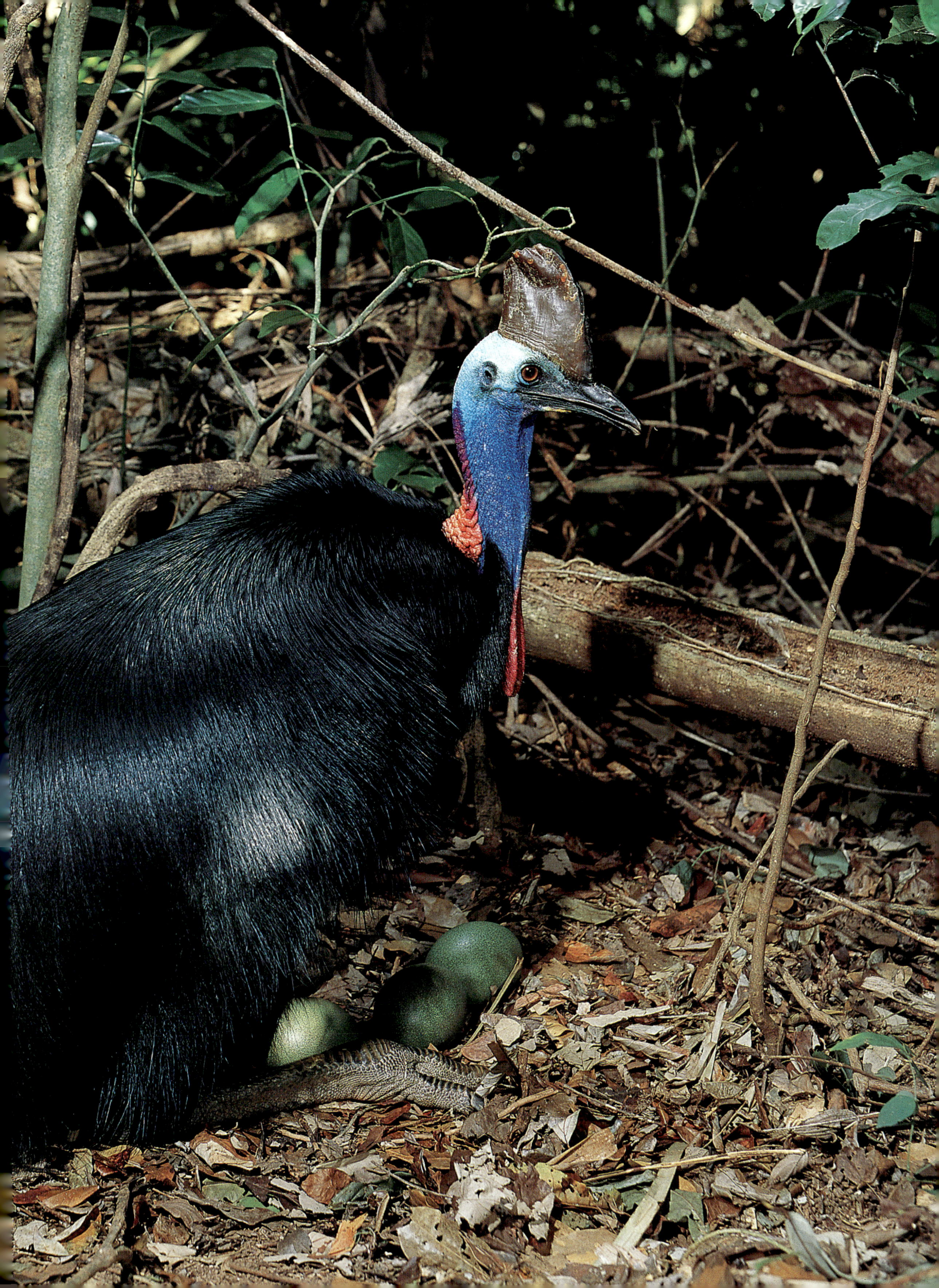

Physical Features

The wet tropical rainforests of north-east Australia are small in extent when compared with rainforests in other parts of the world and account for only about a fifth of one per cent of the world's rainforests. However, what these forests lack in scale they make up for in their antiquity and diversity.

The Wet Tropics World Heritage Area covers three major landform units: the undulating tablelands of the Great Divide, the lower coastal belt to the east and, between them, the Great Escarpment. The Great Escarpment marks the limit between the tablelands and the coastal plain and is a very rugged landscape, featuring deep gorges and spectacular waterfalls, rapidly eroding slopes and diverse environments. Many high points of the tableland and escarpment reach to 900 metres (2950 feet) elevation, with some peaks rising up to 1600 metres (5250 feet) and more.

Queensland's Wet Tropics Area is clothed with a mosaic of vegetation. The various communities which contribute to the mosaic reflect different environmental conditions. Rainforest types range from multi-storeyed vine forests on richer soils in warm, wet areas to simple vine forests on poorer soils in drier areas and fern thickets in the higher, wetter places. The tropical rainforest tracts are bordered, and in places interrupted, by open forests and woodlands, mangroves and swamps. Adjacent to the rainforest margins on the western edge of the region are narrow strips of tall open forests dominated by eucalyptus. The sharp contrast between closely adjoining tracts of rainforest and open forest is a feature unique to Australia.

Sweeping white sandy beaches and fringing coral reefs are found in the northern section of the World Heritage Area and the reefs are at their most extensive between the mouths of the Daintree and Bloomfield rivers. This close juxtaposition of coastal rainforest and coral reef is not seen anywhere else in the world. The sapphire-blue waters and rainbow-hued corals make a spectacular accompaniment to the deep emerald green of the rainforest canopy.

Queensland's Wet Tropics are true to their name, with a number of the region's distinctive features attributable to the high annual rainfall. The region experiences a distinct wet season, with 60% of rain falling during the summer from December to March. Mean annual rainfall ranges from 4 metres (160 inches) near the coast to 1200 millimetres (50 inches) at the western extremity of the area. Still greater quantities of rain fall in the mountain ranges. For example, Mount Bellenden Ker, south of Cairns, which rises to over 1500 metres (4920 feet), has been known to receive 1140 millimetres (45 inches) of rain in a single 24 hour period. During the wet season, tropical low pressure cells and cyclones commonly dump more than 250 millimetres (10 inches) of rain in a day and break the rainforest canopy. Such large amounts of rain falling on a usually saturated landscape often lead to widespread overland flow, something not generally seen in other wet tropical rainforest areas.

Daily temperatures range from between 23° to 31° Celsius (74° to 88° Fahrenheit) on the coast and are roughly 5° Celsius (9° Fahrenheit) lower in winter. The tablelands are cooler, with a range of 17° to 28° Celsius (61° to 82° Fahrenheit) in summer and 9° to 22° Celsius (48° to 72° Fahrenheit) in winter. Coastal humidity is usually high, averaging 78% but frequently soars into the high nineties in summer.

RIGHT The Daintree River meanders through its rainforest wilderness, the home of many of the world's primitive flowering plants.

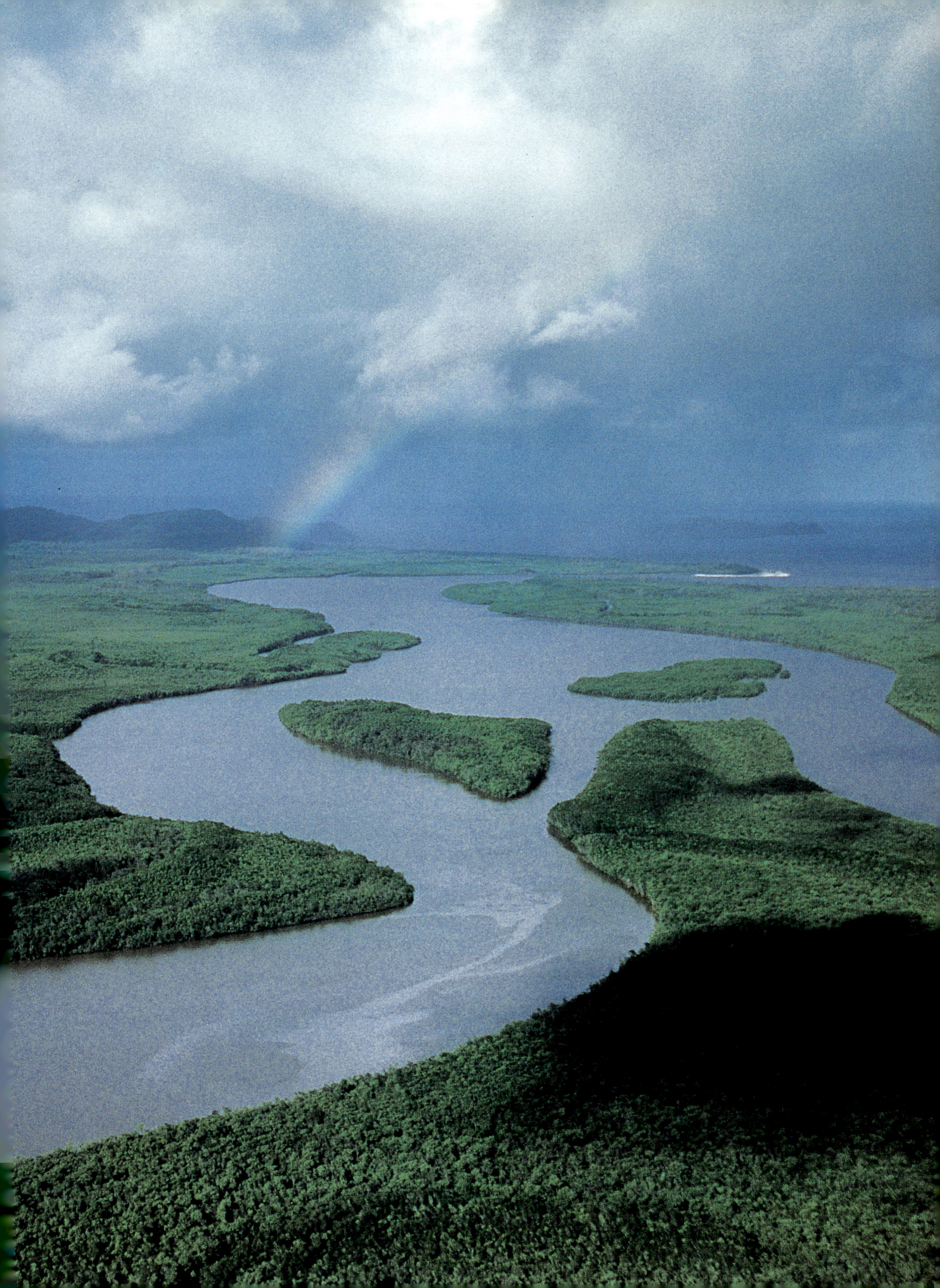

Special Features

The wet tropical rainforests of north-east Australia, although teeming with life, possess a sublime tranquillity. Spectacular landforms are highlighted by extensive forest vistas and there are wild rivers, waterfalls, steep gorges and idyllic coastal scenes. The stark form of Mount Pier Botte, with its massive granite outcrops, towers over sweeping tracts of undisturbed forest.

Precipitous gorges and surging rivers dominate the region. Roaring Meg Creek descends rapidly through a series of magnificent waterfalls and cascades, whilst the turbulent Tully, Russell, Mulgrave and Johnstone Rivers have become popular destinations for canoeists and white-water rafters. Stony Creek plunges 278 metres (912 feet) over the Wallaman Falls, making this the longest single drop of any waterfall in Australia.

The Wet Tropics World Heritage Area also contains abrupt transitions from one kind of vegetation community to another quite different one: rainforest is replaced by open forest, or woodland; or even into mangrove as occurs along the Daintree River and the Hinchinbrook Channel. These associations are unique in the world and are an echo on land of the marvellous complexity of the Great Barrier Reef, which lies just off this coast.

This rainforest region is of great scientific interest as it provides a haven for many ancient and otherwise extinct plant and animal species. Vegetation communities, which were once mixed or in close proximity when Australia formed part of the ancient 'supercontinent' of Gondwana, became geographically separated after the breaking away of the continent. Extensive regional extinction of species occurred due to influences such as climate change, especially the cold and arid conditions brought by successive Ice Ages. However, this reduction of ancient life forms was counteracted within the tropical rainforest of north-east Australia by the northward drift of the continent into the warm and moist tropics. North Queensland is the only large part of Australia where rainforests have persisted since the days when this continent formed part of Gondwana.

The wet tropical rainforests also form an integral part of a delicate ecosystem and help to moderate run-off and siltation of streams in a very wet and erosion-prone landscape.

TOP RIGHT The diminutive musky rat-kangaroo is considered to be the most primitive of the kangaroos and wallabies, and has similarities with tree kangaroos and possums.

ABOVE Boyd's rainforest dragon is a tree-climber and grows to more than half a metre (one and a half feet) in length.

FAR RIGHT Wallaman Falls makes its spectacular leap. This is the longest single drop made by a waterfall in Australia.

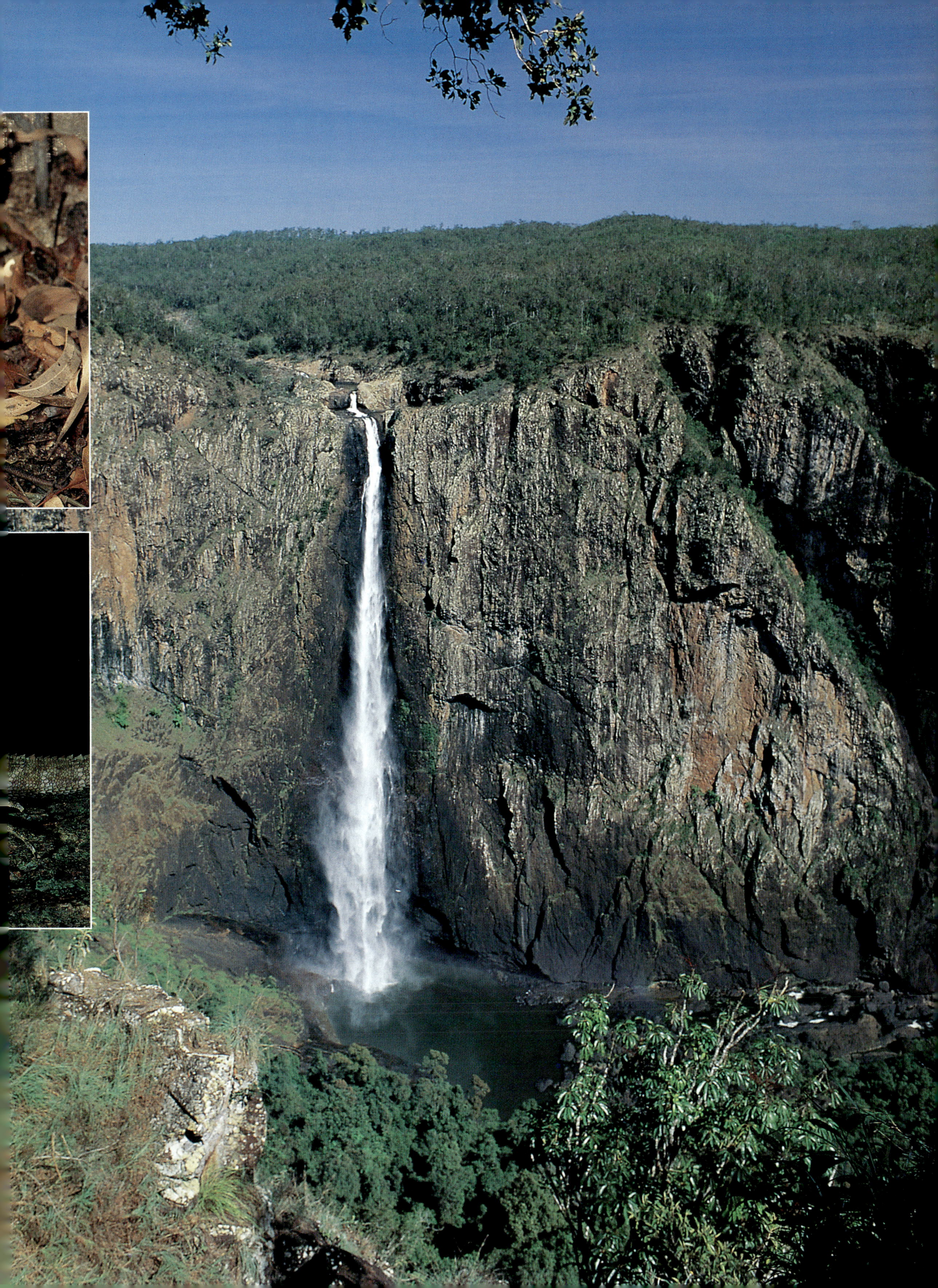

Flora

The plant life of the region is extremely rich and diverse. There are over 3000 species of higher plants, of which over 700 are restricted to the Wet Tropics of the north-east. Many examples of isolated populations of plant species occur both in the lowlands and uplands and the region presents a rich array of native orchids (30% of Australia's orchid species).

The predominant vegetation type in the World Heritage Area is wet tropical rainforest. The nature and type of these forests depend upon the environmental conditions influencing an area. On the upland slopes and summits are the wet forests known as simple microphyll - vine-fern thicket. The canopy is often low and dense and shows the streamlining effects of strong winds. These forests are very different in the plant life they contain compared with other rainforest types within the region and appear to be more closely related to the forests of New Guinea, Indonesia and temperate Australia.

Perhaps the most visually striking rainforest type is that dominated by the fan palm. Fan palm rainforests are restricted to small patches of poorly drained soils on the lowlands. Most of this type of rainforest has been cleared for sugar cane farming and only a few square kilometres remain.

One of the rarer vine forests occur on the very wet lowlands. Small patches may be found between Innisfail and Cape Tribulation but the major stands are at Kurrimine Beach, South Innisfail and at Noah Creek near Cape Tribulation.

The wet tropical rainforests of north-east Australia are home to many plant species that were once widespread and have been reduced in their distribution to refuge areas within the region. Four genera of ancient and primitive conifer, or cone bearing, plants survive in the region. The Wet Tropics are also a major centre for the survival of cycads, an ancient form of plant life with fern-like fronds, of which many types are rare or threatened. This primitive group is believed to have been in existence for 200 million years and the region boasts one of the world's largest, a palm-like plant which grows to a height of 20 metres (66 feet), and also one of the smallest. The rainforests of the region are also an important refuge for primitive spore-producing plants. They contain the richest concentration of fern types in Australia, with more than 240 species occurring in the region.

The unusual tropical plants found in rainforests throughout the world are not lacking in the Australian Wet Tropics. The rainforests of north-east Queensland play a vital role in the conservation of the Australian members of the Proteaceae, a family of plants found only in the southern hemisphere. The rainforest members of this family are thought to be the ancestors of groups such as the *grevilleas*, which form an important part of the modern Australian vegetation. There are also bountiful assemblages of ancient and beautiful flowering plants such as the Magnoliales and Laurales. The region is rich in orchids, too. Like a precious gem concealed in a cave, the jewel orchid is found only in the darkest, densest upland rainforests of the Wet Tropics.

RIGHT Palms dominate the understorey of the lowland rainforest in the Wet Tropics. Stands of tall fan palms like these are no longer common elsewhere due to past clearing.

NEXT PAGE The coils of a carpet python embrace a rainforest palm.

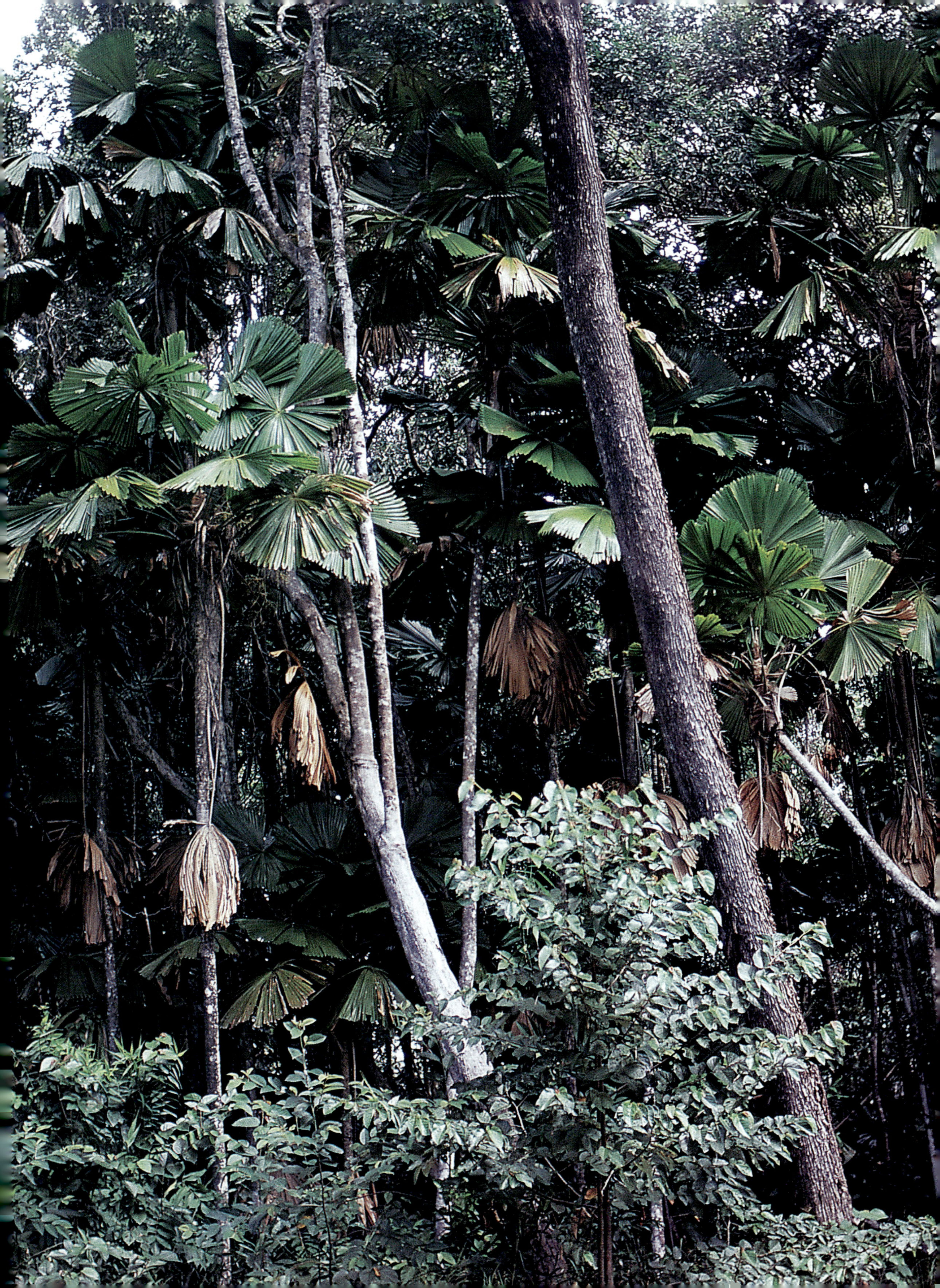

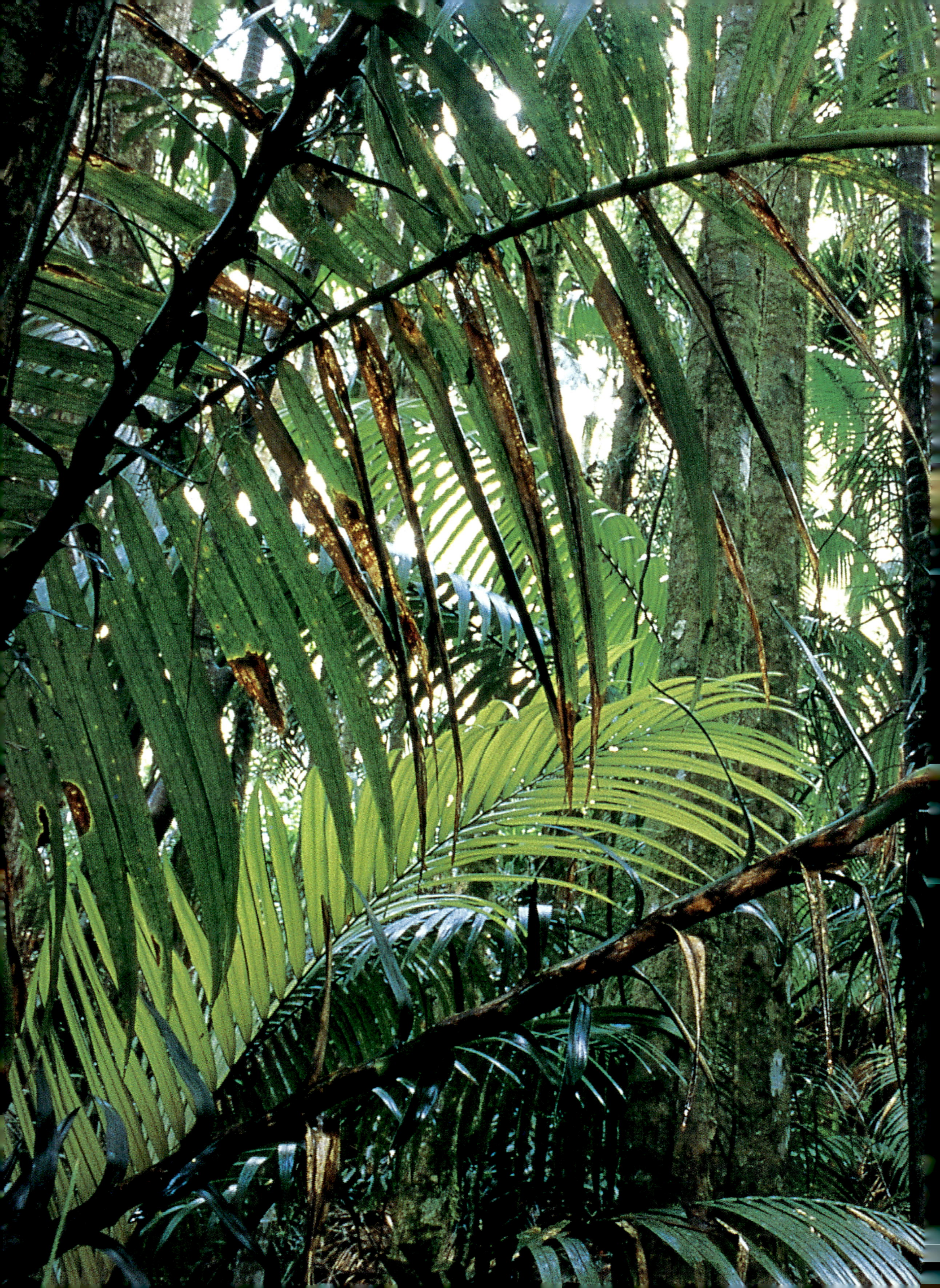

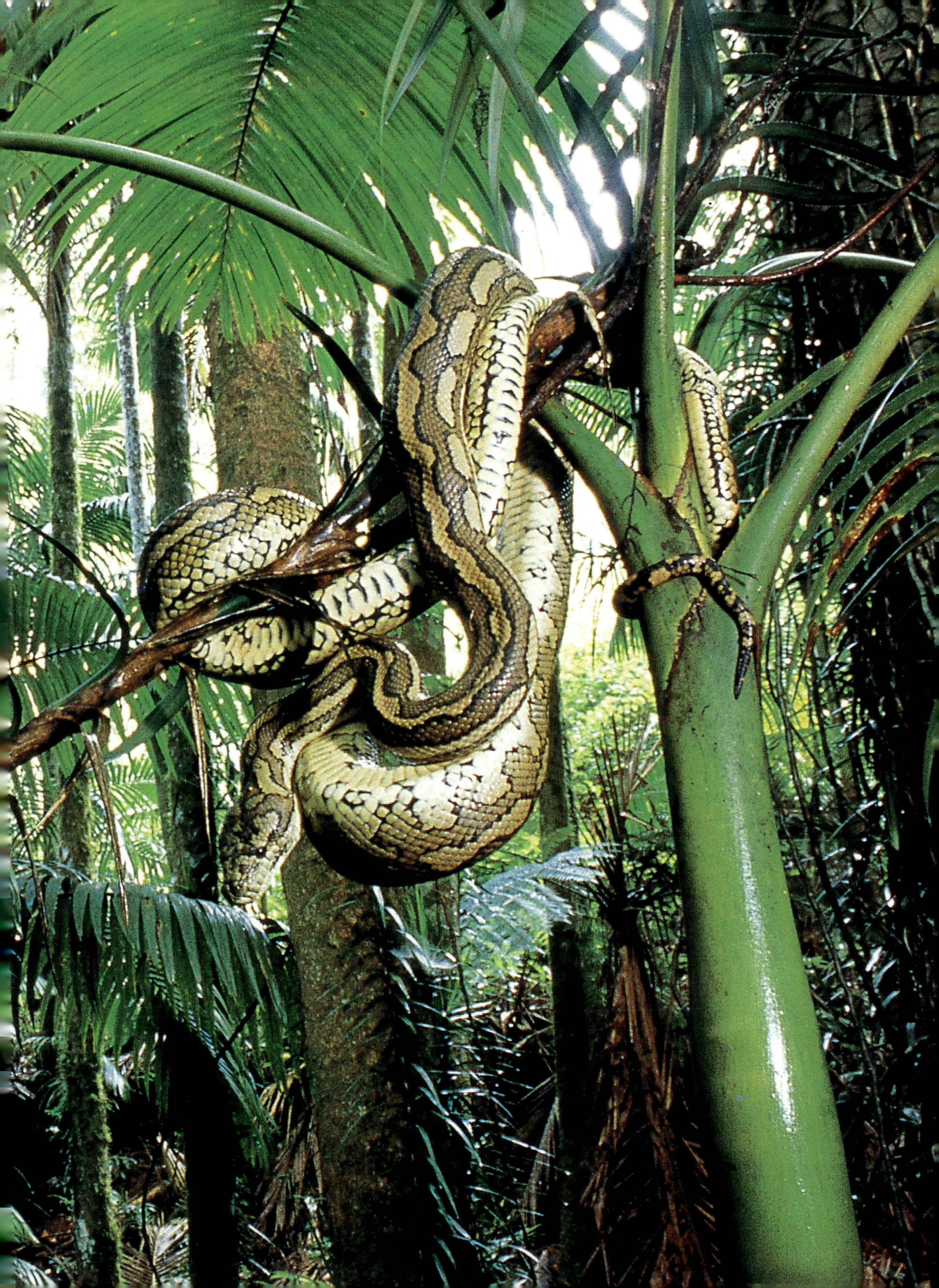

Fauna

Although the Wet Tropics World Heritage Area represents a mere one tenth of one per cent of the land surface of Australia, the region supports extensive and diverse animal life. Surviving within this zoological refuge are 30% of Australia's marsupial species, 58% of the bats, 25% of the frogs, 23% of the reptiles, around half of the bird species and 62% of all Australian butterfly species. Some of these species are found only in this region and some are restricted to a small area. Other species occur in isolated populations which may be separated from their nearest neighbours by thousands of kilometres.

The mammals of the region are a plentiful and varied group and include monotremes or egg-laying mammals, marsupials or pouched mammals, rodents and bats. Eight species are not to be found outside the region. These include the masked white-tailed rat, the Atherton antechinus, four species of ringtail possum and Australia's only two species of tree-kangaroo, Bennett's tree-kangaroo and Lumholtz's tree-kangaroo. It is also the major habitat of the spotted-tail quoll - a ferocious carnivorous marsupial about the size of a small cat. Of particular interest is the musky rat-kangaroo which is the smallest and, in many respects the most primitive, of the kangaroo group, representing an early stage in the evolution of kangaroos from a tree-climbing and possum-like ancestor.

The tropical rainforests of north-east Australia are rich in birdlife, with more than 370 species recorded. Some 13 bird species are not found outside the region. Most of these are confined to the northern uplands and have developed regional features. Included in this exclusive group are the northern log-runner or chowchilla, the little tree-creeper, the Australian fernwren, the bridled honeyeater, Bower's shrike-thrush and the golden bower-bird. One of only three species of cassowary in the world lives in the rainforests of this region; this is the enormous southern cassowary, a formidable, aggressive and flightless bird which stands up to two metres (six feet) tall.

Reptile and amphibian life in the rainforest is also abundant. There are more than 170 species of reptiles, including the chameleon gecko and the northern leaf-tailed gecko. The skinks are a particularly diverse group with several rare and restricted species occurring within the region. Fifty-three species of frogs have been recorded, with a number of rare species of tree frogs restricted to high altitudes.

The Wet Tropics literally crawls with insects. A recent survey of five sites along a 10 kilometre (6 mile) survey line yielded over 4000 species of insects, including 300 species of spiders. Among the rainforests' highly diverse and numerous moth population is the widespread Hercules moth which, with a wingspan of up to 25 centimetres (10 inches), is one of the largest moths in the world. Butterflies are well represented within the region and examples include species found nowhere else, like the evening-flying purple brown-eye, the Australian hedge blue, the Cairns birdwing and more widespread species such as the brilliant blue and black Ulysses. The insect fauna preserved in the cool and moist upland rainforests also contains many primitive species which survive in reduced numbers and distribution, such as the large stag beetle.

TOP RIGHT The Lumholtz tree-kangaroo, seen here eating leaves, is restricted to the highland rainforests. Active at night, it sleeps during the day high up in the tree canopy.

RIGHT A rare tawny-breasted honeyeater feeds its young.

FAR RIGHT The rainbow skink, a denizen of the rainforest.

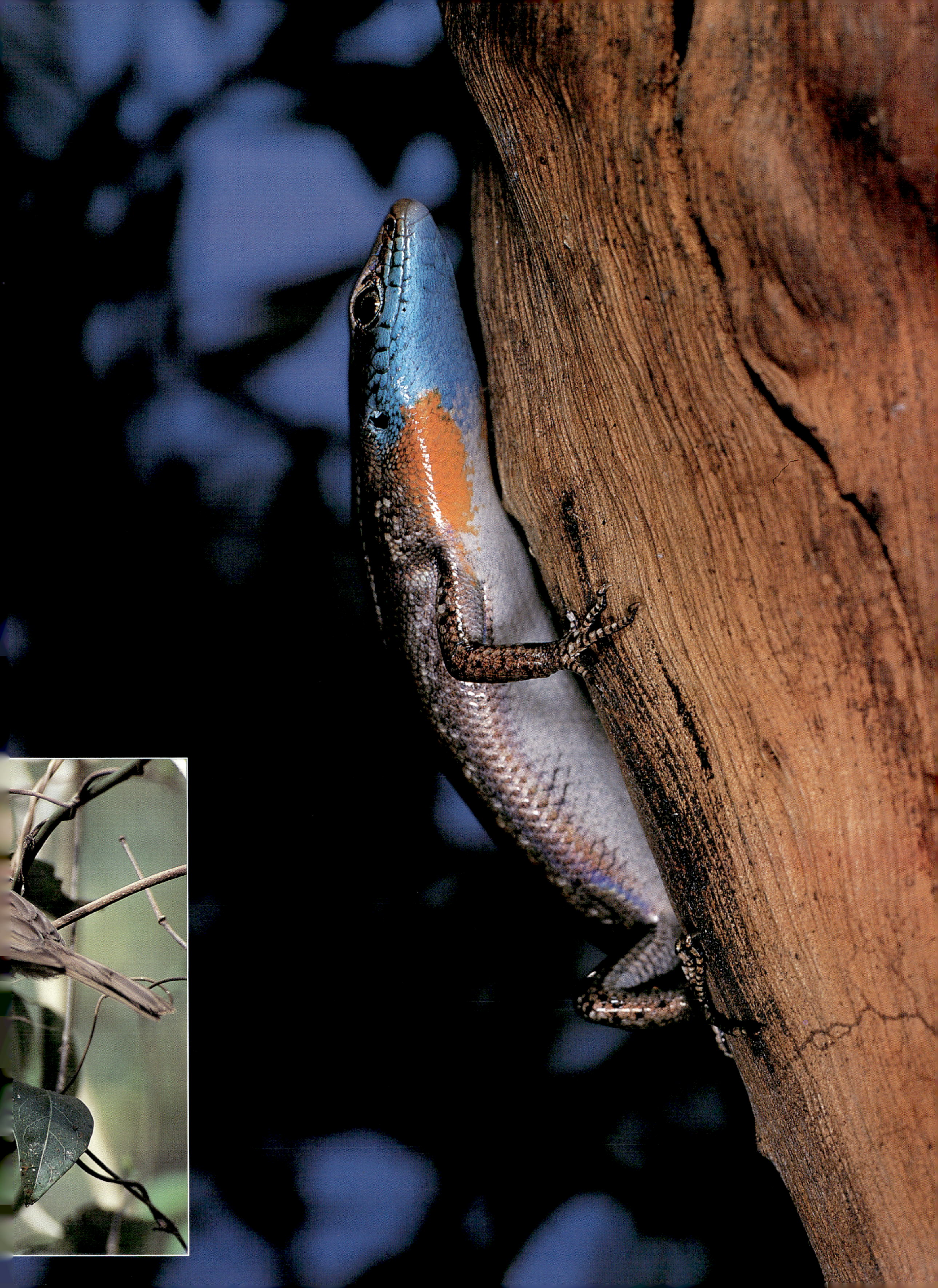

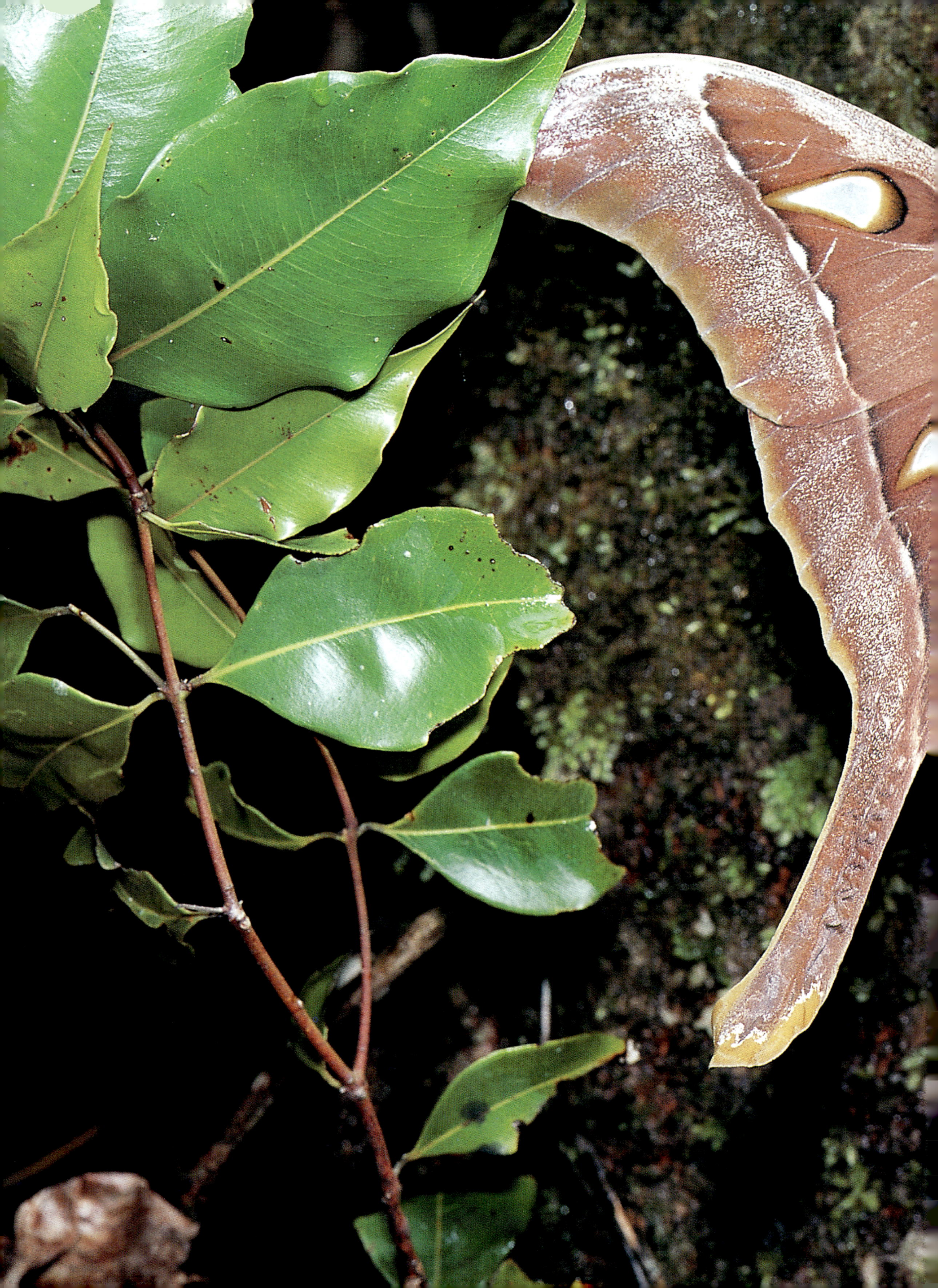

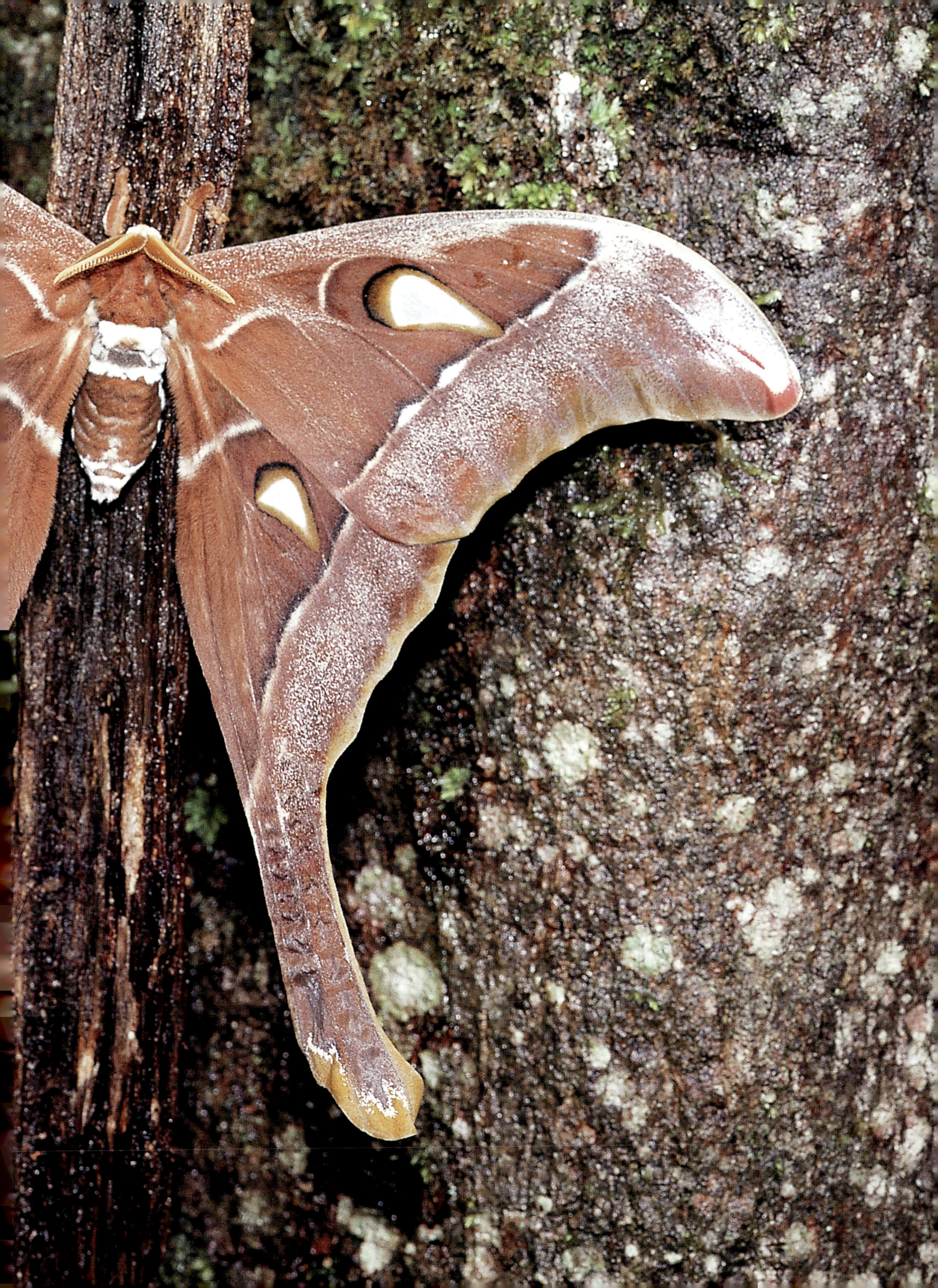

Cultural Heritage

Aboriginal occupation of Australia's north-east dates back to at least 40 000 years. These northern groups are thought by some authorities to represent a first wave of Aboriginal occupation of the continent. This may be the world's oldest continuing human cultural association with rainforests and it is believed that the oral history alone of the rainforest-dwelling Aboriginal groups of the region stretches back 10 000 to 15 000 years.

As with the other indigenous peoples of Australia, the rainforest people were traditionally hunter-gatherers. Rainforest culture, however, differed markedly from that of other Australian Aboriginal groups. Food gathering within the rainforest relied heavily on tree-climbing skills and a knowledge of techniques for removing any toxic elements in plant foods. Spears and boomerangs are of limited use in the heavily wooded rainforest environment, so the rainforest people developed many special tools. Hand-held weapons peculiar to forest dwelling groups included massive wooden swords and stone axes employed for close-quarter combat and hunting.

The way of life devised by the rainforest communities was very successful and continued uninterrupted until the arrival of Europeans. Many elements of the culture continue to thrive today in centres such as Bloomfield River and Murray Upper. Some land within the World Heritage Area is held under various titles by the traditional Aboriginal owners. This land continues to be used for traditional non-commercial purposes by the small number of local residents.

The first European to extensively explore the Wet Tropics of Queensland was the unfortunate Edmund Kennedy who was speared to death by Aborigines at Cape York in 1848. Exploration was followed in the succeeding decades by enterprising timber-cutters and graziers. By 1861, the first north Queensland squatters had taken possession of their runs, while the red cedar cutters worked their way along the coast to reach the Daintree and Mossman rivers by 1875. Tin mining began to impact upon the region in the 1880s. Rainforest was progressively cleared to make way for sugar cane plantations which spread along the entire northern coast by 1885. The less accessible hinterland did not remain untouched for long, with the pioneers entering the Atherton Tableland in 1881.

Since the early days of European settlement, the economy of north-east Queensland has relied almost entirely on primary production. This has had an impact on the rainforests which have suffered both from agricultural clearing and logging. While commercial crops such as coffee, cotton and tobacco were tried with varying degrees of success, sugar production was the industry which secured and shaped the future of the communities of north-east Queensland. The clearing of coastal and tableland rainforest to make way for sugar cane, maize and dairying continues into recent times, although large-scale felling has slowed considerably in the last 20 years. Other industries which are now finding a firm foothold in the region include tourism which has grown rapidly since the 1950s.

PREVIOUS PAGE The Hercules or Atlas moth, with its wingspan of up to 25 centimetres (10 inches), is one of the largest moths in the world.

RIGHT This tube-nosed fruit bat is one of the 58% of all of Australia's species of bats found in the Wet Tropics.

FAR RIGHT The Wet Tropics rainforests are home to many frogs. This giant white-lipped tree frog sleeps in the folds of leaves by day and hunts insects by night. At 14 centimetres (nearly 6 inches), it has the greatest body length of Australian frogs.

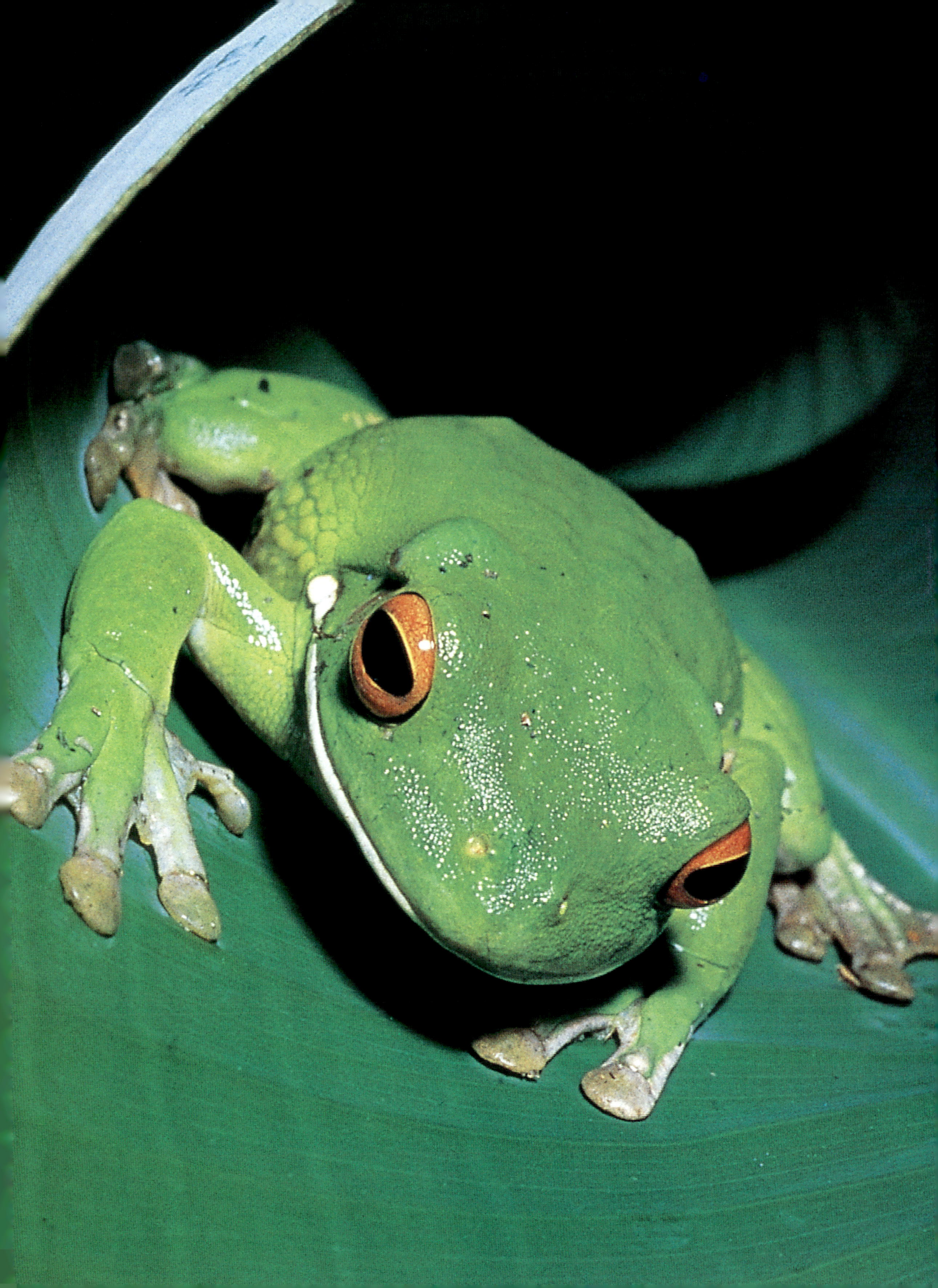

Facilities

North-east Queensland boasts many attractions for visitors: warm climate, miles of white beaches and no less than two World Heritage listed areas, namely the Great Barrier Reef and the Wet Tropics. For these reasons, the area is a popular holiday choice for both local and international visitors. With international and domestic air terminals at Cairns and sealed highways leading from Australia's southern cities, the area is readily accessible. Urban centres such as Cairns and resort towns such as Port Douglas offer accommodation ranging from casual back-packers' hostels to luxurious hotels with all imaginable trimmings.

During the past decade, interest has increased in the natural features of the Wet Tropics and tourism has become a major part of the region's economy. Each year the area attracts over three million daily visits either as the major focus of their trip or, more commonly, as part of a wide range of activities made available to visitors to the region.

Threats

The greatest threats to the wet tropical rainforests of north-east Australia arise from continuing development pressures and from the difficulties of managing such an extensive World Heritage Area containing so many interests and so much complexity. It has proven difficult to co-ordinate the activities of the region's diverse interest groups, many of whom have different and frequently conflicting needs.

The Wet Tropics management plan prohibits commercial logging across all tenures. However, major threats to many of the rainforests' fauna is dry forest clearing, taking place adjacent to the World Heritage Area, particularly around Tully. This is threatening the survival of the mahogany glider on the eastern boundary of the site and a similar pattern is affecting the yellow-bellied glider on the western fringe.

Threats to rainforest areas under various forms of private right or tenure include mining, agriculture and real estate development.

Cleared and disturbed rainforest areas have suffered from the invasion of exotic plant species such as *lantana*. There have also been outbreaks of soil fungus in logged areas, which has lead to patch deaths among the remaining trees and shrubs.

Since the mid 1980s, there has been a marked increase in tourism, concentrated on the region's natural features. Although this has meant a substantial boost to the region's economy and some decline in the dominance of the sugar cane industry, the consequences for the rainforests have not all been good ones. Over 300 000 tourists now visit the region annually. Unfortunately, the increase in visitor numbers has not been matched by a corresponding rise in the standard and provision of infrastructure. There is only a rudimentary support system for visitors and limited active environmental interpretation is provided. As a result, the people virtually flooding into the rainforests remain largely ignorant about the delicate rainforest ecosystem and how best to protect it.

Human Impact

There has been significant human impact on the rainforests of the Wet Tropics World Heritage Area, however it has been moderate compared with some rainforest areas elsewhere in Australia and overseas. These forests are substantially intact, with only an estimated one-third of the cover present at the time of European contact still remaining. A substantial amount of lowland rainforest has been cleared for agriculture and much rainforest has been affected by selective logging.

Scattered human disturbances accumulate to the point where they detract from the overall integrity of the World Heritage area. Examples include transmission lines, quarries, abandoned mines, dams and areas which have been subjected to heavy logging, overgrazing or intensive recreational use. However, these impacts cover only a small proportion of the total area and can be corrected or rehabilitated over time.

There is a long history of research in the area by the Commonwealth Scientific and Industrial Research Organisation and the Townsville-based James Cook University in fields such as rainforest plant classification, ecosystems, catchment studies, research into regeneration and disturbance and wildlife management.

Some areas of the rainforests are currently used by the Commonwealth Department of Defence for the training of military personnel in jungle warfare. As long as they are carefully planned and managed, these activities should not impact significantly on the integrity of the World Heritage Area.

The building of the Cape Tribulation-Bloomfield road through the Daintree rainforests was a serious intrusion upon the region's heritage values and had impacts upon both the Daintree National Park and the Great Barrier Reef. The extent of the impacts was such that in 1984, the area was listed on the Register of Threatened Protected Areas of the World.

Management

The wet tropical forests of north-east Australia were nominated for inscription on the World Heritage List in 1987 and inscribed in 1988. Negotiations between the Commonwealth and Queensland Governments led in 1992 to the establishment of the Wet Tropics Management Authority, a joint Commonwealth-State funded agency based in Cairns. The role of the authority is to co-ordinate funding, planning and management of the World Heritage Area and to monitor activities to ensure that that values that led to its listing are protected.

The public land within the World Heritage Area is administered on a day to day basis by the Queensland State Government through various agencies: primarily the Queensland Department of Environment and the Department of Natural Resources. The Commonwealth Department of Defence manages the areas used for their training exercises.

Private property within the World Heritage Area remains the responsibility of the owners of the land but they are required to comply with relevant laws controlling its occupation, use and development.

THIS PAGE Cape Tribulation. This aerial view shows a line of white sand beaches dividing the azure ocean from the green canopy of the lowland rainforest.

SHARK BAY
Western Australia

Shark Bay is a place of remarkable biological diversity, offering a wealth of scientific and cultural treasures within a largely undisturbed environment. Its exceptional natural values, in particular, won the area an inscription on the World Heritage List in 1991 under all four natural criteria applied by the World Heritage Committee.

The stromatolites of Shark Bay's Hamelin Pool are amongst the Earth's most ancient life forms, and provide a living fossil record of our planet's evolutionary history. Shark Bay's location on the cusp of two climatic and botanical zones, and the fact that offshore islands are free of introduced pests and predators, have resulted in an exceptionally diverse biology and ecology. The area is home to five threatened land mammals and two vulnerable marine mammals. Almost one-eighth of the world's dugongs live here. With its vast seagrass beds, its super-salty waters, its link with the earliest known European landing on the Australian continent and the majesty of its Zuytdorp Cliffs, Shark Bay is one of the world's outstanding coastal regions.

Location

The Shark Bay World Heritage Area is on the extreme western tip of the West Australian coast, some 600 kilometres (370 miles) north of Perth.

The area comprises 2 197 300 hectares (5 429 748 acres) which include the entire 13 000 square kilometres (5000 square miles) of Shark Bay as well as a substantial land component.

The area is bounded to the north by the town of Carnarvon and extends over 200 kilometres (120 miles) to the south to include Bernier, Dorre and Dirk Hartog Islands. The seaward boundary is three nautical miles off the West Australian coast and the landward boundary varies between 70 and 100 kilometres (45 and 60 miles) inland, adjacent to the North West Coastal Highway. Excluded from the World Heritage Area are the township of Denham, situated in the centre, and the land around Useless Loop.

Shark Bay
Western Australia
Vincent Serventy

Many years ago, I camped with my family in the shelter of trees on the shore of Shark Bay's Hamelin Pool. Our daughter paddled in the warm waters while I filmed her against a background of strange, dome-shaped rocks outlined against the rising sun. Over breakfast I remarked, "If I ever make a programme on how life began, I'll start here. This place has a timeless look".

Years later, research by geologists showed those dome-shaped rocks to be stromatolites made by cyano-bacteria - commonly called blue-green algae- which, some three-and-a-half billion years ago, were the first life forms to appear on the young planet Earth. Using the energy in sunlight and the raw materials in the air, these primitive bacteria were able to create oxygen, so taking the first steps on the long path of evolution. Their reign lasted longer than that of any other life form. It took a billion years for the more complicated algae to evolve, followed by animals that grazed on algae and bacteria.

The stromatolites, odd, rock-like masses 'growing' in the shallow waters of Hamelin Pool, were made by countless generations of cyano-bacteria in a manner analogous to the building of a coral reef. The stromatolites were formed from trapped and bound sediments that were shaped by the ebb and flow of the surrounding waters and eventually mineralised. Hamelin Pool, at the head of Shark Bay, is sheltered from tidal flushing by a sand bar and masses of seagrass and is subject to intense evaporation. This makes it too salty for most marine life, and so it is one of the few places on Earth where stromatolite-forming cyano-bacteria survive.

In the words of the World Heritage nomination, this is 'one of the longest continuing biological lineages known. Hamelin Pool remains the most significant known occurrence of shallow marine and intertidal microbial ecosystems living on the earth today . . .'

Ice Ages over the past two million years brought worldwide sea levels down by as much as 150 metres (490 feet) and formed huge dunes along the shore here. There are also dune hollows, known as birridas, that are large and almost perfectly circular. Some of them have filled with sea water and become lakes. Among the area's distinctive landforms are beaches composed of myriads of tiny cockle shells.

Aboriginal people have occupied the Shark Bay area since the time of the last Ice Age. The coastline was then about 40 kilometres (25 miles) further west and Aborigines are known to have occupied the present seabed area until it began to be submerged beneath the advancing sea, about 15 000 years ago. A number of Aboriginal middens have been found, concentrated around Dirk Hartog Island and Peron Peninsula, and these show that the sea and the coast provided an abundance of food, including dugongs, turtles and molluscs.

A colourful early visitor to these shores was William Dampier, an Englishman, whose account of his visit to the coast near Broome aboard the Cygnet in 1688 earned him considerable fame. A decade later he was given command of the Roebuck and returned to explore this little-known south land.

In 1699 he landed at Shark Bay, naming the place in recognition of its abundant sharks. Dutch and English navigators were unimpressed by the barren coastline, with its poor soil, lack of gold and silver, and natives who showed little promise as slaves. Dampier condemned both the land and its inhabitants.

Features with French names are common on the West Australian coast and particularly so at Shark Bay. They are the legacy of early French explorer-scientists who were fascinated by the region's natural history. Zoologists who came in 1801 and in 1803 took away more than 100 000 specimens.

After the early attention of scientists waned, little interest was shown in the Shark Bay area owing to its poor soils, low rainfall and lack of surface water. In 1850, pearls brought the first settlers to Freshwater Camp, which eventually became the township of Denham. The Bay waters, exposed at low tide, were scoured by pearl fishers. Useless Inlet, Denham Sound and the eastern shores of Peron Peninsula were favoured pearling grounds, but over harvesting and the discovery of better grounds further north caused the local industry to decline. There was a modest resurgence in the early 1900s up to the depression of the 1930s, and since the 1980s increased tourism has stirred pearling in the area again.

Arriving with the first pearlers were guano miners, who came in search of fertiliser for the farmlands further south. The first pastoralists arrived in the 1870s, to be followed by fishermen. A fish cannery was built at Monkey Mia in 1912 and, today, the fishing trade also harvests scallops, prawns, crabs, spiny lobsters and edible oysters.

What turned the ugly duckling of Shark Bay into a swan? Mainly a recognition of the importance of the stromatolites, together with the world's largest expanse of seagrass meadows, covering more than 4000 square kilometres (1544 square miles), and the area's extraordinarily diverse assemblage of native animals.

Bernier and Dorre Islands hold species that have become extinct on the mainland owing to the effects of agriculture and the ravages of introduced feral competitors, like the rabbit, and predators, such as the fox and the feral cat.

These islands, separated from the mainland 7000 years ago by rising sea levels, offer the best known sites for the study of marsupial evolution in progress, because scientists have a fairly accurate knowledge of when particular groups of animals were isolated from each other. The rufous hare-wallaby has different forms on each of these two islands, and a third form is found on the mainland.

The boodie, another marsupial, was once as widespread as the rabbit is today. Boodies were burrowers, like rabbits, and lived in the same warrens, but the mainland population was eliminated by foxes and feral cats. The species was saved only by the sea 'moats' surrounding Bernier, Dorre and Barrow Islands.

Using islands as safe havens for endangered species has become a common practice. Plans are now being made to return some of the 5000 boodies living on these islands to the mainland.

Reminders of grim times for the Aboriginal people are also found on these islands, where, in the early years of this century, 'lock hospitals' were maintained as places of internment for those suffering from venereal disease or leprosy.

It was the region's scientific values that led to the protection of an area at Shark Bay comprising 755 000 hectares (1 865 680 acres) of land and sea in one of West Australia's largest regional parks. However, it is impossible to overlook Shark Bay's popular attractions, especially the contribution of successive generations of friendly dolphins at Monkey Mia, which, since the 1960s, have been greeting visitors who flock here in their thousands to see them.

Tourism, a major new industry, has breathed new life into the region's economy, with holidaymakers supplementing the resident population by tens of thousands in the peak seasons.

The great influx of tourists has led to concern, initially among conservationists, then among scientists, and later shared by the fishing industry and the general community, that this prosperity should not endanger the 'resource' on which it is founded and become as transient as the pearl fishery proved to be a century ago.

Commercial whaling began in the region in the early 1900s, but, as with many of these operations around the world, the lack of effective controls led to such a slaughter that whales became scarce and hunting them barely profitable. The whalers here hunted the humpback, a baleen whale that is a giant cousin of the dolphin. Humpbacks swim north to breed in the warmer northwest waters before returning to their near-Antarctic feeding grounds. They were once abundant off the West Australian coast.

Whale numbers have risen to more than 4000 and whale experts estimate they could reach between 10 000 and 15 000 in the next decade. Rules have been formulated to prevent any harm to this novel resource.

The sharks are a more frightening aspect of life in the sea. Tiger sharks 4 metres (13 feet) long and weighing one and a half tonnes are reasonably common, although shark fin hunting could endanger this and other species.

Commercial fishing is important here, employing hundreds of people and earning revenue of tens of millions of dollars a year. The industry is very keen on conservation of the marine environment, aware that intrusions or pollution could put its resource at risk.

The two prevalent turtles of the region are the green and the loggerhead; the latter is the more endangered and its nesting sites at Shark Bay are important to its survival.

There is marine life in abundance to enthrall the visitor to Shark Bay, with eighty kinds of hard coral found at more than thirty locations. The huge area of shallow water has encouraged interest in aquaculture. Cultured pearls, edible oysters and even giant clams, which are of increasing importance as a food resource, are all being farmed.

The birds of the Shark Bay region are as fascinating as the mammals. There are 230 species known, including the brilliant regent parrot and the blue wren. Ospreys hunt along shallow reefs, sea eagles over the sea, and wedgetails on land.

In the hot months, great numbers of waders that breed in the northern hemisphere pass through the region, travelling to or from their breeding grounds. These birds have a passion for daylight and they migrate to where sunlight ensures abundant food.

Birdwatchers are attracted to Shark Bay to see birds common in the south-west of Western Australia together with species that flourish in the arid country.

Many visitors overlook the region's offering of native plants. Shark Bay lies at the northern margin of West Australia's South West Botanical Province, a part of the world that, with the exception of South Africa, is without equal in the splendour and variety of its native flora. Some of that splendour, including the blue-flowered *Dampiera*, named in honour of William Dampier, is found here.

The sandalwood trade has a long history in the Shark Bay region. Harvesting began in the 1880s, when the country was opened up to sheep grazing. Local sandalwood exporters have now offered to replace all trees taken with seedlings and to protect the young plants from grazing sheep and rabbits. The old trade may be reborn on station properties and provide a new source of income for graziers.

RIGHT These strangely shaped masses in the shallow waters of Hamelin Pool at Shark Bay are not rocks but stromatolites, one of the most ancient forms of life on Earth. These mounds were built up by a primitive type of bacteria that reached its evolutionary peak more than two billion years ago. These living fossils offer the visitor a glimpse of the beginnings of life on our planet.

NEXT PAGE The whale shark is the world's largest fish. These monsters of the sea can grow up to 15 metres (48 feet) in length and up to 45 tonnes in weight. Whale sharks can be seen cruising off Shark Bay, feeding on plankton. Their massive bulk and 40 rows of teeth belie their harmless nature.

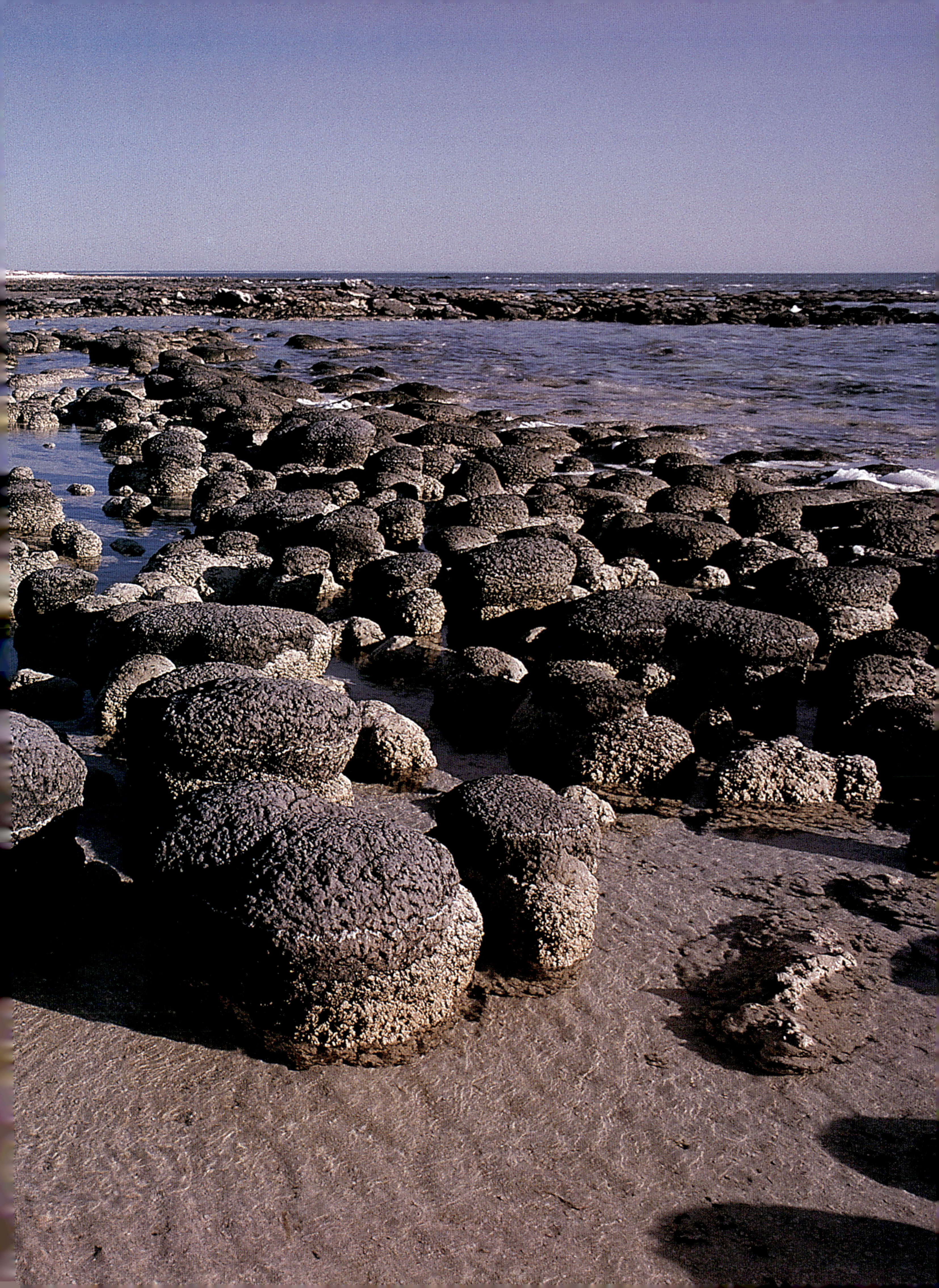

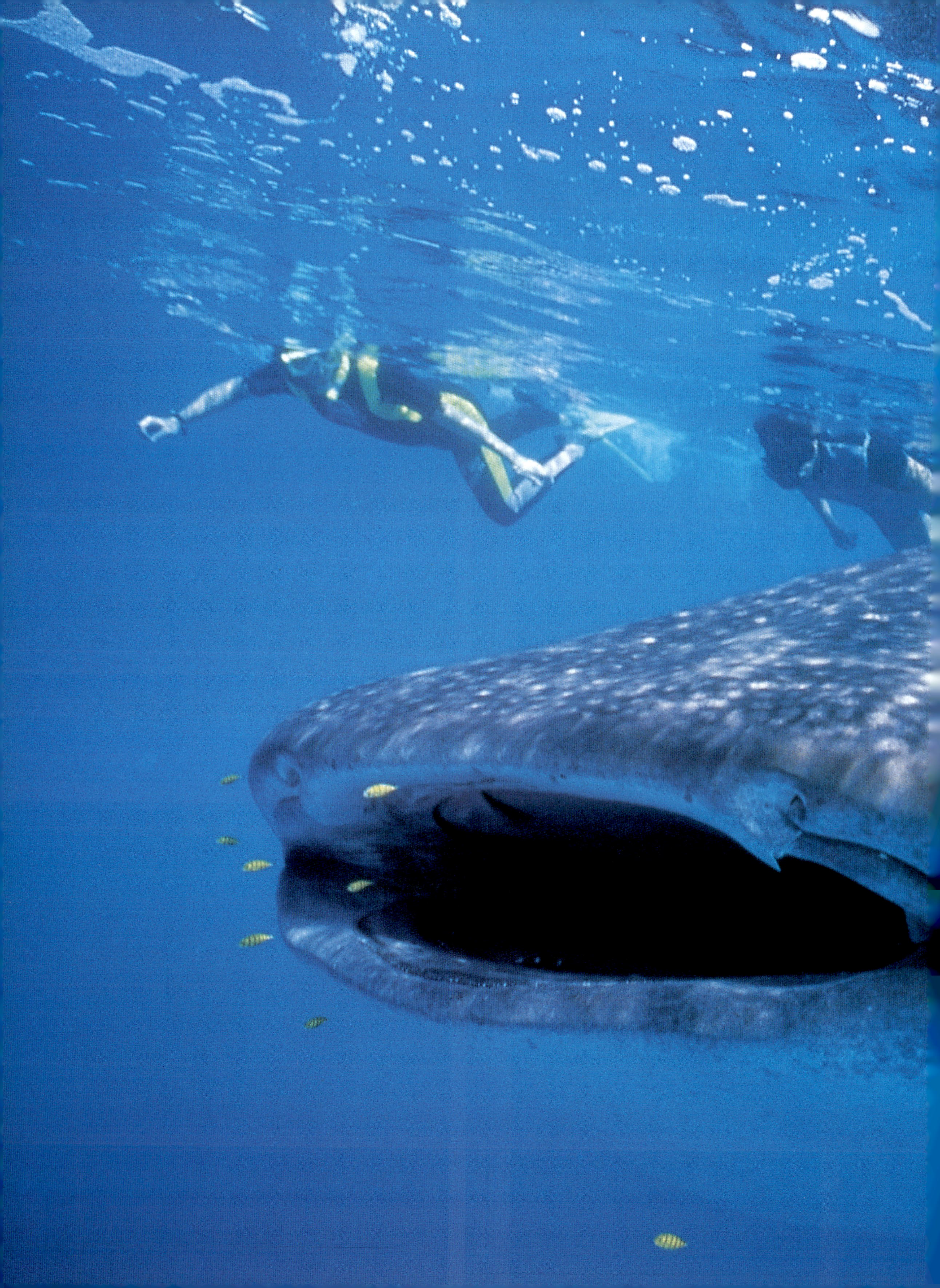

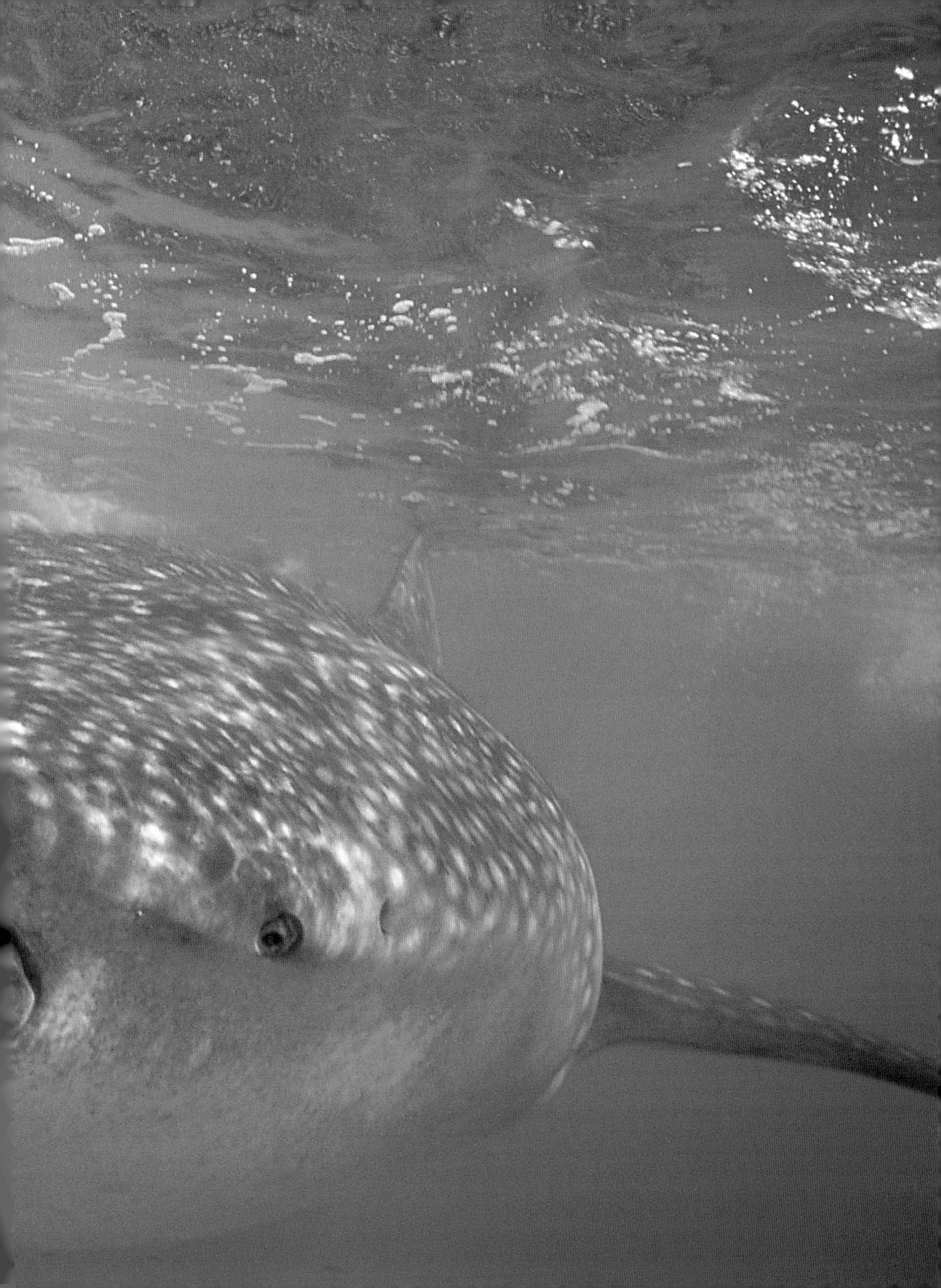

ABOVE Aerial view of the Little Lagoon salt-water wetlands system.

RIGHT Aerial view of Dirk Hartog Island.

BELOW The Dutch navigator Dirk Hartog, the first European known to have landed on Australian soil, left an inscribed pewter plate at Inscription Point on the island now known as Dirk Hartog Island in 1616. His countryman Willem De Vlamingh found the plate in 1697, replaced it with an inscribed plate of his own (pictured), and returned with Hartog's plate to Holland. De Vlamingh's plate is exhibited at the Fremantle Maritime Museum.

Physical Features

Shark Bay is a place of natural beauties both subtle and spectacular. The bay comprises a series of north-south facing peninsulas and islands, threaded between bays, inlets and the Indian Ocean.

For some 130 kilometres (80 miles), the coastline is dominated by the magnificent Zuytdorp Cliffs, which rise 200 metres (650 feet) above the ocean and are amongst the tallest cliffs on the Australian coast. Years of relentless wave action have sculpted the cliffs into an impressive architecture of undercut platforms, blow holes, spouts and sea caves.

The Shark Bay World Heritage Area contains a number of distinctive landscapes, each of which presents an array of natural marvels. The Gascoyne-Wooramel province comprises the low-lying eastern coast of the bay, backed by a limestone escarpment, while the Peron province includes the Nanga and Peron Peninsulas and the Faure Island sill, consisting of undulating sandy plains pocked with gypsum pans that end in narrow, sandy beaches facing the sea. In contrast, the Edel Province is a landscape of elongated dunes cemented to loose limestone, and includes the Edel Peninsula and adjacent islands.

The climate of the area is generally mild to warm. Summer temperatures may reach as high as 35°Celsius (95°Fahrenheit), with winter temperatures averaging between 10° and 20°Celsius (50° and 68°Fahrenheit). The waters of the bay are usually warm but can drop to 17°Celsius (63°Fahrenheit) in the inner bay in winter. The annual rainfall is low, averaging only 200 to 400 millimetres (8 to 16 inches). With an average annual evaporation rate of 2000 to 3000 millimetres (79 to 118 inches), there is little surface water in the region, although saline groundwater is found here. In addition, two rivers drain into the bay, and there are a number of freshwater springs.

The Shark Bay region is an area of major zoological importance, mainly because its oceanic and land ecosystems have been isolated for long periods of time. The marine life ranges from the largest ocean dwellers down to the tiniest micro-organisms. It is also a region of exceptional ecological diversity, which is due in part to the region's transitional location between the temperate and tropical zones.

Special Features

The Shark Bay World Heritage Area is notable for the bay's abundance of primitive, bottom-dwelling invertebrate life forms. Invisible to the naked eye, these microbial organisms thrive on the seagrass beds and carbonate sand flats of the shallows, their great profusion and diversity making them the world's outstanding example of this type of ecosystem. At Hamelin Pool, tiny organisms started growing when the pool formed some 4000 million years ago. Over time, they trapped and held detrital sediment and formed partly organic and partly sedimentary 'microbial mats'. These mats and stromatolites mineralised to form living fossil records of great importance to world science.

The Shark Bay World Heritage Area contains some 4000 square kilometres (1540 square miles) of seagrass meadows, the largest and most species-rich seagrass assemblage in the world. These meadows support such a variety and richness of marine life that they qualify as a site of international importance.

An unusual environmental feature of the park is the wide range of salinity (salt) levels in its waters. These range from a normal oceanic level of 35 to 40 parts per thousand in the northern and western parts of the bay to an astounding 'hypersaline' level of 456 to 470 parts per thousand in Hamelin Pool and Lharidon Bight. The extreme salinity is caused by sand banks and seagrass beds, which prevent the normal tidal flushing of the bay, combined with low rainfall and a high rate of evaporation. The salinity gradient is so marked that it has created three separate biotic zones, which have a profound influence on the distribution of marine life throughout the bay.

RIGHT Aerial view of the mainland coast. Rising sea levels after the last Ice Age, some 10 000 years ago, created the coastline we see today, with its gulfs and shallow bays supporting a rich and diverse marine life.

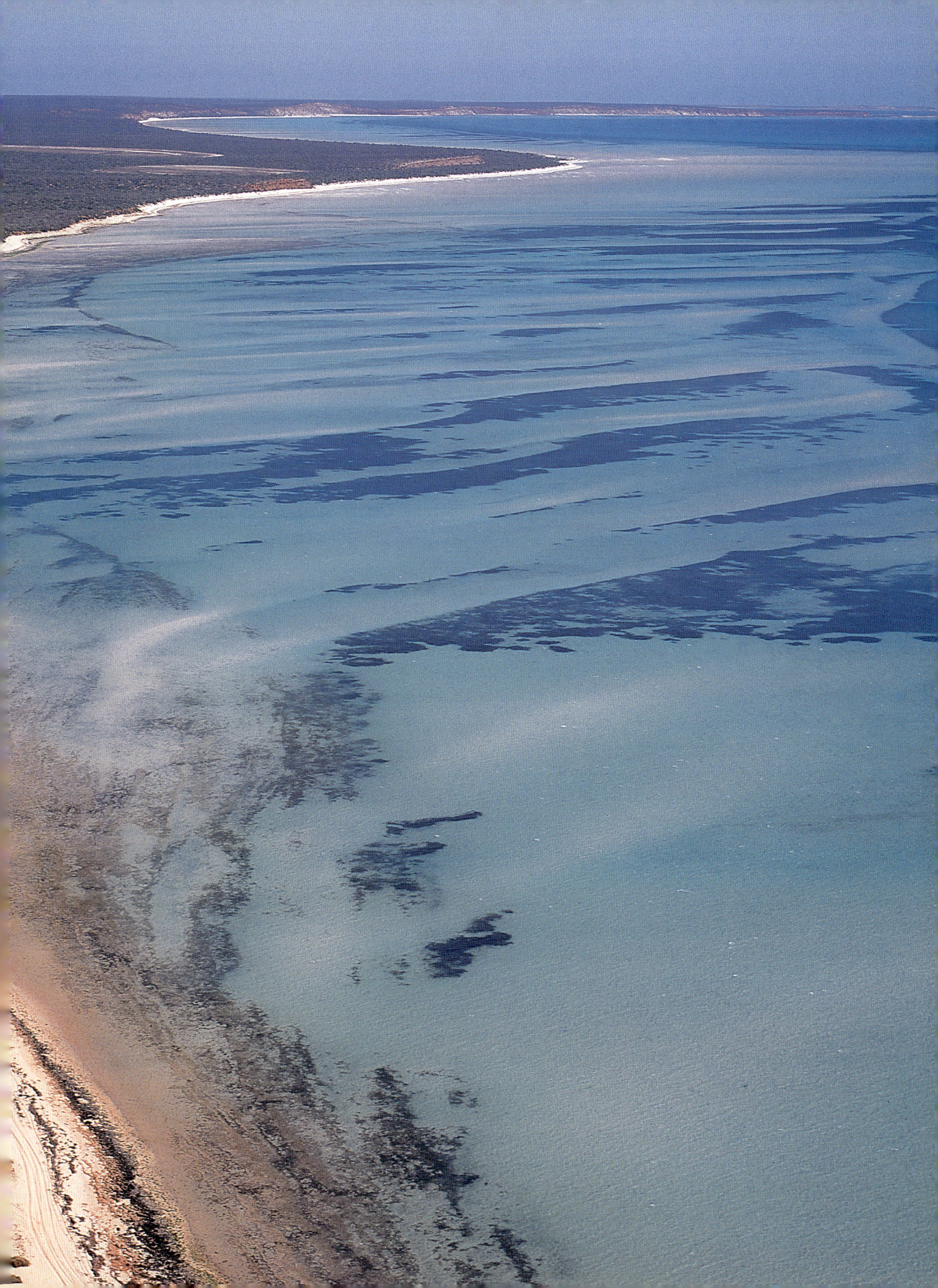

TOP Cape Lesueur, in the Francois Peron National Park. The Peron Peninsula was formerly a sheep station. The 40 000 hectare (99 000 acre) national park is named after the French naturalist who sailed with the Geographe on its scientific expeditions of 1801 and 1803.

LEFT The blue whaler shark, a species first noted in this area by William Dampier during his exploration of this coast in 1699. Also known as the great blue shark, it grows up to three metres (10 feet) long and is known to swim into estuaries and rivers.

ABOVE Covering some 1030 square kilometres (400 square miles), the Wooramel seagrass bank is the largest known structure of its kind in the world. The bank is comprised of carbonate sediment bound by seagrass and is a vital food for the endangered dugong.

INSET Snowy volute seal snail an inhabitant of the seagrass meadows.

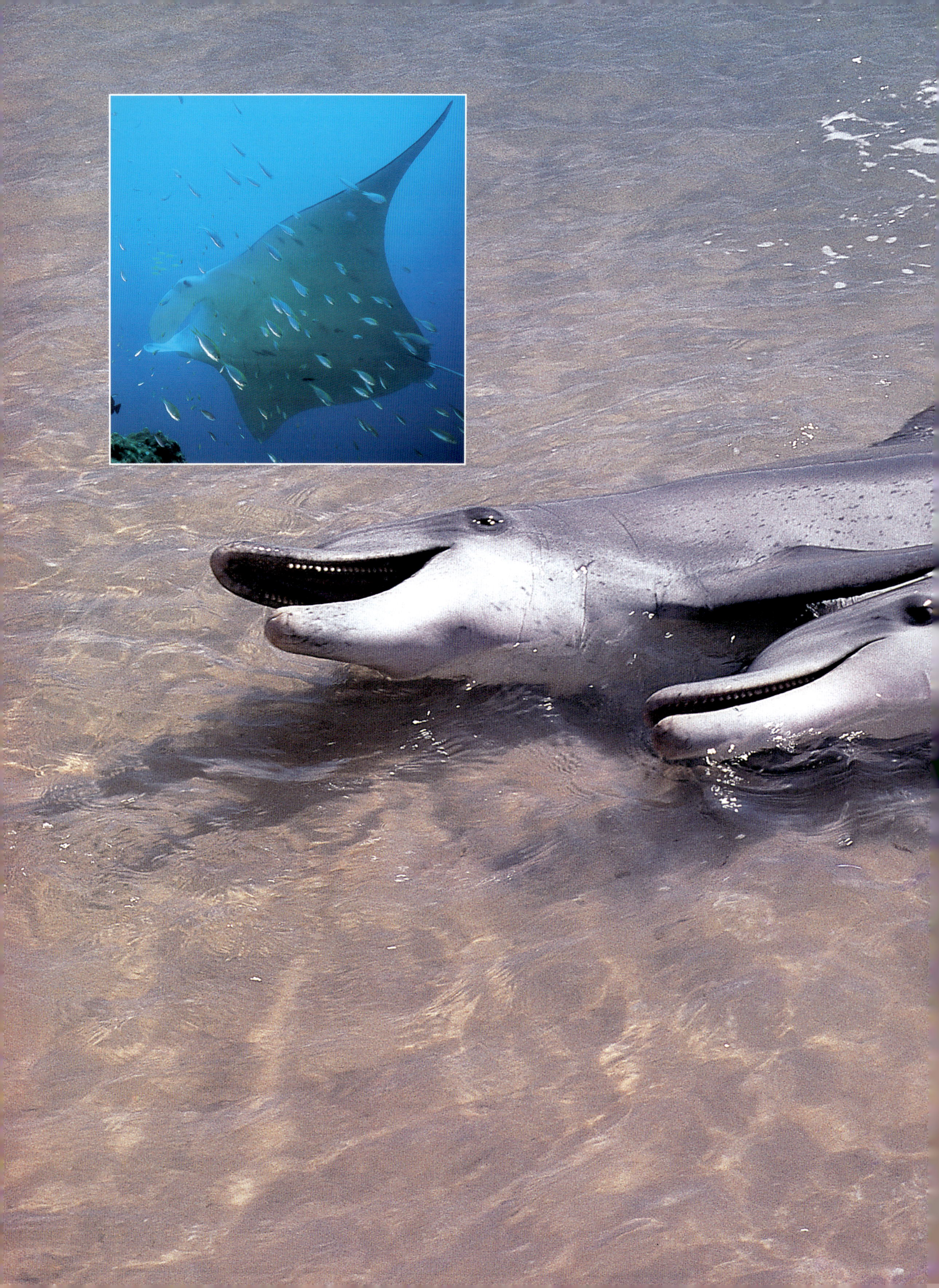

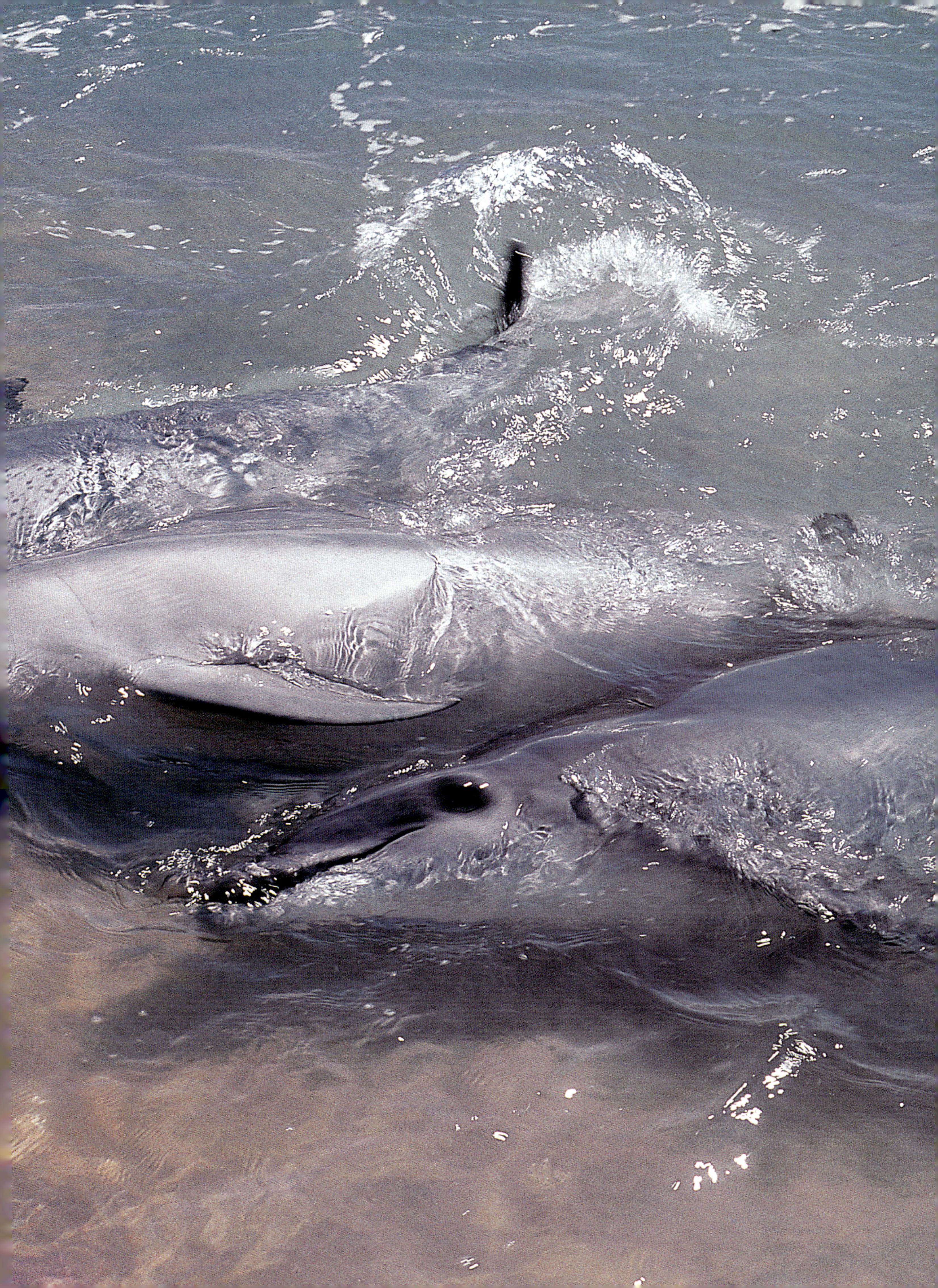

TOP A pair of white-breasted sea eagles nesting along the Zuytdorp coastal cliffs overlooking their hunting domain of the sea.

Flora

Shark Bay straddles the boundary between two great native plant regions of Australia known as the South-west and the Eremaean Botanical Provinces, giving the area an extraordinarily diverse plant life. Over 620 plant species have been recorded, with 145 at the northern limit of their range, 39 at their southern limit, and 25 considered rare or threatened at the national level. The influence of the South-west Botanical Province can be seen in the area's woodlands, which are rich in eucalypt species. These woodlands are characterised by diverse, shrubby understories and heathlands poor in grasses. The Eremaean Province, in contrast, is rich in wattle shrubs and dominated by grasses, especially prickly hummock grasses of the Triodia and Plectrachne genera, commonly known as spinifex.

The Shark Bay area also contains mangroves, which occur in small, isolated pockets in the southern and western areas of the bay, becoming more abundant towards Carnarvon. The southernmost examples, a sizeable stand of white mangrove, are found on the Peron Peninsula.

As well as eucalypts, acacias and grasses, the observant visitor may find plants of rare beauty, such as the aromatic Shark Bay rose and West Australia's floral emblem, the vibrant kangaroo paw.

ABOVE The rare and threatened Shark Bay Mouse is one of the smaller native marsupials on Bernier Island.

RIGHT Sceptre banksia.

PREVIOUS PAGE Bottlenose dolphins playing in a shoal. There are 2700 bottlenose dolphins in Shark Bay, some of which have been given special names, often suggested by the shape of their fins. Regulations now strictly govern how people can interact with these friendly dolphins, to prevent them from being 'loved to death'. Only local fish are fed to them, and 'meetings' are restricted to a supervised area.

PREVIOUS PAGE INSET Manta rays are prevalent throughout the bay, growing up to 6 metres (20 feet) in width. Unlike other rays, the manta (or devil) ray does not have a poisonous tail spine and uses its forward pectoral fins to scoop small fish into its mouth.

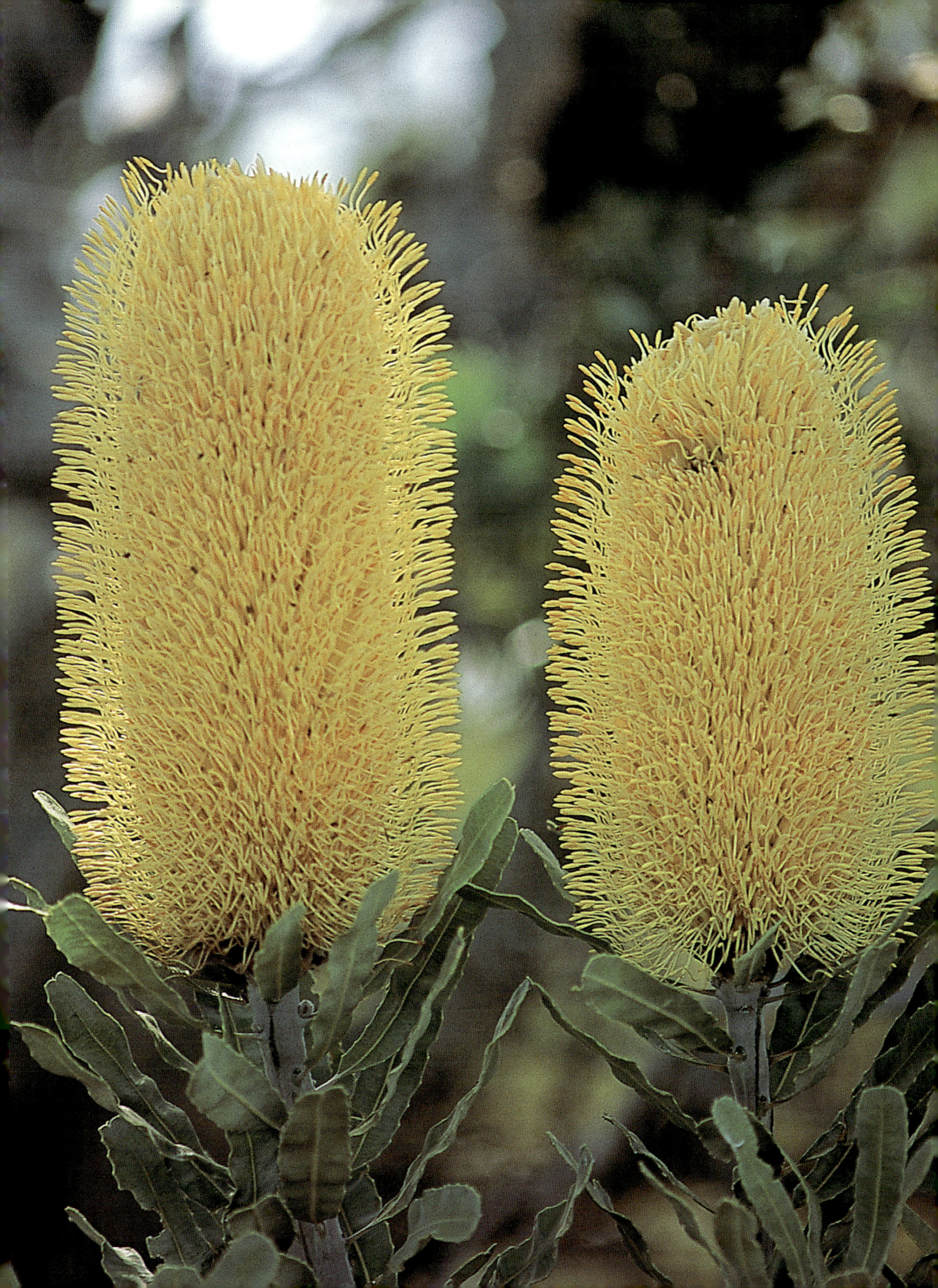

Fauna

Shark Bay's zoological interest lies partly in the fact that it is the habitat of many species at the limit of their geographical range. In addition, Shark Bay contains the only major populations of five of the twenty-six Australian mammal species globally recognised as threatened.

Humpback whales, which numbered some 20 000 in the mid-nineteenth century, were hunted almost to extinction. By 1962 there were only 500 to 800 individuals living off the West Australian coast and the species was placed on the IUCN - The World Conservation Union list of endangered species. Today, humpbacks number between 2000 to 3000 and are prominent in Shark Bay, which they use as a staging post on their migratory journeys from Antarctic waters to the tropics and back.

The bay is also home to some 10 000 dugongs, which make up approximately one-eighth of the world's total dugong population. These gentle 'sea cows' find rich grazing in the extensive seagrass beds, as well as a safe place to bear and raise their young. The only known 'lek' mating system among marine mammals can be observed in the dugong herd at South Cove. The word 'lek' (Gaelic for grouse) is used by zoologists to refer to an area in which males of any species maintain courtship territories to attract and mate with females.

A very special feature of the shallow bay is the schools of bottlenose dolphins. A small group of dolphins come in close to shore to interact with people at Monkey Mia. Although relationships between people and dolphins feature in the mythologies of different cultures, actual cases of dolphins choosing to interact with people over a long period are rare. The phenomenon at Monkey Mia has continued since the 1960s and it comes as no surprise that a quarter of all visitors to Shark Bay come especially to participate in this joyful and magical experience.

In all, more than 320 species of fish inhabit the Shark Bay area, including western king prawns, whale sharks and manta rays. Of the total number, 83% are tropical, 11% are warm-temperate, and 6% are cool-temperate species.

As the bay's name suggests, large numbers of sharks are found here, including bay whalers, tiger sharks and hammerheads. In May 1983, killer whales were seen hunting dugongs at Sandy Point.

The bay is also an important nursery ground for crustaceans (such as crabs and prawns) and coelenterates (such as jellyfish and anemones). The plentiful seagrass beds covering over 4000 square kilometres (1540 square miles) of the bay provide a habitat for 100 species of zoophytes - colonies of microscopic animals - as well as for juvenile fish and sea snakes. At least six species of sea snakes inhabit these waters, including the endemic *Aipysurus pooleorum*.

The faunal rarities of Shark Bay are not confined to the ocean. No less than five of the twenty-six species of threatened Australian mammals are found on Bernier and Dorre Islands; these are a species of bettong, the rufous hare-wallaby, the banded hare-wallaby, the Shark Bay mouse and the western barred bandicoot.

The reptile population of Shark Bay is especially diverse, with over 100 species represented, including a variety of geckos, skinks, lizards and monitors. The islands, peninsulas and gulfs provide a refuge for nine relict or endemic species of legless lizards and skinks. Several turtle species, including the endangered green and loggerhead turtles, nest along the beaches of Dirk Hartog Island.

Shark Bay's location astride the boundary between two climatic zones gives it a diverse and interesting birdlife. Over 230 bird species are found here and 11 species of marine birds breed in the area, including ospreys and Caspian terns. Over 35 Asian migratory species also visit the area, four of them to breed in the bay. Species that have their northern limit in the area include the regent parrot and the western yellow robin.

ABOVE Two bottlenose dolphins at Monkey Mia. In the 1960s, at an anchorage here one hot night, a sleepless Alice Watts watched a group of dolphins splashing around her boat. She threw them a fish from the icebox and the bonding of humans and dolphins began. More animals arrived until finally a group of them took fish from the hands of people on the beach. The Monkey Mia saga had begun.

RIGHT The endangered western hare-wallaby will soon be re-introduced to the mainland from Bernier and Dorre Islands.

NEXT PAGE Mother and calf dugongs with a suckerfish by their side. Sometimes called sea cows, these gentle mammals graze on the seagrass meadows of Shark Bay. The mermaid myth is thought to have arisen from an early mariner's glimpse of a dugong. Once hunted for their oil and bones, dugongs are now protected.

NEXT PAGE INSET A 13 metre (40 feet) humpback whale surfacing for air off the coast at Shark Bay spreads out its giant pectoral fins.

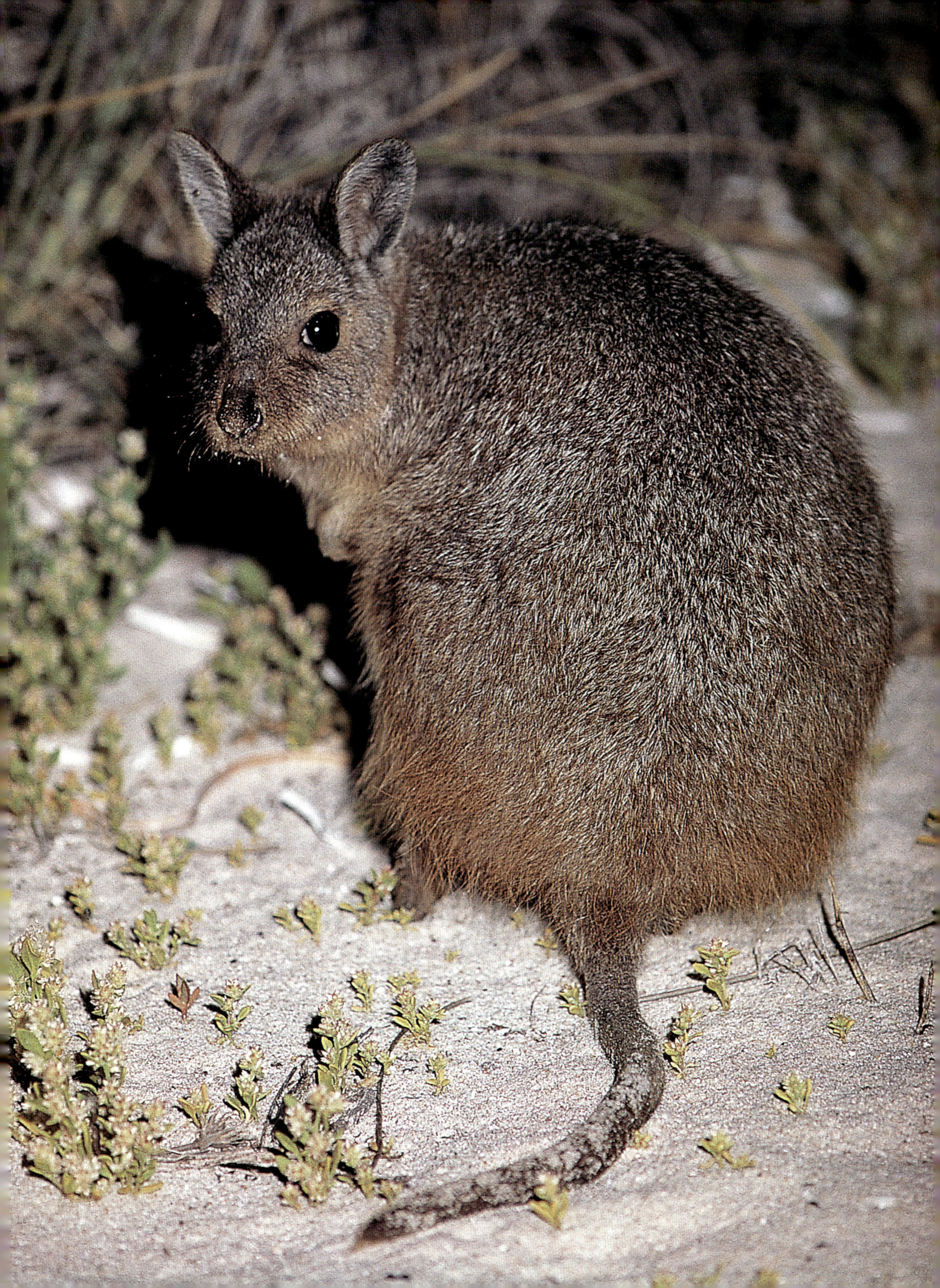

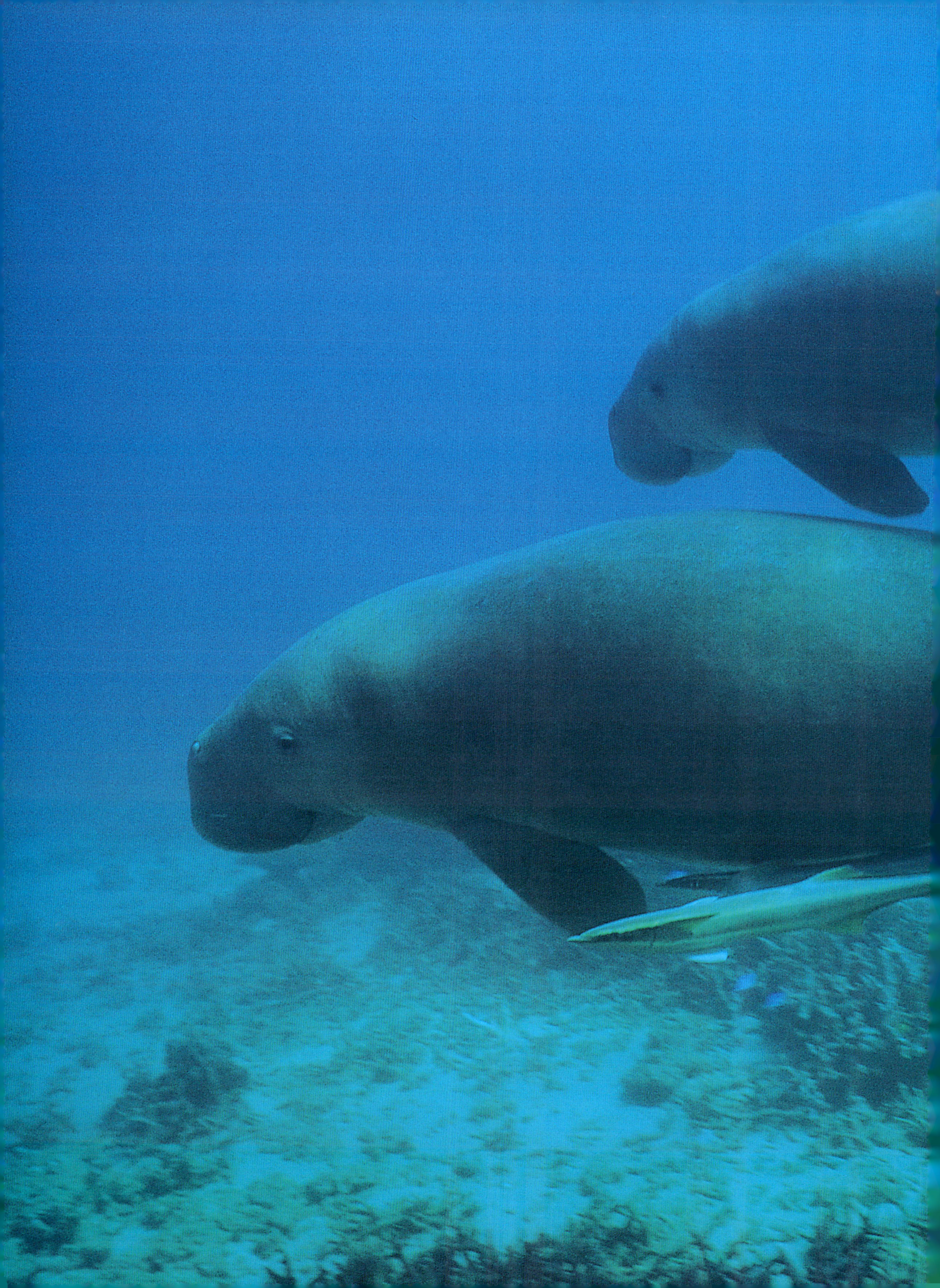

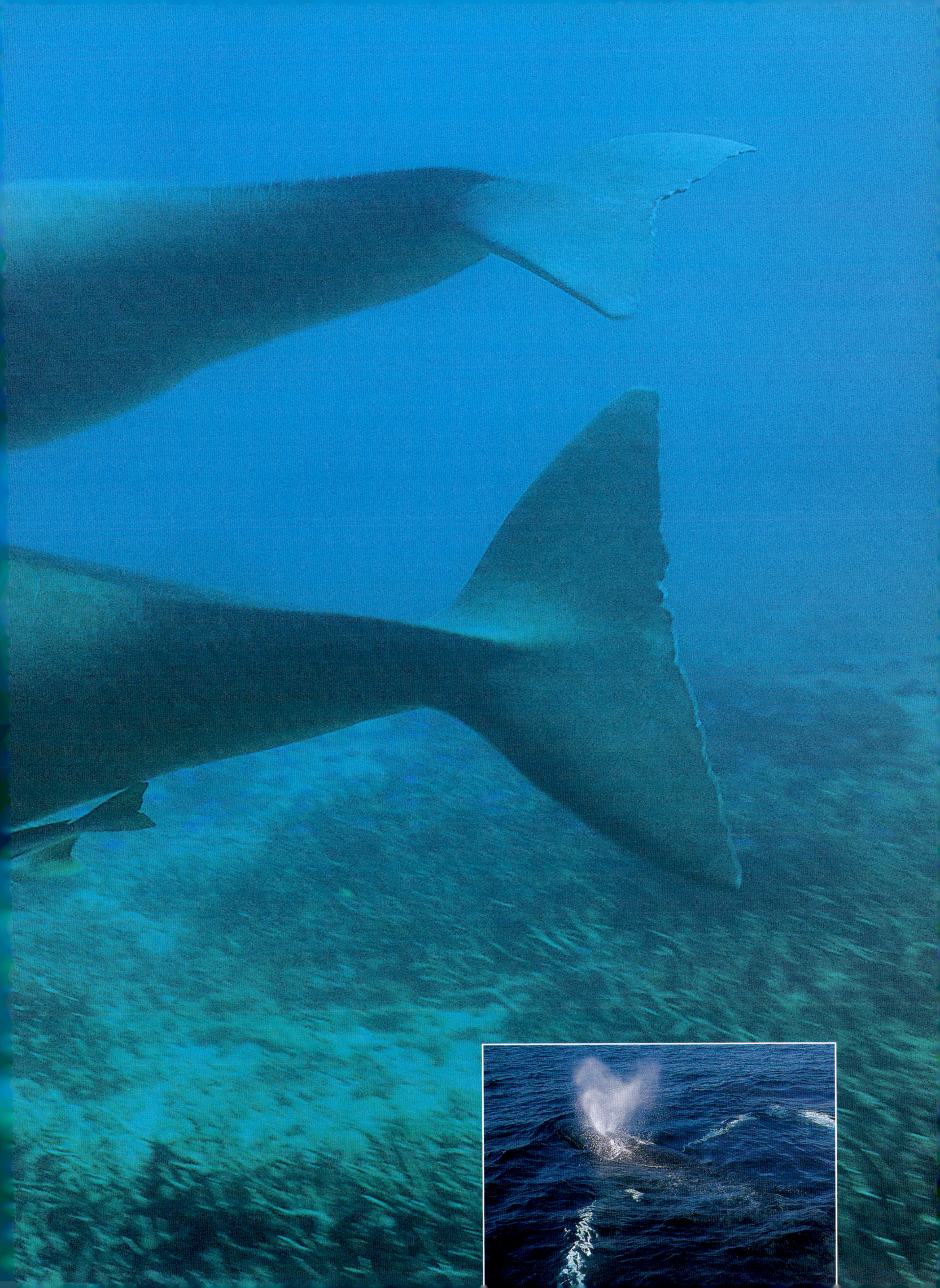

ABOVE From a remnant population on Dirk Hartog Island the western barred bandicoot has been recently re-introduced on the mainland.

RIGHT A honey possum feeds on nectar from native banksia blossoms. This diminutive creature is small enough to fit into the palm of a human hand.

Threats

The township of Denham and the areas around Useless Loop and Useless Inlet are excluded from the Shark Bay World Heritage area but activities in these settled areas could nevertheless affect World Heritage values. Road improvements and tourism have already led to an increase in the local population.

The evaporation salt works at Useless Loop and the gypsum mine at Edel Island may in future prove to have a damaging impact on parts of the bay. The mining of mineral sands either on land or under water could also endanger the park's environmental integrity.

Pressures to enlarge the area's very limited supply of drinking water pose a further threat and might be exacerbated by Shark Bay's World Heritage status, which is stimulating more local development. Suggested solutions to the water supply problem have included desalinisation of local water, using natural gas piped from the northwest shelf as an energy supply. A pipeline carrying fresh water from Lake Argyle, in the Kimberley, to south-western West Australia has also been suggested and, if this comes to pass, Shark Bay could tap into this new supply. Both these measures would disturb the environment to some extent. An increase in fresh water supplies could also act as a spur to local agricultural development and cause problems with herbicides and pesticides leaching into Shark Bay's delicately balanced ecosystems.

Further threats could come from the expansion or intensification of existing mines and fisheries.

Tourism, although essential to improve public appreciation of this World Heritage area, brings its own problems. Recreational boating accounts for more injuries and deaths among dugongs, dolphins and turtles than does poaching. About a dozen dugongs are killed annually for food by the local Aboriginal people but poaching from outside the area is now on the increase. The building of hotels, motels and caravan parks, and the construction of a new road from Denham to Monkey Mia, have increased the pressure on this fragile environment. The semi-tame dolphins have already suffered; in 1989 six adults and a calf were found dead, presumed to have been killed by effluent from a septic tank that has since been removed.

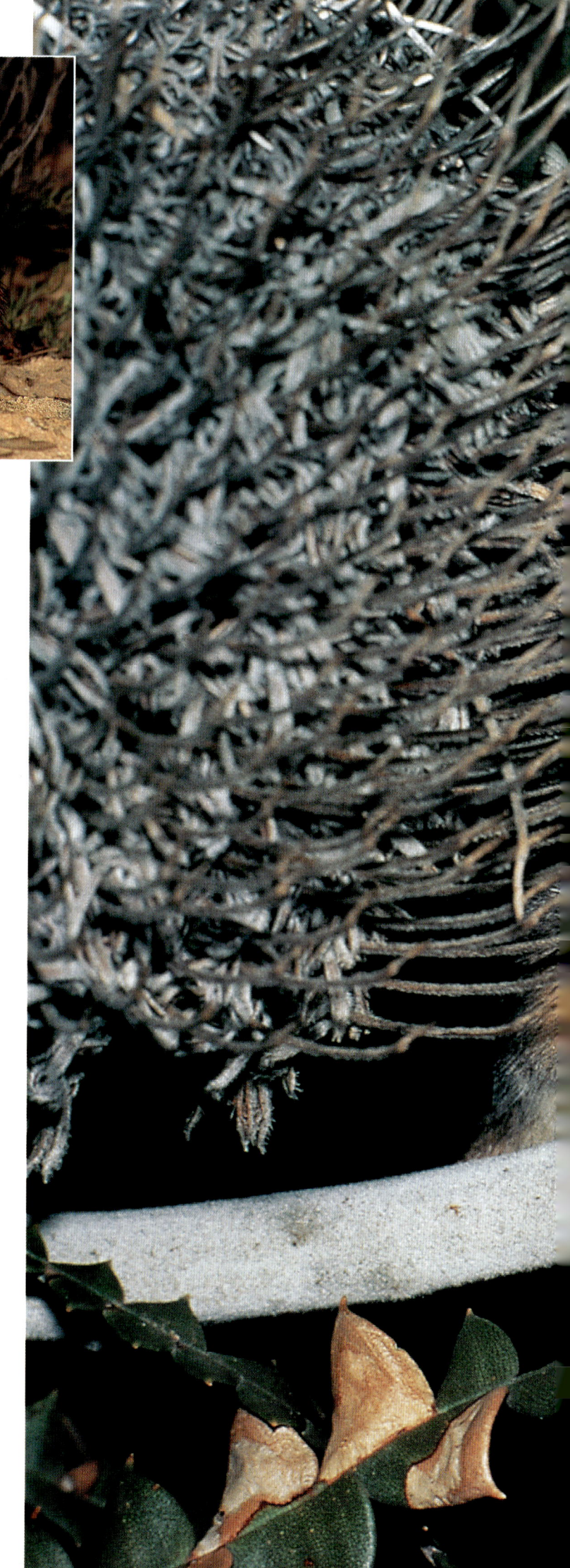

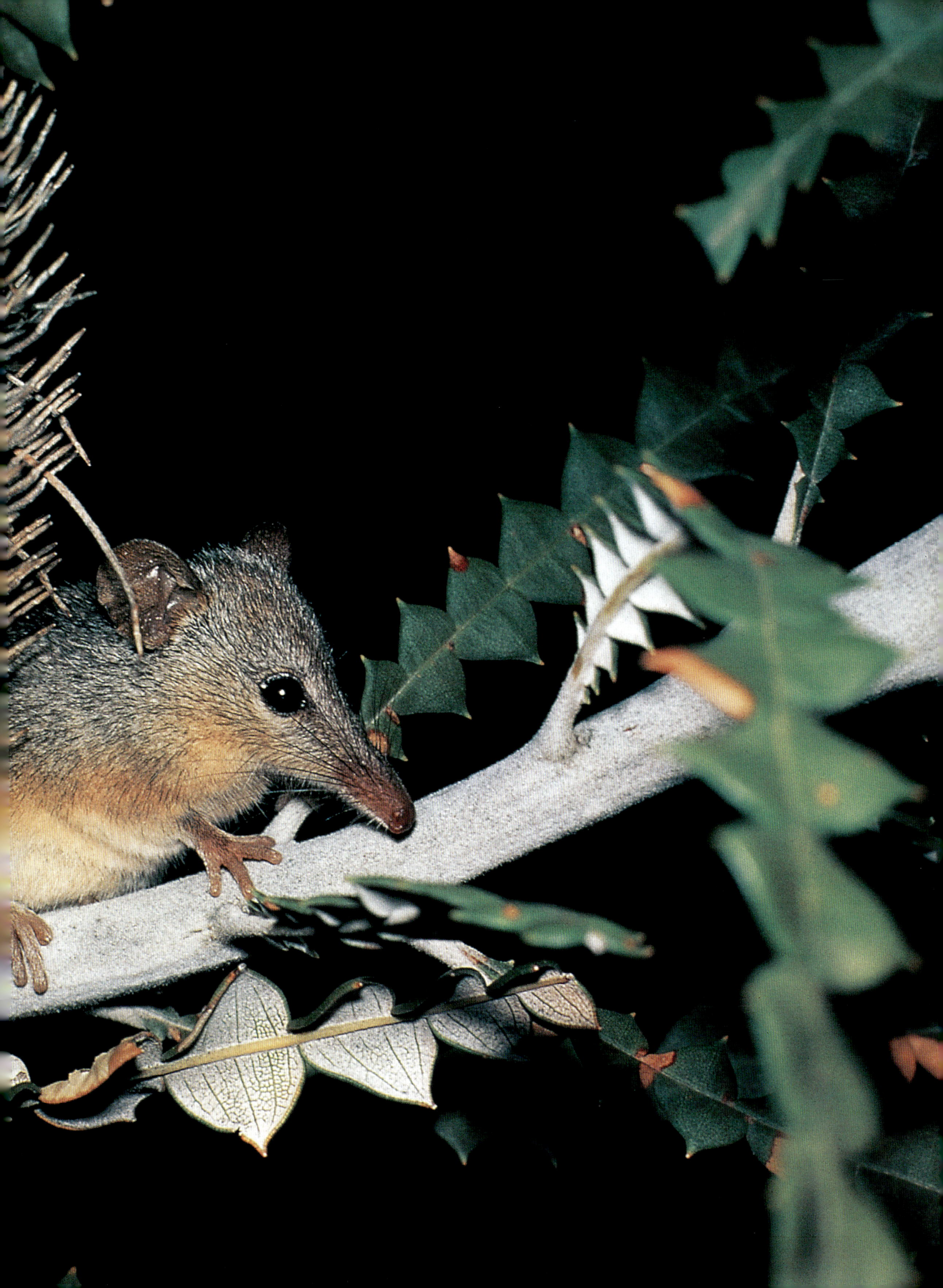

Human Impact

The Shark Bay World Heritage Area has a resident population of 750, of whom 450 live in Denham. The area's arid climate, high summer temperatures, lack of fresh water and lack of transport have generally discouraged settlement. In the 1960s, salt evaporation works were established at Useless Loop and a gypsum mine was founded on Edel Island. These enterprises continue to operate.

Grazing activities, fishing and mining have had some impact on Shark Bay, yet the ecosystems are largely unaltered by human interference.

Oil exploration licences over the area have been issued by the State Government. While these are currently dormant, they pose a possible environmental risk at some time in the future.

Most of the land portion of the Shark Bay World Heritage Area has, over the last decade, been protected as nature reserves or national parks. The remainder is held under pastoral lease and a very small part 700 hectares (1730 acres) is owned as freehold land. The land under pastoral lease has sustained some damage near homesteads and stock watering points, and overgrazing in the past has led to soil erosion. The greatest damage has occurred at Tamala and Peron stations, which were so severely overgrazed that feral pests, such as rabbits and goats, became numerous, along with feral predators, such as cats and foxes. In an effort to minimise further environmental degradation, some former pastoral leases have been bought by the government and incorporated into the protected area.

The pearling, whaling and fishing industries have also had an impact on the marine environment of Shark Bay. Whaling is no longer practised in the region but the fishing industry continues (27 prawn boats and 14 scallop boats, employing 500 local people), using bottom trawling, nets, lines and cray pots. Although the local fishing industry claims to harvest resources at a sustainable level, other people are concerned that trawling is depleting the marine environment, with potentially serious consequences for humpback whales in particular.

Some restrictions have already been placed on commercial fishing in areas where such practices as bottom trawling were seen to have depleted fish stocks below a sustainable level. These so far include limits on boat numbers, regulations specifying minimum mesh sizes and permitted types of fishing gear, closed seasons and protection of nursery areas.

BELOW The Australian thorny devil has the most heavily armed protective spines of any lizard species. The largest thorns are located on its snout and above its eyes.

RIGHT The native Shark Bay Rose.

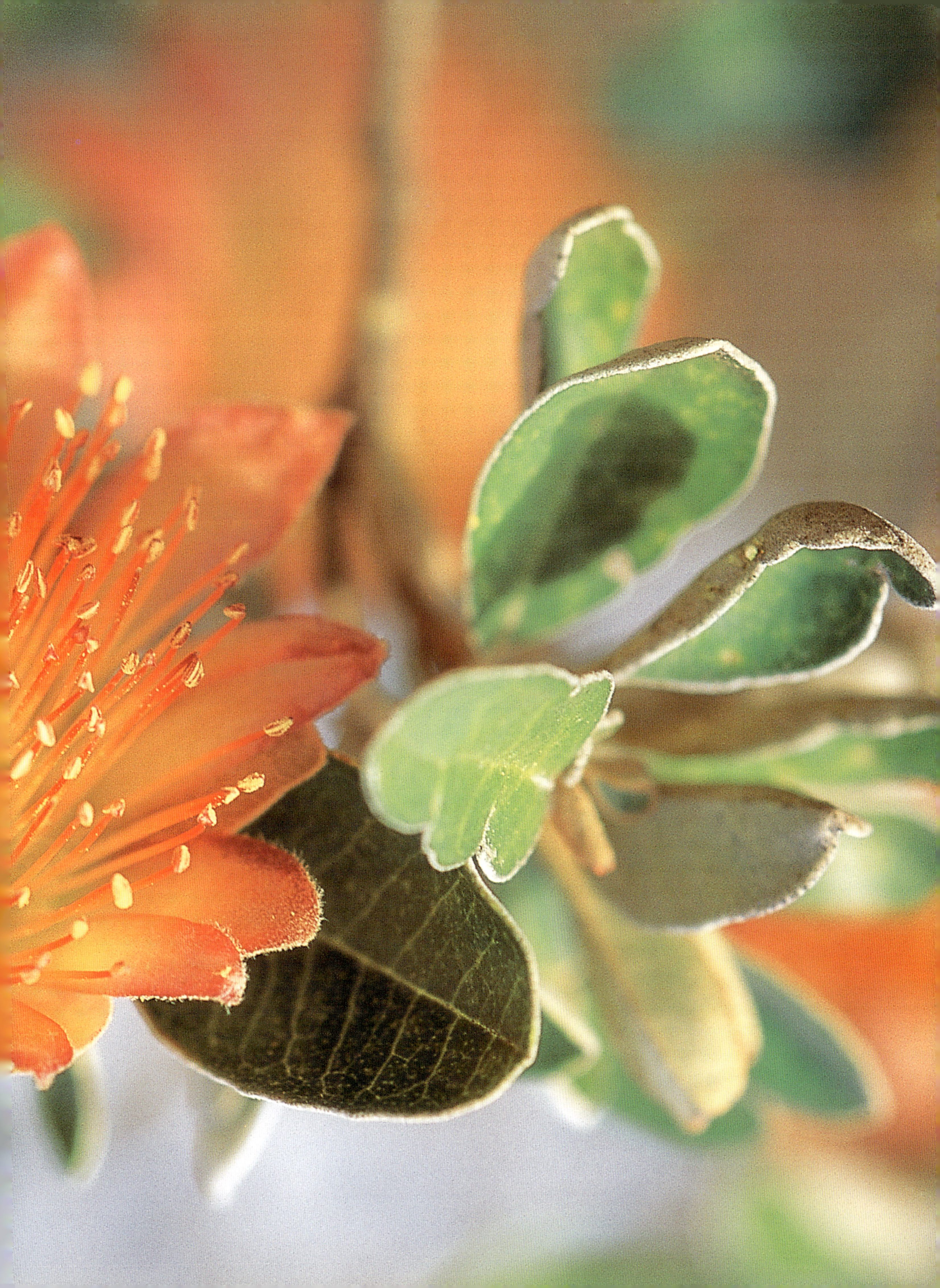

Facilities

Some 160 000 people now visit the Shark Bay World Heritage Area annually and tourism is making an ever-increasing contribution to the regional economy. New facilities are being provided to improve access and accommodation. Developments include a new road from Denham to Monkey Mia, and new hotels, motels and caravan parks. In 1986, a visitor information centre was constructed at Monkey Mia, where each year 100 000 people come to interact with the wild dolphins. The centre plays a valuable role in developing public awareness of the Shark Bay environment and the area's numerous attractions. One of the area's biggest drawcards is recreational fishing in Shark Bay's teeming waters. A range of charter boats and fishing tours cater for sports fishing enthusiasts.

Management

The Shark Bay World Heritage Area is jointly managed by the Commonwealth Government and the government of the State of Western Australia, although much of the day-to-day administration falls to the latter. Most of the work 'on the ground' is carried out by Western Australia's Department of Conservation and Land Management (CALM).

Co-operation between CALM and the Western Australian government's agriculture and fisheries agencies has produced an agreement that provides for environmental protection of the Shark Bay region while allowing appropriate local economic development to take place. Regulation of commercial fishing, the buying back of pastoral leases and a feral animal control programme are some of the state government's initiatives to ensure that Shark Bay's World Heritage values are preserved.

Effective management is made difficult by the ever-present constraints on budgets and staffing. For example, two fisheries officers patrol the waters of the bay, which severely limits the extent to which poaching and illegal fishing practices can be policed.

RIGHT A bay on the south of Peron Peninsula with Eagle Bluff in the distant background.

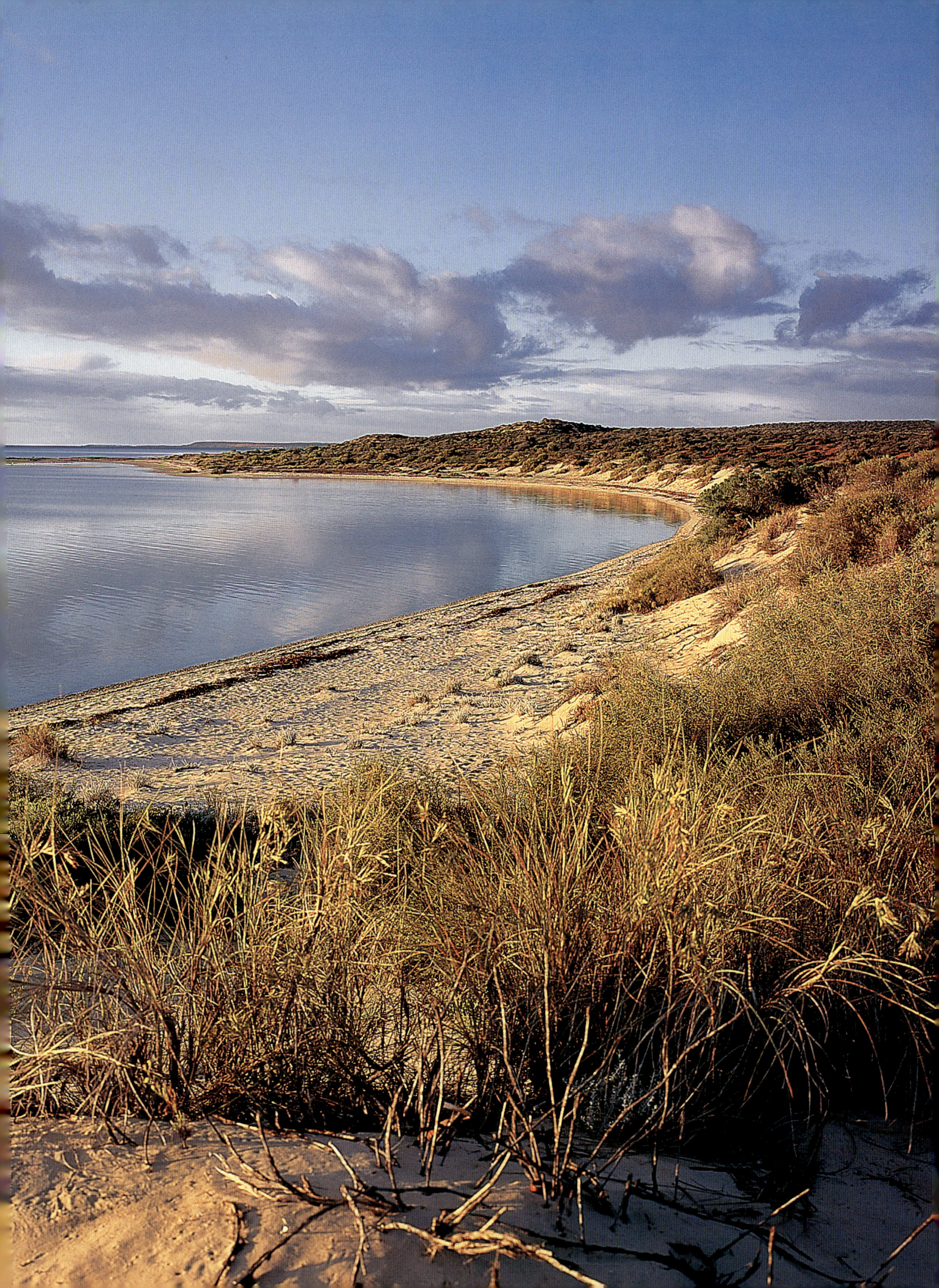

Fraser Island

Fraser Island is the world's largest sand island, yet it is covered with cool, dark rainforests, crystal lakes, robust eucalypt forests, extensive heathlands and thriving mangrove swamps. The island's vast white-sand beaches are washed by the deep, azure waters of the Pacific Ocean. The island forms part of the Great Sandy Region of Queensland, a distinctive and beautiful part of Australia's east coast.

The Great Sandy Region is the end point of a great natural system for the transport of coastal sand by wind, water and tidal currents. This system runs northwards along the south-east coast of Australia and has delivered to Fraser Island more sand than can be found in the entire Sahara. The island displays a greater variety and development of sand dune systems and features than can be seen in any other single sandmass in the world, making it a place of great scientific interest. Fraser Island is also situated at the overlap of two biogeographical zones, giving the island a rich intermingling of temperate and tropical plants and animals.

Location

Located on the south-east coast of Queensland, Fraser Island lies between the latitudes 24°35' to 26°23' South, and longitudes 152°30' to 153°30' East, just off the coast opposite the towns of Maryborough, Hervey Bay and Bundaberg.

The World Heritage Area is approximately 8600 square kilometres (3320 square miles) in area and is 122 kilometres (76 miles) long, with a width varying from 5 to 15 kilometres (three to five miles). It excludes the marine environments of Hervey Bay and the sea coast.

PREVIOUS PAGE The sand masses of Fraser Island are repeatedly renewed by transgressive dunes, or sand blows, which overwhelm the vegetation cover. Sand blows are natural features created by powerful landforming processes. By uncovering buried layers, they reveal the history of the landscape. The sand comes from worn granites, sandstones and metamorphic rocks in river catchments to the south, and from the seafloor. It is transported by marine currents to offshore deposits or trapped on beaches and then blown inland to form a series of overlapping parabolic sand dunes.

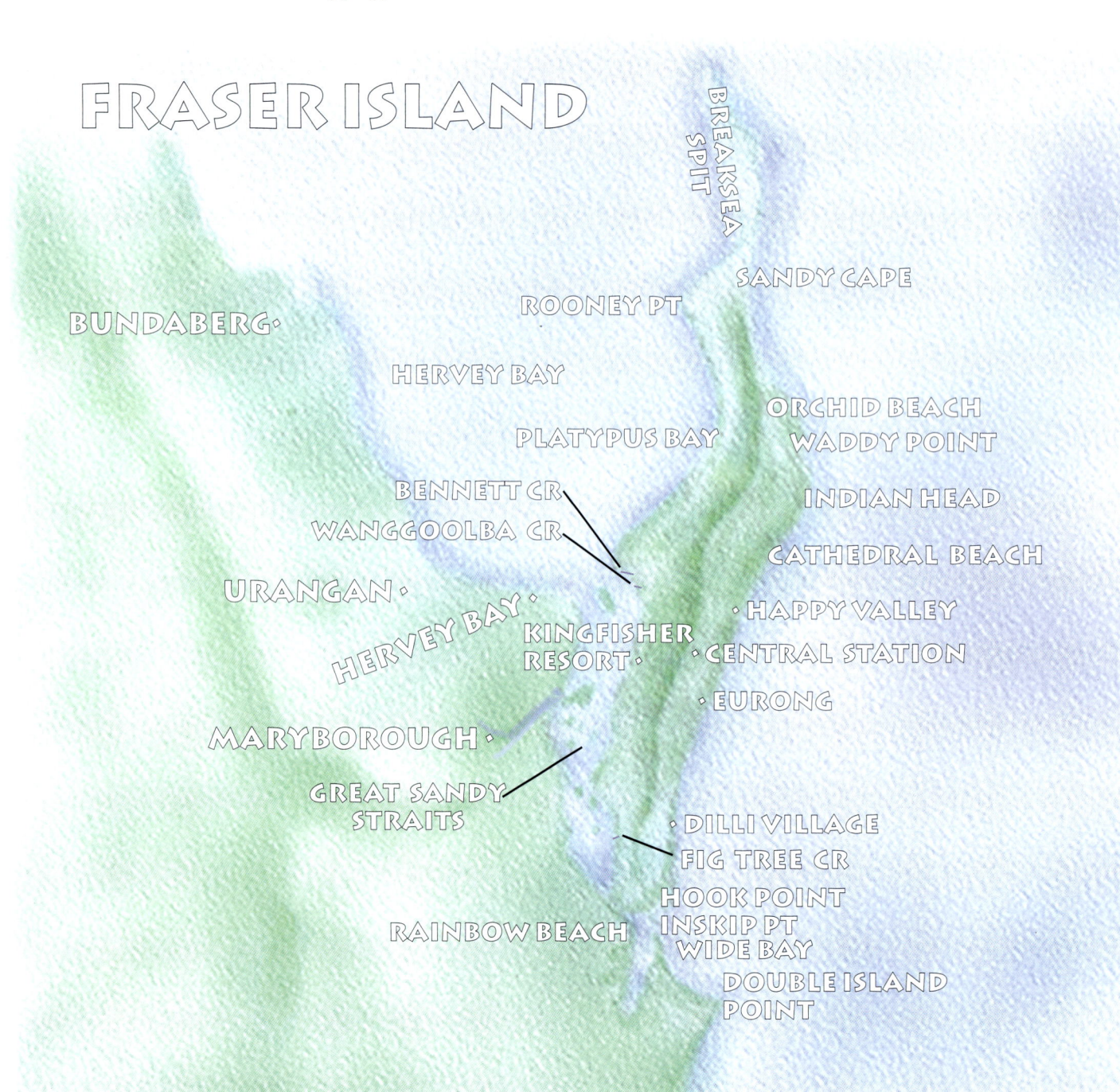

Fraser Island

John Sinclair

Fraser Island is a very large sand island lying just off the north-east Australian coast, some 250 kilometres (150 miles) north of Brisbane. In 1992, the island's credentials as an outstanding natural area were recognised with its inscription on the World Heritage List. This recognition was hard won, the product of a national conservation campaign to protect the island's natural values, that spanned more than 21 years.

It is not hard to understand why Fraser Island has been listed as one of the great natural wonders of the world. It is, after all, the "Mt. Everest" of sand islands: the largest single sand mass in the world, containing 184 000 hectares (455 000 acres) of sand to a depth of 240 metres (790 feet). Fraser Island holds more sand than any of the world's deserts because even though deserts may be vast in area, their sand is just a veneer spread thinly over underlying rocks. In spite of all its sand, Fraser Island is anything but a desert-like landscape; most of it is covered by dense forests and other vegetation and there are even freshwater lakes perched amazingly on the great dunes.

Fraser Island's place on the World Heritage List is justified by more than sheer mass and area alone. The island is to sandmasses what the Great Barrier Reef is to the coral reefs of the world; it has a greater variety and development of dune systems and features than is found in any other single sandmass, a creation that has been more than 800 000 years in the making. The island is of scientific interest for the way its sand dunes have been shaped and developed during many episodes over hundreds of thousands of years, and for the vegetation communities it has supported for the whole of this time. Fraser Island, with its magnificent forests, its surprising perched lakes, vast beaches and sea vistas is also an exceptionally beautiful place.

In spite of Fraser Island's credentials, its nomination to the World Heritage List by the Australian Government was a long time in coming. The island forms part of the territory of the state of Queensland and, for more than a century, the state government saw the exploitation of the island's mineral and timber resources as more important than protecting its outstanding natural values. This entrenched attitude was held more or less uniformly by successive state government administrations and had the effect of discouraging Australia's federal government from proceeding with a World Heritage nomination for Fraser Island.

The outstanding natural values of Fraser Island were first recognised in 1893 when the Australian Association for the Advancement of Science nominated it as one of four natural areas of Australia which should be dedicated as national parks. At that time, there were two obstacles to protecting Fraser Island. The first was the timber industry, based on the island's forests, which had begun in 1863 and was to continue its operations up to 1991. Another and more complex problem was the association of Aboriginal people with the island.

Fraser Island was occupied by Aboriginal people long before the coming of Europeans. The indigenous population was about 3000 when white colonists first settled the adjacent mainland. This population declined dramatically after contact with the settlers. The island was used as a quarantine station for gold miners during the rush to Queensland's Gympie gold field. The Aboriginal community on the island suffered severely from the influence of the quarantined whites, some of whom were sailors addicted to opium and suffering from disease, particularly venereal disease. In 1851, a group of settlers from Maryborough on the mainland was sworn in as special police deputies to assist the authorities in the arrest of two wanted Aborigines who had taken refuge on Fraser Island. This group spent the Christmas and New Year period of that year on Fraser Island, ostensibly attempting to execute a warrant for the arrest of the two Aboriginal fugitives, while in reality, engaged in a massacre of Aboriginal people. By the 1890s, although there were only 200 to 300 Aborigines remaining in the Maryborough district, Fraser Island was seen as a particularly useful Aboriginal reservation where Aboriginal people could be sent into virtual exile, well removed from the lives of the settlers of the mainland. During this period, the Queensland Government was sending Aborigines to the island from many parts of the state and this role was probably seen as more valuable than any benefit that might be obtained from dedicating it as a national park.

In 1905, as the timber industry on the island developed, most of Fraser Island's Aborigines were moved away to other missions in Queensland. However, the island continues to be the repository of evidence of their occupation over thousands of years.

The idea of a national park on Fraser Island languished until 1934. In that year, local people in Maryborough began to press for the reservation of a significant part of the island as a national park. However, the Great Depression and the Second World War stalled further progress. In the post-war period, the timber industry became even more entrenched and mineral prospectors discovered the rich deposits of heavy minerals contained in the Fraser Island sandmass.

It was not until the late 1960s that the voluntary conservation movement began to organise and turn its attention to the task of protecting Fraser Island but, by then, a good deal of the island had been taken up by mineral claims, so the prospects for protecting much of it seemed poor. The lodging of further claims by mining companies in 1971 was the spark for the formation of a new group specifically to campaign for a national park on the island. The Fraser Island Defenders Organisation, in keeping with the word "FIDO" spelled out by its initials, included a menacing-looking bulldog as its logo and the slogan: "FIDO - The Watchdog of Fraser Island."

FIDO's first task was to stop the mineral sands mining on the island. This was not an easy objective as large, multi-national companies were involved and the minerals they mined were in demand. Although FIDO enjoyed substantial public support in its campaign to protect Fraser Island, this seemed to make little impression on the Queensland Government. The organisation received a better response from the Commonwealth Government which established a commission of inquiry into the mineral sands mining industry on Fraser Island. In 1976, this inquiry concluded that Fraser Island was of such significance that it should first be inscribed on the Register of the National Estate and then nominated for the World Heritage List. The inquiry also concluded that the Commonwealth Government should stop further mining on the island by exercising its constitutional power to regulate exports. As almost all the minerals won from Fraser Island were destined for overseas markets, the Commonwealth Government could effectively stop mining by prohibiting the export of Fraser Island minerals. All of the inquiry's recommendations were taken up, although the World Heritage nomination had to wait until some years later.

The Queensland State Government continued to oppose World Heritage nomination of Fraser Island because of the threat this might pose to the island's resource industries, particularly the timber industry. In 1989, a change of government in Queensland brought with it a change in policy towards Fraser Island. The new government established a further investigation into the future of the island, conducted by the Commission of Inquiry into the Conservation, Management and Use of Fraser Island and the Great Sandy Region. In 1990, the commission of inquiry recommended that logging should cease on Fraser Island and that the whole of the island, together with the related sandmass of Cooloola on the adjacent mainland, as well as surrounding marine areas, should be nominated for World Heritage listing.

The campaign to protect Fraser Island was long and arduous and involved complex legal issues which were argued more than once before the High Court of Australia until they were eventually settled. It also involved an enormous effort by the voluntary conservation movement, particularly the local group, FIDO. The Australian Conservation Foundation in 1974 identified Fraser Island as one of the first four Australian natural sites which should be proposed for the World Heritage List.

Following the nomination of Fraser Island to the World Heritage List, its sand dune building processes and resulting ecosystem were judged by IUCN - the World Conservation Union to meet two criteria for listing as a World Heritage site. It was judged to be an outstanding example of significant, on-going, geological and biological processes of world importance. These processes include transport of sand along the seashore by ocean and wind, deposition of sand to form beaches and lagoons, dune building, podsolisation (a type of soil development), rainforest development and biological evolution. The island is significant for biological evolution because of the specialisation of creatures adapted to a sandy environment. Examples include four species of 'acid' frogs living in the wet heathland areas associated with lakes and swamps where unusually acidic conditions prevail.

Fraser Island was also judged to possess superlative natural features and exceptional natural beauty, exemplified by its long uninterrupted ocean beaches backed in some places by coloured sand cliffs, majestic remnants of tall rainforests growing on sand, and crystal clear lakes which comprise half of the perched freshwater dune lakes that exist in the world.

Fraser Island's inscription on the World Heritage List did not include the associated areas in Queensland's Great Sandy Region, including sand dune complexes at Cooloola on the mainland opposite Fraser Island, and the surrounding marine environment of Hervey Bay and Great Sandy Straits. Consequently, concerns remain that the values of the island with its surrounding environs have not yet been fully recognised. Further, some Aboriginal interests believe that Fraser Island's cultural credentials are outstanding and should not have been overlooked.

At Fraser Island, the natural forces of wind and ocean currents have created the largest sandmass and the longest and most complete dune systems in the world. It is the natural beauty of this creation that draws and holds the interest of most visitors. Their anticipation rises from the moment they drive their vehicles onto the ferries plying the routes from Hervey Bay and Rainbow Beach to the island, and their first sensation of the imminent bounty of nature to be enjoyed may be a glimpse of a small school of dolphins passing by. A particular attraction is the opportunity to four-wheel-drive along the 120 kilometres (75 miles) length of beach - the island's north-south 'highway' - which stretches the entire length of the island's east coast, and to camp in beautiful natural surroundings on the way.

Australia's east coast ocean environment is influenced by the width and slope of the continental shelf. The shelf just south of Sandy Cape (the northern tip of Fraser Island) is narrow at less than 40 kilometres (25 miles) wide, and drops off fairly steeply, while further north, the shelf has a more gentle slope and widens to 250 kilometres (150 miles). The shelf's steepness and narrowness to the south of Fraser Island has created strong waves there. A strong northward current caused by the energetic waves and their oblique south-easterly approach, operates along the east coast. This transports northwards huge quantities of sand eroded from coastal areas. The south-easterly onshore winds of the region then deposit the sand on the mainland and Fraser Island. These processes have created coastal masses of wind blown sand which cover 80 per cent of the region's land surface. The dune systems extend well below the present sea level and this shows that both sea sand and wind blown sand have been deposited at different stages, reflecting the higher and lower levels of the sea over many thousands of years.

Fraser Island's dunes are not all alike. There are foredunes or beach ridges up to 10 metres (33 feet) above sea level and stabilised by grasses and spinifex. There are low "transgression" dunes which cut across the line of the foredunes and jut inland for several hundred metres. These dunes are generally stabilised by open scrub and forest woodlands. There are the high transgression dunes rising from 100 metres to 240 metres (330 feet to 790 feet), which slope down to the west (inland) and are covered by low and grassy scribbly gum forests, tall blackbutt forests and rainforests. On the older sand dunes, impressive forests have developed but their fate is to gradually decline into low open woodlands and heathlands. This decline is due to the fact that in older sand dunes, there has been a gradual leaching away and removal of nutrients out of the reach of most plants, starving the plant community which then starts to "go backwards" in its development. The high dunes also hold the perched lakes and local aquifers in which rainwater percolating through these dunes collects. There are, finally, the relic dunes which are commonly called 'coloured sands'. They consist of layered yellow, pink, red and pale grey sediments that are exposed in the cliffs along the eastern, seaward side of the island.

Fraser Island's hydrology is of particular interest. Lakes containing the freshest water to be found naturally in the world can be seen perched on great sand dunes which most people would assume to be too porous to hold water. The process by which these perched lakes are formed and evolve has helped scientific understanding of the important role that organic sediments play in an ecosystem. Here, we can see the processes of dune and soil formation and nutrient exchange in action in very demonstrable ways.

Some perched lakes are up to 300 000 years old and their organic sediments bind the sand, rendering them virtually impervious and providing a continuous record of changes to the island's hydrology and vegetation through cycles of climate from Ice Age to warmer periods. Investigations have shown that most water stays in the dunes of Fraser Island for about 100 years but some of the water could have remained in the sandmass for 200 years or more.

From the beach 'roads' ringing the island, tracks lead off through the banksia heathlands, known locally as wallum scrub, and into remnant stands of majestic rainforest containing trees such as satinay, kauri pine, candlewood, brushbox and hoop pine. These rainforests can be seen thriving on pure sand at elevations up to 240 metres (790 feet) above sea level. The rainforest stands may grow up to 50 metres (160 feet) in height and their trees may have trunks of two to three metres (ten feet) diameter. How does tropical rainforest grow on sand? The sequence of overlapping dunes of different ages up to hundreds of thousands of years old forms the basis of a complex interaction of soil development, micro-organisms, nutrients, hydrology and vegetation. The low-fertility, free-draining sands are firstly stabilised by pioneer vegetation assisted by the hyphae (fungal filaments which enmesh the sand) of soil fungi. Organic matter builds up in the sand, together with other nutrients from weathering, rainfall and the air, and the nutrients are leached downwards through the sand, leaving a bleached infertile level of soil on the surface. Over time, the soil elements move downwards, ultimately producing soil profiles of depths up to 20 metres (66 feet). The extent of this "podsol" soil development in the dunes of the area is outstanding and exceeds that found elsewhere in the world. As nutrients accumulate in the surface level, the ecological succession of plant communities proceeds from bare sand colonies and heathland shrubs to tall forests and rainforests in sheltered, moist dune corridors.

Research has also shown that the plant life of the island is very diverse. Vascular plants, (the kind that transport minerals and foods through a system of vessels analogous to the blood vessels in animals), have been found to number 700 species and additional plant species continue to be found. Many threatened and primitive species of plants exist on the island and this tends to show that Fraser Island is a refuge area where numbers of species, such as king fern, kauri and hoop pines, have been able to survive through climate change and other circumstances, even though the same species has been driven into extinction elsewhere. The island is also home to an extraordinary species of butterfly which highlights the fragility of the relationships between the fauna and flora. The Illidge's Ant-blue butterfly belongs to a genus that is unique in preying on ants throughout its entire larval history. It is dependent on one species of ant that, in turn, depends on one species of mangrove. For these reasons, Fraser Island holds an important place in the story of the evolution of species.

The native heathlands and plant communities of Fraser Island support a diverse fauna distinguished by its variety and specialised adaptation to a large number of habitats, from high dune rainforests and lakes to tidal wetlands and marshes. Some species are restricted to one lake and not others, such as a primitive Chironomid midge found in Lakes Boomanjin and McKenzie, but in none of the other forty lakes on the island. Another example is the fascinating Cooloola propator, referred to as the "Cooloola Monster", so called for its grotesque shape and carnivorous diet. These insects do not construct burrows but literally swim through the sand up to 40 centimetres (16 inches) below the surface, feeding on the larvae of cicadas and other insects. They have evolved for a life underground, with legs adapted for digging, vestigial wings and minute antennae. The sand dunes also host a plethora of ant, termite and earthworm species, and a giant sand-burrowing cockroach.

The island's wetlands also provide roosting sites for 20 species of migratory wading birds such as the eastern curlew, lesser golden plover, large sand plover, red necked stint, bar-tailed godwit and the Mongolian plover. The dune heathlands support a variety of native parrots including one of the world's few ground dwelling parrots, the rare glossy black-cockatoo, the night parrot and the black-breasted button-quail which is the only quail species in the world that lives in rainforest.

Because Fraser Island is an island, it has avoided many of the problems which affect many other World Heritage sites, such as invasions by weeds, feral animals and plant or animal diseases. For example, the island is free of feral pigs and foxes which are the bane of native fauna on the mainland. It is important that Fraser Island's freedom from these injurious influences is maintained.

ABOVE Rooney Point is the only nesting point for the South Pacific loggerhead turtle.

NEXT PAGE Lake Boomanjin, with an area of over 200 hectares (500 acres), is one of the largest perched dune lakes in the world.

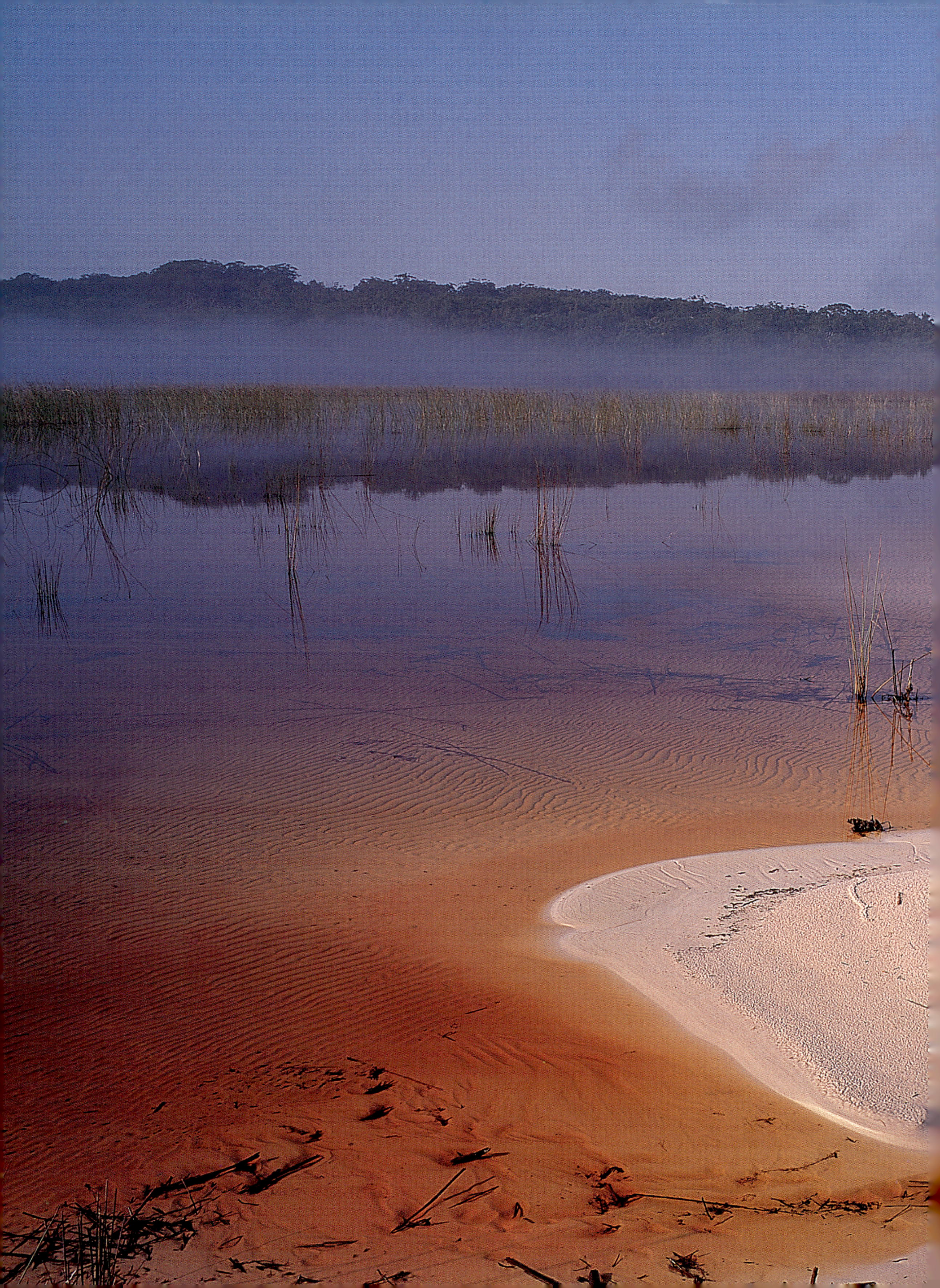

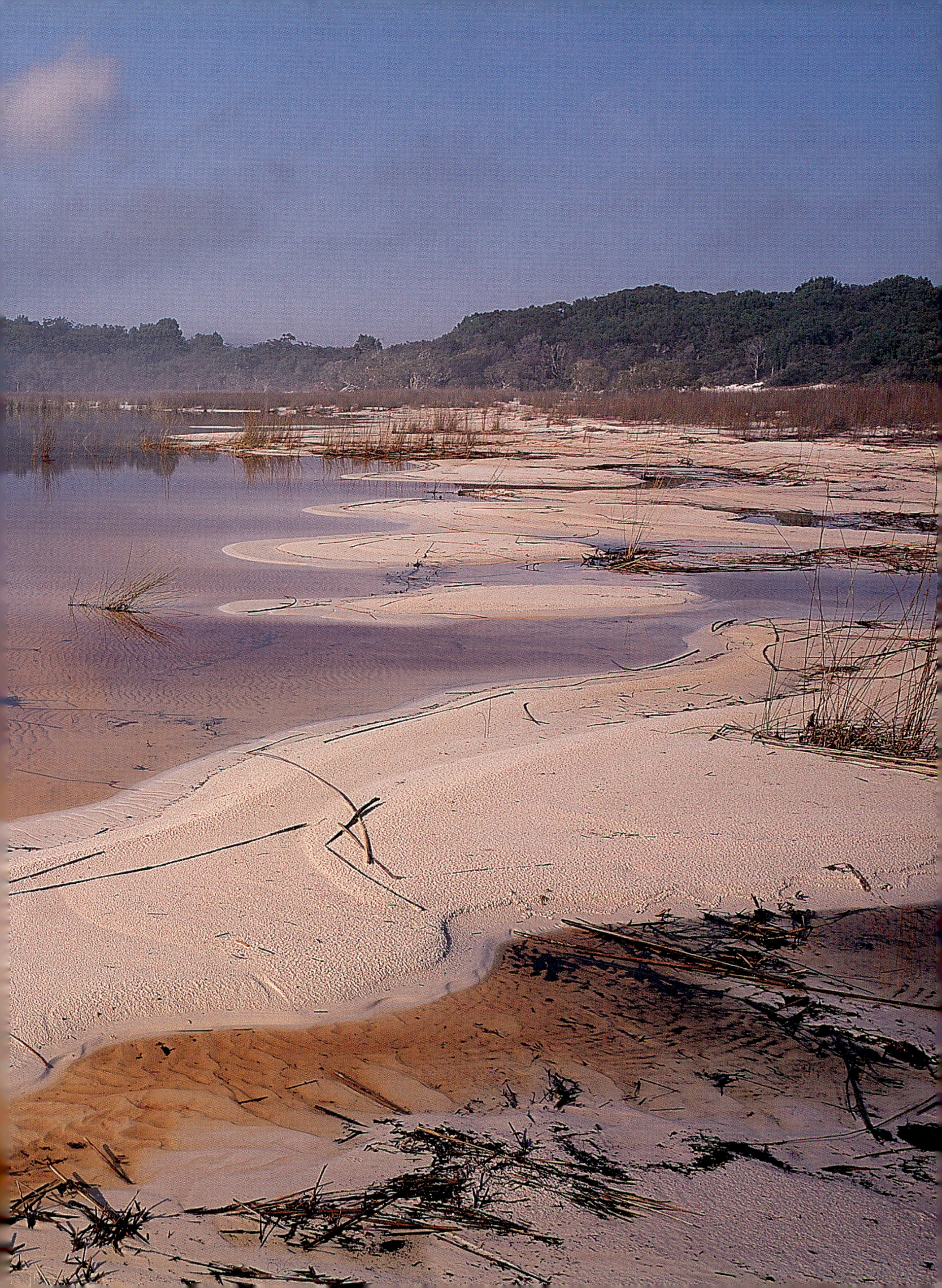

Physical Features

Fraser Island is 122 kilometres (76 miles) long, 5 to 25 kilometres (3 to 15 miles) wide and reaches to 240 metres (790 feet) above sea level. The sand extends 30 to 60 metres (100 to 200 feet) below the present sea level. The Island contains over 184 000 hectares (455 000 acres) of wind-blown sand to a depth of 240 metres (790 feet). Surprisingly, much of this sand is not obvious because most of the island is well covered by vegetation.

The climate is subtropical but moderated by the influence of the sea. Mean annual temperatures range from a minimum of 14° Celsius (57° Fahrenheit) to a maximum of 29° Celsius (84° Fahrenheit). Rainfall is high, reaching 1800 millimetres (71 inches) on the tallest dunes in the centre of Fraser Island. The hottest months are November to March and the coldest, July to August. Light frosts occur in parts of the area, with occasional heavy frosts in winter.

Winds are predominantly from the south-east throughout the year. Fraser Island stands in the path of onshore winds blowing onto Hervey Bay and this gives the bay a wind regime that is variable in direction and speed, making the bay waters rather fickle. The region lies near the southern limit of the tropical cyclone belt and is sometimes affected by cyclones between December and April.

RIGHT An aerial view of one of Fraser Island's perched dune lakes.

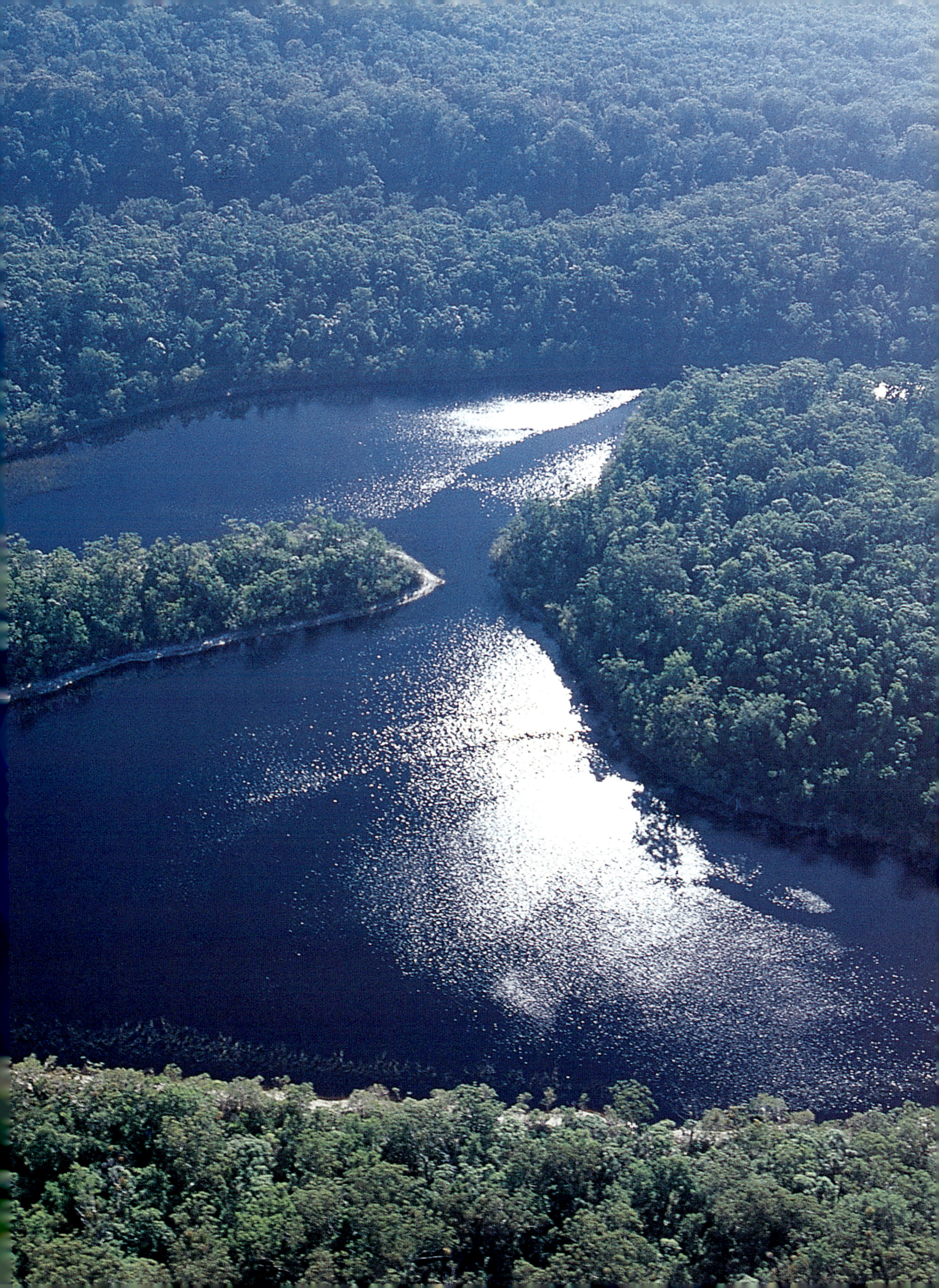

Special Features

The island boasts features of particular scientific value and exceptional natural beauty. Long, unbroken ocean beaches are backed in some places by distinctive multi-coloured sand cliffs which range from white through to yellow, orange, pink, red and black. Long, gently curving beaches are a distinctive feature of the coastal lowlands. These beaches are often 'anchored' to rocky headlands from which they stretch southwards in a characteristic reversed 'J' shape to produce a picture-postcard image of an island paradise.

The hydrology of the sandmasses has contributed to unusual freshwater features such as aquifers, perched dune lakes and associated plains lakes. There is wide variation in drainage characteristics throughout the area, with peaty layers, swamps and lakes, as well as well-drained sands. The soils lack fertility yet support an abundance of vegetation ranging from tall eucalypt forests through to grassy woodlands and wet coastal heaths, with majestic stands of tall rainforest growing on sand in the interior.

ABOVE RIGHT Great Sandy Cape headland is the most northern point of Fraser Island. The harder volcanic material on this headland makes it a 'staging point' for the accumulation of sands transported from southern coastal regions.

ABOVE Fraser Island's dingo population is considered to be one of the most genetically pure. This is due to its relative isolation from other dog breeds on the mainland.

BOTTOM RIGHT Screw pines growing on the banks of Wyuna Creek on the north-east side of Fraser Island.

NEXT PAGE Transgressive dune or sand blow. Sheets of sand migrate inland, covering the vegetation. The advance of sand dunes across the eastern flank of Fraser Island has been in progress for hundreds of thousands of years. Each wave of sand has contributed to building up the island to its present height of 240 metres (790 feet) above sea level.

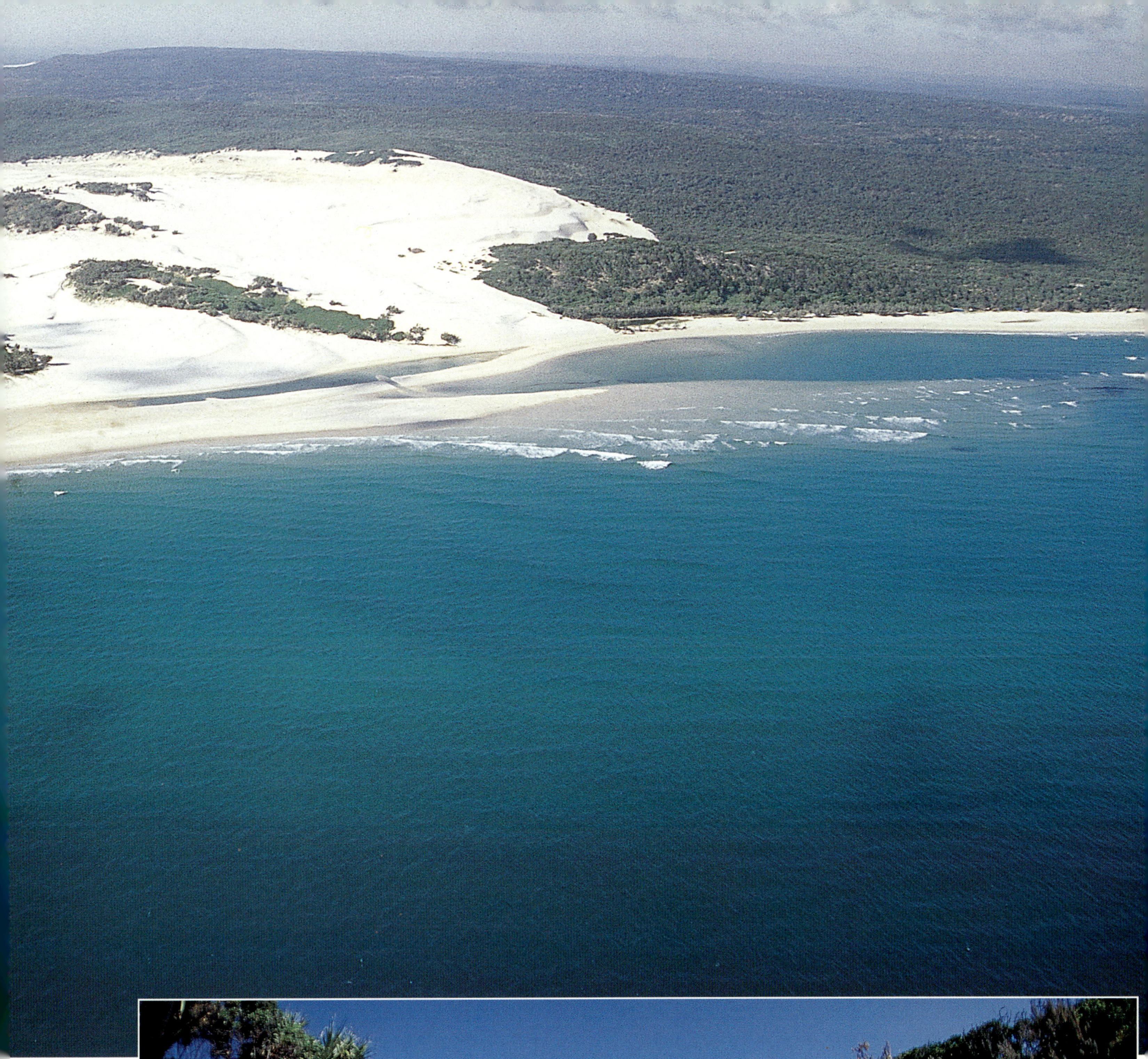

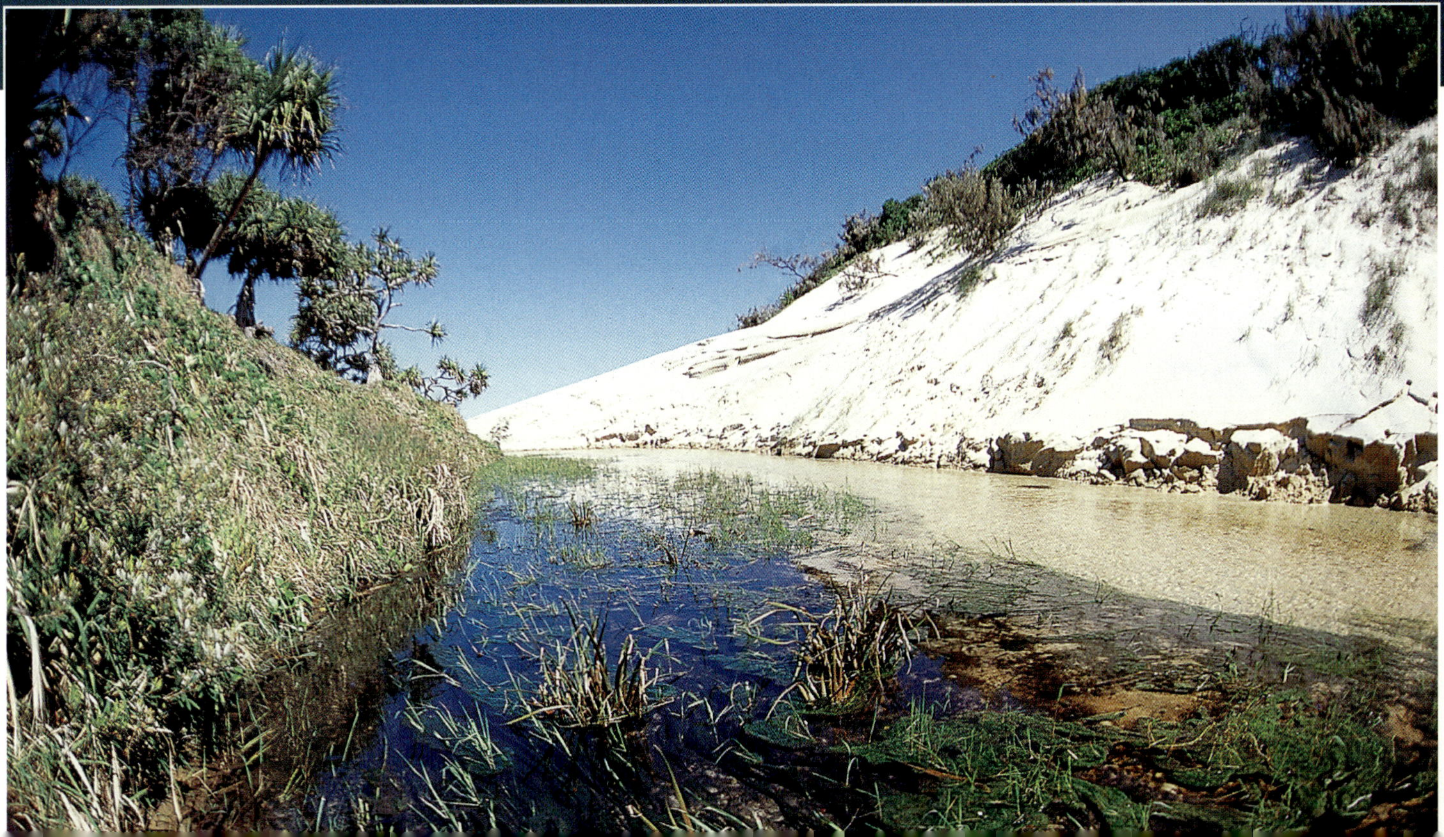

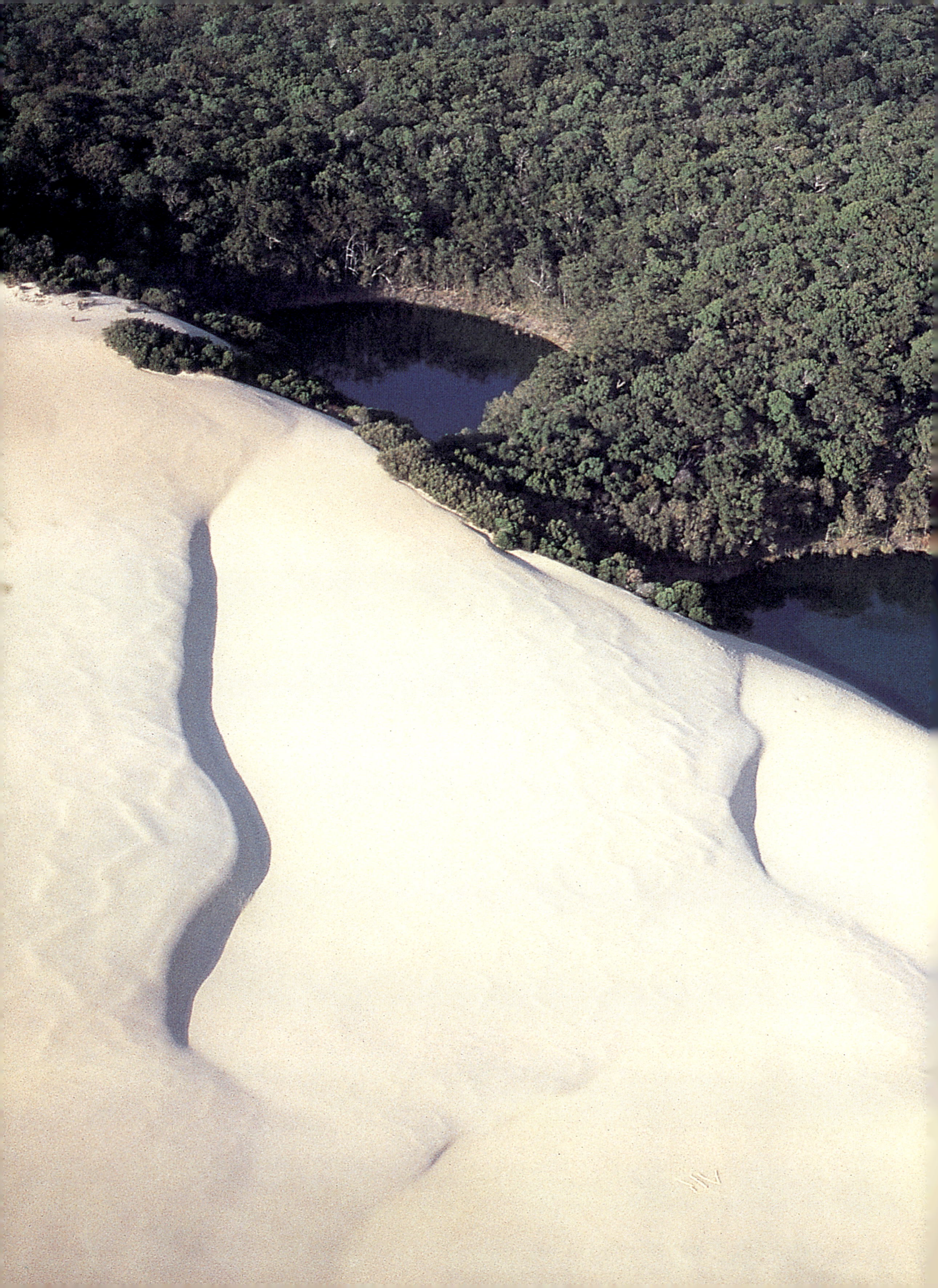

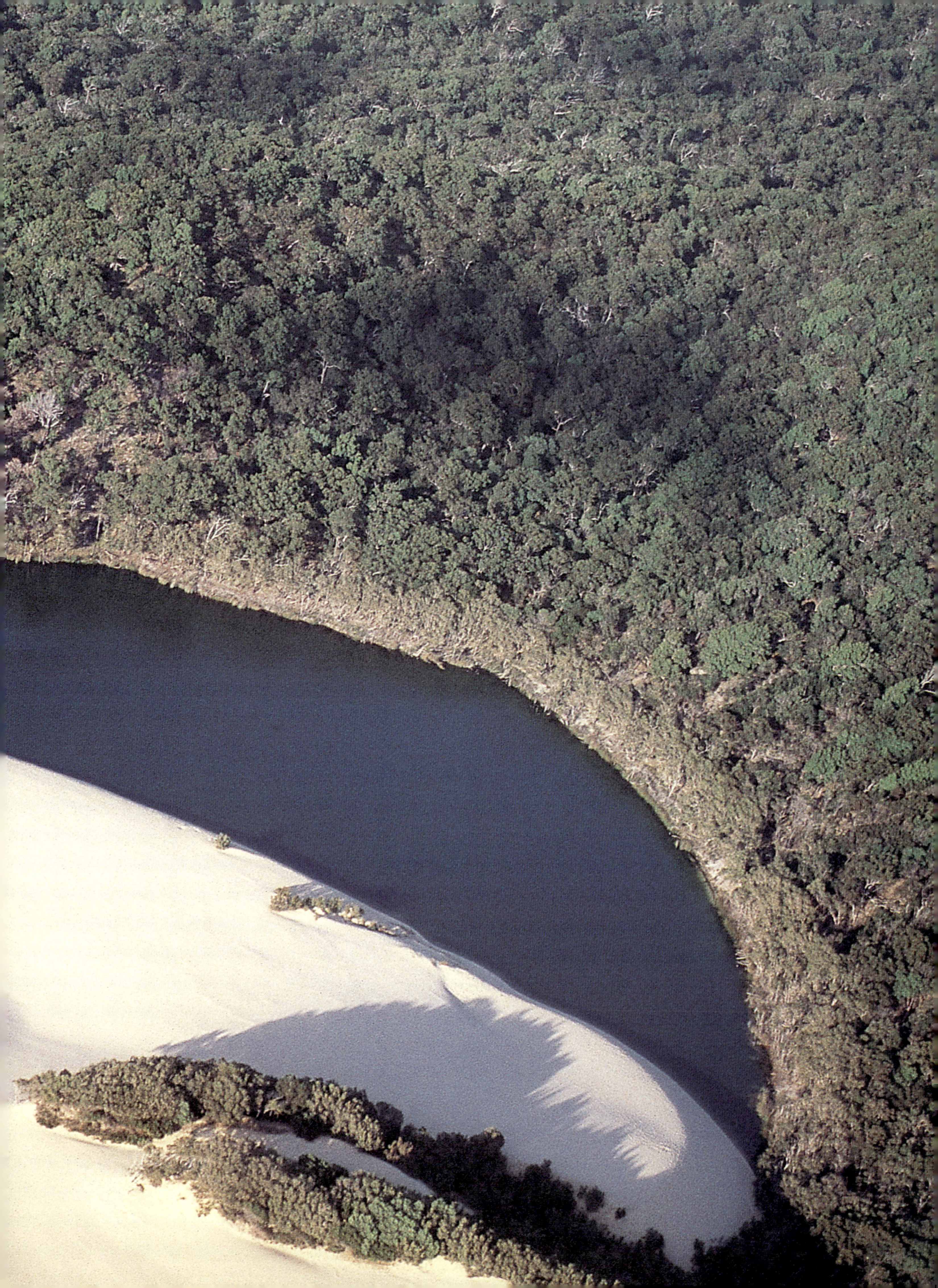

Flora

There is a mixing of tropical to sub-tropical vegetation on the island and this contributes to the great diversity of plant species growing there. The most extensive vegetation types are eucalypt forest and woodland, with patches of rainforest, shrubland, heathland, freshwater swamp, mangrove and saltmarsh. The most characteristic plant communities of the region are known as 'wallum', named after a species of banksia which is dominant in them. On the coastal strip, the vegetation is subject to exposure to strong winds and the influence of salt-laden air from the sea. Bushfires are a major influence on the island's ecosystem, helping to shape its native plant and animal communities.

From east to west, it is possible to clearly discern a sequence of plant communities zoned according to the influence of factors such as salt, water table, the age and amounts of nutrients in the dunes, and their exposure to and frequency of bushfires. Each zone is clearly separated by narrow boundaries and can be broadly grouped according to the successive stages of development of the sand dunes on which they grow.

The sand dunes are heavily vegetated. Fraser Island rainforests retain much of their diversity, while most of the comparable mainland rainforest has been completely cleared. These rainforests include vine forest, palm rainforest and brushbox dominated rainforests, and they merge into tall eucalypt forest dominated by blackbutt and scribbly gum-wallum heath communities.

On flat, low plains bordering the sandmasses, there are paperbark forests and swamps, sedgelands and shrub heaths. The low heaths are known for their spectacular displays of wildflowers and they share, in the composition of plant species, a number of similarities with other fire-adapted eucalypt heaths found on low nutrient soils elsewhere in Australia. Although these heathlands are not as diverse in their species or as extensive as the heathlands of southern Australia, they do represent the northern limit of a well-developed belt of sub-tropical heathland on the east coast of the continent.

Fraser Island has provided, to a significant extent, a refuge for plant species which have been able to survive here when climatic and other changes have made them extinct in most other places. The island is particularly important for surviving populations of ferns, of which some 19 rare or threatened species thrive. At Wanggoolba Creek, there is an isolated population of the giant fern, *Angiopteris evecta*, a member of the ancient group of ferns that first appeared in the Silurian Period, 400 million years ago.

ABOVE RIGHT Key's Boronia, a vulnerable plant species, is restricted to Fraser Island and the Cooloola region.

RIGHT Satinays (turpentines) tower 55 metres (180 feet) above developing rainforest communities containing palms and other understorey species at Pile Valley. Satinays may take centuries to reach maturity. The measured living matter on one rainforest site at Fraser Island is the second highest in the world, exceeded only by the giant Sequoia forests of California. Even more remarkable is that the Fraser Island forests grow on sand.

FAR RIGHT Strangler fig and lianas in rainforest.

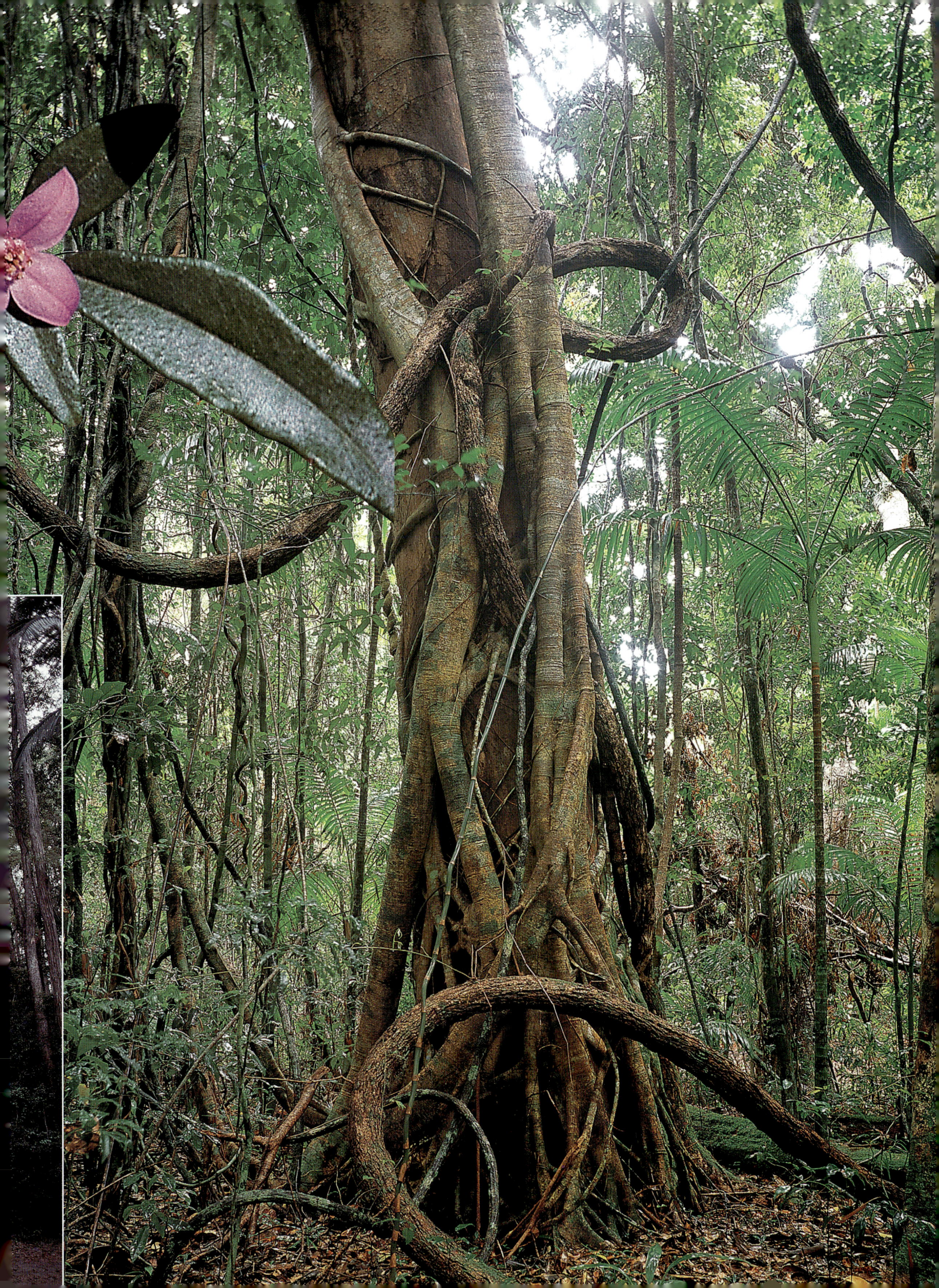

Fauna

The island is situated within a transitional zone between tropical northern and temperate south-east Australia and there is a rich intermingling here of animal species from these two biogeographical regions. The large number of habitats available on the island also contributes to the diversity of fauna; these habitats range from high dune rainforests and lakes to heath and tidal wetlands, as well as the sea. Some animal species have close associations with particular habitat types, while for others, the region is the northern or southern limit of distribution of their kind.

The heathlands and other plant communities that have developed on sandy soils of the coastal lowlands have a low abundance of vertebrates, that is the group of animals, including mammals, that have backbones. There is also a notably low diversity of species within the habitats. Few animal species are confined in their distributions to the sandy coastal heaths of the region, although there are some unusual or localised species to be found in them. There is a noticeable absence of the large plant-eating animals which are common in other parts of Australia. Instead, the island is dominated by a fauna better adapted to the unusual conditions of life in the dunes and, in effect, able to utilise the fluidity of the sand by 'swimming' through it. This explains the numerous ants, termites, worms, cockroaches and other invertebrates which are comfortable moving through the sand and digging and burrowing into it. The island is also home to many species of frogs and reptiles including the four-fingered skink, tiger snake, black whipped snake and short-necked tortoise.

The island supports a great diversity of birds, with more than 230 species recorded. The ground parrot, one of the rarest birds in Australia, is relatively common in the heathlands, while its habitat in other parts of eastern Australia is rapidly disappearing. Peregrine falcons are also present. The freshwater dune lakes and sandy wetlands of Fraser Island provide an important stop-over for migratory birds which fly between the northern and southern hemispheres in order to winter in Australia and to enjoy the northern summers on breeding grounds in Siberia and other places. These long-distance migrants include the eastern curlew, lesser golden plover, large sand plover and the red necked stint.

The freshwater lakes perched on the dunes hold acidic waters that are low in nutrients and support a specialised fauna including four frogs and an internationally threatened species of fish, the honey blue eye.

Adjacent to the World Heritage Areas are the sea grass beds of southern Hervey Bay and the Great Sandy Strait, home to an internationally significant population of the large, grazing aquatic mammals known as dugong. The region is also on the seasonal migration route of humpback whales which can be spotted offshore. Virtually the entire population of southern pacific loggerhead turtles migrates to Rooney Point on the western side of the island, where they court and mate.

ABOVE The carnivorous Cooloola propator, popularly known as the 'Cooloola monster', is found only in this region. Its name reflects its rapacious appetite for the larvae of other insects, which it finds incubating in the sands.

RIGHT Eli Creek on the ocean side of Fraser Island. The nutrients carried by freshwater creeks into the sea help to feed the marine ecosystem. This creek, like others on the island, runs parallel to the beach before entering the sea.

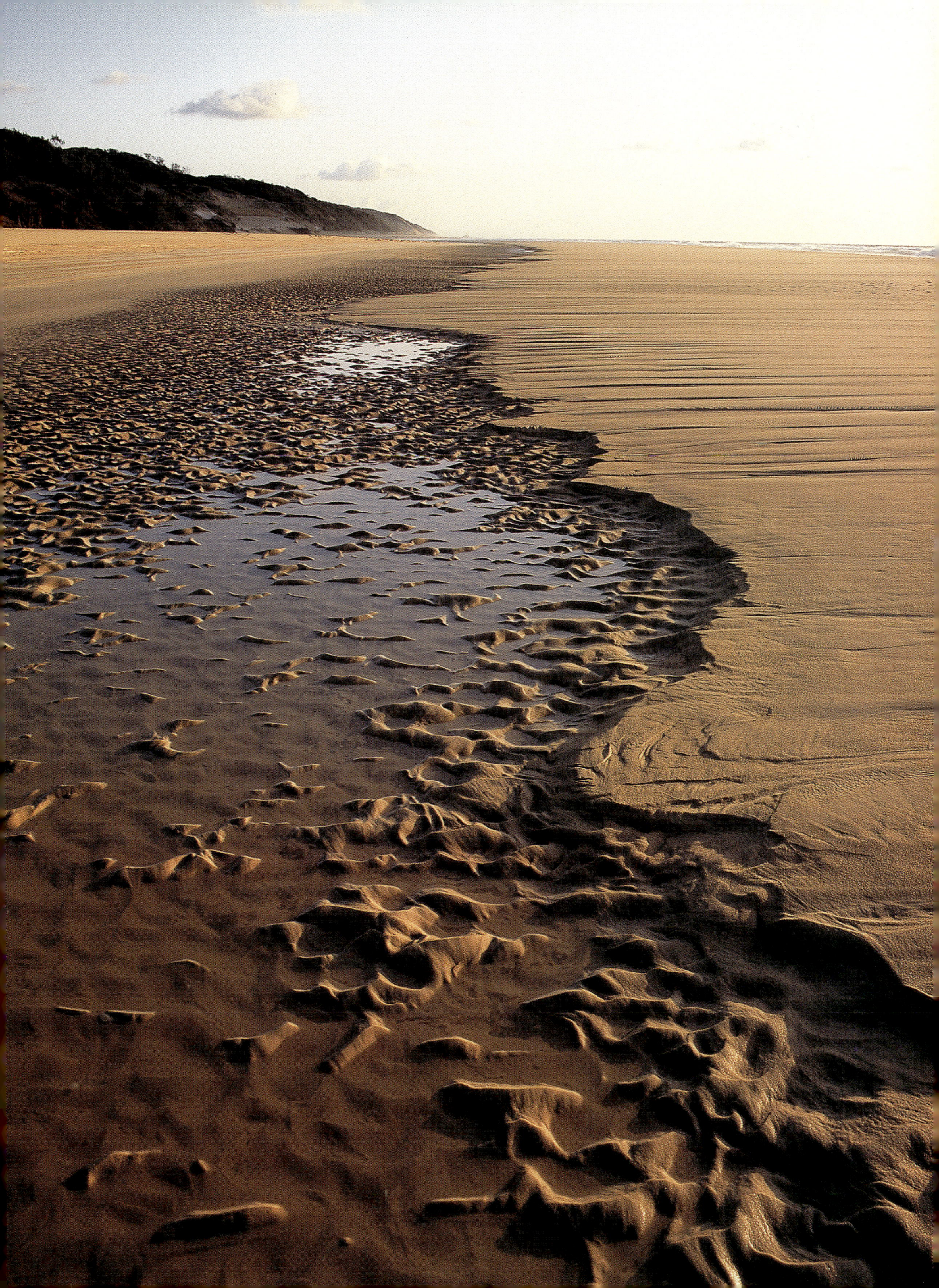

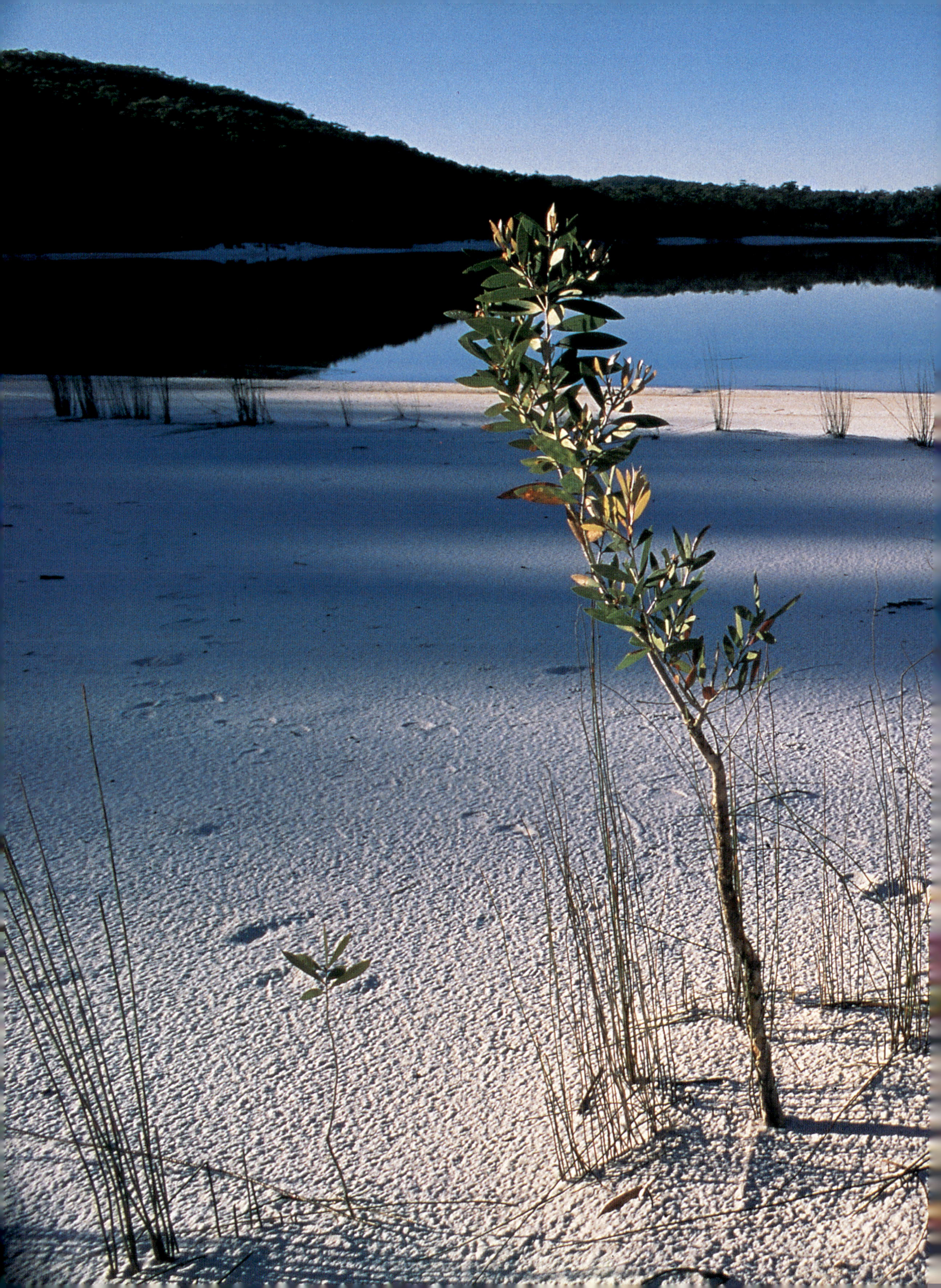

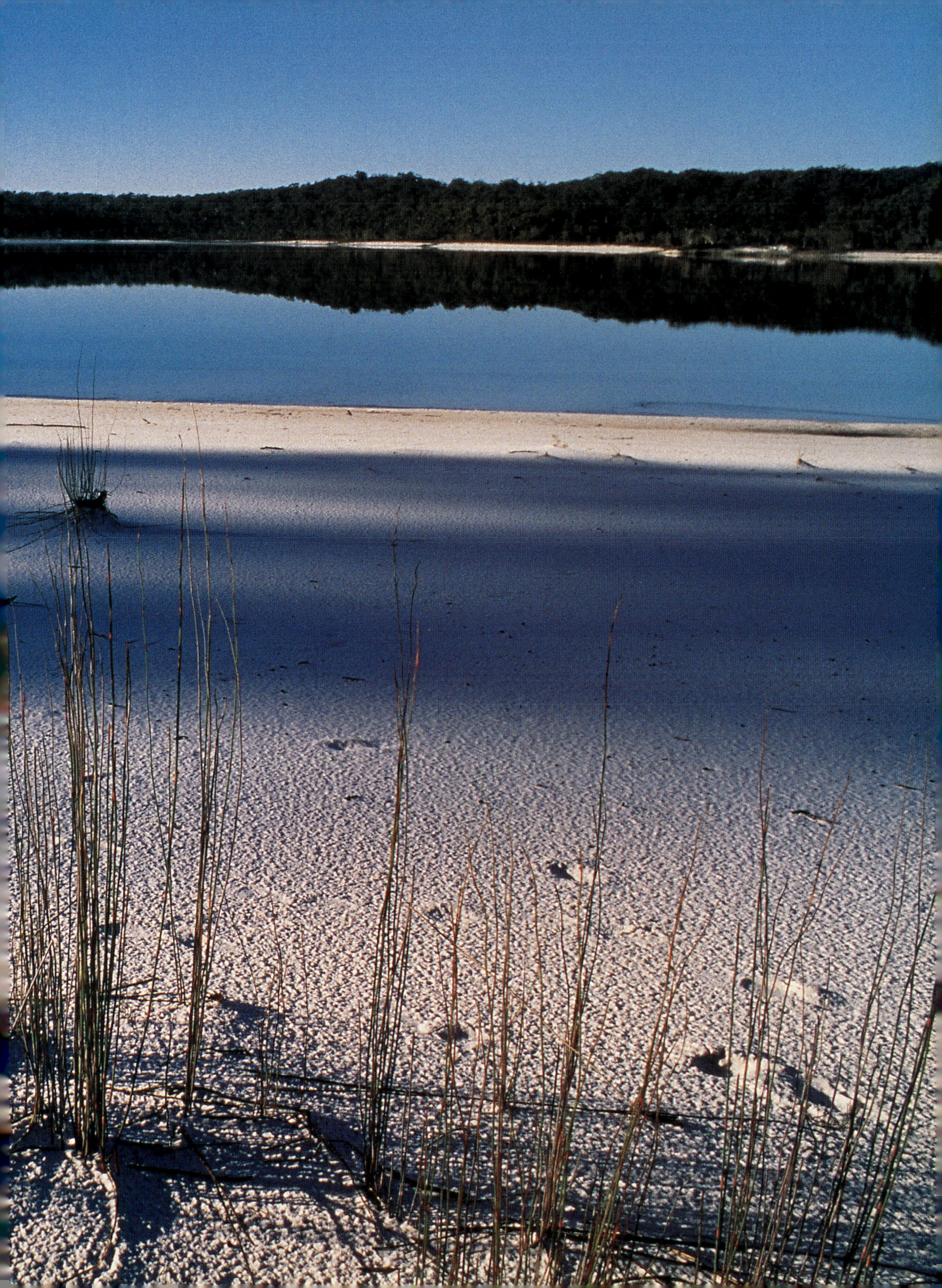

Cultural Heritage

It is thought that Aboriginal people first occupied Fraser Island between 20 000 and 40 000 years ago. The region was the home to four main groups before the coming of Europeans: the Dulingbara in the Cooloola-Noosa River area; the Butchulla who occupied Fraser Island; the Ngulungbara to the north; and the Dundubura. It seems likely that some - if not all - of these people were related clans. It has been estimated that there was a permanent population of 400 to 600 which swelled to as many as 2000 to 3000 during the winter months when seafood resources were abundant.

Hunting and fishing were carried on by the indigenous inhabitants in accordance with their traditions, and their lives encompassed many different social and ceremonial activities. Over 200 shell middens, or waste-heaps, containing the remains of seafood feasting, have been found on Fraser Island. Scatters of artefacts such as tools and the like, fish traps, evidence of permanent campsites in the more sheltered areas, trees stripped of bark to make canoes or gunyah shelters, and scarred trees are reminders of the rich and complex Aboriginal culture that existed here.

As early as 1521, Portuguese sailors charted a landmass corresponding in outline to Fraser Island. Archaeological evidence, in the form of clay pipes found in some Aboriginal middens, suggests that Dutch navigators made unrecorded visits to the region in the seventeenth century. Later, both James Cook and Matthew Flinders sailed along the Australian coastline without realising that the Great Sandy Peninsula was an island, a fact which later maritime explorers discovered.

Flinders met the indigenous inhabitants of Fraser Island in 1802. For several decades after this, contacts were sporadic and limited to explorers, escaped convicts and shipwreck survivors. In 1836, the ship *Stirling Castle* was wrecked off the coast of Fraser Island. A small number of survivors who lived for six weeks on the island included Eliza Fraser, after whom the island is named. Adverse reports of the Aborigines by this group aroused hostile sentiments towards them among the mainland settlers. Frontier settlement and pastoral activity in the Wide Bay and Mary River area led to rapidly-escalating racial warfare in the 1840s and 1850s and to the deaths of many of the Aborigines of the mainland and Fraser Island. After this period of armed conflict, reprisals and disease, 73 Aboriginal people from the adjacent mainland were removed to a newly established Aboriginal reserve on Fraser Island. Many of these people and others sent from other parts of Queensland suffered and died in the poor conditions of the government and church missions in those times. By the 1890s, there were only 200 to 300 Aboriginal people remaining in the district.

In 1900, the Fraser Island reserve became an Anglican mission with up to 180 inmates. The high death rate continued and the mission was disbanded after only 4 years. In 1905, most of the remaining Aboriginal people were moved away to other missions to make way for the island's expanding timber industry. Only 20 of the original inhabitants of Fraser Island remained. Their descendants have maintained and re-established cultural ties with Fraser Island through oral history and, more recently, through a number of Aboriginal organisations.

The magnificent timber resources of the region were first noted in 1842 and the exploitation of timber commenced soon after, in the 1860s. Fraser Island was declared a forestry reserve in 1908. Steam tramways, jetties and sawmills were constructed and the history of settlement and land use in the region until the mid-twentieth century is largely a story of the timber industry.

For over 100 years, forestry and, to a lesser degree, the fishing industry, were the main industries in the region. During the Second World War, Fraser Island was used for secret commando training and, more recently, the region has supported mineral sands mines and tourism industries.

Continued economic use of Fraser Island became increasingly controversial in the post war years. The Fraser Island Defenders Organisation (FIDO) was established in 1971 to protect the island as a national park and to end logging and mineral sands mining. Between 1974 and 1980, Australia's Commonwealth Scientific and Industrial Research Organisation conducted extensive research into the sandmasses at Cooloola and concluded that the region was of international significance to science.

PREVIOUS PAGE Lake McKenzie is a 'perched' lake. It formed in a wind-scoured depression on the dune that was made watertight by the accumulation of layers of decayed plant matter. The beaches at Lake McKenzie are formed from pearly white sand which has been leached of iron oxides.

ABOVE Aboriginal flints. Fraser Island was, for thousands of years, the undisturbed territory of the Butchulla people.

RIGHT Wanggoolba Creek is one of Fraser Island's 'white water' creeks. The clear water is the result of filtering through the island sands. In contrast are the 'black waters' of the island, prevalent in the upper layers of the sands and stained by chemical compounds from decaying plant materials.

NEXT PAGE 'Coffee rock', in wind-blown sands on the eastern flank of Fraser Island, is formed by the leaching and concentration of minerals down through the layers of soil. Wave action on these coastal deposits is eroding them into interesting formations. Remnants of trees, probably thousands of years old, are encased within the coffee rock.

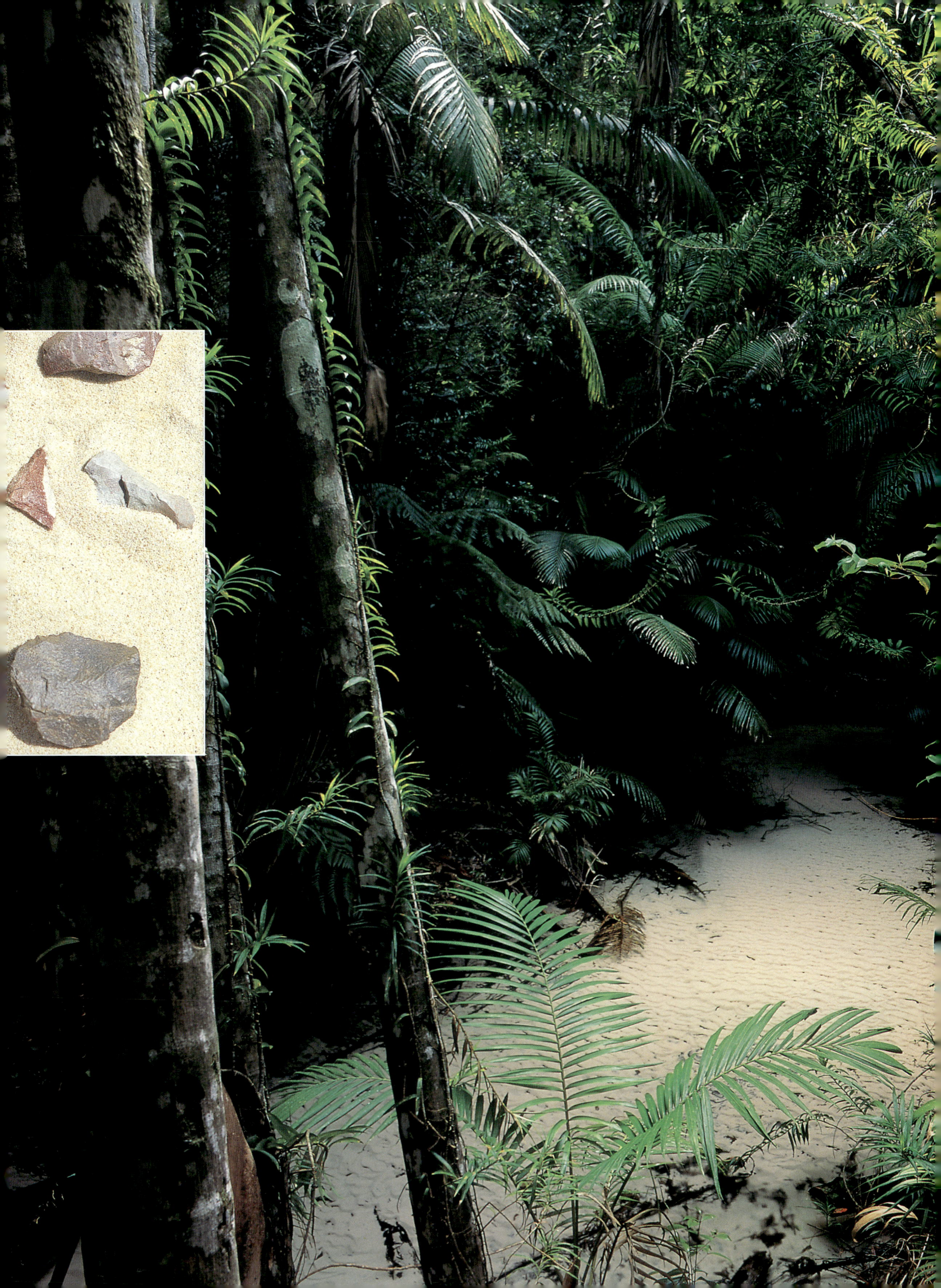

Facilities

Fraser Island is currently estimated to receive around 200 000 visitors a year, this number having increased rapidly since 1975. Facilities for visitors include several resorts and further accommodation for 10 000 campers in developed camp sites. Up to 5000 additional campers may utilise beach areas, fishing camps and other sites at peak times. Access is via vehicular barges at Rainbow Beach in the south, or River Heads, near Hervey Bay, where there is also a fast catamaran service. Air charters are available from Hervey Bay and Eurong on the island.

Human Impact

The impact of human activities on the World Heritage Area has been considerable. Parts of the coastal strip on Fraser Island have been subject to mineral sands mining and the forests have been affected by 130 years of logging, with targeted species including hoop pine, white beech, tallowwood, blackbutt, satinay and brushbox. A comparatively small area of land in the south-east of Fraser Island was mined and, while considerable efforts were made to rehabilitate this area, results are disappointing. The topography of mined dunes on Fraser Island has been irreversibly simplified by mining and by the removal of the original forest cover. Fortunately, these effects are not being extended to further areas as both mining and forestry activities have now ceased. While there is no evidence that any species has been lost from the area due to logging and mineral sands mining, the structure of affected forests, their species composition and the relative abundance of particular species has been irreversibly altered.

Tourism is impacting upon the island. Recreational use of the area is most intensive along the coastal strip. Recreational use of four-wheel-drive vehicles is heavy but the effects are localised and can be addressed through the use of rationalised access and circulation patterns. There are, however, associated impacts on water quality leading to declines in beach shellfish and worm populations. The adjacent marine area continues to be used for commercial and recreational fishing.

Management

Fraser Island is important to many interest groups, including local residents, the tourism and fishing industries and the military, as well as the conservation and scientific communities. The region is an important example of a complex and dynamic biosphere. Management requirements are, therefore, many-dimensional and must incorporate many issues, such as conservation of natural and cultural resources, recreation, tourism and visitor management, marine and wetland management, development, access and infrastructure, water quality, waste management, fire management and research projects.

In 1978, the Queensland Government established an inter-departmental committee to prepare a management plan for Fraser Island. In 1988, the recreational aspects of the plan were replaced by a Recreation Management Plan. The goal of the revised plan was to achieve a high quality, broad-based and economically viable tourist industry compatible with the need to protect the island's natural and cultural resources. The strategy was confused, however, and consisted of a complex set of administrative arrangements involving several government departments, agencies and local authorities, all with different areas of operation and responsibility. The management plans the various agencies produced were typically limited to their own focus and generally promoted the use of resources.

A major turning point in the management of Fraser Island occurred in 1990 when a commission of inquiry recommended that the region be nominated for World Heritage listing. The inquiry also recommended the immediate cessation of logging and the expansion of national park lands. A significant outcome of the inquiry was its recommendation for, and the Queensland Government's subsequent establishment of, a Regional Park Authority, with a responsibility to manage the entire Great Sandy Region. Future developments on Fraser Island are now planned and managed within the wider context of the Regional Park.

Threats

When Fraser Island was being nominated for World Heritage, the significance of some decisions made in 1991, such as the approval of the large Kingfisher Resort on the island, was not widely appreciated. Similarly, many people had not then realised the effects of allowing a new subdivision at Orchid Beach. Both of these developments have intruded in some measure upon Fraser Island's wilderness character and have reduced the sense of remoteness and primitiveness that visitors find so attractive about this place. A better way to cater for the increasing numbers of tourists visiting the island is to accommodate them in resort developments on the mainland and facilitate their daily forays over to Fraser Island. This would be more sympathetic to the island's environment than using it as the site for resort developments. Other adverse impacts on the island have included the clearing of mangroves and the discharge of sewage into Great Sandy Strait. There is an increasing risk, too, that exotic plant animals may one day be introduced.

There is now a consensus among Australian and international scientists who have studied the issue that the Cooloola sandmass should join Fraser Island on the World Heritage List. However, Cooloola, like Fraser Island, suffers from various threatening proposals. Two local authorities have plans to tap the large reservoirs of fresh water which have been stored in aquifers within these sandmasses for up to 200 years, in order to meet the needs of the growing urban populations in the city of Hervey Bay City and in the Rainbow Beach -Tin Can area. The environmental effects of such a scheme on the aquatic and marine environments of the Great Sandy Region would be very grave and a challenge to their future management.

In 1971, the year when the campaign to protect Fraser Island began, the island was visited by just 5500 people. Now the island attracts well over 200 000 visitors a year and the numbers continue to increase. Visitors bring some 70 000 four wheel drive vehicles onto the island each year and most of them establish camps along the foredunes where, as a result of the activities of some of these groups, degradation has occurred. Four-wheel-drive buses carry about 140 000 visitors a year around the island on day trips. The impact of so many motor vehicles driving along sandy tracks has been significant. Vast volumes of sand have moved down the roads, with the effect in one instance of filling one of the island's lakes, Yidney Lake, with sand. Significant siltation has occurred in many other areas and, in places, the four-wheel-drive traffic has been sufficiently heavy to destabilise dunes. While these changes have been gradual, their cumulative effect is severe. The weight of so many tourists and their mode of travel on the island is a threat to what is becoming Australia's most visited World Heritage Site.

To cater for the increasing number of visitors to Fraser Island and, at the same time, reduce their environmental impact, the Fraser Island Defence Organisation has suggested that a light-rail system be developed and that this provide the means of travel around the island for the great majority of visitors. This would remove the need for motor vehicles to travel over the island's loose, unconsolidated surfaces.

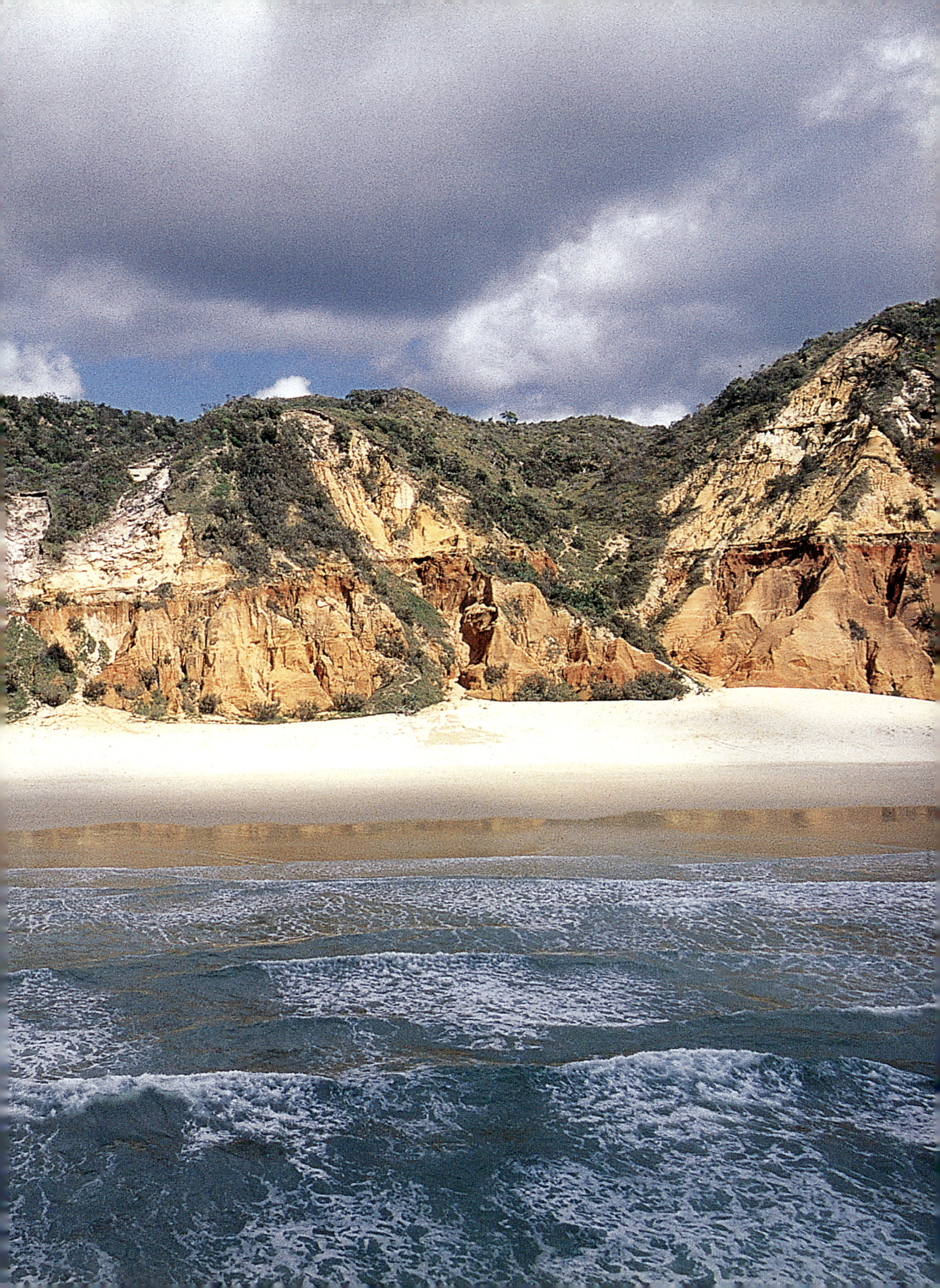

Australian Fossil Mammal Sites
(Riversleigh & Naracoorte)

Australia holds the world's most distinctive plant and animal life and its fossil record shows that this has long been the case, this being the outcome of the continent's almost total isolation for 35 million years, following its break away from Antarctica. A fossil is the remains or the impression of an organism preserved in rock. Imagine a huge fossil 'library' in which we could read the story of Australia's plants and animals over those 35 million lonely years. Imagine if we could read what the land was like then, what kind of animals existed and how they lived.

This is the story that is told in the rich and extensive fossil beds which make up the Australian Fossil Mammal Sites World Heritage Area. In the rocks at Riversleigh and Naracoorte, it is possible to trace almost the entire history of the mammals of modern Australia. These fossil sites are outstanding in their representation of major stages of the Earth's evolutionary history, of significant ongoing geological processes and of the evolution of life.

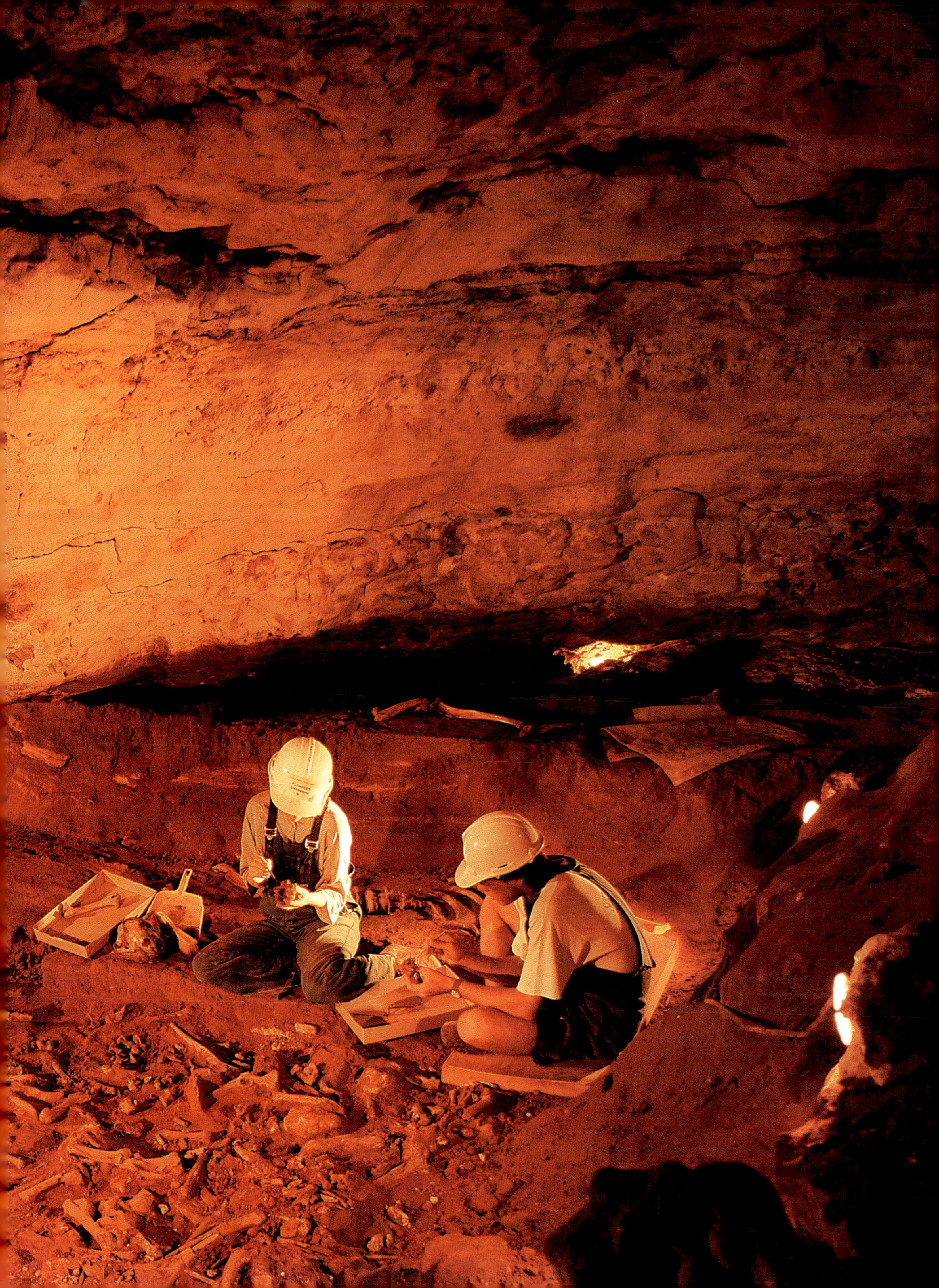

Location

Riversleigh and Naracoorte are widely separated sites in north-east and southern Australia. Riversleigh is situated in north Queensland, while Naracoorte is in South Australia. The distance between them is 2000 kilometres (1250 miles).

The fossil fields of Riversleigh extend over some 10 000 hectares (24 700 acres) in the southern section of Queensland's Lawn Hill National Park and are confined to the watershed of the Gregory River.

The 300 hectares (740 acres) site at Naracoorte lies 11 kilometres (7 miles) south-east of Naracoorte township in South Australia in flat country punctuated by a series of coastal dune ridges running parallel to the coastline. This area's most significant fossil accumulation is found in the Victoria Fossil Cave.

PREVIOUS PAGE Working under powerful halogen lights, Flinders University palaeontology students excavate the bones of extinct marsupials in the Fossil Chamber of Victoria Fossil Cave.

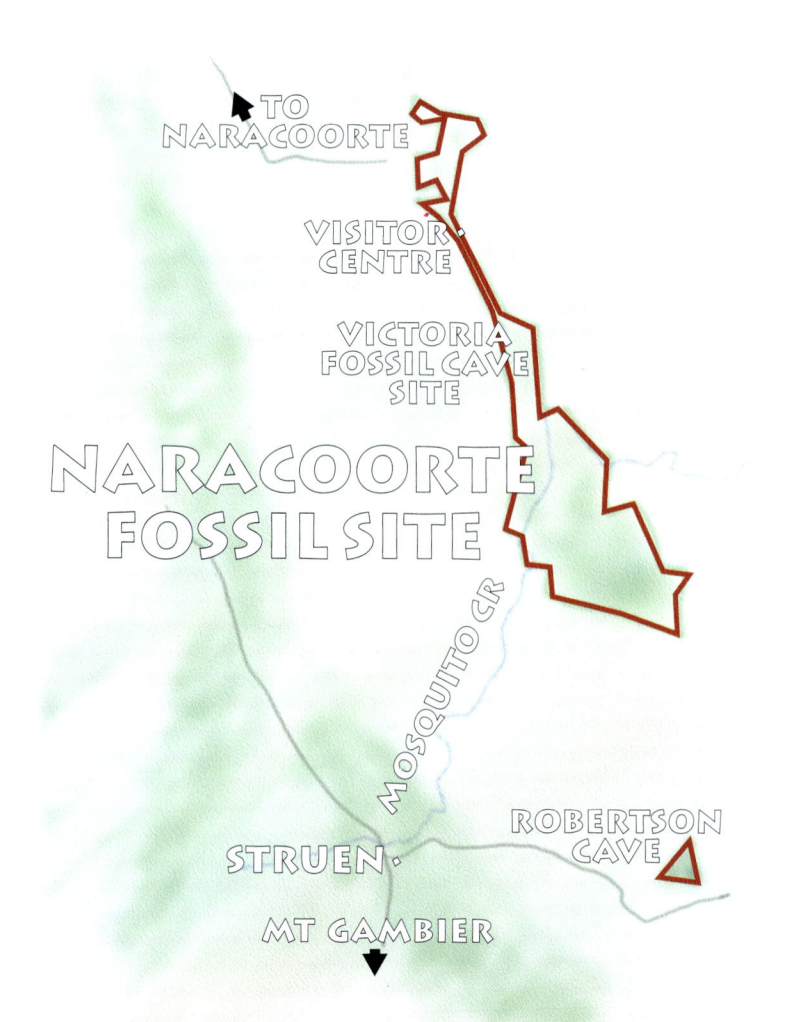

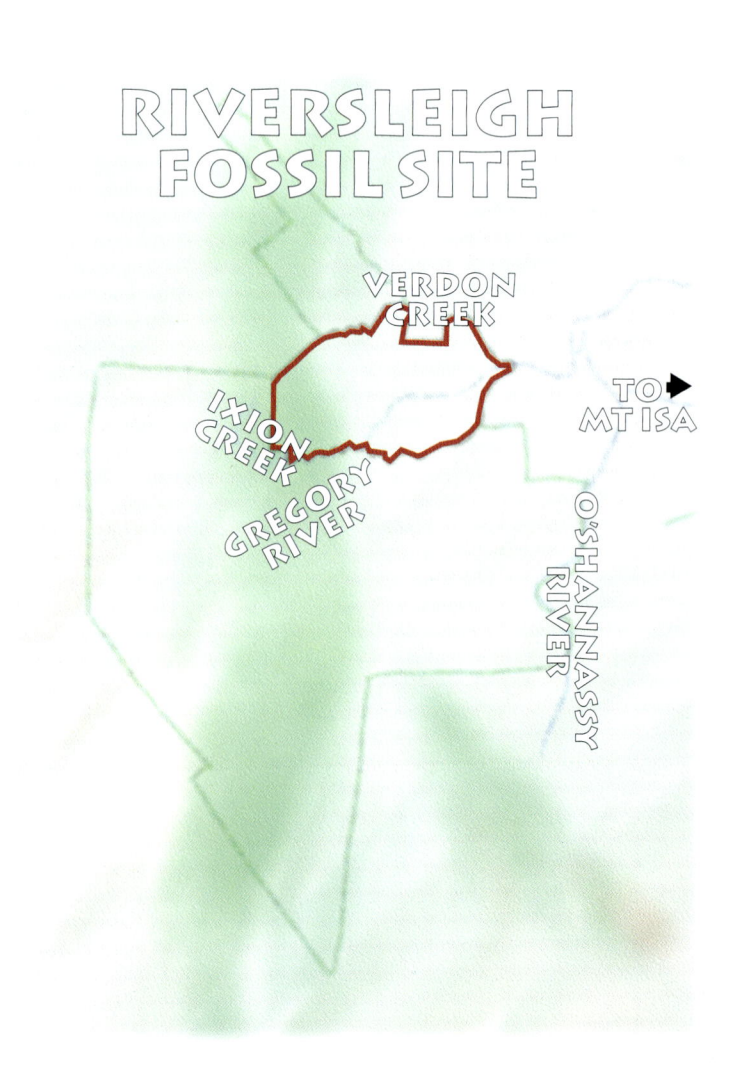

The Naracoorte Fossils
by Rod Wells

Victoria Fossil Cave is one of 26 caves constituting the Naracoorte complex. All these caves exhibit the same pattern of development and in almost all can be found traces of extinct animals. Exploration continues to expand our knowledge of the caves. In some cases, this has led to the discovery of new chambers and, in others, the rediscovery of caves first explored by William Reddan in the 1800s and lost for almost a century.

The whole Naracoorte east ridge consists of a single giant cave, much of it filled in with dune sands during the Pleistocene, effectively dividing it into separate caves. There is a high probability that the system contains several more 'fossil chambers'. It is tempting to speculate that caverns within this system may contain fauna sampled from different periods during the last 700 000 years. Should this be the case, the caves will form an important link with the 'Ice Age' fauna now being described from the Lake Eyre region in Central Australia.

In the past twenty years, about 10 tonnes of an estimated 5000 tonnes of fossil-bearing sediment have been removed from Victoria Fossil Cave. This has yielded almost complete skeletons of some species, while for others we have only a few tantalising pieces. The search for these rarer elements continues. The collection of extinct kangaroo skulls is unrivalled and is the focus of current studies into the evolution of this group. New techniques in analytical chemistry are opening up new ways of dating Pleistocene deposits. The deeply layered deposits in Victoria Fossil Cave have an important role to play in unravelling the events which moulded Australia's modern fauna.

In 1969, a small party from the Cave Exploration Group of South Australia, including the writer, spent a weekend investigating caves in the Naracoorte region. Wandering along narrow paths constructed in the 1890s, we came to the end of a passage and passed through a gate and into a low tunnel. Soon we were crawling on hands and knees along the original floor of a cave. The pale flames of our carbide lamps began to flicker in a breeze emanating from a jumble of rock. This was the telltale sign of a cave beyond.

We found our way into a large dome-like chamber and stood there, eyes straining to penetrate the gloom. There were skulls and jaws! The teeth were kangaroo-like, yet different from those of modern animals. They were from extinct species of kangaroos. I carefully picked up a skull. It was beautifully preserved, short and deep, the eyes set well forward, the braincase elevated over the palate. How long had it lain here undisturbed - 20 000 years, 100 000 years? We picked our way carefully down one side of the passage and saw the remains of marsupial 'lions', their huge slicing premolar teeth grinning from their dusty grave. We had just stumbled upon the greatest collection of extinct Pleistocene marsupials in Australia.

Now, almost 30 years after the discovery of Victoria Fossil Cave, we are able to piece together its story, which began some 20-25 million years ago. During this period, known as the Oligocene and Miocene, a shallow sea covered the area which is now Naracoorte. It stretched from the present day coast north to Loxton and out across the Hay Plain to Balranald and Narrandera in NSW and is known as the Murravian Gulf. Offshore reefs supported oysters, corals, bryozoans, spiny sea urchins and predatory whelks. Fish, sharks, nautiloids and giant toothed whales swam in its warm waters.

When they died, their skeletons joined those of the myriad creatures which burrowed in the sandy bottom or drifted on the currents: snails, scallops, sand dollars, crabs and tiny foraminifera. These remains, mixed with clays washed off the adjacent land, formed an organic ooze. The ooze slowly compressed to form the limestone from which the Naracoorte caves were later hollowed out by running water. Scallop and oyster shells and the ropey bryozoan skeletons are still clearly visible in their walls.

Once the sea permanently retreated from this region, much of the limestone was protected by overlying dunes left by the successive advances and retreats of the sea which had accompanied the Pleistocene Ice Ages. Areas of limestone not protected by sand eroded to form cave systems. Clays covered the floors of the valleys between the dunes or were carried in suspension in the ground water to settle within the lower tunnels of the cave system. This process sealed the floors of some valleys as effectively as one might use clay to seal a dam.

The water level in the valleys rose, finally breaching the dune in the vicinity of the Naracoorte caves. It swept away much of the overlying sand to expose the old entrances to the caves.

Their entrances exposed, the caves now acted as pitfall traps for unwary animals and as homes for others. Often their saucer shaped entrances would temporarily block with sand and plant debris. Water accumulating in these plugged entrances formed small circular billabongs. Sometimes a sodden plug weakened, suddenly giving way. The resulting torrent swept down into the cave, eroding the underlying cone of sediment and its buried skeletons to re-deposit them across an alluvial fan or carry them in a jumbled mess to some deep recess among the rocks. The entrance would once again remain open until, with the inevitable filling, the process was repeated.

Vegetation which stabilised the sands adjacent to the cave entrances hid the shafts leading to the caves. An unwary kangaroo, perhaps pursued by a predator, could easily leap through the shrubbery to suddenly plummet into the depths. Indeed, wallabies, kangaroos and even sheep are today trapped in open caves in this manner. Did all the animals found in the cave simply fall in or were they dragged in by predators? Did some shelter in the cave or use it as a lair? Did birds roost there? What were giant pythons doing in the cave? Research has sought answers to these and other questions.

The normal distribution of age classes among animals found in the cave suggests it is unlikely that the bones are from animals which fell victim to predators and were then accumulated in their lair. Predators normally select as their victims the young or the aged and infirm.

The bones were examined for evidence of chewing by predators. Many large bones have small chisel-like gouges scattered over their surface. These were made by the incisor teeth of rodents as they chewed away the last vestiges of muscle or tendon in their hunger for protein. Sometimes a bone is found with large and deep crescent-shaped cuts. These generally occur on the limb bones of kangaroos and match perfectly the shape of the cutting edges of the gigantic blade-like premolar teeth of the marsupial 'lion'. This indicates some involvement of the 'lion' but is not sufficient to conclude that the cave was the lair of these animals.

The remains of other mammalian predators were also found, but in relatively low numbers. They include the Tasmanian tiger, the Tasmanian devil and the quoll, or native cat. Devils are known to use caves as lairs but their numbers were so low as to give rise to the suspicion that they, along with the tiger and the cat, may have been victims of the pitfall or predators. Snakes are common among the fauna. This is not surprising given the number that fall into caves or live in the boulder strewn entrances today. However, the suspicion that they, along with the tiger and the cat, may have been victims of the pitfall or predators. Snakes are common among the fauna. This is not surprising given the number that fall into caves or live in the boulder strewn entrances today. However, among these snakes are the remains of a very large boa constrictor which may well have been a resident of the cave. Its contribution as a predator to the accumulation of fauna in the cave is unknown.

One quarter of all the species found at Naracoorte are extinct. They are a fauna which existed before man came to this continent. The faunal assemblage indicates much greater species diversity existing in an environment not dissimilar to that of today. The causes of their extinction are a matter of conjecture but man must be a prime suspect. The deposit in the fossil chamber is unlikely to provide an answer to the timing of that extinction but our recent work in the sinkholes near Tantanoola has yielded aboriginal implements and remains of giant marsupials, or megafauna, dated to 14 000 years ago.

Remains of the extinct Diprotodontid *Zygomaturus trilobus* are found at Naracoorte. It is the last in the line of a family of Diprotodontid marsupials that has an ancestry stretching back to the Miocene, 15 million years ago. *Zygomaturus* was found in small herds around the wetter coastal margins of the continent and occasionally extended its range along the water courses into Central Australia. This large, buffalo-sized animal liked to root around near the water's edge, shovelling up clumps of reeds and sedges with its fork-like lower incisor teeth. The creature had a small rhinoceros-like tail to flick back and forth across its mudcaked, bristly hide. The eyes were small and the nose was strangely upturned while its lips were large and fleshy. Its much larger cousin, *Diprotodon*, preferred the drier areas further inland where it fed upon shrubs and wattles.

Naracoorte's fossils include those of an extinct egg-laying mammal, or monotreme, *Zaglossus ramsayi*. This giant echidna lived in the Pleistocene and, in addition to its larger size, it differed in a number of ways from the small anteaters with which we are familiar. It was furrier and had a slightly curved, stronger and much longer beak, while its longer legs gave it an even more rolling gait. With its long snout, it probed the soft soil for worms or searched for insect larvae under logs. This creature resembled the long-beaked echidna of New Guinea, *Zaglossus bruijni*, an animal of the cloud forests and alpine meadows.

RIGHT Pitfall entrance to Robertson Cave, Naracoorte.

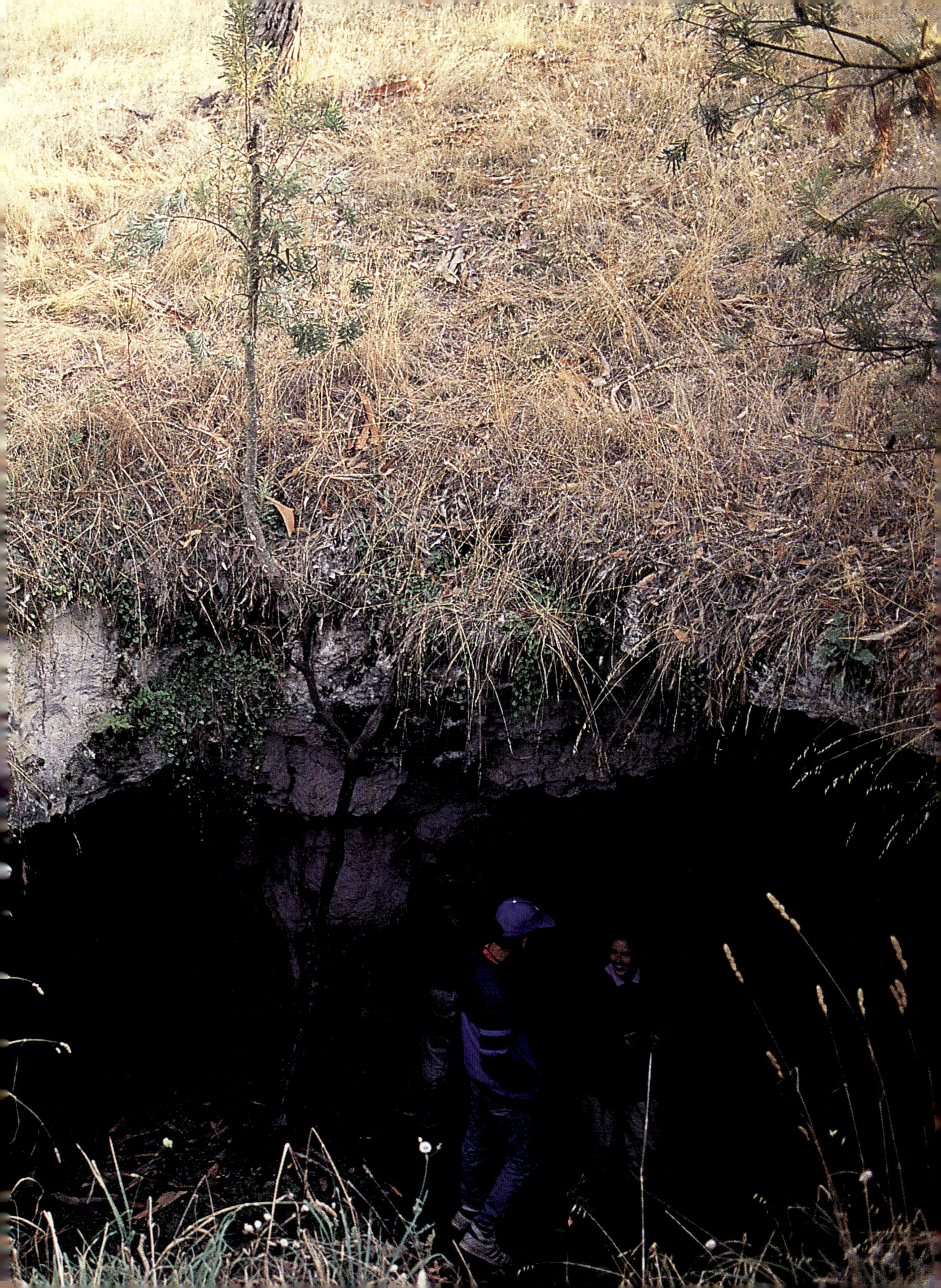

An Extinct Reptile

Measuring five metres (16 feet) a giant python was found at Naracoorte called *Wonambi naracoortensis*. It was not as long as the nine metre (29 feet) Anaconda from the Amazon but its massive ribs suggest a large girth typical of species that live near water. The vertebrae of *Wonambi* are different in size and form, both from modern elapid snakes, like the brown, and also the modern pythons or boids to which it is distantly related. *Wonambi* vertebrae have large facets where the ribs attach - so large, in fact, as to extend beyond the intervertebral articulations. The hole on the top of the vertebra through which the spinal cord passes is relatively small.

Wonambi remains a relatively rare component of the fauna. It is most closely related to boids of the Mesozoic era, of the subfamily Madtsoiinae. Fossils of this family are found in Egypt, Madagascar and Patagonia, suggesting that *Wonambi* is a relic from a time when Australia was part of the great southern landmass, Gondwana. It is not related to the modern pythons of Australia.

ABOVE Fossilised remains of *Wonambi naracoortensis*.

RIGHT Skull of the extinct long-beaked echidna, *Megalibwilia ramsayi*.

FAR TOP RIGHT Tooth row of the giant kangaroo.

FAR BOTTOM RIGHT Painstaking reconstruction of the crushed skull of an extinct leaf-eating sthenurine kangaroo.

NEXT PAGE A weathered pinnacle karst in the 500 million year old Thorntonia limestone of Riversleigh.

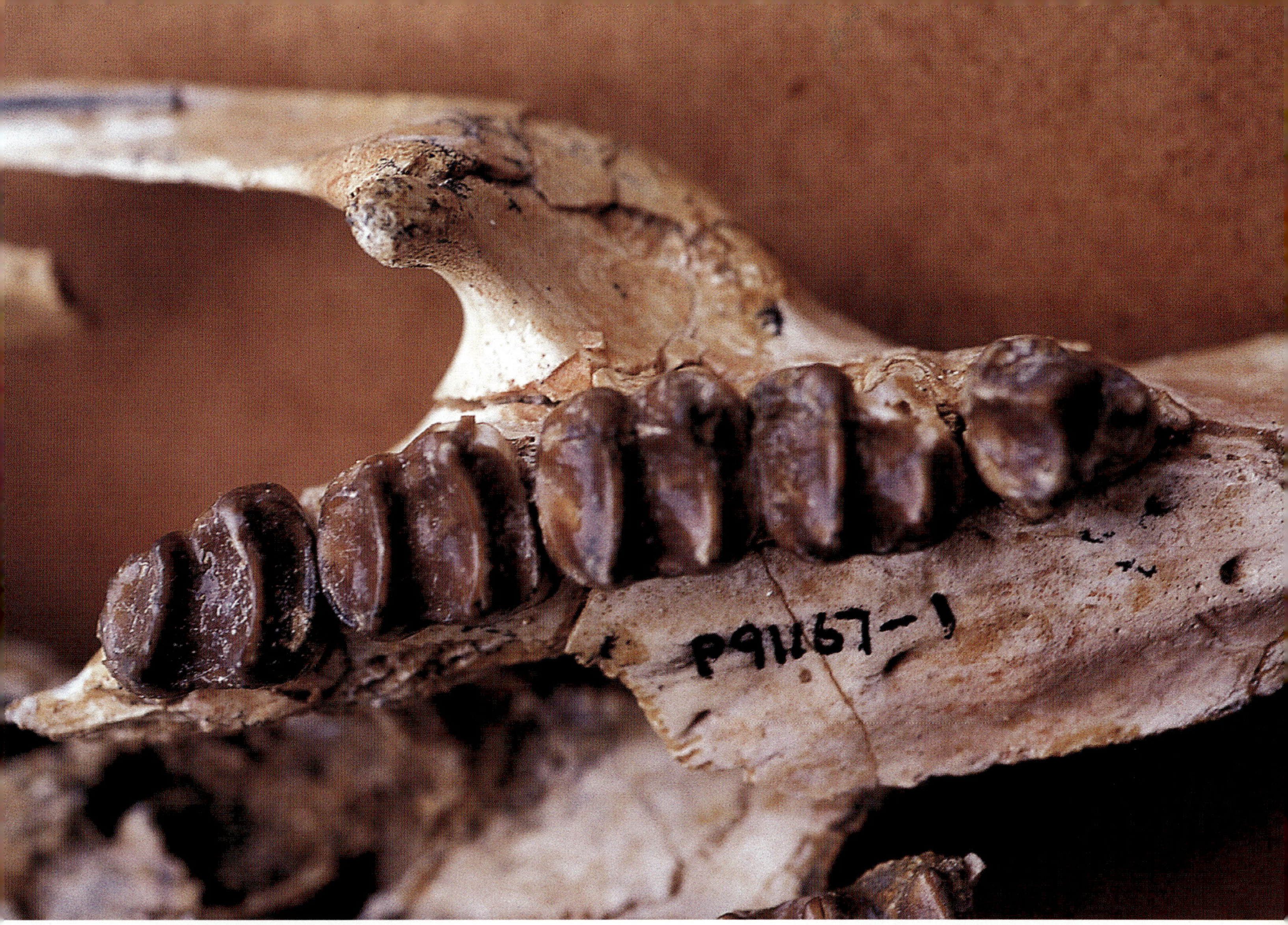
P91167-1

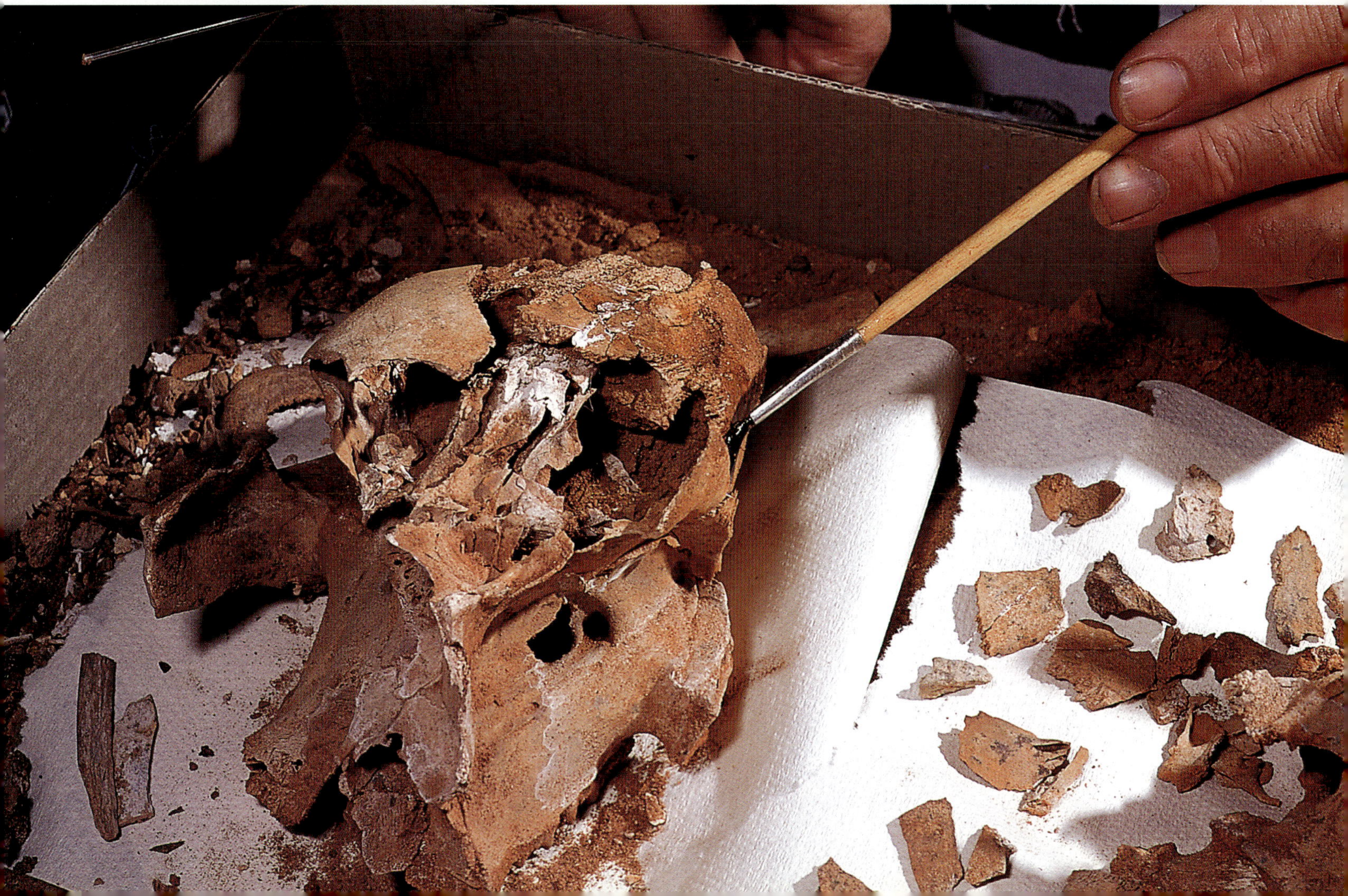

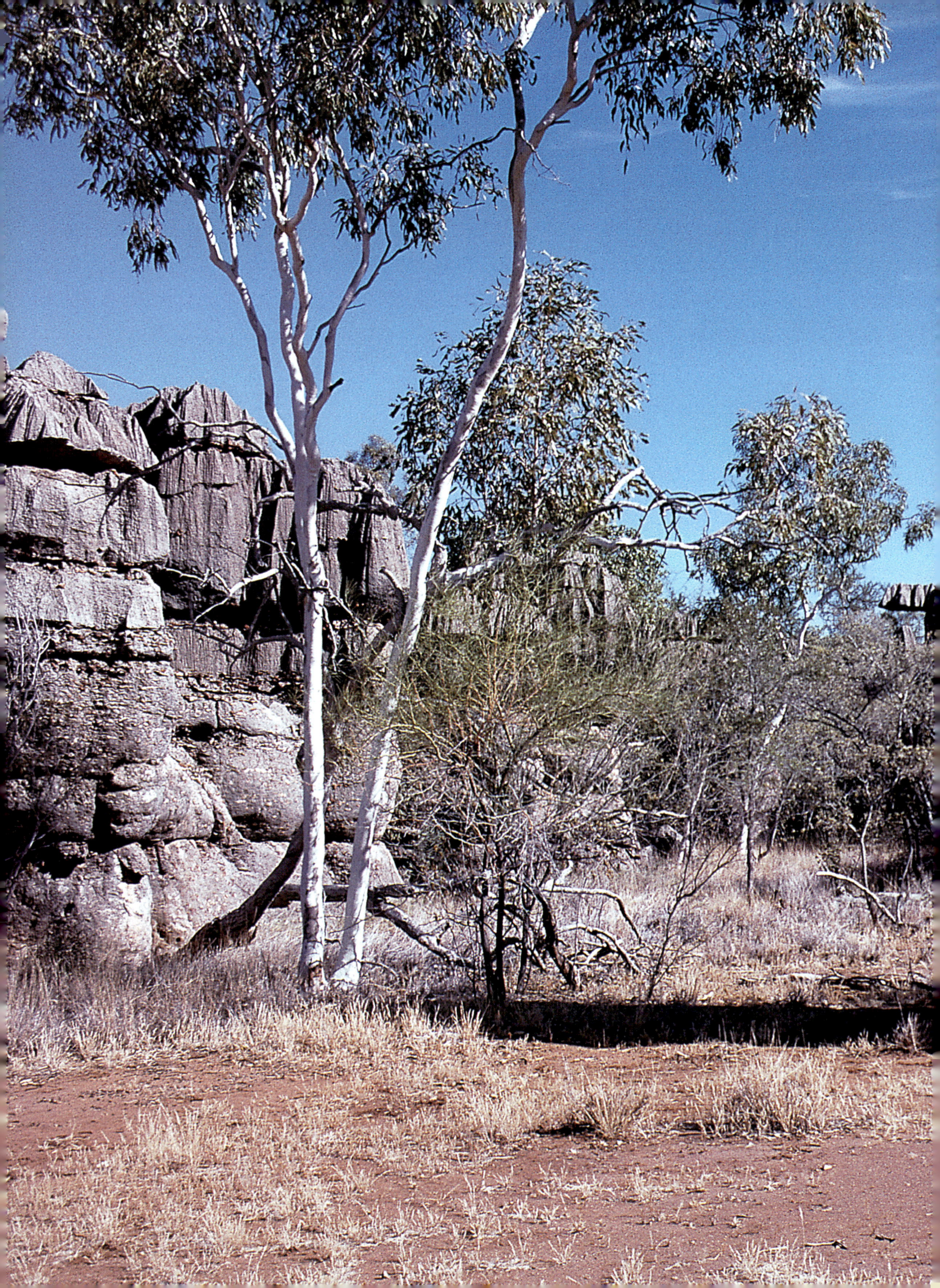

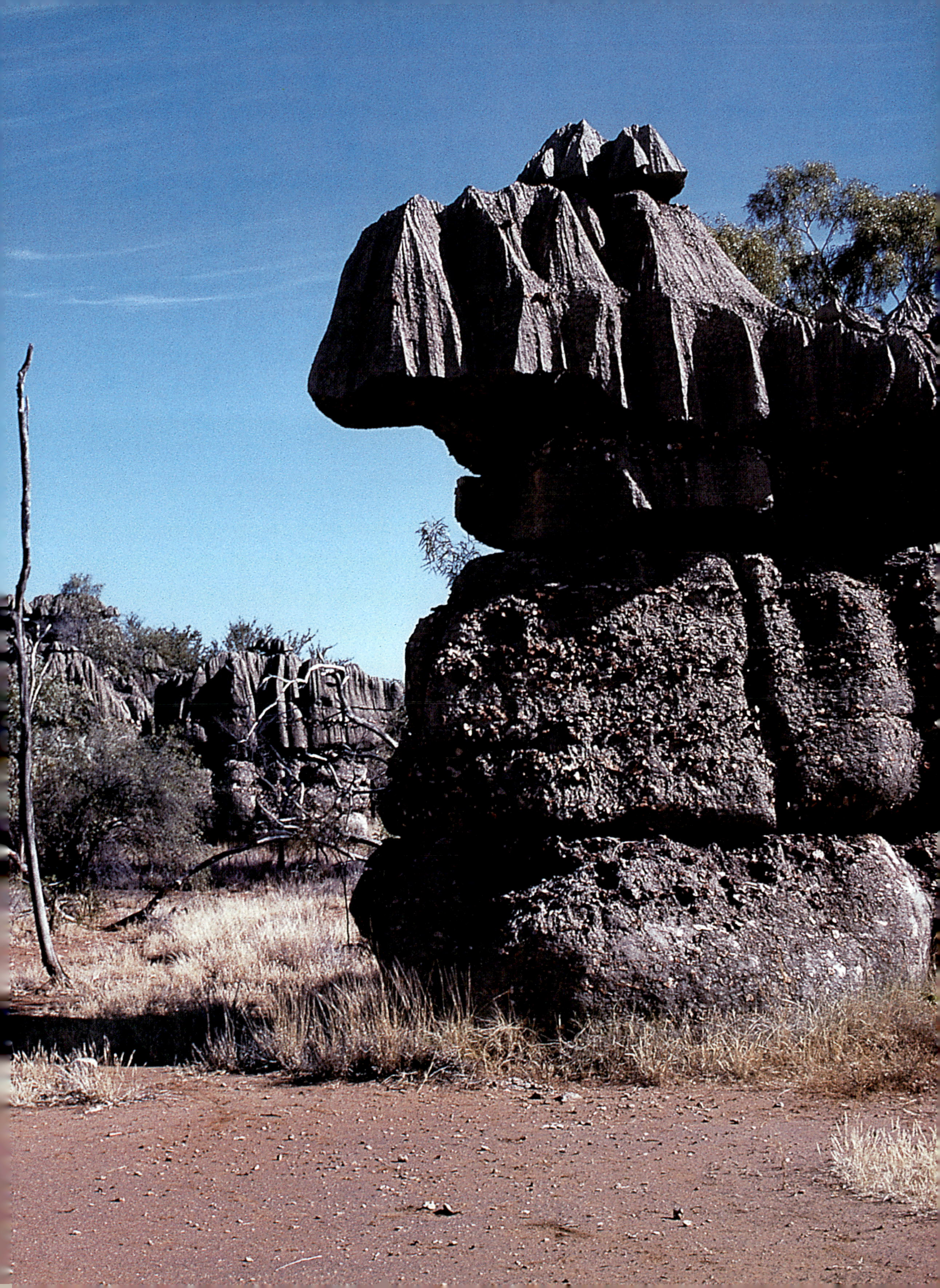

Riversleigh Fossil Site
by Dirk Megirian

In the south-west Gulf region of north Queensland, the Barkly Tableland drops abruptly to the coastal plain. Across the Gulf Fall, as it is called by the geomorphologists who study landforms, the 500 million year old grey limestones of the tableland are eroded and carved into a rugged terrain known as karst, characterised by a barren, rocky surface underlain by channels and sink holes. To the east and north-east, the tableland abuts equally rugged, but three to four times as old, mountain ranges. Emerging from the limestone and cutting through the ranges on Riversleigh pastoral station is the spring-fed Gregory River, its waters charged with dissolved lime, or calcium carbonate. The carbonate builds up in deposits of a material known as tufa and this forms dams along the river and creates a chain of billabongs. These tree-lined bodies of water, separated by rapids and small waterfalls, form cool oases in the otherwise arid landscape.

Within the Gregory River valley, there are tabletop formations of a hard, yellowish limestone, the remnants of a deposit that once filled the valley to a depth of at least 30 metres (100 feet). This is the Carl Creek Limestone, in which is found a remarkable richness and diversity of fossils. For the most part, they accumulated in small pools associated with carbonate springs, in caverns or in fissures eroded into older deposits. The fossils include plants, insects, snails, crustaceans, fish, frogs, lizards, snakes, crocodiles, birds, egg-laying mammals or monotremes, pouched mammals or marsupials, with bats representing the largest mammal group existing today, the placentals. They date from the late Oligocene to the mid Miocene epochs, or from about 24 to 12 million years ago. As faunas of different age are represented, palaeontologists, who study the ancient past, can trace the evolution of Australia's animals over a 12 million year time-span.

Those familiar with Australia's living animals would immediately recognise some of the ancient forms, once they are reconstructed from their remains. Some are noticeably larger or smaller than their closest living relatives and careful inspection might reveal even more significant anatomical differences. Thus, for example, the Riversleigh fossil platypus is more heavily built than its living counterpart and also has permanent teeth. Some of the fish, frogs, lizards, side-necked turtles, birds, bats, possums, koalas, bandicoots and quolls, or native cats, are not so obviously different but, when studied closely, the small differences that do exist help clarify the ancestry and relationships of living species. Other animals can only be loosely aligned with existing forms. Thus, there existed a range of wombat-like animals and diverse groups of kangaroo-like mammals similar to rat-kangaroos but sometimes the similarities between them are only superficial, and the result of independent evolution rather than common ancestry.

Some representatives of now extinct lines of evolution have a fascinating strangeness. Amongst these are small to medium-sized animals which came before the quite recently extinct group of giant marsupials, or megafauna, including trunked marsupials resembling 'tapirs' or 'rhinos' (without the horns), and cat-sized 'lions'. Amongst the small marsupials are rodent-like animals and species with teeth so unusual that it is not yet clear how they fit into the marsupial family tree. They shared the landscape with giant flightless birds and huge tortoises with horned heads and spiked tails - defensive structures retained from the age of the dinosaurs. The dominant predators of the time were not mammals but reptiles. Some of the fossil crocodile species grew as large as the estuarine crocs that now inhabit the coastal plains but were more powerfully built. Others, with box-like heads and flattened, serrated teeth, were not tied to water but hunted on land. Python-like snakes grew to a length of 7 metres (23 feet).

A remarkable feature of the Riversleigh fauna is the close proximity of animal species whose living counterparts are now widely separated. The swamp tortoise is today found only in a couple of swamps in the south-west of Western Australia; thylacines (marsupial 'wolves' or 'tigers') were confined to Tasmania before they recently became extinct; certain kinds of frogs now occur only in New Guinea; and marsupial 'moles' live in the sandy deserts of the interior.

There are currently two theories about what the Riversleigh fossil faunas tell us about Australian environments during the Miocene.

The proponents of one theory observe that the Riversleigh faunas are richer than others of comparable age and also contain, amongst the plant-eating animals, many small, selective leaf-eaters, some of whose living relatives are found only in rainforests. Conditions at Riversleigh were ideal for the fossilisation of both large and small animals and it is maintained that such exceptional preservation provides an unusually complete overview of the Australian Miocene fauna. What kind of ecosystem might have supported such a fauna? Plants form the basis of the food web. Many different kinds of plant-eaters suggest many different kinds of plants. Rainforests are noted for their high diversity of plants, so it is postulated that in the Miocene, the continent was covered by rainforest. Over time, as the Australian climate became drier, animals either adapted to the new conditions or they became extinct, or else they retreated with the rainforests as they drew back into the wetter areas on the edges of the continent. Scientists favouring this scenario see the Riversleigh rainforests as an evolutionary 'cradle'.

Proponents of a second theory accept that a type of 'rainforest' may have been present at Riversleigh but argue that this vegetation was not typical of the whole continent. Evidence is contained in sediments laid down in Australia at the time and since hardened into rock and therefore preserved, which shows products of evaporation and a variety of clay minerals that form only under very dry, desert-like conditions. This indicates that extensive regions were already far too dry to support rainforest. The rainforest at Riversleigh must have been a vegetation restricted to low-lying areas and fed by groundwater discharge and a shallow water table. The Riversleigh faunas are explained as mixtures of animals from a variety of adjacent ecosystems, ranging from rainforest along stream channels through to quite dry habitats on the surrounding plateaux and ranges. Animals occupying the drier country may have entered the rainforest from time to time to drink; those among them that died at the watering holes added their bones to those of rainforest species and thereby contributed to the richness of the fossil deposits. Scientists favouring this scenario see the Riversleigh rainforests as a local refuge for animals that could not adapt to the rigours of a continent already well along the way to becoming the driest on earth.

RIGHT Sediment brushed from around large specimens is bagged, winched to the surface and spread in the sun to dry. Once dry, it can be washed through screens to concentrate the bones of very small marsupials, rodents, birds, reptiles and amphibians.

Special Features

Riversleigh and Naracoorte are sites of outstanding significance in the way they represent major stages of Earth's history, including the record of life. They are outstanding, too, in their representation of ongoing ecological and biological processes in the evolution and development of ecosystems on land.

Riversleigh and Naracoorte are the only World Heritage Property to be listed for fossil values alone. Their listing is unique in that it comprises two sites separated in both space and time. However, this is explained by the fact that together they present the evolutionary history of Australia's remarkable fauna.

At Riversleigh, a combination of factors has given rise to a site where there is an exceptional diversity of superb fossils providing a window into the Oligo-Miocene times from 38 million years to 7 million years ago. Through this window we can 'see' the rainforests which then covered the land, and the fauna living in them, and trace the development of plants and animals as they evolved in isolation after the Australian continent's separation from Antarctica. The animals of that period represent the peak of evolution of the marsupials.

Naracoorte, too, opens a window into a significant period of Earth's history on a continent dominated by marsupials. The last 170 000 years have been characterised by great changes in climate and the Naracoorte fauna provide a key to understanding how marsupial animals responded to these changes. Naracoorte caves are also a source of specimens with potential value in the DNA analysis of extinct species; this is often not the case for fossils recovered from swamps, lakes or dunes.

Riversleigh and Naracoorte each provide a picture of key stages in the evolution of the fauna of the world's most isolated continent and, when these pictures are placed side by side, their value is further enhanced. Among the world's fossil sites, Riversleigh and Naracoorte occupy a place of great importance.

History

Riversleigh and Naracoorte were known to have fossils early this century but it was not until recently that the true scientific significance of these sites was realised.

The Naracoorte Caves were first entered by Europeans in 1856. By the 1870s, Bat Cave was being mined for its deposits of guano, or bat manure. Fossil bones were first documented there in 1859 and a caretaker for the caves was appointed in 1885. Victoria Fossil Cave was found in 1894 and, given the Victorian mania for natural history, was duly developed as a show cave and opened to visitors in 1897. This process involved cutting pathways through the flowstone floor, removing stalagmites and putting them on display in other parts of the cave, and enclosing the whole pathway in a structure of steel pipe and wire netting. By 1908, a total of eight caves were open to the public.

Fossil vertebrates continued to be unearthed from the cave but it was only with the discovery of the Victoria Cave Fossil Bed in 1969 that the real significance of the site became clear. In 1975, the cave was re-named Victoria Fossil Cave. New lighting was installed, an exit tunnel constructed and it was re-opened to the public in 1977. The present visitors' centre was opened in 1979.

The first European to note fossils on what is now Riversleigh pastoral station was W. E. Cameron who published a short paper about the bones he had collected. A second and third phase of scientific interest in the property followed in 1963 and 1976. Small scale research continued until the discovery in 1983 on the Gag Plateau of some 58 species of mammal fossils from the Tertiary period. This made Riversleigh the jewel in Australia's palaeontological crown. Since then, research at Riversleigh has increased steadily as new finds are made.

RIGHT An interdune wetland at Naracoorte. This type was once common throughout the region providing a habitat for many now extinct marsupials.

BELOW Feather wedging (a rock splitting technique) at Riversleigh.

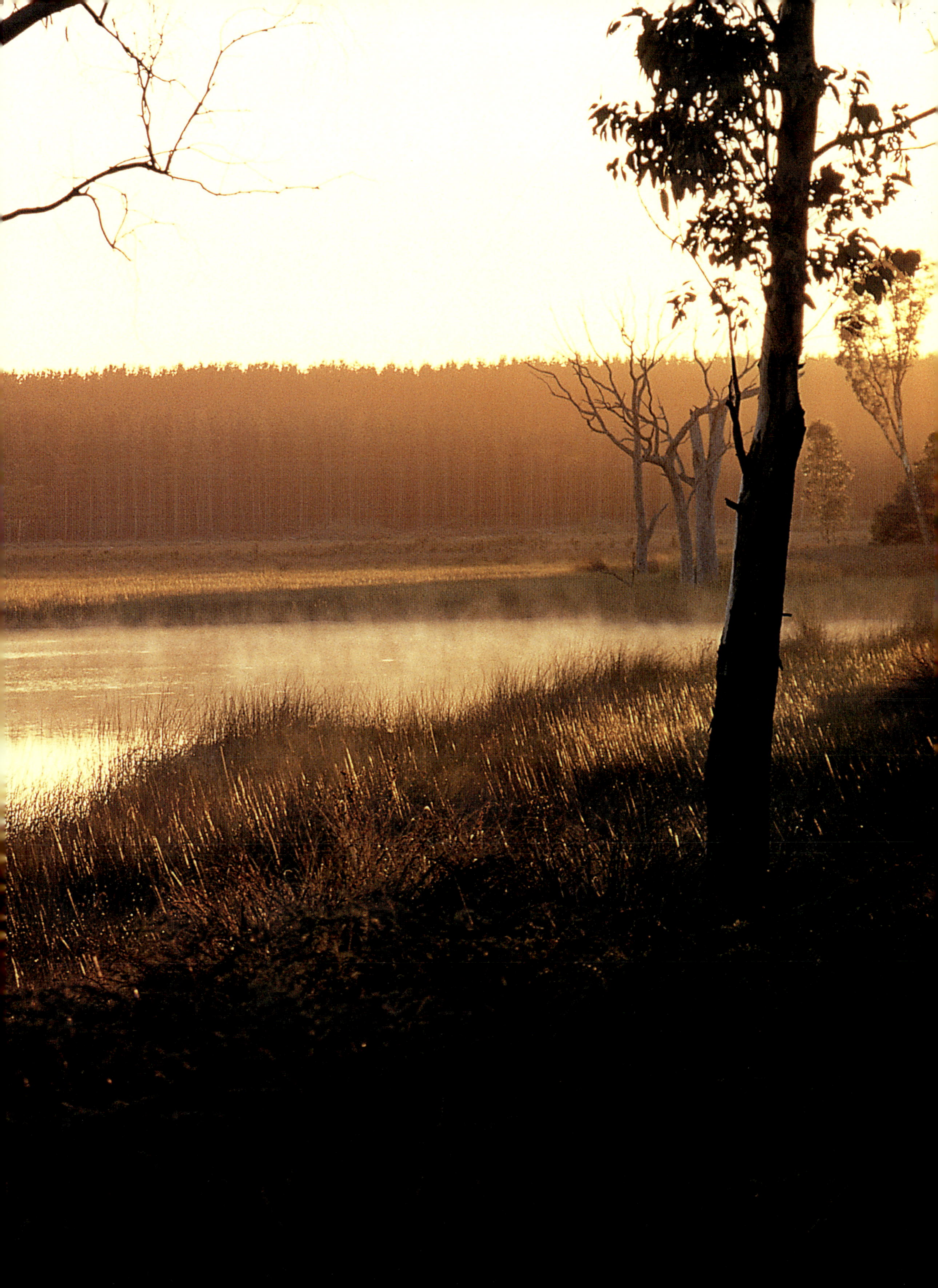

Fauna

Australian fauna during the Cainozoic period stands apart from that of all other continents and animals like those fossilised at Riversleigh and Naracoorte are not to be seen anywhere else on Earth. The fossil record shows the origins of species that have survived into the present but there are other species that evolved, diversified and vanished, leaving no trace of their existence anywhere else in the world.

There have been three key phases in the development of Australia's mammals. They had their beginnings prior to 35 million years ago when Australia was still a part of the ancient supercontinent known as Gondwanaland. Next, came a phase of diversification of species in the lush rainforests which flourished between 25 and 15 million years ago. The final stage came over the last 5 million years, following profound global environmental changes. During this period, these ancient creatures made themselves into the modern species we recognise today as being uniquely Australian.

These three phases are shown in fossil deposits throughout Australia. The phase of species diversification is extraordinarily well documented in the rich fossil deposits at Riversleigh. The reshaping and modernising phase is shown in the diverse and well-preserved fossil mammals of Victoria Fossil Cave at Naracoorte.

Fossil finds at Riversleigh have trebled previous known records for the Australian continent, spanning - with some gaps - a 20 million year period of mammalian evolution. The finds here provide the first fossil record for many distinctive groups of living mammals, such as marsupial moles and feather-tailed possums, and indicate that the majority of animal groups which now occupy arid Australia originated in ancient rainforests which have long since disappeared.

Finds at Riversleigh include the forerunners of today's native cats, marsupial moles, bandicoots and of the recently extinct thylacine. Five fossil koala species have been identified; among them a tiny 'pocket-sized' type. More mysterious discoveries include a group named the thingodontans, ancient marsupials of which no previous trace has ever been found, as well as remains of flesh-eating kangaroos. More strange and unidentified species are found each year. A place for some of these animals can be found in the categories of animal classification currently in use by scientists but others defy classification. For example, a single molar tooth found in 1985 was so peculiar that it was dubbed *Bizzarodonta*. The specimen has been assigned a species and family name: it is the only member of the Yingabalanaridae family and its affinities remain a complete mystery.

Finds from Naracoorte include 5 species of frog - two of which still inhabit the cave today, 12 species of reptile and much well-preserved bird material. Most studies, however, have concentrated on the mammals which make up the bulk of the fauna. Among the discoveries have been the fossils of rat kangaroos, possums, bandicoots and wombats, as well as carnivorous marsupials such as native cats. Fossil echidnas include long-beaked varieties which today are only found in New Guinea.

The fossils of Victoria Fossil Cave are so very well preserved that they have enabled scientists to perform amazing reconstructions of many long-extinct species. The paw of the marsupial lion has been rebuilt to reveal how it worked as a prey-capture mechanism, as has been the creature's jaw. These studies have yielded detailed information about how this leopard-sized carnivorous marsupial caught and ate its food, and about the environmental niche it occupied.

The Naracoorte caves have also contributed significant data to the debate surrounding Australia's extinct megafauna. Giant marsupials dominated the continent during the late Pleistocene but began disappearing around 100 000 years ago for reasons which remain unknown. Theories relating to their demise range from the declining temperatures of the time and the selective pressure to reduce the time taken to produce young, to the impact of humans through direct overkill or through ecological changes brought about by their frequent use of fire to burn the landscape. Giant pythons, wombats, echidnas and kangaroos are represented in the fossils at Naracoorte and they may yet provide information which helps to solve this puzzle.

Through time, the fossil creatures become more clearly recognisable as Australian. In this way, the Australian Fossil Sites World Heritage Area contributes to a time continuum within which contemporary life in World Heritage Areas such as the Wet Tropics, the Central Eastern Rainforests and Kakadu can be better understood.

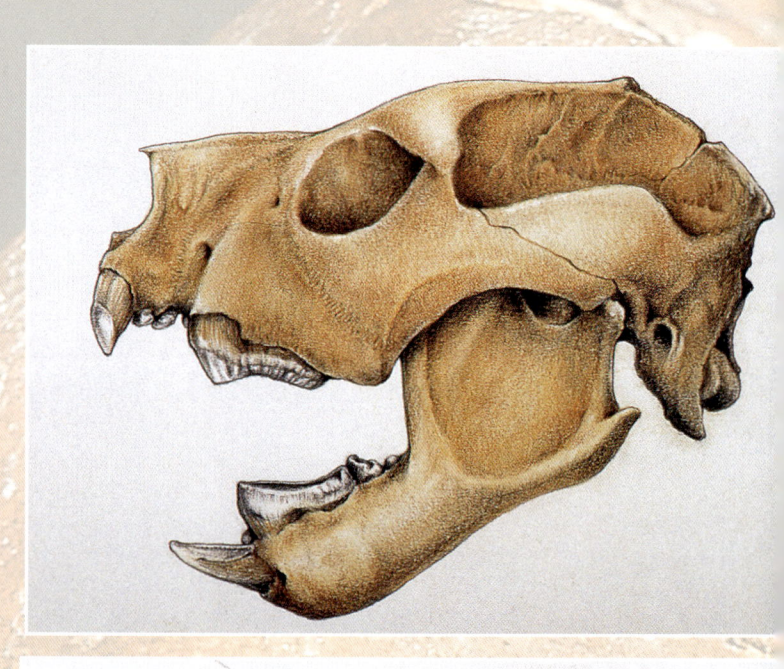

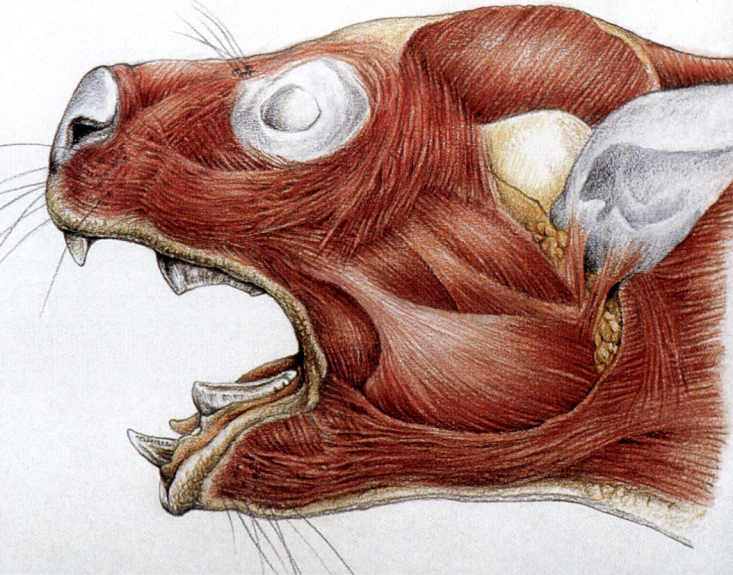

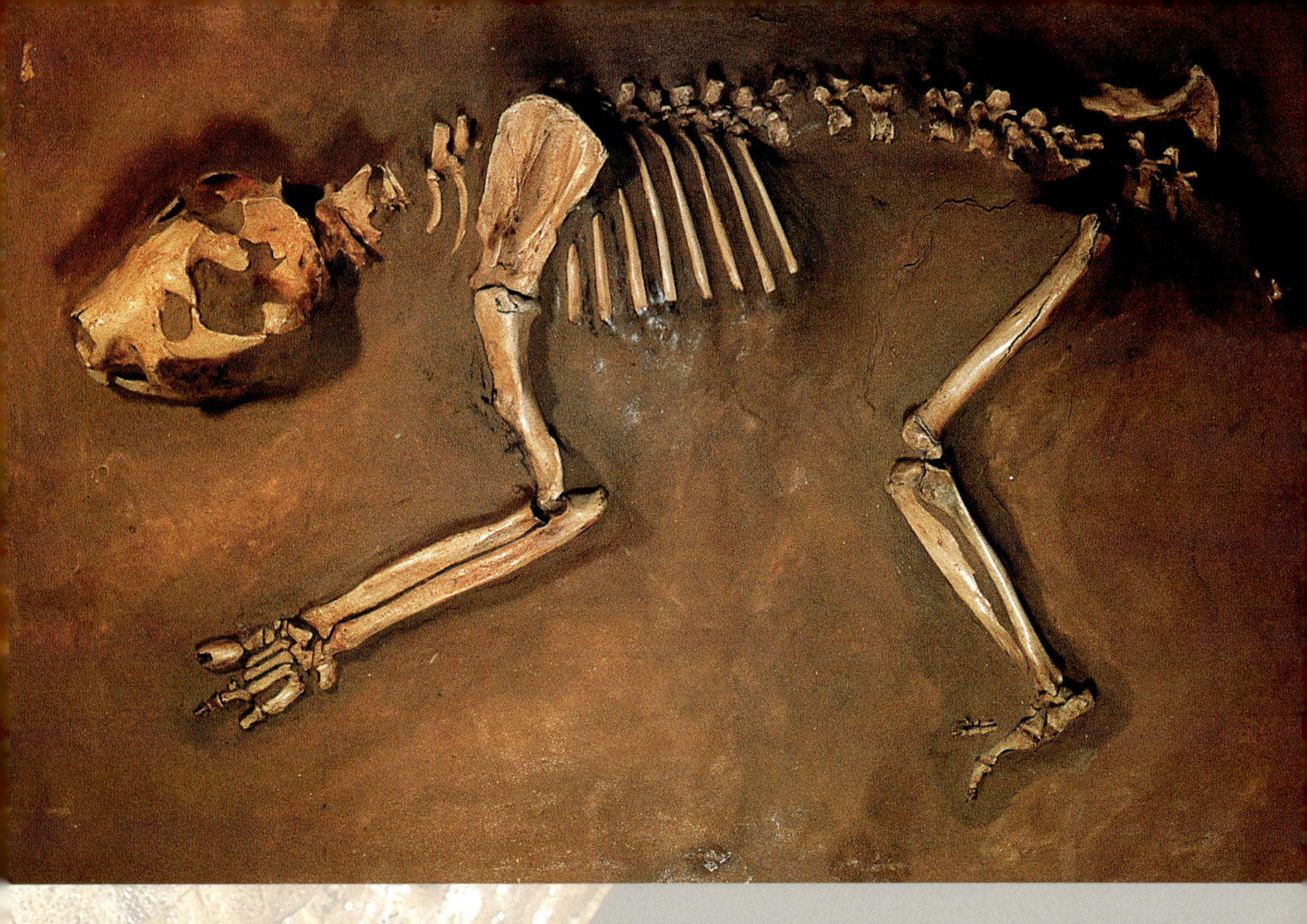

The Marsupial Lion

Few extinct mammals have aroused so much curiosity as *Thylacoleo carnifex*, the marsupial lion. It means literally the marsupial (*thylacis*) lion (*leo*) that cuts flesh (*carnifex*). A glance at the enormous cutting premolar teeth instantly conjures up the image of a formidable carnivore. This image is reinforced by the cat-like nature of the broad skull with its short snout and large eye sockets set well forward. The zygomatic arches sweep around in a great arc attesting to the power of the jaw muscles. The animal was clearly 'diprotodont' (two first teeth), the two first lower incisors being well developed as in all marsupial herbivores.

What has emerged is the picture of a leopard-like animal with exceptionally powerful forelimbs, (similar to a leopard or lion). It had a large heavy head supported on a thick muscular neck. The paws were strong, heavily clawed and probably used in striking at prey and holding it. The thumb had an exceedingly large hooded claw and was partially opposable, not to the remaining digits but to the palm. The remaining digits were long and slender and had small hooded claws similar to those of a cat. The hindfoot resembled that of a brush-tailed possum, the weight distributed along the side of the foot. Toes II and III were cojoined in a sheath like those of a kangaroo or wombat and were clear evidence of its diprotodont ancestry.

The trailing edges of these teeth were microserrate like a steak knife. The huge premolar teeth were crescent in shape so that when they were brought together in a bite the two arcs converged, trapping the food between them while the entire bite force was concentrated at the two converging points. The cutting edges of these teeth also had small serrations. *Thylacoleo* emerges as a large carnivorous marsupial.

We can picture it hunting as it stalks an unwary wombat or ambushes a leaf eating sthenurine kangaroo. *Thylacoleo* springs at its quarry. The sharp thumb-claws plunge deep into the flesh of the startled animal. It holds the victim in a vice-like grip. Powerful forelimbs restrain the struggling prey. There follows a series of plunging bites to the neck of the hapless animal. It is dead within minutes. Holding up a portion of the carcass in its hands, *Thylacoleo* uses its blade-like premolars to shear off strips of hide and flesh which it swallows in gluttonous haste. It pauses now and then to shriek and swipe at scavenging devils approaching too close. Having eaten its fill, it abandons the carcass and retreats to a nearby cave to sleep off its meal.

ABOVE Marsupial lion.

LEFT Illustrations of three stages of the reconstruction of the head of the marsupial lion.

NEXT PAGE Palaeontologists squeeze through one of the narrow passages in Victoria Fossil Cave. The most difficult to negotiate are termed, 'wrigglers'.

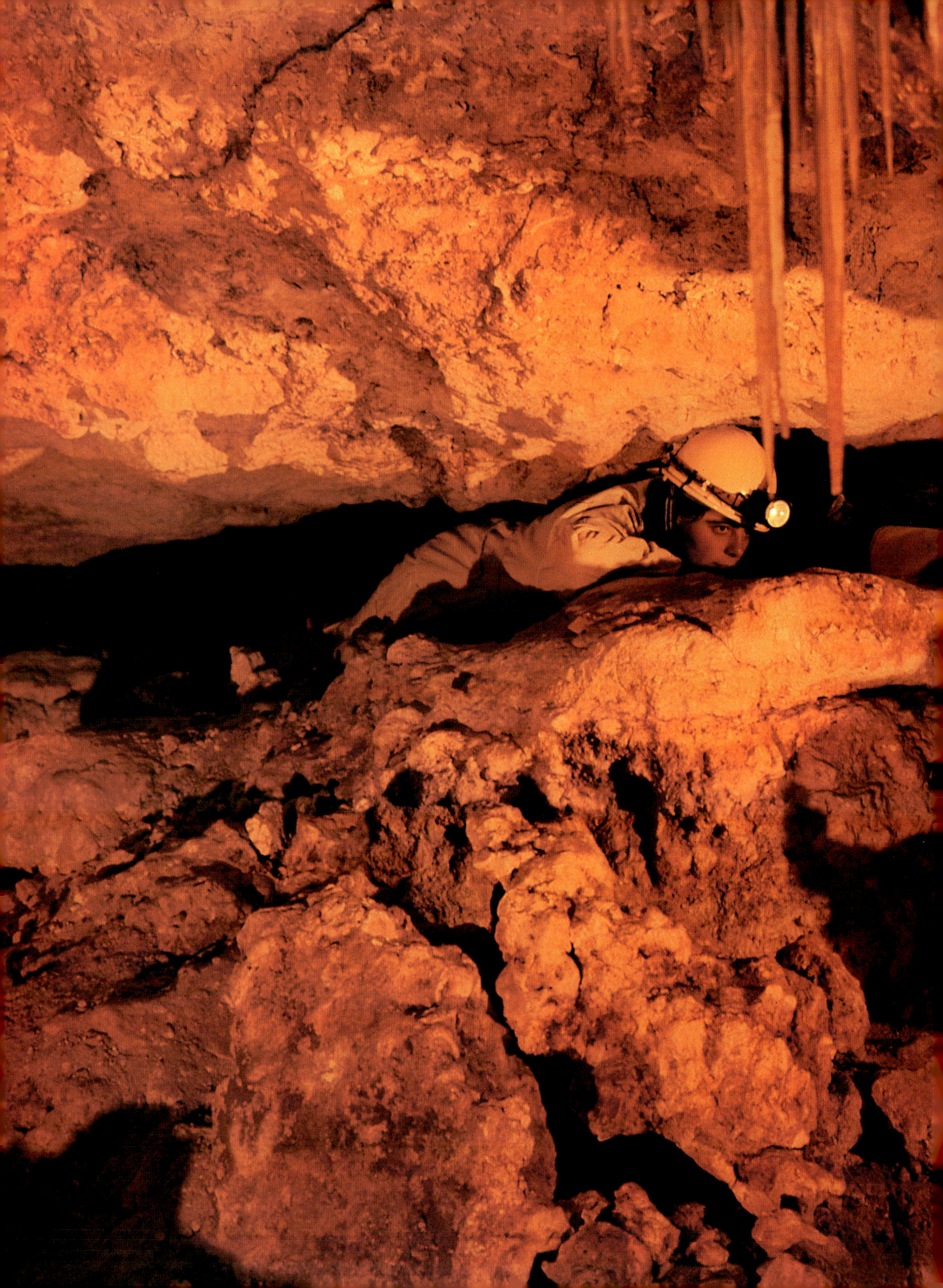

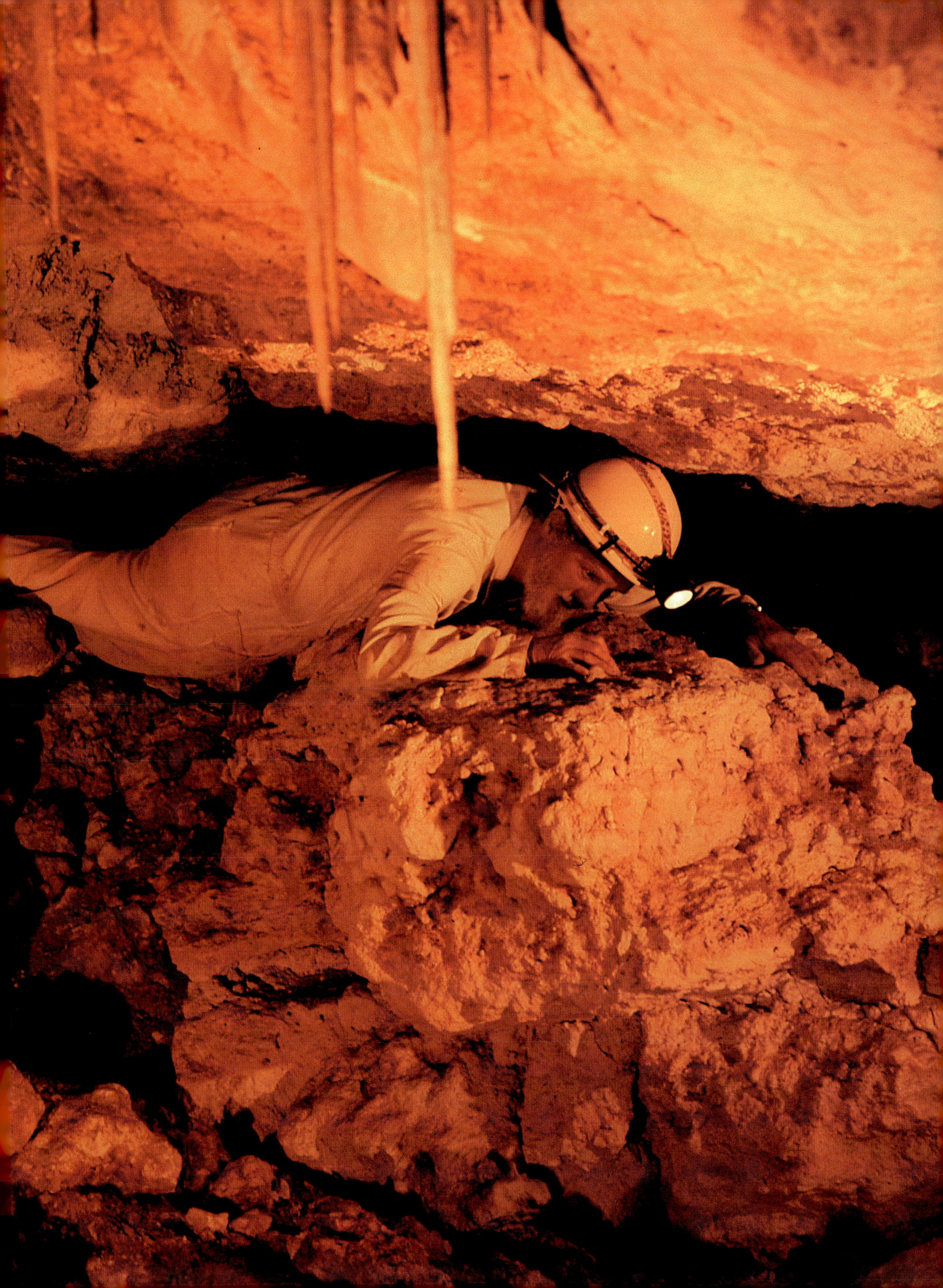

Extinct Kangaroos
The Sthenurines

Sthenurus means strong tailed. When one first glances at the remains of these animals found at Naracoorte, they are undoubtedly kangaroos with powerful hind limbs and strong tails. Although they were usually no taller than the larger modern species, one is immediately struck by the robust nature of the bones, broad pelvis, long arms and short necks. Sthenurines are indeed the heavyweights of the kangaroo family.

These animals were, functionally, single toed. If we carefully examine the undersides of the feet, we find small protuberances or scars where the tendons attached. These are so arranged that the tendons must have crossed over in a similar fashion to the cruciate ligaments of a horse, an adaptation allowing for spring flexion of the foot.

An examination of the broad pelvic region reveals a pair of large spatulate epipubic bones more than four times the size of those of a living kangaroo. These, once thought to function solely as support for the pouch, are now considered to be equally important in supporting the gut.

As we work our way up the back, we notice the human-like form of the shoulder blades and the collar bone. These are so arranged as to allow the animal to raise its arms above its head. Living kangaroos can only raise the humerus to a horizontal position.

To discover the way of life of the sthenurine, we must turn to the skull and jaws, for it is the teeth that give us the essential clues to its diet. The jaw is rather short, as is the gap between the incisor teeth and the cheek teeth. The incisors come together in a tight vee formation and are oriented more vertically than in a grazing kangaroo. In basic shape, the jaw is reminiscent of a koala. The cheek teeth are low crowned, with little allowance for wear, so we may conclude that the diet is not particularly abrasive, like grass. The jaw is heavy and the shape and size of the ascending ramus indicates large and powerful jaw muscles. Even if the diet was not abrasive, its food plants, such as the leaves of woody shrubs, must have been tough. Finally, we examine the nature of the cusps on the molar teeth. They have evolved into a pair of parallel, transverse shearing ridges (lophs). There is no mid-link connecting the lophs as in living species. These were largely shearing teeth, an array of salad dicers.

Now we can reconstruct the sthenurine. It is a leaf eater. We see it hopping through the forest, its short and powerful tail allowing considerable manoeuvrability. It stops here and there to reach up and pull down a branch which is grasped with its long fingers. Delicately, it plucks off the succulent leaves with its incisor teeth and, pausing, slowly chews them. Its large barrel-like belly attests to its bulky diet. Sometimes it spots an exceptionally tasty morsel high up. Standing on tip toe, supporting itself with its tail, it reaches way above its head. Its eyes, set well forward on its short face, give it excellent binocular vision. This aids the animal in visually selecting its food. As it pulls down a small cluster of flowers, a rustle in the shrubbery alerts the *sthenurus* to impending danger. Alarmed, it hops off, body erect, its heavy head on its short, thick neck turning anxiously in search of its adversary.

Protemnodon

Among the extinct kangaroos is a group of animals often referred to as 'giant' wallabies. They belong to the genus *Protemnodon*, once thought to be related to the living swamp wallaby. Although their skulls are similar to modern kangaroos, they are easily distinguished by their simple bilophodont cheek teeth and large cutting premolars. They have a stocky build with robust skeletons. Their feet are relatively short and broad for a kangaroo, having a well developed fifth toe. At Naracoorte, only one species, *Protemnodon roechus*, is represented. They were probably solitary browsing animals of the dense thickets.

RIGHT Skull of *sthenurus*.

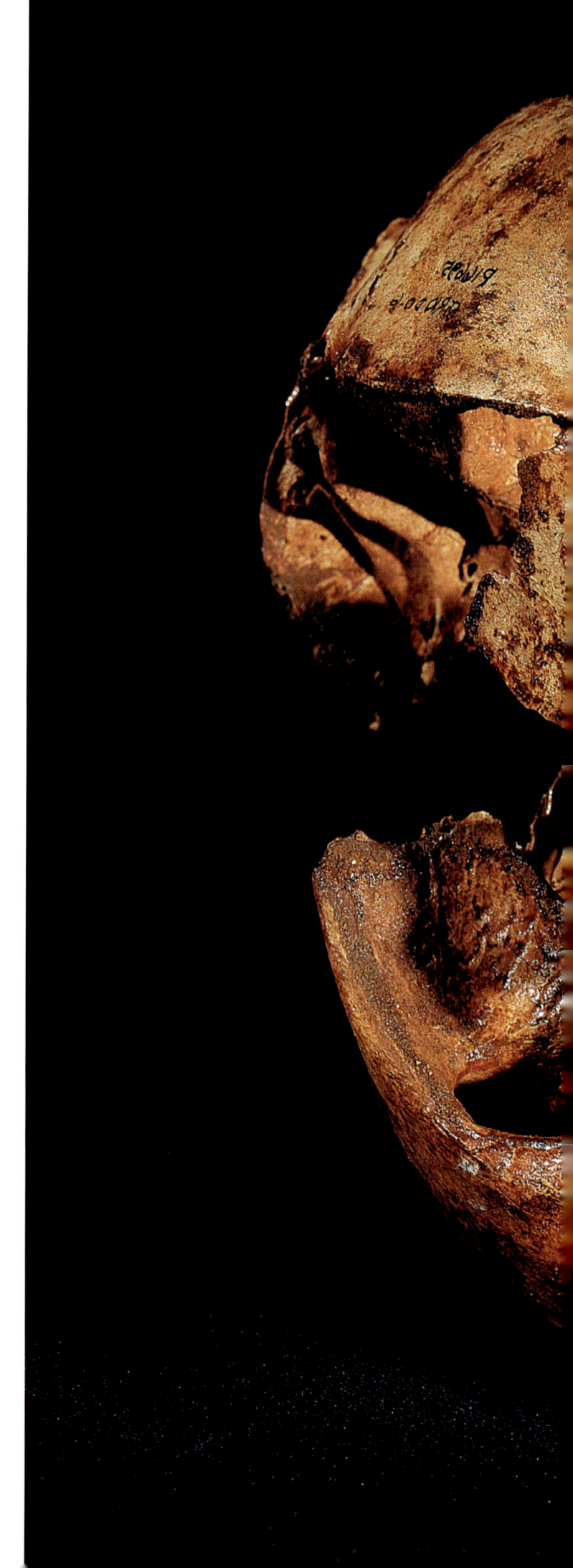

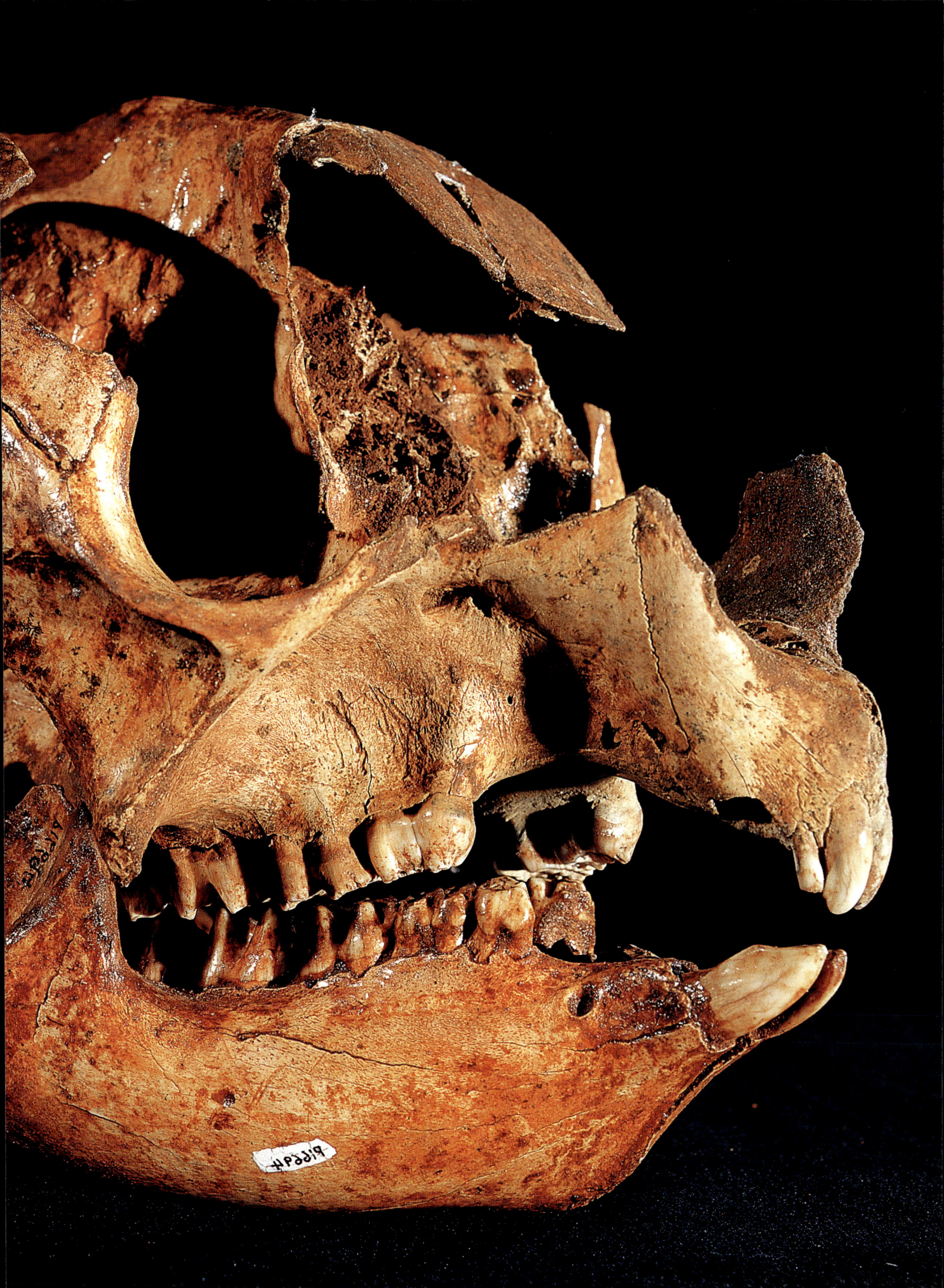

ABOVE The fossilised bones of small vertebrates more than 15 million years old are exposed by the weathering of the ancient limestones, Riversleigh.

RIGHT Skeleton of the extinct giant leaf-eating kanagroo, Sthenurus occidentalis, Naracoorte.

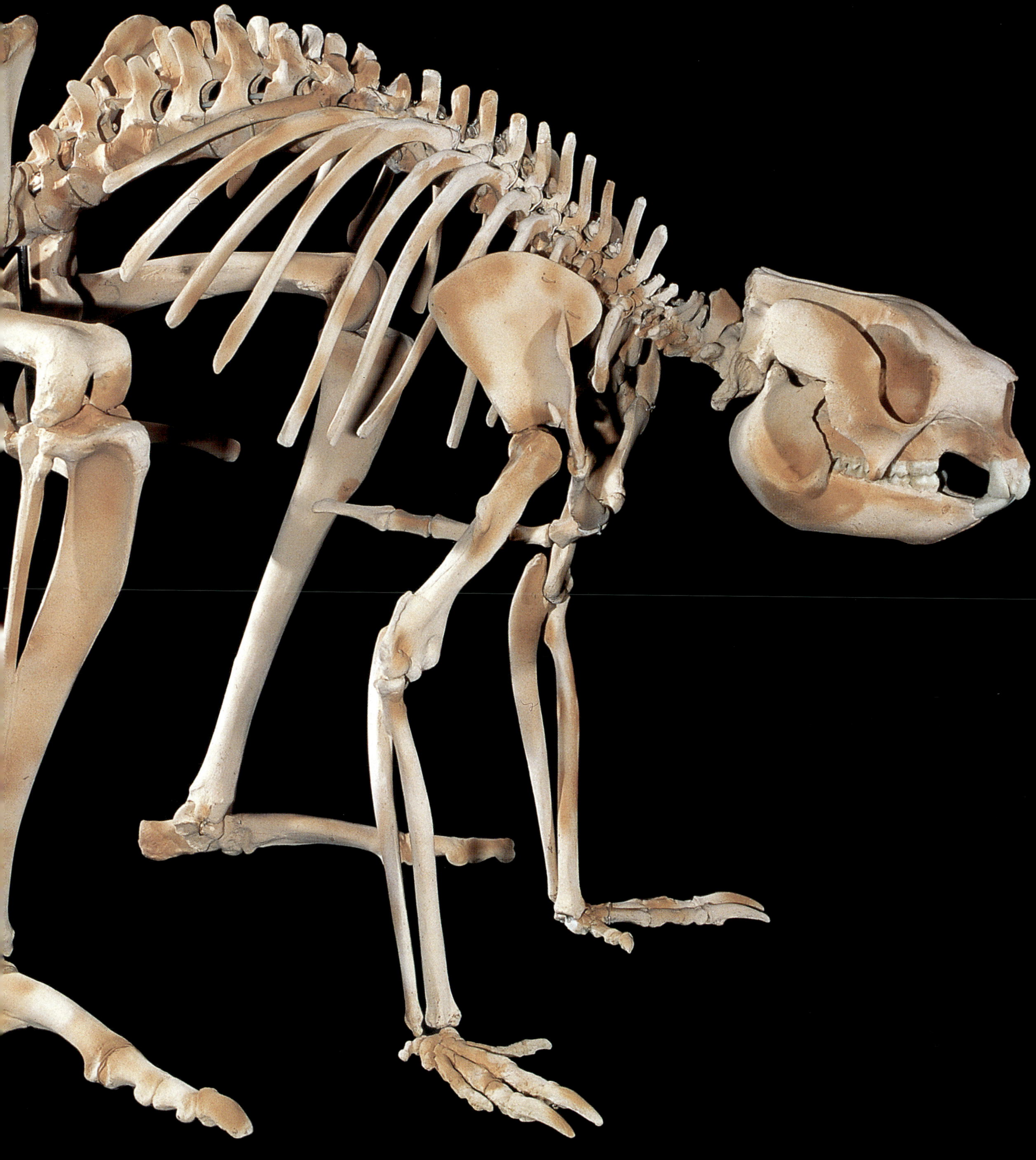

Management

Both Riversleigh and Naracoorte Caves are protected under the provisions of national parks legislation applying in each state. The Riversleigh area is owned by the state of Queensland and was gazetted as part of the Lawn Hill National Park in 1992. The Naracoorte area is owned by the state of South Australia, was gazetted in 1917 as Naracoorte Caves and is currently protected under the provisions of the South Australian National Parks and Wildlife Act. The federal government of Australia is responsible for the World Heritage properties, with day-to-day management responsibility for Riversleigh falling to the Queensland Department of Environment and Heritage and, for Naracoorte, to the South Australian Department of Environment and Natural Resources. Several other government, cultural and research institutions collaborate in the care of these sites.

The Riversleigh site is contained within the Riversleigh management unit of the Lawn Hill National Park. This is rugged limestone terrain and activities are restricted to palaeontological research and education, and some grazing carried over from the land's former use. The Riversleigh World Heritage Area is located in a region of very active mining exploration and although this caused the area's boundaries to be reduced from what was judged to be optimal, they are nonetheless considered adequate. Until recently, Riversleigh was a pastoral property but grazing of the land by cattle has had little impact upon the fossil beds which won the site its place on the World Heritage List. In 1992, the nominated site was acquired for national park purposes with arrangements for cattle grazing to continue under permit for a period of seven years.

At Naracoorte, the limited surface boundaries of the World Heritage Area do not match those of the extensive underground cave deposits. However, protecting the entrance to the caves is the key to protecting the fossils within them and this has been achieved. Naracoorte's fossil caves have been partially modified in the past to allow visitor access and some mining of bat guano was carried out in the years before 1972, when the caves were protected under the National Parks and Wildlife Act. While these impacts were unfortunate, further damage to the fossils is now avoided by the careful control of access to caves containing the main deposits, which remain in an undisturbed condition.

Facilities

Naracoorte: Access via the township of Naracoorte which is only six miles (10 kilometres) away. There is an on-site museum and interpretation centre. An estimated 800 000 people have participated in guided tours of Victoria Fossil Cave since 1969.

Riversleigh: Access via Mt. Isa, where the Riversleigh Museum is located.

Threats

The only significant threat to the Riversleigh and Naracoorte sites is the collection of fossil-bearing rocks by palaeontologists. Palaeontology is an extractive science which depends on the removal of specimens to laboratories for study. This means that the natural condition of the site must be destroyed in order that the information contained in it can be obtained. Great care is taken by scientists in the selection, extraction and care of fossils and, at Riversleigh, less than 1% of the resource is affected by excavation. All specimens taken remain the property of the Queensland Museum. Excavations in Naracoorte affect a higher proportion of the resource but most of the valuable deposits have not been disturbed. Materials collected from each of the sites are kept at a single locality nearby in keeping with a policy of IUCN-The World Conservation Union on the integrity of fossil sites. Explosives are sometimes employed to extract limestone, although their use is controlled to ensure that the impact is restricted to very small areas.

THIS PAGE Dams formed of carbonate tufa on the Gregory River, Riversleigh.

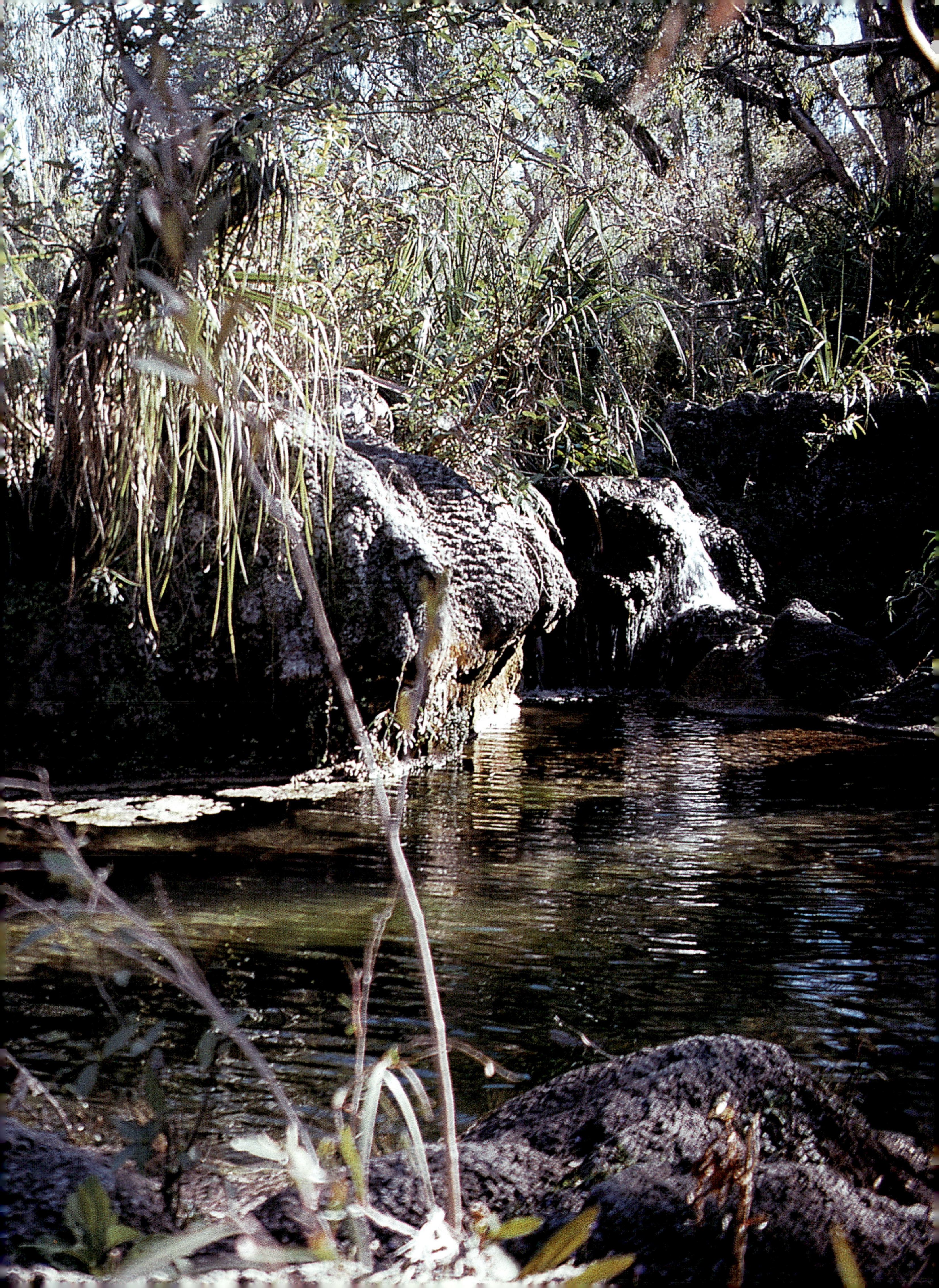

Heard & McDonald Islands

Heard Island's overwhelmingly dominant feature is the Big Ben massif which is capped by the ice-covered and frequently active volcanic cone of Mawson Peak. Heard and McDonald Islands are the world's only volcanically active subantarctic islands and are a window onto major forces in the Earth's crust. There are important opportunities here for scientific study on the mountain flanks, along the coasts and in the adjacent undersea environment.

Heard Island's dynamic glaciers, now in retreat, are outstanding in the speed of their response to changes in temperature. The plant and animal communities of Heard and McDonald Islands are also significant as they have not been altered by the introduction of species from outside the islands. These undisturbed ecosystems are important in the study of natural colonisation of very isolated habitats and will become increasingly so if global warming leads to habitat changes.

Location

The nominated Heard and McDonald Islands World Heritage Area is an external territory of Australia. It comprises a remote group of islands in the Indian Ocean section of the Southern Ocean some 4100 kilometres (2560 miles) south-west of Perth, Western Australia. The nearest land is the Kerguelen Island group, some 440 kilometres (275 miles) to the north-west. The area comprises the lands and all offshore rocks and shoals, extending out to the 12 nautical mile limit. The land area is accounted for almost entirely by Heard Island (368 square kilometres or 142 square miles) and McDonald Island (one square kilometre or one third of a square mile). The total area is 6734 square kilometres (2600 square miles).

PREVIOUS PAGE A massive colony of king penguins. King penguins can grow up to 90 centimetres (3 feet) in height and are only slightly smaller than the emperor penguin, the world's largest.

Heard and McDonald Islands

by William Lines

By far the largest single portion of the world's sea life, as well as much of the world's oxygen, either exists in, or is dependent upon, the Southern Ocean.

Opened up by the separation of the Australian continent from Antarctica and by continental drift, the Southern Ocean extends continuously around the planet, between South America, South Africa, Australia and Antarctica.

Six small islands or island groups dot this vast ocean: Macquarie Island, south of the Tasman Sea; South Georgia, south of the Atlantic Ocean; and the Prince Edward Islands (Marion and Prince Edward), Iles Crozet, Iles Kerguelen and Heard & McDonald Islands, south of the Indian Ocean.

All of these subantarctic islands are remote, mostly more than 2000 kilometres (1250 miles) from the nearest continent. Of their total area of 12 110 square kilometres (4675 square miles), less than four per cent is protected in reserves.

Most of those reserves comprise the Australian sovereign territories of Macquarie Island and Heard and McDonald Islands. They are the only wholly protected islands among the six groups.

The Southern Ocean is the world's last and greatest natural preserve. As the only land in millions of square kilometres of ocean, the subantarctic islands are the focus of life for the millions of birds and hundreds of thousands of seals that rest and breed on them.

The stratified waters of the Southern Ocean, with their cold-warm-cold layers, contain a greater density and variety of living matter than any other ocean waters. Indeed, several other ocean regions owe their productivity to the Southern Ocean. The Antarctic richness is carried up the South American coast by the Humbolt Current and to the waters off South West Africa by the Benguela Current.

The Southern Ocean's influence does not end in the sea. It affects and reflects the atmosphere and climate over the whole planet.

Temperatures at the South Pole are always 10° to 12° Celsius (18° to 22° Fahrenheit) colder than at the North Pole, a consequence of the Antarctic's isolation from other lands. Antarctica's colder temperatures, transmitted through the Southern Ocean, affect not only global currents and the weather, but climate as well.

The freezing of the Antarctic during the last 2.4 million years had the effect of setting climate patterns for the rest of the earth: it exposed the rest of the world to prolonged cold, resulting in widespread ice ages, each lasting about 100 000 years. These Ice Age or glacial periods were broken by much shorter warm periods, known as interglacials. The current warm period began about 18 000 years ago and continues through to the present day.

Causes and consequences can flow the other way as well. Worrying evidence of the effects of global warming is emerging in Antarctica and throughout the subantarctic.

All the subantarctic islands lie within a few degrees of latitude of the Antarctic convergence. This is the region where cold water from the ocean to the south meets warmer water from the north. From the south, surface sea temperatures rise from about 2° to 4° Celsius (34° to 39° Fahrenheit) over the relatively short distance of some 150 nautical miles.

The exact position of the convergence varies, moving within two degrees and four degrees of latitude. Salt levels, temperature and water circulation patterns differ so much on each side of the convergence that it forms a biological boundary. Many organisms, including types of plankton, fish and birds which are typical of either the southern or the northern side of the convergence, are rare on the opposite side. Heard and McDonald Islands lie to the south of the Antarctic convergence.

In the nineteenth century, most of the mammals and birds of the subantarctic islands were hunted and slaughtered in their tens of thousands for their fur-bearing skins, oil-yielding blubber, whalebone and penguin oil. Discovery and exploitation of all the subantarctic islands occurred simultaneously.

In 1853, American captain James J. Heard of the barque *Oriental* made the first sighting of the 368 square kilometres (142 square miles) Heard Island and noted vast colonies of seals and penguins. Next year, Captain McDonald of the British sealer *Samarang* claimed Heard Island for Britain. He sailed 44 kilometres (27 miles) west and discovered the one square kilometre (one third of a square mile) island now named after him, as well as the nearby islets of Flat Island, Shag Island and Meyer Rock.

Captain McDonald did not go ashore to inspect his new discoveries. Like Heard Island, McDonald Island has cliff-lined coasts and rocky shoals that make sea access almost impossible.

Even so, a determined elephant sealer managed to land on Heard Island in 1855. Thereafter, sealing ships called frequently, making the island one of the most intensively harvested in the subantarctic. Sealing led to the near extinction of the Kerguelen fur seal, caused a dangerous reduction in the elephant and leopard seal populations, and did much the same to the king penguins. The harvest collapsed after 1880. On Heard Island, the sealers left flensing platforms, tripots, huts, names on the island map, graves and ship wrecks.

Scientists aboard *HMS Challenger* made the first geological and botanical collections on Heard island in 1874. More comprehensive studies were undertaken in 1902. Sir Douglas Mawson's 1929-1931 British, Australian and New Zealand Antarctic Expedition visited Heard Island and Macquarie Island. Sealing was shortly thereafter prohibited.

In 1947, Britain transferred sovereignty over Heard and McDonald Islands to Australia, which established a scientific research station on Heard Island. The station operated until 1955, conducting meteorological, biological, geoscience and upper atmospheric studies. Scientific interest in Heard Island revived in the 1980s.

The first landing on the McDonald Islands, by helicopter, was made in 1971. A scientific reconnaissance was made in 1980.

Heard and McDonald Islands are oceanic islands. They lie in the path of an almost continuous progression of anti-cyclonic high pressure systems that move around the world in an easterly direction, producing winds and seas that surpass those found anywhere else on Earth. Westerlies blow most of the time.

The westerlies ensure that the subantarctic is one of the cloudiest places on Earth. At Heard Island, relative sunshine, that is, actual sunshine as a percentage of what is astronomically possible, fluctuates between 9 and 15 per cent, probably the lowest amount on Earth. Rain or snow falls on more than three quarters of days during the year. Heard Island temperatures are severe. The island also experiences a transition from winter to summer without an intervening spring.

Snow and ice cover 80% of Heard Island. Some 15 glaciers carry ice from the slopes of Big Ben, the island's dominating, ice-covered volcano. Thin and fast flowing, these are among the most dynamic glaciers in the world, having a relatively short turnover period. They descend from Big Ben, flow between steep basalt buttresses and serrated ridges, and terminate in ice cliffs some 15 to 30 metres (50 to 100 feet) in height at the sea, all in a distance of a mere seven kilometres (four miles). A steep bedrock slope and heavy snow precipitation hasten their travelling speed which may be as much as 250 metres (820 feet) a year.

Heard and McDonald support neither trees nor shrubs. The tallest plants are grass tussocks of Poa or Parodiochloa up to one and a half metres (five feet) tall. Bryophytes, lichens and low-growing vascular plants such as cushion plants, sedges, grasses and forbs are also common.

Low temperatures, particularly during the summer growing season, poor soil and salt air inhibit any species not adapted to the rigours of the subantarctic. Only about 20 per cent of Heard Island is permanently ice-free. Habitats are limited. Tussock grassland, meadow, herbfield, pool and poolside plants, cushion carpet and fellfield grow in favourable areas.

Some bird populations on Heard and McDonald Islands number in the millions; some seal populations number in the tens of thousands. Such reproductive success is possible because these creatures derive all their food from the fertile Southern Ocean.

An estimated one million pairs of macaroni penguin breed on Heard Island and a further one million pairs breed on the McDonald Islands. These colonies are among the world's largest and provide one of the world's great wildlife spectacles.

King penguins, year-round residents on Heard Island, were once heavily exploited for their oil but the population there has been doubling every five years or so.

On Heard Island, gentoo penguins have increased from between 9000 and 10 000 pairs in the early 1950s to 16 600 pairs in 1988. Rockhopper penguins also breed on Heard Island, while the southern giant petrel breeds on both Heard Island and McDonald Island.

Petrels travel long distances. Birds banded on Heard Island have been recorded 14 500 kilometres (9000 miles) away less than two months after release.

Heard Island remains free of introduced feral cats and rats and the nesting there of several species of burrowing petrels makes the island one of the most important habitats for burrowing petrels in the world. In fact, Heard Island is the largest subantarctic island for which there is no record or evidence of introduced plants and animals - one of the values which justify its World Heritage listing.

In recent years, only a single pair of wandering albatross have been nesting on Heard Island. In contrast, both the light-mantled albatross, with 200 to 500 breeding pairs, and the black-browed albatross, with 600 to 700 breeding pairs, are well established on the island.

Seals are the only mammals which are native to the subantarctic islands. Heard Island supports a large population of southern elephant seals.

Virtually exterminated by hunting in the nineteenth century, the Antarctic fur seal has recovered strongly in the last decades of the twentieth century. Small colonies of fur seals began reappearing in mid-century. Thereafter, numbers increased dramatically throughout the subantarctic. Heard and the McDonald Islands all support healthy colonies.

Leopard seals do not breed on Heard Island but concentrate on the island in greater numbers than anywhere else in the world. Around 1000 animals pass the winter there, preying on penguins and young seal pups, as well as fish, squid and krill.

On Heard Island, the glaciers are retreating. In some areas, glaciers and ice caps are up to 65 per cent smaller than in 1947. While a one-degree increase in temperature may sound insignificant, scientists fear it is enough to completely alter the Southern Ocean ecosystem. Evidence that this is happening is abundant and compelling. Throughout the subantarctic, elephant seals are dying. On Heard Island, the elephant seal population has crashed from 60 000 to 30 000, a fall of 50 per cent. Harry Burton, a senior scientist with the Australian Antarctic Division, and an expert on elephant seals, believes that the animals are starving to death due to the loss of their prey, caused by shifting ocean currents and climate changes in the Antarctic and subantarctic.

Cindy Hull, a zoologist at the University of Tasmania, believes that the rockhopper penguins, like the elephant seals, are starving to death. Krill, the tiny creatures on which the penguins feed, are temperature sensitive. Increasing ocean temperatures force krill to move south to colder water and out of the feeding range of the rockhoppers.

Animal deaths and higher temperatures at Heard Island and the scientific base at Macquarie Island are portents of global warming and signal a deterioration in the Southern Ocean. If the Southern Ocean deteriorates, then the whole world will feel the effects.

More than half the Earth's food manufacturing by plants occurs in the sea and the biggest single part of this happens in the Southern Ocean. In terms of plant growth, this ocean must be the largest 'pasture' on Earth. Plankton are the grass, undergrowth, humus and basic living tissue of this 'pasture'. If the plankton fail, so must the species dependent on them. Damage to them is damage to all and none will be immune.

THIS PAGE A view of McDonald Island with the snow-capped form of Heard Island's Big Ben massif towering in the distance.

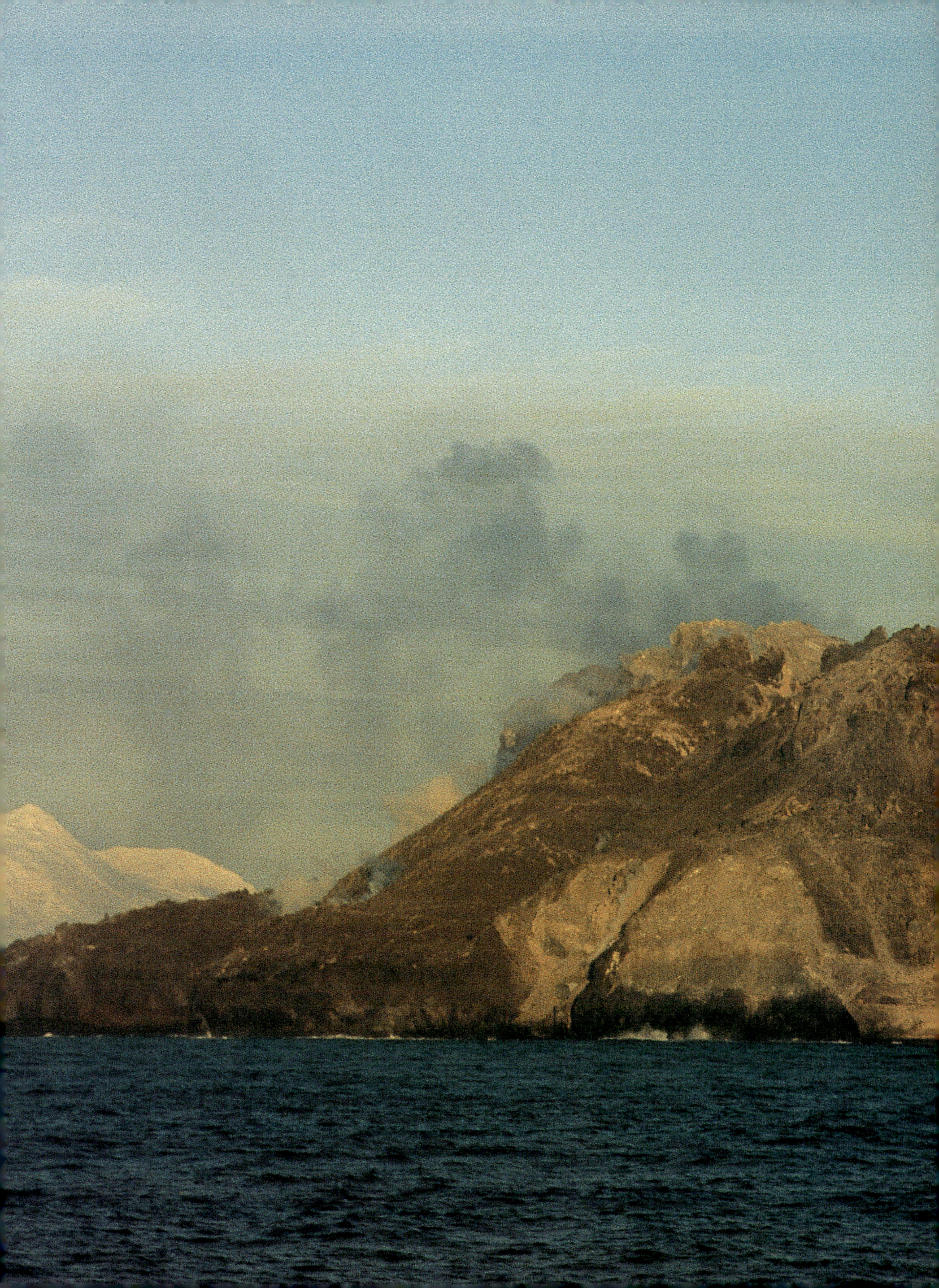

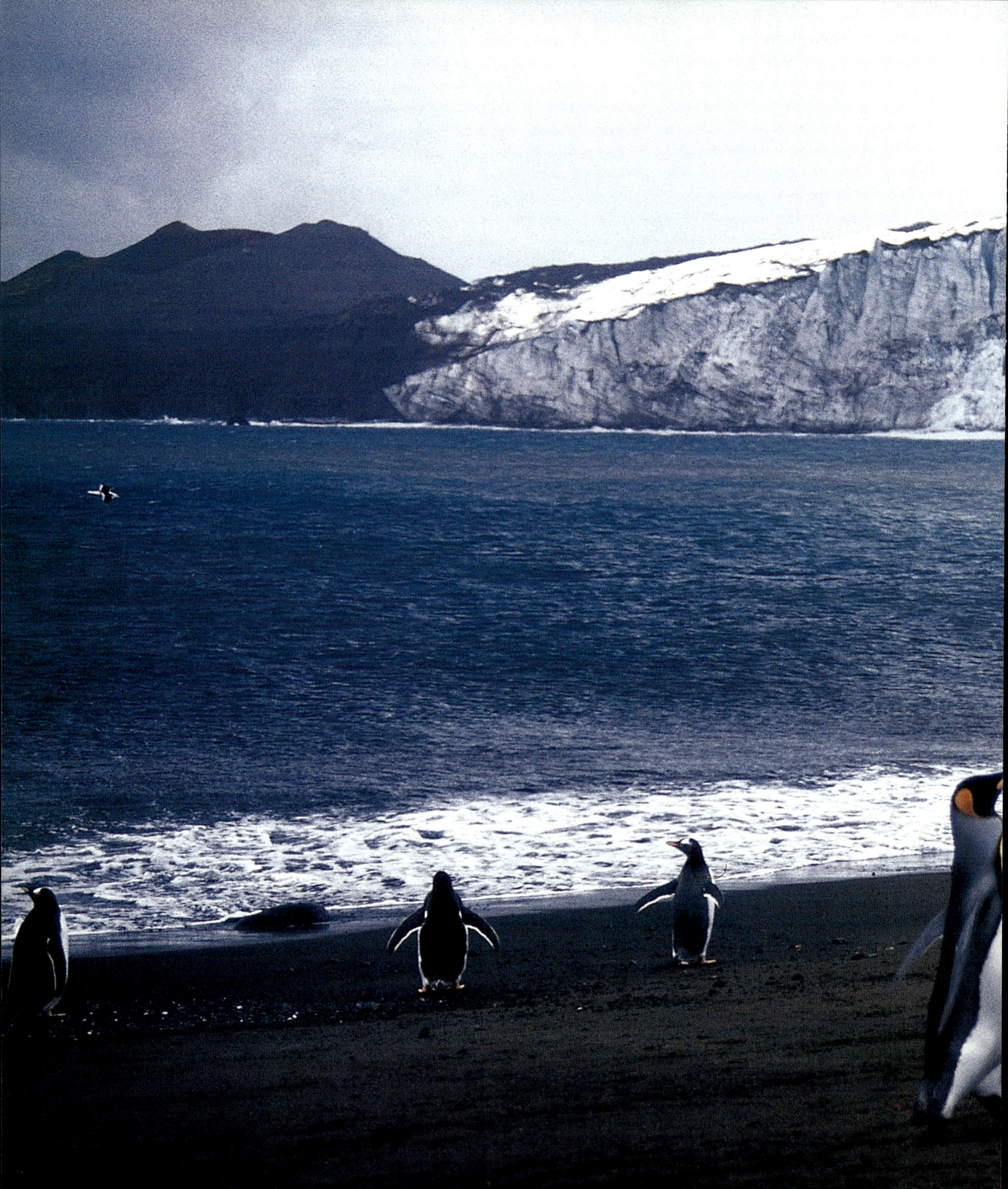

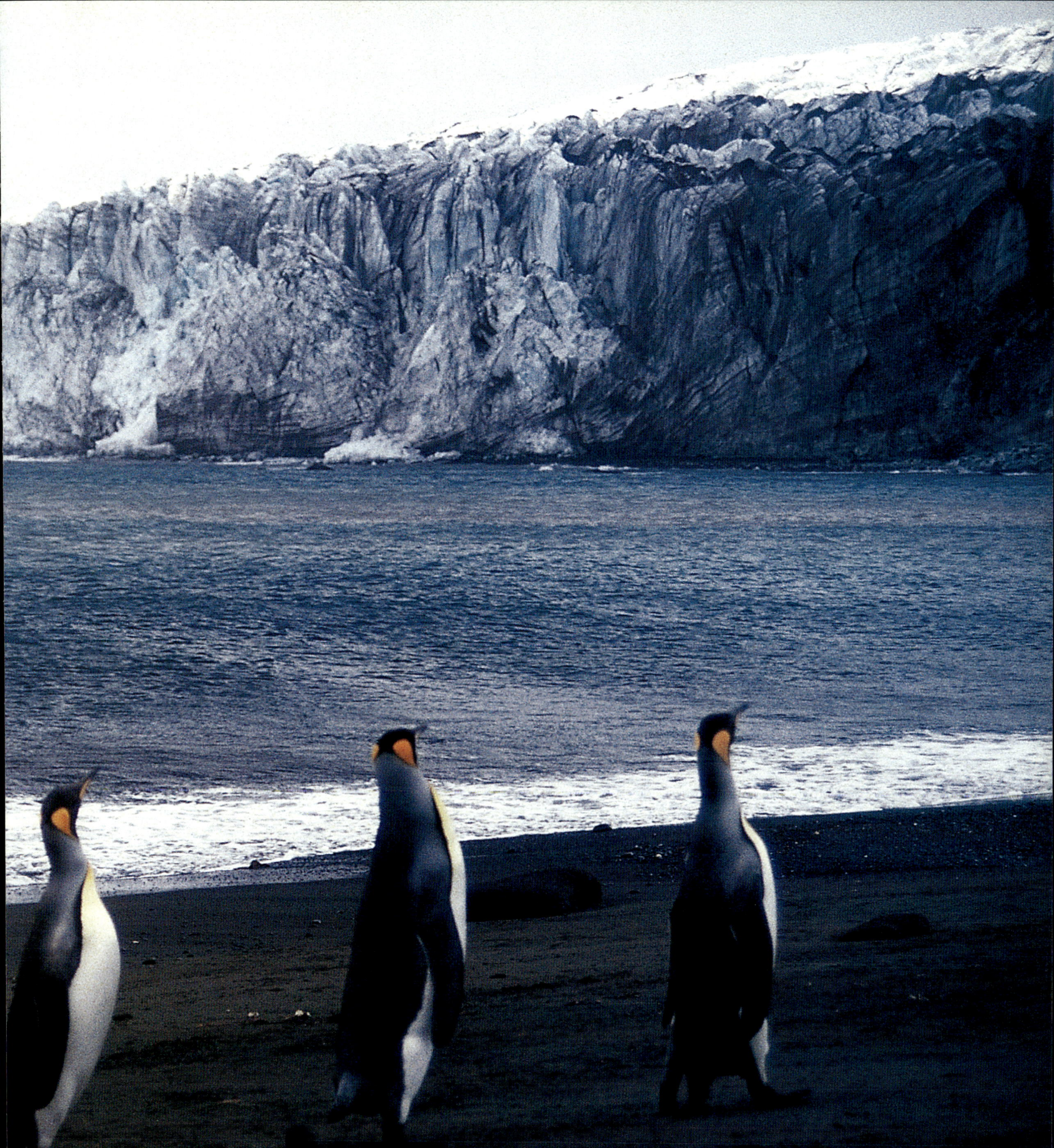

Physical Features

Heard and the McDonald Islands are formed from limestone and volcanic accumulations on the undersea Kerguelen Plateau. Heard Island is a spectacular, glacier-eroded and relatively young volcano, while McDonald is the eroded remnant of another volcanic complex which is lately showing signs of new life.

Recent visits to McDonald Island have observed steam rising from volcanic vents. This makes the island the second active volcano on Australian territory. An interesting, and as yet unexplained, feature observed in volcanic pumice from McDonald Island is that it is of a different chemical composition to that of Heard Island.

Heard Island is dominated by the Big Ben massif which is 20 kilometres (12 miles) wide at its base. The massif is topped by the cone-shaped active volcano, Mawson Peak, which rises to 2745 metres (9000 feet). This volcano is only a few hundred thousand years old. Heard Island is heavily glaciated, with ice cliffs forming a high proportion of the coastline. The glaciers here are very fast flowing as a result of steep slopes and high rainfall but, in recent years, they have been retreating in the face of higher temperatures.

There are numerous outlying islets, rocks and reefs. The McDonald Islands are ice-free and bounded by steep cliffs. This land area is composed of rocks of volcanic origin - basaltic lava and tuffaceous material - that is distinct from Heard Island.

Special Features

A major volcanic zone in the Earth's crust, known as the Kerguelen-Heard plume, has erupted vigorously for 135 million years, longer than any other known. Studies of this feature, which is currently expressed at Heard Island, can improve our understanding of the great plates in the Earth's crust, which support the continents, and of the movement and evolution of the continents surrounding the Indian Ocean.

Heard Island's glaciers are interesting features in their own right. They are significant because of their rapid movement and their quick advance and retreat in response to temperature changes, which make them good candidates for research into the effects of climate change.

It is the absence of introduced plants and animals which gives these islands, in particular McDonald Island, much of their World Heritage value. This pristine environment offers a scientific laboratory in which natural colonisation of extremely isolated habitats may be monitored, especially if global warming leads to habitat changes.

Heard Island, with its active, snow-mantled volcano rising almost three kilometres (two miles) above the world's most turbulent ocean, is one of the most striking landscapes on the planet.

Fauna

Heard Island contains around 34 species of seabird, including four species of burrowing petrel. Nineteen of these seabird species are recorded as breeding in this island group. The islands are home to 16 per cent of the world's macaroni penguins - some 2 million pairs - and significant populations of gentoo, rockhopper and king penguins.

There are also substantial populations of southern elephant seals and Antarctic fur seals. In total, there are seven species of Antarctic seal - five species of true seal and two of eared seals - recorded on the islands.

Low-lying and unglaciated McDonald Island has the least diverse plant and animal life of any subantarctic island. Apart from sharing various species of seabirds, seals and penguins with Heard Island, McDonald has seven insect species found nowhere else. In the surrounding sea, there are 24 species of fish and 128 species of bottom-dwelling invertebrates.

PREVIOUS PAGE King penguins march across the volcanic sands of Heard Island. The Abbotsmith Glacier makes a dramatic backdrop.

BELOW A lava flow pours down the side of McDonald Island. After recently showing signs of life, this is now considered to be the second active volcano on Australian Territory.

TOP RIGHT Aerial view of Laurens Penninsula.

BOTTOM RIGHT Light-mantled sooty albatross.

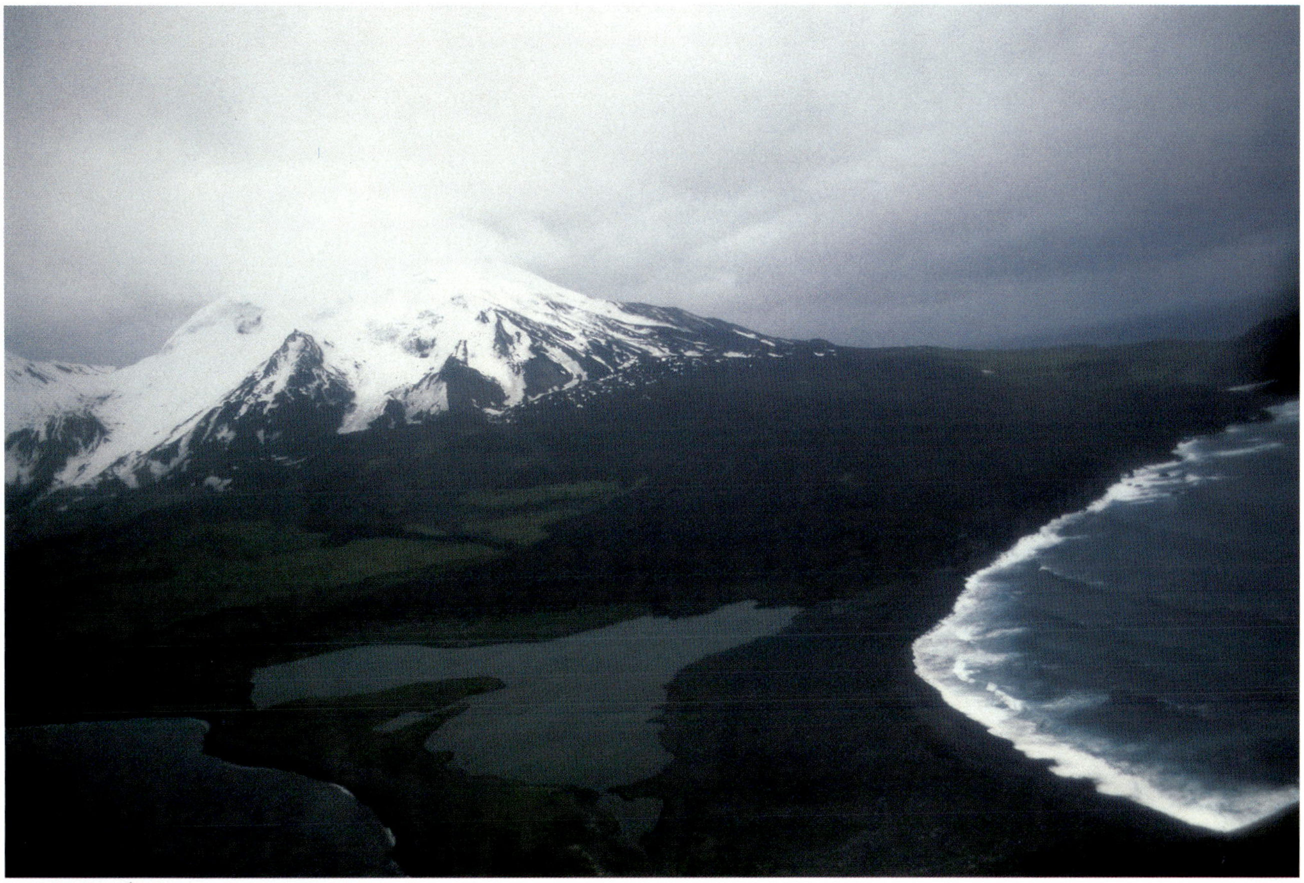

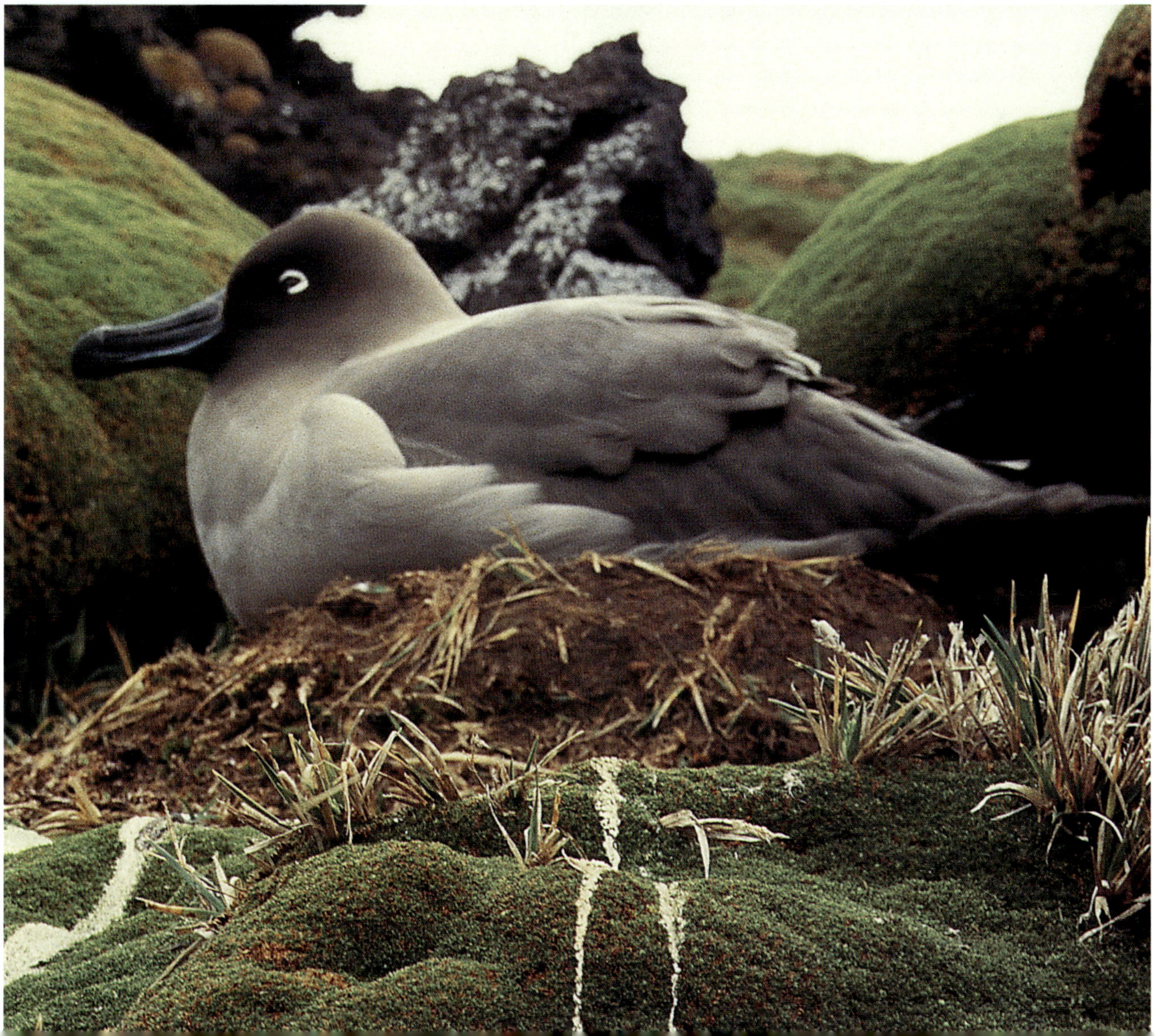

Cultural Heritage

Relics of the grim sealing gangs that roamed Heard Island almost continuously from the first landing in 1855 to 1875, and thereafter sporadically until 1929, are still to be seen. These include barrels, bone engravings and other materials.

Old sealers' camps at Heard Island are the least disturbed and best preserved in the region, with three flensing platforms with tripots (one with an oil cooling tank) still intact. At The Spit, the flensing platform includes bellows, tripots and a blubber press. A further intact blubber press was excavated and now resides in the Queen Victoria Museum and Art Gallery in Launceston, Tasmania. Ruins of a sealers' hut also still exist at Corinthian Cove as well as barrels and the remains of a row boat at Red Island.

The first known landing on Heard Island was made in 1855 by Captain Erasmus Darwin Rogers, an elephant sealer. It is difficult to estimate the number of pelts taken or the quantity of seal oil removed from Heard Island, as early sealers' records are misleading, as they were intended to be. The frequency of sealer visits over 20 years places Heard Island among the most intensively harvested of the subantarctic islands.

Between 1947 and 1955, a scientific research station was situated at Atlas Cove on Heard Island and operated by the Australian National Antarctic Research Expedition (ANARE) to conduct meteorological, biological, geoscience and atmospheric studies. The remains of these buildings (Rondell Huts) and subsequent buildings, which accommodated field parties, represent a 50 year history of construction and sporadic occupation for scientific research.

THIS PAGE Steam plumes rise from volcanic vents on McDonald Island. Meyer Rock rises in the background.

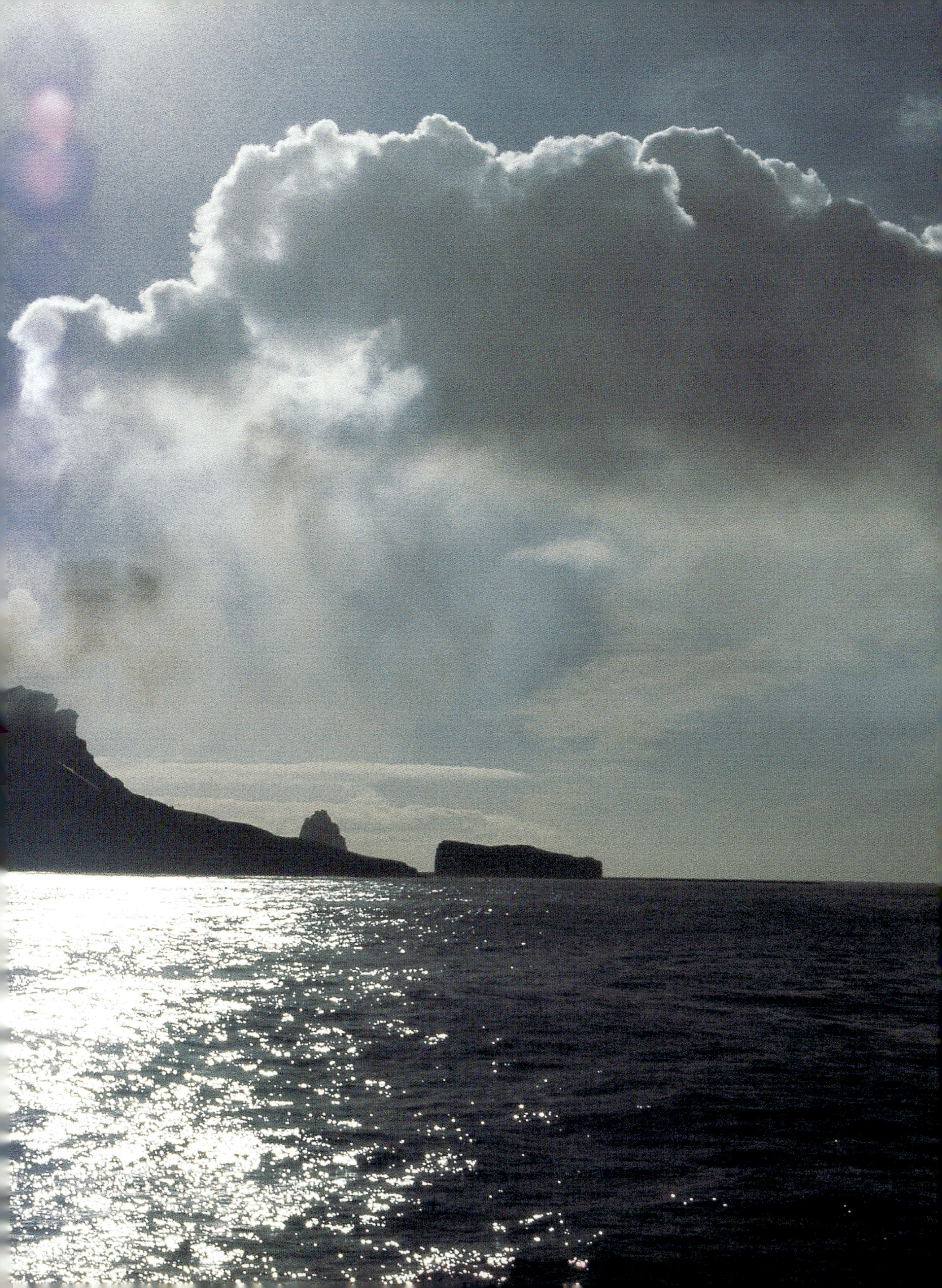

Flora

The principal vegetation communities on the islands are tussock grassland, herbfield and feldmark, with smaller areas of meadow, pool complex and cushion carpet. Eleven species of vascular plants occur on Heard and the McDonald Islands, as well as 42 species of moss and 50 species of lichen. The islands are completely treeless.

Threats

Landings on Heard and McDonald Islands are now strictly controlled by the Commonwealth Government.

There were no recorded landings on McDonald Island until 1971, when a landing was made by helicopter to overcome the severe ocean conditions and the unapproachable coastline. The untouched environment is one of this island's most important scientific and World Heritage values.

The nominated islands are not subject to many human pressures due to their remoteness. The exception is the largely unknown effect of commercial fisheries - including long-line fishing - on the surrounding marine ecosystem. IUCN-The World Conservation Union has recommended that the exclusion of commercial fishing activities be extended beyond the 12 nautical mile limit to the 200 kilometres (120 miles) limit in order to protect the food resource of seals and birdlife.

Facilities

Since the abandonment of the Australian National Antarctic Research Expedition Base at Heard Island's Atlas Cove, there have been no permanent facilities on the islands, a circumstance which helps to maintain their pristine condition. The islands are not near any shipping lane and are visited mostly by fishing vessels which do not land.

Management

The Australian Antarctic Division requires all landings and activities on the islands to be assessed for environmental impact before a visitor permit can be issued.

Heard Island is managed under the regulations of the Heard Island Wilderness Reserve Management Plan and fishing in the surrounding sea is excluded to the 12 nautical mile limit. This provision is not considered adequate by the IUCN for the protection of many of the islands' species or of their food resources.

RIGHT   A huge colony of chinstrap penguins.

NEXT PAGE   An Antarctic fur seal nestles down into the undulating tussock grassland and cushion carpet. Rogers Head can be seen in the distance.

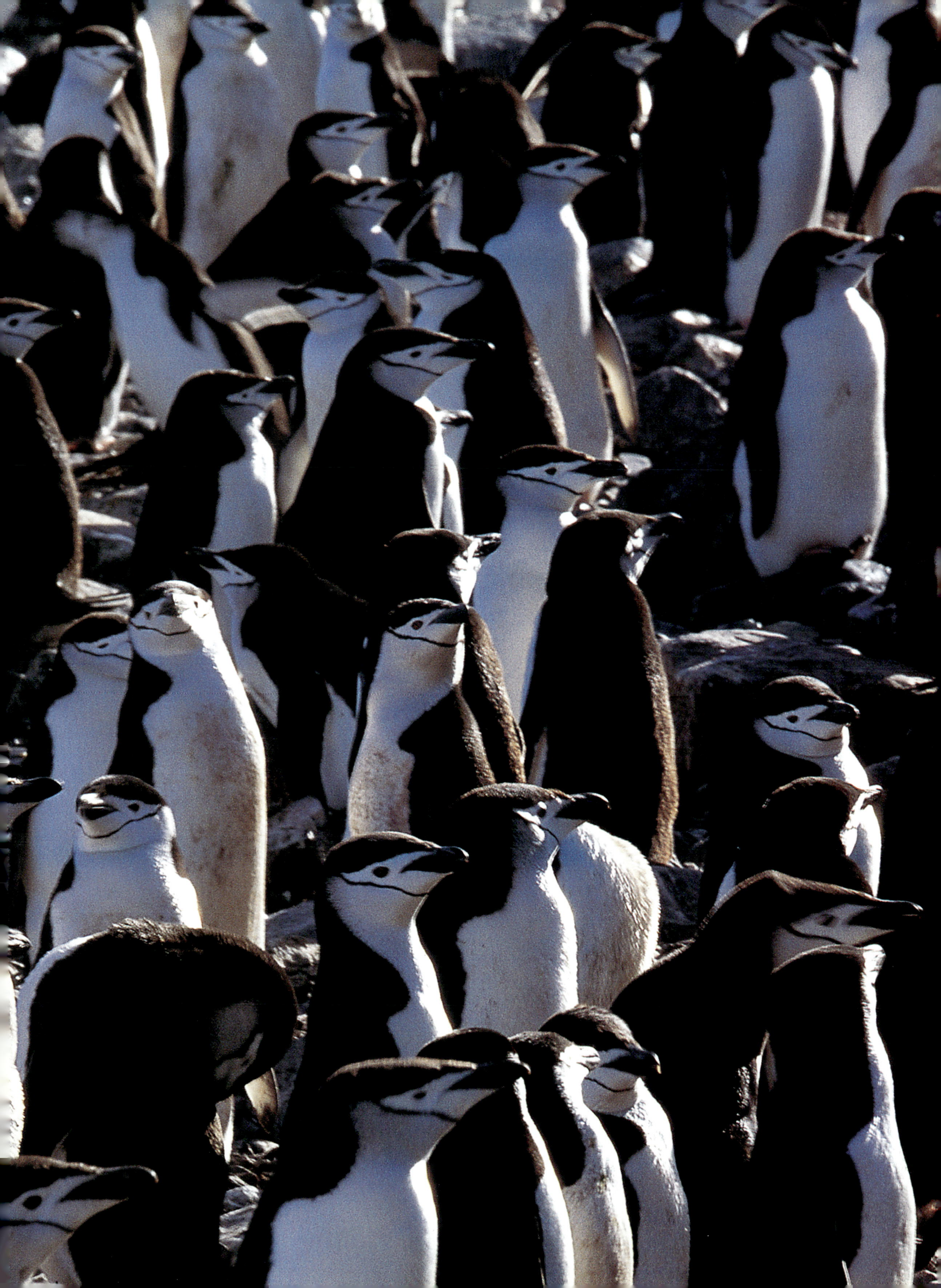

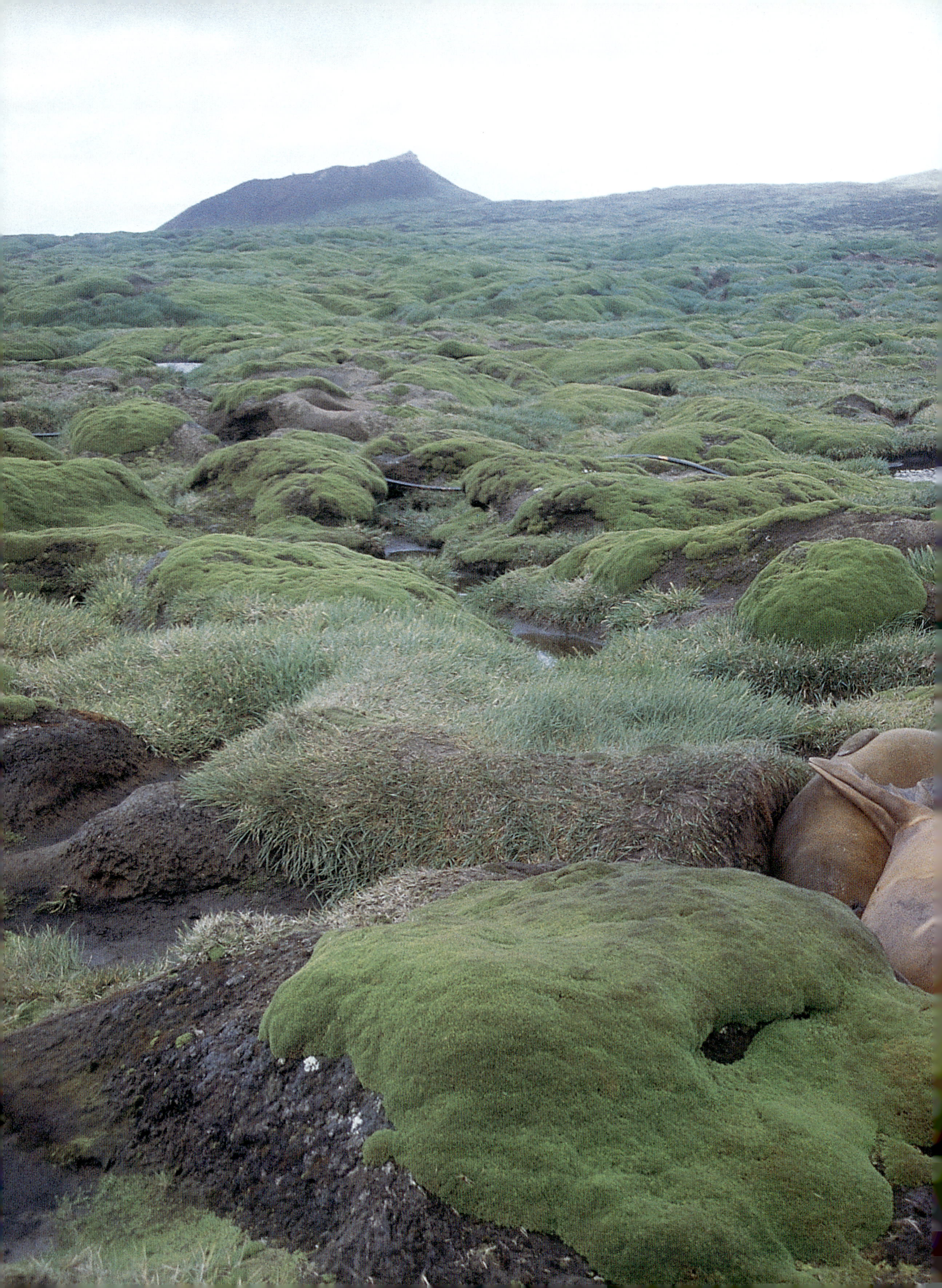

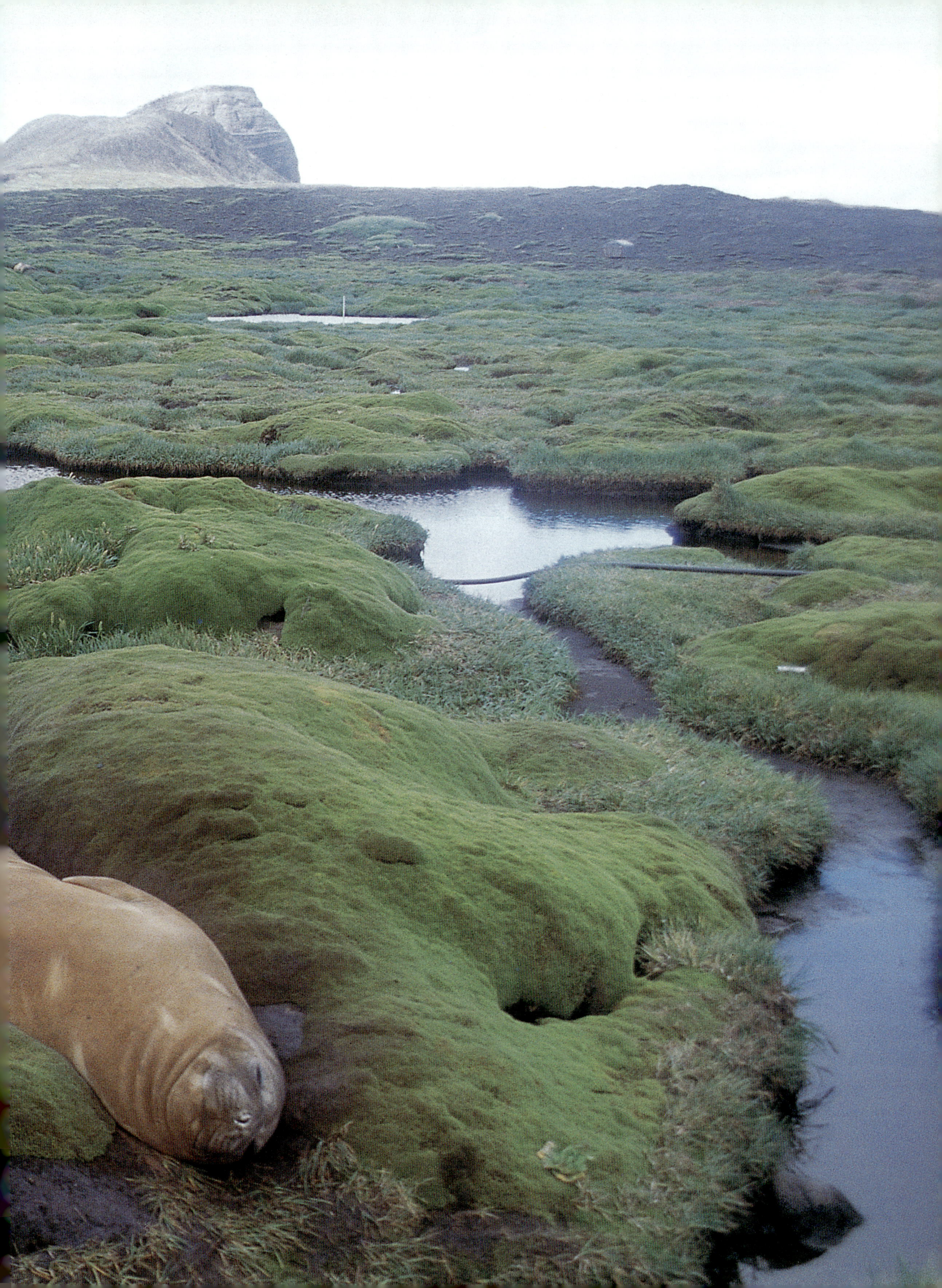

MACQUARIE ISLAND

Tentative Listing

Macquarie Island is included in Australia's indicative list of World Heritage sites and was nominated in 1990 primarily for its landform values. The island is regarded as one of the world's best examples of an ophiolite, a part of the earth's crust underlying the sea which has been thrust up to the surface and exposed. The island supports immense populations of seals and penguins.

The island was again nominated in 1997 but IUCN-The World Conservation Union, in assessing the nomination, considered that equally outstanding ophiolites exist in the world - notably Mexico's Baja, Newfoundland's Bay of Islands, Cyprus and northern Oman. They have recommended inscription of the site be deferred again in the hope and wish that "the nomination be prepared in a wider sense as an oceanic island ecosystem representative of the subantarctic biogeographic realm". Further, their recommendation is that the island be put forward as an international joint nomination with the subantarctic islands of New Zealand, which share similar geological and biological qualities.

Location

Macquarie Island, a territory of Australia, lies 1500 kilometres (930 miles) to the south of Tasmania. The island is 12 785 hectares (31 600 acres) in area and 37 kilometres (23 miles) long. It is only 5 kilometres (3 miles) across at its widest point. Macquarie Island is a nature reserve which also includes the rocky outcrops of Judge and Clerk Islets to the north and the Bishop and Clerk Islets to the south.

PREVIOUS PAGE A sea of royal penguins at the Hurd Point rookery.

Macquarie Island
by William Lines

Huddled at the very bottom of the globe, halfway between the green, temperate island of Tasmania and the frozen and silent expanses of Antarctica lies Macquarie Island. At first sight, the natural marvels of the island may not be apparent; it looks a craggy and uninviting mound, surrounded by cold, grey waters. However, a sense of awe sets in when one realises that the writhing mass of grey is a shoreline alive with elephant seals, and that the pulsating sea of black and white is composed of hundreds of thousands of nesting penguins.

After that, it comes as little surprise to hear of the unique nature of Macquarie Island, of the important marine species that it shelters and of the singular opportunities it provides for research of global significance in many branches of science.

In the nineteenth century, most of the mammals and birds of the subantarctic islands were hunted and slaughtered in their thousands and tens of thousands for fur-bearing skins, oil-yielding blubber, whalebone and penguin oil. Discovery and exploitation of the subantarctic islands occurred simultaneously.

In 1810, the *Perseverance*, a sealing ship out of Sydney, chanced upon a previously unknown island whose shingle beaches abounded with fur seals and sea elephants (southern elephant seals). The captain named the island after the presiding governor of New South Wales, Lachlan Macquarie, and put a gang of men ashore to begin harvesting fur seal pelts.

Other ships quickly followed. Within ten years, the fur seals were wiped out. So ruthless and efficient was the massacre that hardly anything is known about the fur seals originally present on the island, and whether there was more than one type.

With fur seals gone, hunters turned upon the southern elephant seals and, later, the penguins. Both were rendered down for oil to be used for lighting and as a base for paints and lubricants. The slaughter continued for another hundred years.

On Macquarie Island, the sealers left flensing platforms, tripots, huts, names on the island map, graves and ship wrecks. The sealers also left an additional and destructive legacy: mice, black rats, cats, rabbits, New Zealand woodhens and possibly three introduced plant species. The introduced animals disturbed and reduced native vegetation, preyed on native birds and caused the extinction of two bird species found only on this island: a flightless rail and a parakeet.

After the sealers came scientists. Thaddeus von Bellingshausen, commanding an expedition from imperial Russia, visited Macquarie Island in 1820. After a brief stay, he took two albatrosses, twenty dead parakeets, one live one and the skin of an elephant seal. He also gathered specimens of Macquarie Island cabbage *Stilbocarpa polaris* which was used in the diet of sealers, ship's crews and early expeditions to ward off the old sailor's disease, scurvy.

A United States exploring expedition called at the island in 1840. Their specimens were lost in the surf as the men returned to the ship. The commander commented, "Macquarie Island affords no inducement for a visit."

Sir Douglas Mawson, who led the Australasian Antarctic Expedition of 1911-1914, established a wireless relay station and weather observatory on the island. The staff compiled weather reports and surveyed and mapped the island, knowledge that they shared with a few remaining sealers and oil producers.

In 1915, after the base closed, Mawson and other members of the Australasian Antarctic Expedition succeeded in having Macquarie Island declared a wildlife sanctuary. The last legal entitlement for the gathering of animal oil was cancelled in 1920 and the island was proclaimed a wildlife sanctuary in 1933. The Australian National Antarctic Research Expeditions (ANARE) established a base on Macquarie Island in 1948. It has since been staffed continuously.

The island became a conservation area in 1971, a state reserve in 1972 and was declared a Biosphere Reserve under the UNESCO Man and the Biosphere Programme in 1977. In 1978, it was renamed Macquarie Island Nature Reserve when its boundaries were extended to include the entire island and offshore rocks and islets to the north and south, to the low-tide mark. The island became a restricted area in 1981.

Macquarie Island is cold, wet and windy. Because of the moderating influence of the ocean, temperatures hover between 4° and 5° Celsius (40° and 42° Fahrenheit) day in and day out and stay uniform throughout the year, resulting in one of the most even climates on Earth, although not one that people commonly regard as pleasant. One scientist described his existence on the island as like living in a refrigerator with the fan on and a sprinkler going.

Precipitation occurs as mist, rain, sleet, hail or snow at any time of the year, often in several forms on the same day. Snow rarely lies on the ground for more than a week. The only marked seasonal variation is in day length, which ranges from 7 hours in July (winter) to 17 hours in January (summer).

Macquarie Island is an elongated land mass, almost rectangular in shape. It is 37 kilometres (23 miles) long and up to 5.5 kilometres (3.5 miles) wide. Four nearby islets, consisting mostly of barren rock less than 50 metres (165 feet) high, are geologically similar to the main island but, because of difficulty of access, are poorly known.

The main island consists largely of an undulating plateau more than 200 metres (650 feet) above sea-level. Parts of the plateau exceed 300 metres (1000 feet) above sea-level, while three peaks reach more than 400 metres (1300 feet). The highest point on the island, Mount Hamilton, reaches 433 metres (1420 feet). Lakes, tarns, bogs and streams dot the plateau. The scarps bounding the plateau are steep and fall abruptly to a narrow, low-lying coastal fringe. The west coast is more rugged than the east, indented with small bays and coves and fringed with lines of sea stacks and reefs.

Oceanic in both climate and position, Macquarie Island is also totally oceanic in origin. It lies on the boundary of two of the major plates in the Earth's crust, known as the Australian and Pacific plates, and is actually a block of ocean-floor rock raised from great depth in mid-ocean.

The island first emerged from the ocean anywhere between 100 000 and 300 000 years ago. It is still rising between 1.5 millimetres (0.05 inches) and 4.5 millimetres (0.18 inches) a year and is frequently rocked by earthquakes.

Macquarie Island is a spectacular wildlife haven with seas of elephant seals and penguins massing on its shores. It lies just north of the belt in the Southern Ocean, known as the Antarctic convergence, where colder and warmer waters meet, and it is a breeding ground for the albatross and for over 100 000 elephant seals and millions of penguins.

Five species of penguin, by far the most numerous bird, breed on Macquarie Island: royal penguins, the closely related macaroni penguin, king penguins, gentoo penguins and rockhopper penguins.

Royal penguins apparently breed only on Macquarie Island but regularly visit one of Australia's other subantarctic islands, Heard Island. Between 810 000 and 960 000 breeding pairs are scattered over more than 50 Macquarie Island colonies - one of the greatest concentrations of seabirds in the world. They have made a rapid recovery from past exploitation. King penguins were heavily exploited for their oil. One Macquarie Island colony was obliterated and another reduced to about 5000 birds by 1911. Nevertheless, recovery has been strong and, by 1980, the surviving colony contained nearly 250 000 birds.

About two percent of the total world population of the widespread gentoo penguin breed on Macquarie Island where they form several colonies with a total of about 5000 breeding pairs.

Normally, northern giant petrels breed only on islands north of the Antarctic convergence, while southern giant petrels breed only on islands south. Both of them breed on Macquarie Island which lies in the zone of overlap. On Macquarie Island, about 1000 breeding pairs of northern giant petrels nest singly or in loose aggregations, while about 4000 breeding pairs of southern giant petrels nest in colonies. Large congregations of both species remain more or less in the same areas from year to year. They are scavengers and predators on land and at sea.

Cats and skuas take unguarded petrel eggs. Predation by cats has caused the burrow-nesting grey petrel to cease breeding on Macquarie Island.

After hunting by sealers in the nineteenth century, wandering albatrosses slowly recovered. By the 1960s, there were more than 30 nests on Macquarie Island. Since then, with the rise of longline fishing, the population has again declined. At present, only ten nests or less per year are occupied. In 1995, the wandering albatrosses of Macquarie Island were listed as an endangered species. In recent years, a single pair of wandering albatrosses has been nesting on Heard Island.

Up to 1000 pairs of light-mantled albatrosses nest along the coast on the steep slopes and cliffs of Macquarie Island. This long-lived species appears to mate for life. One pair, breeding in 1954-55, was still together in 1996, aged 41 and over 50 years old.

Like the wandering albatross, the light-mantled albatross does not necessarily breed every year. If a pair successfully rears a chick, it will not nest the following season. Breeding success of Macquarie Island light-mantled albatrosses has declined over the past 25 years, possibly due to predation by cats and disturbance by visitors.

Cats probably came ashore on Macquarie Island with the first sealers. They have been found on over 65 per cent of the island and, at their peak, probably numbered between 350 to 500. There is currently a campaign to eradicate cats, primarily through shooting. This may well succeed but it seems less likely that the island will ever be made free of rodents.

Rabbits were introduced in the 1870s to provide a source of food for sealing gangs. Since then, numbers have fluctuated between 50 000 and 150 000. Heavy grazing by rabbits has devastated some areas and changed the plant composition of grasslands and herbfields elsewhere. Introduced *myxoma* virus has reduced numbers but the rabbit is still present. In areas where rabbits have been eradicated, vegetation has recovered.

New Zealand woodhens, known as Wekas, once numbered around 500 but an eradication program by shooting and trapping has reduced their numbers. However, the survivors have become more secretive in their habits.

However, just as the dangers from introduced species decline, larger threats to life loom on Macquarie and the other subantarctic islands. Rubbish from every continent is now floating in the currents of the Southern Ocean and much of it ends up on the beaches of Macquarie Island: wooden beer kegs, soft drink bottles and shampoo bottles. Rubbish is just one of the ways the industrial world affects the pristine order of life in the subantarctic; other threats, however, are more insidious and more destructive

On Campbell Island, a small island south of New Zealand, the number of rockhopper penguins crashed by 94 per cent. Macquarie Island's rockhopper population is also collapsing. In the 1970s, there were 6000 pairs scattered around the island; now there are less than 3000 and numbers continue to decline.

Cindy Hull, a zoologist at the University of Tasmania, has suggested that the rockhoppers and, indeed, the elephant seals, are starving to death. Krill, the tiny creatures on which the penguins feed, are temperature sensitive. Increasing ocean temperatures force krill to move south to colder waters and out of the feeding range of the rockhopper.

RIGHT Chinstrap penguins leaping into the icy sea at Macquarie Island. These penguins are recognisable by the narrow black strip across the white of their throats. Chinstrap penguins occur throughout the subantarctic islands.

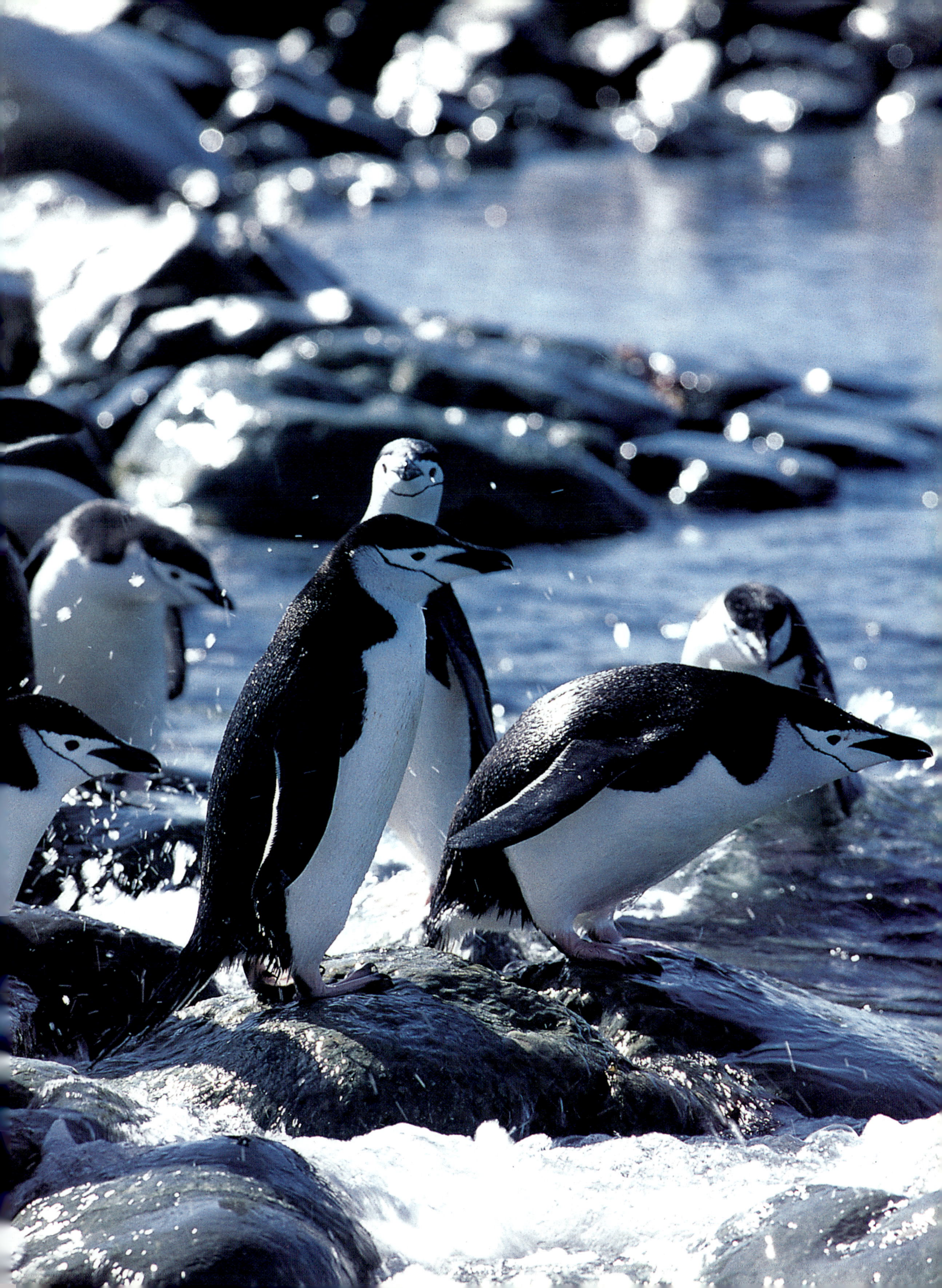

Physical Features

The coast of Macquarie Island is wild and beautiful, consisting of narrow beaches bordered by rocky headlands and sharp, rugged inclines that reach up to the lake-studded plateau. The forbidding, battered landscape of the west coast takes the brunt of mountainous ocean swells urged on by powerful westerly winds.

At a latitude of 54° South, Macquarie Island lies in the region known as the 'Furious Fifties' for its strong winds and stormy seas. The island has an oceanic climate with small annual variations in temperature and rainfall, and no marked extremes. Average seasonal temperatures range from 6.6° Celsius (44° Fahrenheit) in summer to 3.3° Celsius (38° Fahrenheit) in winter. Annual rainfall, which falls over an average of 308 days each year, averages 901 millimetres (35.5 inches).

Macquarie Island derives much of its character from its situation in the subantarctic biogeographical province. This is a body of water surrounding the pole and dotted with six island groups. All of these groups lie within a few degrees of latitude of the Antarctic convergence - the oceanic boundary where cold water from the south meets warmer water from the north.

Macquarie Island's dominant physical feature is its elevated and undulating lake-studded plateau which is best developed in the northern part of the island. The plateau stands about 300 metres (1000 feet) above sea level and is cut off abruptly at the seaward margins by sheer scarps. Neither above-ground volcanoes nor glaciers - both features of other subantarctic islands - are found on Macquarie. The present landform has resulted mainly from a combination of faulting, uplift, sea-level changes and erosion processes.

In very exposed, windy places such as the plateau, the soils are mainly gravelly loams. Elsewhere, acid peats predominate. The low temperature and moisture levels on the island mean that plant material decomposes very slowly. On low altitude terraces, peat has accumulated to at least 5 to 6 metres (16 to 20 feet) in some areas.

Flora

The plant life of the subantarctic region generally displays low diversity. It has established slowly by colonisation over vast expanses of cold ocean.

The Macquarie Island vegetation can be considered in several habitat zones, ranging from beach to plateau.

The intertidal zones around the island are inhabited by marine algae. Above this, is a zone dominated by lichens and several small flowering plants, including a cushion plant and a species of grass. Grasses also sprout on the caps of many coastal rock stacks, along with hardy flowering plants.

Grasses of various species predominate on the island. The upper margins of the beaches are fringed with tall tussock grass, with shorter grasses and herbs occurring on the coastal slopes. Boggy mire and herbs cover the sodden raised beach terraces, while sheltered gullies harbour the less common fern-dominated communities. The plateau supports a range of plant communities, such as tall tussock grassland, herb fields and feldmark.

Native animals can have a significant impact on the island's vegetation. Royal and king penguins have stripped some coastal and inland areas, removing the underlying peat as they establish permanent colonies. However, the nutrients produced by these large bird colonies can have beneficial effects for some plant life.

RIGHT Royal penguins share the dark, volcanic beach sands of Macquarie Island with southern elephant seals. The penguins are dwarfed by the huge marine mammals which can grow as long as 7 metres (23 feet) and weigh over a tonne. These female elephant seals are easily distinguished from the males which have an inflatable trunk through which they make the elephant-like trumpeting sounds that give them their name.

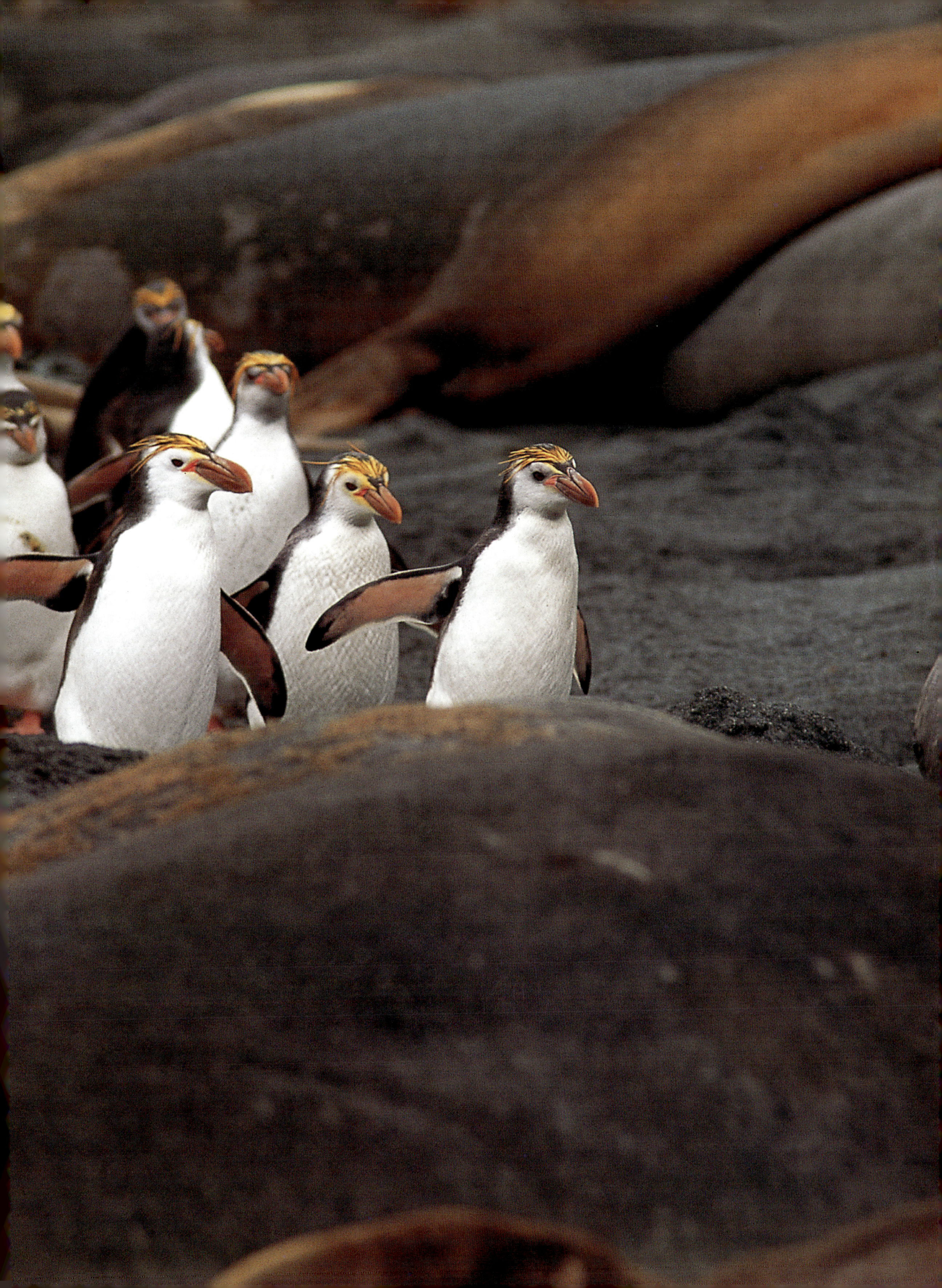

Special Features

In its origins, Macquarie Island is unique. It is an ophiolite complex - a piece of oceanic crust in a relatively pristine condition. This is the only known exposure above the sea of a section of the floor of a major oceanic basin. This gives the island outstanding universal value. Major ocean basins cover approximately 65 per cent of the Earth's surface but the study of their rock structure is difficult and limited by the tools available. Studies by camera, dredge, corer, drill and submersible have produced much valuable data but they are no substitute for a hands-on investigation of oceanic crustal rocks conveniently brought to the surface.

Macquarie Island is also the only known case where a segment of an active and clashing tectonic plate boundary, in an oceanic setting, has appeared above the waves. It is therefore a remarkable example of a significant and ongoing geological process. The Macquarie Ridge, as it is called, results from the compression of the Australian and Pacific oceanic plates at their common boundary, which has resulted in frequent earthquake activity.

Macquarie Island is a site of global significance for meteorological research and upper atmosphere studies. There are few places in the world better suited to the study of the aurora phenomenon. The spectacular atmospheric occurrence - known as the Aurora Australis in the Antarctic, and the Aurora Borealis in the Arctic - takes place in opposite hemispheres on the same magnetic field lines. Finding corresponding points which both lie on dry land is very rare; in almost all cases, one of the points will fall in the ocean. However, Kotzebue in Alaska and Macquarie Island form a pair of conjugate points which offer unsurpassed opportunities for studies of events in the upper atmosphere.

Macquarie Island is currently an important site for the monitoring of ozone levels. This site is vital in monitoring the extent of the northward movement of ozone-deficient air from Antarctica, following the annual spring break-up of the ozone "hole" which lies over the continent.

History

The recorded history of Macquarie Island began in July 1810 when the sealing brig, *Perseverance*, chanced upon it. This discovery was followed by the merciless exploitation of the island's wildlife for over a century.

Such was the pace and intensity of commercial activity that fur-sealing was forced to cease in 1820, as the seals had been slaughtered to the point of virtual annihilation. Economic interest in the island resumed in 1873, with the killing of elephant seals and penguins for oil. It is estimated that 8548 tonnes (8380 tons) of elephant seal oil were produced on the island, and that as a consequence, the elephant seal population was reduced by about 70 per cent.

The island has been the subject of scientific research since 1820 when a Russian expedition made the first known collections of plants and animals. Between 1911 and 1914, the Australian Antarctic Expedition, under Sir Douglas Mawson, established a wireless relay and scientific station on the island. Personnel of the Australian National Antarctic Research Expeditions (ANARE) have operated a research station on Macquarie Island continuously since 1948, with research concentrated on biology, geology, upper atmosphere physics, cosmic ray physics and weather.

In 1978, Macquarie Island was declared a nature reserve under the laws of the Australian state of Tasmania. The major purpose of the reserve was the conservation of the island's plants, animals, natural beauty and cultural resources. The reserve was designated a restricted area in 1979 and intending visitors must obtain permits from the managing authority.

BELOW   King penguins on the volcanic shores of Macquarie Island.

Facilities

Although access to Macquarie Island is difficult, this is as much due to poor transport links as conservation policy. Commercial airlines very occasionally advertise scenic flights over the Antarctic and subantarctic region but these are infrequent and expensive.

It is part of a management plan for the proposed Macquarie Island World Heritage Area that limited tourism should be catered for in the future, but only within the capacity of the island and its wildlife to sustain it. With this in mind, some accommodation and support facilities will be built near the existing ANARE station on the isthmus.

Existing facilities include the research station, its workshops, stores and outbuildings, as well as field huts and walking tracks. It is proposed to construct further limited facilities and experimental sites elsewhere on the island and the adjacent sea stacks.

Fauna

All of Macquarie Island's indigenous animals are marine and, in common with all animals in the subantarctic region, they depend on the sea for food. The southern elephant seal has recovered from the uncontrolled hunting of former years and can now be seen basking on the beaches in huge colonies. There are also three or four species of fur seal which breed on the island and, although numbers are low, it is a miracle that any of these creatures exist after their near-extermination at the hands of fur traders. Since the mid-1970s, small numbers of subantarctic and Antarctic fur seals have been found in breeding groups on the island and, interestingly, there is some evidence of hybridisation between the two species. Individual Hookers sea lions and leopard seals are frequently found on the island.

Whales can be spotted in the waters around Macquarie Island. The most common, by far, are the killer whales - sometimes called "wolves of the sea" for their habit of hunting in packs among the penguin colonies along the shore.

The birdlife of Macquarie Island is varied and abundant, with 70 recorded species. Of these, the breeding colonies include four species of penguin, four albatrosses, eight petrels, one cormorant, two ducks, one rail, one skua, one gull, one tern and two passerines, plus four other species which may breed on the island but have not yet been proven to do so. The island also provides a welcome rest-stop for 38 occasionally visiting bird species.

The most spectacular sights on Macquarie Island are the enormous penguin colonies, some of which contain hundreds of thousands of birds. Penguins are easily the most numerous birds on the island. Royal penguins, king penguins, gentoo and rockhopper penguins all live here in large colonies. The king penguin population suffered a catastrophic decline last century but has recovered well and continues to expand. The royal penguin, found only on Macquarie Island, is estimated to have a population of some 850 000 breeding pairs.

A species of king shag is also restricted to the island. There are estimated to be 660 breeding pairs located in 19 colonies. Their feeding grounds are in waters close to the island and are limited in area.

In addition to the conspicuous mammal and bird life, Macquarie Island hosts 113 land invertebrates, some 30% of which are believed to be found nowhere else. The invertebrate animals include earthworms, over 20 species of nematodes (worm-like parasitic and related organisms), a native land snail and a slug that was probably introduced by sealers.

Two species of kelp fly play an important role in the island's ecosystem. Huge piles of rotting kelp can be seen littering the beaches after a storm. The kelp flies help to break down these stinking masses, and also to recycle the beached bodies of dead seals.

Human Impact

Over the years, ignorance and carelessness have resulted in the introduction of exotic species, with severe consequences for Macquarie Island's indigenous plant and animal communities. Although the smaller islands in the listed area have happily escaped these effects, animals introduced to the island by sealers during the nineteenth century included cats, rabbits, rats, mice and the flightless New Zealand woodhen, or Weka. Many of these animals remain on the island today and, because of this, the white-headed petrel, Antarctic prion and sooty shearwater are now the only burrow-nesting native birds left on Macquarie. Rabbits have had a devastating impact on the island's vegetation and Wekas have been implicated in the demise of the native rail and parakeet.

Efforts to eradicate introduced species are now being made and some success has already been reported. It is possible that Wekas have been eliminated on the island, while the cat population has been reduced to 100, or so, individuals. Studies into the diet and habits of the mice and rats have revealed that the mice feed mainly on invertebrates and the rats eat mostly plant matter.

Increased human activity on the island has had affects such as increased wastes, the creation of walking tracks and the construction of field huts; it has the potential to introduce serious pest species. Concerns over these issues have been addressed in the nature reserve's management plan and strategies are being developed to protect the island's outstanding environment.

Management

The Australian state of Tasmania owns Macquarie Island, Bishop and Clerk Islets and Judge and Clerk Islets and the surrounding water to three nautical miles and these areas have been declared a nature reserve under Tasmanian legislation. The Australian Commonwealth Government has jurisdiction over the marine area from the limit of Tasmania's territorial waters to 12 nautical miles.

The day to day administration is the responsibility of the Tasmanian Department of Parks, Wildlife and Heritage, which began to take an active role in the island's management in 1972. Collaborating agencies include ANARE and other agencies of the Commonwealth.

The management plan for the proposed World Heritage Area aims to provide a high degree of protection for the natural and historical assets of the reserve, to repair past damage where possible and practicable, and to encourage research and data-collecting programs on the natural and historical features of the island, providing they have no long-term detrimental effects. While it is part of the management plan to extend research facilities and to allow for some tourism, these developments will be small-scale. It is envisaged that the Bishop and Clerk Islets and the Judge and Clerk Islets will be preserved in a pristine state, with no facilities or experimental sites, and visits will be permitted for limited scientific purposes only.

Research and management programs involving native and introduced plants and animals are under way. Intensive control programs are also being carried out with considerable success against introduced species. Long-term studies to monitor changes in the status of native and exotic species have been instigated. Where possible, eradication or control programs are undertaken. Stringent precautions are being established to prevent the further introduction of exotic species.

NEXT PAGE Chinstrap penguins are found at Lusitania Bay on Macquarie Island. The massive colony shown here occupies the raised coastal platform right up to the escarpment.

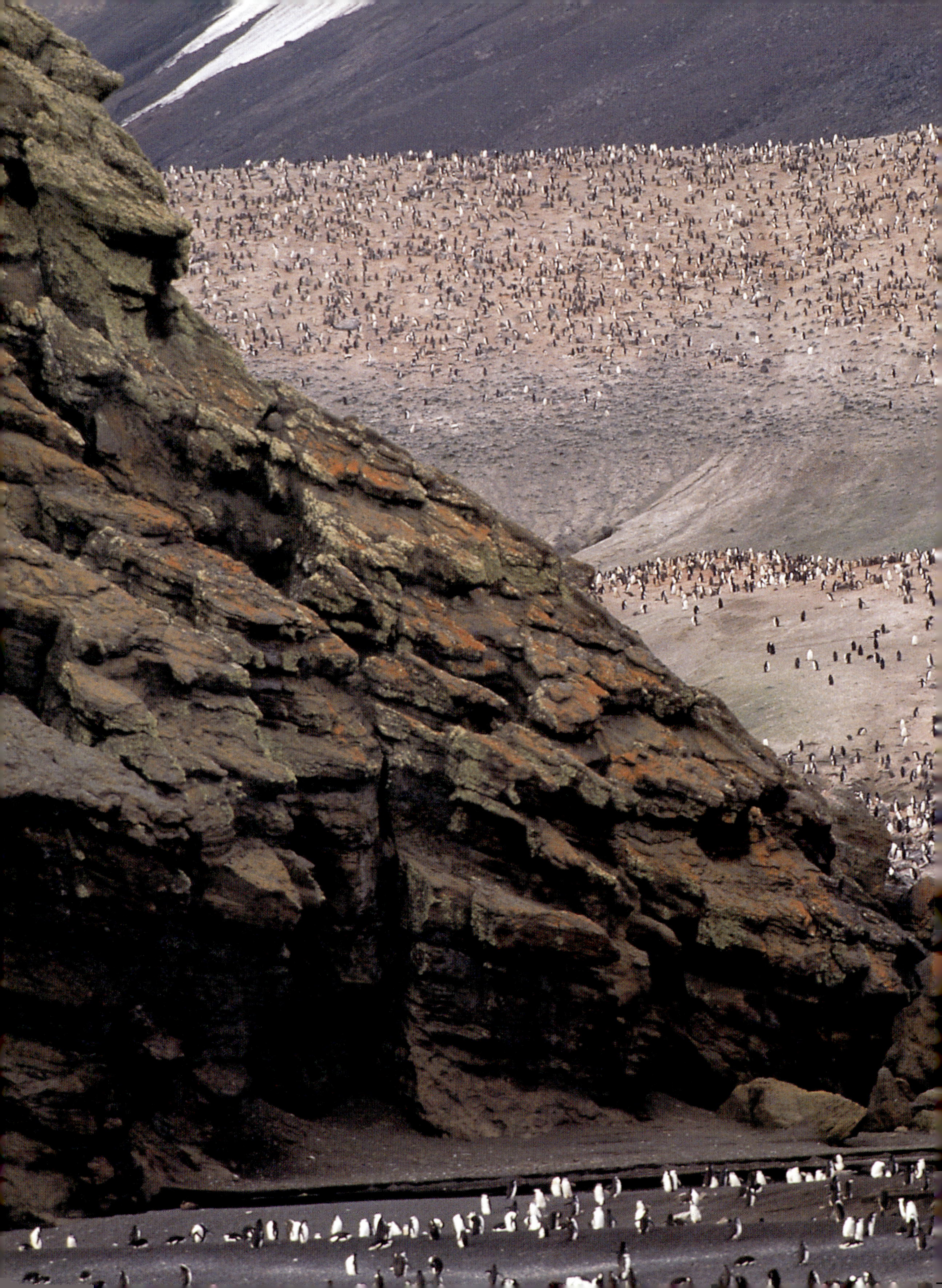

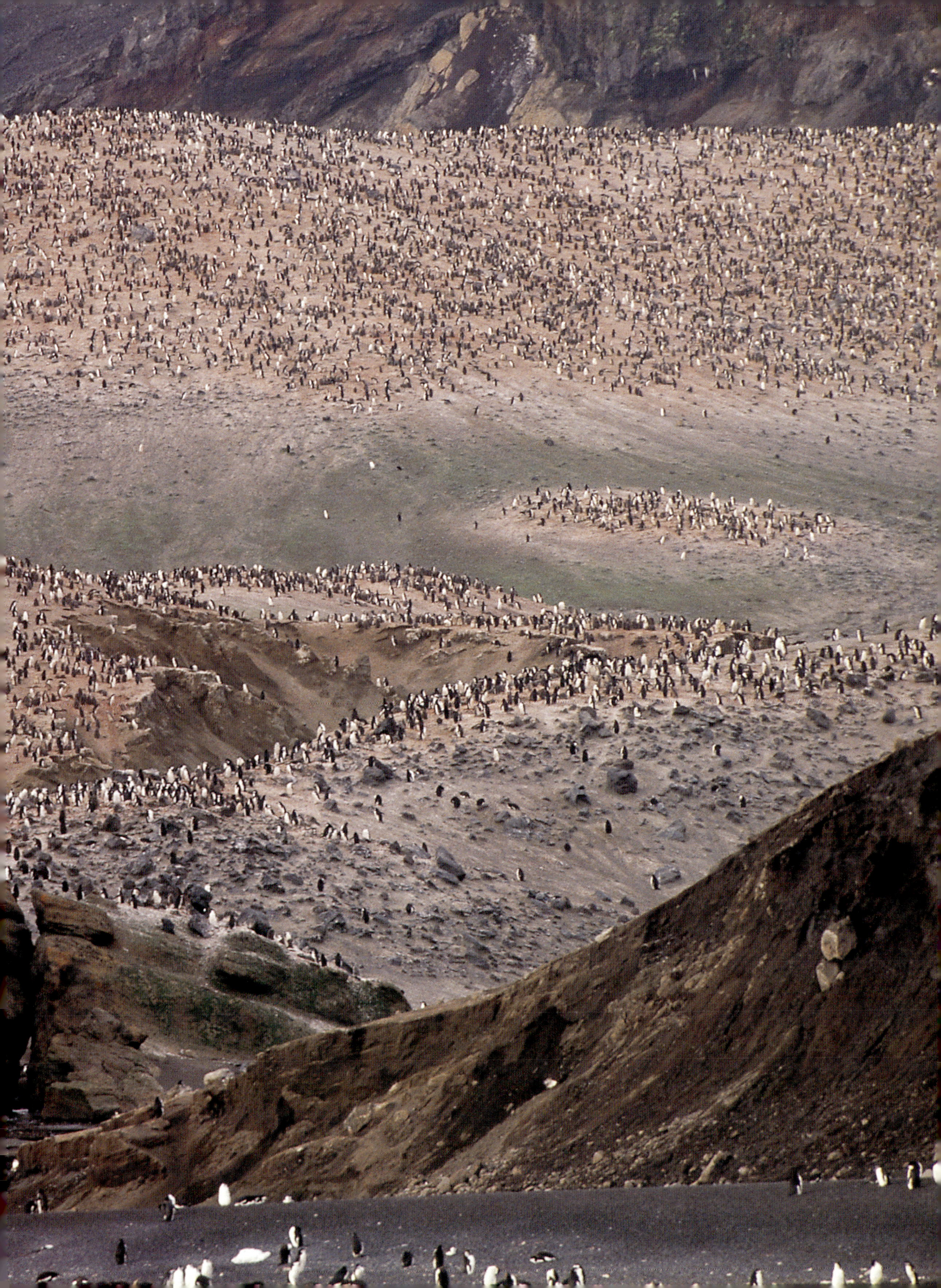

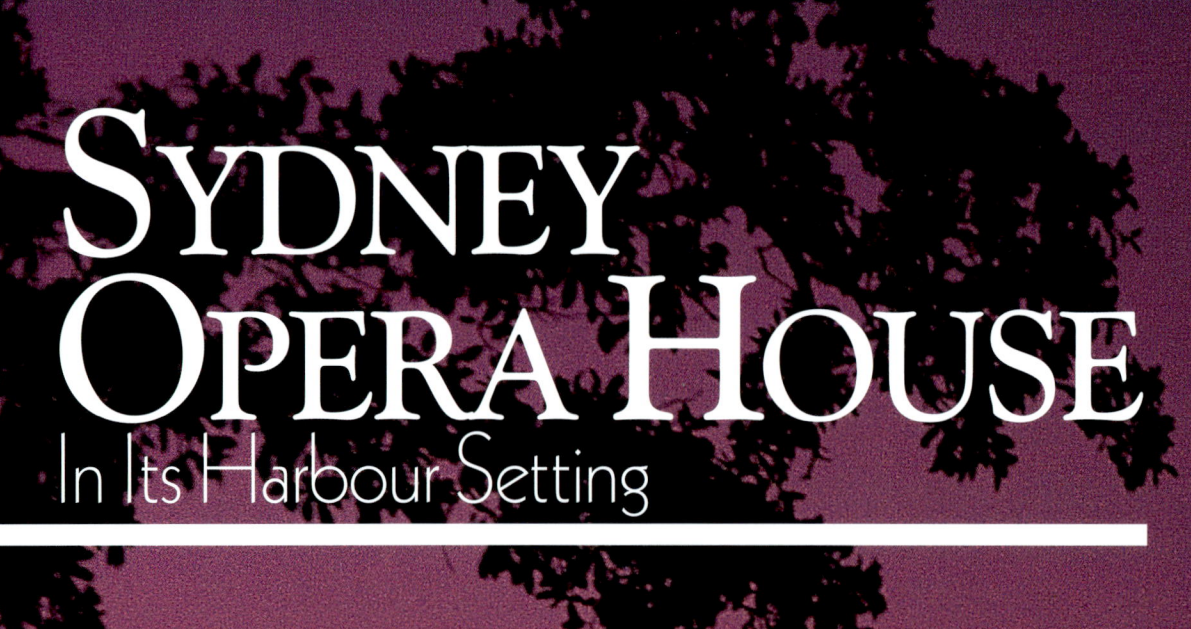

SYDNEY OPERA HOUSE
In Its Harbour Setting

Tentative Listing

The Sydney Opera House is an architectural monument, which represents a masterpiece of human creative genius. It is inextricably tied to its setting.

Sydney's inner harbour, which surrounds and includes the Opera House, is an outstanding continuing landscape which illustrates significant stages in human history. It is both directly associated with a cultural encounter of outstanding universal value and enriched by the quality of artistic and literary works it has inspired.

Furthermore, Sydney's inner harbour, with its built components of Opera House, Fort and Bridge, meets the test of authenticity in its distinctive character and in the design, material, workmanship and setting of its parts.

Adequate legal protection and management mechanisms are in place to ensure the conservation of the cited values of Opera House, Fort, Bridge and the surrounding waters of the nominated area.

Location

Situated on Sydney Harbour, the indicative property includes the Sydney Opera House and surrounding waterway environs to the mean highwater-marks of the foreshores and encompassing the Sydney Harbour Bridge and the island of Fort Denison. The boundary of the site stretches from the shoreline at Dawes Point on the south side of the harbour to Mrs Macquaries Chair in the Botanical Gardens, across the harbour to Robertson's Point at Cremorne Reserve and around to Blues Point.

PREVIOUS PAGE A panoramic view from the east. Hues of a glorious sunset enhance this scene of the Sydney Opera House and harbour environs. The night-lit Sydney Harbour Bridge is further illuminated with light from the City of Sydney's business centre.

Sydney Opera House in its Harbour Setting

by Joan Domicelj

"...the Sydney Opera House is a house which one will see from above, will sail around - because it sits on a point sticking out into a harbour, a very beautiful harbour, a fjord with a lot of inlets. This point is in the middle of the city and the city rises on both sides of the fjord so the Opera House is a focal point... Furthermore, people will sail around it, there are ferries sailing past and large ships coming in - the big harbour is just outside and the large bridge nearby..."

- Jørn Utzon, 1965

Sydney Opera House in its harbour setting has been officially included on Australia's tentative list of properties for possible future inscription on the World Heritage List. A nomination, with supporting documents, has been prepared and positively reviewed nationally and internationally but has not, at this stage, been forwarded to UNESCO for consideration by the World Heritage Committee.

Sydney Harbour

"Sydney Harbour... one of the finest, most beautiful, vast and safe bays the sun had ever shone upon"

- Conrad, 1906

Sydney is the oldest and largest city in Australia. Its harbour and surrounding lands were inhabited and cared for by Aboriginal people over millennia and evidence of their occupation remains in shell middens, rock paintings and engravings. The arrival of the first fleet of British colonists in 1788 lead to the disruption of traditional patterns of life in the region.

From its inception, the European settlement spread rapidly and reshaped the foreshore landscape as an active port. We can see today many layers containing the evidence of each stage of Sydney's development: from eighteenth and nineteenth century penal and defence structures, colonial villas, wharves, shipwrecks and public gardens to the twentieth century's great steel-arched bridge and the poetic shells of the Opera House.

Bennelong Point (named Tu-bow-gule by local Aboriginal people) projects north into the inner harbour, flanked by Sydney and Farm Coves. This was a place in constant use during the early settlement - for cultural relations, scientific inquiry, harbour defence, warehousing and commerce. In the mid-twentieth century, Bennelong Point was selected as the site for Sydney's future opera house.

During the last Ice Age, some 20 000 years ago, the present Sydney Harbour was a river valley which extended some 25 kilometres (15 miles) further east before meeting the ocean. Material in rock shelters shows that Aborigines inhabited the surrounding region at least from that time.

By six to seven thousand years ago melting ice had flooded the river valley, creating Sydney Harbour in the form we see today, with its islands and foreshores. Evidence of earlier human occupation along the valley floor was submerged under water. Over the next millennia, plants and animals adapted to their new coastal environment of sandstone ridges, streams and swamps, and fire was used to modify the environment to suit human needs. This Aboriginal land husbandry was noted in the journals of British officers who, on arriving in 1788, described parts of the landscape as having a park-like appearance.

Captain Phillip, who became the first governor, referred to his 'colonists' as 'guests' of the Aborigines and attempted, to treat his 'hosts', "... well and fairly" - except with regard to land ownership. This exception is so profound that it continues to lies at the heart of unresolved tensions between the two cultures. The general impact of the British arrival on Aboriginal life at that time - through disease, competition and incomprehension - was immeasurable. The harbour landscape is directly associated with that eighteenth century encounter and continues to represent human life before it, through occupation and art sites, and after it, through its extensive reshaping by the newcomers.

The inner Harbour abuts the site of the proclamation of British rule and of the first buildings of the penal settlement and naval base. In response to the concentration of shipping in the area - importing convicts, free settlers and goods, exporting whale oil, gold, wool and wheat - maritime structures sprang up along the waterfront. Below the waters lie wrecked or scuttled ships.

Aware of foreign competitors and distant conflicts, the colony built batteries to defend the inner harbour at Dawes and Bennelong Points, Kirribilli and the island of Fort Denison. Later came the naval dockyard: great finger wharves embarking and receiving cargoes, passengers, migrants and warships; and, later still, a torpedo and submarine base. Along ridges and promontories, established society built stone villas. On lower slopes and along every new transport line, less substantial housing appeared in brick, timber and fibro. Rough outcrops of sandstone sheltered patches of native vegetation from development, so that the footpaths skirting the harbour now link remnant bushland reserves with more formal parklands and buildings. The inner harbour and its foreshores provide a legible record of this history. The words of poets and novelists, as well as the images of visual artists in paint, photograph and woodcut have enriched our understanding of the place.

The Historic Encounter

The bays and headlands of the inner harbour of Sydney are the site of an encounter between their Aboriginal custodians, nourished by the land and waters for thousands of years, and a foreign fleet carrying British colonists from the other side of the world - officers, convicts and seamen - with very different ideas of society. At the time, in January 1788, it is thought that similar numbers of European colonists and Aboriginal inhabitants, some fifteen hundred each, met on the harbour. The place seemed strange and isolated to the newcomers; the bond between the landscape and the Aboriginal people who inhabited it and who had, with their ancestors, cared for it over millennia, was extraordinarily strong. The impact of this event on the lives of such culturally distant groups, and on their descendants, makes it one of outstanding significance. It epitomises the universal drama of meetings between cultures.

The arrival and continuing encounters were much documented by the British colonists of the day, giving their various versions of half the story. Interpretation now is, and must be by its nature, ambivalent in attempting to add the other half and to assess long term results. The World Heritage Committee's determination of "outstanding universal value" need not imply celebration. The Island of Goree in Senegal, symbol of African martyrs to the slave trade, was inscribed in 1978, as were the World War II Auschwitz concentration camp, Poland, in 1979, and the Hiroshima Peace Memorial, Japan, in 1996.

Landmarks: Fort Denison and Sydney Harbour Bridge

Fort Denison stands on a small island (previously named Mat-te-wan-ye, then Pinchgut) to the east of Bennelong Point. It was a small, well-vegetated sandstone pinnacle much visited by Aboriginal people, but soon converted by the British to an island gaol. From 1796 to 1815, a gibbet was erected on its crest, where felons hanged for capital offences were displayed as a salutary warning to new arrivals.

The present form of the island fort results from major works through the colonial period. Its first battery was cut and built from the existing rock, in 1840, by convict labour. In 1856-62, a semi-circular bastion, a castellated Martello tower, barracks and loophole chambers were built as one of a planned series of four batteries around the inner harbour. In the first half of the nineteenth century, many towers were built in Europe for coastal defence but this is one of only two in the southern hemisphere. The island was designated 'Fort Denison' in 1857 in honour of the Governor General of the day.

Because of its strategic location guarding the entrance to the settlement from the sea, the island was given a navigational role. Its first light was established in 1858, the tide gauge by 1870 and, from 1906, the One O'clock Cannon was fired each day from Fort Denison as a mark of time and authority. The fabric of the island fort illustrates the history of defence and navigational systems for colonies remote from Europe, as well as later stories, such as the episode in World War II, when an American shell, fired during a Japanese submarine attack, cracked the tower wall.

The Sydney Harbour Bridge spans the inner harbour at its narrowest point, framing the Opera House to the east. It is monumental - a steel two-hinged arched structure, flanked by huge, granite-faced pylons and abutment towers, with the largest arch and the second longest span (503 metres or 1650 feet) in the world. As the heaviest rivetted steel structure ever built, it is the culmination of early twentieth century pre-welding steel technology. The International Committee for Conservation of Industrial Heritage, in its 1995 study on World Heritage bridges, listed the Sydney Harbour Bridge as one of seven outstanding steel bridges and as one which embodies the spirit or character of a people.

Sydney Harbour Bridge was opened in 1932, amidst much ceremony and excitement, after 16 years of planning and over five years of active construction. It was an immensely significant public work, towering over the city. During its construction, the connection of the two arms of the arch had been awaited by the public with bated breath.

Visible from great distances, Sydney Harbour Bridge is a powerful landmark of Sydney Harbour. From its roadway, bicycle and footpaths, there are spectacular views of the inner and outer harbour and of the sculptural form of the Sydney Opera House. Its great arch provides the perfect foil for the Opera House. The promenade of the Opera House, in return, provides an ideal viewpoint for the bridge. A symbiosis, or mutually supporting existence, has grown up between these two great structures, each extending the visual impact of the other.

Sydney Opera House

"... this transcendent geometry of house and harbour have touched and transported many. It is an enchanted place."

- Emmett, 1995

In 1957, the Danish architect, Jørn Utzon, was selected from over 220 entries as the winner of an international competition for the design of an opera house with two main halls, on the site of former tram sheds at the end of Bennelong Point. His daring, yet harmonious design, of a massive platform (Stage 1) with paired series of tiled roof shells (Stage 2) of two halls placed side by side was elaborated, perfected and implemented by Utzon over the next few years. This was done in collaboration with Ove Arup engineers, other specialists and a small design team. The brilliant solution to the construction of the roof shells, a technical breakthrough, was achieved in 1961.

By early 1966, tensions between the architect and his government client forced Utzon to leave the project amidst public and professional outcry. Much of the controversy centred on questions over Utzon's design solutions for Stage 3 of the building - specifically for the two main halls and the glazed walls closing the shell roofs. What seems clear is that Utzon envisaged the exterior and the interior of the Sydney Opera House as a single, harmonious whole with the halls designed as a spectacular, visual climax to the experience.

Stage 3 of the project was subsequently redesigned to an amended brief from the client - with the main hall changed from multi-purpose to concert performance - and the newly designed halls and glass walls completed by the Australian architects, Hall, Todd and Littlemore. The building was opened in 1973 as a centre for the performing arts and has functioned successfully ever since.

Many regret the break in continuity of the creative process and consider that the building's completion did not fulfil Utzon's vision. Nonetheless, the Sydney Opera House has, since its opening in 1973, continuously provided an acoustically excellent international venue for orchestral music, theatre and festivities. The Opera House is viewed as a sculpture that completes the harbour environment of fort, bridge, ferries and public foreshores. It embodies the integration of sophisticated geometry, technology and art and demonstrates the creative potential of assembled prefabricated components.

The monumental platform of the Opera House, a great granite-clad podium, provides a base for the two main auditoriums. The southern pedestrian concourse, with its 86 metres (282 feet) wide approach stair, is supported on prestressed folded beams spanning 49 metres (161 feet).

Utzon said in 1993: "The platform as an architectural element is a fascinating feature. I first fell in love with it in Mexico on a study trip in 1949. A great strength radiates from them . . . It's a tremendous experience to see how an architectural idea must have evolved in order to create contact with their gods."

The shapes of the roof shells, soaring above the platform, are derived from the surface of a sphere of common radius. Each vault is made up of precast rib segments radiating from a concrete pedestal and rising to a ridge beam. The concrete shells are clad in chevron-shaped tile-lids covered in a pattern of white glazed and matt tiles, like ice and snow.

Utzon said in 1965: "... one could not design a building for such an exposed position without paying attention to the roof ... in fact one must have a fifth facade which is just as important as the other facades ... I have made a sculpture."

The halls and multiple facilities within the Sydney Opera House provide for performances of music, theatre, opera, dance and film, as well as catering for dining, conferences, exhibitions and private functions.

The largest venue, the Concert Hall, with seating for some 2700 people, is used principally for musical events, while the smaller Opera Theatre, with some 1500 seats, is used mainly for opera and dance. The exterior of both halls is clad in Australian brushbox

RIGHT View of Bennelong Point circa 1965. "If you take a palm leaf... that was exactly what inspired me", Jørn Utzon 1993.

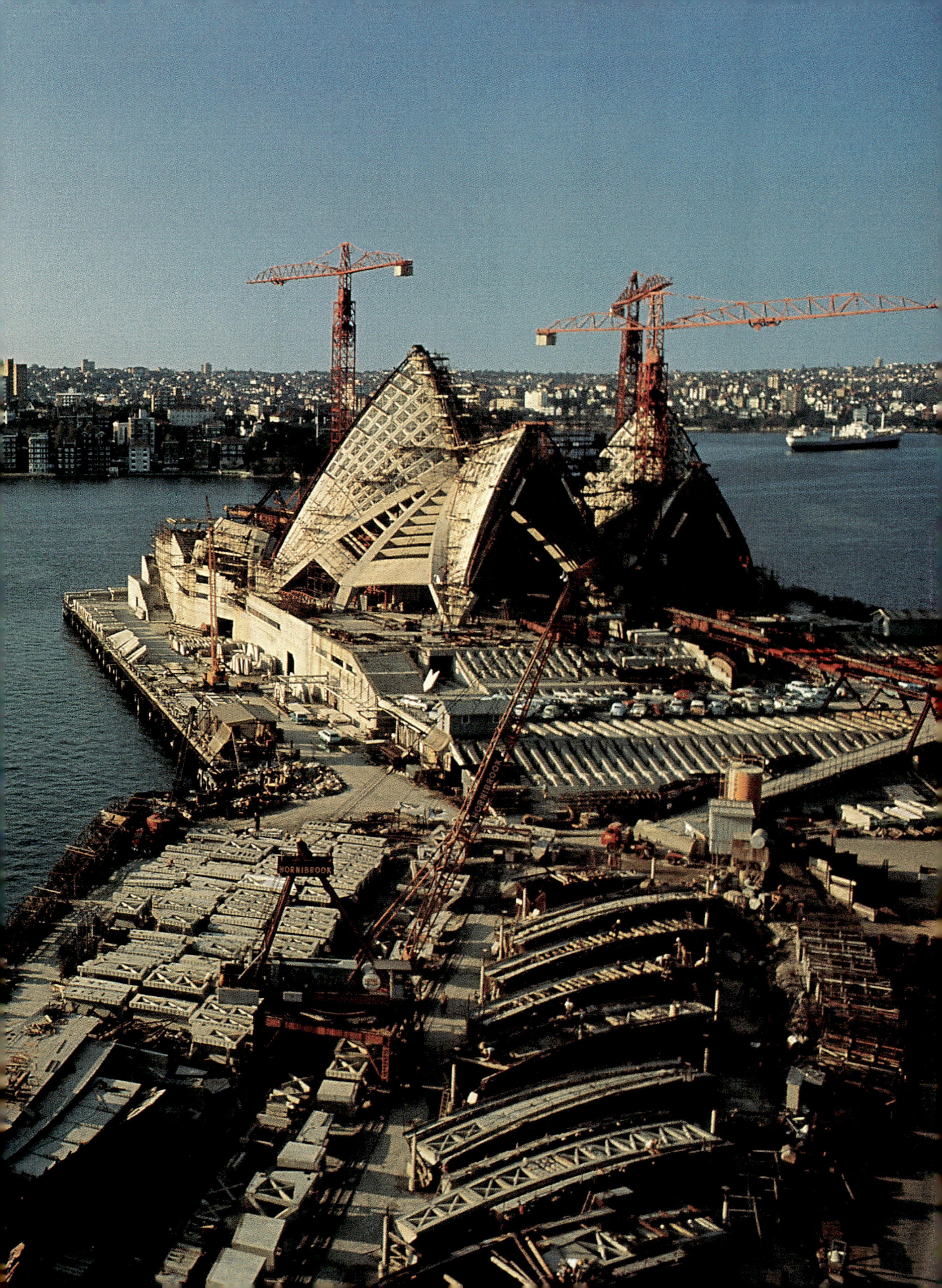
HORNIBROOK

timber, in contrast with the precast concrete finish of the underside of the ribbed shells. The ceiling of the Concert Hall is also ribbed, radiating down to the brushbox timber walls from a crest above the stage. The stage is surrounded by stepped banks of seating.

In 1962, Utzon explained his intention to create elaborately shaped halls built of light plywood, visually separated from the arching structural shell: "... the two halls hang from the shells visibly as a piece of furniture from the outside, and ... the halls and the stage tower in forms and colour will stand out like a big exotic bird..."

Architect, Ken Woolley, has said that in completing the interior, Peter Hall, the principal of the Australian firm of architects responsible for its design and execution, was "... able to achieve an excellent medium size opera theatre... (with) the wonderful Coburn stage curtain and the brilliant red seats, the interior is striking and a fine representative of 60s design. The Concert Hall is one of the top halls in the world acoustically and functionally. It is also a beautiful interior. Only, perhaps, Scharoun's Berlin Philharmonic has more architectural character, of all the post war concert halls."

From the point of view of history, the significance of the Sydney Opera House lies in the seminal nature of much of its design and construction techniques, in its place as the expressive culmination of modern architectural philosophy, and in its emergence as a national and international cultural icon of the twentieth century.

From the point of view of art, the Opera House is a spectacular creative response to Sydney Harbour. Its design is so appropriate for its setting. Utzon said in 1965: "... we worked six months using sea charts and imagining it from the bridge that it acts as a pivotal sculpture in the round, day and night." In 1993, he said: "The art of the building lies in its form and in its life. It is a performing arts centre of world renown and a popular gathering point... a building must have a soul, so that your mood corresponds to what you are doing there."

From the point of view of science, the Sydney Opera House embodies within its structure the integration of sophisticated geometry, technology and art. It epitomises the extraordinary creative potential of the assembly of pre-fabricated, repeated components. Utzon said of this aspect of his creation in 1965: "Because I have moulded space with geometrically defined shapes, the whole enclosure of the void is fully defined and the surface is divisible in a number of similar elements (which) can be assembled like a big jigsaw puzzle in space."

Utzon, in 1992, endorsed claims that the Opera House, although not completed by him, is the highlight of his extraordinary creativity and pursuit of excellence:

"This was the most brilliant building any architect could wish to work on. When I see my models and all the sails on the harbour, I simply soar into paradise. It is my idea of perfection... There was this feeling of a new epoch, a new school in architecture... with industrial techniques, with fantastic constructions that were being invented and it was happening there in Australia. The building itself forced the people on it, everybody, to live up to an extraordinary standard."

Comparative Evaluation

The Sydney Opera House, as a twentieth century architectural monument, lies within an under-represented field in the World Heritage List. Of twentieth century cultural properties inscribed in the list, the Auschwitz Concentration Camp, Poland, and the Hiroshima Peace Memorial, Japan, are clearly not identified for their architectural significance but rather for the strength of their war-time associations. This leaves only the outstanding architectural works of Gaudi, Niemeyer/Costa and Asplund in Parque Guell, Palacio Guell and Casa Mila, Barcelona in Spain, the City of Brasilia in Brazil and the Skogskyrkogarden cemetery in Sweden, together with the architects associated with the Bauhaus movement and its sites in Weimar and Dessau, Germany. The Sydney Opera House was built more recently than these listed properties and so provides a sequel which complements their outstanding values.

Steps have been taken by both the International Council on Monuments and Sites (ICOMOS) and the International Working Party for Documentation and Conservation of Buildings, Sites and Neighbourhoods of the Modern Movement (DOCOMOMO) to prepare an international comparative study of the modern movement in architecture and of the broader topic of twentieth century architecture, to assist the World Heritage Committee in identifying examples of outstanding universal value. The work is, however, incomplete.

An ICOMOS expert meeting on contemporary architecture in Paris in 1985 produced the first tentative list by building type, identifying the Sydney Opera House as one of four theatres or opera houses of outstanding universal value. The others were Sullivan & Adler's Auditorium Building in Chicago (1889), Perret's Theatre des Champs-Elysees in Paris (1911) and Scharoun's Philharmonic Concert Hall in Berlin (1963).

The eminent Norwegian architectural historian and critic, Professor Christian Norberg-Schulz, was invited, in 1995, to evaluate the position of Utzon's Sydney Opera House in the history of modern architecture. His analysis discovers in this building, and in its powerful relationship with its setting, the synthesis of the principal strands of modern architectural thought.

Norberg-Schulz confirms the prediction by Sharp in 1972 that Utzon's Sydney Opera House, being so tied to its site, would take upon itself the role of a symbol for the city, if not the whole continent. He explains that, whereas in the past, living spaces were seen as closed and static, modern space became open and dynamic. Utzon's work relates to Lloyd Wright's destruction of the box, transforming traditional building into a juxtaposition of vertical and horizontal planes between an earthbound base and a hovering roof. Wright's early works inspired European architects such as Le Corbusier and Mies van der Rohe. The former defined the new conception of space as a free plan; the latter emphasised its clarity of structure. Aalto and Kahn introduced the dimension of locality and meaning to modern architecture.

Norberg-Schulz concludes

"Jørn Utzon was the first to realise a true synthesis of the achievements of the pioneers... In Utzon's works, the earthbound base has become a free man-made continuation and interpretation of the site, whereas the roof is understood as a visualisation of the qualities of the sky. Between the two, space moves about as a varied and articulate response to measurable as well as non-measurable demands."

The Sydney Opera House thus fulfils the basic aim of the modern movement: the resolution of the split between thought and feeling. It accomplished the humanisation of modern architecture, advocated by Giedion.

RIGHT The spectacular interior of the concert hall which seats 2700 people. The ribbed ceiling is birch-veneered and radiates down to the brushbox-timbered walls from a crest above the stage.

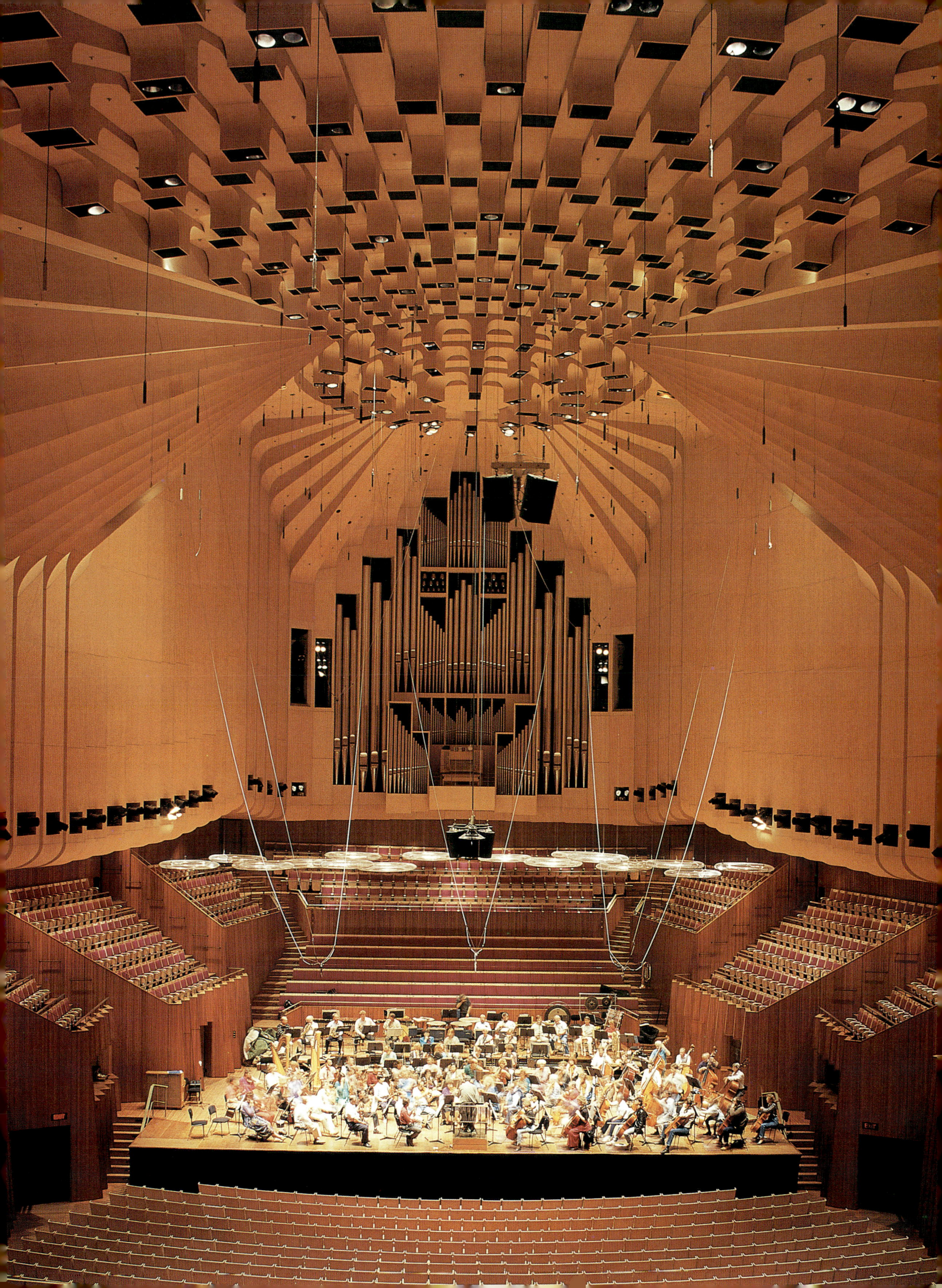

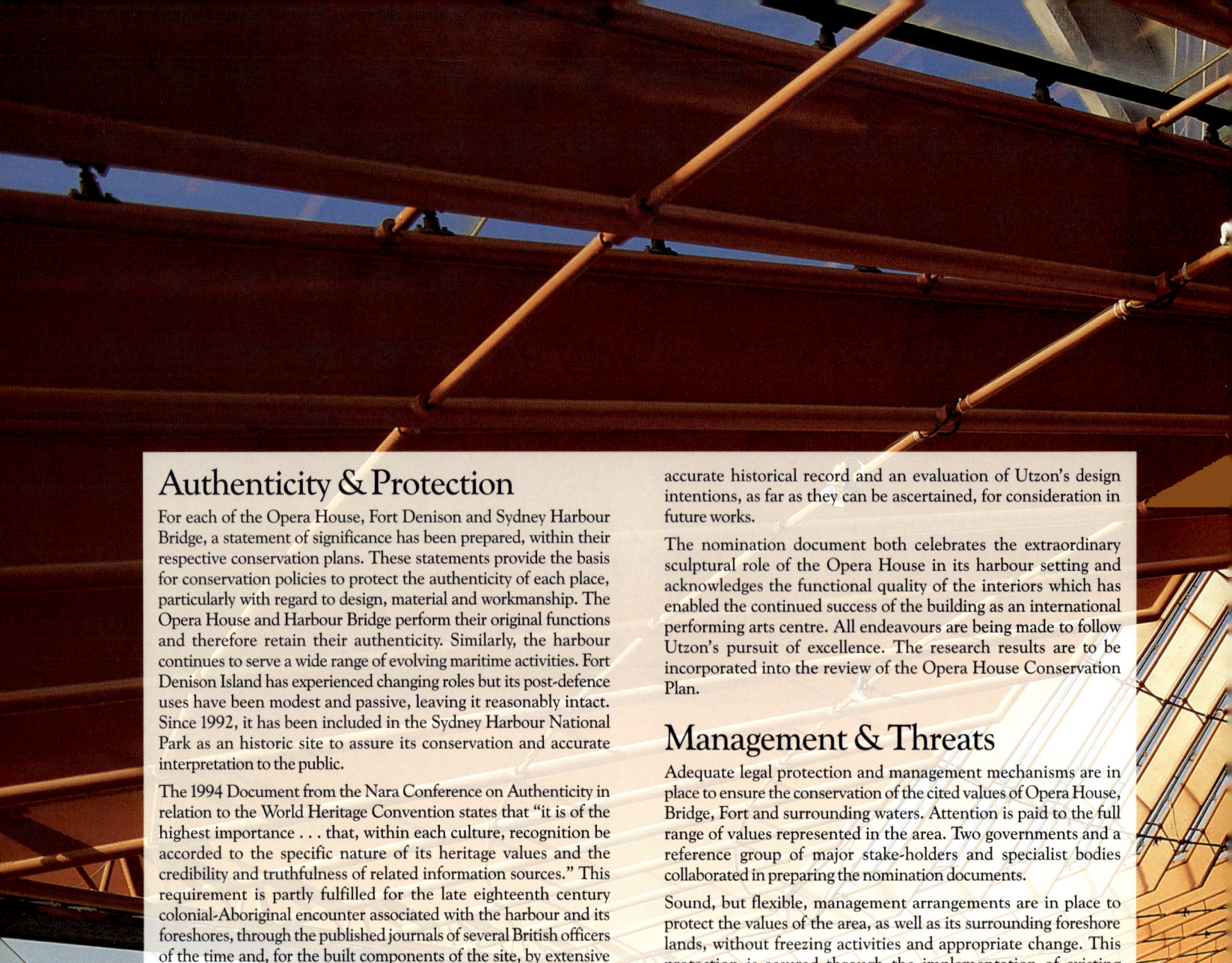

Authenticity & Protection

For each of the Opera House, Fort Denison and Sydney Harbour Bridge, a statement of significance has been prepared, within their respective conservation plans. These statements provide the basis for conservation policies to protect the authenticity of each place, particularly with regard to design, material and workmanship. The Opera House and Harbour Bridge perform their original functions and therefore retain their authenticity. Similarly, the harbour continues to serve a wide range of evolving maritime activities. Fort Denison Island has experienced changing roles but its post-defence uses have been modest and passive, leaving it reasonably intact. Since 1992, it has been included in the Sydney Harbour National Park as an historic site to assure its conservation and accurate interpretation to the public.

The 1994 Document from the Nara Conference on Authenticity in relation to the World Heritage Convention states that "it is of the highest importance . . . that, within each culture, recognition be accorded to the specific nature of its heritage values and the credibility and truthfulness of related information sources." This requirement is partly fulfilled for the late eighteenth century colonial-Aboriginal encounter associated with the harbour and its foreshores, through the published journals of several British officers of the time and, for the built components of the site, by extensive and detailed documentation.

One issue concerning authenticity persists. This is the design of the Sydney Opera House as a masterpiece of the creative genius. Jørn Utzon designed and supervised the erection of the great stair and podium and the soaring shells which, together, establish the spectacular exterior of the building. He selected the sheen of tiles and, with Arup, designed the rib and repetitive lid system by which they were fixed. Although he had worked for considerable time on complex designs for the halls and the glazed walls, these elements were, following much controversy, designed and built by Australian architects, Hall, Littlemore and Todd. Opinion differs over how close Utzon was to resolving the technical problems of his design intentions when he left Australia - and over the significance of the interiors and glass walls as built. The question is whether future work on the Opera House should conserve Peter Hall's interiors, glass and other details, or should seek to recapture Utzon's concepts.

This issue will be addressed. In 1972, Utzon presented his personal archive of plans and files to the State Library; related files are held in the National Library and elsewhere. This resource fulfils the 1994 Nara requirement of credibility and truthfulness of related information sources. A major exhibition of plans for the interiors, the "Unseen Utzon" (Nobis), was shown at the Opera House in 1994-1995. In recognition of the significance of the architectural questions raised, a research project into the Utzon and related collections is proposed. Its purpose is to complete, in accordance with the building's Interim Conservation Plan, a consolidated catalogue and to assess graphic and archival material to provide an accurate historical record and an evaluation of Utzon's design intentions, as far as they can be ascertained, for consideration in future works.

The nomination document both celebrates the extraordinary sculptural role of the Opera House in its harbour setting and acknowledges the functional quality of the interiors which has enabled the continued success of the building as an international performing arts centre. All endeavours are being made to follow Utzon's pursuit of excellence. The research results are to be incorporated into the review of the Opera House Conservation Plan.

Management & Threats

Adequate legal protection and management mechanisms are in place to ensure the conservation of the cited values of Opera House, Bridge, Fort and surrounding waters. Attention is paid to the full range of values represented in the area. Two governments and a reference group of major stake-holders and specialist bodies collaborated in preparing the nomination documents.

Sound, but flexible, management arrangements are in place to protect the values of the area, as well as its surrounding foreshore lands, without freezing activities and appropriate change. This protection is assured through the implementation of existing environmental planning and heritage conservation regimes. A process has been set in train to offer the three significant structures in the area the State's highest legal protection. Fort Denison is offered the full protection of an historic site under the State's National Parks and Wildlife Act, 1974; protection will be sought for the Opera House and Harbour Bridge by permanent conservation orders under the Heritage Act, 1977.

Debate has raged over changes to a site adjacent to the nominated area. Three linked slab buildings, with ground level shops and cafes along the promenade south of the Opera House, were permitted, under stringent guidelines, to replace earlier high rise offices separating east Sydney Cove from the Botanic Gardens. In 1997, there was a public outcry when the earlier buildings were demolished and new construction rose to obstruct previous views of the Opera House, from the ferry wharves of Circular Quay, as well as the new open views to the gardens.

Initiatives of the Sydney Opera House Trust, its managing body, to maintain the Sydney Opera House in good condition and conserve its outstanding values include an upgrade program, asset management plan and interim conservation plan. The latter will be reviewed and may require future works to take into account the unfulfilled design intentions of Jørn Utzon.

THIS PAGE The northern glass walls designed by Peter Hall. A special feature is the canting out of the lowest sheets which allows views out without reflections.

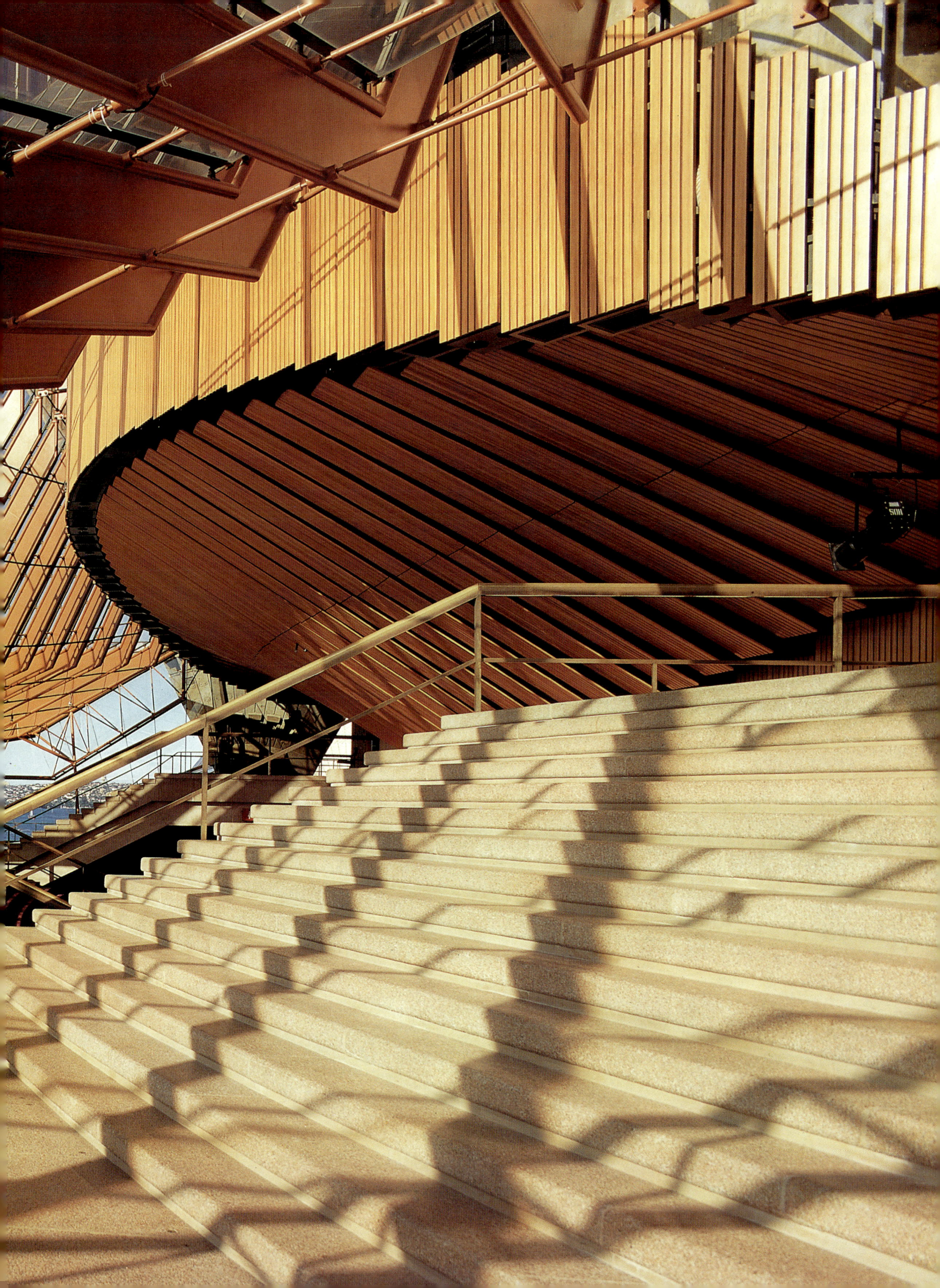

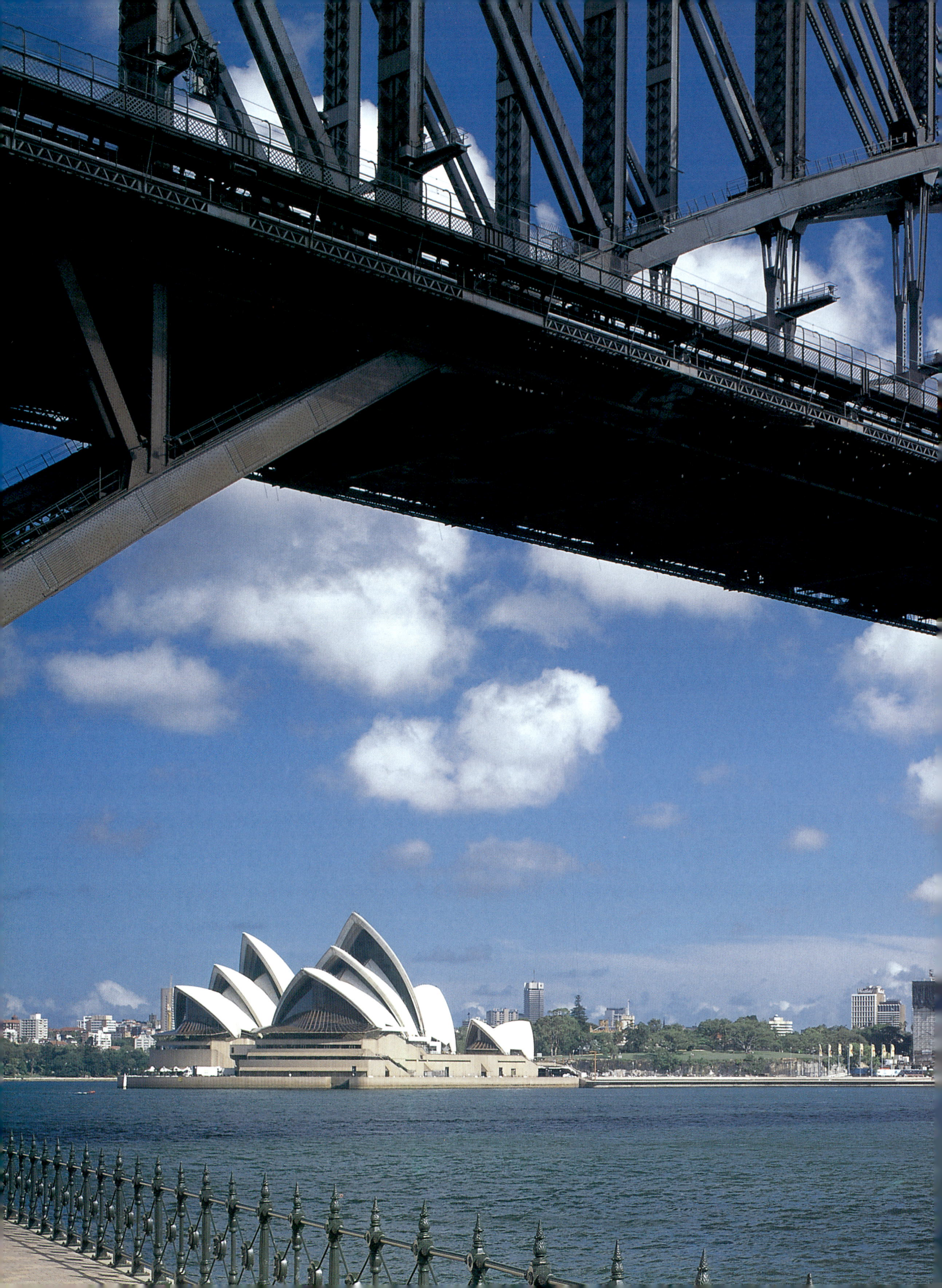

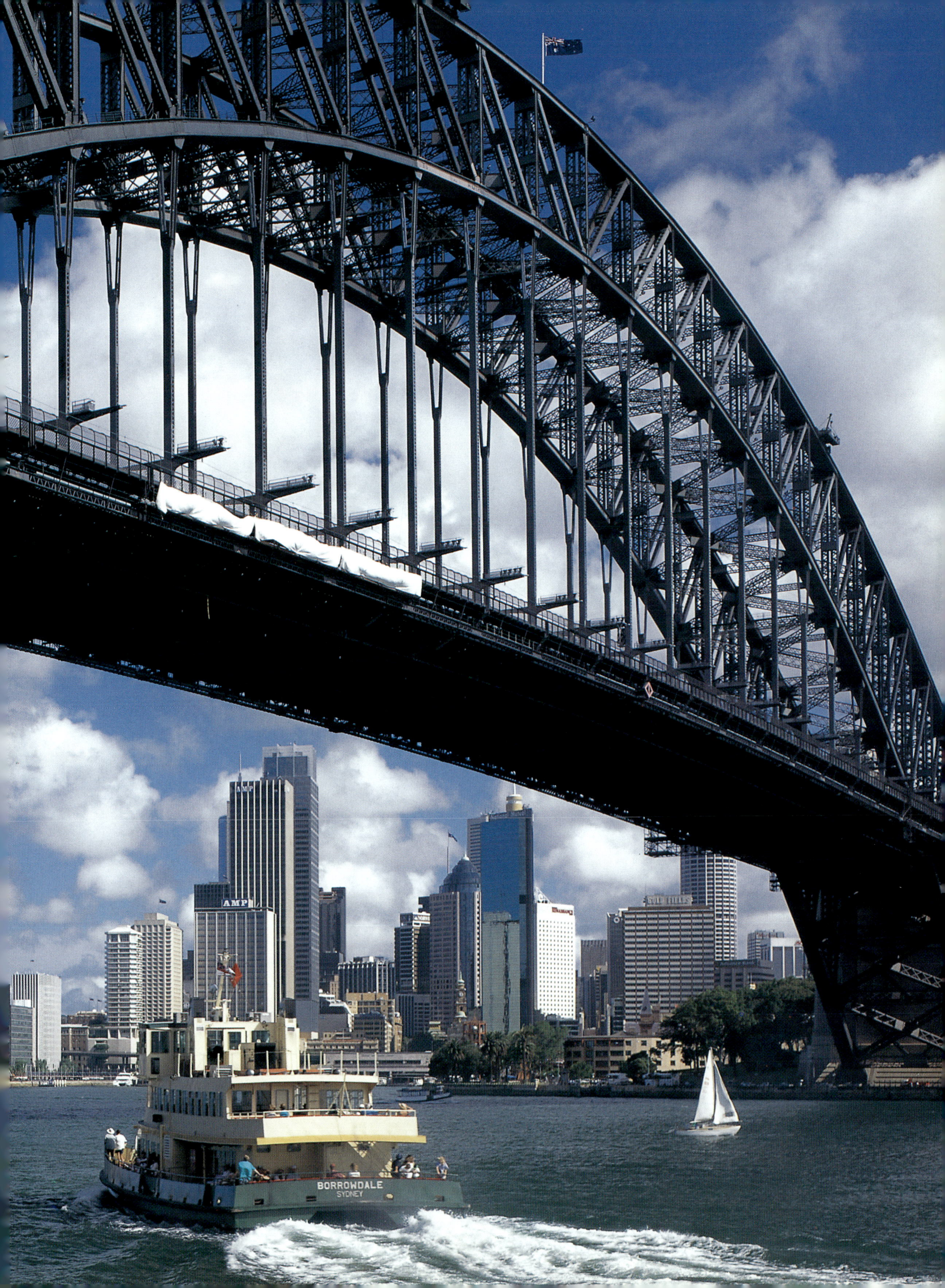
AMP
AMP
BORROWDALE
SYDNEY

The Australian World Heritage Properties Conservation Act (1983) - An Overview

by Atticus Fleming

Foreword

This article is an extract from a paper written in 1995 and presented at Richmond in New South Wales for a conference organised by the IUCN-The World Conservation Union on World Heritage management in Australia. The article has not been updated to reflect some recent developments including decisions in the Federal Court regarding consents granted under the World Heritage Properties Conservation Act. However, the information presented in the article is consistent with the Federal Court decisions and remains an accurate description of the law.

Introduction

The World Heritage Properties Conservation Act 1983 ('the World Heritage Act') implements some of Australia's obligations under the Convention for the Protection of the World Cultural and Natural Heritage ('the World Heritage Convention'). The World Heritage Act was enacted by the Commonwealth in 1983 in response to the proposed construction of the Gordon-below-Franklin Dam in Southwest Tasmania which, if completed, would have substantially destroyed a significant part of the World Heritage values of the Western Tasmania Wilderness.

The World Heritage Act ultimately saved the World Heritage values of South-West Tasmania by preventing construction of the Gordon below Franklin Dam. The Act has subsequently been effective in protecting other World Heritage areas, including the Wet Tropics in Queensland.

Constitutional Basis for the World Heritage Act

There is no power in the Constitution granting the Commonwealth Parliament specific power to legislate with respect to 'the environment'. The World Heritage Act relies for its constitutional validity upon a number of Commonwealth legislative powers. The most significant of these are the external affairs power (paragraph 51(xxix) of the Constitution), the corporations power (paragraph 51(xx)) and the races power (paragraph 51(xxvi). The constitutional validity of the World Heritage Act was considered by the High Court in 1983 in the case of the Commonwealth v Tasmania ('the Tasmanian Dam case'). In the Tasmanian Dam case, a majority of the High Court confirmed the constitutional validity of most provisions of the World Heritage Act.

Operation of the World Heritage Act

The World Heritage Act does not automatically operate to protect World Heritage properties - that is, properties forming part of the 'natural heritage' or 'cultural heritage', as defined in the World Heritage Convention.

Before the protective provisions contained in the World Heritage Act apply to any World Heritage property, a number of steps need to be taken:

* the property must satisfy the definition of 'identified property';
* the Governor-General must make a Proclamation (or Proclamations) declaring the property to be property to which one (or more) of the protective provisions of the World Heritage Act apply;
* once relevant Proclamations are made:
   - it is unlawful for corporations to do certain acts in relation to the proclaimed property (section 10);
   - it is unlawful for any person to do certain acts in relation to the proclaimed Aboriginal site, including any relic or artefact on that site (section 11).
* the Governor-General may make regulations for the purposes of section 9 in relation to the proclaimed property. It is then unlawful for any person to do an act specified in the regulations.
* the Minister administering the Act may consent to the doing of an otherwise unlawful act.

Identified Property

The World Heritage Act potentially applies to any property in respect of which one or more of the following conditions is satisfied:

* the property is included in the World Heritage List, provided for in paragraph 2 of Article 11 of the World Heritage Convention;
* the property has been nominated for inclusion in the World Heritage List;
* the property forms part of the cultural heritage or natural heritage (as defined in the World Heritage Convention) and is declared by regulations made under the World Heritage Act to form part of the cultural heritage or natural heritage; or
* the property is subject to an inquiry established by a law of the Commonwealth whose purpose, or one of whose purposes, is to consider whether the property forms part of the cultural heritage or natural heritage.

A property, or any part of a property, that falls within one of the above paragraphs is referred to as 'identified property': section 3A of the World Heritage Act. A property is not, however, protected by the World Heritage Act simply by virtue of the fact that it is identified property.

The Making of a Proclamation

The sections in the World Heritage Act which provide substantive protection for an identified property are sections 9, 10 and 11. However, these sections apply only to an identified property, in respect of which a Proclamation has been made by the Governor-General under sections 6, 7 or 8 respectively.

The Governor-General may make a Proclamation under section 6 and section 7 in relation to any identified property if satisfied that the property "is being or is likely to be damaged or destroyed". (There is an additional requirement in subsection 6(2), which must be satisfied before identified property that is in a State may be the subject of a Proclamation under section 6 - however, it is likely that if a property is identified property, it will satisfy this requirement.)

The Governor-General may make a Proclamation under section 8 if satisfied that an Aboriginal site within an identified property, or any artefacts or relics situated on such a site, are being, or are likely to be, damaged or destroyed. There is an additional requirement that the protection or conservation of the site must be of particular significance to the people of the Aboriginal race.

The critical point to note is that a Proclamation can be made only if there is evidence of a threat to the World Heritage characteristics of the identified property - that is, if the property is being, or is likely to be, damaged or destroyed.

The Application of Section 9

Section 9 of the World Heritage Act will apply to an identified property in respect of which a Proclamation is made under section 6. Section 9 provides that it is unlawful, except with the consent in writing of the Minister administering the Act, for a person to do any act that is identified in regulations made for the purposes of that section. Accordingly, section 9 will protect an identified property only if:

* a Proclamation is made declaring the property to be property to which section 9 applies; and
* regulations are made identifying the prohibited acts.

Section 9, and the regulations made for the purposes of section 9, rely upon the external affairs power for their constitutional validity. It is not intended to exhaustively define here the scope of the external affairs power. However, it is important to note that the protective regime established by section 9 and any regulations made in relation to a particular property must be capable of being considered "reasonably appropriate and adapted" to the purposes of discharging Australia's international obligations under the World Heritage Convention (for example, to protect or conserve that property).

In particular, the external affairs power is unlikely to support a scheme of controls and prohibitions that apply uniformly to all Australian World Heritage properties: this is clear from the Tasmanian Dam case, especially the judgements of Justices Brennan and Deane. In that case, Justice Brennan said:

"The fact is that protection and conservation are functions that can only be performed with respect to an individual property; those functions have to be performed according to the condition of the property at the time and with reference to any threat that may then be posed by specific dangers."

To ensure that the legislative scheme is supported by the external affairs power, the acts which are identified in the regulations - and which are therefore prohibited by section 9 - must be directed toward the particular threat which is faced by the particular World Heritage property. There must be a sufficient relationship between the prescribed acts and the nature and source of likely damage to the World Heritage property.

Identifying and defining those acts, the prohibition of which would be reasonably appropriate and adapted to the protection and conservation of a World Heritage property, may be a complex task. For example, in the case of Richardson v Forestry Commission, decided by the High Court in 1988, the Court was required to consider whether the external affairs power would support a provision in the Lemonthyme and Southern Forests (Commission of Inquiry) Act, 1987 (section 16) that made it unlawful to do any of the following acts in the Lemonthyme and Southern Forests area of Tasmania:

"(a) for the purposes of, or in the course of carrying out, forestry operations, to kill, cut down or damage a tree in, or remove a tree or a part of a tree from, the protected area;

(b) to construct or establish a road or vehicular track within the protected area;

(c) to carry out any excavation works within the protected area;

(d) to do any other act prescribed for the purposes of this paragraph, being an act capable of adversely affecting the protected area."

Chief Justice Mason of the High Court, and Justice Brennan, acknowledged that some of the prohibited acts "may be so trivial that they do not present a significant risk of real impairment to the World Heritage characteristics of the land in question". Nevertheless, the Chief Justice and Justice Brennan concluded that the class of acts prohibited by the provision were "generally speaking, acts involving a potential risk of injury" to the property. Accordingly, it was appropriate to single these acts out as objects of prohibition. The judges therefore held each of the paragraphs to be valid - there was a sufficient relationship between the prescribed acts and the nature and source of likely damage.

In contrast, Justice Deane held that the prohibition of acts identified in paragraphs (b), (c) and (d) was not capable of being considered reasonably appropriate and adapted to achieving the discharge of Australia's obligations under the Convention and, therefore, was not supported by the external affairs power. Justice Deane noted, for example, that "no vehicular track, however narrow, temporary or short, or for whatever purpose, could be constructed". For the same reason, the judge held that paragraph (a) was invalid to the extent it prohibited the removal of a tree or part of a tree from the property. However, Justice Deane concluded that the prohibition of active logging operations in paragraph (a) was valid because these activities were "obviously capable of being seen as constituting a threat to the preservation of any actual or potential World Heritage Areas in which they were carried on".

The operation of section 9 may be illustrated by reference to the action taken in 1994 in relation to a proposed resort development near Hinchinbrook Channel in the GBRWHA. The action taken included:

* under section 6, a Proclamation was made by the Governor-General, after he was satisfied that a part of the GBRWHA was likely to be damaged or destroyed, declaring that part of the GBRWHA to be property to which section 9 applied; and
* regulations were made, for the purposes of section 9, identifying prohibited acts - it was necessary to ensure there existed a sufficient relationship between these acts and the threat created by the development (for example, the prohibited acts include constructing a breakwater and dredging).

The Application of Section 10

Section 10 applies to an identified property in respect of which a Proclamation has been made under section 7. Section 10 relies upon the corporation's power (and to a lesser extent, the Territories' power) for its constitutional validity. Accordingly, the effect of section 10 is limited because it applies only to a body corporate that is:

* a trading corporation (as that term is used in paragraph 51(xx) of the Constitution);
* a foreign corporation (as that term is used in paragraph 51(xx) of the Constitution); or
* incorporated in a Territory.

Here, corporations to which section 10 apply are referred to as 'constitutional corporations'. Section 10 applies also to servants and agents of a constitutional corporation.

It is, of course, possible that acts which damage a World Heritage property will be carried out by an entity other than a constitutional corporation - for example, an individual, a partnership or an unincorporated trust. Acts carried out by such entities will not be prohibited by section 10. However, relevant acts may be prohibited by section 9 and section 11 of the World Heritage Act.

Once a Proclamation is made under section 7, section 10 operates as follows:

* It is unlawful for a constitutional corporation to do any of the acts specified in paragraphs 10(2)(d)-(k) on the proclaimed area. These acts include:

(i) to carry out any excavation works or use explosives;

(ii) to carry out operations for, or exploratory drilling in connection with, the recovery of minerals;

(iii) to erect a building or other substantial structure or to do any work in the course of, or for the purpose of, the erection of a building or other substantial structure;

(iv) to damage or destroy a building or other substantial structure;

(v) to kill, cut down or damage any tree;

(vi) to construct or establish any road or vehicular track;

* it is unlawful for a person to do any act which is specified in regulations made for the purposes of paragraph 10(2)(m) of the World Heritage Act; and

* it is unlawful for a constitutional corporation to do any other act that damages the proclaimed area (see subsection 10(3)).

Unlike section 9, section 10 uniformly prohibits the carrying out of certain acts in relation to all proclaimed properties. The prohibition comes into force in relation to a property immediately upon a Proclamation being made in respect of that property - it is not necessary to take the further step of making regulations (although regulations may be made adding to the list of prohibited acts). Section 10 may operate in this way because the corporation's power is not subject to the same limitations as the external affairs' power, in particular, it is not necessary to ensure that the prohibited acts are sufficiently related to the source of damage to the property.

The Application of Section 11

Section 11 applies to an Aboriginal site in respect of which a Proclamation has been made under section 8. Section 11 relies upon the race's power for its constitutional validity.

Once a Proclamation is made under section 8, section 11 operates as follows:

* it is unlawful for a person to do any of the acts specified in paragraphs 11 (1) (a)-(h) of the World Heritage Act in relation to the proclaimed Aboriginal site. (These acts are similar to those identified in paragraphs 10 (2) (d)-(k) in relation to corporations);

* it is unlawful for a person to do any act which is specified in regulations made for the purposes of paragraph 11 (1) (j) of the World Heritage Act; and

* it is unlawful for a person to do any other act:

- that damages or destroys; or

- that is likely to result in damage to or the destruction of any proclaimed Aboriginal site or any artefact or relic on that site.

Section 11 operates to prohibit relevant acts, immediately upon a Proclamation being made.

Consent

The Minister administering the Act may consent (in writing) to the carrying out of an act that is otherwise unlawful under section 9, section 10 or section 11 of the World Heritage Act. It is not unlawful to do an act with the consent of the Minister.

It is important to note that subsection 13(1) of the World Heritage Act provides that, when deciding whether to give consent for the purposes of subsection 9(1), the Minister may have regard only to the 'protection, conservation and presentatio' as those terms are used in the World Heritage Convention, of the relevant property. This means that when deciding whether to give consent for the purpose of section 9:

* The Minister may not have regard to general economic, commercial or political factors.

* The Minister may not have regard to general environmental effects unrelated to the World Heritage values of the proclaimed area.

In having regard to 'protection, conservation and presentation', 'protection' and 'conservation' should be given their ordinary meanings. The term 'presentation' conveys the intention that the parties to the Convention should encourage people to appreciate and make use of World Heritage Areas, provided that such usage does not damage their cultural or natural values. This is consistent with the view of Justice Brennan, who, in the Tasmanian Dam case, after noting that presentation implies bringing out a property's "potentialities to best advantage", states that "nevertheless, conservation of the property is an element of its presentation and is not to be sacrificed by presentation".

In deciding whether to give consent for the purpose of section 10 or section 11, the Minister is not restricted to consideration of the 'protection, conservation and presentation' of the property.

Other Acts Not Unlawful

Section 12 of the World Heritage Act effectively provides that it is not unlawful to do any act that is authorised by:

(a) a zoning plan in operation under the Great Barrier Reef Marine Park Act, 1975; or

(b) a plan of management in force under the National Parks and Wildlife Conservation Act, 1975.

Section 12 also allows for regulations to be made which would have the effect of providing that it is not unlawful to do any act authorised by a law of a State or Territory which is identified in those regulations.

Enforcement

The World Heritage Act does not provide that it is a criminal offence to do an act that is unlawful under section 9, section 10 or section 11. However, the Commonwealth Attorney-General or an 'interested person' may apply to the Federal Court or the High Court for an injunction to restrain a person from doing an unlawful act.

Subsection 14(3) provides that, in relation to an act that is unlawful by virtue of section 9 or 10, a reference to an 'interested person' includes:

(a) a person whose use or enjoyment of any part of the property is, or is likely to be, adversely affected by the doing of the unlawful act; or

(b) an organisation or association of persons, whether incorporated or not, the objects or purposes of which include, and activities of which relate to, the protection or conservation of the property, or of property of a kind that includes the property.

Accordingly, certain environmental groups will have standing to seek an injunction to prevent the doing of an unlawful act.

In relation to an act that is unlawful by virtue of section 11, the reference to an 'interested person' includes a reference to any member of the Aboriginal race.

Index

Abbotsmith Glacier *278-279*
Aboriginal artefacts 40, *74*, 244, *244*
Aboriginal culture 123, *138-139*
    erosion of 100, 123, 138, 142, 227, 244, 303
    face painting *40*
    protection of 142
    rainforest 176, 192
Aboriginal custodians 142, 192, 303
Aboriginal environmental mgt *130*, 138
Aboriginal languages 41, 123
    disappearance of 42
Aboriginal occupation 32, 40, 54, *75*, 83, 84, 176, 192, 199, 227, 244, 303, 303
Aboriginal rock art 39, 40, 41, *42-43*, 46, *54*, 83, 100, *100*, 124, 130, *138*, 138, 303
Aborigines 15, 37, 78
    rainforest 176
    forced re-settlement of 100, 140, 176, 227, 244
    Tasmanian 100
    traditional economy of 34, 40, 66, 83, 84, 121, 192, 218, 244
acacia 130, 212
Admiralty Group 106
Admiralty Islands 110
aestivating amphibians 132
agriculture 168
    damaging effects of 118, 152, 218
agricultural clearing 192
albatross 292, 297
    light-mantled sooty 281
    wandering 276
algae 15, 30
    blue-green 199, 206
    marine 294
    valona *20-21*
Alice Springs 122, 140
Alligator Rivers 42
Alligator Rivers Wildlife Sanctuary 56
alpine vegetation 90
Amadeus Basin 124, 128
Anangu 123, 124, 142
    rock art *138*
anemone *30, 112-113*
anemonefish *30*
Angbangbang Billabong *44-45*
angle-headed dragon - southern *160-161*
Anne-a-kananda 88
Antarctic beech *168-169*
Antarctic convergence 294
Antarctica
    fossil leaf from 90
    separation from 259
ants 72, 240
apostle birds *68*, 72
aquifer 128, 234
archaeological evidence 46, 54, 67, 100, 244
archaeological sites *75*, 130
archaeology 40, 63, 74, 83, 84, 138
Arnhem Land 48
Arnhem Land plateau 39, 44
Atherton antechnicus 188
Atherton Tablelands 182,
Arthur Ranges *84-85, 86-87*, 88
Atila 123, 128
Atlas Cove 282, 284
Atlas moth *190-191*

Aurora
    Australis 296
    Borealis 296
Australian and New Zealand Antarctic Expedition 275
Australian fernwren 188
Australian Fossil Mammal Sites (Riversleigh/ Naracoorte) 248-271
Australian Museum 117
Australian National Antarctic Research Expeditions (ANARE) 282, 284, 296, 291, 297
Australian Core Tool and Scraper Tradition 66
Australian World Heritage Properties Conservation Act (1983) - An Overview 312-314
Ayer's Rock (see Uluru)

Ball, Lieutenant Lidgbird 107
Ballawinne Cave 83, *100*
Balls Pyramid 106, 107, 108, 110, *110-111*, 116
banded
    fruit dove 52
    hare-wallaby 214
bandicoot 66, 151
    western barred *218*
Bang Gerreng 40
bangalow palm *157*
banksia - sceptre *213*
banyan fig 107
barramundi - in rock art *42*
Barrine Falls 175
Barrington Tops National Park 146, 148, *166, 168-169*
Barron Gorge 175
Barrow Island 199
bar-tailed godwit 116, 229
bat 40, 52, 132, 151, 160
    Australian false vampire 132
    fossil 116, 250
    large forest eptesicus 116
    long-eared 72
    tube-nosed insectivorous fruit 188, *192*
bêche-de-mer 32, 54
beech - Antarctic 151, *168-169*
    southern 150
beekeeping 102
bees 52
Beginner's Luck Cave 83
belah 70
Bellinger Valley 148
Benguela Current 275
Bennelong Point 303
Bennett's tree kangaroo 188
Bernier Island 198, 199
bettong 66, 214
    burrowing, skeletal remains of 70
Big Ben 273, 276, *276-277*, 280
Big Scrub 168
bilby 66, 132, *134-135*
biological integrity 148
    preservation of 168
bird of paradise 160
birds of prey 39, 132
birrida 199
Bishop and Clerk Islets 290, 297
bittern 52
Bizzarodonta 262

black
    butcher birds 39
    currawong 96
    flying fox 52
    footed rock wallaby *137*
    wallaroo 52
    winged petrel 116
black-breasted
    button-quail 229
    buzzard 39
Blackburn (Rabbit) Island 106
blackbutt forest 228
bleeding heart 152
Bligh, Captain William 16, 32
bloodwood 130
Bloomfield River 176, 192
blow holes 205
blue
    flowered Dampiera 200
    plum 107
    tongue lizard *126*
    whaler shark *208*
    wren 200
bluebell 70, *158*
bluebottles 16
bluebush 72, *72-73*
Blues Point 302
boa constrictor 251
boating
    commercial 34, 118
    recreational 34, 218
boids 254
Bone Cave 83
boodie 199
Boomanjin Lake *230-231*
bottlenose dolphin 26, 210, *210-211, 214*
Border Ranges 150
Border Ranges National Park *144-145*, 148, *158-159, 168-169*
Botanical Gardens 302
bowerbird 151, 160
    golden 188
    spotted *136*
Bower's strike thrush 188
Bowes, Arthur 107
Boyd's rainforest dragon *182*
box jellyfish 16
Brahminy kite 39
bridled honeyeater 188
Brindle Creek *144-145*
brolga 52
broom bush 130
brushbox *157*, 228, 238
bryophytes 276
budget constraints 224
buffalo industry 42, 56
Bundaberg 226
burials 54, 63, 66, 74
burrowing
    bettong *72*, 132
    petrel 280
Burton Harry 276
brush turkey 160
bustard 39
Butchulla 244
butterflies 52, 116, 188, 229
    orchard *178*
    white nymph 160

315

butterfly - Illidge's Ant blue 228
butterfly fish 26
buttongrass 90
buttressing 90, 148

C.S.I.R.O. 244
Cahill Paddy 42
Cainozoic Period 262
Cameron W.E. 260
Campbell Island 292
candlewood 228
cane toad 40
canoes 32, 54
Cape Lesueur *208*
Cape Tribulation 184, *194-195*
Cape York 14, 15
Capricorn and Bunker Islands 20
Capricorn-Bunker Group National Park 14, 15
Carnarvon 198
carpet python *186-187*
Caspian terns 214
cassia 130
cassowary 175, 188
    southern *178-179*
Cave Exploration Group of South Australia 251
cave paintings 84 (see also rock art)
caves 83
cays 15,
    formation of 22
cedar 176
Central Eastern Rainforest Reserves 144-171,
    1, 2-3, 262
central netted dragon *126*
ceremonial sites 54
    damage to 56
Ceremony Beach 184
charter boats 222
chestnut quail-thrush 72
Chibnalwood lunette 68
Chinocochloa conspicua 114
chinstrap penguins *284-285, 292-293, 298-299*
Chironomid midge 229
chowchilla 188
climate change 83, 147, 151, 182, 258, 276
coachwood tree 168
coastal
    blackbutt 151
    heath 234
cockatoos
    pink *136*
    red-tailed black 39
    sulphur crested 39
coelenterates 214
coffee rock *246-247*
Concert Hall 306, 307
conifers *88*, 175, 184
Conrad 303
conservation 102
conservationists 39, 152, 175, 227, 244
convicts 100
Cook, Captain James 15, 16, 32, 147, 244, 112
Cook's scorpionfish *112*
Cooktown 16, 174
Cooloola 244
Cooloola propator 229, *240*
coral 15, *31*, 108, 110, 200
    yellow *26*
coral polyps 16, 22
coral reefs *12-13, 22-23, 35*, 104, 112, 180, 240
Coral Sea 175
Corinthian Cave 282
cormorant 52
Coxen's fig-parrot 151
crab 251
Cracroft River 100

Cradle Mountain *94, 98-99*, 100, 102, *103*
crayfish - Lamington spiny blue *152*
cremation - earliest record of 65, 67
Cremorne Reserve 302
crocodiles 39, 52
    estuarine or saltwater *44*, 52, 240
    shooting of 42
crown-of-thorns starfish 16, 34
crustaceans 214
cultural change 83-84
curlew 39
currawong
    black *96*
    Lord Howe Island pied *117*
curtain fig tree 175
cushion
    carpet 276
    plant *286-287*, 294
cycads 175, 184
cyclones 152, 232
cypress pines 70

Daintree 175, 176
Daintree River *180-181*, 182, 184, 192
Dampier, William 199, 200
damsel fish 26
darter 52
Darwin 38
Darwin glass 83
dating (carbon) 40, *41*, 61, 63, 67, 83
Dawes Point 303
Deaf Adder Creek 46
Denham 198, 199, 218, 222
    population of 220
Denham Sound 199
Department of Conservation and Land
    Management Western Australia
    (CALM) 222
Desert Creek 157
desert oak 125
dillon bush 70
dingo 40, 125, 132, 151, *234*
    poisoning of 42
Diprotodon 66, *255*
Diprotodontid 252, *255*
Dirk Hartog Island 198, 199, *204-205*, 214
Dirk Hartog's Plate *204*
discharge of sewage 218, 246
diving *35*
dolphins 199
    bottlenose 26, 210, *210-211*, 214
    deaths among 218
    Indo-Pacific humpback 26
    Irrawaddy 26
    spinner 26
Dorre Island 198, 199
double-banded dotterel 116
Dove Lake *98-99, 103*
Dreaming 123, 138
Dreamtime 41
drip-tip leaves 90
drought 78, 125, 142, 143
Du Cane Range *88-89*
duck 52
dugong 26, 30, 197, 199, 210, *216-217*, 240
    deaths among 218
Dulingbara 244
Dundubura 244
dune heathlands 229
dunes 63, 124, 199, 205, *224-225*
    clay 68
    destabilisation of 228
    formation of 228
    transgressive *236-237*
Dutchman's pipe *158*

Eacham Falls 175
East Alligator River 38
eastern
    bristlebird 150
    curlew 229
    golden plover 116
echidna 52, 151, 160
    ancient 252, 262
    short-beaked 72, *170-171*
    short-nosed 132
    skull of long-beaked *254*
echinoderms 26
Edel Island 218, 220
egret 39, 52
elephant seal 291, *294+295*
Eli Creek *241*
El Sharana 56
emu 39, 72
    in rock art 46
endangered species 13, 37, 40, 52, 114, 116, 214
endemic species 90, 96, 104, 107, 114, 214, 240,
    291, 297
engravings 130
epiphytes 90, 148, 150, 156
eptesicus 116
Eremaean Province 212
erosion *68-69*, 182, 194
eucalypts 48, 90, 130, 212, 238, *234*, 244
euro 124
Eurong 246
Exit Cave 88
exotic plants 40, 125, 143, 194
    control of 143
exotic weeds - damage done by 56, 114, 168
extinct species 67, 107, 118, 125, 147, 199, 291
    DNA analysis of 259
    reintroduction of 132

Fairfax Island 14, *18-19*, 20
falcon - peregrine 132
fan palms *184-185*, 184
Farm Cove 303
fat-tailed dunnart 72
Faure Island 214
fawn footed melomys *150-151*
feather wedging 260
Federation Peak *84-85*
feldmark 294
fellfield 276
feral animals 40, 72, 118, 125, 143, 229
    control of 143, 224
    damage done by 56, 78, 199, 220, 292
    eradication 292
ferns 114, 156
    king 228
    rare 238
fire stick farming *130*
firewheel flower *162*
firing practices 39, 124, 138, 143, 303
    suppression of 125
fish 30
    bottom dwelling 26
    threatened 240
fish traps 244
fisheries - commercial - human pressure 284
fishing 246
    commercial 34, 199, 200, 220, 244
    recreational 32, 34, 222, 224
    regulation of 224
    tours 222
Flat Island 275
Flinders, Matthew 32, 244
flintstone *74*
Florentine Valley 84

316

flycatcher 39
foraminifera 251
Fort Denison 302, 303, 304, 308
fossil chamber *248-249*
fossil leaf Antarctica 90
fossils 90, 110, 116, 250-270
four wheel drive vehicles 228, 246
Frankland Range 88
Franklin River Valley 100
Fraser, Eliza 244
Fraser Island 224-247, 14, 15
Fraser Island Defenders Organisation (FIDO) 227, 228, 244, 246
Fraser Island Lake 228
Frenchman's Cap 88
Freshwater Camp 199
frigatebirds 16, 26
frill-neck lizard *54-55*
frogs 96, 151, 188, 240
    giant tree *193*
    green and golden *102*
    hip-pocket 151
    harmonious 151
fungus
    bracket *156*
    root rot 102
fur seals *286-287*
fuschia - native 130

Gag plateau 260
Galawan (sand goanna) *46-47*
Gascoyne-Wooramel Province 205
gecko 39, 214
    chameleon 188
    northern leaf-tailed 188
    soft knob-tailed *132-133*
geomorthology 41
giant clams 16, 200
giant leaf-eating kangaroo *255, 266, 267, 268, 269*
giant stick insect 108
giant tree frog *193*
Gilbert, Captain Thomas 108
Giles, Ernest 124
gin's whiskers 152
glaciers 84, 273, 275, 276, 280
global warming 152, 273, 276, 280
glossy black-cockatoo 229
goanna *138-139*
golden orb spider *164*
golden perch 66
Goldsborough Valley 175
Gondwana 88, 90, 145, 148, 156, 173, 182, 262
goose 52
Gordon River *80-81*, 100
Gordon-below-Franklin Dam 102, 312
Gosse, William 140, 124
Gouldian finch 52
Gower Island 106
grass 212
grasses 294
grassland - tussock 276
grassy woodland 234
graziers 78, 192
grazing (see also pastoralism) 168, 220, 270
    damage done by 56
grazing animals 125
Great Barrier Reef 12-35, 108, 112, 227
Great Escarpment *158-159*, 180
Great Sandy Cape *234-235*
green and golden frog *102*
green catbird *163*
Green Island 15, 32
green rosella *92*
greenshank 39

Gregory River 258, *270-271*
grevillea 184
    desert 125
grey ternlet 116
grindstones 74
ground parrot 240
groundsel bush 70
guano 22
gulls 26
Gunumeleng 40
gunyah shelters 244
Gurrung 40

hakea 130
Hall Peter 308
Hall Todd and Littlemore, architects 304, 308
Hamelin Pool 197, 199, *200-201*, 206
hand stencils (see also rock art) 83, *100*
Hartz Mountains 88
Hastings River mouse 156
hawk 151
Heard and McDonald Islands 272-287
Heard Island Wilderness Reserve Management Plan 284
Heard James J. 275
hearths 66, 67, 74, 83
heathland 228, 238
herb fields 294
Herbert River ringtail possum *177*
Hercules moth 188, *190-191*
hermit crab *30-31*
heron 39, 52
Heron Island 14, 15, 32
Hervey Bay 226, 228, 246
Hinchinbrook Channel 175, 182
Hinchinbrook Pass 16
honey possum *218-219*
honeyeater 39
hoop pine 228
Hoskyn Island 14
Howea palm 107, *108-109*, 118
Hull Cindy 276, 292
Humboldt Current 275
humpback whale *217*
hunter-gatherers 83, 84, 100, 192
Hunter Valley 148
hunting - modern methods 124
Huon pine 90, 100
hydro-electric power 102
Hydro-Electric Commission 84, 102
Hypipamee Falls 175

ibis 52
Ice Age 15, 32, 62, 63, 74, 83, 88, 175, 182, 199, 228, 250, 251, 303
Illawarra 168
Iluka Nature Reserve 148
Indo-Pacific batfish *33*
International Committee for Conservation of Industrial Heritage 304
International Council on Monuments and Sites (ICOMOS) 306, 308
International Working Party for Documentation and Conservation of Buildings, Sites and Neighbourhoods of the Modern Movement (DOCOMOMO) 306
introduced species 96, 107, 116, 118, 246, 291, 297, 297
invertebrates 96, 116, 132, 151, 229, 240, 297
Ironbound Range 88, *94-95*
IUCN-The World Conservation Union 32, 78, 123, 148, 214, 270, 284

Jabiru *50-51*
Jabiru - township of 56

Jane River goldfield 102
jellyfish 16
Jim Jim Falls 39, *58-59*
Johnstone River 182
Jones, Professor Wood 16
Judd, Henry 83
Judds Cavern 83, 100
Judds Glacier *101*
Judds Lake *101*
Judge and Clerk Islets 290, 297
Jurassic Era 88

Kakadu 262
Kakadu escarpment *41, 58-59*
Kakadu National Park 36-59
kangaroo 125
    ancient 251-252, 266
    giant leaf eating 255
    Lumholtz tree *188*
    musky-rat 175, *182*
    red *72-73, 132, 140-141*
kangaroo paw 212
Kata Tjuta 122-123, *128-129, 130-131*
kauri pine 228
kelp 297
kelp fly 297
Kennedy, Edmund 176, 192
kentia palm (see Howea palm)
Kerguelen Island 2743
Kerguelen Plateau 280
Kerguelen-Heard Plume 280
Kermadec petrel 116
Key's boronia *238*
killer whale 214
King Billy pine 90, *94, 101*
king shag 297
kingfisher 39
king penguin *272-273, 278-279*
Kings holly 90
Kirribilli 303
koala 66
kookaburra 39
Koolpinyah Surface 44
Koongarra - uranium mining 56
Kotzebue 296
krill 276, 292
Kuku-Yalanji 176
Kutikina Cave 83, 100

Lachlan River 63, 64
Lady Elliott Island 32
Lady Musgrove Island 14, 20
Lake Boomanjin 229, *230-231*
Lake Chibnalwood 64
Lake Garnpung 63, 65
Lake Leaghur 65
Lake McKenzie 229, *242-243*
Lake Mulurulu 64, 67
Lake Mungo 63, 64, *64-65*, 65, 67, *70, 72-73, 78-79*
Lake Mungo lunette *72-73, 78-79*
Lake Pedder *97*, 102
Lake St Clair 88, *88-89*, 100, 102
lakes - perched dune 228, *230-231, 232-233, 234, 236-237, 240, 242-243*
lamb's tail 130
Lamington National Park *2-3, 9*, 148, 149
Lamington spiny blue crayfish 152
land rights 124, 142 (see also native title)
lantana 194
large-billed scrubwren *162*
large sand plover 229
Laurales 184
Laurens Peninsula *281*
Lawn Hill National Park 270

leaching 148
legless lizards 214
Leichhardt, Ludwig 54
lesser golden plover 229
Lharidon Bight 206
liana 107, 150, *239*
lichen 276, 284, 294
lighthouses 32, 102
limestone 22, 70, 83, 205, 251, 258, 280
little
    red flying-fox 52
    shearwater 116
    tree-creeper 188
Little Lagoon *204*
lizard
    blue tongue *126*
    Burton's snake 72
    frill-neck *54-55*
    Galawan (sand goanna)*46-47*
    shingle-back 72
Lizard Island, 16, *32-33*
lock hospitals 199
loggerhead turtle *229*
logging 100, 102, 152, 168, 168, 176, 192, 194, 227, 246
long-beaked echidna 254
Lord Howe Island Group 104-119,
Lord Howe Island *118-119*
Lord Howe Island
    currawong 116
    golden whistler 116
    pied currawong *117*
    woodhen 104, 108, 116, *116*
lorikeet 39
lotus flower *46-47*
Lumholtz tree-kangaroo 188, *188*
lunettes *60-61*, 62, 64, *64-65, 66-67, 68-69, 72-73, 78-79*
lungkata 124, *126*
lyrebird 151, 160

Maccassans 32, 54
mackerel 26
Macquarie Island 288-299, 275
Macquarie Lachlan 291
Macquarie Ridge 296
macropods - in rock art 46
Madagascar 175
magpie geese *36-37*, 40
Magnoliales 184
Main Range 146, 148
mallee 65, 70, 78
mallee ringneck parrot *76*
mammals 40, 96, 116, 132, 188
    placental 250
    threatened 214
    rarest 188
mangroves 20, 39, 175, 180, 182, 212, 238
    clearing of 228
manta ray *210*
Maps
    Australian Fossil Mammal Sites (Riversleigh/Naracoorte) 250
    Central Eastern Rainforest Reserves 146, 147
    Fraser Island 226
    Great Barrier Reef 14
    Heard and McDonald Islands 274
    Kakadu National Park 38
    Kata Tjuṯa 122
    Macquarie Island 290
    Shark Bay 198
    Sydney Opera House In Its Harbour Setting 302
    Tasmanian Wilderness 82

The Lord Howe Island Group 106
Uluṟu 122
Uluṟu-Kata Tjuṯa 123
Wet Tropics of Queensland 174
Willandra Lakes Region 62
marine worms 108
marlin 26
marsupials 52, 72, 96, 160, 188
    ancient 258, 262
    lion 251, 262, *262, 263, 263*
    mole 132, 258
    mouse 151
    tiger cat 151
Maryborough 226
masked
    booby bird 116, *116*
    white-tailed rat 175
Mawson Peak 273, 280
Mawson, Sir Douglas 275, 291, 296, 297
Maxwell River 100
McDonald Captain 275
McDonald Island (see Heard & McDonald Islands) *276-277, 280, 282-283*
Meg Creek 182
megafauna 66, 250, *70-71*, 83
    extinction of 74, 262
melomys - fawn footed *150-151*
Mesozoic Era 254
Meyer Rock 275
microbial mats 206
mining 32, 102, 143, 152, 220
    damage caused by 56, 218
    gold 56, 176
    guano 199, 260
    gypsum 218, 220
    sand 227, 244, 246
    tin 176, 192
Miocene 251, 258
missions 140, 176, 227, 244
molluscs 16, 26, 30, 108, 199
    terrestrial 116
Mongolian plover 229
monitor 214
monitor lizard 132
Monkey Mia 199, 210, 218, 222, 224
monotremes 52, 72, 160, 188, 250
Mossman Gorge 175
Mossman River 192
Mossman River grass 142
moths
    daymoth *162*
    Hercules or Atlas moth *190-191*
Mount Anne 88, *101*
Mount Bellenden Ker 180
Mount Conner (see Atila) 123, 128
Mount Gower *104-105*, 107, 108, 110
Mount Hamilton 291
Mount Lidgbird *104-105*, 107, 108, 110, *114-115*
Mount Ossa 88
Mount Pier Botte 182
Mount Warning 146, *154-155*
Mrs Macquaries Chair 302
Mt Isa 270
mulga 124, 125, 130
mulga parrot 72
mulgara 132, *142*
Mulgrave River 182
mulla mulla, tall *4-5, 130-131*
Mungo Lady 65, 67
Mungo Lake wool shearing shed *76-77*
Mungo National Park 62
Murrávian Gulf 251
Murray
    cod 66
    pine 67

Murray Upper 192
Murrumbidgee River 63
musky rat-kangaroo *182*
Mutijulu community 124, 142
Muttonbird Point *116*
Muttonbird Rock 106
Myrtaceae 148
myxoma virus 292

Nanga Peninsula 205
Nanwoon Cave 84
Nara Conference on Authenticity 308
Naracoorte 250, 251-252, 259-262, 270
Naracoorte Caves 260, 270
narbalek 52
native title 176 (see also land rights)
New Caledonia 175
New River Lagoon *94-95*
Ngulungbara 244
night parrot 229
Nightcap Range 148
Noah Creek 184
noddies 16
noddy 116
Norberg-Schulz Professor Christian 306
North Reef Island 32
northern
    log-runner 188
    shield shrimp *132*
Nourlangie - Brockman massif 46
Nourlangie Rock escarpment *44-45*

Oakleigh Creek 102
Oakleigh Creek Conservation Area 100
ochre 46, 54, 63, 66, 74, 83, 84
Oenpelli 56
oil exploration 32, 34, 220
Olduvai Gorge 63
Oligo-Miocene 259
Oligocene 251
One O'clock Cannon 304
One Tree Island 16
Opera House Conservation Plan 308
ophiolite 289, 296
orange-bellied parrot 96
orange brush 125
orchids 150, 156, 184
    jewel 184
Orpheus Island 15
ospreys 26, 39, 200, 214
Ove Arup engineers 304
overgrazing 194, 220
Overland Track 102
owl 151
oyster catcher 39
oysters 200
ozone hole 296

pademelon
    red legged 160
    red necked 160
palaeomagnetism 67, 74
palaeontology *259*, 270
palm 107, 156
    fan *184-185*
    Howea *108-109*
Pandani *88-89, 90-91*
Pandanus 118
paperbark 48
pardalote *165*
parrot 39, 132
pastoralism 42, 140, 176
pastoralists 42, 123
patch burning (see also firing practices) 142
pearling 199, 220

pearls 200
pelican 26
penal settlement 100
penguins 280, 291, 294, 297
    chinstrap *284-285, 292-293*
    gentoo 276, 280, 291, 292, 297
    king *272-273*, 276, *278-279*, 280, 291, 297
    macaroni 276, 280, 291, 297
    rockhopper 276, 292
    royal *288-289*, 291, *294-295*, 297
    slaughter of 296
perched dune lakes 228, *230-231, 232-233*, 234, *236-237*, 240, *242-243*
peregrine falcon 132, 240
Peron Peninsula 199, 205, 210, 212, *222-223*
Peron Province 205
petrels 276
    northern giant 292
pigeon 107, 160
    banded 39
    crested 72
    fruit 151
    rock 39
    topknot 151
    wonga 151
pigs 108
pink cockatoo 72, *136*
Pitjantjatjara 123, 142
plains lakes 234
plankton 276
plateau - lake-studded 294
platypus 151, 160
    ancient 258
Pleistocene 54, 63, 68, 112, 251, 262
plover 39
plumed frogmouth 151
plumed whistling duck 39, *52-53*
podsol 228
Point Lookout 148
porcupine grass 65
Port Essington 54
Portuguese men-of-war (see bluebottles) 16
possum
    brush-tail 132
    Herbert River ringtail *177*
    honey *218-219*
    ringtail 188
    rufous ring-tail 151
    short-eared bobuck 151
potato cod *28-29*
Precambrian Era 88
prickly hummock grass 212
primitive plants 228
Prince of Wales Range 88
Procoptodon 74
Proteaceae 147, 148, 184
Protemnodon 66, 266
protestors 152, 176
providence petrel 108, 116, *117*
python
    carpet *186-187*
    Ramsay's 132
quarantine station for gold miners 227
Queen Victoria Museum and Art Gallery 282
Queensland Museum 270
quoll 251
    spotted-tail 188

rabbits 125, 292
rail 39
Rainbow Beach 228, 246
rainbow
    bee eater 39
    skink *189*

Raine Island 15
rainforest 48, 107, 145, 147, *153*, 173, 180, 228, 234, 238
    ancient 258
    antiquity of 90, 147, 152, 175
    coachwood 150
    cool temperate *93, 168-169*
    evolution of 154
    littoral 148
    palm 238
    strangler fig and lianas *239*
    sub-tropical 114, 145, 148
    temperate 114
    tropical 176, 184
Ranger Uranium Inquiry 39
Ranger Uranium Mine 56
rare species 104, 150, 188
rat-kangaroo - musky 188
rats 107, 118
rattlepod 125
recreational activities 34, 142
red cedar 192
red goshawk 52
Red Island 282
red
    capped robin 72
    kangaroo *72-73, 140-141*
    necked stint 229
Reddan William 251
reef heron 26
reefs 15
    formation of 22
regent parrot 200, 214
Register of the National Estate 227
relict species 96, 214, 238
reptiles 125, 188, 240
River Heads 246
Riversleigh 250, *256-257*, 258, 260, 270, *270-271*
Riversleigh Museum 270
road building 102, 142, 152, 176, 194
Roaring Forties 88
Robertson Cave *252-253*
Robertson's Point 302
Robinson, George 100
rock art 39, *40-41, 42-43*, 46, *54*, 83, 100, *100*, 124, 130, *138*, 138, 303
    Anangu *138*
    damage to 56
    degradation of 143
    protection of 143
rock ringtail possum 52
Rogers, Captain Erasmus Darwin 282
Rooney Point *229*, 240
rosewood 68
rosy dock 125
Royal penguin *288-289*, 291, *294-295*, 297
rubbish 292
rufous
    hare-wallaby 132, 199, 214
    scrub-bird 150
Russell River 182

sacred sites 54, 130, 143
    disturbance of 143
    protection of 143
Sail Rock 106
salinity 206
saltbush 68, *72-73*
Salutation Island 214
samphire 48
sand dollar 251
sand dunes *224-225*, 227
    red *127*
sandalwood industry 200

sandpiper 39
sandstone 125, 130
Sandy Cape 228
Sarah Island 100
satinay 228, *238*
savannah 48
scalybark 107
scarred trees 244
sceptre banksia *213*
scientific expeditions 117
scleromorphic plants 147
sclerophyll forest 90
scorpionfish - Cook's *112*
screw palm 107
screw pine *235*
scribbly gum forest 228
scrub bird 160
sea
    caves 205
    eagles 26, 200, *212*
    lions
        Hookers 297
    slugs 16, 26
    snakes 214
    urchin 30, 108
seabirds 26, 90
seagrass 30, 197, 199, 206, *209*, 214, 240
sealers' camps 282
sealing 291, 297
seals 280, 291
    fur 275, 276, *286-287*, 291, 297
    southern elephant 276, *294-295*, 297
    leopard 276, 297
    near extinction of 275
    slaughter of 296
seastar *16*, 108
sedgeland 238
sedges 130
Shag Island 275
Shark Bay, Western Australia 196-223
Shark Bay mouse 210, *212*
Shark Bay rose 212, *220-221*
shark 15, 200, 210
    blue whaler *208*
shearwaters 26
    fleshy-footed 108, 116
    wedge-tailed 116
sheep grazing - damage done by 78
shell middens 66, 83, 100, 244, 303
shield shrimp 132
shipwrecks 32, 107, 244, 303
short-beaked echidna *170-171*
shrimp 132
    fairy 132
    northern shield *132*
siltation 182, 228, 246
Silurian Period 238
silver-eye 116
skeletal remains 63, *74*
    state of preservation of 66
    largest 151
    Pedra Branca 96
skink 39, 214
    four fingered 240
    rainbow *189*
slugs 116
snail 116, 118, 251
snakes 39
    ancient 251, 258
    black whipped 240
    death adder 39
    giant python 254
    king brown 39
    taipan 39
    tiger 240

western brown 132
snowgum *166*
snowy volute sea snail *209*
soft knob-tailed gecko *132-133*
sooty tern 16, 108, 116
South Alligator River *36-37*, 38, *57*
    mining at 56
South Coast Track 102
South-west Botanical Province 200, 212
southern
    angle-headed dragon *160-161*
    cassowary *178-179*
    hairy-nosed wombat 72
Southern Ocean islands 275
Spanish dancer (see also sea slugs) 16
spinifex 65, 68, 124, 125, 130, 212
spinifex hopping mouse *126*, 132
splendid fairy wren *143*
spoonbill 52
spore-producing plants 175, 184
spotted bower bird *136*
spotted snake *132*
spouts 205
Springbrook National Park *153*
starfish 16
sthenurine (see kangaroo) 255
Sthenurus 66, 266
    skull of *266-267*
    skeleton of *268-269*
stilt 39
stone arrangements 54
stone tools 54, 66, 74, *74*, 83, 84, 138
Stony Creek 182
strangler fig 148, 156 *166-167, 239*
striated grass wren 132
stromatolites *196-197*, 197, 199, *200-201*
    formation of 206
sugar-cane growing 175, 184, 192
Swain, Edward 176
Swain Reefs 20
swamp 234, 238
swamp wallaby *164*
Sydney 303
Sydney Cove 303
Sydney Harbour Bridge *300-301, 302*, 304, 308, *310-311*
Sydney Harbour National Park 308
Sydney Opera House In Its Harbour Setting 300-311
Sydney Opera House *300-301, 310-311*
    comparative evaluation 306
    concert hall 306, *307*
    construction 304, *305*
    design 304
    features 304, *308-309*
Sydney Opera House Trust 308

Tantanoola 252
Tasman, Abel Janzsoon 100
Tasmanian devil 96, *96*, 250, 251
Tasmanian tiger 96, *96*, 250, 251
Tasmanian Wilderness 80-103, 145, 147
    Conservation Areas 82
    Forest Reserves 82
    National Parks 82
    Wilderness Areas 82
tawny-breasted honeyeater *188*
tea-tree 130
tectonic plate 296
termites 72, 125
tern 26, 39
Tertiary period 260
The Font 88
The Olgas (see Kata-Tjuta) 122-123, *128-129*
thingodontan 262

thornbill 132
Thornton Peak rat 188
thorny devil 132, *220*
thylacine 250, 258, 262
thylacoleo carnifex (Owen) 66, *262, 263*, 263
timber industry 227, 244 (see also logging)
Tjalkalyiri 124
Tjukurpa (see also Dreaming) 123, 124, 138, 142
tortoise
    short necked 240
    swamp 258
tourism 34, 56, 78, 118, 142, 176, 192, 199, 218
    damage caused by 34, 102, 143, 218, 228
    effect on economy 224
    pressures of 40, 194, 246
Townsville 16, 174
trawling 34
    damage caused by 220
tree-kangaroo 188
Tropic of Capricorn 14
tropicbird 16
Truganini 83
tube-nosed insectivorous fruit bat *192*
turnstone 39, 116
turtle 26, 30, 107, 199, 240
    deaths among 218
    flatback 15, 26, 52
    giant horned 110
    green 15, *17, 24-25*, 26, 52, 200, 214
    hawksbill 15, 26
    leatherback 26
    leathery 15
    loggerhead 15, 26, 52, 200, 214
    Pacific Ridley 26
    pig-nosed 52
    South Pacific loggerhead 229
Tweed Caldera *154-155*
Tweed Range 148
Twin Falls 39

Ubirr (Rock) 46, *48-49*
Uluru *120-121, 127*
    creation of 123
Uluru - Kata Tjuta National Park 120-143
uranium mining 39, 40, 56
    damage done by 56
Unseen Utzon (Nobis) 308
Useless Inlet 199
Useless Loop 198, 218, 220
Utzon, Jorn 303, 304, 306, 308

valona algae *20-21*
vandalism 56
vascular plants 228, 276, 284
Victoria Fossil Cave *248-249*, 250, 251, 260, 262, *264-265*, 270
vine forest 184
volcanic activity 107, 175, 273, *276-277*, 280, 282-283
volcanic exposures 110
von Bellingshausen Thaddeus 291
wader 200
wallaby 40, 66, 72
    ancient 266
    black-footed rock *137*
    black-striped 160
    fossil 83
    parma 151, 160
    red-necked 100
    swamp *164*
    western hare *215*
Wallaman Falls 175, 182, *183*
wallaroo 72
    common 132

Walls of China *60-61*, 62, 67, *68-69*, 78
Walls of Jerusalem 88
wallum 238
Wanggoolba Creek 238, *245*
Wargata Mina 100
Warragarra 84
Washpool National Park 150, *157*
wasps 52
water buffalo 54
water quality - deterioration of 34, 246, 276
water-holding frog 132
waterfalls 37, 175
waterholes - maintenance of 123, 138
wedgetail eagles 200
Weld River 100
Werrikimbe National Park 148
Western Desert 122
western barred bandicoot 218, *218*
western hare-wallaby *215*
western yellow robin 214
Wet Tropics 262
Wet Tropics of Queensland 172-195, 145, 147
wetlands 37, 39, 52, 229, *260-261*
whale shark *202-203*
whales 297
    humpback 26, 199, 214, *217*, 240
    hunting of 214
    killer 26, 297
    minke 26,
    numbers of 200
whaling 32, 100, 199, 220
whimbrel 116
whistling duck - plumed 39, *52-53*
whistling kite 39
white cypress pine 65
white-bellied storm petrel 116
white-breasted sea eagle *212*
white mangrove 212
Whitsunday Islands 27
wide-buttressed carabeen 156
wild raspberry 152
Wildman River 38
Willandra Lakes Region 60 - 79
Willandra Lakes Visitor Centre *70-71*
Willowie Scrub 150
Wiyai Kutjara 123
wombat 72
Wonambi *254*
woodlands 228
Woolley, Ken, architect 306
woollybutt, Darwin *48*
Woolwonga Aboriginal Reserve 39, 56
Wooramel seagrass bank *209*
World Conservation Union - The (IUCN) 32, 78, 123, 148, 214, 270, 284
wren 132
    grass 39
    splendid fairy *143*
Wurrgeng 40
Wyuna Creek *235*

x-ray art rock paintings *42-43*, 54

Yakunytjatjara 123, 142
Yegge 40
yellow carabeen *149*
yellow coral 26
Yonge, Sir Maurice 16
Yulara 142
    tourist resort 122

Zuytdorp Cliffs 197, 205
Zygomaturus 70

Photo Credits

FRONT COVER Vincent Serventy; INSIDE FRONT COVER Glen Threlfo; BACK COVER Jiri Lochman, Lochman Transparencies; ENDPAPERS Peter Halton Photography, The Photo Library, Sydney; Andi Islinger; 1 Art Wolfe, Art Wolfe, Inc.; 2 QLD Dept of Environment and Heritage; 4 Jiri Lochman, Lochman Transparencies; 9 QLD Dept of Environment and Heritage; 12 Bill Wood, Bruce Coleman Limited; 16 G. Sauerbacker, Lochman Transparencies; 17 Vincent Serventy; 18 Ron & Valerie Taylor, Ron Taylor Film Productions; 20 Ron & Valerie Taylor, Ron Taylor Film Productions; 22 Ralph A Clevenger, Westlight; 24 Great Barrier Reef Marine Park Authority; 26 Michael Aw, The Photo Library, Sydney; 27 Rob Jung, The Photo Library, Sydney; 28 Ron & Valerie Taylor, Ron Taylor Film Productions; 30 G. Sauerbacker, Lochman Transparencies; Vincent Serventy; 31 Eva Boogaard, Lochman Transparencies; 32 Norman Quinn, The Photo Library, Sydney; 33 Ron & Valerie Taylor, Ron Taylor Film Productions; 35 Ben Cropp, Ben Cropp Productions; 36 Glen Threlfo; 40 Art Wolfe, Art Wolfe, Inc.; 41 Vincent Serventy; 42 Vincent Serventy; 44 Ted Mead, The Photo Library, Sydney; Glen Threlfo; 46 Jiri Lochman, Lochman Transparencies; 47 Vincent Serventy; 48 Jiri Lochman, Lochman Transparencies; 49 Glen Threlfo; 50 Glen Threlfo; 52 Glen Threlfo; 54 Vincent Serventy; 55 Marie Lochman, Lochman Transparencies; 57 Glen Threlfo; 58 David Hancock, Lochman Transparencies; 60 Geoff Higgins, The Photo Library, Sydney; 64 Jiri Lochman, Lochman Transparencies; 66 Jiri Lochman, Lochman Transparencies; 68 Jiri Lochman, Lochman Transparencies; 69 Jiri Lochman, Lochman Transparencies; 70 Vincent Serventy; 71 Vincent Serventy; 72 E. Slater, NSW National Parks & Wildlife Service; 73 Vincent Serventy; 74 Peter Clark, Dept of Land & Water Conservation, NSW; 75 Peter Clark, Dept of Land & Water Conservation, NSW; 76 Jiri Lochman, Lochman Transparencies; 77 Jiri Lochman, Lochman Transparencies; 78 Marie Lochman, Lochman Transparencies; 80 Vincent Serventy; 84 Ted Mead, The Photo Library, Sydney; 86 Ted Mead, The Photo Library, Sydney; 88 Ted Mead, The Photo Library, Sydney; 90 Vincent Serventy; 92 Tasmap Photographics; 93 Ted Mead, The Photo Library, Sydney; 94 Tasmap Photographics; 95 Ted Mead, The Photo Library, Sydney; 96 Clay Bryce, Lochman Transparencies; John Cancalosi, Bruce Coleman Limited; Sean Davey, Westlight; 97 Jocelyn Burt, The Photo Library, Sydney; 98 Tasmap Photographics; 100 Tasmap Photographics; 101 Tasmap Photographics; 102 Tasmap Photographics; 103 J. Fennell, Bruce Coleman Limited; 104 Vincent Serventy; 108 Vincent Serventy; 110 John & Val Butler, Lochman Transparencies; 112 John & Val Butler, Lochman Transparencies; 113 John & Val Butler, Lochman Transparencies; 114 Vincent Serventy; 116 David Austen, Bruce Coleman Limited; Vincent Serventy; 117 Ben Miller, NSW National Parks & Wildlife Service; 118 Vincent Serventy; 120 Paul Mevin, The Photo Library, Sydney; 126 Wade Hughes, Lochman Transparencies; Jiri Lochman, Lochman Transparencies; 127 Michael James, The Photo Library, Sydney; 128 Jiri Lochman, Lochman Transparencies; 130 Jiri Lochman, Lochman Transparencies; 132 Jiri Lochman, Lochman Transparencies; 133 Jiri Lochman, Lochman Transparencies; 134 Jiri Lochman, Lochman Transparencies; 136 Roger Brown; 137 Jiri Lochman, Lochman Transparencies; 138 Craig Lamotte, Lamotte Editions; Art Wolfe, Art Wolfe, Inc.; 140 Glen Threlfo; 142 Jiri Lochman, Lochman Transparencies; 143 Jiri Lochman, Lochman Transparencies; 144 Andi Islinger; 149 Marie Lochman, Lochman Transparencies; 150 Jiri Lochman, Lochman Transparencies; 152 Glen Threlfo; 153 Trevor Horden, The Photo Library, Sydney; 154 Bob Wickham, The Photo Library, Sydney; 156 Marie Lochman, Lochman Transparencies; Geoff Biddle, NSW National Parks & Wildlife Service-Nth Region; 157 Rob Jung, The Photo Library, Sydney; 158 Glen Threlfo; Glenn Leiper; 159 Andi Islinger; 160 Glen Threlfo; 161 Glen Threlfo; 162 Glen Threlfo; 163 Glen Threlfo; 164 Jiri Lochman, Lochman Transparencies; Andi Islinger; 165 Raoul Slater, Lochman Transparencies; 166 NSW National Parks & Wildlife Service-Nth Region; 167 Jiri Lochman, Lochman Transparencies; 168 Marie Lochman, Lochman Transparencies; 170 Glen Threlfo; 172 QLD Dept of Environment and Heritage; 177 Fritz Prenzel, Bruce Coleman Limited; 178 QLD Dept of Environment and Heritage; 179 C. B. & D. W. Frith, Bruce Coleman Limited; 180 QLD Dept of Environment and Heritage; 182 QLD Dept of Environment and Heritage; 183 QLD Dept of Environment and Heritage; 184 Vincent Serventy; 186 Norbert Wu; 188 C. B & D. W. Frith, Bruce Coleman Limited; D. Jew, QLD Dept of Environment and Heritage; 189 P.C., QLD Dept of Environment and Heritage; 190 Frithfoto, Bruce Coleman Limited; 192 D.G. Mc G, QLD Dept of Environment and Heritage; 193 Norbert Wu; 194 QLD Dept of Environment and Heritage; 196 Vincent Serventy; 200 Marie Lochman, Lochman Transparencies; 202 Ben Cropp, Ben Cropp Productions; 204 Jiri Lochman, Lochman Transparencies; Clay Bryce, Lochman Transparencies; 205 Vincent Serventy; 206 Richard Woldendorp, The Photo Library, Sydney; 208 Jiri Lochman, Lochman Transparencies; 209 Clay Bryce, Lochman Transparencies; John Butler, Lochman Transparencies; 210 Eva Boogaard, Lochman Transparencies; 211 Jiri Lochman, Lochman Transparencies; 212 Jiri Lochman, Lochman Transparencies; 213 Jiri Lochman, Lochman Transparencies; 214 Jiri Lochman, Lochman Transparencies; 215 Jiri Lochman, Lochman Transparencies; 216 Geoff Taylor, Lochman Transparencies; 217 Lynn Cropp, Ben Cropp Productions; 218 Jiri Lochman, Lochman Transparencies; 219 Jan Taylor, Bruce Coleman Limited; 220 Jiri Lochman, Lochman Transparencies; 221 Jiri Lochman, Lochman Transparencies; 222 Ted Mead, The Photo Library, Sydney; 224 Glen Carruthers, Chris Wilcox/Mantis Wildlife Films; 229 QLD Dept of Environment and Heritage; 230 Ted Mead, The Photo Library, Sydney; 232 Glen Carruthers, Chris Wilcox/Mantis Wildlife Films; 234 QLD Dept of Environment and Heritage; Glen Carruthers, Chris Wilcox/Mantis Wildlife Films; 235 Densey Clyne, Chris Wilcox/Mantis Wildlife Films; 236 Glen Carruthers, Chris Wilcox/Mantis Wildlife Films; 238 Glenn Leiper; 239 Ted Mead, The Photo Library, Sydney; 240 Densey Clyne, Chris Wilcox/Mantis Wildlife Films; 241 Geoff Higgins, The Photo Library, Sydney; 242 QLD Dept of Environment and Heritage; 244 Glen Carruthers, Chris Wilcox/Mantis Wildlife Films; 245 Geoff Higgins, The Photo Library, Sydney; 246 Glen Carruthers, Chris Wilcox/Mantis Wildlife Films; 248 F. Coffa/R.T. Wells, Flinders University, SA; 252 F. Coffa/R.T. Wells, Flinders University, SA; 254 F. Coffa/P. Rich, Flinders University, SA; D. O'Carroll, Flinders University, SA; 255 D. Megirian, NT Museum; F. Coffa/R.T. Wells, Flinders University, SA; 256 D. Megirian, NT Museum; 259 F. Coffa/R.T. Wells, Flinders University, SA; 260 D. Megirian, NT Museum; 261 F. Coffa/R.T. Wells, Flinders University, SA; 262 Dr Peter Murray, N.T. Museum; F. Coffa/P. Rich, Flinders University, SA; 263 D. O'Carroll, Flinders University, SA; 264 F. Coffa/R. T. Wells, Flinders University, SA; 266 F. Coffa/R.T. Wells, Flinders University, SA; 268 Rod Wells, Flinders University, SA; 269 F. Coffa/R. T. Wells, Flinders University, SA; 270 D. Megirian, NT Museum; 272 Art Wolfe, Art Wolfe, Inc.; 276 Dick Williams, The Antarctic Division, DEST; 278 DR Graeme Wheller; 280 Dick Williams, The Antarctic Division, DEST; 281 DR Graeme Wheller; 282 Dick Williams, The Antarctic Division, DEST; 284 Art Wolfe, Art Wolfe, Inc.; 286 DR Graeme Wheller; 288 Vincent Serventy, The Photo Library, Sydney; 292 Art Wolfe, Art Wolfe, Inc.; 294 Art Wolfe, Art Wolfe, Inc.; 296 The Photo Library, Sydney; 298 Art Wolfe, Art Wolfe, Inc.; 300 The Photo Library, Sydney; 305 David Beal, The Photo Library, Sydney; 307 David Messent, The Photo Library, Sydney; 308 The Photo Library, Sydney; 310 Paul Thompson, The Photo Library, Sydney.

Abbreviations:

DEST Department of Environment, Sports and Territories
     (Commonwealth Government)
QLD State of Queensland
NSW State of New South Wales
SA State of South Australia